D0891934

He's Got Rhythm

HE'S
GOT
RHYTHM

The Life and Career of

GENE
KELLY

*Cynthia Brideson
& Sara Brideson*

UNIVERSITY PRESS OF KENTUCKY

Editorial and Sales Offices: The University Press of Kentucky
663 South Limestone Street, Lexington, Kentucky 40508-4008
www.kentuckypress.com

Unless otherwise noted, photos are from the authors' collection.

Cataloging-in-Publication data available from the Library of Congress

ISBN 978-0-8131-6934-7 (hardcover : alk. paper)
ISBN 978-0-8131-6935-4 (epub)
ISBN 978-0-8131-6936-1 (pdf)

This book is printed on acid-free paper meeting the requirements of the American
National Standard for Permanence in Paper for Printed Library Materials.

Manufactured in the United States of America.

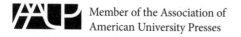 Member of the Association of
American University Presses

This book is dedicated to our father, Mark Brideson (March 19, 1962–October 14, 2015). Though not typically a fan of musicals, he loved Gene Kelly's work and would never miss a chance to watch one of Gene's films with us. Thank you, Daddy, for all the encouragement and love you gave us.

In memory of Sara Brideson, who passed away on January 23, 2017. Sara's passion for Gene Kelly's work was the spark behind this book. Her love for and loyalty to her family and friends will never be forgotten.

Contents

Part 4. Ambassador of His Art: 1972–Present

Photographs follow page 232

Introduction

Ballet Dancer and Swaggering Tough

"There is about him and his artistry the wonderment of childhood, the sad searching loneliness which seeks companionship in the fairyland of the imagination. It is an abiding, cherished faith in make-believe."[1] This portrait of Gene Kelly, penned in 1946 by a columnist for *Photoplay* magazine, seems inapplicable to a man who had a "worldly, hard quality," according to lyricist/playwright/screenwriter Adolph Green, and the propensity to come across as "cocky" and "jaw-jutting."[2] Even more alien to a land of make-believe was the man's appearance. He bore a small, crescent-shaped scar on his left cheek; his five-foot-nine, 155-pound frame was muscular and compact. His reedy tenor voice bore traces of his urban Pittsburgh roots. He dressed in khakis, T-shirts or sweatshirts, loafers, and a baseball cap pulled over his slick black hair. Even when dressed in top hat and tails, he, in his own words, still looked "like a truck driver."[3] If provoked, his brown eyes could shoot "a lethal glance that packs a wallop."[4]

However, columnist Alyce Canfield noted, "There [was] a certain gentleness about him . . . he's a kind man, a sincere and honorable person. A gentleman." He was the type who removed his cap when ladies were present in an elevator. The moment he grinned, his lethal glance and worldly hardness vanished. His teeth were perfectly white; his eyes crinkled at the corners. With the appearance of his smile, suddenly, he had about him a "mischievous likeability. . . . His eyes twinkle and you forgive him anything."[5] Pair his smile with the impromptu balletic pirouettes or athletic jigs he was inclined to do at any given moment, and one might be persuaded that this man could indeed cross into the "fairyland of the imagination."

Equally adept at ballet and straight hoofing, he was also a formidable

1

player of nearly every American sport. In addition, he was a master choreographer and actor, could speak several languages, and might spend hours discussing politics, philosophy, and American history. He called himself an average Joe, but he was anything but ordinary for more reasons than his remarkable intellect: he single-handedly made dance one of America's favorite pastimes. Melding his athletic prowess with his balletic training, he altered the notion that dancing was only for women or effete males.

Gene himself went so far as to call his brand of dancing "a man's game." He explained: "I knew I couldn't stay with straight classical ballet. I had to create something of my own. . . . I had to express manliness and strength and Cokes and hot dogs and football and basketball and jazz. You can't do it with a *port de bras*."[6] Though Gene Kelly did indeed create his own style, he took inspiration from dancers and choreographers before him. He admired the common-man persona, cocky strut, and integration of dance and plot that Irish American dancer/playwright/producer George M. Cohan developed in his productions of the 1900s–1920s. Gene expanded the ideas of Russian-born choreographer George Balanchine, who introduced modernistic balletic expressionism on Broadway in the 1930s. Finally, he adopted choreographer Robert Alton's thesis that every dance should tell a story and have a purpose for being, a theory Alton put to use throughout the 1930s and 1940s onstage and in film.

Still, Gene Kelly was not a copyist. He perfected his art into a uniquely American style—one that combined rhythms from Harlem to Ireland and the grace of ballet with the earthiness of folk. His style was so broad in scope that he was in his lifetime and remains to new generations of admirers one of the few stars "adored by young people and old, men and women."[7] Gene's wife of fifteen years, Betsy Blair, concluded that he wanted to "democratize dance. He wanted to bring it to the whole world."[8]

From 1942 to 1956, Gene Kelly came to symbolize the American Dream and the confidence and optimism of the postwar nation. Through his films, he spread more happiness and hope than any other dancer of his time. In *Cover Girl* (1944), he urged audiences to "make way for tomorrow" while skipping down a Brooklyn street. In *Anchors Aweigh* (1945), he banished worry from a somber cartoon kingdom through song and dance. As a sailor on twenty-four-hour leave, he cavorted through Manhattan in *On the Town* (1949). He tapped through bistros in *An American in Paris* (1951) and laughed at clouds while splashing through a storm in *Singin' in the Rain* (1952). More than anything else, his mass appeal stemmed from his ability to transform the commonplace into the spectacular. A rain puddle, a mop, or a newspaper could reach the status of art when incorporated in his dance. Just as he could dance with anything, Gene could dance with anyone: girl-next-door Judy Garland, femme fatale Cyd Charisse, Jerry the Mouse, a group of French children, and even himself in his double-exposure "Alter Ego" routine in *Cover Girl*.

Gene was arguably the most winning screen personality of the twentieth century—a man "men wanted to be and women wanted to be with" and whose lack of pretension immediately put children at ease.[9] But he was a man of unusual complexity. He shunned Hollywood society, studio politics, and glamour yet fumed at those who scorned the film industry that had made them rich. In spite of the wealth he amassed in Hollywood, he maintained a humble lifestyle and was a devoted family man. Wary of any sort of regimentation, Gene questioned set religious and political beliefs but still called himself a Catholic and a Democrat. Yet, "whatever the subject, [he] supports an open mind without for a moment yielding his own convictions."[10]

Gene's complexity only grows upon further examination. Though willing to hear all viewpoints and believing that prejudice was akin to cowardice, he was exclusive when it came to whom he did and did not accept into his social circle. To gain Gene's acceptance, one had to possess both talent and intelligence. Gene made his Beverly Hills home a haven for ex–New Yorkers or any creative person who was in but not of Hollywood. At parties he hosted, often he sat back and drank whiskey, performing only if others performed. Contrarily, the "cocky, jaw-jutting" side of his personality often emerged. He would engage in fiercely competitive games of charades or volleyball. Gene, who once said that to him second best was nothing, could not abide losing—and he never hesitated to show his temper when he did. Film historian Rudy Behlmer admitted that "Kelly could be difficult" but argued that "he was not alone, good people, really good people, could be difficult on occasion."[11]

Gene rarely became "difficult" unless he was dissatisfied with himself. According to his frequent co-director Stanley Donen, "He was aware that he had a very special gift and that he wanted to show it in the best possible way. He drove himself very hard. He was very nervous about his singing voice though, and would get hoarse from nerves when he had to record."[12] As hard as he was on himself, he was equally hard on his colleagues. He had little patience for amateurs, which earned him the reputation of a taskmaster. MGM musical director/composer/lyricist Johnny Green observed, "Gene is easygoing as long as you know exactly what you are doing when you're working with him. . . . If you want to play on his team you better love hard work too. He isn't cruel but he is tough."[13]

Though Gene's screen presence is nearly always ebullient, his intensity particularly comes through in his solo numbers. The dances he choreographed himself possessed a dimension of introspection that numbers by other musical performers of the era lacked. For instance, at the close of his "Alter Ego" number in *Cover Girl,* he smashes a window to rid himself of his argumentative reflection. Other notably meditative routines include a tap dance in a barn in *Summer Stock* (1950) and portions of the cinematic ballets he designed for *On the Town, An American in Paris,* and *Singin' in the Rain.* During these sequences, he stands alone in darkness, suddenly separated from a merry crowd or amid people and things he feels are unobtainable. Betsy Blair explained that he "wanted to express the simplest but also the most complex emotions" through dance.[14]

Gene was similarly subject to introspection offscreen. Friends and family noted that he could sometimes lapse into silence and stare ahead, broodingly. Nevertheless, his eldest daughter, Kerry, claimed Gene was the only adult she ever knew who was never in analysis.[15] For Gene, the process of creating was his therapy. Staging dances was essentially a way for him to make sense of both his own personal demons and the greater problems of the world. "Dancing is much more than mere exhibition. It's a complete art in itself, both visually and emotionally," Gene asserted.[16]

Gene succeeded in making dance more than show; indeed, he was a pivotal player in the creation of the integrated film musical. Because he worked at the greatest studio of Hollywood's golden era, Metro-Goldwyn-Mayer, and was part of the studio's most prestigious production unit, led by producer Arthur Freed, Gene had ample opportunity to innovate. He combined his talent with those of directors such as Vincente Minnelli, Stanley Donen, and Charles Walters and composers and screenwriters including Alan Jay Lerner, Betty Comden, and Adolph Green. At the height of his success at MGM, he had become, according to musical director Johnny Green, "the Neil Armstrong of MGM. He enjoyed great respect and admiration, and in [producer] Arthur Freed he had a powerful ally. It was almost a father-son relationship with the father having a near-reverence for the son."[17]

Freed's career-long goal was to change the formulaic stories and stage-bound look of musicals. He found in Gene an enthusiastic avenue through which to do it. Interviewer Graham Fuller stated in 1994 that "Kelly's streetwise, Everyman figure" did most "to liberate the [musical] genre from its 'putting on a show' tradition."[18] Gene brought the musical into the real world; the plots of his films took on more weight and the characters had more dimension. It was at his insistence that *On the Town* became the first musical to be filmed on location. Aside from adding authenticity to the settings of his pictures, Gene changed the look of musicals by creating dances that could not be replicated on the stage—a technique now known as cinedance. Director Busby Berkeley preceded Gene in the creation of musical numbers meant solely for the screen, but Berkeley's routines are less dance and more brilliant use of camera angles. Gene took Berkeley's work a step further by employing both dance and innovative camera work.

Today, the remarkable breadth of Gene Kelly's work is overshadowed by the singular image of a euphoric man "dancin' and singin' in the rain." Similarly, Gene Kelly's life and achievements, particularly after he left MGM in 1956, are all but forgotten. He was a man who wore as many hats professionally as he did personally. He was a choreographer, director, comedian, dramatist, singer, ballet dancer, and tap dancer. He was a father, husband, devoted son, naval lieutenant, and political activist. His character was complex: he has been variously described as a brutally competitive sportsman and a pensive intellectual, an egotist and a shy, self-deprecating man. No matter what hat he wore, Gene's overarching goal in whatever endeavor he undertook—personal or professional—was to make the world a place where fascination, idealism, and sincerity were not just for children.

"If you're making musicals for a mass audience, with few exceptions your goal is to bring joy," Gene explained. "And if you can lift the audience and make them happy for a few minutes, then the dance has done its work."[19] It is telling that Gene, in spite of his social conscience, quick temper, and occasional dark moods, chose as the ideal musical not one of his own works or a weighty, moralizing picture. The picture to hold that title was Vincente Minnelli's nostalgic work *Meet Me in St. Louis* (1944), a story told through the eyes of an impish five-year-old child. "That is a picture that is seamless, touching, marvelous—the wedding of song and story," Gene told interviewer Michael Singer.[20]

Gene Kelly's life, remarkably scandal free, was a highly private one and thus presents an exceptional challenge for biographers. However, by utilizing previously untapped primary sources and hundreds of newspaper and magazine articles written during and after his lifetime, this book, the first comprehensive biography written since Gene Kelly's death in 1996, endeavors to give a balanced, in-depth view of one of filmdom's most enduring icons. The text focuses not only on his most famous work but on his lengthy career before and after his time in Hollywood. Above all, the book ventures to illustrate the many dimensions of Gene Kelly the person. He never stopped believing in the fantasies of boyhood, but at the same time he was grounded in reality by a deep-seated compulsion to push himself and others to achieve a perfection he claimed never to have found. Little wonder it is, then, that his daughter Kerry noted that the resolution of any story in her father's life and work "always takes place through fantasies and dreams."[21] And yet, what made Gene Kelly a true original was his ability to take the world of imagination and make one believe it was tangible. This is the story of the dreamer, the realist, the "ballet dancer and swaggering tough" who was Gene Kelly.[22]

Part I

"Who wants a choreographer from Pittsburgh?"

1912–1941

1

The Reluctant Dancer

When one thinks of Pittsburgh, Pennsylvania, almost inevitably the first image summoned is that of an industrial city built on steel and coal. If the context is entertainment, one's mind naturally wanders to the Pittsburgh Pirates, two-time World Series champions. Eugene Curran Kelly, an intellectual ballet dancer endowed with equal parts charm and temper, is not a man one would think of as the typical Pittsburgh citizen. However, according to one journalist in 1993, Gene Kelly is one of Pittsburgh's "favorite sons."[1]

In history books and to scholars of American history, the names Andrew Carnegie and J. P. Morgan may spell Pittsburgh, but those men were not native to the city and thus can never hold as cherished a place in its history as Gene Kelly. Among the many reasons Pittsburghers still revere Gene is because he, until the day of his death, never lost his regard for the city. "Pittsburgh's a swell town," he said. "I was born there and I love the town and I love the people. And it isn't so doggone dirty as people make out, either."[2] Gene's most vivid—and fondest—memories find their source in Pittsburgh. "I don't think adult experiences can come up to childhood for sheer excitement. Everything is an adventure then, imagination is unfettered."[3]

From its beginnings, Pittsburgh was a magnet for those with boundless ambition and a remarkable scope for imagination. Before the construction of canals and railroads in the mid- to late nineteenth century, the Ohio and Mississippi rivers acted as highways to the city, opening it up to America's heartland. Exporting precious natural resources such as wood, coal, limestone, and sand enriched the area. From 1870 to 1910, Pittsburgh experienced an economic golden age thanks to a proliferation of entrepreneurs, most notably J. P. Morgan and Andrew Carnegie, who made the city an international power through the creation of U.S. Steel.

The late 1800s and early 1900s saw not only an influx of industry in Pittsburgh but also of immigrants, primarily Irish. Because of Pittsburgh's booming industry, it seemed there would be plentiful work opportunities for all. The area around Fort Pitt Blockhouse became known as Little Ireland. More Irish communities developed in the South Side, Strip District, North Side, Oakland, and Lawrenceville. The majority of these settlements were cramped and very poor, leading to an intense distrust of Irish immigrants among politicians and employers. Many factories sported "Irish Need Not Apply" signs on their doors.[4]

Discrimination against the Irish did nothing to dampen the spirits of Gene Kelly's grandfather, a "wild Irishman called Billy" Curran.[5] Billy had immigrated to New York from Londonderry in 1845 after experiencing a brush with the English authorities. He worked sweeping the porches of general stores until he decided to move to West Virginia, where he hoped to make his fortune as a coal miner. However, ignorant of geography, Billy instead found himself stepping off a train in Huntington, Pennsylvania, where there were, ironically, no coal mines. He did not regret landing in Huntington; there he met the young Mary Eckhart, whom he made his wife after a brief courtship. The Eckharts, heralding from Alsace-Lorraine, were financially secure. Now with enough money to pursue the mining career that had been his original intent, Billy headed with his wife to Houtzdale, Pennsylvania. There he promptly discovered the presence of coal. He bought the piece of land but, oddly, rather than mine it, he opened a general store. The enterprise flourished, as did his offspring, one of whom was a fiery, dark-eyed girl named Harriet. Harriet was unlike Billy in one distinct aspect—she was a devout Catholic who strove to live as clean a life as possible. Gene later explained that Harriet often spoke with more pride when referring to the Eckhart side of her heritage and alleged that her family had a connection to the first US Catholic bishop, John Carroll.

After saving enough money, the family moved to Pittsburgh and opened a saloon. It was a respectable establishment, but Harriet loathed her father's choice of business, feeling that it represented all that outsiders disliked about the Irish. At times, she even refused to admit that her father was the son of an Irishman. Harriet, now nearly twenty years old, continued to build a refined life for herself, pursuing music, dancing, and the theater. She relished performing in local stock productions and singing in a chorale group. In 1906, just as the Currans reached the peak of their success, Billy, walking home one night with his pockets full of the night's receipts, was brutally attacked and robbed by two reprobates. He lay in the gutter for hours before being discovered and died of pneumonia days later. Though his exact date of birth remains vague, Billy was in his eighties at the time of his death.

He left behind him nine children. Each received a $50,000 inheritance ($133,202.99 in 2015 dollars). However, the children all lost their fortunes through inadvisable investments or alcoholism. Harriet lost hers during the Panic of 1907 when the New York Stock Exchange fell 50 percent from the previous year. The loss of her money came at a most inopportune time—she had just married James Kelly the year before.

James Patrick Kelly was more like her father than Harriet liked to admit. The grandson of a poor blacksmith, he was born in Peterborough, Canada, and grew up in Ontario. James's father was a landscaper who owned several acres of land—though the veracity of this story is questionable and may have been invented to lead Harriet to believe she was not marrying a "shantytown" Irishman. James became an American citizen at age twenty-eight and worked on the East Coast as a traveling sales executive for Thomas Edison's Columbia Phonograph Company. He eventually settled in Pittsburgh, where he met Harriet in 1905 at an amateur concert in which she was performing. Gene later called his father a "doll of a man" and his mother "an artist" and a "frustrated actress."[6] Gene's first wife, Betsy Blair, wrote, "I think Gene's ambition and a lot more of his character came from [Harriet] . . . but his charm definitely came from Pop." Betsy claimed that James "was an alert and quiet man. He was like an old wood burning stove, radiating warmth at the heart of the family."[7] James and Harriet did share one character trait: they were both loose with the truth, particularly when it came to their ages. Harriet never revealed her true age and therefore never wished James to reveal his for fear that people would be able to estimate hers based upon it. Though born in 1875, until his death, James would always reply, "Sweet sixteen" when asked his age.[8] Harriet was born somewhere between 1887 and 1891.

After honeymooning in Ontario, the newlyweds moved into a house on the corner of Portland and Bryant streets in the Highland Park area of Pittsburgh. There Harriet Joan (nicknamed Jay) was born in 1910, and James Kelly Jr. followed in 1911. Harriet raised her family alone most of the time; James was gone five days out of the week traveling from city to city selling phonographs. "My mother was proud he wasn't a blue collar worker," Gene reflected.[9] But he wasn't exactly a white-collar worker, either. His earnings fluctuated, ranging from $75 to $125 a week, a tidy sum in this era. According to Fred Kelly, Gene's younger brother, James became the top salesman at Columbia. "He made the largest single sale in music that ever happened. He went out to the Midwest and sold the first phonograph ever in the state to the governors of Missouri, Nebraska, and Kansas. . . . These were the first phonographs ever to be [sold] on the other side of the Mississippi. It was the arts coming to the Wild West." Fred claimed that as a child, he thought the story was "blarney," but later he found newspapers with front-page spreads telling about the one hundred trains and one hundred boxcars it took to ship all the phonographs and records James had sold.[10]

With James's career on the upswing, he and Harriet saw no reason why they should not expand their family. Their second son, Eugene Curran Kelly, was born on August 3, 1912. For a man whose life and art were defined by rebellion, rhythm, and creativity, there could have been no year more fitting than 1912 in which to be born. The Progressive Era, a period characterized by sweeping improvements to workers' rights, sanitation, and civil liberties, was still very much in evidence. Suffragettes marched down the streets of New York, fighting for the right to vote. In August, the month of Gene's birth, dissident Republicans formed the Progressive Party and nominated Theodore Roosevelt as their presidential candidate. Though Roosevelt did not win, the Progressive Party took enough votes away from the incumbent William Howard Taft to result in democratic candidate Woodrow Wilson winning a landslide victory. On the international front, the year's big news centered on the tragic sinking of the RMS *Titanic* on April 14, 1912, in the North Atlantic. The ship's foundering served as a sort of symbol that the once all-powerful United Kingdom was not unsinkable. America was fast emerging as the dominant world power.

However, Gene Kelly's year of birth was most appropriate for one very special reason: it ushered in a new, innovative era of dance called ragtime. Ragtime, influenced by the syncopated rhythms found in St. Louis or New Orleans African American dance clubs, was accepted by all sectors of society after the 1912 publication of Irving Berlin's song "Alexander's Ragtime Band." Ragtime was among the first styles of music and dance to originate in America, completely free of European influence. The dances that accompanied "rags" were accessible because they required no formal training and encouraged individual movement.

The entertainment industry was also undergoing massive growth.

Carl Laemmle founded Universal Studios and Mack Sennett formed Keystone, which specialized in slapstick comedies. Director D. W. Griffith created several short subjects, many starring a girl with blond curls and a rosebud mouth named Mary Pickford. On the stage, large-scale spectacles exemplified by the popular *Ziegfeld Follies* drew eager audiences. Among the most popular entertainers of the time was a first-generation American son of Irish immigrants, George M. Cohan. In 1912, he produced seven Broadway shows, including a revival of his famed *Forty-Five Minutes from Broadway.*

Harriet kept herself far more abreast of developments in entertainment than politics. One of her favorite pieces of advice was: "Never talk about politics or religion, and never ask anyone their age . . . it only ends in argument."[11] Still, Harriet could have been a suffragette. Indeed, she wore the proverbial pants in the family and was the primary decision maker when it came to raising her children. This can partly be attributed to the fact that James was traveling much of the time and that he had a more retiring nature than his wife. Harriet was determined to involve her children in the arts during their formative years. But in 1914, the Kellys' mounting expenses left little chance for the children to dabble in the world of fine art. The family moved to a more affordable home at 722 Mellon Street, where they lived until 1924. Two more children were born shortly after the move: Louise on July 6, 1914, and Fred on June 29, 1916. To help with expenses, Gene later explained, "a spinster aunt and a bachelor uncle shared the house [on Mellon Street]. Both were in full time employment."[12] The crowded home on Mellon Street was located in the East Liberty District, which was not as upscale as Highland Park.

Mellon Street was an active area where people got to know each other whether they wanted to or not. The street was lined with homes so close together that one could carry on a conversation with a neighbor through a facing window. The homes had little in the way of front lawns, leaving the children to use the street or nearby parks for play. Gene claimed East Liberty was known as "a ghetto," partly due to its high Jewish, Polish, and Irish population.[13]

James Kelly made the most of their humble property. Each winter, he flooded the backyard in order to transform it into a miniature ice-skating or hockey rink. "A lot of people look back on their childhoods as unhappy. I had a marvelous one, and the utmost care and attention and good will paid to the children. But also our duties and obligations were clearly felt,"

Gene remembered.[14] Despite James's tendency to drink and his frequent business trips, he instilled decent morals in his children. Both he and Harriet were regular churchgoers at Sacred Heart Parish. James did not allow anyone to return to the dinner table if he or she left it and insisted on immaculate fingernails. He took every "No Trespassing" sign literally, even if it meant walking an extra mile home instead of cutting through an obviously abandoned lot. One law he did not abide, however, was Prohibition. He managed to keep liquor in the basement throughout the country's dry years. One Christmas, all of James's sons gifted him a case of beer. Harriet wagged her finger at him and cried, "See what your sons think of you?" Though he deeply respected his father, one rule that Gene did not later follow was James's edict that formal attire was mandatory at the dinner table. Throughout Gene's adulthood, he could be found at home in khakis and a sweatshirt looking, as he admitted, like a "walking slum."[15]

Gene's preference for informal attire may have been acceptable at the Fulton Grammar School on Mellon Street, but at the St. Raphael Grammar School, he was required to dress like a little gentleman. A brand-new structure built in 1915 in the East End of Pittsburgh, the school was led by the Sisters of St. Joseph of Baden. Though Gene had spiritual doubts throughout his entire life, the virtues of justice, peace, and reverence instilled in him at St. Raphael remained with him, particularly justice.

Peers and teachers alike at St. Raphael held great esteem for Gene and his siblings. "We were a very orderly group. Not that we didn't fight a lot . . . [but] we never thought of disobeying our parents. . . . It was an old-fashioned bringing up," Gene explained. In a 1991 interview, Gene stated that he never wished to be an only child. He liked sharing—including the responsibilities of chores. "Everybody had their turn. One day, someone did the dishes, and the next day, someone made the beds," he recalled.[16]

St. Raphael provided the Kelly children with "old-fashioned" education, but Harriet felt it would not be complete without added lessons in the arts, especially dance. Harriet sent her children to Blinsky's Dancing School at Sixth and Penn streets beginning when Gene was seven. "My brother and I went to dancing school because my mother—a far-seeing woman well ahead of her time and, incidentally, my Inspiration—sent us," Gene told Hedda Hopper in 1954.[17]

Dancing school meant budget cuts elsewhere; Gene especially noticed the lack of desserts at the dinner table. He had a remarkable sweet tooth— as an adult, he often had candy bars for breakfast. Like many children, he loathed vegetables. Aside from sweets, he liked sandwiches with bologna and cheese, potato and onion, or even the unlikely combination of pickle, cheese, liverwurst, and peanut butter. He enjoyed steak and potatoes; in general, the simpler the food, the better. Gene's sweet tooth was only fully indulged on his birthday. In the Kelly home, Harriet made it a tradition that on each of her children's birthdays, the child could decide on the family's dinner—no matter how unbalanced it might be. Gene's birthday dinner of choice was course after course of cakes.

Gene's hearty appetite gave him ample fuel to pursue all manner of sports. James's determination to make sportsmen of his sons matched Harriet's to make them artists. Harriet predicted that Fred would be the star in the family. Gene showed less potential as an entertainer in Harriet's eyes due to his overarching interest in sports and his tendency to catch every illness that came to the neighborhood, even those that passed his siblings by. His illnesses did not, however, affect his ability to master sports. Ironically, he could thank his sickliness for some of his athletic prowess. He suffered for many years with sinus issues and, at age seven, developed a near-fatal case of pneumonia. Harriet's brother Gus suggested that Gene try gymnastics to strengthen his lungs after he recovered. Gene took the suggestion and, as with every pursuit, dedicated himself to it wholeheartedly. No physical ailments could keep the mischievous boy out of trouble. As well as being the sickliest, Gene was the most accident prone of the Kelly children.

The enumeration of Gene's youthful mishaps reads like the story of an Irish American Tom Sawyer. In one instance, Gene, inspired by the trolleys running up and down the streets of his neighborhood, constructed one himself (likely modifying a tricycle or wagon). On the "trolley's" maiden voyage, an enormous truck came barreling down the street. Gene, riding the little trolley, disappeared beneath the truck's wheels. He and the trolley emerged, miraculously unscathed, out the back. Another time Gene fell and broke his arm. This occurred during a brief period when Harriet had decided Gene would become a violinist. Gene considered the broken arm a blessing in disguise. "There's something about a boy carrying a violin case in a poor neighborhood that brings out the very worst in every kid," he later said.[18]

Though Gene could be the target of bullying on Mellon Street, at other times, he and his siblings were the ones bringing mayhem to the neighborhood. According to Gene, "In a family with three boys and two girls anything can happen—and did." He recalled that when he was six, he received a BB gun for Christmas, "and we Kelly kids took Pittsburgh by storm. One of the neighbors finally called the police. Luckily, the police got the wrong address and instead of coming to our house, arrived at the Doyles' next door . . . the BBs were donated—much against our will—to a society for the Improvement of the Poor."[19]

One neighbor, a mailman, was not as patient as the Doyles. Gene recalled that the man had had enough of the Kelly children after they pulled a Halloween prank. He "whacked" them, leading James to march next door and punch him hard enough to account for every slap he had given Gene and his siblings. "That was very Irish, no one could lay a hand on your kids."[20]

Gene was the primary instigator in another incident that caused the neighbors grief. It began when the Kelly children constructed a three-story shack in their backyard. "We . . . had it for several weeks, meeting every day like conspirators to make *plans*. Don't ask me plans for what. Just plans," Gene reminisced. When winter came, the children hung burlap on the walls for warmth. During one of their "planning" sessions, one child held a candle too near the burlap. The "place went up like tinder" and the flames traveled to the backyard fence. "Men, women and children rushed out to form a bucket brigade and we finally managed to get the blaze under control, just about the time the fire department arrived. After that we were limited to one-story shacks."[21]

The only childhood mishap to leave Gene physically damaged for the rest of his life took place when he was, by his account, age five, but others' accounts suggest he was seven. While riding his tricycle with no handlebars, he fell forward into an exposed piece of cast iron, which punctured his left cheek. The accident sent the entire family into a state of panic, and Gene was left with a noticeable slightly curving scar to the left of his mouth. According to one reporter in 1943, the scar "still turns white when he gets fighting mad." When Hollywood columnists asked about the scar in his adulthood, Gene wryly replied: "I'd love to ascribe that scar to some great dramatic event . . . but actually I fell off my tricycle when I was a sprout of five."[22]

Gene's accidents made Harriet all the more adamant that he continue attending dance classes—a pursuit she hoped would keep him out of trouble. Thrifty as ever with the household budget, she managed to set aside money to take him and his siblings to the theater whenever a Broadway show came to Pittsburgh. She had never forgotten her girlish hopes of being on the stage, and she hoped to transfer her youthful ambitions to her children. Among the luminaries Gene and his siblings saw were Billie Burke (wife of Florenz Ziegfeld Jr.) and George M. Cohan, a man Gene declared to be one of his first major influences. Rather than tell stories of royalty and wealth, Cohan wrote and starred in plays focusing on middle-class characters who were plucky embodiments of the American Dream. Though Gene committed Cohan's style to memory, he did not see himself as the next Yankee Doodle Dandy. He envisioned himself as a shortstop for the Pittsburgh Pirates.

His weekly dance lessons and the long walk to and from the studio were a source of dread. The way Harriet insisted Gene look when attending lessons, dressed in a "prim" suit with an "Eton collar, hair slicked and his ears scrubbed pink," did nothing to discourage bullies from targeting him and his brothers. "The route to [the dance] school was lined with kids whose mothers held less aesthetic views," Gene said. "Invariably the divergent schools of thought clashed and I had to do battle on each of six corners to prove I was no sissy."[23] Because Gene was smaller than other boys his age, he felt he had to prove himself, "and the best way to do this was with my fists."[24] According to Fred, "Gene would start the fight and Jim would finish it. Jim was our protector. But it was sort of our daily routine."[25] Gene was especially angered when he was taunted by older boys with whom he played football; these boys knew he was a superb athlete and most certainly not a "sissy."

After one too many weeks went by with Gene, James, and Fred coming home from dancing lessons with limps, bruises, and "shiners," Harriet forgot her frugal nature and paid to have them take a taxi to and from school. "Fighting, that was the style in Pittsburgh in those days," Fred reflected. "But aside from being a fighting town it was a real show business town."[26]

Fred's assessment was correct. Theatrical companies and acts passed through town regularly, prompting Harriet to make her children a part of the city's show business world. By 1921, nine-year-old Gene and his siblings had become so proficient at dance that Harriet entered them in amateur night competitions under the name the Five Kellys. Harriet took inspiration from the popular family group, "Eddie Foy and the Seven Little Foys," which had become a national sensation on vaudeville beginning in 1910.

Vaudeville reigned as arguably the most popular entertainment during Gene's early childhood. In historian John Kenrick's words, it was a "hodgepodge of songs, sketches and specialty acts" that could vary from family dancing troupes to performing seals.[27] Unless vaudevillians made it to the "big time," meaning they would be paid up to $1,000 a week, they were relegated to small- or medium-time theaters at whistle-stops around the country that paid only $15 a week. The epitome of a big-time venue was New York's Palace Theatre, which opened in 1913.

The Five Kellys were not the Foys, and though audiences met their efforts with enthusiasm, it was clear they were not going to the big time. According to Michael Kelly, Gene's nephew, "The five dancing Kellys used to replace the seven little Foys when they couldn't get to town."[28] As the children grew older, they refused to participate any longer. James Jr. was most adamant against it, openly declaring his hatred for amateur theatricals.

Each summer, Harriet gave the Five Kellys a much-needed break from their lessons and professional engagements. Between 1916 and 1924, the family rented a vacation cabin on Lake Erie in Ripley, and later on Lake Conneaut in western Pennsylvania. Harriet took her children from school two weeks before the term came to a close and did not bring them back until two weeks after the new term began, arguing that little work was done at these times anyway. James, like Harriet, relaxed a number of his rules during these halcyon summers, most notably his insistence on formal dress.

The children thrived in the unstructured atmosphere at the lake. Gene would always run out of allowance before any of his siblings because, as the most active in the family, he spent more to rent a horse or canoe for the day. In later life, Gene recalled summers at the lake as the most idyllic periods of his youth. He retained the love of nature and recreation, and for the rest of his life always left time for camping, picnicking, and other leisure activities, even during periods of hard work.

Though far removed from the world of show business, Gene still enjoyed tastes of it while at the lake. Fred wished to put on amateur shows for the other vacationing children and enlisted Gene as director. Gene relished this more authoritative role and, after each show, tried his hand at being a businessman by offering—for a fee—to teach other children how to sing, dance, and recite.

One of Gene's most thrilling experiences at the lake was meeting lightweight boxing champion Harry Greb, who was training at a camp nearby.

Greb gave Gene a few lessons. The boy put his newly learned skills to good use on the unsuspecting bullies in East Liberty. "Boxing was a ghetto kid's dream, for fame and easy money," Gene explained. "But an uncle took my brother and me down to the gym and showed us guys who were punched out, talking out of the side of their head. That kept us dancing."[29]

When Gene returned in the fall of 1924 to St. Raphael, the school's nuns pressured him to continue his involvement in the theater. They placed him in several school productions, including *Babes in Toyland*, simply because he was the only boy his age who could tap-dance. Gene was not enthusiastic. "As a kid . . . if anyone had told me I'd grow up to be a dancer, I'd have socked him in the jaw," he later said.[30]

Though the Kelly children had, for the most part, lost interest in performing, Fred remained eager, staging miniature vaudevilles in the Kelly basement. He arranged puppet and dog shows as well as a magic show that had Gene playing Houdini. Predictably, Gene suffered a head injury after falling in the chair from which he was unable to loosen himself during the routine. Still, Gene grudgingly helped his younger brother with his efforts, though he, like James Jr., disliked "small-time show biz."[31] Harriet insisted that Fred charge 3¢ admission for his neighborhood productions. However, she knew his talents were worth more, so she proceeded to book him at various venues in Pittsburgh. According to Fred, "corny comedy" was one of his specialties.[32] Gene's biographer Alvin Yudkoff asserted that Fred was Harriet's favorite son and the one among her five children she believed had the most potential as an entertainer.[33]

Unbeknownst to Harriet, Gene had stopped resenting his dance lessons. In truth, he wanted to outshine Fred when they performed together, but the younger boy invariably won more applause. Gene's boyhood friend Jules Steinberg recalled that Gene kept his dancing ambitions to himself. "We would discuss sports most of the time."[34] Not until years later did Gene confess that he hated to see dance lessons come to an end. "We [Gene and his siblings] loved the dancing," he said. "The younger a child is when exposed to dancing the better his or her chance is to respond instinctively to the music."[35]

2

A Depression-Era Kid

The period following World War I led to an explosion of creativity in show business that made the time ripe for new performers, the Kellys included. America's isolationism in the 1920s led artists to refine uniquely American music, dance, and theatrics. Despite the postwar rise of the Ku Klux Klan, much music of the era was inspired by new forms of jazz introduced by black musicians. Jazz, like its predecessor, ragtime, was fully accepted only once audiences heard it on Broadway. One of the first examples of a modern American musical to blend "hot" jazz with "sweet" romantic tunes was Florenz Ziegfeld Jr.'s *Sally* (1920). Ziegfeld's masterpiece used music *and* dance to further the plot and reflect the characters' feelings and intentions.

Aside from Ziegfeld's production, two of the biggest hits of the 1920s were *Lady, Be Good* (1924) and *Funny Face* (1927), both of which were typical of the decade's light, witty musical comedies. George and Ira Gershwin's scores distinguished the plays, as did the immaculate performances of Fred and Adele Astaire. Together, the Gershwins and the Astaires brought jazz fully into the mainstream. The new refinement found in jazz dance as exemplified by the Astaires led more and more parents to enroll their children in dancing schools.

The prosperity that defined the 1920s did not leave the Kellys unaffected; indeed, in 1924, they were able to move from Mellon Street to 7514 Kensington Street, approximately three miles south. The bachelor uncle and spinster aunt who had lived with the family on Mellon Street apparently found other lodgings, as the Kellys were now able to make ends meet without the aid of relatives. Aside from James's income, eight-year-old Fred often brought in anywhere from $10 to $50 for performing in amateur shows in and around Pittsburgh. Nevertheless, the house was heavily mortgaged.

Kensington was only a few miles east of the city center and mere yards from the opening of Frick Park near Homewood Cemetery. Gene and many of the neighborhood children enjoyed using the cemetery as a skating venue during the winter months. The Kensington home was aesthetically pleasing, with a large porch, two stories, and a third-story attic that Gene and Fred used as their room. For the rest of his life, Gene looked upon this period of his childhood with the most nostalgia.

One of the most vivid memories of Gene's childhood was seeing his beloved hometown team, the Pittsburgh Pirates, win four of the seven games in the 1925 World Series. "We were delirious," Gene declared. Of all sports, he held baseball in the greatest esteem. "I loved to play in the field, that's where I shone," he asserted. "I was a dazzler. I remember that all the other fellas wanted to get up to hit, but I loved better being in the field. Maybe a lot of that was ego, because any ball hit near me in the infield I could get."[1]

Another memory of Gene's adolescence stands out due to its impact on his development as both an athlete and a dancer. Like most teens, Gene idolized famous figures of the time, particularly those on the silver screen. On one frigid, overcast day in 1925, Gene decided to cut school and sneak to the local movie house. In an account he gave to *Parade* magazine in 1957, he explained that he went into the theater, angry over an argument with his mother. But he came out

> anxious to get home and say I was sorry. The picture was *The Mark of Zorro* starring Douglas Fairbanks, and in one scene Fairbanks said something I'll always remember—"When you are in the wrong admit it—when you are in the right, fight." I . . . have also often thought what a power for good movies can be, and I don't think it's exaggerating to say that had the movie I saw that day been a gangster picture or, let's say anything other than a Doug Fairbanks picture, my life might have taken a different course. For Doug Fairbanks was my ideal from that day on and his dashing athletic prowess was what really inspired me to become a dancer.[2]

The Mark of Zorro was a 1920 film, so the showing Gene saw was likely a re-release. However, Fairbanks remained active in films during Gene's formative years, starring in pictures such as *The Three Musketeers* (1921), *The Thief of Baghdad* (1924), and *The Black Pirate* (1926). Gene later named

Buster Keaton as another of his heroes. "A lot of his moves I certainly intuitively copied in doing certain numbers."[3] Because of his dark good looks, Gene was not as convincing a comedian as Keaton, though he did possess a talent for wit and mimicry that he expanded throughout his career.

As Gene was preparing to enter high school in the fall of 1926, he endeavored to become less like Buster Keaton and more like a junior Douglas Fairbanks where his athleticism and budding romanticism were concerned. For his freshman year, Gene attended Sacred Heart School. Located at 325 Emerson Street, the school was attached to the church in which Gene had been baptized. After only one term, he transferred to the public Peabody High School on North Highland Avenue. Peabody, though not a private school, was a stately, three-story brick structure whose front was graced with Ionic pillars. There, Gene was pleased to be the only Kelly boy in attendance. Finally, he would not have to compete with Fred for center stage. He began to pursue dancing in earnest, but not because he wanted to prove he was as talented as Fred. His driving force was, in one word: "girls." Gene elaborated: Dancing "gave me a chance to put my arm around their waists without getting my face slapped."[4]

Gene possessed a reverence for women from an early age. His regard for the opposite sex began with his strong love for Harriet, whom he referred to in later life as a saint, and his close bond with his sisters. Like many a youth, however, he was still unsure of himself with girls.

Gene's confidence grew with his success in theatrics and sports. He sealed his interest in dancing upon discovering that it helped him win substantial parts in school plays. Unlike his attitude toward St. Raphael productions and his brother's basement vaudevilles, Gene was eager to be a part of the world of show business at Peabody High School. In his junior year, he joined the Masque and Wig Society as well as the Assembly Squad. Gene and another dancer, Jimmy Brenner, performed physically challenging dance routines in the school auditorium designed to persuade other boys to join the school shows. Although he was involved in theater throughout his three-year tenure at Peabody, most of Gene's stage appearances took place in his senior year, at which time he joined the Senior Dramatics Society. Perhaps Gene's most memorable—if most embarrassing—high school theatrical experience was his portrayal of Bottom in *A Midsummer Night's Dream*. His pants fell down during the performance, sparking much laughter from the audience. Overall, however, Gene found acclaim in his stage endeavors.

At home, Harriet noted that Gene was particularly adept at playing charades, a game requiring a great deal of acting skill. Harriet acknowledged Gene's cleverness at showmanship, but she did not foster his dancing and theatrics in the way she did Fred's. She decided Gene would have a better future as a lawyer. Gene, loyal son that he was, did not refuse Harriet's plans. Such a career was not entirely unsuited to Gene's talents; a lawyer employs a certain amount of theatrics in convincing judge and jury to agree with him. Gene, though shy, lost inhibition when arguing about his convictions. His talent for persuasion was evidenced when he joined the debate team at Peabody as well as a debate society, the Toreadors. The group, composed of a dozen students of diverse backgrounds and opinions, met at the YMCA each week. "I was the only Catholic, the others were Protestants and Jews, but we could discuss the tenderest subjects and understand each other," Gene reflected in 1962. "We could even criticize each other—the criticisms leveled at me were usually that I was conceited. We all were. We were also deeply religious, atheistic, and agnostic by turns, and pretended we knew too much about sex to even discuss it!"[5]

Gene's involvement with the Toreadors began his lifelong interest in philosophy and politics. Harriet and James were greatly perturbed at one result of his broadening mind. He began to rebel against his strict Catholic upbringing. Instead of choosing "the funny papers" as his primary reading material, he would bring home tomes such as H. G. Welles's *Outline of History*, in which Welles criticized religious and political figures such as Alexander the Great, Mohammed, and Woodrow Wilson for their failures to unify humanity. Gene found the book especially compelling due to national events that occurred during his sixteenth year.

In 1928, progressive New York governor Al Smith became the first Catholic to run for president. He won the support of nearly every Catholic in America, including women who had heretofore neglected to utilize their right to vote. However, Smith's candidacy led to a surge of anti-Catholicism, especially in the South. Pittsburgh was not immune to such prejudice. Gene witnessed anti-Catholic cross burnings on the hillsides of his hometown. By Gene's senior year, he was again a devout Catholic, perhaps because of the intolerance he witnessed against the faith he had known all his life. He even went as far as to consider becoming a man of the cloth. In 1962, he recounted to the *TV Radio Mirror* his fondness for "the young parish priests who had such an influence on us when we were kids in Pittsburgh. Father Tynan for example—a handsome, tough, well-educated fellow, virile and energetic, who played third base like crazy and had a way with kids, tough or otherwise."[6] He discussed the idea of entering the church with a priest, "who advised him to take his time, probably seeing that the monastic life wasn't for Gene."[7]

Gene remained alternately agnostic and religious for the rest of his life, but no matter how his spirituality changed, he never disparaged others' belief systems. Still, he claimed that the greatest shock he received when he entered college was "not the birds and the bees or even the theory of evolution. . . . It was the discovery that some fellows could not believe in God and still be just as nice, if not nicer, than those who went to church."[8] This realization left Gene not an atheist but a "very ecumenical" Catholic. No matter how religious he was at a given time, Gene did not discount omens and superstitions. "When I was a boy I used to have troubled dreams. I dreamed one night about my dog and the next day he was dead. After all these years, I've never forgotten it," Gene told an interviewer in 1944.[9] In his later career, he always insisted on wearing his "lucky shirt" in at least one scene in each of his movies.

During Gene's time of religious exploration and crisis, he funneled much of his confusion, anger, and budding philosophy into his writing. Though he did not yet break the news to Harriet, who still favored a legal career for him, he considered majoring in journalism once he entered college. He gained experience as the associate editor for his high school newspaper, the *Citivan,* and also served as associate editor of the Peabody yearbook. As well as writing journalistic pieces, Gene wrote poetry. Many of his verses were published in the *Citivan,* revealing the shy, sensitive side to his dynamic and forceful nature. His poems often described working-class people and neighborhoods—in essence, the environment and people he knew.

Gene's reading material now included Yeats, his favorite poet. His choice is not surprising; Yeats, like Gene, was of Irish descent and politically minded. According to a reporter in 1943, Gene was "a poetry addict."[10]

One would not immediately assume that a poet would be a varsity letter winner on the gymnastics and football teams. But Gene had not neglected his first love, sports, during his years at Peabody. He may have ceased attending formal dance lessons, but his teachers and classmates recognized his superior ability in movement. He was a self-proclaimed "Mozart" in hockey, gymnastics, track, football, and baseball. Because of his relatively short stature (he did not reach his full height of five feet nine until his senior year in high school), he was deemed unfit for basketball. Yet he excelled at that sport as at all others. "He was in a furious rush to ... become a 130-pound, tough-as-wire high school athlete. He made his letter as a peewee half-back at Peabody High, and by the time he was fifteen, he was working out with a semipro ice-hockey team, the Pittsburgh Yellow Jackets," wrote a journalist for the *Saturday Evening Post* in 1950.[11]

While Gene worked at honing his athletic skills, Harriet still held high hopes that her sons would continue to perfect their dancing skills as well. Noting the downturn in James's phonograph sales, Harriet took an administrative job at Lou Bolton's Dance Studio on 5858 Forbes Street in the Squirrel Hill area of Pittsburgh. Bolton was no stranger to Harriet; Fred had been taking lessons at his studio ever since he outgrew the offerings at Blinsky's Dancing School. Fred was still demonstrating the most promise in the world of show business; in addition to performing in amateur nights, Fred danced every summer from the time he was thirteen to eighteen (1929–1934) on a showboat that toured the Mississippi and Ohio River ports from Pittsburgh to New Orleans. Though Bolton was not a dancer himself, his school offered lessons superior to those at Blinsky's. Bolton knew how to judge a good dancer and thus hired the crème de la crème of teachers. Yet the establishment was failing to turn a profit. Harriet initially received no salary for her work at Bolton's, but Fred earned free lessons in return for her work. "This was 1928, and there was no general Depression yet. Everything was going well," Fred explained. "People wanted to take dancing. When the arts do well, it means the country's doing well."[12]

Though the country was in an upbeat period, the Kellys were beginning to experience financial worries. The two eldest children were in college and Gene was about to matriculate. He would major in economics at Pennsylvania State University before proceeding to law school at the University of Pittsburgh. Gene graduated from Peabody with honors in spring 1929. A class questionnaire amusingly summarized the impression he left on his classmates: he won third place as wittiest and first prize for boy who thought he was wittiest. Most tellingly, he tied with two boys as best dancer and was "destined to be a great entertainer."[13] Gene's yearbook as well as all source material available about his youth list 1929 as his graduation date, indicating that he graduated a year early. No previous biographer has illuminated how this happened; it is possible he began school early or that he took a heavier course load than his classmates to graduate in 1929.

The semester Gene entered college, his family and the country at large suddenly and irrevocably changed. Gone was the ebullience that characterized the Jazz Age. On October 24, 1929, the stock market crashed. Gene may have been majoring in economics, but no amount of education on the subject could remedy the national financial crisis. Americans did not need another economist or lawyer. They needed "a great entertainer."

In 1931, historian Frederick Lewis Allen asserted that prosperity was more than an economic condition; it was a state of mind. Americans' "compulsion for idealism was gone and realism was in the ascendant." They were sickened by President Herbert Hoover's erroneous statement that the country had "passed the worst and would rapidly recover."[14] Hoover's pronouncement rang especially false for James Kelly. He lost his job with the Columbia Phonograph Company after the Crash. James attempted to work solely on commission, selling everything from hammers to hats, but each night he came home penniless. Gene remembered that his father's permanent unemployment left him so depressed that outwardly, he appeared to have had a stroke. Gene's first wife, Betsy Blair, explained her impression of James nearly ten years later. The Depression had weakened him, but not broken him. He was "old before his time, defeated. . . . But he was loving and gentle with wit in his blue eyes and the Irish gift of the gab. . . . He sat in his kitchen, clean shaven and well-dressed, with a constantly renewed pot of tea for most of the rest of his life."[15] But the tea came later—immediately after the Crash, James's drink of choice was alcohol, a habit that revolted his daughters and wife.

Gene later said that he was fully aware of the gravity of his family's situation only in retrospect because at the time he was so occupied at college. Since Pennsylvania State was roughly 130 miles from Kensington Street, it was no simple task for Gene to commute home. He could not have known that James was resorting to borrowing on his insurance to make the monthly mortgage payments. Gene, still freewheeling, had "joined a fraternity and spent so much money that I wish my father had kicked me."[16]

It was he who felt like doing the kicking when his fraternity refused admission to Eddie Malamud, one of his Jewish friends. Gene soon discovered that all fraternities were segregated. Pledges experienced discrimination from their "brothers" based on their social and financial status. Gene also found the entire system of initiation ceremonies disgusting. He promptly quit his fraternity and with Eddie and Johnnie Napoleon, a Protestant boy, banded together to fight against prejudice. They called themselves "rebel activists."[17] But they were before their time; their efforts ultimately bore no fruit and the fraternities continued as they always had. Gene claimed this experience did not affect his career, but it did deeply affect his outlook on life. If he could not help improve conditions on his college campus, he could at least help those closest to him. Learning of his family's plight, Gene turned his efforts to earning whatever money he could. "I dug ditches. Puddled concrete. Laid bricks. Jerked sodas. Worked in gas stations."[18] He also found a job with the Firestone Tire and Rubber Company, where he "learned to roll as many as eight tires at once."[19]

After only one year at Pennsylvania State, Gene transferred to the University of Pittsburgh. His two elder siblings then attended the university and the two younger would go on to graduate from there. Here, Gene was much closer to home and thus could help his family to a greater degree. "I could live at home and all I had to do was earn my tuition,"[20] Gene explained. The summer after his freshman year, Gene found an ideal opportunity to earn tuition for the more expensive University of Pittsburgh: counseling children at the YMCA's Camp Porter. Additionally, he was hired to stage weekly shows for the organization. He received $150 for his efforts. He saw himself in many of the reluctant boys at the camp who assumed dancing was for "sissies." Gene knew it would not be simple to show boys that dancing was a sport, too, but his manner of convincing them was ultimately successful. He won the younger boys over by shooting baskets with them and persuaded the older boys that learning to dance would win them girls. Soon, "news got around that this Kelly guy was terrific."[21]

Gene, discovering that he was a natural-born teacher, showed more interest in Fred and Harriet's work at Lou Bolton's Dance Studio. Somehow, the studio remained open in the economic crisis. Americans, it appeared, still had the enthusiasm to dance in spite of the national gloom. Indeed, before and immediately following the Crash, audiences could not get enough of the musical films released in swift succession with the advent of talking pictures. The first talking film to win Best Picture was in fact a musical; Metro-Goldwyn-Mayer's *The Broadway Melody*. The picture was not escapist—it contained enough realism and grit to be relatable to audiences. Yet its score, penned by future MGM producer Arthur Freed and his co-writer Nacio Herb Brown, was uplifting and allowed audiences to focus on romance rather than finance. The same year *The Broadway Melody* premiered, MGM released the *Hollywood Revue of 1929*, a movie most notable for introducing Freed and Brown's "Singin' in the Rain" to the American public. The tune was an optimistic melody that acted as encouragement to audiences during a challenging time in America's history.

As much as moviegoers needed the reassurance musicals offered them, they no longer felt like laughing "at clouds so dark above" as the 1920s rolled into the 1930s. In 1932, movie studios released fewer than fifteen musicals, compared to seventy in 1930. Broadway shows, too, reflected a downturn in conventional musicals. Composer Alan Jay Lerner wrote that "the legitimate theater became a theater of protest and musicals became brash and satiric."[22]

Gene's confidence was high even if the nation's was low—he had already gained a reputation among the young women at the University of Pittsburgh as the most entertaining boy and best dancer on campus. "Some of them thought I was bloody marvelous and pretty soon I began to believe them," Gene said with a laugh years later.[23] Not wishing to lose his reputation, he ensured that his talent did not stagnate. He began attending any show that passed through town. At Loew's Penn Theatre, he was particularly enthralled by the performance of a black hoofer who called himself Dancing Dotson as well as by that of Bill Robinson, another black entertainer. Gene and Fred went to the local Stanley Theatre and Nixon Theatre and wrote shorthand notes of routines they liked. If Gene was going to imitate anyone, he only wished to imitate the best.

Harriet encouraged Gene and Fred to create a routine they could perform at theaters or country clubs. Sometimes Gene performed with Fred; other times he danced with his elder sister Jay. Gene and Jay danced the "obligatory ballroom bit and then a kind of jazz ballet item" that Gene recalled as "pretty awful." Audience members often asked if they were brother and sister like the Astaires, but they replied: "No, we're a professional dance act touring the country."[24] The self-proclaimed professionals made as much as $150 a night. When Gene performed with Fred, he styled their act less in the ballroom and more in the vaudeville style. They staged one ill-fated routine on roller skates: though they landed on "their rear bumpers . . . they did some pretty astonishing back-flips and nip-ups," a journalist wrote in 1950.[25] Though vaudeville virtually died on the professional circuit during the Depression, theater managers kept it alive via amateur nights that they hoped would attract more people to movie show-ings following the live acts. If Fred ever felt unsure of his chances at win-ning an amateur contest, he would bring in Gene as his partner and they would invariably merit first prize. Gene and Fred's performances brought in up to $15 per engagement, much less than the $150 Gene earned with Jay, but the brothers welcomed any income.

Gene and Fred performed in every venue, from mob-owned night-clubs to clubs with flooded dressing-room floors. Gene dubbed both sub-standard locales "cloops," a combination of "club" and "chicken coop." At one particularly seedy cloop, "ringside drunks would snigger 'Hello, honey,'" to Gene and toss coins at his feet.[26] Gene stated that he felt like a prize cow on display. It humiliated him to stoop and retrieve coins, espe-cially as accusations of being "a fag" drifted to his ears. In 1990, Gene recalled: "You can do two things [when heckled]: shout back at them, which is undignified, and not particularly satisfying; or you can belt them, which isn't very dignified either, but very satisfying. . . . One night . . . I jumped off the stage and hit [a guy]. But I had to make a run for it, because the owner of the place and his brother took after me with a couple of base-ball bats."[27] After Gene suffered a broken finger as a result of punching an agent who demanded more than his share of commission, he realized he was losing as much money as he was earning due to medical bills.

The cloops were degrading, but nothing now could move Gene from his interest in dance. All he needed was a more appropriate venue and people who would appreciate his and his partners' efforts. Harriet was of the same mindset. Seeing the talent her two sons possessed, she realized it had been her foresight and determination that made them such promising entertainers. Harriet, always enterprising, was aware that Lou Bolton had an offshoot of his dancing school in Johnstown, Pennsylvania, sixty-five miles from Pittsburgh. She also intuited that Bolton was growing weary of the commute. Her brother Gus, who lived in Johnstown, asserted that the city needed a good dance school; if she were to take over Bolton's, she would likely find willing pupils. Harriet convinced Bolton to "put up the capital" for the enterprise and opened the new school (though it was still under Lou Bolton's banner) in the American Legion Hall on Main Street. Staffing the school posed no obstacle. Harriet decided Gene would be the school's primary teacher. Gene, looking at his resourceful, deceivingly diminutive mother, marveled: "She has more energy than any of us."[28] Gene seemed to have just as much energy; he managed to maintain his grades at college while teaching dance, devising new steps for his routines, and working odd jobs about town.

The boy who was supposed to be on the road to law school was drifting further and further away from anything college had to offer. "The more you do, the more you learn," Gene claimed, and he decided he could do more and learn more off campus.[29] Though he had no intention yet of dropping out, his primary focus at the university shifted to staging Cap and Gown shows rather than honing his skills at economics and law. Cap and Gown, an all-male organization, wrote and produced musical variety shows each year at the university. Gene began to see the Depression not as a time when there was no place for music and dance but rather as an era that needed a new style to reflect the changed mood of the nation. "When I was growing up, dance in movies was a means of expression for the wealthy," said Gene in 1994, his eyes still flashing with wry disdain at age eighty-one. "But I didn't want to wear rich people's clothes and become a victim of the shiny-floor syndrome. I wanted to dance like the man in the street, like the ones I met while working my way through college, pumping gas in Pittsburgh."[30]

Yet as Gene leapt from one activity to another, his path for the future remained uncertain. In a 1974 interview, a reflective Gene observed: "I've never had a plan in my whole life."[31]

3

Kelly Mania

In 1931, nineteen-year-old Gene Kelly already had more responsibility than many grown men. "It didn't take the Depression to make a man out of him [Gene], but it certainly rounded him out," a journalist later noted in 1945.[1]

On top of his full load of classes at the University of Pittsburgh, Gene was performing in clubs with his brother Fred nearly every night of the week and instructing students on weekends at Lou Bolton's Dance Studio. Despite moviegoers' ongoing apathy toward musicals, Gene was able to rally interest in dance. At both the Pittsburgh and Johnstown locations of Lou Bolton's studios (the latter run by Harriet), it was Gene who drew in clients. Parents wanted him to teach their children and children wanted him as their teacher. Gene put as much—if not more—effort into his work at the dance studios as he did into earning his bachelor's degree.

"My extra-curricular activities were curtailed . . . the only study group I was connected with in my college days was the French Club," Gene recalled. As was becoming his modus operandi, Gene sought to learn more by doing than by passively studying. Observing people from all different social worlds taught him more than any class in sociology. In the precious little time Gene had to relax, he snuck to a nearby speakeasy, Bakey's, with his friend Jules Steinberg. Steinberg remembered that Gene found people-watching at Bakey's more diverting than flirting with girls or seeing a show. By spending time there and engaging in conversation with the dominantly Italian clientele, he claimed to have learned the language more quickly than he could have at school. By the end of his college career, he could carry on conversations in Italian as well as Yiddish, French, and Latin.

Gene remained remarkably levelheaded during the relentless activity of his college years. Perhaps because he'd seen his father overindulge in drink, he never used excessive alcohol intake to decompress. However, Gene did not always exert the same control over his temper. The only instance in which Steinberg saw Gene get his "Irish up" was one night at Bakey's when two traveling salesmen began to disparage priests. He promptly gave them black eyes. He then left the bar and, as he did most nights, attended an early-morning Mass.

Gene's adoring pupils were not subject to his temper. They saw only his affable side, and it was not long before he became a sort of Pied Piper. Part of the key to Gene's success was that he allowed the students to choose what type of dance interested them. If they wished to learn the jitterbug, he would teach them the jitterbug. If they wished to learn a Viennese waltz, he would oblige them accordingly. "Plenty of times I was only one step ahead of my pupils; I'd go to a nightclub, watch the routines, pick up a couple and teach them the next day in class," Gene explained.[2]

Gene further utilized the routines he learned when staging the university's Cap and Gown shows. "He had a burning desire to put on better shows than . . . previously produced. . . . Gene made them [members of Cap and Gown] sweat," one journalist wrote.[3] The college's twenty-fourth annual show, entitled *What's Up?* premiered on April 20, 1931, at Pittsburgh's Nixon Theatre and ran for one week. Gene choreographed the production and appeared in two numbers. The show was a hit and won unanimous praise.

The leaders of the YMCA's Camp Porter asked Gene back in the summer of 1931 to again stage and write the organization's annual revue. He enlisted the aid of Fred for several numbers. The show, *High, Wide, and Handsome,* debuted at Conneaut High School on August 14, 1931, with Gene acting as emcee and Fred as a drummer and dancer. Gene seemed to have had as much fun acting in the show as his pupils. Gene performed "a challenge tap" with Fred and then appeared in two more numbers, both of which required Gene to dress in drag. Despite Gene's quickness to fight when accused of being effeminate, he did not have any qualms about appearing fey for theatrical, comic purposes. Gene was comfortable in his own skin and did not need to prove his masculinity.

The year 1931 continued to be a prolific one for Gene. In September, he found himself choreographing, starring in, and directing a revue for the Beth Shalom Synagogue in Squirrel Hill. The job had originally been offered to Lou Bolton but, as was his way, Bolton inexplicably disappeared from town before fulfilling his responsibilities. Harriet lost no time in suggesting Gene as his replacement. The revue was not to take place until spring of 1932, allowing Gene time to hone his students' skills.

Ruth Portnoy, the wife of the cantor, was the first to call Gene "Pied Piper." The affection his young pupils felt for their teacher was mutual. Gene often claimed that working with children was most fun because they danced purely from emotion rather than constricting their styles to cerebral theories. One student recalled that Gene taught her to do an Irish jig with her arm behind her back in order to hide the large cast around it. "He made me laugh, joking about how he was even more accident-prone than I was. . . . Although I was basically a klutz, he always made me feel I could truly dance," she said.[4]

Though Gene was much occupied with the business at Beth Shalom, he remained no less active at Lou Bolton's Dance Studios. By mid-1931, Harriet was disappointed that enrollment at the Johnston dance school had failed to increase. She and Gene faced competition from another studio in town run by what Gene called a "schmuck" who told parents that their children were "little geniuses" after only one lesson. The "schmuck" tried to discredit the Kellys by pointing out to potential clients that neither Gene nor his family were members of the Dancing Teachers Union and thus had no right to open a school. Gene, enraged, decided that he would "run the school so well that his opposition would be forced to close rather than compete with him."[5] Nonetheless, Gene did apply to become a member of the Chicago Association of Dancing Masters to enhance his credibility. The institution turned him down, but Gene was determined to be accepted the following year.

The Kellys' first method of rallying interest in their school was to spread news by word of mouth, as they did not have the means to pay for advertisements. Gene endeavored to gain a reputation in town that could not help but attract clients. He found that he would have to overcome the same obstacles he had faced in Pittsburgh as a child—bullies. "Johnstown seemed an unlikely place for such an enterprise [a dancing school]. Since it was a steel town, 'effete' was hardly the word for it. When its male citizens saw Gene coming, they placed hand on hip derisively and waved at him with simulated daintiness," a *Saturday Evening Post* journalist wrote in 1950.[6] Gene had little difficulty winning over the men of Johnstown after interacting with them in terms they understood: sports and fighting. Gene explained, "I couldn't get around to licking everybody in town, so I played baseball and basketball every chance I got, and that convinced them I was a real guy."[7] He also won "a bruising fist fight at the Y.M.C.A. pool [that made him] known in the local pubs."[8]

From June to December 1931, Gene cemented his high standing in Johnstown not through sport or fights but a series of exceptional revues starring the students of Lou Bolton's Dance Studio. Harriet often wrote the elegant descriptions in the revue programs, such as: "Dancing is the loftiest, the most moving, the most beautiful of the Arts, because it is no mere translation or abstraction from life: it is life itself."[9]

Dancing did not always seem distinguished to Gene, particularly when he had to play in cloops. However, all this changed when Gene and Fred, through a series of extraordinary circumstances, landed a gig with one of the most talented jazz musicians of the era. The job was at an all-black club in Altoona, Pennsylvania, where the legendary Cab Calloway and his Cotton Club Revue were scheduled to perform. Harriet was able to secure Fred and Gene an audition with Calloway by the simple expedient of failing to mention they weren't black. Calloway's representative had called Harriet, asking if she had any recommendations of a black brother act that could fill the place of the Nicholas Brothers. The brothers, a talented acrobatic dancing duo, had abruptly left Calloway after they were offered work in Hollywood.

"Well, I know of a great brother act, the Kelly Brothers, playing at the Nixon and Stanley Theatre," Harriet told Calloway's representative.

"Send them over!"

At the theater in Altoona, the club manager asked Fred and Gene with raised eyebrows: "*You're* the Kelly brothers?" Calloway strode over. In Fred's words, he "took one look at us, looked at his manager, and in a real Amos and Andy put-on said, 'Somebody done make a big mistake!' Did you know this was an all-black show?"

"Yes, but I thought you needed a dance team," Fred told him, handing Calloway's band their arrangements.

The brothers were surprised to receive a standing ovation from Calloway and his band after their performance. "That was really something. The guys we were nuts about were applauding us!" Fred recalled. As Fred and Gene left the theater, they saw two men changing the marquee to read: EXTRA-SPECIAL ADDED ATTRACTION—GENE AND FRED KELLY—THE KELLY BROTHERS. "What a time that was; just kids and having the time of our lives," Fred reflected in 1989.[10]

The Kellys proved to be so popular at the club that Calloway asked them to stay with the act when he played for three days in Johnstown. Throughout his career, Gene had a remarkable rapport with black dancers. Because of his intolerance for racial prejudice, he was a nonthreatening presence and truly appreciated what other cultures had to offer. Indeed, he later named black dancers John Bubbles and Bill Robinson (Bojangles) as two of his early influences. Bubbles is commonly credited as the father of "rhythm tap," a style of tap dance that, as opposed to Robinson's style, did not emphasize clean phrases and toe taps. Rather, it melded tap dancing with the emerging improvisatory style of jazz.

In 1958, Gene explained why tap dance was the ultimate "indigenous American type" that "exists here and only here. . . . It is like America itself. It's the real melting pot of the folk dances of several countries." Gene asserted that tap was even more definitive of America because it used jazz as its inspiration—a type of music born completely in the United States. Gene concluded that tap was especially appealing to the male dancer because "men, like small boys have always enjoyed making noise, stomping their feet to music; it makes them feel more a part of it."[11]

Aside from tap dancers like Robinson and Bubbles, Gene admired another distinctly American performer, Martha Graham. Graham, a fellow Pittsburgher, impressed Gene because she "danced to percussive sound and to poetry [rather than music]. The popular classic ballets were fairy tales. It was necessary to express something more and in stronger terms. That resulted in a revolution in dance." Though Graham's style impressed him, Gene was not interested in pursuing modern dance.

In complete contrast to the influences of modern American innovators, Gene took inspiration from California native Isadora Duncan (1877–1927), a mother of American modern dance; and Russian Vaslav Nijinsky, a contemporary balletic performer. Gene was struck by Duncan's incorporation of fantasy and spontaneity in her dance as well as her dedication to teaching young people her philosophy. Nijinsky epitomized Gene's thesis that dance was an athletic pursuit. Known for his gravity-defying leaps, he was also a talented choreographer. For the rest of his life, Gene spoke reverentially of the Russian view of dance as a virile form of expression for men.

No matter how much he took from other cultures, Gene could not forget where his evolving dance style first found its roots: Ireland. In 1990, Gene told a journalist for *Irish America* magazine: "The Irish really dominated the popular dance in twentieth century America. . . . [Irish

Americans] blended the tap dancing of the Irish—as I call it—with the syncopation of the music of the blacks and created a whole new form of tap dancing."[12]

The mélange of different dance styles and music from other cultures not only helped Gene's style evolve but widened his appeal to the diverse clientele in Pittsburgh. Indeed, a sort of "Kelly mania" overtook Squirrel Hill. Parents of children at Beth Shalom were shocked when their sons and daughters begged to be sent to dancing school with "that handsome Irish fella."[13] Interest grew stronger after Beth Shalom's long-anticipated *Revue of Revues* opened on April 15, 1932. The show was created on virtually no budget; the parents of the more than two hundred students made most of the costumes, and Harriet provided scenery and props from odds and ends gleaned from the Kelly attic or bargain stores. For the show's musical accompaniment, Gene assembled a band from the local high school. The show's program gave advance rave reviews for Gene's contributions: "His work with the children speaks for itself. He has presented clearly and thoroughly every type of dancing in a manner that cannot be surpassed."[14] The *Revue of Revues* earned an impressive $1,100, more than enough to allow the synagogue to retain the services of their rabbi. Those at Beth Shalom were so delighted with the outcome that they asked Gene to stage a show each summer for the next seven years.

With Gene in such good graces at the synagogue, he gained permission from the caretaker to offer one-on-one private lessons in the establishment's basement. After he had collected a sizable number of students, he transferred his lessons to the ballroom of the Pittsburgh Hotel. However, the marble dance floor was "murder" on the feet, so he continued to search for an ideal spot in which to teach his private students. In the meantime, the Kellys fell into a regular weekend routine: the family left Pittsburgh on Friday (Gene hired a chauffeur for $2 a week so the family could rest during the commute), spent the night at a boardinghouse in Johnstown operated by Harriet's friends, and began classes on Saturday morning. The classes went until ten at night, at which point the family climbed back into their Chevrolet and returned to Pittsburgh in time for Mass and Sunday classes at Beth Shalom.[15]

During the time Gene was working at Beth Shalom, he found a new location for the dance studio in Johnstown reflective of his and his family's success. The venue, located in a two-story building on Vine Street, offered a much larger space than the third-floor room in the American Legion

Hall.[16] Optimistic that enrollment would rise, the Kellys planned an elaborate gala opening. On the day of the party, all the Kellys, even James, assembled proudly in their new studio, representative of "years of struggle, hard work, and an unfaltering belief in their abilities." A table covered with plates of cookies, bottles of soda, and bowls of candy gave the room even more appeal. The Kellys waited and waited for clients to come through the door. An hour passed. Finally, a pair of twins who had been with the school since its beginnings came inside. They were two of the students whose tuition Harriet "carried." The girls looked back and forth in confusion at the empty hall and the listless Kellys, wondering if they had the wrong date. Harriet, in an uncharacteristic show of vulnerability, burst into tears. James murmured: "We went too far, too fast."[17]

Gene, unfazed, began to arrange a publicity campaign to attract clients. He went to all the newspapers and radio stations in town and offered the owners' children free lessons if he could place advertisements in their periodicals or on their programs. He next engaged high school students to place flyers in every Johnstown mailbox announcing the upcoming presentation of a children's musical show he claimed was as high quality as anything on the renowned vaudeville circuit of theaters owned by B. F. Keith. He called the revue *Gene Kelly's Kiddies' Vodvil* and also renamed the new Johnstown studio the Gene Kelly School of Dance. If nothing else, he hoped his name would entice his old pupils to come back. The Herculean efforts Gene put into building interest in his school made him feel, as he put it, as if he had celebrated his own bar mitzvah.[18] Before, he felt he had merely been a boy helping his mother. Now, at twenty years old, he was a man ready to move from adolescence into adulthood.

Within two weeks, it was clear that "Kelly mania" was as alive in Johnstown as in Pittsburgh. The bulk of Gene's former students returned to his school plus a plethora of new ones. Gene observed that an inordinate number of the newcomers seemed to be attractive females. He claimed that Johnstown boasted an extraordinary number of young women who could "dance like devils. Even at thirteen or fourteen, they were knockouts and certainly the best advertisements of the school we ever had."[19] One such student was twelve-year-old Jeanne Coyne, a "lithe, exotically attractive" brunette whose crush on her teacher developed into a secret love that she carried with her for over two decades. "I remember the first time I saw him," Jeanne later recounted.

My heart, which had been thumping at the prospect of meeting the maestro himself, slid back into normal as the young man with the broad smile approached us.

"You have good legs for a dancer," he said. "You'll have a lot of fun here."

It *was* fun, too, for Gene had a way with youngsters.[20]

Gene, though he was constantly surrounded by beautiful girls, never became unprofessional with them. After witnessing one too many managers' "casting couch maneuvers" at cloops, he sought to be the opposite of such men. Instead, he cultivated an attitude of "old-fashioned gallantry" like that of his hero, Douglas Fairbanks.[21]

As much as Gene was able to put his students at ease, his pupils never forgot he was in charge. "The teacher was the absolute King. When you were teaching, you were not interrupted. A class was one hour, and you danced. You did not sit down," Fred Kelly explained.[22] Gene's insistence on a professional work ethic and environment in his classes extended to his arrangements for the school's revues. He made them virtual imitations of legitimate theatricals and organized the Johnstown Youth Orchestra to provide music for the shows, which gave students a "taste of the big time and lent stature to his productions."[23] Though Gene was the dominant figure in arranging all events at the school, he stated, "It wouldn't have amounted to a damn if it hadn't been for Harry [Harriet]. She really ran it."[24]

By this time, the Kellys had acquired the Pittsburgh location in addition to the Johnstown school from Lou Bolton. Thanks to Harriet's business acumen and Gene's dynamism, both studios were enjoying brisk business. Business was so brisk, in fact, that James, unemployed for three years, was now put to work as the schools' accountant. To the family's relief, the job replaced alcohol as his pastime.[25] At Gene's studio, female students wore loose, button-up blouses and velvet trunks with three pearl buttons on each side. The mothers embroidered "K" on the blouse as a proud emblem that their girls attended the Kelly studio. Male students simply wore street clothes for uniforms. "Gene wanted to have a masculine image," Fred stated.[26]

Almost the entire Kelly family became a part of the studio after Gene employed siblings Louise and Fred as teachers. "My job was to take any of the kids who had missed a lesson and teach them the new material. I think we were the only dance studio in the world that did this," Fred asserted. Aside from Gene, Louise proved to be the most indispensable member of the studio. "It was called the Gene Kelly Studio, but Louise was really the architect," Jay commented of her younger sister. Louise taught ballet and beginning dance while Gene instructed advanced students. "Louise was the closest to Gene of all the siblings," Jay continued. "He just adored her. There was an extreme warmth about Louise." Even as Gene's skill increasingly developed, he depended on his sister's criticism. "She would call out when he had missed the mark. She would sit there and very, very patiently go through and watch him rehearse," Jay explained.[27]

While Louise acted as Gene's critic, Fred was akin to his understudy. When either of the brothers was engaged for gigs, they often stepped in for one another if the other found a better job. "We were never jealous of each other. . . . I've always been very proud of him, and he of me," Fred stated.[28]

Jay and James Jr. did not pursue careers at the dance studio or any other area of show business; James became an aeronautical engineer and Jay a schoolteacher. Despite the help of his two younger siblings, Gene needed more aides for the studio. He spent most of his spare time poring over theater magazines, viewing local acts, and even traveling hundreds of miles to inspect a potential teacher.

The Gene Kelly School of Dance presented its first revue in February 1932 at the State Theatre in Johnstown. When Gene and his students played for benefits or at out-of-town venues, he charged $35 for his services. After expenses, this left him a $20 profit—a small fortune in the bleakest year of the Depression. One of the dominant reasons Gene's productions found such success was because, just as he tailored dance to his pupils' tastes, he customized his shows to the audiences that would see them. He and his students played in primarily working-class towns built on the steel industry. Gene later stated that "subtlety was a dirty word" to many of these theatergoers. He became familiar with his potential audience members via Bakey's speakeasy, where he shared beers with workers in the production lines. At the same time Gene immersed himself in learning about the work and mindset of blue-collar laborers, he also took on the lofty pursuit of learning French. He proclaimed that he would travel to France someday and get a taste of what he imagined was the most innovative dance in the world.[29]

In tailoring shows to his working-class audiences, however, Gene omitted French-inspired dance. One such show, a less than subtle revue titled *Hits and Bits of 1932,* opened in Lilly, Pennsylvania, for the benefit of volunteer firemen. Initially, the revue seemed like a flop—no seats sold at the theater because, according to Gene, the "firemen were smashed out of their minds at the local bar." Gene devised a solution. He borrowed a fire engine, picked the most attractive girls in the show, and had them stand on the truck while he "rang bells like hell." Through a megaphone, he yelled that if patrons came to the Liberty Theatre they would see "the best girlie show of their lives." "Which," Gene later admitted, "wasn't true, of course." However, the firemen did not know this, and by eleven o'clock, seats at the Liberty Theatre had sold out. Gene feared that the house would empty when the audience discovered there was no girlie show. Still, the production did include a degree of suggestive humor. One skit had a girl walk across the stage, saying to Fred: "Why does a chicken cross the road?" "To get to the other side, everyone knows that," Fred replied. "Wrong," the girl retorted. "To get some ice cream." "Chickens don't eat ice cream!" Fred declared. The girl then put her finger in her mouth and said provocatively: "This chicken does." Years afterward, Gene said: "Believe it or not, I actually wrote that."[30]

The audience met *Hits and Bits* with enthusiasm; nonetheless, Gene and Fred realized that its weakest points were Fred's magic act and Gene's comedy. They dropped both from future productions. Dancing was what made Gene's shows exceptional; consequently, that became his sole focus. The manager of a theater in nearby Ebensburg was so impressed with the dancing in the revue that he asked Gene to open another branch of his school in town. Gene relished the idea and began to envision a chain of Gene Kelly Schools of Dance from coast to coast. He could not help but think of how Harriet would delight in the financial windfall such an enterprise might bring. Gene and his mother immediately rented a hall in Ebensburg and the best of the city's dancing talents enrolled. However, two months later, only three students remained. Gene and Harriet were left scratching their heads. Gene closed the studio, but the failure did not leave him discouraged. The Pittsburgh location was "finally beginning to take off" and rival Johnstown in enrollment and profits.[31]

In the early summer of 1932, Gene, tireless and soon to be twenty, returned to the Pittsburgh YMCA and produced a revue, *Waiting for the Ships That Never Come In.* He also staged another Cap and Gown show, *Silver Domino.* In addition to all his other productions, Gene added a second annual revue to the *Kiddies' Vodvil* series titled *Johnstown on Parade.*

In June, the show opened at the Nemo Theatre in downtown Pittsburgh. A local journalist noted the remarkable professionalism of all 150 children in the show. The first edition of *Johnstown on Parade* won such accolades that Gene raised his fee from $35 to $75.

His confidence was higher than it had ever been thus far in his young life. He even began to think, "I'm better than that" as he took notes on professional acts. Now, when Gene frequented Bakey's speakeasy with Jules Steinberg, he was less apt to engage in fistfights and more apt to launch into impromptu pirouettes. Steinberg recalled numerous occasions when, walking out of the establishment, Gene would leap, tapping into the street, much to the confusion of late-night pedestrians and the ire of drivers. Despite Gene's sometimes flamboyant behavior and his nonexistent love life, his masculinity was now unquestioned. Steinberg stated, "There was something very private and secretive about Gene. He didn't have many close friends—only acquaintances."[32]

Additionally, Gene was quite selective about the type of woman to whom he was attracted. In 1944, when columnist Helen Hover asked him what qualities he most admired in a female, he replied: "Sweetness and reticence, coupled with brains." The trait he claimed he found most obnoxious in a girl was "a general air of loudness. That is, women who try to talk loud, dress loud or try to monopolize the attentions of everyone in the room by their conduct." He disliked overdone lipstick and elaborate hairdos as well. Gene concluded that what he most hoped to find was a woman who was "a good sport."[33] He knew exactly the type of girl he wanted and he was willing to wait for her, so he did not engage in superfluous relationships he knew would have no future.

In the later summer of 1932, work remained of utmost importance in Gene's life. The Gene Kelly School of Dance went into recess, but he did not take time off. He and Fred drove the Chevrolet to Chicago where preparations were being made for the World's Fair, set to open in May 1933. The fair's opening was months away, but people flocked to the fairgrounds anyway to gawk at the construction. Already, producers and entertainers, Fred and Gene included, were giving audiences a preview of what was to come. The fair, titled A Century of Progress, was designed to give Americans hope for the nation's future. When not at the fair, Gene and Fred tap-danced in six to ten shows a day at local cloops. Gene found he still had much to learn about pleasing an audience; his dancing had become so advanced in two short years that it was too highbrow for much of the clientele. They wanted a straight hoofer to come out, tell them dirty jokes, and sing an equally dirty song. Gene took it as a personal affront when the audience laughed, talked over, or simply ignored him as he performed.

Though Gene tried to mold his dances to audiences' preferences, there was only so far he was willing to stoop. He was not about to halt the evolution of his skill to cater to base tastes. He returned home to Pittsburgh with plans to travel to Chicago the following summer and take lessons there from great dance masters. In the 1930s, Chicago was the dance hub of America, primarily due to a cluster of Russian refugees who had set up several academies in the city. Gene reapplied at the prestigious Chicago Association of Dance Masters and this time was accepted. (Coincidentally, the association was formed in the month and year of Gene's birth: August 1912.) His teachers there included Serge Diaghilev of the Bolshoi and Ballet Russes, Alexander Kotchetovsky, and Angel Cansino, the uncle of Rita Hayworth, who specialized in Spanish dance. Gene Kelly held the distinction of being the youngest member ever accepted by the association.

Over the course of 1933, business at the Gene Kelly Schools of Dance continued to flourish. The Depression was still in full swing, but Americans' desire to dance and watch others dance became unquenchable. After a three-year slump, the Hollywood movie musical returned, reinvented and full of fresh, exciting talents both onscreen and behind the scenes. On March 11, 1933, Darryl Zanuck of Warner Bros. released a new type of musical that was both stylistically innovative and tailored to Depression-era audiences. The film was *42nd Street*. Starring young hoofers and singers Dick Powell and Ruby Keeler, *42nd Street* appealed to the masses due to its relatable depiction of men and women absorbed in working their way out of poverty. What truly set *42nd Street* apart, however, was its cinematography. The musical numbers—and the camera—were in constant movement, unlike the stagnant production numbers of early musicals.

The man responsible for freeing film from the confines of a stage was thirty-eight-year-old dance director Busby Berkeley. According to Berkeley's biographer Jeffrey Spivak, "Dance was an end to itself in Berkeley's films. He didn't choreograph . . . the 'purpose' of a Berkeley number was to escape reality with an imaginative tableau with canted angles."[34] Berkeley's numbers, because of their focus on interesting formations and angles, actually did not include a great deal of dancing in them. The title number, with its vivid depictions of "naughty, gaudy, bawdy, sporty" 42nd Street, was a realistic rendering of blue-collar life in the big city.

Musicals' shift toward stories about working people rather than socialites was a reaction both to the Depression and to the inauguration of America's new president from the Democratic Party: Franklin D. Roosevelt. Roosevelt did not whitewash the fact that the nation was still far from recovery. He stated in his inaugural speech on March 4, 1933, that "only a foolish optimist can deny the dark realities of the moment" but stressed the importance of unity if America hoped to rise from the economic crisis.[35] Roosevelt's plans for revitalization included federal work programs, including the Works Progress Administration, which employed artists, actors, and musicians. Partly due to Roosevelt's work programs, the entertainment industry survived and actually experienced a renaissance during the Depression. Gene, as a liberal, was an adamant supporter of the new president and for the next decade proudly called himself a "Roosevelt Democrat." He believed in Roosevelt's philosophy that giving people meaningful work rather than handouts was the best way to end the Depression.

Gene continued to work, both at school and at his studios. Though an instrumental part of his family's dance enterprises, Gene did not know how much revenue the studios were actually bringing in. Like Gene, Harriet was secretive, and she maintained a "none of your business" attitude about the financial side of the schools. She still doled out allowances to Gene, Fred, and Louise. Still, Gene could deduce that the studios were reaping more income than the Kelly family had ever enjoyed before. For the first time in his memory, Harriet hired a housekeeper.

The bulk of Gene's allowance went to tuition; he was now nearing the end of his senior year at the University of Pittsburgh. In April 1933, he staged and appeared in another Cap and Gown show. Off campus, he put together a new production with his Johnstown pupils. The revue included a rendition of "Young and Healthy" from *42nd Street*. Gene also won a small role in *On with the Show*, a revue at Pittsburgh's Florence Fisher Parry Theatre. A local reviewer wrote: "Last night's star was a young dancer, Eugene Kelly. . . . Unfortunately we saw no more of him, and that was a pity, for the moment he sprang upon the stage it was electrified. Now I hope I have his name right. His smile was dazzling and his body was one with the music, quite free of the shackles of self-consciousness."[36]

The reviewer would have been disappointed to learn that Gene still had law in mind for his career. After his graduation with a degree in economics, he was accepted into the University of Pittsburgh Law School. He met the news of his acceptance not with happiness but with doubt. He had made a name for himself as a dancer and knew his schools were reaping more money than he could ever hope to make in the near future in another endeavor. His economics degree suddenly seemed irrelevant, but Gene did not regret the years he spent earning it. Reflecting on his time in college, Gene stated: "It not only made me more of a person, but it aided me in everything I did as a creative artist." He quipped that his economics degree, if nothing else, would allow him "to discuss intelligently certain things with the IRS."[37] Gene held true to his belief that real-world experiences were more valuable than mere study. "People can't give you education. You can't get knowledge or learning by having it stuffed down your throat. You have to want to know things."[38]

At age twenty-one, Gene thirsted for more knowledge—about dance, that is. Before his acceptance to law school, he had been toying with the idea of pursuing a career as a choreographer or a serious ballet dancer. His imminent return to Chicago to study with the dance masters only furthered his conviction that law would not be part of his life. Gene claimed the creation of his own dance studio in the midst of the Depression had made him a man. If he was truly to become his own man, he had to decide what he wished to do, even if it clashed with his mother's long-held vision for his future.

4

"It wasn't elegant, but it's me"

"Dedicated to the elevation of the art of dancing and the promotion of the welfare of the profession." So read the mission statement of the Chicago Association of Dance Masters upon its founding in 1912. The association also sought to give its members "a guide to the fundamentals and correct methods of teaching dance . . . [and to] promote good will and mutual help among its members."[1]

Such a description could have well applied to the Gene Kelly School of Dance or, later, to the Arthur Freed Unit at MGM. Thus, Gene's studying in Chicago in the summer of 1933 was the first step on a transformative path that directed the rest of his life. "I got some of my best dance training in Chicago," Gene stated in 1970.[2] "I . . . found a good teacher, and in my spare time read every book on the ballet that they had in the Chicago Public Library. Yeah, I even read the ones that were in French, and that was strictly labor because my French is just school French."[3]

Gene had to pack a semester's worth of reading into a very limited time frame. The association convened for only two weeks each summer and allowed members to take as many classes as they wished for a few dollars. Beginning in 1933 and continuing throughout the 1930s, Gene attended every summer's meeting. To earn money for food and board, he performed many gigs at local clubs, which were inundated with customers now that the Chicago World's Fair was in full swing.

Gene, though his physical build did not mesh with the ideal for ballet, spent the bulk of his first year's two weeks perfecting his balletic skill. One of his favorite ballet teachers at the association was Berenice Holmes, who had danced with Adolph Bolm's companies in the United States. Bolm, a former member of Sergei Diaghilev's Ballets Russes, "epitomized the kind of virile Russian male ballet dancer Diaghilev had unleashed upon Paris in 1909," wrote journalist Anna Kisselgoff in 1985. "Berenice Holmes was really remarkable," Gene recalled. "She could do double *tours en l'air* better than a man."[4] Gene also remembered her as a kindly and patient teacher— and found the blond, graceful, and intelligent twenty-eight-year-old woman very attractive.

Gene had a fine rapport with the rest of his teachers, though some were less innovative than others. One instructor, an eighty-year-old man known simply as Senor Gambelli, drilled all of his pupils solely in the Cecchetti Method. This method, developed in the early nineteenth century, held that students could best learn to dance by studying and absorbing the fundamental principles in an effort to become independent rather than imitative of their teacher's movements. Aside from Gambelli, Russian ballet master Alexander Kotchetovsky (a colleague of Nijinsky) further helped Gene refine his balletic talent. "A lot of them [my teachers] . . . were real down-to-earth, even tough guys," Gene explained. "We used to go out and drink together in Chicago and have a ball. They were terrific men, and at the same time their whole life was the dance."[5]

Aside from ballet, Gene learned another form of movement new to him: Spanish dance. His instructor was Angel Cansino, uncle of future film star Rita Hayworth. Cansino taught ballroom dance as well as flamenco. As a tap dancer, the rhythm and footwork necessary for Spanish dancing came easily to Gene. Cansino was so pleased with Gene's performance that he gave the young man lessons for free. Gene learned two more European dances as well while studying in Chicago: the Rumanian chain dance and Polish mazurka. As adept as Gene became in European folk dances, however, he still found himself more absorbed in the world of ballet.

After his two weeks of study in Chicago were over, he vacationed in a cabin on Lake Erie. The locale, which reminded him of his idyllic lakeside summers as a boy, was a perfect, distraction-free environment in which to reevaluate his future. He decided he would attend law school in the fall but still devote all his spare time to honing his dance skills at the Kelly dance studios. By this time, Gene had found a trustworthy staff of instructors to take over his classes on weekdays. In Harriet's view, the most important thing for him to do now was to earn his law degree in order to be a part of a reliable and "proper profession."[6]

Gene purchased the pricey textbooks for his first semester and spent almost two months pretending to be enthusiastic over lectures on corporate and mercantile law and torts. However, when his professor informed the class that they'd be using their books on torts for the rest of their lives, Gene snapped out of the half-anesthetized state into which he tended to fall during law classes. He could not, in any capacity, imagine spending the remainder of his life trapped with dense books of legal jargon. With his mind firmly settled on dance as his chosen profession, Gene sold his textbooks at a loss. Harriet was crushed that Gene quit law school; no reports exist that James Kelly disapproved. He remained, for the most part, a passive presence in the Kelly family after the Crash of 1929. Harriet granted Gene her approval only on the condition that he become the best dancer and teacher in the country. Gene felt more than prepared for the challenge. In 1958, Gene reflected on the motivation behind his decision: "What drives a man to take dancing as a profession? The same things that drive painters, sculptors—he wants to express himself and he has a basic love of movement."[7]

Gene still took no part in the business end of the family dance schools. Gene, who so easily mastered almost every other subject, admitted that when it came to law and business dealings he was "lousy." In an interview with Edward R. Murrow in 1958, he elaborated: "I'm pretty much bored with business. . . . I guess I am at the creative end of doing just about anything I can get my hands on."[8] All he had to do was what he loved—dance, teach, and choreograph. Gene's future costar Frank Sinatra later voiced his opinion about Gene as a teacher. His words reflected the feelings of nearly all those Gene taught. "He was a born teacher," Frank said. "I felt really comfortable working for him and enjoyed his company in spite of his manic insistence on hard work."[9]

Gene endeavored to infuse his schools' annual revues with more inspired movement than ever before. Additional opportunity to flex his teaching/choreographing skills came his way when the University of Pittsburgh asked Gene back to stage the yearly Cap and Gown show. When not otherwise occupied, Gene spent an hour each day after classes rehearsing the ballet steps he had learned in Chicago. He had come to see it as a form of self-expression that nonetheless had a universality about it. Gene held that ballet "leaps over boundaries of language and politics; it is a language that can be understood by anyone, anywhere."[10]

Gene rarely needed sleep at this point in his life, nor did he crave it. Even if he had wished for it, rest would have eluded him. He was far too excited about an upcoming performance the Ballet Russes de Monte Carlo was to give in Pittsburgh. Gene attended the recital dressed in unusually formal attire for him. Garbed in a smoking jacket, polished black shoes, and slacks, he looked as dapper as John Barrymore. After the performance, Gene went backstage to speak to David Lichine, the company's lead dancer. "Is there any chance I could give you an audition tomorrow morning?" Gene asked. Lichine looked him over with much scrutiny. "I cannot tell if you have the build of a dancer under all those clothes," he commented.[11] He advised Gene to come the following morning wearing a simple outfit.

Gene arrived the next day in his customary clothes of a tight T-shirt, khakis, and moccasins. Lichine was not present, but the more genial company ballet master was there to evaluate Gene's skill. "I could use you in the male ensemble once we go to Chicago in two weeks," the master informed Gene. Gene, overwhelmed, thanked him and returned home to discuss the offer with Harriet. If he joined the ballet, he would only be earning, in his words, "two dollars a week and a donut."[12] He earned more playing at cloops. Like many young people, he was restless and forever changing the definition of his goals and tastes. He decided he did not wish to be tied to one form of dance for the rest of his professional life. Additionally, he recognized that the marriage of tap and modern dance he was striving to perfect was unique; his skill in ballet, on the other hand, was not. The Chicago Association of Dancing Masters recognized where his expertise lay and consequently asked him to teach his style of tap dancing to students during one of its annual summer workshops.

Gene now made it his primary aim to develop his own brand of modern movement. He could not envision "doing 'Swan Lake' every night."[13] He "wanted to dance to the music of Cole Porter, Rogers and Hart, Irving Berlin and others. . . . I set out to find what I then called 'American Dance.'"[14]

Gene had already integrated elements of modern dance into tap, incorporating an emphasis on masculine strength and jazz-inspired free movement; now, with his balletic skill, he saw no reason why tap and ballet could not be blended in some capacity. Gene saw that this was possible, for one popular tap dancer was already integrating the grace of ballet into his movements. "The only dancer in the movies at that time with any success was Fred Astaire. . . . He did very small, elegant steps in a top hat, white tie and tails," Gene stated.[15]

Gene knew of Astaire from his fame on Broadway in, most notably, Gershwin shows. But Gene had not seen him dance until 1933 when

Astaire appeared in his breakthrough film, RKO's *Flying Down to Rio*. His dance partner in the picture was a bright young talent named Ginger Rogers. Like Astaire, Rogers had also made her name on Broadway through a Gershwin production, *Girl Crazy* (1930). Astaire and Rogers's number, "The Carioca," a new type of ballroom dance with a South American flair, invented for the film, electrified the nation. The most distinct part of the carioca was that the partners' foreheads had to touch throughout the entire dance. What further prompted movie audiences to applaud after Astaire and Rogers performed in the movie was their "red-hot" chemistry. The duo starred together in nine pictures through 1939.

As well as performing innovative dances, Astaire and Rogers gave purpose to dance itself in their films. Astaire demanded that all his song and dance routines be used to move the plot along. In contrast, Busby Berkeley (who directed nearly all of the other most notable musicals of the early 1930s) created numbers filled with aerial shots, quick takes, and close-ups that, when put together, had nothing to do with the plot of the film. Though Astaire and Rogers's romantic musical comedies were more sophisticated in fluidity, critics viewed them as lightweight because they, unlike many of Berkeley's films, failed to make allusions to societal woes of the time. But as film studies professor Dr. Philip DiMare has explained, "Singing [in most musicals] is a joyous thing, not a political thing."[16]

Gene found Fred Astaire's screen work inspirational, particularly the solo numbers reflective of his character's emotional dilemmas included in each of his films. Gene also admired that Astaire, like himself, was a choreographer as well as a performer. In his memoir, Astaire wrote: "When working on my own choreography, I am not always receptive to outside suggestions or opinions. I believe that if you have something in mind in the way of creation . . . you can have damaging results if you go around asking for opinions."[17] Despite arguments to do otherwise, Astaire insisted that his dance routines be shot with a mostly stationary camera that kept him and/or his partner in full view at all times.

Gene and Astaire had similarities as dancers, but Astaire lacked the athletic prowess Gene saw as vital to American expression. "I was too big physically for that [Astaire's] kind of dancing, and I looked better in a sweatshirt and loafers anyway. It wasn't elegant, but it was me," Gene noted.[18] According to writer Anna Kisselgoff, "Astaire came from the era of ballroom teams and was a class act. Kelly saw himself as a soloist and never identified with a steady partner."[19]

Another male dancer in film in 1933 was, like Gene, muscular and more athletic than Fred Astaire. He paralleled Gene in a number of ways. His name was James Cagney. Cagney, the son of an Irish bartender raised in the slums of Manhattan, started tap-dancing as a boy. He was also a formidable boxer. By the mid-1920s, Cagney was a successful vaudevillian and had choreographed a few of his own revues. Additionally, he opened his own professional dancing school. Despite his musical talent, in his earliest screen roles, Cagney was typed not as a dancer but as a street tough. In 1933, he turned musical man in Busby Berkeley's *Footlight Parade*. He brought the same brazen charm to his dancing style that he lent to his portrayals of gangsters. Cagney and Gene, unlike Fred Astaire, represented the working class and gave the impression that they had to fight for everything they got.

Gene, intently watching what these two men were accomplishing, hoped to meld Astaire's polish with Cagney's bravura. One thing he knew for certain: he favored basic time steps and Maxie Ford tap steps and was in his element when he was at his simplest, unhampered by partners, sets, costumes, or heavy concepts—when he could just create something himself.[20]

From 1933 to 1938, Gene proved to be a master of all trades, whether teaching, acting, dancing, choreographing, or learning. In the summer of 1934, he returned to Chicago to study with the dance masters and again perform at the World's Fair. The fair had been such a success the year before that President Franklin Roosevelt requested it be brought back. Several promising performers aside from Gene performed at the event, including twelve-year-old Judy Garland and nine-year-old Donald O'Connor.

Back in Pittsburgh, Gene's annual productions *Johnstown on Parade* and the *Kiddie Revue* (formerly called *Kiddies' Vodvil*) remained major attractions. Audiences increasingly demanded that Gene not only choreograph but appear in his shows. Thus, he found ample opportunities to create dances solely for himself in a number of his revues. His equal talent as a director and a performer allowed his students to see him as both an authority figure and a trouper. He was as hard a taskmaster as ever, but he put as much pressure on himself as he did on those he taught. Commenting on a spring 1935 Cap and Gown show, *In the Soup*, one journalist said of a typical Gene Kelly rehearsal: "Rehearsals usually last about two hours and give a vivid picturization of a forty-man track meet, every man for himself."[21]

When *In the Soup* premiered, the students evidently bore no grudges against Gene for putting them through endless rehearsals. After the final curtain, the cast carried him on their shoulders, cheering.

In his hometown as well as Johnstown, Gene had become well known as a "sort of an act doctor." He claimed that established players "would call on me to spruce up their dancing, and occasionally, I would get as much as a hundred dollars to devise a new routine."[22] After watching them perform, Gene would silently rise and "present a version of the 'disaster' he had just seen."[23] He would exaggerate the dance moves that went wrong, even to the point of burlesquing them. The entertainers would bristle and prepare to leave, but then Gene would give them his winning smile and begin encouraging them with supportive suggestions and ideas for improving their acts. He even allowed them to borrow his favorite moves, such as handstands and airplane propeller motions with his arms. He would then rehearse with the performers for hours, without any concern if they went overtime.

Gene's name became so prominent throughout the city that nearly every organization in town requested his services, including the prestigious Pittsburgh Playhouse, the prime symbol of culture in the city. The owners of the Playhouse asked Gene to prepare shows that combined the talents of amateurs and professionals. VIPs from Broadway began to take notice of the Playhouse, particularly of Gene's offerings. One such person was choreographer Robert Alton, a foremost representative of American popular theater dancing. Thus, it was a great honor when Alton agreed to stage a Christmas show at the Playhouse.

One evening, after both he and Gene were done rehearsing for their respective shows, Alton visited Gene backstage and urged him to come to Broadway. "If anybody's ready for it, you are."[24] Gene thanked Alton for his encouragement but said he was comfortable where he was at the moment. He did not want to give up what he had built in Pittsburgh. Furthermore, although the products of the Gene Kelly School of Dance were acclaimed in Pittsburgh, Gene's efforts might pale next to the work of people like Alton and his colleague John Murray Anderson. Despite Gene's refusal, Alton gave him his phone number and the two remained in contact for the next several years. Alton continually told Gene that if he ever decided to come to New York, he could be sure there was a job for him.

If Gene was already uncertain he had what it took to make it anywhere other than Pittsburgh, any hopes along those lines were completely dashed in the summer of 1935. While he and his family were visiting relatives in Southern California, an executive at RKO Studios (who, like Alton, had given Gene his contact information when passing through Pittsburgh) arranged a screen test for Gene. Gene was firmly against the idea; he was a dancer, not an actor. But the moment Harriet heard about it, she insisted he do the test. Gene, who could seldom say no to his mother, agreed. In Pittsburgh, reporters blew the test into a greater event than it was, claiming that Gene was going to undergo not just one, but an entire series of screen tests. When Gene arrived at RKO, he found the preparation for the test more taxing than the test itself. He was ushered into the makeup department and by the time the technicians had finished working on him, Gene claimed, "I looked like a raving fag. . . . I'm sure they [studio heads] just took one look at it and laughed."[25]

Indeed, RKO executives never contacted Gene again. Gene stated that the only enjoyable part of the entire humiliating experience was meeting actor Fredric March. Pittsburgh journalists, ever loyal to one of their favorite sons, wrote that Gene turned down Hollywood rather than the other way around.

Gene found more than enough work awaiting him upon his return home. The combined number of students at his two schools had reached 350. Though both studios had always attracted a high rate of preadolescents, in the mid-1930s this age group saw the largest increase in enrollment. Why the uptick? Beginning in 1934, Americans found a new obsession in the form of singing and dancing child actors after the appearance of a six-year-old Shirley Temple in the musical *Stand Up and Cheer*. Franklin Roosevelt hailed her as "Little Miss Miracle" for raising the nation's spirits during the Depression. Her success resulted in dozens of imitators who, according to columnist Hedda Hopper, descended on Hollywood "like a flock of hungry locusts." From all the young hopefuls, a handful of enduring stars were born, including Judy Garland, Deanna Durbin, and Mickey Rooney.[26] Shirley Temple mania was not infecting just stage parents in Hollywood; plenty of ambitious mothers and fathers in Pittsburgh also imagined their children were going to be the next big thing—with Gene's help. "By the mid-1930s, every time Shirley Temple made a movie, our studio enrollment doubled," Fred Kelly recounted. "We had a hundred girls in our studio who all looked exactly like Shirley Temple!"[27]

The nearest Gene's pupils came to movie stardom was when the star of *42nd Street*, crooner Dick Powell, honored Pittsburgh's Stanley Theatre by acting as master of ceremonies for Gene's annual *Kiddie Revue*. The show, due to the combination of Powell's presence and the town's loyalty to Gene, found eager audiences. When Powell called for Gene to take a bow at the end of the show, Gene "was in a spot. He had no tie. A stage-hand gave the embarrassed Kelly one of Dick's ties and Gene went on." In a 1943 article for the *Pittsburgh Press*, a journalist recorded that when Gene reunited with Powell for a radio broadcast, he "came to the first rehearsal tie in hand, and returned it to its owner. 'It took eight years and a film contract to make this possible,' [he said]."[28] In 1935, Gene was still far from winning a film contract. For the time being, he contented himself with doing what he did best: teaching young performers.

All things connected with Gene and his studio seemed blessed. Maybe, Gene decided, he would try Broadway. Then, as if to renew his doubts, two catastrophic floods hit Johnstown. The disaster destroyed entire neighborhoods, killed twenty-five people, and displaced hundreds of families—among them some of Gene's students. During the emergency, Gene suspended all classes and turned his studios as well as his family's home on Kensington Avenue into "emergency hostels" for the families of his students. Still a firm believer in omens, Gene saw the floods as confirmation of "the utter unpredictability of life. It reminded him starkly that there was no guarantee he could gradually rise in show business and achieve his ambitions."[29]

Gene remained in safe territory, staging yet another Beth Shalom revue and Cap and Gown show. The latter, titled *Trailer Ho!* was so successful that the company took its title literally and "[hit] the trail to Johnstown, Bradford and Erie."[30] It was the first University of Pittsburgh show to tour since 1930—a testament to Gene's ever-growing popularity outside of his hometown.

Harriet was highly pleased with her middle son's success and was now almost glad that he had rejected law school. However, in one aspect, Gene was a disappointment to her. He was twenty-four years old, yet he had not brought home one girl to introduce to her as a potential fiancée. She wanted him to reach his highest potential in both his personal and professional lives. Failing to find a nice Catholic girl and maintaining the status quo in Pittsburgh did not mesh with her ambitious visions for him. She feared he was "drifting in a sea of passivity" too similar to that of her husband's after the Crash of 1929.[31] But, as those closest to him knew, Gene was difficult to know on an intimate level. He had a secret inner life he shared with no one. He had not dismissed pursuing a career outside of Pittsburgh, nor did he dismiss the possibility of falling in love.

One day, Harriet Kelly overheard that Gene and a lovely, dark-haired showgirl in the cast of his latest production for the Pittsburgh Playhouse had been seeing quite a bit of each other. Harriet set out to find out who this girl was and what her family was like. The only information Harriet could glean was the girl's name: Helene Marlowe. She waited, feigning patience, for Gene to mention Helene. Weeks passed without a word. Finally, Harriet resorted to asking a gossipy neighbor for the reason behind Gene's taciturnity. Helene was of Russian Jewish heritage, the neighbor informed her, and the Marlowes wished Helene to marry a Jewish boy, preferably a lawyer, doctor, or banker. An Irish Catholic dancer and law school dropout was completely unsuitable. The Marlowes' disapproval of Gene infuriated Harriet. Still, she proved to be more intolerant than the Marlowes. When at last she broached the subject of Helene to her son and discovered that their relationship was far more serious than she'd imagined, she advised that Helene convert to Catholicism if she had any intention of marrying into the Kelly family. Gene bristled at his mother's assumption that a wedding was imminent and, for the present, ignored the subjects of marriage and religious conversion.

Helene Marlowe, though four years Gene's junior, was a strong personality who, unlike his other girlfriends over the years, did not submit to his usual role as director in a relationship. Betsy Blair later wrote: "I admit he was old-fashioned and paternalistic, but then so were most men at that time."[32] After hours at the Playhouse, they would dine together and practice modern dance to the music of Gershwin. Helene told Gene that she was ready to try her luck in New York, even if he was not. She urged him to come to the city and study with her, but he still wished to remain in Pittsburgh. Harriet was relieved to see the girl go; however, unbeknownst to her, Helene and Gene's relationship was far from over. According to Helene's son, Bruce, his mother and Gene were engaged for five years (1937–1942). "It was a long romance."[33]

Gene never hurried relationships, and his affair with Helene was no exception. If they were engaged, Gene's behavior in 1937 gave no clue to anyone that this was the case. That summer, he did find himself in New

York City, but not because of Helene. Rather, he traveled to the city to accept an offer for what could possibly be the most important job of his career thus far: choreographing a specialty number in a new Broadway revue. Gene was thrilled. Harriet shared his excitement and bought him a round-trip ticket to New York. But Gene's anticipation turned to disillusionment. On his first day of work, he was bewildered to find that the producer of the revue looked at him with puzzlement when he introduced himself as the choreographer from Pittsburgh.

"What? You're not choreographing. You're here to work as a chorus boy," the producer told him, barely restraining laughter. Clenching his fists and fighting the desire to hit the producer or anyone else within arm's reach, Gene stormed from the theater. His first impulse was to see Helene, but he took a train back to Pittsburgh without so much as calling her. The disheartening New York trip plus the disappointment of the failed RKO screen test made Gene again doubtful of Robert Alton's claim that if anyone was ready for the big time, it was Gene Kelly. His neglecting to see Helene hurt her, but he did not feel ready to face her after the blow of losing the choreographing job. Also, she was beginning to pressure him about setting a date for their marriage. Gene was having second thoughts; he did not like being rushed or nudged into things, and he was not altogether certain he was ready to take such a step.

Home again, Gene fell easily back into his routine. After staging another Cap and Gown show in April 1938, Gene took on the task of staging his most large-scale revue yet: *Hold Your Hats*. The production, also premiering in April, was to be staged at the Pittsburgh Playhouse. Harriet believed that if the show were successful, Gene would have a second chance at Broadway.

In an interview with the *Pittsburgh Press* regarding the ambitious show, Gene explained, "My idea is to do dances that are different, and I believe the chorus will give the show just that." He created no fewer than ten dance routines, "ranging from tap and comedy to modern ballet" for the revue and performed in six of them himself.[34] He drew on all the techniques he had learned in Chicago, putting his training in Spanish dance to notable use in one number, "La Cumparsita."

The show proved to be one of the Playhouse's most successful productions to date. According to a writer for the *Pittsburgh Press*, the lyrics, music, and sketches plus Gene's choreography added up to "an original, sophisticated revue . . . packed with laughs."[35] One local reporter, in acknowledging Gene, simply wrote that he "originated all the chorus routines [and] hoofs and warbles."[36] Gene, always self-conscious about his singing, was not thrilled to have his voice described as a "warble." Fred Kelly maintained that his brother "had a great singing voice," but the fact that he was a tenor "embarrassed him to no end."[37] Apparently Gene's warble was not a detriment to the show. The play, which ultimately ran for a month, was "the high spot in Playhouse entertainment this season" specifically because of "the [snappy dance routines] of Gene Kelly."[38]

As the show continued its run, Gene finally gained the recognition for which he had been searching outside his hometown. The success of the show was so visible and its quality so high that *Variety,* the most widely read national show business periodical, heaped praise upon the production, in particular its choreographer. Moreover, Gene's picture appeared in the June 1938 issue of *Stage,* a leading magazine in the entertainment world. Robert Alton phoned Gene after the premiere of *Hold Your Hats* and again urged him to come to New York. Gene did not yet tell Harriet about Alton's call, but this time, he did not dismiss outright his friend's suggestion.

As Gene rose in the entertainment world, so did the prestige of his dance studios. Gene's schools were now making approximately $10,000 a year ($170,000 in 2015 currency). The family had never been so financially secure. Even without Gene's presence, the studios could function successfully because of the exceptional teachers he had employed (including his own siblings). Years later, Gene said of himself in 1938 that he was doing "too well."[39] He felt, at last, that it was "time to move. You reach that spot and you either move or you stay where you are and end up wearing a flowing black tie and being called 'Professor.'"[40] "I had done everything that I could do in my line in Pittsburgh, and I couldn't see a life that was just more of the same."[41]

Harriet met Gene's announcement that he was ready to take another try at Broadway with joy, relief, and sadness. His family, pupils, and friends would miss him, but Gene could not abide standing still in either a figurative or a literal sense. He left Fred and Louise in charge of the schools. Louise had graduated from the University of Pittsburgh in 1936 and later earned a master's degree there in elementary education. When the United States entered the Second World War in 1941, Fred enlisted and Louise officially took over the dance studio. She would run it for nearly fifty years with her husband, Bill Bailey.

No matter who ran the studio, it was Gene whom pupils remembered and his reputation that continued to draw students after he left. His memory boosted enrollment, and later his fame as the screen's most innovative dancer kept hopefuls interested in learning. One young lady missed Gene perhaps more than any other: fifteen-year-old Jeanne Coyne. She recollected that Gene had established such a close bond with his students that she sensed he would like to remain in touch. "Through the next few years I wrote to him—and almost always, a gay letter filled with hope and encouragement was my answer. More than anything else, those letters made me keep up with my dancing."[42]

On a humid morning in August 1938, Gene, with a mixture of pain and anticipation, prepared to say good-bye to his family and his students for an indeterminate amount of time. Harriet accompanied him to the Pittsburgh Railway Station, giving him an envelope containing $200 and his train ticket. Gene, in going to New York, may have been leaving behind his family, but in an unfamiliar city of millions, he at least had Helene Marlowe and Robert Alton as contacts. Just how he planned to proceed with his and Helene's relationship was a matter he had yet to determine.

As Gene settled into his seat on the train, he opened the envelope and discovered that the ticket his mother had purchased for him was one way. He would not visit home, he decided, until he had become as important on Broadway as he had been in Johnstown and Pittsburgh. Gene watched his hometown dwindle to nothing outside the window. Within a few hours, he could see the skyline of New York City growing larger as the train drew near. He remembered his last experience in the metropolis when his credentials as a Pittsburgh choreographer had been a source of laughter. Choreography was a difficult field to break into even for experienced professionals. But Gene held on to his conviction that the New York theater scene could benefit from his ideas. He felt time was on his side as well. True, the theater season was over in August, but that meant producers would be holding dozens of auditions as they prepared for the next season's shows. Surely he would find a spot in one of these productions. He would even become a "chorus boy" if necessary, though he dreaded the thought. What mattered was that he would be in a Broadway show. Gene, with an unwavering determination "only Harriet Kelly's son could have," felt certain of success.[43]

5

The Time of His Life

"New York in the thirties was indeed a 'Wonderful Town,'" Hugh Martin, a young composer with whom Gene Kelly later worked, asserted. "[It was a] Utopia . . . [where] everything was challenging and new."[1] Challenging and new—both words were as irresistible to Gene as the courses of cake he enjoyed on his birthdays. Filled with compelling juxtapositions, New York provided no shortage of inspiration for dancers, writers, and composers. Grand hotels stood only blocks away from shabby boardinghouses. Opera played at the Metropolitan while the rhythms of Gershwin and Berlin played at the Music Box Theatre.

Arguably, the most inspired activities in 1930s New York took place on Broadway. The theater was undergoing a period of great prolificacy unparalleled since the mid-1920s. Broadway historian Stanley Green remarked that the lighter yet still timely musicals of the late 1930s "discovered that a song lyric, a tune, a wisecrack, a bit of comic business, a dance routine could say things [about modern times] with even more effectiveness than many a serious minded drama simply because the appeal was to a far wider spectrum of the theatregoing public."[2] In 1937 and early 1938, Adolf Hitler had not yet annexed Austria into the Third Reich, President Roosevelt had not written the dictator a letter pleading for peace, and Germany, France, and Italy had not signed the Munich Agreement to appease Hitler. Thus, the lighter tone of musicals on Broadway, even when spoofing dark political matters such as fascism, was not inappropriate. Pioneering director Vincente Minnelli, a relative newcomer to Broadway in the 1930s, claimed that in his naïveté he felt that "fascism could be laughed away."[3]

Shy, inarticulate, and a maddening perfectionist, the slender, dark-haired, pop-eyed Italian American Minnelli made his involvement in any project total. According to lyricist and playwright/screenwriter Alan Jay

Lerner, "His enthusiasm [was] limitless and irresistible."[4] Minnelli's most prestigious assignment to date was as art director and costume designer for the *Ziegfeld Follies of 1936* (produced after Ziegfeld's death in 1932). Minnelli, Robert Alton, and George Balanchine (who in 1934 had opened the American School of Ballet in New York), worked together to create a surreal ballet in the new *Follies*. The ballet was so successful that it helped to make the medium a part of mainstream theater. "With the full range of ballet movement, anything is possible," Lerner later remarked.[5]

Alton's unconventional ideas changed Broadway choreography by molding the chorus from a simple precision line into small groups with featured vocalists. Balanchine and Agnes de Mille are usually credited with perfecting the integrated dramatic musical. But Alton had "his champions as the leader in the field, and Mr. Kelly is clearly his prime supporter," Anna Kisselgoff, writer for the *New York Times,* stated in 1985. "There was no one who could top Bob Alton," Gene asserted. "Anytime [he] put on a dance number, he stopped the show."[6] Like Minnelli, Alton prized elegance and attention to detail. His most recent hit as of 1938 was another Minnelli-directed production, *The Show Is On.* In the play, he trained a young dancer, Charles Walters, whose style was in the same vein as Gene's. Walters became a "minor sensation" under Alton's guidance, giving hope to Gene that he might have the same success. Walters's thoughts on American dance, expressed in 1937, sound remarkably similar to Gene's: "A clever synthesis of the variety of forms—tap, specialty, ballet—would prove a striking novelty."[7] Alton saw in Gene what he had seen in Walters. Gene hoped to become a part of this new generation on Broadway.

If Broadway's trailblazers had a home base in New York, it would be Vincente Minnelli's apartment, fondly dubbed "the Minnellium," on West 53rd Street next to the Museum of Modern Art. Parties that began at Minnelli's would move to the second hub for Broadway's elite: the residence of lyricist Ira Gershwin at 33 Riverside Drive. Among those in Gershwin and Minnelli's set were mordant comedian and pianist Oscar Levant, Robert Alton, songwriters Harold Arlen, E. Y. Harburg, Hugh Martin, Ralph Blane, and Irving Berlin, and musical arrangers Kay Thompson and Lennie Hayton. These artists imprinted American attitudes into musical comedy and set a teaching example for Hollywood of how to integrate music and dance into story.

The year 1938 was an ideal time for Gene Kelly to arrive on Broadway.

Minnelli and Gershwin's set appealed to Gene's intellect, but he, in finding his own definition of American movement, wanted to apply the finesse of their productions to everyday, working-class settings and characters. However, he found no immediate opportunities awaiting him. Gene swiftly became disenchanted upon his arrival in New York. "Nobody wanted a choreographer from Pittsburgh, so I got a job as a dancer just to keep going," he explained.[8] Though he still cringed at the memory of that New York producer laughing at the thought of him as anything but a chorus boy, this time, Gene was not going to let the same experience send him packing.

Gene settled into an inexpensive hotel at the 44th Street Hotel on West 44th Street between 6th and 7th Avenues. He lost little time in calling Helene Marlowe, who was struggling to find work herself, and informing her of his new residence. She was pleased to hear his voice but chided him for not saving money by staying with her. "It was the kind of decisive action she tended to propose," Gene's biographer Alvin Yudkoff wrote. Gene, as he had from the beginning of their relationship, admired her spirit, but "her strength and certainty made him uncomfortable. . . . He was not proud of his behavior with Helene."[9] Gene had no intention of breaking off their relationship. He simply wanted to keep his career his top priority—and dating cost time and money.

The morning after he arrived in New York, Gene scanned *Variety* for audition announcements. He also called Robert Alton, who advised him to wear a T-shirt, slacks, blazer, and tap loafers to tryouts. Gene was immediately drawn to an advertisement for a new show, *Sing out the News,* by producer Max Gordon with a book by George Kaufman and Moss Hart. What further attracted him to the show was that it was staged by Dave Gould, who had been the choreographer (along with the young dancer Hermes Pan) for Fred Astaire and Ginger Rogers's first joint film, *Flying Down to Rio* (1933).

Gene arrived early at the theater on a Saturday morning but found that three hundred others were as prompt as he. As he waited in line, perspiring in the un-air-conditioned room, he watched every dancer audition, hoping that the producers would see what he believed—that his ability was superior to the bulk of his competitors. After an hour, his turn finally came. Gene performed a buck and wing and added his own flourishes—leaps, jumps, pirouettes—everything but a hand walk across the stage. The producer conceded that Gene was the best dancer in the bunch and offered him a featured spot in the show for $35 a week.

"Thirty-five dollars?" Gene asked, incredulous. "Seventy a week and you've got a deal."

"Thirty-five is the going rate for the chorus," an assistant choreographer told him.

"Sixty dollars," Gene tried again.

"Good-bye, Mr. Kelly," the producer said. Gene stood, frozen, then gathered his blazer and left the theater.

"A very discouraging business, this trying for a role," Gene reflected in 1947. "You stalk out on the stage . . . [and down in] front are a bunch of guys who look at you like you were in a sack of lemons. They pick 'em up, they squeeze them, and some they kick into the corner. One they grab and nibble on."[10] Though disheartened, Gene kept true to his resolve not to return to Pittsburgh after his first defeat. Instead, he asked Robert Alton for advice. Alton sent Gene to Johnny Darrow, Charles Walters's agent. Darrow, a thirty-one-year-old former star of B pictures in Hollywood, now ranked as one of the entertainment world's top talent agents.

"Gene Kelly—Gene—you know that's a girl's name?" Darrow asked during their first appointment. "What would you say to changing your name to Frank Black?"

Gene stiffened. He had built his reputation on his name. He thought of how hurt his mother would be if he shunned the Kelly surname. The idea that Darrow might be trying to fool anti-Catholic casting agents and producers also crossed his mind. Gene shook his head. "Gene Kelly is good enough," he declared.[11]

Darrow did not argue. He arranged an audition with the Shubert Brothers, the most prolific producers on Broadway. The Shuberts' dance director was impressed with Gene's tryout, particularly his masculine style, which stood in such contrast to the fey quality he saw in the majority of the other chorus boys. The director called Darrow, saying he would give Gene $150 a week. Without consulting Gene, Darrow decided to negotiate for $300—and in the process lost him the job.

When Darrow saw Gene the next day, he noted how desperate the dancer was for money. Gene could have used the money his schools in Pennsylvania were earning—or accept Helene Marlowe's invitation to board at her apartment—but he intended to "start from scratch" and "rough it for as long as he could." Darrow tried to call the Shuberts and accept the $150 offer, but J. J. Shubert bluntly told him: "We don't need Kelly anymore."[12] When Gene heard of Darrow's blunder, he remained calm, much to Darrow's relief. Gene, like Darrow, had "overplayed his hand" in an attempt to get as much as he felt he was worth.[13] Darrow persuaded Alton to hire Gene for a small featured role as a secretary and specialty dancer in Cole Porter's new show, *Leave It to Me!* For his services, he received $75, half of what the Shuberts had offered.

The show, a political satire, revolved around a befuddled American ambassador sent to Russia because no one in Washington could abide looking at him. The stars of the show were vaudeville veterans Victor Moore and Sophie Tucker. Aside from Gene, another promising newcomer in the cast was twenty-five-year-old singer/dancer Mary Martin. Fortuitously, one of Gene's spots in the show was in Martin's standout number, the suggestive "My Heart Belongs to Daddy." Martin played "a dumb cluck who had urgently to be shipped out of town all the way to Siberia." Her character came onstage dressed "to the teeth" in furs and was met by six male dancers wearing Eskimo suits. One of the Eskimos was Gene Kelly. The boys were required to "lift, sling, and pass Martin from hand to hand" as she did "a mock strip tease, removing her wraps and singing in a baby voice." Martin recalled that Gene worked every day at the theater and practiced for hours after all other cast members had gone home. "I've never known anybody who worked so hard perfecting his art. . . . I knew he was going to be somebody very great."[14]

Cole Porter also noticed Gene's individuality. When he was not practicing dance steps, Gene sat backstage reading the *New York Times* or Aldous Huxley's novel *Point Counterpoint.* Porter was impressed that Gene was reading something other than trade papers and was not focused solely on flirting with the chorus girls. One afternoon, Porter, who was confined to a wheelchair as a result of a riding accident, rolled over to Gene and asked him what he thought of Huxley. Though married, the composer was known by many to be a homosexual. If Gene was aware of this fact, he did not let it affect his high opinion of Porter. Gene claimed that the composer was "charming and very polite . . . he never actually gave me any advice about my career, but he seemed to take interest in what little I had to do." Porter may very well have been attracted to the young dancer; Alton reported that upon first seeing Gene, the composer had asked to be introduced to "that unusual man."[15]

Porter was so struck by Gene's uniqueness that he invited him to attend exclusive cocktail parties at his townhome. At the soirees, Porter treated Gene to champagne, caviar, witty conversation, and a general sumptuous atmosphere that was glamorous "beyond his wildest imagination." Though Gene was generally not fond of formal affairs, he was grateful to be included as a guest. The wealthy backers of the show, unlike Porter, invited only chorus girls to their gatherings. "They treated the young men in the show like second class citizens," Gene explained, "and this brought out my resentment of the establishment."[16]

During the rehearsal period and throughout the run of *Leave It to Me!* Gene continued to see Helene Marlowe. Helene, according to Gene's biographer Clive Hirschhorn, became "a sort of oracle to him."[17] He asked her for advice about his future plans, and she spent hours listening to him talk and watching him demonstrate his new routines. Though he still refused to share an apartment with her, they did share a pet, according to Helene's son, Bruce: "One fond memory [she] spoke of was a Cocker Spaniel she and Gene bought and named . . . Michael. They trained him to use the bathtub."[18]

Throughout the month of October, Gene saw less of Helene as *Leave It to Me!* toured in New Haven and Boston for its pre-Broadway tryouts. On November 9, 1938, the show premiered at New York's Imperial Theatre. Brooks Atkinson, the difficult to please theater critic of the *New York Times,* called it "a handsome carnival" with the "wittiest score" Porter had yet penned. Gene's work garnered no special mention in any review; the closest thing to notice he received was via Robert Alton; Atkinson deemed his staging "clever dancing." "My Heart Belongs to Daddy," which the reviewer called "a broad piece of ribaldry," became the drawing point of the show and seldom failed to win applause from the audience.[19] On April 30, 1939, during the run of the show, the New York World's Fair opened. The event drew 44 million people and created stiff competition for Broadway plays. *Leave It to Me!* played for 291 performances; one can only wonder if it might have enjoyed a longer run without the diversion of the fair. The production closed on July 15, 1939—without Gene.

During the run of the show, Johnny Darrow informed him that he had the opportunity to play a leading role in an upcoming Little Theatre musical revue entitled *One for the Money.* The Little Theatre Movement (which, since its beginnings in the 1910s, was a sort of precursor to the Off-Broadway Movement of the 1950s) produced intimate, noncommercial, and reform-minded shows. Though officially a "little" production, *One for the Money* was slated to premiere at a Shubert-owned theater, the Booth. Also, Gene's salary was guaranteed at $115 a week, a hefty upgrade from the $75 he was currently earning in the Porter production. The producers of *Leave It to Me!* told him that if he quit the show, he would never work for them again. Such news gave Gene pause; if *One for the Money* failed, he would be back where he started. However, choosing the new show seemed judicious. After all, it was to be directed by John Murray Anderson and choreographed by Robert Alton. The show, presented by Guthrie McClintic and Stanley Gilkey, allowed Gene to meet their colleague, legendary stage star Katharine Cornell, who took an interest in his career. Gene would appear in seven different numbers, some of which required him not only to dance but to speak lines. Gene later stated: "You never get paid much for just dancing. In that second show, somebody gave me a line to say and I realized they'd have to pay me more to speak. And I thought, hey, this is easy." What was not so simple was for Gene to lose his Pittsburgh accent. Cornell engaged a dialogue coach to help him. "In 1939 my flat Pittsburgh accent must have sounded really terrible," Gene admitted. "This teacher would ask me to say 'water' and I'd say 'wadder' . . . just like the Jean Hagen character in *Singin' In The Rain*. . . . After a few months of hard work, I felt I was ready to play Shakespeare."[20]

Even with his newly refined speech, Gene seemed out of place in *One for the Money*. Indeed, one number required him to be costumed à la Fred Astaire in white tie and tails. On the surface, the revue seemed a vehicle for right-wing propaganda. However, upon closer inspection, it was revealed to be a parody of elitist lifestyles. Sidney Whipple of the *Pittsburgh Press* observed, "There are . . . sketches that lampoon the pseudo-culture of the brainless rich."[21]

The production was light and modestly staged, but Gene approached it as if it were the most prestigious Broadway spectacle. He tirelessly rehearsed with Robert Alton on his dance numbers, hoping to find ways to bring new dimensions to them. During one practice session, Alton asked Gene to improvise a soft-shoe routine to brighten an otherwise wordy and slow-paced scene. Gene ran into the dancer's equivalent of writer's block, lamenting, "Nothing comes. There's no *reason* for the dance, no motive. A dance is supposed to say something, and here there's nothing to say." Alton argued that the dance did have a purpose: "You want her [the girl in the number] to know that you have a kinship of spirit . . . that you think she is beautiful." According to a 1946 *Modern Screen* article, in ten minutes, Gene created a dance "that said all those things, and more."[22]

Gene found a new teacher in the show's director, John Murray Anderson. "No one has had as great an influence on my work as John Murray Anderson. The biggest compliment I ever had, certainly up to then, was his approval of my work on *One for the Money*," Gene revealed. What Gene took from Anderson was his creative use of lighting to suggest mood and his ability to "watch a song and make one simple suggestion that would turn a good number into a hit." Even more than Vincente Minnelli, Gene claimed, Anderson knew "how to construct a scene." As Gene's biographers Sheridan Morley and Ruth Leon put it, "With Minnelli . . . you could see the seams. . . . With Murray you saw all the magic and wonderment of the effect."[23]

Gene made three more contacts during the run of the show. First, he met the sensitive Hugh Martin, the vocal arranger and understudy to all the male members of the cast. Next, there was the boisterous Keenan Wynn, a chorus boy and son of the famous vaudevillian Ed Wynn. Finally, Gene befriended another member of the chorus, William Archibald. Archibald, five years Gene's junior, was making his Broadway debut in *One for the Money*.

One for the Money's run had a rocky start. Wynn became ill with the flu and Martin was required to take his place without having gone through a single rehearsal. In one number he was required to lift leading lady Maxine Barrat gracefully upward, a feat Wynn could accomplish without effort. However, Martin, forty pounds lighter than Wynn, found it impossible. The orchestra members became so amused by "the circus" occurring on the stage that they set their instruments in their laps and watched. People began to laugh so hard that many "cried real tears."

"Bring down the curtain!" the harried stage manager called. Martin fled backstage, attempting to make it to the restroom before he became sick. Gene interrupted him, giving him, as Martin recalled, "that famous Kelly grin and a bear hug to go with it."

"Hugh!" he cried. "You were a smash. They oughta keep that in the show."

"Not with me," Martin said and ran the rest of the way to the bathroom.[24]

Though the embarrassment made *One for the Money* "a classic exercise in humiliation" for Martin, the show was a highly positive experience

65

for Gene.[25] The production, which had opened on February 4, 1939, played for 132 performances. The revue excited little critical attention, but what notices it did receive were respectable. Brooks Atkinson noted that it opened to an "extremely enthusiastic audience" but that during many stretches, the revue seemed like a "private joke" that author Nancy Hamilton wrote for her friends rather than the general public. Atkinson gave Gene his first nod in a New York review, mentioning him by name and adding that he "can dance."[26] But Gene would soon receive greater notice.

By June, *One for the Money* was ready to go on tour. Robert Alton faced a dilemma; he had commitments in New York, as did several members of the troupe. Who would coach the replacements? John Murray Anderson called upon Gene to take the job. The replacements, more experienced as actors than as dancers, were eager to receive Gene's help. Viewing Gene's work with the new performers, Anderson was pleased to see he had added his own touch to the routines without "compromising Alton's work."[27] On June 5, *One for the Money* premiered in one of Gene's favorite cities, Chicago, where it played at the Selwyn Theatre until July 15, 1939. Gene's hometown paper, the *Pittsburgh Post-Gazette,* reported of the Chicago tour: "[The show is] a glittering rib of café society, which is two-thirds first-rate and just a third dull. . . . [Gene's] hoofing comes under the general heading of distinguished. Some of the Chicago reviews have even caught in him a combination of Fred Astaire and Georgie Tapps, and they aren't far wrong, either."[28]

Though he enjoyed the tour, Gene desired to return to a simple lifestyle for the rest of the summer of 1939. After *One for the Money* closed, he and Bill Archibald drove to Orr's Island in Maine and rented a weather-beaten cottage by the ocean. In a 1941 interview, Gene explained why he seldom saw a profit after the run of any show: "What I like to do when I have any money is to go to Maine for six weeks. I know an island there where I can do anything I want to. It's a swell place to be."[29] The excursions to Maine were akin to his lakeside vacations as a child. The time Gene spent in the outdoors seldom failed to replenish him after the frenetic pace of city life.

With little to worry about for six weeks, Gene's adolescent desire to write was reawakened. Bill Archibald was a serious author and spent several hours a day practicing his art. Gene, attempting to follow his friend's work ethic, began to draft a three-act drama. The plot dealt with a young out-of-towner who arrives in New York and "finds himself in serious trouble." Gene wrote one and a half acts but abandoned the project when he could find no way to proceed. Undaunted, he set to work on a comedy, which he called a "very sophisticated S. N. Behrman sort of thing."[30] However, as had happened with his drama, he was at a loss as to how he should continue the story after the second act. Gene became restless, and the sound of the wind and the waves outdoors was an endless distraction. He now remembered why he had not chosen to pursue writing: writing was a sedentary, lonely business, and he had to be in motion and in contact with fellow creatives. He later admitted: "Writing was beyond me."[31]

When their Maine idyll ended, Gene and Bill found that they did not share as much in common as they had thought. After squabbling over one too many issues, both petty and serious, they parted ways forever upon returning to New York. Bill went on to a successful writing career on Broadway, working both as a lyricist and playwright for shows such as *The Innocents* (1950) and *Portrait of a Lady* (1976).

Before the next theater season began, Gene went to see his family in Pittsburgh. He had made a promise to himself that he would not go home until he had reached some level of success in New York. In the eyes of loyal publicists in Pittsburgh, the fact that he had appeared in two Broadway shows made him a bona fide celebrity. Louis Little, an acquaintance of Gene's who had offered to finance him through law school, threw a party for him. Gene, who assumed it was going to be a small, informal gathering, appeared at the event in his customary T-shirt, khakis, and loafers. He was startled to find the Pittsburgh Symphony Orchestra, the mayor, and several prominent citizens in attendance. He tried to mingle for a time before settling down on the floor (his favorite spot at parties, perhaps because it freed him from circulating, requiring people to come to him). After a short while sitting there amid the festivities, he looked down at his shoes and mumbled, "Well, I think I gotta go now." Gene's friend Jules Steinberg later asked him why he had left so quickly. "Little was exploiting me. I don't want to be exploited. I thought the party was just for me and my pals. If I knew strangers were going to be there, I wouldn't have accepted."[32]

More pleasant were Gene's visits to his family's two dance schools, which were thriving under Fred and Louise's direction. The studios now had over five hundred pupils and were bringing in $12,000 a year.[33] The Kelly family reunion was short-lived and incomplete—Gene's eldest brother, James, was living in Cleveland and his older sister, Jay, was busy working as a schoolteacher and was no longer involved in the dance studios at all. His father seemed more tired than Gene remembered. Only Harriet remained unchanged. She listened eagerly when Gene told her about the new job awaiting him. Johnny Darrow had contacted the stage manager of the Theatre Guild, Johnny Haggott, and suggested Gene as chief choreographer for the summer season at Connecticut's Westport Country Playhouse. Though the job did not take Gene back to the New York stage, it provided him with a more important position than he had thus far won on Broadway. Harriet could not have been more pleased.

"For a boy from the streets of Pittsburgh (and aggressively proud of it too) it was ironic that his first real break in show business happened in the 'toniest' of summer theatres," author Richard Somerset Ward commented of Gene's work at the Westport Country Playhouse.[34] The Playhouse, which opened in 1931, had gained the highest of reputations and become an established stop for summer stock companies. The theater was located in a converted tannery that, nestled among red barns, bore a look of rusticity. Those involved in productions took an active part in painting scenery and sewing costumes. "It was like a musical about doing summer stock," actress Ruth Warrick observed. "It's like belonging to an exclusive club, to play Westport."[35]

Despite the lofty reputation of the Playhouse, Gene's pay was less than what he had been earning on Broadway (no records exist on what the exact pay was, but it was likely between $35 and $75 a week). However, the experience of working at Westport was comparable to taking a college course. Gene was assigned one project after another at a frenetic pace. The variety of duties initially overwhelmed him, and he wondered if the job was too much for him. But he did not wish to add to his failures in 1939—failed writing endeavors, a failed friendship—so he threw himself into his multitude of tasks.

His first assignment held the most prestige—staging Eugene O'Neill's *The Emperor Jones,* starring Paul Robeson of Ziegfeld's *Show Boat* (1927) fame. Gene had a mere three days to devise dances for an all-black theater troupe from Harlem. Gene found a firm supporter in Robeson. Robeson admired Gene's political opinions, though his own were further left than the young choreographer's. The week-long run of *The Emperor Jones* in August was considered a success.[36]

Gene's next assignment, *Green Grow the Lilacs,* was a rural drama utilizing traditional folk songs. The show, like *The Emperor Jones,* was a monumental success and was held over for a second week. The heads of the Theatre Guild, Theresa Helburn and Lawrence Langner, adopted the play as their pet project for the next few years. Though other guild members referred to it as "Terry's [Theresa Helburn's] Folly," the play evolved into *Oklahoma!* the first collaboration of Richard Rodgers and Oscar Hammerstein II.

But the production for which Gene received most recognition during his summer at Westport was a revue entitled *The Magazine Page.* Gene took on three assignments for the production: master of ceremonies, performer, and choreographer. The sketch in which Gene participated was essentially a satire showing a series of different types of dancers attempting to interpret the same tap routine. Gene's personable, tongue-in-cheek send-ups won over audiences and led Armina Marshall, wife of theatre producer Lawrence Langer, to later reminisce: "I remember I told Gene Kelly he had talent. . . . I said to him, 'Just work at it and you'll go someplace.'"[37]

The revue proved to be the highlight of the season not only because of Gene but also thanks to the talents of Betty Comden and Adolph Green, who acted in the show and wrote its clever lyrics and dialogue. Also in the cast was fledgling actress Judy Holliday. Comden, Green, and Holliday were the primary members of a popular theater troupe (which later included another young musical talent, Leonard Bernstein) called the Revuers. Green and Comden in particular took an immediate liking to Gene. Green explained, "There was a certain element of boyish ingenuousness along with an element of [a] worldly hard quality [in Gene]."[38] "What I remember most was the effect he had on an audience. They just loved him."[39]

Gene found Comden and Green as intriguing as they found him. Gene, who had a lifelong love of word games, discovered that Comden's and Green's exceptional mastery of wordplay made for stimulating conversations. At this time in his life, Gene began to actively befriend bright, creative types like Comden and Green. "He was always smart enough to surround himself with wonderful exciting people," Green stated.[40] Gene's time in Westport did more than introduce him to influential personal and professional contacts in the theater world; he said his experience in summer stock taught him "how to be an actor." He elaborated, "I learned to do it all, some of it maybe not so well, but I learned a lot that year."[41]

As an ending to his unusually active summer, Gene decided to go to Mexico. The trip turned out to be less a vacation than a test of faith. Betsy Blair wrote that the Kelly clan "was a good Catholic family but Gene was no longer a good Catholic, or so he believed. [In] Mexico [he was] appalled by the extremes of wealth and poverty." Gene was so riled by what he saw that when he returned home he invited his father, who never doubted the church's integrity, to visit the country with him. There, Gene tried to show James "the gold inside the churches and the beautiful, dignified people living in clay shacks." He assumed that James would understand why he had lost his faith. "It didn't work. Pop only saw the good the Church does, but they had a great trip and enjoyed the beers," Betsy concluded.[42]

Though he deemed himself an atheist during this period, Gene still essentially lived the life of a good Catholic boy. His time in Westport had been an eye-opening experience; there, he had seen much sexual freedom and experimentation among his colleagues. According to many of his fellow thespians' accounts, he was one of the few who didn't join in these extracurricular activities. Upon returning to New York, Helene Marlowe was still his only girl.

After such a productive summer, Gene was perplexed to find no immediate prospects awaiting him in New York. He subsisted for nearly two months on $15 a week from Social Security. No longer able to afford his Village apartment, he relocated to a tiny room at the Woodward Hotel on West 55th Street he shared with a struggling playwright and musician, Dick Dwenger. According to Betsy Blair, Dwenger was "blond and slight with glasses. He had a quiet authority and wit about him, and he played the piano."[43] Rather than ask him to pay half the rent at the Woodward, Gene requested that his friend act as his rehearsal pianist at a "squalid, depressing, and rat-infested Masonic Hall" that he rented as a rehearsal spot for a quarter an hour.[44] Dwenger was one of the many artists Gene met at his favorite haunt, Louie Bergen's Bar on 45th Street. The clientele there were "other ambitious young actors, writers, and directors. Their group was intellectual and left-wing."[45] A few in the group were card-carrying members of the Communist Party, among them actor Lloyd Gough. Gene was open to all political ideologies, but he did not align himself with Communism, primarily due to his abhorrence of regimentation.

Gene kept his mind and social life active during his lull in employment, but nothing made him feel as fulfilled as work. As luck would have it, by September 1939, Johnny Darrow had a possible job for him. The

Theatre Guild was staging William Saroyan's new play, *The Time of Your Life*. The action of the play takes place at a San Francisco bar owned by an Italian American, Nick. His establishment is a gathering place for those who "can't feel at home anywhere else." Among the outcasts are a Greek newspaper boy who sings Irish ballads, a black piano player, an Arab harmonica player, and an Assyrian pinball wizard. Finally, there is an American vaudevillian, Harry, who delivers unfunny comic sketches, performing interpretive dances to express the point he is trying to make. In Saroyan's words, Harry is "a dumb young fellow whose philosophy is that the world is full of sorrow and needs laughter."[46] Darrow thought the character would be perfect for Gene.

Gene was not the first or even the second choice for Harry the Hoofer. Before him, Martin Ritt landed the role, but Saroyan ultimately found him wrong for the part. Saroyan needed someone who could make people laugh. Before suggesting Gene, Darrow brought choreographer and dancer Charles Walters to Saroyan's attention. However, Walters deemed the $175 a week salary too low. Now Gene's name came up as a possibility. Lawrence Langner, head of the Theatre Guild, recalled Gene's polished performance in white tie and tails at the Westport Playhouse and declared: "He's too clean cut, too posh to play Harry the Hoofer." Apparently, Gene's diction lessons had worked too well. Saroyan, not having seen Gene act at Westport, had no preconceived notions. When Gene appeared for an audition, Saroyan wanted to sign him immediately. He looked precisely like Harry: he wore pants that were "too long, a coat too large and too loose," and he was unshaven. What finally clinched the role for Gene was the fact that he could speak loudly. In the text of the play, Harry is described as having "great energy, both in power of voice and in force and speed of physical gesture."[47] Out of the crowd of aspiring dancers who came to audition, Gene yelled, "I can shout!" Langner found Gene's assertiveness off-putting, but Saroyan saw it as an attribute perfectly attuned with the character of Harry.

Gene found in Saroyan both a cheerleader and a friend. A reporter for the *Pittsburgh Post-Gazette* recorded: "Ever since *Time of Your Life*, Gene Kelly and William Saroyan have been bosom pals. When Gene speaks of him, there's idolatry in his voice. 'That guy's writing gets you down here. . . . That Saroyan is out of the world.'"[48] Harry the Hoofer was in many ways like Saroyan. Because Gene became such close friends with the author, he was able to better mimic the characteristics Saroyan took from his own personality and put into Harry. Gene saw himself in certain aspects of the character as well; Harry was struggling to gain recognition in a world that placed too much emphasis on wealth rather than integrity. In one scene, Harry declares: "I've been poor all right, but don't forget that some things count more than some other things . . . talent for instance counts more than money. . . . And I've got talent. I get new ideas night and day."[49]

What Gene found most fulfilling in his work in the play was returning to his first love, choreography. He devised his own dance numbers as well as those of the other characters in the show. He explained the evolution of his seemingly impromptu routines for *The Time of Your Life* as "an accident." In 1980, he stated: "Bill Saroyan had an Armenian mouth organ player do some of the music. I said, 'Americans can't dance to Armenian music.' And he said, 'Go ahead, you can do it.' And then he had a black pianist playing a 12-bar blues and I wondered how you could relate these styles. One day it hit me, because I learned you can do anything with dance if you do it through the character."[50]

The Time of Your Life premiered at the Booth Theatre on October 25, 1939. Audiences and critics readily accepted its characters as believable, flesh-and-blood people. *New York Times* critic Brooks Atkinson penned what could have been the production's tagline: "It is innocent at heart and creative in art." Despite Gene's conspicuous role in the play, Atkinson gave him only a cursory mention, including him among the list of cast members who added to "memorable scenes."[51] Theatergoers, however, took more notice of the young dancer. In a 1950 article for the *Saturday Evening Post* recounting Gene's theater days, one writer recorded that Gene made Harry's improvised dances "so convincing that, although he had worked the dance out down to the last clean tap and never varied it, seasoned playgoers who saw the show not once but several times marveled at his ability to 'create a new dance for every performance.'"[52]

The play spoke to Depression-era audiences, who related to its "undistinguished characters" who have "rubbed their elbows in life without soiling [their] spirits."[53] Saroyan's work won both the 1940 Pulitzer Prize for Best Play and the New York Drama Critics' Circle Award. The show enjoyed a long run, closing on April 6, 1940. As part of the most lauded production of the season, Gene was now firmly removed from "small-time" show business.

During the run of *The Time of Your Life*, Gene received an unexpected visit from the lyricist of such classic tunes as "Singin' in the Rain" and "The Broadway Melody," who also happened to be MGM's most influential producer of musical films: Arthur Freed. On one of his yearly "scouting expeditions" to Broadway, Freed caught a performance of the play and wanted Gene to join the ranks of Hollywood's greatest "dream factory." Such an offer was tempting; according to writer Alan Jay Lerner, Freed was "the producer who had taken the studio [MGM] by the hand and guided it through the bustles and breeches of operetta into the modern world of screen musicals."[54]

Though Freed was a true artist, he was unremarkable from the outside. Journalist Murray Schumach described him as a "tidy, conservatively dressed man with thinning gray hair and a voice that is a chronic growl, ranging from the gentle to the ominous."[55] Ironically, this somber, nondescript man gave audiences more to smile about than any other producer of film musicals. Indeed, his first (albeit uncredited) producing effort was *The Wizard of Oz* (1939). With *Oz*, he began to create his own brand of musical in which plot and character are dependent on songs and musical numbers. Freed's films were lavish glorifications of the American Dream, American music, and the American family. If ever there was a film producer who could artfully utilize Gene's all-American, Everyman persona and dance techniques on screen, it was Freed.

After a performance of *The Time of Your Life*, Freed came backstage and tried to convince Gene of his film potential.

"You want to test me? 'Cause I'm not a handsome guy," Gene stated.

"No tests. You're not going to look any different if you do one," Freed replied.[56]

Gene mulled over Freed's offer. He had not forgotten his humiliating experience at RKO in the summer of 1936. He did not want to repeat it and was certainly not ready to leave Broadway just as he was earning a name there. "I'm not ready to try pictures. My place is here in New York," he told the producer.

Freed accepted Gene's rejection, but he was not about to admit defeat. He felt he could persuade Gene to come to Hollywood—eventually.

Arthur Freed was not the only influential producer to take notice of Gene after the success of *The Time of Your Life*. Billy Rose saw possibilities in him, too. Like Freed, Rose had begun as a songwriter. But unlike Freed, he looked and played the part of a flamboyant producer to the hilt. Betsy Blair described him as "short, with slick black hair, his stubby body encased in a very expensive suit with matching silk polka dot tie and handkerchief. Rose radiated energy and power."[57]

Simultaneous with the run of *The Time of Your Life,* Rose was preparing a new show for his luxurious nightclub, the Diamond Horseshoe. The club was located in the basement of the Edison Hotel on 47th Street between Broadway and 8th Avenue. Near the entrance "across the whole width of the room was a Gay Nineties–type bar, brass railed and mirrored. The walls were red velvet, there were crystal chandeliers." Protruding from the stage was a horseshoe-shaped runway; the inside of the horseshoe lowered between shows and transformed into a dance floor. Enough tables to accommodate four hundred people flanked the stage.[58]

Rose originally wished to engage Robert Alton as choreographer of his show; however, Alton was otherwise committed, so Rose turned to his director, John Murray Anderson, for suggestions. Anderson recalled his work with Gene at Westport and immediately recommended him. Though he respected Anderson's suggestion, Rose was doubtful about Gene's ability to choreograph the show, especially given that he was performing on Broadway at the same time. Gene could hear the dubiousness in Rose's voice when the producer called him to offer him the job.

"I can handle it," Gene declared defensively.

Rose asked Gene for a complete description of how he would stage each part of the show. Gene spoke without pausing for breath for over an hour, then waited for Rose's reaction. All he heard was silence at the other end of the line. Gene assumed he had either walked away from the phone or hung up the receiver.

Just as he was about to hang up himself, Gene heard Rose's voice: "Great. That's exactly what I want. I'll give you $100 a week." Gene balked. He had been paid more for his last two shows. "So I swore at him," Gene recalled years later. "'Don't you talk to me that way,' he said. 'I wouldn't work for you anyway!' I said."

At the peak of their argument, Rose suddenly burst into laughter and said, "Okay, $115 a week."

"I won't work for that," Gene said.

Rose laughed again. "Okay, $135," he conceded.

"I'll take it."[59]

The choreographer from Pittsburgh whom no one had previously wanted had won a plum assignment—and exceptional pay—from one of the most renowned producers in New York. As well as Rose and John Murray Anderson, Gene would be working with an acquaintance he had met at Louie Bergen's, art director Raoul Pene Du Bois. Before Gene, Du Bois, Rose, and Anderson could execute the show, they had to complete one last but crucial task: auditioning six hundred girls Rose had personally invited to try out.

The day before the marathon of auditions, Gene was alone in the club, moving chairs and tables to make room for the girls. He heard a light step behind him and turned to see a sixteen-year-old redheaded girl with long legs and wide blue eyes standing in the entrance. He froze, if only for an instant. The Irish American girl had an attractively cocky way of holding herself. Yet there was a vulnerable naïveté about her that struck Gene. It was clear she had dressed to appear older, in a lavender four-gore flair skirt, polka-dot blouse, gray squirrel coat, pillbox hat, and high-heeled shoes that accentuated her long legs. Raising her chin high, she looked past Gene, who was dressed in "an open-necked white shirt, a dark long-sleeved sweater, dark trousers, and moccasins." Assuming he was a busboy, she approached him and asked about the auditions for dancers.

"You're in the right place, but you're a day early," Gene explained. The girl frowned and turned to leave. Gene called after her: "Are you a dancer?"

"Yes," she replied with a haughty air, as if she were speaking to an underling.

"Are you a *good* dancer?"

"Very," she replied, and left hastily.[60] Gene smiled after her.

The next day, the red-haired girl returned, but she came without her previous self-assurance. Six hundred girls were competing with her, and they all had the same personal card from Billy Rose that she thought had been given to her alone. After the stage manager corralled the girls into groups of twenty, he introduced them to Rose, Anderson, Du Bois, and "our choreographer, Gene Kelly." The girl suppressed a gasp. The "busboy" was the choreographer. "I felt the blush begin in the pit of my stomach. [But] when I happened to catch his eye, he grinned at me," the teenager, whose invitation bore the name Betsy Blair, later recalled. Through her mortification, she felt previously untouched emotions stir within her. "The combination of sensitive Irish face and slim muscular body was spectacular enough, but he was also the only one . . . who looked at us as individuals," Betsy explained. Despite Gene's encouraging grin, she felt certain she had no chance of securing a job. As she showed her dancing abilities to the four men, Betsy heard the stage manager mutter: "She's got no tits. She looks twelve years old." Rose argued that her "long stems" made up for her flat chest. Gene ultimately convinced Rose to hire her: "She can dance. We need good dancers."[61]

Betsy was thrilled to be under Gene's care. Billy Rose was known to make inappropriate advances toward chorines, but she had no fears in that direction working at the Diamond Horseshoe with the choreographer, who urged the girls to "just call him Gene." He was a strict professional, concerned only with how hard the girls were willing to work.[62]

Gene worked as hard as Betsy and the other chorus girls in trying to make real the ideas he had explained to Rose over the telephone. For the first show, which Gene named *Nights of Gladness,* he devised an Irish number that blended swing and traditional Irish clog dance. Gene deemed the number "the most tangle-footed to direct, and the most rhythm-wrecking to score."[63]

In Betsy Blair's 2003 memoir, she described other numbers Gene designed. Striving toward his goal of creating balletic dance that was accessible to everyday Americans, he planned a football-themed number and a schoolyard ballet that included "identifiable characters" such as a boy, a girl, a bookworm, and a bully. However, Rose vetoed the rather unglamorous schoolyard number and instead demanded "almost obligatory can-can and South American numbers." "They don't come to the Diamond Horseshoe to see a fucking ballet!" Rose shouted.[64]

Gene obeyed Rose's orders. He enjoyed his work for Rose in spite of the producer's less refined taste. After all, he was among friends at the Horseshoe. He had secured his roommate Dick Dwenger a job as a rehearsal pianist at the club.

It did not take long after the revue's opening for the nightclub to reach capacity each evening. According to syndicated columnist Walter Winchell, the crowds were drawn more by Gene's numbers with the chorus than the club's various headliners. Winchell stated that Billy Rose's "American Beauties" were the "youngest, prettiest, chorus line in New York—and some swell numbers they do. Go see them!"[65]

Gene was dazzled by the great Winchell's praise of his numbers, but the columnist's words did not cloud his vision: not everything and everyone involved with the Diamond Horseshoe was perfect. He was becoming swiftly disillusioned with his mentor, John Murray Anderson, who was making Betsy Blair the target of vicious humor. Noting the girl's infatuation with Gene, he nicknamed her "teacher's pet" and made her, as she recalled, "his chosen scapegoat." Betsy had a habit of tossing her head when she danced, which prompted Anderson to shout: "Teacher's Pet, come here! Your head was bobbing like a cork in the ocean again. Kneel down before me and apologize!" Rather than give way to tears, Betsy made an elaborate, medieval curtsy and murmured, "I'm sorry, Sire." Several chorines began clapping, but Gene clapped the loudest.[66]

Betsy felt victorious where Anderson was concerned, but she was still confused as to where she stood with Gene. She did not wish him to view her as merely amusing. She realized she was in love with him one night during the can-can finale, when she spotted Gene with a beautiful brunette at the bar watching the show. The woman was, as she later learned, Helene Marlowe. Betsy recalled that as she high-kicked and smiled through the number, tears streamed down her face.

Little did Betsy know that she need not have worried about the brunette. Though Gene did not immediately intend to woo Betsy, he could not ignore the fact that he felt something for her deeper than a teacher's appreciation of an apt pupil. She was markedly different from Helene Marlowe; she was a girl who needed him, one to whom he could offer guidance. And he was a man who needed to feel useful.

Gene realized his relationship with Helene Marlowe had been in a state of limbo for too long and showed little promise of moving forward. They parted amicably. Back in Pittsburgh, Harriet was relieved to learn of Gene's severed ties with Helene—especially after she discovered that the girl refused to convert to Catholicism as a condition of marriage. One journalist, visiting Helene in 2011, wrote, "I've tried to get her talking about Gene but have not been very successful, except for memories of Michael, the dog. . . . Helene Marlowe did not go on to laugh and be teased about her serious relationship with Gene. She went on to marriage and a child and a happy life, but the heartbreak about Gene is still with her at ninety-five, some seventy years later."[67]

Gene buried any sorrow he felt over finally ending his relationship with Helene in his work. While still employed at the Horseshoe, Gene took jobs on two smaller shows that were in closer alignment to his proletariat sensibilities. *Two Weeks with Pay*, a musical revue, opened in June 1940 at the Ridgeway Summer Theatre in White Plains, New York, before an audience of five hundred. Gene staged all dances for the revue, which had "vacation merrymaking" as its theme. Fred Kelly was in the cast, though a reporter for the *New York Times,* oddly, referred to him as "Maurice."[68] The show included contributions from twenty renowned writers and composers, including Cole Porter, Rodgers and Hart, Ira Gershwin, Johnny Green, and Johnny Mercer. Intended to reach Broadway in September, it never progressed past the summer theater season. In July, Gene appeared in *The Royal Roost,* a show penned by Dick Dwenger about a group of indigents who inhabit an abandoned mansion. It opened at the Stamford Connecticut Community Playhouse. Both shows garnered mention in the *New York Times,* tangible proof that Gene's rise in New York theater, as one *Times* reporter stated, "has assumed meteoric proportions."[69] The reporter had ample reason to make such a claim. By the end of the summer, Johnny Darrow came to Gene with the news that he was the front runner to play the most coveted role of the upcoming theater season, and arguably, the entire decade: Joey Evans in *Pal Joey.*

6

Bewitched, Bothered, and Bewildered

"He . . . set theatrical fire to the theatre, to 44th Street and Broadway, and to all of New York before the first week was out."[1]

Who was the young man responsible for such an incendiary performance? Twenty-eight-year-old Gene Kelly, better known on stage to his friends and foes as Pal Joey.

Gene's casting could not have come at a more fortuitous time. Indeed, it coincided with what was, as far as the show business world was concerned, the end of the Depression. According to film scholar Mark Vieira, 1939 had been "a watershed year. The Great Depression was barely over, but America was again feeling the chill winds of change. Politics, economics, and art braced for war. There was a lull before the storm and Hollywood, as if expecting to be judged by posterity, produced a portfolio of classics. . . . In 1939 every week was a cinematic cornucopia."[2] *Gone with the Wind, The Wizard of Oz, Mr. Smith Goes to Washington, Babes in Arms,* and *Wuthering Heights* were only a few of the year's notable releases. The following year, 1940, Broadway theatergoers enjoyed a similar "cornucopia." Ethel Waters starred in the all-black show *Cabin in the Sky,* Ethel Merman belted out Cole Porter tunes in *Panama Hattie,* Monty Woolley was an acerbic curmudgeon in *The Man Who Came to Dinner*—and Gene Kelly was a heel with a heart in Richard Rodgers and Lorenz Hart's *Pal Joey.*

Pal Joey, arguably the most innovative and fresh Broadway production since *Show Boat* (1927), seemed tailor-made for Gene. The following passage, penned by writer John O'Hara, could have been written for him: "I don't know whether you're the right man for the job or not," nightclub manager Mike tells Joey at the opening of the play. "This job calls for a young punk about your age. About your build—about your looks. But he has to be master of ceremonies . . . he has to introduce the acts, such as they are—he has to have a lot of self-confidence. He has to be able to get up and tell a story. He has to be sure of himself in case he gets heckled."[3] Although he had been unable to cope with hecklers as a fledgling dancer, Gene had grown markedly more self-assured now; he had even acted as master of ceremonies in Westport the previous summer. Gene, for all intents and purposes, had been working toward *Pal Joey* for his entire career.

Richard Rodgers, with his partner Lorenz Hart, took on the task of writing the score for the musical adaptation of two short stories by John O'Hara. Rodgers later wrote that the idea of doing a show with a hero who was not "a conventional clean-cut juvenile" would "open up enormous possibilities for a more realistic view of life than theatregoers were accustomed to." They had never before written a show like *Pal Joey*, but Rodgers and Hart proved to be ideal composers for the production. Rodgers claimed that Hart had spent "thousands of hours" in clubs like those depicted in the play and thus was "thoroughly familiar with the Pal Joeys of the world."[4] The blend of Rodgers's refined melodies and Hart's harder-edged lyrics succeeded in capturing the characters' attempts to enter high society without first reforming themselves.

Pal Joey is set in a cheap nightclub on the South Side of Chicago. "Not cheap in the whorehouse way, but strictly a neighborhood joint," O'Hara explained. The play depicts the manner in which Joey Evans rises to prominence as owner of his own posh nightclub by taking advantage of the affections and patronage of Vera Simpson, a wealthy, married, older woman. He has little respect for women, whom he refers to as "mice," and never stops to consider their feelings (in this aspect, Joey is a complete departure from Gene, who felt protective of women). Joey is undeniably a heel whose heart, in the words of the show's only likeable character, Linda English, seems to be "asleep."

Yet somehow, the audience feels sympathy for Joey. He is gullible, desperate for approval, and oblivious of the malapropisms he uses in his efforts to sound intelligent. He invents elaborate stories about himself to impress Linda and Vera, and he is the only one who does not realize the transparency of his tales. After trusting a shady agent, losing his club, and being abandoned by Vera Simpson, Joey's heart finally awakens. He finds himself penniless and, only half joking, declares that he plans to imitate Larry Renault, John Barrymore's character in *Dinner at Eight* (which he incorrectly calls *Dinner at Eight Thirty*), by committing suicide via gas. The new manager of the club demands that he leave immediately. As he slinks out, he is aware of Linda looking on. He tries to retain an air of bravado as he accepts her invitation to supper at her sister's house.

After dinner, Joey and Linda walk past the pet shop where they first met. Joey is still spinning tales, though he now lacks conviction as he tells them. He plans to enter "those big New York shows." Continuing with a shrug, he states: "I don't know. They [Broadway plays] might bore me . . . I may shoot you a wire and let you know how things go."

"Oh, that would be wonderful," Linda says. "Goodbye."

As Joey leaves her, he utters his first sincere words. "And thanks. Thanks a million."[5]

Rodgers, in his concluding theory on *Pal Joey,* wrote, "While Joey himself may have been fairly adolescent in his thinking and his morality, the show bearing his name certainly wore long pants and in many respects forced the entire musical-comedy theatre to wear long pants for the first time."[6] The most sophisticated aspect of the play was its use of lyrics in place of dialogue to move the story forward and define characters. "Bewitched, Bothered, and Bewildered" serves to characterize Vera Simpson while the title song shows Joey the Heel. "I Could Write a Book," on the other hand, allows a small glimpse into his human side. In the first verse, he admits to Linda that he "never learned to spell and never learned to count" but that he wishes to write a book about how to make "two lovers of friends."[7]

The show's dances served to create atmosphere and further deepen characterization. Certain numbers that were representations of entertainment at the nightclub were "shows within shows." For instance, the song and dance routine "Chicago" represented the low caliber of the club at which Joey works before Vera sponsors him. The dance steps are tired and the lyrics are clichéd. More refined dances take place after Joey sings the title song. He launches into a dream ballet illustrating the grandeur of "Chez Joey," his own club.

> It's going to be the right club for the swell gentry
> It's elementary
> I'll wear top hat and cane
> in Chez Joey.[8]

When Robert Alton was hired as dance director for *Pal Joey,* he immediately thought of Gene for the title role. Rodgers was of the same opinion.

After seeing Gene in *The Time of Your Life,* he informed O'Hara that "we had our Joey." Gene received a call from his agent, Johnny Darrow, urging him to find a singing coach as soon as possible. He would be auditioning at the Century Theatre before producer George Abbott, Robert Alton, John O'Hara, and the composers. The fact that he would have two allies in the audience, Robert Alton and Lorenz Hart (with whom he often drank at his haunt, Louie Bergen's), boosted his confidence. When Gene arrived at the theater and noted that Hart was absent, he claimed to have felt suddenly terrified. Rodgers, O'Hara, and Abbott did nothing to defuse Gene's anxiety during the audition. Their faces remained immobile as he sang "I Didn't Know What Time It Was," a tune from the Rodgers and Hart catalogue. Gene had not stopped to consider that he had made an enormous error in his choice of audition song. "This kind of thing looks like you're currying a favor," Gene dryly acknowledged years later.[9]

When he finished, Rodgers was the first to respond. "Sing something with a faster tempo." Gene nodded and launched into "It's the Irish in Me," a "lively ditty" he used to perform in cloops. Only after Gene sang the last note in the Irish tune did O'Hara show a sign of life. "That's it. Take him!" he burst out.[10]

And yet, in spite of O'Hara's overwhelming approval, Gene had not yet secured the part. Abbott was hesitant to sign a dancer who had never carried an entire show himself. Discouraged, Gene escaped to Maine for his semi-annual vacation. Three weeks passed. Gene heard unsettling rumors that another dancer had already been signed as Joey. However, Abbott surprised Darrow when he called with an offer to sign Gene for $350 a week. Darrow was aware that such a figure was too low for a leading part. But the agent recalled the unsuccessful negotiation he had tried to make for Gene with the Shuberts in 1938. He did not argue with Abbott: he accepted the offer. Gene rushed back from Maine upon hearing Darrow's good news. Accepting the role did mean he would have to leave the cast of *The Time of Your Life* just as it was ready for a national tour. The producers were at a loss as to who could fill the role of Harry the Hoofer as ably as Gene. Gene knew of one dancer who could: his younger brother. Fred Kelly successfully took over the part, much to the relief of William Saroyan and all involved in the play. Indeed, Fred secured permission from Saroyan to add five new dances to his part; he went on to win three Donaldson Awards (precursors to the Tony Awards) for his performance.

Harry the Hoofer and every other stage role Gene had filled thus far were decidedly supporting parts; Joey Evans was onstage for almost the entire running time of *Pal Joey*. Though Gene explained in 1990 that he "was not intimidated" by the role of Joey, because he was young and "grateful just to be getting a chance," he admitted that "once I started playing it, I found it was a very demanding role . . . there were so many songs and dances in that show that I had to keep in training like a boxer."[11] Gene found the singing especially trying. The part required him to deliver five songs, one of which was a solo, "I Could Write a Book." "There is no use my trying to let my voice out because there is not enough to it to show," Gene sighed.[12]

Gene, as dubious as he may have felt about his capabilities, was a stage veteran compared to other members of the cast. Only Vivienne Segal, who filled the role of Vera Simpson, was a truly seasoned performer. Leila Ernst, as Linda English, had appeared in only one previous show, Rodgers and Hart's *Too Many Girls* (1939). Also in the cast of *Too Many Girls* had been twenty-four-year-old Van Johnson, who was engaged as a dancer in *Pal Joey*. Alongside Johnson in the chorus and in a small walk-on role was sixteen-year-old Stanley Donen. Donen, though he was later Gene's protégé and close collaborator, dispelled the rumor that he and Gene became fast friends during the run of *Pal Joey*. In actuality, they hardly crossed paths or spoke during rehearsals.

During the run of *Pal Joey*, a small community similar to that fostered by Vincente Minnelli and Ira Gershwin among Broadway's elite formed among the young members of the cast. Van Johnson and Stanley Donen lived in the same building as Gene's acquaintance from his summer at Westport, composer Hugh Martin, and another young songwriter, Ralph Blane. On many nights after rehearsals, Van took chorine June Allyson out to dinner at the automat. June was currently performing in *Panama Hattie* with another up-and-coming dancer, Vera-Ellen. June happened to share a room at the Henry Hudson Hotel (only women tenants permitted) with Betsy Blair, who was also dancing in the chorus of *Panama Hattie*.

Billy Rose had been dismayed and angry when both Betsy and Gene left the Diamond Horseshoe for better jobs. "You'll never work on Broadway. I can stop you. And you won't be receiving your last paycheck!" Rose had screamed at Betsy. "You keep the money. You act as if you need it!" Betsy retorted. She fled to Louie Bergen's, where she was to meet Gene. Eventually, they "fell about laughing" over the entire incident. Then, growing serious, he raised his drink to her and said, "You're some brave kid."[13]

Gene, as the eldest in the crowd of the new "kids" on Broadway, was an inspiration to the younger performers. But he too had yet to cement his place in New York. "We all shared a wonderful camaraderie, Gene was just one of us," Van Johnson recalled. "Trying to get along and loving his work, every minute of it. Gene was always very serious, very tense, very bright, about his work."[14] Gene's intensity, however, did set him apart from the others. Arguably, the only other young hopeful with his level of ambition was Betsy Blair.

For a time, it seemed that Gene's and Betsy's careers were in sync. When one found a role in a bigger play, so did the other. Thus, the two found themselves continually drawn together. "It developed gradually, our romance . . . over after-theatre suppers at Bergen's," Gene explained. "And we found out we liked the same things . . . and each other."[15]

Betsy Blair may have only been sixteen years old, but she already knew what many adults never discover: what she wanted from life. Born on December 11, 1923, as Elizabeth Boger, she was raised in a large Catholic family in a diverse neighborhood in Cliffside, New Jersey. Betsy's interest in politics was cultivated in her childhood due to the juxtaposed ideologies of her parents. Her father, William, was an insurance broker and a staunch Republican while her mother, Frederica, was a schoolteacher and a Democrat. Betsy more often than not followed her mother's beliefs, partly because she grew disillusioned with her father from an early age. After he became aware that Betsy knew he was carrying on an affair with another woman, he became hypercritical of her. Frederica, however, was Betsy's strongest supporter. She was as hard-working as Harriet Kelly in her efforts to keep her family together. But Mrs. Boger, unlike Harriet, was far less outspoken and kept her feelings to herself.

In this way, Betsy did not wish to emulate her mother. She strove to establish her independence at as young an age as possible. She saw herself doing this by becoming a dancer/actress. Because of her single-minded vision for her future, Betsy sped through her childhood, entering high school at age twelve and graduating at age fifteen. Throughout her adolescence, she honed her dancing skills and regularly modeled in catalogues. Betsy was most often the youngest member in whatever group she found herself, but she thrived in the company of more experienced show people. Consequently, Betsy was thrilled when her parents gave her permission to live in New York and work at the Diamond Horseshoe in the summer before she would presumably enter college.

In that summer of 1940, Betsy explained, she felt "everything was possible. And besides, it [the hotel where I lived] was two blocks up and three blocks over from Gene's hotel. I was in heaven." Gene, barely showing signs of fatigue after his long hours rehearsing for *Pal Joey*, would invite her out on the town almost every night with Dick Dwenger. "I was their project. Oh, lucky girl that I was," Betsy remembered.[16]

Gene yearned to pour into her young, untutored mind all the culture and philosophy he had absorbed and was impatient to share. One of his first missions was to escort Betsy to the Museum of Modern Art and the Metropolitan Museum of Art. Then he took her on a tour like that in the famed opening of his 1949 film, *On the Town*. He showed her every area of their "wonderful town"—the Battery, the docks, Little Italy, Chinatown, the Village. Betsy remembered many a night that she, Gene, and Dick attended the Apollo Theatre and the Cotton Club in Harlem and enjoyed performances by Gene's acquaintances Cab Calloway, Buck and Bubbles, and the Nicholas Brothers. She sipped ginger ale while Gene drank beer. Other nights, they frequented the Vanguard in Greenwich Village to watch Gene's friends Betty Comden and Adolph Green perform with the Revuers.

Gene did not neglect to show Betsy the opulent side of New York at clubs such as the Copacabana, the El Morocco, and the Rainbow Room. When Gene brought Betsy to the Rainbow Room, he was slated to make an appearance at the venue. However, the club's choreographer, Jack Cole, recalled that Gene "just wasn't suited for so sophisticated a spot."[17] According to Betsy, her and Gene's "best place" was the Polish Folk Hall. There, Gene utilized a few moves he had learned during his summers in Chicago—most notably the mazurka and the polka. Betsy reflected that, in taking her to every conceivable corner of the city, Gene gave her New York.[18]

It was often six o'clock in the morning before Gene would return with Betsy to his and Dick's room at the Woodward Hotel. Gene would proceed to make tea and toast for everyone. Many nights, he played hours of classical music on their turntable after discovering that Mozart, Beethoven, Copland, and Stravinsky were "just names" to Betsy.

Had she not met Gene, Betsy may have attended Sarah Lawrence College, where she had already been accepted. But she did meet Gene Kelly "and lived instead the life that housewives and young girls alike paid money to inhabit, via the silver screen, for two hours at a time."[19] Betsy wrote that she guessed "it was obvious to everyone but Gene and me that I was besotted."[20]

Betsy claimed that while Gene nourished "the romantic, dreaming part" of her, another actor and regular at Louie Bergen's, thirty-three-year-old Lloyd Gough, rounded out another part of her "education."[21] The most passionate member of Gene's left-leaning friends, Gough habitually bombarded Betsy with questions about current events such as the Spanish Civil War or asked her if she had read liberal texts such as *The History of the Communist Party in the Soviet Union*. Without Gene, she attended Marxist study groups at Gough's apartment every Wednesday and Friday.

Though Betsy was easily drawn in by the ideas and lifestyles of those close to her, she still maintained her own opinions and an independence remarkable in one so young. However, at sixteen, she found herself torn between self-reliance and becoming dependent on a man—Gene. She reflected in her memoir:

> Although I wasn't conscious of a big hole in my life, I sure set about filling it quickly. I'm not saying that I saw Gene as fatherly. . . . He was too vital and sexy to be cast as a father. But I find myself wondering over and over why that twenty-eight-year-old man wanted the child I was at sixteen. . . . Gene was a natural carer, a smart, creative, and benevolent boss type. . . . [Yet he] enjoyed my spirit and smiled with indulgence at my quirks and radical ideas. But it was *his* life that I was becoming part of, not my life nor even our life, but his.[22]

After months of hearing their daughter rhapsodize about "Mr. Kelly," Betsy's parents finally had the opportunity to meet him. His friendly demeanor and genuine interest in their daughter immediately won their approval.[23] Though the Bogers assumed Betsy's interests in Gene and the theater were merely summer fancies, Betsy was already planning to postpone college another year. "I couldn't leave New York and Gene. Everything was too exciting."[24]

If Betsy ever came to resent Gene for being part of her choice to forsake college, she never spoke of it. Show business was her life, just as it was Gene's. Gene, like Betsy, was a motivated self-learner. He read two books a month, most often on history or philosophy. Gene could have become a law or economics professor, just as Betsy could have become a schoolteacher, but they both thrived on challenge—and few places offered more challenges than the theater.

"Those were wonderful days," Gene later reflected on the period when he simultaneously worked on *Pal Joey* and fell in love with Betsy.[25] They were equally uncertain days—depending on the failure or success of the show, it could either open or close potential new worlds for Gene and for his future with Betsy.

"I watched him rehearsing, and it seemed to me there was no possible room for improvement. Yet he wasn't satisfied. . . . It was midnight. I could see a single lamp burning on the stage. . . . Under it a figure was dancing. He was Gene Kelly."[26] Van Johnson's reminiscences offer proof that Gene was as invested in *Pal Joey*, if not more so, than its producer and composers. George Abbott, John O'Hara, Rodgers, and Hart began to see the play as representative of a troublesome rather than a wonderful time in their lives. After it went into rehearsals at the Biltmore and Longacre on November 11, 1940, both O'Hara and Hart often disappeared for days or even weeks at a time. The two artists' absences left Rodgers and Abbott to shoulder the burdens of rewriting and last-minute casting before the premiere on Christmas Eve 1940. Though Gene admitted that on many nights after rehearsals he would go to a cloop with O'Hara and Hart (when they were in town, that is) and stay there until four in the morning, he was always up early for the next day's work. Gene did not drink to excess and claimed to have "practically gone on the wagon" for the run of *Pal Joey*.[27]

As elated as Gene was to be part of a Rodgers and Hart production, he could not ignore the physical toll it was taking on him. During rehearsals, his weight dropped from 163 pounds to 147. Though he later claimed never to have seen a vitamin pill in his life, he consulted a doctor, who promptly gave him a course of vitamin B-1 tablets.[28] The strenuousness of his role did not keep Gene from endeavoring to interpret and gain an intimate knowledge of his character, just as he had when playing Harry the Hoofer. "Joey isn't bad—he just doesn't know the difference. . . . By all his standards, and the standards of the people he's been brought up with, it's . . . an accomplishment to land a rich society dame and work her for all he can," Gene stated in one interview.[29] In another he noted with a wry grin, "When my mother comes to New York to see the show, and sees the kind of a no-good skunk I'm playing, she'll probably yank me off the stage and drag me home by the ear."[30]

After weeks of exhausting rehearsals, Gene and the rest of the cast were ready for an out-of-town tryout in Philadelphia. Gene, with a strained voice and frayed nerves, felt that the "freshness" he had originally thought he could bring to the role had left him; the part had become a "burden." However, Gene's sudden pessimism ended after act 1 of the tryout. Johnny Darrow rushed backstage after the curtain fell to inform Gene that his Joey was already so wonderful that "by the time you get to New York you'll be knocking the shit out the part."[31]

On December 24, 1940, Gene prepared to make his entrance on the stage of the Ethel Barrymore Theatre. In the audience were the harshest of New York's theater critics as well as Gene's mother, who was wringing her hands with anxiety. Gene mentioned in subsequent interviews that his mother was in the audience, but he never said whether his father or siblings came to see the show. Betsy Blair was also there, with Dick Dwenger as her escort. For Gene, the performance went as if he "were in a dream."[32] By the end of the show, critics and audience members alike realized that the dancer had come forth as an actor.

The first person he saw after the curtain closed was his mother, weeping with happiness. After kissing her, Gene ran to Betsy, who had rushed backstage as the audience was still applauding. The couple went to Lorenz Hart's to celebrate Christmas. Ordinarily, as is the custom on a show's opening night, the group would also have been awaiting the first reviews. But the next day was a holiday—Gene would have to wait an excruciating twenty-four hours to read critics' reactions. However, Hart and the rest of the company were sure the show was a hit and felt it was not premature to celebrate.

They were correct: on December 26, critics released almost unanimously positive reviews. "Take my tip and don't miss *Pal Joey*. . . . Gene Kelly is terrific as Joey. He acts, he sings, he dances superbly," raved Robert Morris of the *Mirror*. The *New York Times* ran an advertisement with various reviews for *Pal Joey*, including one by Louis Kronenberger of *PM*: "*Pal Joey* is the most unhackneyed show since *Of Thee I Sing* . . . superbly illiterate and full of rich and gamey spade-calling."[33] But Brooks Atkinson of the *New York Times*, the critic notorious for the "morning after put down," had little praise for *Pal Joey*.[34] Atkinson did concede: "If it is possible to make an entertaining musical comedy out of an odious story, *Pal Joey* is it." But his concluding statement, "Can you draw sweet water from a foul well?" has become one of the "most quoted lines in the annals of Broadway theater criticism."[35] Rather than sap theatergoers' interest, Atkinson's review drew audiences curious to see what made the show so loathsome. Gene later admitted that after certain scenes in the play, he "could feel the waves of hate coming from the audience." Undaunted, he devised clever ways to defuse their revulsion. "I'd smile at them and dance and it would relax them. It was interesting to use the character to manipulate the audience," he explained. "The audience would think 'This jerk isn't such a jerk after all. The jerk!'"[36]

The press grew more positive as the weeks passed, virtually erasing the effects of Atkinson's words. By March, four months into the show's run, Gene had become a regular guest at parties where he mingled with musical comedy masters including Victor Moore and George M. Cohan. In June 1941, *Pal Joey* was still receiving full-page spreads in the *New York Times*, though journalists now focused specifically on Gene's work. John Martin, dance critic of the *Times*, wrote with enthusiasm: "A tap dancer who can characterize his routines and turn them into an integral element of an imaginative theatrical whole, would seem to be pretty close, indeed, to unique."[37]

The importance of *Pal Joey* in Gene's career cannot be overstated. In this production, he created a blueprint for all of his succeeding works. "Dancing and character are far more closely united than in the majority of ballets, and through both there runs a penetrating line of comment which makes it possible to laugh at Joey instead of shooting him forthwith," Martin observed.[38] Since his earliest days learning from the dance masters in Chicago, Gene strove to give his dances meaning and allow them to communicate more than dialogue. He had accomplished his goal in *The Time of Your Life*, but in *Pal Joey*, he took it a step further through his dream ballet. It was the first time Gene had used such a device—but in subsequent years, he would seldom fail to include one in his projects. Because Gene made the original Joey so special, he could never quite dissociate himself from the part. Indeed, in the 1952 revival of the show, the writers inserted Gene's slang term *cloop* into Joey's vocabulary.

Gene's peers had seen the risk *Pal Joey* held for him early on. "My friends said 'Don't do it.' They said I would get myself marked as a lousy heel," Gene noted. "Well, if that is to be, let it."[39] In one cast member's estimation, Gene actually absorbed some of Joey's personality traits. Stanley Donen was "astonished" by Gene's "cockiness" and "confidence in himself." He found Gene "egotistical and very rough," alleging that he had "a ruthlessness in the way he went about things."[40] Gene's success could have easily bred vanity, especially given that, in Van Johnson's recollection, each time Gene walked on the set, "the ladies and gentlemen of the ensemble . . . [prodded] each other in the ribs and [said], 'There's Kelly,' with more than a little awe in their voices."[41]

Though Gene's dominating presence was off-putting to Donen, he was not the self-involved star he appeared to be. Van Johnson asserted that Gene carried "no swank, no pretense."[42] In truth, Gene held the struggling members of the chorus in high regard. He took special note of Donen, considering him the dancer with the most promise in the show. Additionally, Gene did not begrudge the production's bit players their moments of glory. He recalled that "the kids would line up knee-deep outside the Ethel Barrymore Theatre where we were playing. The first night I thought those kids were for me, supposedly the star of the show. I learned differently. It was that red-haired chorus boy they were after."[43] Gene, rather than resent the redhead—Van Johnson—became closer friends with him. With Van, Donen, Keenan Wynn (Gene's friend from the Westport Stock Company), and Charles Walters, Gene would often catch midnight shows of whatever Fred Astaire movie was showing at the time. Walters recalled: "We all used to go up to the balcony so we could smoke, talk, and dream out loud."[44]

Gene, behind his cockiness and confidence, was still a dreamer, fantasizing about possible outcomes of his uncertain show business future. "I know I'm lucky now," Gene said. "But what if my next show is lousy and I am shown up as being not too good? You don't get a book and songs like [Pal Joey] every year, you know."[45]

In spring 1941, Gene received a most unexpected visitor backstage after an evening performance of Pal Joey: MGM's fastest-rising musical star, Judy Garland. Judy, like Gene, was one of producer Arthur Freed's discoveries. He had insisted she be cast as Dorothy in The Wizard of Oz (1939) when studio head Louis B. Mayer pushed for Shirley Temple. Judy became a sensation not only in Oz but also in a subsequent string of backstage musicals in which she costarred with top box office attraction Mickey Rooney. As a result of Judy becoming (with Mickey) the nation's first teenage idol, Mayer's respect for Freed's hunches increased exponentially.

Gene admired Judy's film work, particularly The Wizard of Oz. Despite his propensity for playing streetwise, unsentimental characters, he held a reverence for childhood throughout his entire life. At his and Judy's first meeting, he saw that she was unlike the archetypal insincere Hollywood personalities who had made him disdain the idea of ever making movies. She was earnest, down to earth, and had talent comparable to the most highly regarded Broadway singers. Like Gene, she had taken on the role of breadwinner for her family at an early age and worked her way through unsavory vaudeville houses until she attained stardom. For these reasons, Gene respected her as a true professional.

During a brief respite Judy had earned between motion pictures, she chose New York as her vacation destination. She was eager to be considered an adult; thus, her choice to see a mature show like *Pal Joey* did not come as a surprise. Still, Judy's mother, Ethel, and members of the MGM press team chaperoned her to the theater. By the time the curtain closed, Gene had the nineteen-year-old actress thoroughly entranced. Judy and her entourage of press aides went backstage to see the star after the audience finally stopped applauding. Judy and Gene exchanged compliments on one another's work.

Never missing an opportunity for publicity, the press agents suggested that Judy and Gene dine at the Copacabana together. In agreeing, Gene broke a date with Betsy. After spending an hour or two at the nightspot dining and dancing, Gene suggested he and Judy go out alone together.

"I don't see how I could get away," Judy said.

"Don't you trust people or is it your press agents that don't trust people?" Gene asked.[46]

Judy escaped from her minders long enough to reach East 52nd Street, where she and Gene danced at Leon and Eddie's nightclub. The fairy-tale evening continued with a horse and buggy ride through Central Park. "It'd be great if we could make a picture together!" Judy declared.[47]

For the next few days, all Gene could speak of was Judy, Arthur Freed, and Hollywood. But he had yet to win Louis B. Mayer's approval. The man whose vision of the world was defined by the apple pie world of Andy Hardy films bristled at the darkness of *Pal Joey* and its antihero. "Too short, too sexy, not sympathetic, not for us," Mayer concluded after seeing Gene perform on Broadway.[48]

Arthur Freed had observed in his experience that performers with unconventional looks—like Fred Astaire, Mickey Rooney, or Judy Garland—often exuded an indefinable star quality on camera. Because of Judy's and Freed's relentless persistence, Mayer finally agreed to invite

Gene to work at his studio.[49] When Mayer told Gene he would like to have him at MGM, Gene replied: "I'll wait until the show [*Joey*] is through. Then I want to take a test out here [in New York], not there." Gene was aware that MGM was famous for its unflattering screen tests. "You don't need to take a screen test. I'll hire you when you're ready," Mayer assured him.

The mogul's offer certainly made Gene's future less uncertain—if he accepted it. The proposal was more tempting because he would not have to undergo a screen test—he was still smarting from the humiliation of shooting one at RKO five years before. "I was sure Arthur Freed was behind all this," Gene reflected years later, recalling the producer's eagerness to sign him after *The Time of Your Life*.[50] MGM was hard to resist. Although it was the youngest of the major studios in Hollywood (it began functioning in 1924), it already enjoyed more prestige than any other production company. According to historian Peter Hay, "The world of MGM is brighter, darker, and more romantic than real life because MGM cinematographers worked with directors and the art department to enhance the mood of the scripts and increase the illusion of reality."[51]

Gene accepted Mayer's offer, but not without trepidation. As a self-proclaimed liberal and part of "the sweatshirt generation," he was uncertain how well he would fit in the conservative, rarefied atmosphere of MGM.[52] Moreover, despite the opportunities MGM presented, Gene found it painful to contemplate leaving his social circle in New York. Betsy Blair shared his hesitation. In fact, she hoped to dissuade him from accepting Mayer's offer. She and Gene enjoyed the rich, full lives they had made for themselves in New York.

Thus Gene and Betsy were both, to varying degrees, relieved when Gene found a reason to reject Mayer. Several days after Gene agreed to work for the studio, he "got a notice from MGM . . . it said, 'You must take a screen test.'" Gene's temper immediately flared and he shouted over the phone at the MGM lackey that Mayer was a liar. He then proceeded to write Mayer a livid letter letting him know there would be no Gene Kelly in Hollywood for the time being. At MGM, Freed and Mayer were shaking their heads. Freed had in fact ordered stills of Gene, not a screen test. He intended to persuade Gene to come back, but such a task was more difficult than he expected.[53]

Gene was stubborn; he would not hear of working for Mayer, "that right wing punk who lied to me." As Gene's friend Jules Steinberg explained his mindset: "If he had an idea in his head about something, he wasn't going to let anything come between it and him."[54] Gene refocused his energy on *Pal Joey* and Betsy Blair.

Betsy, like Gene, had continued to ascend on Broadway. She had "inherited" June Allyson's part in *Panama Hattie,* which gave her one line: "Hello, sailor!" However, a far better opportunity soon came her way: one night at Louie Bergen's during dinner with Gene and Dick Dwenger, William Saroyan offered her the chance to audition for a role in a production she came to view as her career's *Pal Joey,* the ingénue in Saroyan's new play, *The Beautiful People.*

When Betsy met with Saroyan and the show's producer, Pat Duggan, Gene was with her. Betsy recalled that Gene "was being very protective— almost as if he were my agent." Duggan was dubious that the seventeen-year-old Betsy could fill the part and would not cast her until he heard her project her "tiny voice" onstage. Gene took the script home and stayed up all night to prepare himself to work on two scenes with Betsy the following day. On the morning of the audition, Gene went with Betsy onstage. They had spoken only six or seven words from the scenes they had rehearsed when Saroyan rose from his seat in the auditorium and exclaimed: "Okay, that's enough!" Gene, clenching his fists, shouted: "Give her a chance, Bill!" Saroyan laughed, defusing Gene's anger. "I said 'okay.' She's okay," he clarified.[55]

When *The Beautiful People* premiered at the Lyceum Theatre on April 21, 1941, Betsy's notices were positive; one writer stated, "This is one 'mouse' Kelly better do right by." Betsy's performance in the show was enough to make a talent scout from Twentieth Century-Fox offer her a contract; but, like Gene, Betsy ignored the studio's pleas that she make a screen test. "I foolishly decided not to accept," Betsy reflected in 2003. "I didn't want to be a 'starlet.'" Betsy saw her opportunities in her future stage career—and her relationship with Gene—as boundless. "Gene and I were in love . . . the horizon glowed with a golden light," she reminisced.[56]

To their friends, Betsy and Gene were a puzzle. They knew she was more than a "kid sister" to him, but how much more? The two themselves were well aware that their relationship had moved beyond that of teacher and protégée or big brother and little sister. Before they became physically intimate, Betsy explained, they had developed a ritual at the close of each evening. Gene would walk her to her door, at which point she would say, "Thank you. Now I'll walk you back to your hotel, and you can walk me back. I promise after that I'll go in and go to bed." By the end of summer, they often walked until dawn. One night, Betsy was too exhausted to return to her room. "I'll lend you a toothbrush and pajamas," Gene said, motioning for her to come inside his hotel. Betsy followed him upstairs, and they fell asleep in each other's arms. "I don't know what he [Gene] thought. I don't know when he fell in love with me," Betsy wrote. "But Gene was an honorable young man. What remained of his Catholicism manifested itself in his attitude toward women." Though he began to invite her to spend the night at his apartment, Gene never went beyond giving her a kiss before she went to sleep. "You're too young for more than that," he told her. Betsy later admitted that she was impatient to be more than "looked after."[57] His "*not* making love to me was his way of showing me that he *did* love me, though at the time I didn't understand that and wondered what the hell was wrong with him. . . . I wasn't used to being treated with such consideration by men—particularly not men in the theater," she reflected.[58]

Aside from his moral values, Gene did not wish to take their relationship to the next level until he was certain he had a reliable income in New York. Betsy may have thought he had completely forgotten Hollywood, but he could not help wondering if he had been hasty in his decision to reject it a second time. He mulled over missed opportunities and Judy Garland's words, "It'd be great if we could make a picture together!" He did not have to ruminate for long; only weeks after Gene turned Mayer down, the mogul's son-in-law and rival, David O. Selznick, paid the dancer a visit.[59] "Your father-in-law is a son-of-a-bitch because he lied to me," was Gene's greeting to the producer. Unfazed, Selznick chuckled and admitted he had a strong dislike for Mayer, too. Selznick offered him a contract—no screen test required. He added that Gene would be committed only to five pictures, with the option of returning to Broadway for several months per year. Gene softened, especially after Selznick concluded his visit by telling Gene he would receive $750 a week beginning in October 1941. This would give Gene financial security and allow the producers of *Pal Joey* time to find a replacement for the rest of the season (the appropriately named Georgie Tapps took over the part).[60]

Before Gene headed west, he was in talks with William Saroyan to possibly star with Betsy in a play entitled *Sweeney in the Trees*. Saroyan stated that he had written it with the couple in mind. Though they never did the play (and it never made it to Broadway), Gene adopted the nickname "Sweeney" for Betsy. Betsy retaliated, calling him "Geney."

As he prepared to move to Hollywood, Gene completed one last gig in New York—one that, at last, fulfilled his first, true ambition—to be a choreographer. The production, George Abbott's musical *Best Foot Forward,* was no small show. Gene, who in later years spoke of what a lucky man he considered himself, was already aware of his unusual blessings at the age of twenty-nine. A reporter for the *Hartford Courant* recorded that Gene, though he "considers himself too intelligent to be superstitious . . . still touches wood when he talks about the good fortune that has come to him."[61]

"I want little guys, a new fresh team of songwriters on this show," George Abbott announced as *Best Foot Forward* went into production. Van Johnson, who was still rooming in the same apartment house as Hugh Martin and Ralph Blane, suggested that the two musicians "be a team." Martin and Blane heeded Van's suggestion with superior results, although they drove the fellow tenants mad by endlessly pounding out what became the production's theme song, "Buckle Down, Winsocki," on the piano.[62]

It was Martin's suggestion that Gene be considered as choreographer. With only five weeks remaining before the show premiered, Abbott was panicking that he still had no dance director. When Martin told Blane of his idea to suggest Gene, Blane told his partner he was "off his rocker. . . . Gene Kelly's appearing eight times a week at the Shubert Theatre two blocks away. How can he do both?"

Martin took a chance and visited his old colleague during an intermission of *Pal Joey.*

"Hugh, you old stinker, come ona my dressing room. Want a Coke?" Gene asked the songwriter.

Martin, ignoring his question, blurted out: "Will you do the choreography for *Best Foot Forward?*"

Gene, perplexed, asked Martin how he knew he had wanted to work as a choreographer since his arrival in New York.

Martin, feigning omniscience, claimed, "I just know."

"Hmm. Clairvoyant," Gene said, smirking. "Well, I have a four-week vacation coming up. I could stage your show then. That'd be better than a vacation for me."

Martin "raced" to tell Richard Rodgers, a silent partner and music advisor for the show, of the news. Rodgers approved, but Abbott bellowed, "Can't this show be first class without robbing me of my star? *Joey* is our biggest hit yet! How do you know this man has any gift for choreography?"

95

Abbott went to see Gene himself, and whatever words they exchanged succeeded in convincing the producer to give his star the job. Gene was in his element choreographing *Best Foot Forward*. He saw to it that the cast was composed of real teenagers, seven of whom were from the Gene Kelly School of Dance. Martin recalled that by the end of Gene's first day on the set, he had already begun to remedy the problematic show. The songwriter explained that Gene had the pivotal gift of adding "life and humor" to a number, which made the difference between it being well received or "laying an egg." Even more than his directorial talent, Gene's rapport with dancers impressed Martin. There was always "more than a little laughter" when Gene was present during the rehearsals, and the dancers' limbs seemed "supercharged" with energy.[63]

Gene's friendly relationship with the performers made him better able to create dances suited to them, for he took the time to know their personalities. Gene's technique was to "build a number around the particular talents of a performer, then match the individual movements to the music for maximum effect."[64] The cast boasted unique talents who needed special dances; among the performers were June Allyson; Nancy Walker, a sassy "black Irish" girl; and *Pal Joey* alum Stanley Donen.

Gene enlisted Donen's help in his efforts. Gene and the young dancer were well matched, sharing determination, precision in their work, and a strong, if at times "put-down" style of humor. As much as they shared, Donen did not have Gene's brooding quality. "He was not totally serious, far from it. When you're with Stanley, be prepared to fall to the floor giggling," actress Audrey Hepburn later said.[65]

Gene may have been pleased with Donen's help, but Abbott grew weary of the enterprising youth. Several weeks before the show premiered, Abbott ordered his stage manager to dismiss Donen. Gene turned to his brother Fred to assist him in the remaining time before the show opened. *Best Foot Forward* was ready for its tryout period in September 1941.

Gene had accomplished all he had set out to do upon his arrival in New York three years earlier. Once *Best Foot Forward* opened, he could leave for Hollywood with no regrets in his professional life. But he felt more than a little regret at the thought of leaving Betsy Blair. Never before had he been involved with a girl he could not envision living without. Now, with a film contract signed and impressive Broadway credits to his name, marriage seemed a viable—and appealing—option. "I am glad we waited,"

Gene later wrote. "I do not believe in hasty marriages. Nothing so vital, so important, so for-all-your-life, should be a quickie."[66]

In Betsy's memoir, she recalled that Gene's proposal came "one moonlit night" when they were sitting on the edge of a fountain in front of the Plaza Hotel. "He said he wanted me to be the mother of his children, and besides he couldn't leave me alone at the mercy of New York. . . . I said 'Yes yes yes yes yes yes.'"[67] They planned to marry in September after *The Beautiful People* closed and while *Best Foot Forward* was in its tryout period. Because Betsy had not yet turned eighteen, Gene needed her father's permission for marriage. Mr. Boger consented. Betsy and Gene initially planned to be married by a justice of the peace, but after they agreed that the ceremony would take place in Philadelphia with Gene's family in attendance, he decided they should be wed in a Catholic church. Betsy, who still harbored Marxist political convictions, was hesitant. "It has to be in a church. Do you want to kill my mother?" Gene asked, only half joking. Before the ceremony, Betsy (with her fingers crossed behind her back) saw the local priest, promising to convert to Catholicism and raise her children as Catholics. On September 24, 1941, seventeen-year-old Betsy and twenty-nine-year-old Gene wed, with both their families present. The Bogers gave the couple an elaborate breakfast afterward.[68]

The newlyweds spent two weeks in Philadelphia while *Best Foot Forward* was trying out. They enjoyed room service, sightseeing, and visiting museums, although they looked more at each other than the paintings on the walls.

After *Best Foot Forward* wrapped, Betsy and Gene returned to New York for its Broadway premiere. On October 1, 1941, the show opened to rave reviews—even from Brooks Atkinson. Atkinson deemed the play "fresh" and "good-humored," with "none of the sleazy nightlife of Broadway" (one can assume he directed this last comment at *Pal Joey*). Atkinson lauded Gene's dance direction for the production as "droll and whirling."[69] The play ultimately outran *Pal Joey* by more than fifty performances. Hugh Martin claimed that without Gene, "the show would have failed and I would have had no career whatsoever."[70] Martin hardly exaggerated; based on the success of the play, he and Ralph Blane received an offer from MGM for a seven-year contract. Their first assignment? A film adaptation of *Best Foot Forward* produced by Arthur Freed with dance direction by Charles Walters. Stanley Donen traveled to Hollywood as well and snagged a spot as a chorus boy in the film.

At Louie Bergen's, Gene and Betsy's friends arranged a gathering that served as a farewell party, a celebration of *Best Foot Forward*'s success, and a toast to Gene and Betsy's marriage. They ate a chocolate devil's food wedding cake amid "riotous . . . love and laughter."[71] Lloyd Gough made Betsy promise that, once in Hollywood, she would not buy a house with a swimming pool. The most difficult person to whom they bade farewell was Dick Dwenger. He, Gene, and Betsy had become like the Three Musketeers over the past year and a half, and now they wondered if they would ever see each other again. Dick waved good-bye to Betsy and Gene, watching their car embark on a long honeymoon journey to New Orleans and points beyond before proceeding to Hollywood.

Now that he was leaving Broadway, Gene was seized with sudden anxiety that he was making the wrong decision in pursuing films. However, because Selznick's contract allowed him to accept Broadway roles if he so wished, his departure from New York theater did not have to be permanent. Over a decade later, Gene expressed his enduring fondness for life on the stage. "It is one of the strange and wonderful qualities of the theater that once you have been part of it, once you have known it intimately, it always stays the same," Gene reflected. "Coming back to the theater is coming back to reality, to human contacts. . . . These are the things that instantly make the prodigal feel at home when he returns."[72]

No matter what doubts Gene had about his move to Hollywood, he assured himself he had done everything he could in theater for the time being. Indeed, in *Pal Joey,* dance critic John Martin credited him as "surreptitiously" forcing the "high brow columns" to view a musical as a work of art that was "considerably better than most of the works that frankly admit to being art."[73] Now was the time to bring the same transformation to the Hollywood musical. Gene's goals for his life on the West Coast went beyond changing the look of film; he wanted to change the entire idea of Hollywood society, bringing to it the intellectualism he and Betsy had found so fulfilling in New York. With Betsy's support and the collaboration of fellow New York transplants, Gene emerged as one of the first of a new order working to redefine Hollywood moviemaking.

Part 2

Riding on a Rocket

1941–1957

7

At the MGM University

After Gene Kelly proved he was a triple threat—dancer, actor, and singer—in *Pal Joey,* Broadway critic John Martin opined that the "only fear one has for the future is that a young man who can act as well as Kelly can will gradually be weaned away from dancing."[1] Martin's fear almost became a reality. As Gene discussed his future in films with David O. Selznick in the fall of 1941, the producer informed his new star that he intended to make him the next Fredric March. Gene was surprised but intrigued by the prospect. Thirty years later, he reflected: "Selznick only wanted me to be a legitimate actor; he wasn't interested in making musicals—he said he didn't know how to do them!"[2] But Selznick did not intend to pull Gene away from dancing forever. Because of Selznick International's lofty reputation, rival studios often requested "loan-out" services of the actors employed there. Consequently, Gene could be asked to perform in an MGM or Twentieth Century-Fox musical. Selznick International had very few actors under contract but was responsible for introducing such screen legends as Ingrid Bergman and Katharine Hepburn to filmgoers. Among the male stars who regularly worked for Selznick were Fredric March and later Joseph Cotten. If Metro did request Gene's services, he would find far more competition there than at Selznick International. Under contract to MGM were reigning musical actors like George Murphy and Mickey Rooney.

Given the customary breathless pace of Gene's work, MGM would have been a better fit for him. Indeed, beginning in 1940, the studio released more than twenty-six films a year while Selznick produced only two to three "prestige pictures." MGM had the distinction of releasing both prestige pictures and low-budget films (think of the quickly made yet highly entertaining Andy Hardy or Thin Man serials versus meticulous masterpieces like *The Wizard of Oz* or 1940's *The Philadelphia Story*).

By 1940, Selznick International was the highest-grossing studio in Hollywood, thanks largely to *Gone with the Wind*. The following year, however, the studio fell from grace as precipitously as it had risen. Without a major studio in which to reinvest his profits, Selznick and his partners encountered major tax issues that ultimately led to a deal with the Internal Revenue Service to liquidate the studio within three years via dividing and selling the company's assets among the partners. At a profit, Selznick and his partners resold the rights to the studio's most valuable property, *Gone with the Wind*, to MGM. Selznick, who despised Louis B. Mayer, could not have been pleased.

At the time, Gene was unaware of Selznick International's financial woes. At every overnight stop during his and Betsy's trip west, he compulsively telephoned his new employer. "Am I going to be late for an assignment? Am I missing any casting calls?"

Selznick's casual reaction only intensified Gene's anxiety. "There's no hurry. Just enjoy yourself," the producer told him.

Gene had no idea what, if any, definite assignments awaited him in Hollywood—nor, it seemed, did Selznick.

Gene, though riddled with apprehension and anxiety, enjoyed his honeymoon. "We were happy and rich," Betsy reminisced. "We stopped when we wanted to, we ate when we were hungry, we made love wherever we were, we drove through the night if we felt like it . . . [but nothing] could stop us on our appointed way." The newlyweds spent hours on the road playing endless word games, keeping score over the course of each week. "Since we were both such competitive game players, it was a real contest, and the result was usually very close," Betsy remembered.[3]

The couple spent ten days in New Orleans, dining on Cajun food in the French Quarter and enjoying jazz music and dance. Then they took a banana boat to Mexico, where they would spend a few weeks before proceeding to San Francisco for a week-long stop. From there, they would drive down to Hollywood, arriving in mid-November 1941. Photographs from the honeymoon reveal that Betsy was still wearing the plaid skirts, bobby socks, and saddle shoes of a schoolgirl and Gene was still wearing his uniform of khakis, sweatshirt, and loafers. Both looked like freewheeling teenagers on a post-graduation road trip. Like typical fun-loving teens, they allowed their imaginations to run wild when observing their fellow passengers en route to Mexico. They were particularly fascinated with the "gigantic Chinese cook" on board who seemed to speak every language on the planet. "He was the first of the hundreds of strangers Gene and I invented stories about for the next sixteen years," Betsy wrote.[4]

On one occasion in Mexico, as Gene and Betsy drove in the car, drinking thermoses of tea and snacking on Oreo cookies, they ran out of gas. Gene went to get help while Betsy slept on the floor of the car. Awakened by the sound of horse hooves and slowly turning wooden wheels, Betsy looked out the window to see Gene riding in a donkey cart beside a farmer in a sombrero. Gene jumped from the cart and held out his hand in an ornate gesture reminiscent of Douglas Fairbanks in *The Three Musketeers* (1921). From behind the farmer, a somber eight-year-old girl with long black braids appeared. She took Gene's hand and he twirled her in a circle, set her down, and danced around her, ending with a bow. She watched with a "grave little smile" and curtsied to him. The farmer then handed Gene a can of gas before he and the girl rolled away down the street. Gene filed the image of the serious little girl away in his memory as a source of future inspiration.[5]

In Mexico, the newlyweds gazed at Mayan temples, swam in the Gulf and Acapulco Bay, and visited museums, churches, bars, and dance halls. When they moved on to San Francisco, they enjoyed the luxury of the Fairmont Hotel. The establishment was an opulent treat after camping in the car or sleeping at roadside inns. "I could see how easy it is to get used to luxury," Betsy admitted. In the bayside city, Gene and Betsy caught up with their friend William Saroyan, who took them on a day trip to his hometown of Fresno. Amid the flurry of activity and new experiences, Betsy later reflected that Gene must have "been aware of what was going on. It was the start of what was to be his life—his career—and he'd chosen me to share it. For me, it was just life itself with colored ribbons on it."[6]

When they arrived in Hollywood, Gene and Betsy discovered that all they had heard about the royal treatment movie stars received was true. Selznick had arranged for them to stay at the Hollywood Roosevelt Hotel, site of the first Academy Awards ceremony in 1929. The producer met them armed with a basket of oranges for Gene and a bouquet of flowers for Betsy. "You're both invited to my home for dinner and a movie screening tonight. And I've set up a membership at the tennis club for you," he began. He then gave them a typed list. "Here's the name of a bank manager, a doctor, a dentist, a place for Betsy to take driving lessons. . . . By the way, Betsy has access to the studio hairdresser . . . and here are the names of real estate agents to help you find a home."[7]

The overwhelmed couple thanked Selznick, though neither had any intention of taking up the tennis club membership. Betsy later wrote that Selznick was a "generous man who spoiled us both for any future producer and we were about to embark on the 'studio will take care of it' syndrome."[8] Betsy, who had hitherto earned only $35 a week, now had a weekly allowance of $100 from Gene. Gene's biographer Clive Hirschhorn wrote that if ever Gene felt Betsy was being a spendthrift, he lectured her on the "eternal verities," but in general he did not question how she spent her money.[9] In any case, Betsy's spending spree was short-lived. The Marxist theories she had embraced in New York came back to her and she wondered how she could justify living in such an excessive manner. She began shopping, even at elite department stores, in blue jeans or a cotton skirt, as if her casual garb negated the fact that she was giving patronage to an upscale shop. She also began to donate her money to various charities, predominantly those that supported leftist causes. Gene, too, did not buy into the Hollywood system. To him, Hollywood was less a place than a state of mind—and it was a state of mind he refused to embrace. Betsy explained: "The studio system was geared to keep them [stars] childish. If an actor wasn't as tough and intelligent as Gene, he was likely to believe his own publicity and lose track of himself."[10]

Gene could easily have "gone Hollywood"; he and Betsy were receiving invitations from Hollywood's royalty, including Norma Shearer, Claudette Colbert, Charles Boyer, and Lewis Milestone. Betsy recalled that at Shearer's home, the actress urged her to come along with the other women to powder their noses while the men enjoyed brandy and cigars. Betsy said, "I'll stay with Gene." Gene "gave my hand a squeeze and sat me in a chair. I hadn't meant to be rebellious . . . but Gene loved it. . . . He had no pretensions, no society aspirations." According to Betsy, she and Gene were "in it together" during the difficult period in which he acclimatized himself to the world of film. They visited cutting rooms and watched movies being shot, tap-danced in Gene's private rehearsal room, and viewed every picture released either in screening rooms or executives' homes. However, Gene preferred attending local movie houses rather than hobnobbing with moguls. "He wanted to sit in the theatre in the dark with everyone else and experience the public reaction and his own."[11]

Gene and Betsy's first home was as free of ostentation as they themselves strove to be. They rented a furnished one-bedroom chalet in Laurel Canyon surrounded by wooded hills and wild lavender. They often woke to see deer in their yard. The major drawback to the home, however, was the series of ninety-nine stepping-stones they had to climb to reach the front door from the street. Its small size also posed a problem; Gene and Betsy's ping-pong table took up the entire downstairs.

As Gene waited for his first film assignment, he and Betsy filled their time playing ping-pong—and playing house. Gene did most of the housework, including cooking and ironing. He told Betsy that all he wanted her to do was "pick flowers and read by the fireplace and sing around the house—my little white dove with the burnished feathers that wakes up every morning smiling." The angelic image Gene projected onto Betsy was one that she accepted—for now. "He wanted to have and keep forever the girl I was, shaped by his care and love," Betsy explained. "I spent my adolescence as a married woman and the inevitable forces of nature, growth and rebellion, were postponed." As much as Gene had lectured Betsy on the "eternal verities," he did enjoy "spoiling her." On their first Christmas together, he gave her a bagful of fur samples. "I want you to pick out the style of the coat," Gene told her. She burst into tears of happiness but could not help feeling that the coat made her a symbol of success—his success.[12]

Gene and Betsy, settled in their modest home, opened it up to fellow New York transplants. Writer Arthur Laurents, an acquaintance of the Kellys, facetiously dubbed the Kellys' guests "the Real People." "The Real People didn't dress up, they sat on shaggy rugs; they talked politics as well as the movies (that was Betsy); they were liberal (also Betsy) and only the exception made a sexual pass (that was Gene). They were slapdash potluck meals for the faithful: writers and directors, actors and dancers."[13] Laurents's claim that Gene made sexual passes is likely exaggerated or completely false; Laurents, a homosexual, harbored a personal dislike for Gene, alleging he was homophobic. Gene did make off-color jokes at times, often about homosexuals, yet many of his friends and the colleagues he admired most (for example, Charles Walters, Cole Porter, and Vincente Minnelli) were homosexuals.

The worst behavior in which Gene engaged at this time was related to alcohol, not sex. He went on occasional all-night drinking binges with Selznick, often running up liquor tabs of $200. Betsy would awaken when he arrived home at dawn and brew black coffee for the drunken men. She later stated that she ignored or denied what she called "the manly side" of Gene, instead choosing to recognize only "the tender, indulgent side of him."[14]

The fantasy life Gene had created with Betsy could not go on indefinitely. He needed a creative outlet; if he did not find one soon, would he become like his father, defeated and reliant on drink? It took a tragedy of epic proportions to push the movie industry into an unprecedented period of productivity that ensured Gene would not be idle in the near future.

Early on Sunday morning, December 7, 1941, the Japanese bombed Pearl Harbor. The toll was severe: 2,403 Americans were killed and 1,178 wounded. What President Franklin D. Roosevelt called "a day that will live in infamy" shook America from the neutrality it had maintained since World War II began in 1939—Roosevelt declared war on Japan on December 8, 1941, and three days later on Germany and Italy.

Hundreds of actors and behind-the-scenes artists were eager to enlist. Among those to don uniforms were top box office attractions Henry Fonda, Clark Gable, Robert Taylor, and James Stewart. Directors Frank Capra, John Ford, and John Huston also enlisted. In less than a year, 12 percent of all employees in the film industry had entered the armed forces. Other Hollywoodites, including Hugh Martin and Mickey Rooney, wanted desperately to fight but were rejected for health reasons—the army deemed Rooney's blood pressure too high and Martin's weight too low. Stars who did not enlist helped the war effort by selling war bonds, performing in USO shows, and participating at the Hollywood Canteen, an organization that provided food and entertainment to servicemen. Judy Garland was among the first Hollywood entertainers to sing for enlisted servicemen at camps across the country.

Gene's daughter Kerry explained in 2014, "The way it was always described in the family was that he had wanted to enlist [in the navy] early on."[15] He was dissuaded by Selznick, who claimed he was more useful on the home front, boosting morale through films. Gene accepted the argument, but it did not fully ease his agitation as he watched his friend Dick Dwenger enlist in a navy combat unit and his brother Fred join an army entertainment unit. Fred eventually became a sergeant.

Betsy, though she had initially planned to pursue serious acting either on the stage or screen in Hollywood, did not join in the entertainment industry's boom. In January 1942, she discovered she was two months pregnant. "I never lost my dream of becoming a serious actress, but the time for that was not now."[16] Gene, delighted at the prospect of becoming a father, discussed parenting plans with Betsy. She wanted a natural childbirth and no nanny to take care of the child; she and Gene would raise the baby themselves. The prospect of becoming a father alleviated Gene's feeling that he should be overseas rather than at home.

As Gene and Betsy began to read books on childcare, Gene also began to read a script. He was relieved that Selznick was finally considering him for a role—the lead in *The Keys to the Kingdom*. The film tells of a young Scottish priest and his struggles to establish a Catholic parish in China. Selznick also told Gene in no uncertain terms that he was to be in Alfred Hitchcock's next picture, but that never materialized.

Gene was so eager to begin working that he finally agreed to a screen test. He reasoned: "I wanted to look at the camera to see what it was about." Gene later admitted that the tests "weren't very good; as a matter of fact, I think they were pretty bad." Viewing the tests, Gene, as he was prone to do when nervous, began to giggle. He turned to Selznick, but the studio head remained impassive. A second later, however, he could not help breaking into laughter, too. Gene later remembered falling on the floor with the mogul in convulsive chuckles. "That's the best comic performance I ever gave," Gene concluded. Selznick, once he regained his composure, told Gene to see a coach to help him with the Scottish brogue required for the role. However, no amount of lessons could made the Irish American from Pittsburgh speak with a believable Scottish accent (the film was eventually released in 1944 by Twentieth Century-Fox with Gregory Peck in the lead). Selznick instead offered Gene the supporting role as the priest's best friend, an atheist doctor. Although he was dropped from the project, Gene never resented the time spent on the lessons, believing it was "something well learned, if just for a nebulous future."[17]

Excused from *The Keys to the Kingdom*, Gene's future was again uncertain. Uncertain, too, was his and Betsy's new home base. The ninety-nine steps leading to their chalet had washed away in a downpour. The mother of Betsy's cousin, Lois Moran, provided the Kellys with temporary housing for eight weeks. At the end of that time, Gene found himself with not one new home but two: 506 North Alta Drive and Metro-Goldwyn-Mayer Studios.

If the Depression, as writer and lyricist Alan Jay Lerner explained, "killed the sentimental musical . . . WWII killed satire and revived the sentimental musical. The mood of the country switched like a traffic light to escapism, nostalgia, and fantasy."[18]

Producer Arthur Freed had a new picture in mind for Judy Garland filled with plenty of nostalgia but also enough reality to make it relevant to wartime audiences. The film was of the utmost importance to Judy; she saw it as her opportunity to transition into adult roles. Thus far, almost every one of Freed's vehicles for her had cast Judy as a teenager alongside Mickey Rooney. The duo's backstage musicals, sometimes dubbed "Let's put on a show!" films, were seemingly simple but had helped release pictures from the stage-bound look of early 1930s musicals. Also, they created characters that, according to Freed, were "real people." Director Vincente Minnelli asserted: "The true revolutionary [at MGM] was Arthur. . . . Arthur's desire to make musical pictures about back-home America with its homely values seemed to anticipate the public's shifting interest. Suddenly the climate at Metro was ripe for innovation, and many of us were being given the opportunity to show our stuff."[19]

Freed's picture for Judy, an intimate black-and-white musical entitled *For Me and My Gal,* centers on three characters: an ambitious, egotistical heel, a self-sacrificing young actress, and a noble yet bland actor. Freed already had George Murphy for the latter character. But he knew of no one already under contract to MGM who could satisfactorily fill the part of the self-centered actor. "He [Freed] was not interested in the already established crop of Hollywood talent . . . their scope and style were rapidly becoming passé," historian Hugh Fordin explained.[20] Fifty years later, author John Updike wrote in the *New Yorker,* "In Hollywood it was producer Arthur Freed's unit at MGM, staffed mainly by sophisticated refugees from the East that carried the torch [of New York's cutting-edge strides in show business]."[21]

In Gene, Freed saw a leader—the best that Broadway had to offer to Hollywood. The producer wanted an unprecedented brand of leading man, not the one-dimensional hero of the old guard of musicals. Gene was a rogue, but a sensitive, charming, and even likeable one. This rascal with balletic skill was a man whom audiences could envision defeating the Germans with one high kick and the Japanese with a mad pirouette.

"He *would* be perfect for the role of Harry," screenwriter Fred Finklehoffe commented to Freed, looking over his script of *Gal* one afternoon.

"I don't see any motion picture potential in Kelly," Eddie Mannix, MGM's studio manager, argued. "He's the wrong kind of Irishman."[22]

"Everybody is telling me I'm wrong about Kelly," a discouraged Freed told Louis B. Mayer later over lunch in Mayer's private dining room.

"Do you still feel he's the right man for the part?"

"I love him," Freed said without hesitation.

"Well then, don't listen to all those shmucks," Mayer advised, grinning.[23]

Gene could barely restrain his enthusiasm when his agent, Johnny Darrow, called him with the news that he would be Judy Garland's costar in Freed's next musical. As he had nothing to offer, Selznick consented to loaning the rival studio his star's services. Gene still bristled at the mere thought of Louis B. Mayer—a man he saw as a complete phony. Mayer, known for his over-the-top showmanship during conferences, demanded he have an office large enough for him to "do a proper act for the people of the studio . . . to convey to them his ideas and inspire them."[24] Carey Wilson, a writer at MGM, recalled that despite Mayer's less appealing qualities, he "contributed a reasonable optimism, tremendous vitality, *salesmanship* . . . shrewd judgment of character."[25] In judging a picture's merit as well as a potential star's character, Mayer was equally shrewd—though he often needed the input of producers like Arthur Freed to stop him from relying too heavily on his own preferences. He liked "cornball pictures" and judged a picture's quality based on its ability to bring tears to his eyes.[26] Freed was the ideal liaison for Mayer because he too preferred sentimental stories, but he knew how to insert enough realism and humor in them to prevent them from being saccharine.

Gene, in spite of his street-smart exterior, was also easily moved by nostalgia. He saw that MGM was in truth better equipped for his talents than Selznick's much smaller company, though he still disliked Mayer. Working at MGM did not mean he would have to be "chummy" with Mayer. "I never had any creative contact with Mayer. I don't know anybody who did, except when he told them not to write about toilets or bathrooms because it would offend some mother in Illinois!" Gene declared in 1974.[27]

Even more than Selznick International, MGM took the "we'll take care of everything" syndrome to a new level. Among MGM's first orders of business was to find Gene and Betsy a new home. The house, located at 506 North Alta Drive in Beverly Hills, was leased from lyricist E. Y. "Yip" Harburg (composer of "Over the Rainbow"). The abode was considerably roomier, allowing Gene and Betsy to expand their open-house parties and keep their ping-pong table in a more convenient place outside. The studio also set the Kellys up with a housekeeper, a plump and cheerful black woman named Mamie who, Betsy claimed, "cooked up a storm."[28] Between Mamie's meals, Gene snacked on "a steady supply of [his] favorite chocolate peppermints [shipped] from his favorite candy store in Pittsburgh."[29] At the same time the Kellys moved into their new home, Betsy passed her driving test and received a gift from Gene that served as both a Valentine and a congratulatory present: a blue and white Pontiac convertible.[30]

As Gene and Betsy were settling into their new house, Gene explored the sprawling MGM lot in Culver City, approximately half an hour by car from the Hollywood district of Los Angeles. (Most major studios were not in Hollywood; Warner Bros. was in Burbank, and Universal was in Universal City.) Alan Jay Lerner described Culver City as "a town of well-to-do squalor, gas stations, and oil derricks."[31] The communities of stars and moviemakers in the Hollywood area functioned, for all intents and purposes, like company towns. "When I say . . . company town, I mean that everything revolved around the filmmaking," Betsy explained. "Social life was dictated by shooting schedules. . . . It was only natural and sensible to eat early and be home in bed by ten."[32]

MGM itself was like the land of Oz—a strange place that nevertheless had all the amenities necessary for living. Actress Debbie Reynolds described her initial impressions of the studio in her 1988 memoir: "It didn't occur to me then but being at MGM was like going to a university. You could get out of college in four years, but some of us were at this university for ten or fifteen. . . . It was a small town of very creative people."[33] The self-contained lot included a main street that even accommodated a trolley to shuttle its employees from one end of the lot to the other. The thoroughfare fed onto other streets, which housed rehearsal halls, a hospital, a fire station, and a schoolhouse. Studio gatekeepers monitored the moment each employee arrived and left. If an actor was late more than once, he or she received a visit from the studio manager, who was comparable to a school principal in his disciplinary talks. MGM was magical, but studio executives made it difficult for stars to forget that they were in essence pieces of studio property, used only for as long as they were profitable.

Gene still believed Hollywood was only a state of mind; he was not about to adhere to its cliques or be infantilized by the studio system. His and Betsy's Saturday night parties became a sort of rebellion against the notion that actors must abide by a child's bedtime. They lasted into the early hours of the morning and were a welcome change from the formal gatherings at the homes of Norma Shearer or Louis B. Mayer and at swanky nightclubs where conversations were drowned in superficial amiability. In an interview for *Screenland,* columnist Paul Marsh made an observation that held true for Gene's entire film career: "There's one Hollywood institution he'll [Gene] have no part of—nightclubbing. 'Too rugged for me,' [Gene said]. 'I can't take all that bumping and pushing in noisy little rooms filled with smoke. I'd rather stay home.'"[34] Gene's home was his nightclub and, as much as he professed to hate cliques, he made his establishment as select as Hollywood's most exclusive social circle. Johnny Green, director of music at MGM, stated that "if you didn't possess . . . 'special abilities,' he [Gene] found it difficult to have time for you . . . a lot of people disliked him for this, but that didn't bother Gene. . . . [He] demanded nothing from anyone that he didn't demand from himself—perfection, whether in the studio during the week, or on Saturday night at home."[35]

Among those accepted for membership in Gene's "club" were new friends such as Saul and Ethel Chaplin, Jessica Tandy and Hume Cronyn, Lena Horne and Lennie Hayton, Phil Silvers, and Judy Garland. Old friends included Evie and Keenan Wynn, Hugh Martin, Ralph Blane, Van Johnson, and Stanley Donen. Guests usually arrived at five thirty for a game of ping-pong and a potluck dinner, but the highlight of a given evening was when Chaplin, Martin, or Hayton would sit at the piano and play while guests (most conspicuously Judy Garland) belted out Gershwin, Porter, Mercer, and Arlen tunes. Gene would perform only by request or if others were performing. With his guests, he drank wine, sang, and laughed until two in the morning, at which time those who were still awake would have a calming snack of milk and Oreos.[36]

As low key as Kelly soirees may have appeared, an evening at Gene's home was certainly not an opportunity to allow one's wits and alertness to take a vacation—especially if one wished to take part in Gene's favorite indoor sport. Gene and his friends called it "the Game," a complicated version of charades he had learned in New York. The Game required two teams to separate into different rooms. The team leaders would then receive a hint from the designated captain and return to their team's room to share the hint. Then it became a matter of who was fastest at guessing and running from his or her room to receive the next clue. Betsy recalled, "We ran and screamed and shouted, tempers were lost, we occasionally collapsed on the floor laughing."[37] Gene played to win and usually succeeded. His side often won not only because of his own talent but also because of his shrewd selection of team members. British character actress Gladys Cooper's daughter, Sally, was only nine years old, but Gene found her to be a prodigy at the Game and was always eager to have her in his group.

In her memoir, Betsy explained the comic side to her husband's intimidating competitive nature: "There was a characteristic gesture he had—sort of a family joke. When there was an argument about a date in history or the meaning of a word, we would look it up. When the correct answer—more often than not—was found to be his, he would leap to his feet, throw his arms into the air, grin, and twirl around, crowing 'Right again.'"[38]

Gene's compulsion to be the best—the leader in any realm he entered, whether in show business or games—seemed like a primary ingredient for a temperamental star. However, on the set of *For Me and My Gal*, he brought only the benign dominance that, in his career thus far, had made him both admired and emulated. One columnist gushed: "There has never been anyone on the Metro lot less temperamental than the Kelly boy, who is liked by directors, writers and publicity men."[39]

According to John Updike in his essay "Genial, Kinetic Gene Kelly," it is in *For Me and My Gal* that "we are most fully persuaded that the Kelly character is loved by the heroine."[40] This is no easy feat; "the Kelly character," a World War I draft-dodging and opportunistic actor, is decidedly difficult to love. The film tells the story of Jimmy Metcalfe (George Murphy) and Jo Hayden (Judy Garland)—a vaudeville team with a stale routine. In walks the brash Harry Palmer, who promptly asks Jo to team with him. Jimmy lets her go despite his feelings for her and goes on to become a success on his own. As Harry and Jo struggle to find bookings, they fall in love and plan to marry. They then work their way up to a booking at the Palace, the greatest vaudeville playhouse in America. Just when they secure their booking, Harry is drafted. Determined that nothing will stand in the way of his big break, he purposely breaks his hand by slamming it in a trunk. Jo learns her brother has been killed in action the same day she sees Harry's broken hand. "You'll never be big time because you're small time in your heart," she tells him before she leaves to entertain troops overseas. Harry, devastated, tries to enlist but is told his hand will never properly heal. He goes on to perform for army camps in France. There he runs into Jimmy, who is again friendly with Jo and waiting for her to reciprocate his affections. Harry and Jo reunite in New York after the Armistice is declared. Jo, now heralded as the sweetheart of the armed forces, is playing at the Palace. She sees Harry in the audience and runs to him. They embrace; all is forgiven. She brings him onstage and they sing "For Me and My Gal" as Jimmy looks on, jilted but content that Jo has found happiness.

When filming commenced on *For Me and My Gal* in April 1942, Gene became immersed in every aspect of its production. Though Busby Berkeley sat in the director's chair, Gene, in a sense, took over his job. In Pittsburgh Gene had been dubbed "the dance doctor," similar to Berkeley's Broadway nickname: "the show fixer." Both men were known for putting original twists on ordinary concepts, though their approaches were in complete contrast to one another. Berkeley's approach was rapidly becoming a relic of the past, but Arthur Freed's intense loyalty to the director helped keep the man employed over the next decade despite his well-known alcoholism. Berkeley and Gene shared similarities, but they did not immediately have a rapport. Berkeley still thought Murphy would be better as Harry, but the director eventually came to acknowledge Gene's abilities.

Murphy, however, did not change his opinion of Gene. Unlike his placid character onscreen, he was upset that Gene, a "nobody," had won the lead role over him, a veteran of such profitable Metro musicals as the *Broadway Melody of 1938* and *1940*. "This [*For Me and My Gal*] was the film that disappointed me most. . . . I got the part of the schnook who never gets the girl," Murphy lamented.[41] Murphy, however, had one opportunity to dominate over Gene. One day, the tired Berkeley ordered Murphy rather than Gene to oversee a number he was unable to complete. To Murphy's chagrin, Gene was not a complacent subject and interjected ideas of his own. Murphy watched with a scowl as Gene approached Berkeley and heard the director sigh, "Okay" in acquiescence to the young actor's requests to experiment. Gene tried different camera angles, much as Berkeley had done more than ten years before. By minimizing the background of a scene, he was able to focus the camera on the individual dancer. Placing vertical props in the background created the illusion of movement from left to right. In order to convey momentum and speed, he tested the effect of having the dancers rush forward toward the camera.[42]

The one-on-one dance Gene developed with Judy for the film's title song is a simple yet highly original routine. Gene's intimate choreography in the sequence focuses solely on the two players in the scene dancing to an understated song in an unassuming diner. Only a mustachioed waiter acts as their audience. Watchful film viewers will notice a sign above the piano reading, "Where there's music there's love." John Updike articulated why Gene and Judy's dance routines were so effective. "An intensity of mutual regard [burns] through when they gaze each into the other's shining black eyes or crisply tap dance side by side. . . . Both have a slightly troubled, orphaned air which lends believability . . . to the film."[43] Previously, only Mickey Rooney had been able to match Judy's personality onscreen. Now, with Gene, Judy found a "grown-up" Mickey Rooney. Their banter in the film is also more sophisticated but retains the casual ease Judy and Mickey had shared on camera. One particularly comical piece of repartee occurs when Jo and Harry first meet at a snow-laden train station. "Good morning, Springtime," the foppishly dressed Harry says after whistling at Jo. "Aren't you a little out of season?" Jo shoots back, hugging her coat around her. Her barb does nothing to dissuade Harry from pursuing her. Instead, he looks after her, grinning and tilting his derby at a jaunty angle. Jo says to Jimmy, loud enough for Harry to hear, "Who's the want-ad with the squirrel around his neck?"[44]

Gene's worldliness was in complete contrast to the innocence Judy conveyed onscreen, yet somehow they were ideal partners. Indeed, their opposing screen personae aided their growth as actors. He helped Judy become a woman and she softened the lingering influence of Joey Evans in his characterization. "Judy was my first booster," Gene stated. "She is a real trouper, a brilliant actress, and one of the nicest people I've ever met. . . . She's able to work out another person's problems at the same time she's working on her own."[45] Gene followed Judy's lead during all dramatic sequences. He later asserted that the best acting he ever did was in his first film. "She . . . gave him [Gene] hints about how little projection of emotion is necessary, not like in the theater—and she made him laugh," Betsy Blair reflected.[46] For the rest of his life, Gene never uttered Judy's name without expressing his gratitude to her. The feeling was mutual. Just as she had taught Gene how to emote for the camera, he taught her how to dance at a professional level. Gene spent hours coaching Judy, and she would not settle until she was satisfied that she had the steps down perfectly. Although she went home with a sore back and blisters on her feet, Judy was thrilled to become a more than competent dancer. "She was the quickest study I've ever known," Gene declared.[47]

Judy managed to lighten the mood on a set laden with tension between

Murphy, Berkeley, and Gene. "The joy of working with Judy was her capacity for laughter," Gene commented. "She laughed . . . and she wanted to laugh. All I had to do was snap my fingers. When I made a goof, this made her laugh too."[48] In Gene, Judy found a kindred spirit. She, too, shunned Hollywood artificiality and enjoyed poetry, classical music, and complicated word games. During filming, she invited Gene and Betsy to dine with her and her husband, musician David Rose, at their home. Rose was eager to show his guests the elaborate toy train he had set up in the backyard. Judy indulgently allowed her husband to expound on his hobby, though she, Gene, and Betsy found his obsession odd. "We thought some aspects of Hollywood were strange, but we loved Judy," Betsy said.[49] "Judy saw no difference between us. . . . She was a joy to know."[50]

Though filming on *For Me and My Gal* wrapped in late May 1942, Judy and Gene remained regular guests at each other's homes. Louis B. Mayer had high expectations for the movie's success despite his reservations concerning Gene's picture potential. A columnist for the *Pittsburgh Post-Gazette* wrote on June 8, 1942: "Metro's all excited about the teamwork of Judy Garland and Gene Kelly in *For Me and My Gal* and is thinking about building them up into a Rogers-Astaire combination."[51]

MGM's potential Astaire-Rogers combination seemed a doubtful prospect after the film's first preview. When asked their opinion of the picture, 85 percent of preview audiences declared they were disgusted that Gene's character won Judy's love rather than George Murphy's. The movie, as it stood, did not meet the Office of War Information's specifications for what a film should communicate if it was to aid the war effort (specifically in the area of self-sacrifice done voluntarily and cheerfully). Mayer had already invested too much in *For Me and My Gal* to let it be a box office flop. He ordered Fred Finklehoffe to rewrite the entire ending so that Gene's character becomes a war hero by saving a transport of ambulances before they drive into an area under enemy fire. The revised conclusion was filmed in June 1942, adding twenty-one extra days of shooting and sending production costs up to $802,980.[52] However, the film's profits more than made up for its costliness. When the new and improved *For Me and My Gal* made its Los Angeles premiere on November 26, 1942, it became Judy's biggest box office hit yet, grossing $4,371,000.

Judy was the film's primary attraction, but Gene proved to be a draw in his own right. Eddie Mannix, the executive who had been most opposed to casting him, told Freed after viewing the film: "Arthur, remind me not to tell you how to make pictures." Busby Berkeley was also ecstatic about the film and shook Gene's hand "until it was almost embarrassing." Berkeley concluded that of all his films, *For Me and My Gal* was his "top favorite."[53]

Gene, for all his outer bravura, was not without self-doubt. When he first saw himself onscreen, he was miserable. "Shocked is a better word," he amended. "The sight of my funny Irish kisser magnified that many times sent me out of the theater with the screaming meemies!"[54] "I had an awful feeling I was a tremendous flop, but when I came outside [at the premiere of the revised film] executives started pumping my hand and Judy came up to me and kissed me. . . . It was a new world and quite different from the theater. In the theater, you can chug along for years, but being a success in the movies is like suddenly being turned into a rocket."[55] A writer for *Time* magazine raved that Gene "has flashes of acting intuition which should rate him a special berth, or perhaps a drawing room, in Hollywood," but Bosley Crowther of the *New York Times* argued that the newcomer was "pressed a bit too far [dramatically] in his first film role."[56] Gene was swift to admit that he never felt he was an exceptional actor. In 1975, he mused: "I would have loved to have been as good an actor as Spencer Tracy or Marlon Brando. I was a very good stage actor, but in films I never was quite as good, just passable."[57]

Gene worked to refine his acting skills throughout his career, and many critics took note of his improved abilities. Even early in Gene's film career, a writer for the *Chicago Tribune* went so far as to call him "a combination of Cagney—Tracy—Astaire."[58] In his critique of Gene's career, John Updike called him "a gentler younger brother to James Cagney's sassy George M. Cohan" whose generally "immobile face" gave him the sulky "bruised appeal of John Garfield or Humphrey Bogart."[59]

Louis B. Mayer now viewed Gene as an asset to the studio and thus decided to buy out the remainder of his contract from Selznick. He offered Gene a seven-year contract with MGM with a starting salary of $1,000 a week (paltry compared to major Metro stars like Spencer Tracy, who was earning $4,400 a week). The new contract did not carry the stipulation that Gene could return to Broadway if he wished. Signing the document was a serious commitment, but Gene, with a child on the way and a promising start in film, felt it was one he was willing to make. At this point in his career, Gene was no longer under Johnny Darrow's management. The legendary and charismatic agent Leland Hayward became Gene's representative. He represented nearly every big name in Hollywood at various times in their careers, including Judy Garland, James Stewart, and Henry Fonda.

Few were happier about Gene's decision to sign an MGM contract than Arthur Freed. To him, Gene Kelly was the future of musical films. As actress Nina Foch explained, "It was a different world, suddenly we [Americans] were defending ourselves. We were macho, this country. Along comes this muscular young man who takes dance and puts it somewhere that all Americans could appreciate it."[60]

Gene's next two films were a step down from his stellar beginning of instant celebrity status after the release of *For Me and My Gal*. His first follow-up assignment, a low-budget, rather stilted war drama directed by George Sidney entitled *Pilot #5*, is notable only because it offered him his first "straight role." Filmed immediately after *Pilot #5* was another Arthur Freed musical, *Du Barry Was a Lady*, an entertaining if fluffy picture directed by Roy Del Ruth elevated by a Cole Porter score and lush Technicolor. In spite of Gene's disappointment in these two films, he valued them as learning experiences. In a press book for *Pilot #5*, Gene stated: "When it comes to acting and dancing, there's no reason at all why the two should be divorced. Both are great mediums of expression. And dancing helps acting. I'm sure I never would have been an actor if I hadn't first been a dancer."[61]

Pilot #5 began shooting in July 1942 and was slated to wrap in August. Though a "programmer" that would be the second on a double bill, the film at least cast Gene alongside his friend Van Johnson. The movie tells the story of five American pilots in a bomb-blasted air base in Java. The senior officer has only one usable aircraft and must choose one of the pilots to attack the Japanese in a deadly mission. According to Gene's biographer Tony Thomas he, in his role as a "moody Italian-American . . . surprised those who had little reason to consider him as an actor on the basis of his work in *For Me and My Gal*." Gene felt the film could have left a stronger political message, claiming that it began as "a statement against fascism . . . but . . . we were in the entertainment business and this was wartime. So the script was changed [to be more entertaining rather than moralizing]."[62] When the picture premiered on June 24, 1943, a critic for the *New York Times* deemed it "tedious" and "overlong" but singled out Gene's acting as "convincing."[63]

Du Barry Was a Lady gained Gene far more notice than *Pilot #5*. It went into production in August; shooting came to a close in November 1942. The film was a screwball confection starring Lucille Ball and Red Skelton with Gene, Virginia O'Brien, and Rags Ragland as the supporting cast. Gene balked about receiving third billing, but as consolation, Freed allowed him to request a dance director for the picture. Gene felt the man assigned to the job, the elderly Felix Seymour, was not the best selection. He asked for Robert Alton, but Gene's agent, Leland Hayward, informed him that Alton had Broadway commitments.

"Well then, where's Charlie?" Gene asked, using a nickname for Charles Walters that allegedly made the choreographer "bristle." "I have one big number in this picture and I need him." Walters agreed to do the picture with an "oh well, what the hell?" shrug.[64] Because *Du Barry Was a Lady* was dominantly a Red Skelton comedy, it offered Walters, and thus Gene, fewer opportunities to demonstrate their skills. However, Walters worked to make what dance routines the picture did contain the most memorable parts of the film.

Du Barry Was a Lady, adapted from the Broadway show by Herbert Fields, B. G. DeSylva, and Cole Porter, tells the story of a coatroom attendant, Louis (Skelton), who is hopelessly in love with nightclub singer May Daly (Ball). However, she is in love with Alec (Gene), an emcee at the club. One evening, Louis accidentally drinks a laced beverage and falls into a dream in which he is Louis XVI, chasing after Madame Du Barry (also played by Ball). In the dream, Alec is "the Black Arrow," the leader of a revolutionary group. Just as Louis is about to be put to death, he wakes up—safely back at the nightclub, where he discovers that he actually loves the cigarette girl (O'Brien) who works there.

Gene called the project "atrocious." He told Freed: "Arthur, you know, you don't want to do this."[65] Freed promised better assignments in the future and Gene made the best of the situation. One redeeming part of the project was that as the Black Arrow, Gene had the opportunity to play a swashbuckling character similar to his boyhood idol, Douglas Fairbanks.

The rest of the film gave Gene little to do with the exception of one solo dance sequence. The dance finds Gene in top hat and tails, emceeing at a nightclub not unlike Chez Joey. Charles Walters was the ideal choreographer for the number, for he rivaled Fred Astaire for "tuxedoed grace."[66] But Walters chose not to choreograph the number like an Astaire routine. Instead, he and Gene decided to juxtapose Alec's elegant appearance with Gene's trademark performance of athletic dance moves—he moved across a stage by bouncing on the balls of his hands (he had also used this technique in *For Me and My Gal*). Arthur Freed praised Walters as the only dance director "who had ever read a script to find out what the characters are all about."[67]

Because he had indeed read the script, Walters knew that immediately preceding Gene's number, Alec and May share a romantic moment during which Alec serenades her with "Do I Love You?" "Wouldn't it be fun to start the number inside the dressing room and then pow, out through the door, through the audience, and onto the stage to continue it?" Walters asked.[68] Freed and Gene took his suggestion; once Alec leaves May's dressing room, the Tommy Dorsey Orchestra takes up the tune of "Do I Love You?" as Gene launches into his dance solo. Through the device of the number beginning in May's dressing room, the audience feels that the energy and enthusiasm Alec gives his dance is fueled by his love for her. Walters's brainstorm added much-needed authenticity to the love scene between Gene and Lucille Ball, whose onscreen chemistry was almost nonexistent. Walters became an integral choreographer and director at MGM for the next two decades.

Du Barry Was a Lady received generally positive reviews upon its release on August 19, 1943. Bosley Crowther praised Gene and Walters's collaboration, proclaiming Gene's solo to be "screen magic."[69] A writer for *Photoplay* called Gene's dancing "something to shout about."[70] The production, which required a hefty $1,239,222 to shoot, grossed $3,496,000.

Working with old friends like Walters went far toward making Gene feel more at home both at MGM and in Hollywood. "When I first went out to Hollywood from New York I was an effete Eastern snob. I only went into films to make money. Then, when I got there, I found I liked it," Gene reflected in 1980.[71] He shared his newfound love for Hollywood with anyone he could, including Mamie, his housekeeper. He often took her to the best restaurants or to the MGM commissary (which was like a restaurant itself, complete with menus, waiters, and waitresses), where he introduced Mamie to her favorite movie stars.

A large part of Gene's growing taste for Hollywood was due to the fact that he had won acceptance into the "Freed Unit," an honor few on the MGM lot could add to their list of accomplishments. Hugh Martin, who was working with Ralph Blane on Freed's film adaptation of *Best Foot Forward* at the same time Gene was filming *Du Barry*, did not have Gene's extroverted personality or thick skin. He found the Freed Unit a formidable group, especially after he and Blane were shunned when they tried to sit at Freed's table in the studio commissary. Freed's coldness and unpredictable temper were enough to drive the introverted Hugh Martin away from the cafeteria for the rest of his tenure at MGM.

Unlike Martin, the self-assured Stanley Donen had little trouble making himself at home in the commissary as well as in the Freed Unit. Donen had been in Hollywood less than a week before he managed to land his first assignment, as a dancer in Freed's *Best Foot Forward*. Van Johnson recalled that one of Donen's first moves at MGM was to call him and ask, "Can you get me into the commissary?" Donen well knew the cafeteria was the best place to meet influential people. Van obliged and later stated that after Donen gained access to the commissary, "the rest is history. Only wouldn't you know it, when the son of a bitch got to be a big director, never once did he hire me."[72]

The fact that Gene included both Martin and Donen in his group proved that, as much as he had grown to embrace Los Angeles, he was still independent minded. True, he befriended only those he felt possessed talent and intelligence, but he did not judge them based on the opinions of others, or on their personal style—quiet and delicate or raucous and blunt; Gene made room for them all.

Just as Gene had settled comfortably into his new life in Hollywood, an entirely new role came his way—one that required sensitivity, discipline, intelligence, and plenty of talent: fatherhood.

While Gene was filming *Du Barry Was a Lady*, Betsy checked into the Good Samaritan Hospital on October 15, 1942, the day before the baby, if it arrived on time, was due. Betsy's mother, Frederica, had arrived in the first week of October to help her daughter and son-in-law through their first months of parenthood. Though he knew Mrs. Boger was there for Betsy, Gene still found it nearly impossible to focus on his work. "Every time the phone rang he jumped. He said a man who was about to become a father ought to be pardoned for nerves," a journalist visiting the set of *Du Barry* reported.[73]

Immediately after work, Gene drove to the hospital. He played the board game Battleship with Betsy for an hour and sang to her before visiting hours were over. The doctor promised to inform Gene when Betsy was ready to deliver. The moment he received word that Betsy had gone into labor, Gene rushed to the hospital. But by the time he arrived, his baby had already been born. Though disappointed he had missed the birth, Gene was overcome with joy when the doctor placed his daughter in his arms. Gene and Betsy gave their daughter a name to acknowledge their shared Irish heritage: Kerry.

Gene, Betsy, and Kerry became nearly inseparable. When Gene was rehearsing or shooting, Betsy often brought Kerry in a padded laundry basket to the studio for lunch. Five years later, a reflective Gene told *Silver Screen* magazine that he did not "agree that children can't be raised 'normally' in the environment of Hollywood. That depends on the parents. It's their job and it's one that is shirked by a lot of people who yip about 'phony atmosphere' and simultaneously raise brats because they don't take the time to give them a normal home life." Gene strove to protect Kerry from publicity as much as possible. He balked at "home sittings" and the "family portrait" type of publicity. "Our home and home life are our own," he declared.[74] Nevertheless, he fulfilled his contractual obligation to pose for a small number of publicity shots with his family. "We were photographed in the kitchen, with Kerry on Gene's knee and me at the stove pretending to cook in an apron borrowed from our housekeeper," Betsy recalled.[75]

Gene soon discovered that not everything about fatherhood was idyllic. When Kerry was three weeks old, her first all-night wailing fit sent Gene into a panic. He had sixty pages of a script to study and a seven o'clock call scheduled at the studio the next morning. "She hates me," he told Betsy in despair. "I can see it in her eyes." However, Gene soon grew accustomed to the behavior of babies and stopped taking it personally.[76]

Gene had been in Hollywood for just over a year, and already he had established a family, an intimate circle of friends, and stardom. According to one *Movieland* report, he was "the hottest thing in town" whose personality "hits an audience like a three-alarm fire."[77] A writer for *Photoplay* summarized his swift ascent in the film world: "He came to Hollywood devoid of the supposed essentials of handsome looks and personal glamour; his subordinate role in *For Me and My Gal* created such an instant sensation he was rushed into top roles in two top MGM pictures and then was handed the starring part opposite Kathryn Grayson in *Private Miss Jones*. Not bad for a young man who just has skimmed by his thirtieth birthday!"[78]

"Starring part" was no exaggeration. *Private Miss Jones,* later renamed *Thousands Cheer,* placed him as the male lead in a Technicolor, star-studded wartime extravaganza under the direction of the versatile George Sidney. Yet in spite of his remarkable professional progress, Gene did not, as Betsy had feared, lose track of himself. Neither she nor Gene, she claimed, took his stardom "very seriously yet."[79]

8

New Heights

Now that Gene Kelly was a star, MGM publicists capitalized on his appearance and persona—the very attributes that had initially made studio executives question his future in Hollywood. The crescent-shaped scar on his cheek, his unremarkable height, his solid build, reedy voice, and regular Joe dancing attire became hot topics in fan magazines. "Everyone's been trying to get me to cover that scar up," Gene told a writer for *Motion Picture*. "But why should I? Just covering the scar wouldn't turn me into a glamour boy." The columnist admitted that nothing about Gene spelled "glamour boy." "His voice is not romantic. . . . It hasn't the tone or timbre that make women dream of being with Boyer on a tropical island."[1] A *Seventeen* reporter commented on Gene's carriage, which was not stereotypical of a dancer. "If you saw Gene walking down Main Street you would not be likely to say, 'There goes a dancer.' He has a compact, purposeful walk with long, vigorous strides. You might think him a cop—genial and tough."[2]

Gene later dubbed himself the "Marlon Brando of dance." Just as Brando would later set a new trend in acting—intense, raw, and physical—so Gene set a new style in dancing. The men also shared an unconventional fashion sense; one could argue that Brando was actually influenced by Gene in this area. "I may have been the first to look like a slob," Gene said in 1972. "I rolled up my sleeves and danced in blue jeans and sweat shirts and moccasins when those things weren't . . . so fashionable."[3]

What set Gene apart from later antiheroes, however, was his unabashed sentimentality and, as the *Seventeen* reporter noted, his geniality both onscreen and off. He was a city kid and a rebel, but he was also a "good Catholic boy" and a traditional family man.[4] His far-reaching appeal increased his value to MGM as a star of morale-boosting pictures for the home front; this was a boon to his career but a barrier to his hopes of donning a uniform not provided by the costume department.

Gene had to be content with such a uniform for the time being. In his next picture, *Thousands Cheer*, he wore the khakis of an army private. The film was among the first in a resurgence of film revues, a genre that had almost gone extinct after the early 1930s. Revues made a comeback during the war due to their entertainment-dense format. The fact that 1940s audiences were music crazy and accepted any excuse to see another song or dance in a picture certainly helped the genre's popularity.

Despite Hollywood's loss of foreign markets, film production reached its peak of efficiency and profits from 1943 to 1946. Gas and rubber shortages curtailed travel; consequently, Americans had few other places to go but movie houses within walking distance of their homes. Movie attendance soared to near-record levels of 90 million a week. MGM films, *Thousands Cheer* included, continued promoting American values. In 1942, Mayer's pet project, the Andy Hardy series, received an honorary Oscar for "furthering the American way of life."[5] Rather than release gritty war epics, MGM found its forte in producing pictures portraying the bravery of those on the home front that "affirmed a sense of national purpose" and "emphasized patriotism, group effort, and the value of individual sacrifices for a larger cause. They portrayed World War II as a people's war."[6]

Joe Pasternak, the other major musical producer at MGM besides Arthur Freed, had signed to produce *Thousands Cheer*. "Pasternak had an interest in kind of sentimental stories and liked what people . . . refer to as classical music," director Stanley Donen explained.[7] Pasternak, a self-made immigrant from Hungary, had built his career mainly on productions starring Deanna Durbin, Universal Studio's popular young opera star. Once at MGM, Pasternak found his niche producing films that blended classical and modern tunes, such as in the musical comedy *Presenting Lily Mars* (1943), which showcased both Judy Garland's swinging style and Marta Eggerth's operatic one. *Thousands Cheer* promised to follow the same pattern.

The film was essentially a revue with a thin plotline running through it; opera by soprano Kathryn Grayson and concertos by pianist José Iturbi dominated the classical side of the picture's score, while swing by Bob Crosby's big band orchestra filled the modern one. Gene, by this time in danger of being typecast, plays Eddie Marsh, a sharp-talking, lone wolf soldier who is the adopted son of an Italian family of circus performers. He is moved to show his soft side by the love of Kathryn (Kathryn Grayson). She pursues him despite the fact that her father, a colonel in the army, disapproves of Eddie's vocation as a trapeze artist. She also helps teach him the value of teamwork and how accepting help from others does not make him weak. Gene had the opportunity to show off his gymnastic skills during a scene in which he does warm-up exercises on a pull-up bar, but a professional trapeze artist doubled for Gene in long shots. The thread of the engaging story is lost during an overlong extravagant camp show staged for the servicemen.

The picture went into production in November 1942 and proved to be a pleasant experience for all involved. Gene found friends in the cast and crew, including Judy Garland, Lena Horne, and vocal arranger Roger Edens. The rest of the cast was composed of almost every single musical or comedic MGM star under contract. Mickey Rooney, Red Skelton, Eleanor Powell, Lucille Ball, and Margaret O'Brien were among the scene-stealers in the picture. Pasternak, upon watching Gene during rehearsals, observed that he was unperturbed at the prospect of being upstaged by the other performers. "And believe me, this made a change because most actors are ignorant people who let success go to their heads. . . . Kelly . . . took success in his stride."[8] As well as winning the producer's approval, Gene also impressed Kathryn Grayson, who revealed in 2001, "My favorite dancer was Gene Kelly." She added, "His mannerisms were pretty much the same in each picture. If you look at his films, one after the other, his expressions were very much the same."[9]

Gene's expressions were consistent in each of his films because he established his stage/screen persona so early in his career. From the time he portrayed Harry the Hoofer in *The Time of Your Life,* Gene's character was that of a self-made, ambitious proletarian whose hardened exterior covers passionate convictions, an inner vulnerability, and a search for approval. The lines Gene speaks as Eddie in *Thousands Cheer* prove that he is playing a variation of the same character. After describing to Kathryn's character how he became "the King of the Trapeze," he asks: "Do you think I got to the top overnight? Do you know how long I spent working at it?"[10]

The authenticity Gene brings to his character adds much-needed dimension to the picture. Gene was able to make Eddie Marsh so believable because the character's outlook was similar to the actor's own. The film was, in essence, a message picture in that it showed the importance of people working together. Despite his independent nature, Gene believed that everyone in a given organization, from the lowliest employees to the bosses, should cooperate.

Gene's dance routines for the film were what made *Thousands Cheer* more than a formulaic wartime musical. Pasternak gave him permission to do what was necessary to elevate the film. "I told him from the start: 'You want to steal the movie? All you have to do is one dance that is new and original . . . you be different,'" Pasternak recalled. "So he came up with the mop dance, which is the best number in the picture."[11] The "mop dance" became Gene's most important cinematic contribution in his career to date. Indeed, it marked the first solo film routine he created and choreographed himself. In his first two screen musicals, he had performed with others, often in routines not fully indicative of his unique style. The mop dance established many of Gene's trademarks, such as casual wardrobe, utilization of props, and a setting that is not stage bound. Critic Karel Reisz wrote that the movement of musical numbers away from the stage and into the outside world was the transition from the old to the new.[12]

Gene's solo takes place after Eddie Marsh is confined to quarters as punishment for insubordination. As he carries out his penalty—mopping the local PX—he wears army fatigues consisting of a white T-shirt and loose-fitting denim pants. The task of mopping seems anything but unpleasant once Gene turns it into a dance. In choreographing the routine, Gene ensured it could not be duplicated on the stage. Biographer Clive Hirschhorn wrote of its "complicated rhythms and skillful synchronization of beats."[13] Gene's use of as many props as were handy added even more intricacy. First he dances with the mop while singing "Let Me Call You Sweetheart," then he times his steps to working soda fountain gadgets. At the heart of the sequence, Eddie picks up his broom and uses it as a rifle to mime shooting at a poster of Adolf Hitler. Gene considered the dance his first contribution to the war effort. Though one could say Gene's routine was not completely original because Fred Astaire, too, used props in his solos, Gene's daughter Kerry articulated why her father's approach was new to the screen: "His ability to maintain the leading-man role while still dancing has to do with his particular style of dance and his own personality. The style was athletic and that made it masculine. And also . . . it was unabashedly sexy."[14]

Thousands Cheer, in spite of its overwhelming cast of stars, was Gene's picture, as Howard Barnes of the *New York Herald Tribune* appreciated: "Gene Kelly . . . is so superb in the role of a distinguished draftee who discovers a few things about discipline and teamwork that he dominates the proceedings."[15] The picture, budgeted at $1,568,000, made an astounding $5,886,000 upon its release on September 13, 1943.

Gene's success in *Thousands Cheer* did not earn him what he had hoped it would: a green light from the studio to put his contract on hold and join the navy. Though he was still invested in his home and family life, he could not ignore his patriotic itch to defend the country. Instead of letting him enlist, MGM again cast Gene as a soldier in his next film. The picture, to be directed by Tay Garnett, was a propaganda piece with a mostly male cast entitled *The Cross of Lorraine*. The film tells the story of a group of French soldiers held prisoner in a German camp. They eventually stage a successful rebellion and take back the Nazi-occupied French village. Gene was relieved he was not required to adopt a French accent for the film, given his failure to acquire a proper Scottish dialect for the aborted *Keys to the Kingdom* project at Selznick International.

The Cross of Lorraine was a B picture, but it was an improvement over *Pilot #5*. In the cast were talented actors including Sir Cedric Hardwicke, Hume Cronyn, and Peter Lorre. Gene, again in the part of a rebel, established his persona early in the film's proceedings. During a Nazi interrogation, he gives a facetious salute and asks, "Heil, er—what's his name?" For his disrespect of "Der Fuhrer," an officer knocks him unconscious and throws him into solitary confinement. The Nazis work night and day to break his spirit, which they succeed in doing after much physical and mental torture. The picture required significant dramatic acting on Gene's part. Film critic Jeanine Basinger wrote in 1978, "In the prison torture scenes in particular Kelly's close-ups revealed his brooding intensity and he conveyed realistic internal suffering by the subtlest of changes in his face."[16] Gene told *Screenland* magazine in 1947 that he deemed *Lorraine* "one of the best things he has done in Hollywood."[17]

Gene, as much as he relished taking on a dramatic role, accepted that his name meant more in musical pictures. But he firmly believed that musicals could be as thought-provoking as dramas like *The Cross of Lorraine* and carry in them food for American thought.

Gene may have wished to perform in more realistic pictures, but audiences were tiring of such films. *The Cross of Lorraine,* released on December 2, 1943, received positive critical reviews but, according to Gene, only "about three people saw it."[18] A critic for the *New York Times* warned audiences: "This is a harshly realistic film drama . . . unsullied by the usual 'softening up' ministrations of Hollywood." The reviewer singled out Gene as rising above the uneven screenplay. "Like the picture itself, Mr. Kelly's character (a conventional tough hero type) goes all to pieces toward the end. The writers and the director are at fault in this instance, not the actor."[19] The film, budgeted at $1,010,000, grossed only $1,248,000.

Another small Metro picture produced in 1943 fared much better. *The Human Comedy*, based on the novel by Gene's friend William Saroyan, told the story of a telegram delivery boy (Mickey Rooney) who sees first-hand the effects of war on the people in his hometown. The picture, budgeted at $1 million, grossed $3 million. Playing the ghost of the protagonist's older brother who died in the war was Van Johnson, who was quickly rising as MGM's most popular new male star. According to reports from the *New York Times* and St. Petersburg, Florida's *Evening Independent*, Gene was supposed to play the part of a wounded soldier who adopts Johnson's family and hometown as his own. Why his role in the film was abandoned is unclear. It may have been because Gene was occupied with *Thousands Cheer* or simply because *The Human Comedy* was not a musical, which was clearly the direction in which the studio wanted to push Gene.

Gene did not mind that his future lay in musicals. Indeed, from his experience on Broadway in *Pal Joey*, he knew that genre could provide plenty of "solid food for American thought." "Kelly believes that screen musicals are still child's play, their possibilities largely ignored," Philip Scheuer of the *Los Angeles Times* reported. He quoted Gene: "The way I see it . . . dance can be used to express emotions phonetically—in movements that 'speak.' It's too soon to expect it yet, but it'll come."[20]

As it happened, Gene found an opportunity to bring more depth to musicals sooner than he expected. Harry Cohn, head of Columbia Pictures, had begun filming a Rita Hayworth Technicolor spectacle—with no leading man yet cast. The film boasted Charles Vidor as director, Jerome Kern and Ira Gershwin as composers, and Arthur Schwartz as producer. To Schwartz's mind, no one at Columbia was appropriate to play Rita Hayworth's love interest. Only one man in Hollywood, Schwartz argued, could play the part: Gene Kelly. Cohn grew apoplectic each time the producer brought up the possibility. "That tough Irishman with his tough Irish mug? He doesn't belong in the same *frame* as Rita!" he stormed. "Besides, he's . . . too goddamn short."

Without informing Cohn, Schwartz went to MGM and negotiated with the studio to loan Gene out for four weeks. Schwartz returned to

Cohn's office, grinning as he said: "Your problems are over! I just got Gene Kelly for the role."

Cohn rose from his desk, put his arms around Schwartz, and uttered, "Thank God."

"Strange man, Harry Cohn," Schwartz dryly concluded.[21]

Why was Schwartz so set on casting Gene as the male lead? Reading the plot of *Cover Girl,* one can see that Gene was an obvious choice for the role given that, as in *Pal Joey,* he plays a nightclub host. However, his new assignment had him portraying a conscientious man (Danny McGuire) rather than a heel.

"If you can get there [to the top] quicker, why shouldn't you?" Danny's girlfriend, Rusty (Rita Hayworth), asks.

"Look, when you get there quick, you get out quick. Easy get, easy lose. You have to work for what you get . . . you've got to get there on your feet, not on your face," Danny replies.

"Old hard-way McGuire," Rusty teases him.[22]

Cover Girl follows Rusty's dilemma of choosing the easy way or the hard way to become a star. The film begins with Rusty working as a chorus girl at a small club owned by Danny. She is content with her job and her friends there, though she, Danny, and his pal, the star comic Genius (played by Phil Silvers) all dream of bigger things. Every Friday night, they order oysters at their favorite haunt (reminiscent of Louie Bergen's in New York) and chant, "Come on, pearl!" Rusty does not consider leaving her job until she hears of a contest to become a cover girl for the popular *Vanity* magazine. The magazine's editor John Coudair (Otto Kruger), who years earlier had been in love with her grandmother, Maribelle Hicks, gives Rusty the chance to be a star. Once she is *Vanity*'s cover girl, Danny's club becomes the hottest spot in town—a Chez Joey, so to speak—but only because Rusty is a performer there. After arguing with Danny, Rusty leaves and finds success on Broadway in a musical produced by Coudair's wealthy friend Noel Wheaton (Lee Bowman). Danny closes his club when Rusty leaves and he and Genius enlist as USO entertainers. Hesitantly, Rusty decides to marry Wheaton. At the last moment, she flees the altar after Coudair gives her a pearl Danny found (and Genius had delivered to Coudair) the previous night. Rusty and Danny reunite at their old haunt, presumably with plans to marry and resurrect their act together.

The four weeks MGM gave Gene to complete the film continually extended as he grew more and more involved in its creation. As an assistant, Gene enlisted his apprentice, Stanley Donen. Since his arrival in Hollywood in 1942, Donen had been the most frequent visitor at Gene's open-house parties; he was at the Kelly home so often that another occasional guest, director George Cukor, asked, "Who is that young man who's always asleep on your floor?"[23]

Donen had been floundering in his attempts to gain a foothold in movies, and only after *Cover Girl* did he consider his career "really swinging."[24] Gene later claimed that it was he who had asked Donen to work on *Cover Girl* after MGM fired him, promising the young man that he would receive equal billing. At this point, Gene explained that he and Donen became close friends. Gene's claim is not completely true. Donen was not fired from MGM. Columbia borrowed him. Nor did Donen receive "equal billing" with Gene. Biographer Stephen M. Silverman argues that Gene's paternalistic attitude toward Donen (whom he said was "like a son to me," although he was only twelve years younger), and Gene's assertion that he had virtually rescued the younger man from unemployment "demonstrate Kelly's longstanding attempt to diminish Donen's contribution to their collective work."[25] Whether or not Gene was purposely trying to minimize Donen's input is debatable. Gene did have a far more prominent place in Hollywood at the time, which inevitably cast him as the leader. By his account, Gene did allow Donen to play a part equal to his own in directorial duties. He valued the young man's opinion to such a degree that he did not view any shots of the film without Donen present.

With Cohn's approval, Gene and Donen took over supervising the musical numbers in the film. Fred Kelly apparently also assisted with choreography, albeit uncredited. When Gene and Donen first arrived at Columbia to view the footage of what had already been shot (incidentally by Seymour Felix, whom Gene had vetoed as dance director for *Du Barry Was a Lady*), they were taken aback, especially by the kitschy opening number, "The Show Must Go On." To ensure that Gene was not credited for the routine, he and Donen inserted three "reaction shots" showing Danny in the wings covering his face and shaking his head in horror. The other routines that lacked Gene and Donen's touch were flashback numbers showing Maribelle Hicks in the 1890s: "Sure Thing" and "Poor John." The numbers seriously impeded plot continuity, a problem of which Gene was well aware and hoped to remedy in the numbers he and Donen designed.

Each morning, Gene came to the set with more script revisions or ideas for further enlivening the dance numbers. Those on the set of this film, as on Gene's others, watched in amazement as he jumped from behind the camera to check the viewfinder, bolted to watch the dailies, and then ran back to the set to perform in front of the cameras. The next day, he would begin the entire process over again.

One of Gene's numbers was notable less for its choreography than for the depth of emotion it conveyed. The routine takes place after closing hours at Danny's club as Danny is putting up chairs, distracting himself from the fear that Rusty and he are growing apart. He quietly sings Kern's "Long Ago and Far Away," soon joined by Rusty, who has been watching him from the doorway. The number that follows utilizes simple ballroom steps. The song was by far the best in the film and the only one that won enduring popularity. Gene was not a crooner on a par with Frank Sinatra, but the feeling he gave the song brought tears to Jerome Kern's eyes. Gene later spoke of the number "with special fondness, calling it 'Really more of a mood than a dance.' . . . It tells its own story of nostalgic love. Kelly says that he and Miss Hayworth worked longer and harder on getting the right feeling into those thirty seconds [of dance] than they did on any of their longer and more exuberant numbers."[26] Gene and Rita had a great rapport onscreen and off. She was no amateur dancer, and Gene held a special regard for her in part because he had learned invaluable techniques from her uncle, Angel Cansino, at the Chicago Association of Dancing Masters in the mid-1930s. Betsy Blair called her "sweet and gentle" and recalled Gene complimenting her for working "like a real trouper."[27]

Gene likewise admired the abilities of his other costar, Phil Silvers. Phil, incidentally, was another frequent guest at the Kelly open-house parties. Phil, with his slightly chubby build and bespectacled face, was not a typical musical star. Nevertheless, he successfully performed in several dance routines with Gene and Rita. When a friend remarked to him: "Phil, I didn't know you were a dancer," he quipped: "I'm not, Kelly hypnotized me."[28] Gene's friend Saul Chaplin (who worked uncredited as assistant musical director) was assigned to write a humorous song for Gene and Phil to perform during a USO scene. Discussing his ideas for the number with Chaplin, Gene surprised him by saying: "Make Phil as funny as you can, and don't worry about me—I'll take care of myself." Chaplin concluded that "Gene . . . would always maintain this attitude. And he would *always* be able to take care of himself."[29]

In the midst of filming *Cover Girl*, Gene received word that his friend

Dick Dwenger's ship had been torpedoed off Salerno on October 9, 1943. Dick was declared missing in action. A year would pass before he was officially declared dead. In an interview from 2014, Gene's daughter Kerry explained that Gene "lost his very best life-long friend . . . and it had a big impact on him. . . . My father wanted to go to war right then."[30] Still bound by his contract, however, Gene worked out his grief in the only way he knew: work. He turned a number in *Cover Girl*, "Make Way for Tomorrow," into a sort of tribute to Dick.

The routine is an optimistic one danced and sung by Danny, Genius, and Rusty as they traipse about the streets of New York in the early hours of the morning. The number is a prime example of the shift toward musical sequences in open-air settings rather than stage-bound ones. It also served to establish camaraderie between a threesome, which became a hallmark of numerous Kelly-Donen numbers. As in the mop dance, "Make Way for Tomorrow" utilizes many props. For instance, a breadstick becomes a baton and a mailbox becomes a tom-tom. With arms linked, the trio then chuckles at a couple kissing on the landing of a walk-up, dances around a friendly drunk, and salutes a milkman. "I think Gene honored his [Dick's] memory and commemorated the three of us and our wonderful time together," Betsy Blair asserted. "Dick would have loved" the number.[31]

The most intricate number Gene and Donen designed for *Cover Girl* was reflective of the era's most cutting-edge Broadway production. Rodgers and Hammerstein's *Oklahoma!*, which premiered on March 31, 1943, ushered the stage musical into what Alan Jay Lerner called the "belle époque" of the genre.[32] *Oklahoma!* picked up where *Show Boat* had left off in 1927, perfecting the weaving of songs and dances into a strong story that summons a broad range of emotions beyond laughter. Gene had not forgotten that in 1939 at the Westport Country Playhouse he had created the choreography for *Green Grow the Lilacs*, the show that evolved into *Oklahoma!* Agnes de Mille's choreography in *Oklahoma!* however, replaced most of what Gene had conceived in *Green Grow the Lilacs*. De Mille's greatest achievement in the play was a fifteen-minute "dream ballet" illustrating the heroine's feelings for two men. Despite the fact that most of Gene's work had been discarded, his ideas were the inspiration behind the final, polished product on the Broadway stage. Gene was indignant that he never received credit for his part in the creation of *Oklahoma!* According to his biographer Alvin Yudkoff, "From then on, he would always fight for credits and proper recognition. Anonymity simply doesn't pay."[33] In truth, Robert Alton and Gene had already designed something similar to de Mille's ballet two years before *Oklahoma!* opened: the fantasy ballet in *Pal Joey*. Now, for *Cover Girl*, Gene needed to take what he had used in *Pal Joey* and meld it with de Mille's more psychologically charged model.

The resulting dance routine, in stark contrast to the joyousness of "Make Way for Tomorrow" and the romance of "Long Ago and Far Away," was sorrowful and introspective in tone. Donen later took credit for conceiving the idea of having Danny McGuire "fight it [his dilemma] out with his inner self in a double-exposure dance." Donen claimed that the concept came to him after he decided a number with a lone dancer was far less "powerful" and "fun" than one with two dancers.[34] Gene, however, maintained that he was the first to envision performing an angsty duet.

Regardless of who was responsible for devising the number, it evoked equal enthusiasm in both Gene and Donen. Director Charles Vidor did not share their excitement. "It won't work," he said after listening to Gene and Donen describe what they now dubbed the "Alter Ego" number. Executives at Columbia were also against the idea. "For one thing, you can't pan and dolly in double-exposure," they said. "It's never been done." "About time then," Gene declared.[35]

Saul Chaplin described Charles Vidor's mounting impatience with Gene's brashness. "Charles Vidor had never done a musical before, but that would not have mattered if he had not been so totally humorless. . . . Gene's latent towering Irish temper would get the better of him every now and then until he and Vidor had a fistfight. Cohn . . . had to be called down to the set more than once to settle their disputes."[36]

Gene finally reached a truce with Vidor after Cohn agreed to give Gene and Donen a chance to experiment. At first, the studio head had been as unconvinced as Vidor about the possibilities of the "Alter Ego" dance. Gene went home and stayed up until five a.m. for two consecutive nights, sipping coffee and working out the dance in his head and on paper. After consulting with the cameramen and technicians, he went back to Cohn, who finally said: "All right. Go ahead. Just get the fucking hell out of here."[37]

Before plunging into filming, Gene and Donen had to devise a clever transition into the sequence. Gene knew he could not begin the dance without a bridge. "You have to state your thesis in a song first and then go into a dance," he explained. "So, what I decided to do was state my thesis not in a song but in a few words which came over the soundtrack as if they were my stream of consciousness, and then go into the dance."[38] As is true of nearly everything involved in the "Alter Ego" routine, it remains murky whether it was actually Gene or Donen who formulated the bridging statement. Donen has stated that he told Gene to drop "McGuire" in the following line because he had never heard anyone refer to himself by his full name: "Wait a minute, Danny McGuire, she [Rusty] stood you up and you know it."[39]

The scene continues with Danny nervously pacing back and forth on the sidewalk while his self-satisfied reflection looks on from a window, arms crossed over his chest. "Don't be such a hard-headed Irishman. If you love Rusty you'll let her go." The real Danny ignores his reflection, provoking his twin to jump from the window and engage in a dancing duel.

Gene later said the number was "the most difficult thing I've ever done. Technically nobody knew anything at the time, so it was done under very primitive conditions."[40] To create the number, Gene had to match one dance with another on a prerecorded sound track, synchronizing every muscle he moved to beats of music. Each time his feet touched the stage, they had to land on a certain spot marked off with chalk and tape "to a quarter-of-an-inch exactness."

The scene ends with Danny throwing a garbage can through a window and shattering his inner self into shards. Columbia executives called in a glass expert, who warned that if Gene threw such a heavy can through the glass, it would "cut [him] to pieces" and "put out [his] eyes." News spread around the studio that day, and all who had the chance slipped onto the set to watch "Kelly kill himself."[41] Gene came away unscathed by the glass.

During rehearsals, Donen acted as Gene's alter ego, tirelessly helping him work out his moves in time to a "twin." At times, Donen had trouble keeping up with Gene. He had the most difficult time during a shot in which Gene and his alter ego slide down a telephone pole. Gene reached the floor before Donen and shouted in front of the cast and crew: "Stanley, move your fat ass!"[42] This exclamation may have been part of Gene and Donen's well-known "put-down humor," or it might have been an example of Gene's temper. But, joke or not, at this time Donen was "the happiest guy in town" to be working with Gene.[43] In 1943, Gene and Donen's collaboration was in its "honeymoon phase," so to speak. Donen's biographer Stephen M. Silverman characterized Gene and Donen's working relationship as indeed like a marriage. "While Stanley did have the technical prowess and knowledge, I think [the success of their work together] was really a magical combination of Gene Kelly's charisma and Stanley Donen's chutzpah."[44]

By the time filming completed on *Cover Girl* in November 1943, Metro was already calling Gene for another loan-out assignment. Consequently, Donen spent seven days a week in the dubbing and cutting room, completing the "Alter Ego" number himself. The picture, slated for its New York release in March 1944, took several months to edit. Because of his intense involvement in the film, Donen termed it "his baby."[45] Still, Gene claimed the picture as primarily his creation. "I was captain. . . . He [Donen] was never a real choreographer in the inventive sense but he had a great faculty for criticizing," Gene explained in 1980. "It's good to have another opinion from a dear friend and a trusted colleague who's not a yes-man."[46]

Gene and Donen had created a dance that had initially been dismissed as impossible; now, all they had to do was wait to see if audiences and critics appreciated their efforts. The picture premiered at New York's Radio City Music Hall on March 30, 1944. To the two men's disappointment, Bosley Crowther of the *New York Times* did not so much as mention the "Alter Ego" dance, instead penning the dismissive words that the film "is so frankly familiar that it must have come from the public domain."[47] Crowther was in the minority. Other critics, not to mention audiences, met the film with overwhelming enthusiasm. A writer for *Modern Screen* recorded the tremendous response to Gene and Donen's first collaborative effort: "When Gene Kelly's amazing dance ended, and one of the biggest thunders of applause any Hollywood star has ever earned died down at last, an expert on the dance turned to his companion in the audience. 'That's the greatest dancing since Nijinsky!'"[48] Critics also noted Gene's developing acting skill. One critic raved: "Few cinema actors can match his reticence, exact evocativeness and sincerity, or carry such acting abilities into dancing and singing."[49]

Cover Girl became the nineteenth-highest grossing film of 1944 and was one of the great morale boosters during the final year of the war. In England, the British Ministry of Information's film division ran the picture every morning for their troops as a morale booster.[50]

Today, historians credit *Cover Girl* as the film that turned Gene into a top Hollywood star and marked his "promotion from hoofer to dancer."[51] Film writer Jeanine Basinger commented in 1985 that "before Kelly, whenever a dance number came along . . . it had somehow seemed extraordinary. There was a self-conscious quality to it, from the 'here it comes' opening music on through the 'ta-da' finale. . . . Kelly began to experiment with ways to bring the audience into the dance. . . . They felt the dance as movement, and thus became not just viewers of dance, but dancers."[52] As in his numbers with Judy Garland in *For Me and My Gal*, Gene employed the idea that dancers moving toward the camera provide a sort of 3-D effect that engages filmgoers. *Cover Girl* bore this signature trademark as well as two others: the use of a threesome to play off one another and a solo lacking a garish finale. The "Alter Ego" number set a formula for all of Gene's future solos. Emotionally charged, it begins on a note of introspection, reaches an energetic climax, and ends in quiet sorrow with Gene alone in the dark.

A *New York Herald Tribune* writer best summarized Gene's fine piece of work: "The human race has been having trouble with its conscience since time immemorial. It remained for Gene Kelly, however, to get his still, small voice out into the open and dance with it."[53]

After *Cover Girl*, Louis B. Mayer fully realized what an asset he had in Gene Kelly. He would no longer be so willing to loan his new star to other studios, despite frequent requests for his services. Harry Cohn was so pleased with the box office returns for *Cover Girl* that he called Metro asking for Gene every three months for several years. He often discussed pairing Gene again with Rita Hayworth in a screen version of *Pal Joey*. However, Mayer demanded an exorbitant sum of money for Gene's service and thus the project was continually put on hold. Much to Gene's disappointment, he never reprised his role as Joey Evans (the picture was finally made, with lackluster results, in 1958 with Rita Hayworth as Vera Simpson and Frank Sinatra as Joey). Mayer, before he knew how successful *Cover Girl* would be, had made another loan-out agreement he now could not break. Gene was to work for Universal Studios in a straight dramatic picture starring Deanna Durbin and directed by Robert Siodmak, *Christmas Holiday*. Though Gene's next film was a project for which he had no enthusiasm, Mayer told him he would be suspended if he did not agree to do the role. Gene, who saw unemployment in wartime as unpatriotic, acquiesced.

In November 1943, Gene reported for work on *Christmas Holiday*. Based on the 1939 short novel by W. Somerset Maugham, the picture tells the story of Abigail, a woman who marries a southern aristocrat, Robert

Manette. Manette is a seemingly weak yet malevolent character who is dependent on his possessive mother. Abigail goes into the marriage oblivious that he has inherited his family's streak of mental instability. After discovering that Manette has committed murder and his mother helped him cover it up, Abigail runs away, gets a job as a hostess in a brothel, and changes her identity for her own safety.

Christmas Holiday is notable in that it cast both Gene and Deanna Durbin against type; Gene was an unusual choice for the disturbed southerner Robert, while Durbin was the last actress one would consider to play a fallen woman. Up to 1944, Durbin had been primarily an operatic musical star in Joe Pasternak's confectionary musicals. She almost single-handedly saved Universal from bankruptcy due to the success of her films. Not to disappoint Durbin's fans, she did sing two songs in *Christmas Holiday*, "Spring Will Be a Little Late This Year" and "Always," though they were torchy rather than classical in style. Upon its release on June 28, 1944, *Christmas Holiday* went on to gross more than $2 million. Durbin considered it her only film of any true merit.

The fact that it, one of the darkest film noirs of the 1940s, was so popular during wartime is a testament to both Gene's and Durbin's star power. This is not to say that film noir pictures were unpopular in the 1940s. On the contrary, the genre saw a renaissance. Film noir of the 1940s, unlike the crime films of the 1930s, did not glorify criminals or loose women. Instead, detectives, policemen, or victims of circumstance were the heroes. Humphrey Bogart's films best typified the genre, namely, *The Maltese Falcon* (1941, in which he plays a detective) and *To Have and Have Not* (1944, in which he portrays a fishing boat captain drawn into the French Resistance movement). Noirs spoke to the disillusionment and dark introspection of World War II–era Americans, thus providing a different kind of release than musicals and romances.

Gene, despite his lack of enthusiasm about *Christmas Holiday*, gave a convincing performance. A critic for the *Evening Independent* wrote that he "plays naturally and with sincerity."[54] Bosley Crowther of the *New York Times* was less complimentary: "Gene Kelly performs her [Durbin's] no good husband in his breezy, attractive style, which is thoroughly confusing, considering the character that he is supposed to be."[55] Gene's performance has become more appreciated with time. Biographer Clive Hirschhorn commented that he brought an intriguing, "slightly homosexual" quality to the role.[56]

After finishing *Christmas Holiday,* Gene received a wire from the Hollywood Victory Committee telling him to report to its headquarters in New York. Assuming that they planned to send him overseas to entertain, he "was a pretty excited fellow." He discovered the organization had only a home-front project for him. "I was deeply disappointed at first," he admitted. "Having set my heart on going overseas. But then I realized it was a terribly important and worthwhile job they had selected me for."[57]

From the beginning of the war, Gene had found much fulfillment in his USO activities. He helped at the Hollywood Canteen as well, where hundreds of other stars performed and served complimentary doughnuts and coffee to servicemen on leave. In early 1944, Gene had completed a successful tour for the Hollywood Victory Committee, garnering favorable reports. In several, columnists noted that Gene attracted squealing audiences of girls and autographed bonds, which sold before the ink on his signature could dry.

For his latest home-front project, the committee asked Gene "to organize a unit and go out on a planned itinerary of Army and Navy hospitals." Gene enlisted several entertainers to go on tour with him and "built the show so that the boys in the hospitals could feel that they were seeing a regular Broadway revue. I sang with the girl singer and danced with the girl dancer, and I played in sketches, and M.C.'d the whole show." Gene worked as hard as a traveling vaudevillian, playing up to three shows a day in hospital auditoriums for an average of 550 servicemen per show. Then, he and his team would perform in all the wards for soldiers who were unable to leave their cots. "Their enthusiastic applause did my hammy heart good. After playing to the electricians in Hollywood for two years it was swell having a real audience, not that I don't like electricians." There was no publicity in connection with the tour—just as Gene wanted it. "The hour it would have taken us to give interviews to the local press in each town, we could use to much better advantage by giving a show to the wounded," he explained.[58]

Gene's return to New York and live entertainment reminded him how much he missed the theater. A reporter for the *Los Angeles Times* quoted Gene as saying: "Sometimes I get the urge to . . . direct dance numbers in a play like I used to. But I realize a big movie corporation can't adjust its schedules to suit me. . . . Maybe Freddie March can do it, going back and forth, but I couldn't. The economical dent," he grinned, "would be too big."[59]

However, his return to Hollywood in May 1944 did not seem so dismal a prospect. MGM had major plans for him in two upcoming pictures. Both films were again replacements for active service in the military: morale-boosting, big-budget, Technicolor musicals as only MGM could produce them. One of the films, *Anchors Aweigh,* would reunite him with producer Joe Pasternak, director George Sidney, and leading lady Kathryn Grayson. He was pleased to find that the other film, *Ziegfeld Follies,* was to be produced by Arthur Freed with Vincente Minnelli acting as director for the skit in which Gene would perform. He had watched what the Freed Unit had produced in his absence and itched to be a part of it again. Freed's most recent release was a simple story set in 1903, following a year in the life of an ordinary family. The film, titled *Meet Me in St. Louis,* starred Judy Garland, was directed by Vincente Minnelli, and included original songs by Gene's friends Hugh Martin and Ralph Blane. The picture marked the beginning of the Freed Unit's golden period. The circle of people with whom Freed was working, some since his beginnings as an MGM producer, was now a cohesive team, dedicated and faithful to one another. He had Vincente Minnelli and Charles Walters as directors, Lennie Hayton, Conrad Salinger, Roger Edens, and Kay Thompson as musical arrangers, Hugh Martin and Ralph Blane as songwriters, and Gene Kelly and Judy Garland as his leading stars.

"Arthur Freed was such a brilliant man to establish a cabinet around himself like a president. He had the most money to spend. Other producers didn't get that kind of attention," actress Ann Miller later remarked.[60] To work for Arthur Freed was not just a job; it was an appointment to join a royal family. Freed's brilliance also showed through his consistent production of films that suited the precise need of the nation at any given time. Though the Allies were closer to winning the war with the triumph of D-Day on June 6, 1944, the loss of over ten thousand lives that came with it left theatergoers in need of a film depicting happy endings in a peaceful era of American history—like *Meet Me in St. Louis.* The film's theme of fondness for one's childhood home touched the nation, Gene included.

Vincente Minnelli was disappointed that the Academy failed to nominate him as Best Director or the movie for Best Picture at the 1945 ceremony. Gene was so indignant about the snub that he called Judy Garland and Minnelli (who were engaged to marry by this time) after the nominees were announced, declaring: "Goddamn it, they don't appreciate what a fine thing it is. They don't realize all that went into it."[61]

Gene was as much a perfectionist as Vincente Minnelli when it came to his own work, and he was ready to bring such preciseness to his upcoming assignments. As had been the case since US involvement in the war, his new projects helped assuage the pain he felt at not fighting overseas. "He managed somehow . . . to focus fiercely on his work. I think now that his work was never out of his mind. . . . For Gene, his work was the most important part of his life," Betsy Blair commented in 2003. She was quick to add: "This is not in any sense a complaint."[62]

Gene's work was in truth the center of his life, but the devotion he showed to Betsy and Kerry indicate that they were vital parts of his existence. Betsy strove to keep her marriage as idyllic as fan magazines made it out to be. When she and Gene first met, she was five feet five, but she continued to grow for the first two years of their union, reaching her full height of five feet six and a half inches. In three-inch heels, she was "no longer looking up to Gene." She later wrote that she "liked looking up to him. . . . So, I sadly put my high heels in the closet. It was flats and sneakers from then on. I think Gene noticed, although it was never mentioned. I know he was glad. . . . I think he liked me to look up to him—actually and metaphorically. Perhaps it was even a necessary element for us as a couple."[63]

Gene, both consciously and subconsciously, did not want Betsy to grow up and become a sophisticated (and perhaps cynical) woman of the world. Many reports noted that Gene preferred her to wear almost no makeup. Following a snide remark "to the effect that it was about time Mrs. Kelly started using make-up and dressing smartly to keep from hurting her husband's reputation," Gene replied. "Of course my wife doesn't use makeup. She doesn't need to."[64]

Columnists allowed Gene to have human weaknesses but seldom made Betsy out to be anything but a saint—a characterization that secretly chafed her. Commenting on Gene's shortcomings, one reporter wrote: "He won't write letters. Would love to live on meat, potatoes and thick slabs of white bread. He demands candy for breakfast and a heavy meal at bedtime. He stays awake all night and sleeps till noon. 'He's impossible,' Betsy tells you. But for her dough, he can boss her into endless sweaters and skirts, bawl her out for making the car gears grind and forbid her wearing any make-up but just a little lipstick."[65]

Though Betsy scoffed at Hollywood's notions of glamour and thus willingly gave up high heels and makeup, she did not know how long she could remain the bobbysoxer Gene had married. "He treated me like a little angel, like his beloved playmate to share his bed and his life—and perhaps the eldest daughter in a motherless house," Betsy commented. "Gene paid the bills. Gene took care of everything."[66]

In her memoir, Betsy claimed to bear no grudges over her delayed maturation. She confided that at age twenty she needed and welcomed the protection and guidance Gene offered. "I had no responsibilities except for the one I'd chosen: taking care of Kerry. . . . I know now that it was the most wonderful thing of all. . . . She was always central to our happiness." Nonetheless, Betsy did not plan on being a docile wife and mother forever. When Kerry was old enough to enroll in school, she planned to pursue her dream of becoming a serious actress. In the meantime, she attended auditions "just for fun," but her unconventional beauty and understated quality fit few producers' notions of the ideal actress. She remained a spectator of the theatrical world, Gene's booster—her "growth and rebellion" dormant.[67]

Gene provided a sort of "hothouse environment" for Betsy, but he too lived in his own glass house. At times, the all-powerful studio system became suffocating. Gene later called it "a form of serfdom." He continued without any apparent bitterness: "At the same time we were able to create a musical repertory group at MGM unlike any other in the world. . . . We had advantages working in musicals—all the script would say was 'A dance number follows.' We had the freedom to make it up as we went along."[68]

As Gene plunged into his new assignments, he engaged in a competition with himself like that depicted in the "Alter Ego" dance. In Stanley Donen's estimation, "When Gene's on the job there's no kidding around. . . . Gene has a creative genius that is never satisfied with a first attempt. He is constantly striving for new heights."[69]

9

"I'm asking for the Navy"

Louis B. Mayer recognized that his studio was the best producer of musicals in Hollywood and therefore planned to funnel more money into producers and stars of musicals—Gene Kelly and Arthur Freed included. "They [MGM and Americans] wanted more musicals," Arthur Freed reflected of Hollywood's climate in 1944. "Musicals were selling."[1]

Following the phenomenal success of *Meet Me in St. Louis,* Mayer appointed Freed as head of all musical productions on the Metro lot. Rival producers Joe Pasternak and Jack Cummings were displeased at the threat Freed's power posed over their own endeavors. Director Vincente Minnelli later recalled Gene observing that, rather than worry about competing with each other, Freed, Pasternak, and Cummings should have "considered their real threat, those units specializing in dramatic films. A Greer Garson or Katharine Hepburn picture could be made at half the cost of a musical and grossed twice as much." Minnelli asserted, "The only touchstone of the studio was success at the box office."[2] Because Freed's track record at MGM had been full of record-breaking hits, he was appointed to head his own official unit, an honor usually given only to producers of high-grossing Hepburn- or Garson-type dramas.

"They [Pasternak and Cummings] weren't units really in the sense that mine was," Freed explained. "Every producer is different. . . . A creative producer like Irving Thalberg . . . *made* the picture."[3] Freed considered himself such a creative producer while Pasternak and Cummings were more passive and did not do a "lot of research" to make a superior end product.[4] Freed's appointment as head of musicals was good news for Gene Kelly; not only was Freed one of Gene's greatest champions, but the men shared the same picture-making philosophy. Gene was never passive in creative matters. Also, both men were not afraid to fight for untraditional ideas that they believed would elevate a picture.

Gene and Freed meshed for more reasons besides their shared integrity. Like Gene, Freed shunned Hollywood norms when it came to personal appearance. From the flawless visions he put onto film and the romantic lyrics he penned, one would expect Freed to be suave, articulate, and immaculately dressed. However, according to his daughter, Barbara, Freed "was not someone you would have picked out as a writer of romantic lyrics."[5] Freed's brashness, clumsiness, and untidy eating habits often overshadowed his romanticism. Members of his production unit were all too familiar with his less attractive characteristics. Each time Judy Garland saw him coming into the commissary, she declared: "Here comes the tank!"[6] Betsy Blair recalled that the producer's car was full of old food wrappers.[7] Gene could also appear untidy, mostly due to his casual attire and general dislike of shaving. And yet the moment Gene began to dance, he became the embodiment of gracefulness and vigor, just as Freed became the personification of fine taste once he was in the producer's seat. One way in which the men did differ was that Freed had a wandering eye whereas Gene was faithful to his wife. Freed carried on an affair with actress and dancer Lucille Bremer (who had appeared in *Meet Me in St. Louis*) and ensured she was conspicuously featured in his next film, *Ziegfeld Follies*.

Gene and Freed were ideal candidates to bring *Ziegfeld Follies* to life and make it reflective of MGM's motto: *Ars gratias artis*. The film, designed to celebrate MGM's twentieth anniversary, was studded with even more stars than comparable revues disguised as romantic musicals such as *Thousands Cheer* and the two 1944 pictures *Two Girls and a Sailor* (starring June Allyson, Gloria DeHaven, Van Johnson, José Iturbi, Lena Horne, and Jimmy Durante) and *Bathing Beauty* (starring Esther Williams, Red Skelton, Harry James, and Xavier Cugat). Given an unprecedented $3 million budget, the *Follies* had every reason to live up to its tagline: "Greatest Production since the Birth of Motion Pictures!" The alleged "greatest production" paid homage to Florenz Ziegfeld Jr., the Broadway producer commonly referred to as Freed's theatrical predecessor.

"Arthur wasn't just going to do a revue [with] the *Ziegfeld Follies*. He was going to go one step further. He was going to try his wings in other directions," biographer Hugh Fordin commented.[8] Ballet, satire, opera, and experimental modern dance—Freed's revue included them all. The *Follies* was unique among World War II–era revues in that it made no allusions to the war. The picture was also distinct because, true to the spirit of

Ziegfeld's *Follies*, it carried no pretense of a plot. Rather, it was simply a progression of beauty and humor utilizing the best talents on the Metro lot. Aside from Gene, Judy Garland, Lena Horne, Lucille Ball, Red Skelton, Keenan Wynn, Kathryn Grayson, Fanny Brice, and Fred Astaire had signed to appear in the picture. Gene's friends Robert Alton, Charles Walters, and Lennie Hayton were among the talents behind the scenes.

Directing the majority of the film was Vincente Minnelli. Like Gene and Freed, he was obsessive about his work and put research and every available ounce of energy into it. Though Gene and Freed found in him a kindred spirit, not everyone could cope with his work habits or outward appearance. Many whom Minnelli directed claimed they could never work with anyone else again because of his unparalleled artistic talent and ability to bring out actors' best performances. But others refused to work with him a second time, so infuriating was his compulsive attention to detail. His odd appearance was enough to repel a number of actors and other colleagues as well. Minnelli's weak chin, large nose, pop eyes, nervous facial tics, and use of makeup were enough to make Kathryn Grayson admit, "To tell the truth, I couldn't really look at him." The studio eventually had to request that Minnelli refrain from wearing obvious cosmetics on the set, particularly his favored green eye shadow. Most assumed he was a homosexual, but Judy Garland argued, "It's just his artistic flair!"[9]

Minnelli's fey quality seemed the norm in the Freed Unit. Red Skelton, strolling past a patch of pansies blooming on the MGM lot, pointed and quipped: "Look! It's the Freed Unit!"[10] Not only Minnelli and Roger Edens but also composer Conrad Salinger, Robert Alton, and Charles Walters were known or thought to be gay. Gene, despite his decidedly masculine dance style and personality, felt comfortable working with gay colleagues. Minnelli was no exception. He found in the director a fellow New Yorker who was as driven and intelligent as himself and who shared his goal of giving musicals more dimension. Their collaboration on *Ziegfeld Follies* was the beginning of a fruitful professional association.[11] Though Minnelli and Gene became close friends, the director was seldom present at the Kellys' open-house parties, preferring instead the quieter gatherings at Ira Gershwin's home, to which most of his former New York colleagues (and Arthur Freed) gravitated. Minnelli and Judy Garland were not yet married at the time *Ziegfeld Follies* was in production; Judy was still a regular at Gene's parties.

When *Ziegfeld Follies* began shooting in April 1944, Minnelli declared he was "eager to plow into more hard work."[12] His hardest task on the film proved to be directing Gene's number, and for one extraordinary reason: Gene's dancing partner was Fred Astaire.

"An urgent call came from my agent," Fred Astaire recalled in his memoir. "Arthur Freed wanted to talk to me about several films and a term contract. I was soon to be a Metro player and very pleased about it."[13]

By 1944, Fred had appeared in only one Metro film, *Dancing Lady* (1933), which also marked his screen debut. MGM executive Eddie Mannix, who had claimed Gene had no film potential, had felt the same way about Fred Astaire in the 1930s. A decade later, Mannix still held the same opinion of Fred. When Freed announced he was going to star the dancer in his new revue, Mannix demanded: "How can you photograph him? He's so ugly!"[14] Freed ignored him, just as he had ignored the man's condemnations of Gene. Freed had every reason to be smug and self-assured of his own intuition; indeed, Gene was now a heartthrob and, in Minnelli's words "the hottest male dancer in town."[15]

As different as forty-five-year-old Fred and thirty-two-year-old Gene were in appearance and dance style, critics made constant comparisons between the two. Both were well liked by their coworkers at the studio, even if their personalities contrasted as much as their techniques. Gene had an easily ignitable temper and used his work as a means of sorting out troubles in his private life. Fred Astaire was, according to actor/musician/wit Oscar Levant, not "in the least temperamental and he's very considerate. . . . [He] would never use profanity. He's rather prudish—a very cautious fellow about everything."[16] Gene observed that Fred conveyed his personality through his less demonstrative dance style. "Fred's style is more introverted, close, tight, while mine is wider and more open. . . . My style is more proletarian while Fred's is aristocratic."[17]

Essayist John Updike further explained the men's differing methods: "One cannot imagine Astaire . . . [doing] the sidewise scuffle on hands and feet that Kelly agilely lowers himself to in several films—and his screen persona was less partnerable. . . . His image left no space around it into which the moviegoing wife could project herself."[18] Gene's image versus Fred's was indeed the area in which they differed most. Fred was ethereal and buoyant whereas Gene was tangible and had gravity. Housewives may have been able to imagine themselves in Fred's celestial onscreen world, but it was offscreen that they could see themselves with Gene. Jeanine

Basinger concluded that women gave their hearts to Fred Astaire but saved their bodies for Gene Kelly.[19]

Neither Gene nor Fred was comfortable with the incessant comparisons between them. They had no desire to compete, but columnists could not help but set up a rivalry. Take, for instance, the following lines from *Photoplay* in June 1944: "After *Cover Girl* Gene Kelly is hailed as the greatest dance sensation since Fred Astaire and Mr. Astaire, cold to the press and aloof with the natives where Gene is warm and friendly, is looking slightly worried. He should."[20] Gene and Fred did what they could to defuse the fascination with their supposed competition. Fred claimed that Gene, unlike most dancers, gave him a kick while Gene, in a statement to *Modern Screen,* explained: "I think [Fred's] a great artist. There's a lot of things in his dancing I wish I had."[21]

Perhaps columnists so enjoyed pitting Gene and Fred against each other because the men really did not have substantial competition from other male dancers at Metro or any other studio. Other musical stars, such as Bing Crosby, Bob Hope, and Frank Sinatra, won fame more through their singing than their dancing. George Murphy's career was winding down and up-and-coming tap dancer Dan Dailey Jr. was barely starting to garner notice. Thus, Fred and Gene could easily have become unfriendly rivals for the place as top dancer in Hollywood.

Fred and Gene, in spite of their stylistic differences, shared some similarities. For one, both found that their height raised difficulties beside particularly tall costars. (Fred, at just over five nine, was only half an inch taller than Gene.) Though Fred exuded an air of gentility, he, like Gene, had been brought up in a humble Catholic household. Both also had controlling mothers who had prodded them to attend dancing schools against their wills. Finally, both climbed from performing in small-time settings to working for the crème de la crème of Broadway. Fred could list the Shubert Brothers and Florenz Ziegfeld Jr. among his ex-employers; Gene could name Billy Rose and George Abbott.

As his fame grew, Fred developed a dogged drive for perfectionism on a par with Gene's. He spent seven to eight weeks perfecting any routine, yet was always convinced his talents left something to be desired.[22] Fred also did not think highly of his social skills. He was shy around strangers and embarrassed when acquaintances or fans nodded to him on the street. Like Gene, he seldom frequented nightclubs and preferred to entertain in his own home.

For all Fred's timidity, he was not hesitant to assert himself with Gene on the set of *Ziegfeld Follies*. "Fred was the senior partner and if I felt that there was any conflict or any doubt about any step, I would certainly defer to him," Gene explained.[23] His relationship with Fred was a reversal of that between himself and Stanley Donen, requiring Gene to take on a role he rarely filled—follower rather than leader. Fred insisted they do a skit based on a George Gershwin number entitled "The Babbitt and the Bromide." Originally, he and Adele Astaire had performed it in *Funny Face* (1927). The routine shows two rather boring people meeting in a park at various stages throughout their lives. In Gene and Fred's skit, they first meet as clean-shaven young men in white summer suits and straw boater hats. Then they meet as mustachioed middle-aged men in bow ties and derbies. Finally, they meet in heaven, bearded, dressed in evening clothes with carnations in their lapels and harps in their hands. With each meeting, they engage in the same banal conversation (in song, of course):

Hello!
How are you?
How's the folks?
What's new . . .[24]

Gene felt the number lacked vitality. In an attempt to avoid making the skit as boring as the men depicted in it, Minnelli enlivened the piece by changing the demeanor of a horse statue in the park with each meeting. He left the remainder of the scene for the dancers to choreograph. Fred was adamant about executing it in the same way he had in 1927. Arthur Freed later recalled that during filming of the sequence, Fred would come to him and say: "Gene's so wonderful, but why does he want everything his own way?" Later the same day, Gene would unwittingly echo Fred: "I admire Fred so much, but why does he want everything his way?"[25] If Gene had had his way, he and Fred would have abandoned the number altogether, instead dancing to a lively, modern Hugh Martin and Ralph Blane tune, "Pass That Peace Pipe."

Minnelli declared that the fact Fred and Gene never again did another original feature film together was the "movie-goer's loss." Though he and Freed tried to interest them in future projects, "they didn't work out."[26] One such project was *Three Little Words,* which was ultimately produced by Jack Cummings in 1947 with Astaire and Red Skelton as the stars. Still,

Fred and Gene remained on friendly terms for the rest of their lives. Almost ten years after *Ziegfeld Follies,* Hedda Hopper quoted Gene as saying, "Fred and I [still] get together to crab a little and talk a little. We chat like two men on a desert island."[27]

Gene did not hold it against Fred that he had more screen time and better-quality numbers in *Ziegfeld Follies.* Besides his skit with Gene, Arthur Freed assigned the elder dancer two more lengthy sequences that utilized the most cutting-edge dance and cinematography techniques in the picture. Both numbers were devoid of dialogue and used solely dance and lyrics to tell a story. One, "Limehouse Blues," was an abstract, fantastical ballet costarring Freed's mistress, Lucille Bremer, while the other was a ballroom dance set to Freed's tune, "This Heart of Mine." Historian Hugh Fordin commented that in his numbers, Fred "changed from his marvelously unique style of dancing to a more balletic expression."[28] His sequences elevated the film from being a mere "cream puff" to "some kind of Freed Unit nirvana."[29] Fred proved to be far more adaptable to modern times than anyone, most of all himself, could have guessed. His new style took cues from the balletic elements in Gene's technique, but his methods remained his own because his airy steps lacked Gene's athletic prowess and sensuality.

After a series of costly setbacks, *Ziegfeld Follies* was ready for its first preview on November 1, 1944. Freed and Minnelli knew that the film would need much cutting, considering that its running time was 273 minutes. Re-takes and more editing elongated the shooting of the film until February 6, 1945. The picture, meant to be Metro's twentieth anniversary celebration, ultimately honored its twenty-second anniversary.

Upon its release in March 1946, *Ziegfeld Follies* lost money. Though it brought in $5,344,000, the costs incurred from advertising left the studio a deficit of $269,000. By the time the film finally premiered, the revue's temporary resurgence in popularity had begun to wane. Nonetheless, reviews were genial. Edwin Schallert of the *Los Angeles Times* deemed the picture "splendiferous."[30] Bosley Crowther of the *New York Times* wrote glowingly of Fred Astaire's ballets and concluded: "A third number, done by Mr. Astaire, with Gene Kelly as his twin, settles one point of contention: Mr. Astaire has the reach."[31]

Whatever reach Fred had over Gene proved to be isolated to his work in *Ziegfeld Follies.* The film was released after another Astaire-Minnelli-Freed picture, *Yolanda and the Thief* (1945), which proved to be a major flop, leaving Fred again feeling that he was completely out of sync with modern times. Fred complained that *Yolanda* was "inventing up to the arty"—his term for the approach of those, like Minnelli, who went into a picture with the priority of creating art. Fred was of the opposite mindset; he believed artistry could emerge only as an unplanned result of a relentless pursuit of perfection.[32] Gene fell somewhere in the middle. He went into projects with the intention of creating art—but at a level children, housewives, and highbrows alike could appreciate.

Fred had been considering retirement ever since his screen separation from Ginger Rogers in 1939, and now seemed the right time to bow out. He formally announced his retirement after making one more picture, *Blue Skies* (1946), a pleasant Technicolor musical by Paramount costarring Bing Crosby. Bosley Crowther had written that Astaire had "the lead" in *Ziegfeld Follies,* but, with Astaire's retirement, Gene stepped into his place as the number one male dancer in Hollywood. He secured this place largely due to one factor: *Anchors Aweigh.*

"Gene Kelly, the one male musical comedy dancer who has sex appeal, has the picture all wrapped up for himself," asserted Wanda Hale of the *New York Daily News.*[33] "Gene Kelly, MGM's triple-threat man, holds together a mammoth production. . . . This is . . . Gene Kelly's film. The fun lets down a little when he is not on the screen," concurred Eileen Creelman of the *New York Sun.*[34]

The columnists were not speaking in superlatives. Gene received third billing in *Anchors Aweigh,* and yet he enjoyed more screen time than his costars and gave a deeper, more varied performance than any thus far in his screen career. Those billed above him, Frank Sinatra and Kathryn Grayson, exceeded him in the singing department, but neither were triple threats. Frank may have been the top crooner in the nation—the idol of thousands of bobbysoxers—but as a relative newcomer to films, his acting was self-conscious and tentative. He was not a dancer, either, until Gene convinced him he could be. Nor was Kathryn Grayson a dancer. Her impressive coloratura was what truly allowed her to stand out. Gene's sheer personality combined with his threefold talent made him the undisputed star of the picture. From the moment he appears onscreen, wooing an elusive girl named Lola on the phone, he establishes his charisma. "Baby . . . Forgotten you? Aw, honey, with the picture of you I've got in my mind, why, even across the phone I can see every . . . ," he purrs into the receiver.[35]

Anchors Aweigh seemed a failsafe hit not only because of its cast but also because of its timely patriotic plotline. The story revolves around two sailors on leave in Hollywood. Gene portrays the "wolf of the navy," Joe Brady, while Frank is cast as Clarence Doolittle, a meek sailor who trails Joe in hopes he will teach him how to be a ladies' man. Joe allows Clarence to tag along with him only from a sense of duty:

> Clarence: Look, I didn't ask you to save my life [when I fell overboard], but you did. So now I feel you are responsible for me.
> Joe: Well, I don't!
> Clarence: Well, what's the good of having a life saved when you can't have any fun with it?

A particularly humorous scene ensues in which Joe pretends to be a "dame" and instructs Clarence to practice "picking him up." A policeman walks by and eyes Joe, who is sashaying down the street, with much suspicion. This was one of many comical female imitations Gene performed throughout his film career.

During their first night on the town, the two sailors find themselves babysitters instead of "wolves." They meet a little boy, Donald (Dean Stockwell), who has run away from home to join the navy. When they return him home they meet Aunt Suzy (Kathryn Grayson), an aspiring singer, with whom Clarence promptly falls in love. The girl's great goal is to audition for composer José Iturbi who, Joe declares, is a good friend of Clarence's. The film follows the sailors as they try to track down Iturbi in hopes of securing a screen test for Suzy. During their struggles, Joe discovers he loves Suzy while Clarence transfers his affections to a waitress (Pamela Britton) who comes from his hometown of Brooklyn. The film concludes with Suzy singing "Anchors Aweigh" with José Iturbi's orchestra before Joe and Clarence return to their ship.

The film was superior to Gene's earlier picture with Joe Pasternak and George Sidney, *Thousands Cheer,* because of its stronger storyline and its better-integrated musical numbers. Gene's influence in the production of the film prevented it and its dance numbers from being overly (in his words) "hackneyed." He also relied on the second opinion of Stanley Donen, whom he again enlisted as his assistant on the project. Pasternak began to avoid Gene on the set because the actor "seemed to be constantly at him like a terrier with constant calls for revisions and improvements."[36] Isobel Lennart, the film's screenwriter, had a similar experience working with Gene. "Gene read the first twenty pages [of the script] and liked them. He had a thousand ideas, a thousand suggestions—and, worst of all—a thousand questions. . . . My answer to all of the questions was 'I don't know—and please—I'm busy now—.' He'd nod and go away. But next day, there he'd be again, tapping at the office door. . . . We never stopped Kelly. He just rapped until we *un*-locked the office door." As had been the case on *Cover Girl,* Gene was concerned with improving the whole production, not only his own role. Lennart recounted that "a number of his suggestions actually cut his own part to build others."[37]

Gene was particularly interested in building up the part of Clarence Doolittle. Frank was initially unaware of Gene's behind-the-scenes work on his behalf; consequently, when he and Gene first met, Frank admitted, Gene intimidated him. According to Frank's biographer James Kaplan, Gene swiftly eased Frank's anxiety. He "looked him in the eye, and decided to help him out. . . . [He] maturely decided that if he held Frank Sinatra's hand rather than kick his ass they would come out the better for it. . . . Sinatra saw his self-assurance and respected it. . . . The two men decided to like each other."[38]

Frank performed in only one of the picture's four major dance numbers. Nevertheless, his routine took eight weeks to perfect, longer than the entire shooting schedule of his previous films. The number takes place in a sailors' bunk room where Joe and Clarence do a tap dance and then jump in sync over a series of mattresses. Gene assigned Stanley Donen to work on another dance number while he personally took on the task of teaching Frank to hoof. Frank later told his daughter Nancy that he had felt like a child during the process. "I didn't even know how to walk let alone dance." Gene spent hours coaching him until Frank finally had to demand an afternoon off from sheer exhaustion. However, Frank appreciated Gene's help even if his rehearsals and demand for faultlessness were, in Frank's word, "insane."[39]

"We became a team only because he had the patience of Job, and the fortitude not to punch me in the mouth because I was so impatient. . . . He managed to calm me when it was important to calm me," Frank explained.[40] He later reflected: "When I arrived at MGM to do *Anchors Aweigh,* I was a nobody in movies . . . but after working with Gene . . . I felt I actually had some talent."[41] By helping Frank realize his abilities and potential in motion pictures, Gene was returning the favor Judy Garland and Arthur Freed had done for him when they guided him through *For Me and My Gal.*

In spite of Gene's ongoing patience and boosting, he was not always able to calm Frank's feelings of depression and humiliation. Frank's lack of confidence extended beyond his acting and dancing abilities to include his appearance. Gene looked and felt wonderful in a sailor suit whereas Frank swam in his wide-legged pants and roomy shirt. "The Navy made the best dance costume ever," Gene stated. "The proportions, the fit were perfect."[42] "If I thought I looked odd in a gob's uniform, all I had to do was look at Sinatra and I felt fine again!" He added with a rueful grin, "Just wait till Sinatra sees that in print!"[43] In Frank's future films, he required padding on his bottom and legs to disguise his thinness.

When Frank was depressed and embarrassed, "his first reaction was to bark commands." Stanley Donen admitted that he and Gene played "mean, nasty" tricks on Frank because he "was always a pain in the neck." Gene and Donen concocted one practical joke that took place in the commissary where they lunched with Frank each day. All the tables in the room were square shaped and pushed against the walls, cafeteria-style—except one. The single round table in the cafeteria belonged to Louis B. Mayer's brother, Jerry, who ran the studio's physical operations.

"Wouldn't it be wonderful if we could have a round table? It's so much nicer that way because then we could sit closer together," Donen remarked to Frank.

"You watch. I'll get us a round table," Frank replied.

"There was no way Frank was going to get us a round table. We knew that," Donen later said.

"Just forget it," Gene told Frank. Gene's assumption that Frank could not rise to the challenge sent him into a rage: "He steamed and he fumed and threw fits and said he was going to quit."[44]

Such pranks stood in contrast to Gene's usual professionalism and maturity. Researcher Susan Cadman asserted that when Gene and Donen were together, "Donen was the troublemaker who brought out the worst in Gene. I think perhaps they were rather tiresome at times, with their practical jokes and silliness."[45] Despite Gene's ribbing, he and Frank maintained a fond relationship. Looking back on his experience in *Anchors Aweigh* three years later, Gene claimed it held a special place for him because it introduced him to Frank, "who became one of my best friends."[46]

Kathryn Grayson did not remain so friendly with her costar. Though she did call Gene her "favorite dancer" in a 2003 interview, this did not mean she liked him on a personal basis.[47] During the filming of a scene in which Clarence, Joe, and Suzy are dancing up the front walk of Suzy's home, Gene continually pushed Kathryn and made her trip, which was not hard considering she was wearing a floor-length gown. Such behavior was confusing coming from a man who was usually generous to his costars and treated women with care. Kathryn, however, was strong willed and not in awe of Gene in any way—perhaps she posed a threat to Gene's self-appointed role as leader/mentor. Finally, Kathryn had had enough of his shenanigans when she fell to the ground. Gene bent over her and said, "Gee, sorry, Katie, I didn't mean to make you fall." Kathryn grabbed the tie of his sailor suit and pulled it tighter and tighter until he screamed for her to stop. After this display of temper, Gene never bothered Kathryn again. "I didn't know you had it in you," he told her.[48]

Throughout his career, Gene pushed people to their limit. Whether he did this out of a need to exert power or to test a person's character is debatable. Patricia Towers, Kathryn's daughter, commented, "He was very egotistical. Everything had to be where he was the focus of attention."[49] Kathryn admitted she had no talent for dance, and Gene had little patience with people who had no potential in the art that came so naturally to him. Frank Sinatra, though he initially had little ability, had proved that he had promise and willingness to learn; consequently, he won Gene's favor.

The routine in *Anchors Aweigh* that Gene performed with Frank in the soldier's bunk room may have been the most challenging part of the film for the singer, but for Gene, it was the simplest of the four main dance numbers in the production. "The three major dance numbers Gene devised for himself are brilliantly characteristic of his personality and clearly show the way his mind was working and the progress he was making towards formulating a personal style," biographer Clive Hirschhorn commented.[50] All three numbers he created seemed specifically designed to appeal to children.

Gene's first solo in the picture shows him wandering about Olvera Street, the Mexican settlement in Los Angeles, after leaving Clarence alone with Suzy. As he contemplates his own feelings for Suzy, he sees a solemn little Mexican girl watching him (she was inspired by the child with long black braids he had met when he and Betsy were honeymooning in Mexico). Joe proceeds to use pots, copper pans, and fluted clay pieces being sold at a street stand as props to aid him in a dance routine to entertain the girl. He and the child then perform the Mexican hat dance and skip rope. The number, like Gene's iconic "Singin' in the Rain" routine, shows him engaging in childlike activities as an expression of his discovery that he is in love. The number bears another trademark of Gene's solos: it ends on a quiet note with him walking introspectively into darkness.

The task of teaching child actress Sharon McManus the dance routine went to Stanley Donen. The young man was pleased to be working with Joe Pasternak, whom he called a "dear man," but he was less thrilled with the picture itself. "I thought his [Pasternak's] movies were real crap." Stronger than his distaste for Pasternak's pictures was his dislike of young Sharon. Allegedly, Donen spent three hours in the morning and four more in the afternoon going over a single step involving the jump rope. Donen claimed after the experience that he never wanted to see another young girl or jump rope again—"unless the rope was for hanging the little girl."[51] Every half hour, Gene strode into the rehearsal room to inquire whether Sharon had gotten the "rope bit" down yet.

"No," Donen would reply, grimacing.

Gene took him aside and whispered, "The secret is to make her believe you *love her*."

"But I loathe her," Donen declared.[52]

In contrast, children on the set found Gene "endlessly funny," proving that he was as much a Pied Piper as ever.[53]

Gene had always found pleasure working with children, but it had increased since he had become a husband and father. No matter how hectic his filming schedule, Gene devoted Saturdays to Betsy and Kerry. They could be found at an amusement park on Beverly Boulevard, the Santa Monica beach, or picnicking in their own backyard. "His excitement, his commitment to his work, and his pride in 'my two girls' as he called us, was irresistible," Betsy shared in her memoir.[54]

The third major dance in *Anchors Aweigh*, though it did not include children, appealed to their imaginations with its fantasy setting and vibrant use of color. The routine constituted the now obligatory dream sequence found in Gene's pictures and most musicals of the period. The number comes about after Suzy shows Joe around the MGM lot. Joe then imagines how he would court her if he were in a costume picture. He envisions himself in a Spanish courtyard dressed as a toreador, swinging from vines and rooftops à la Douglas Fairbanks to reach Suzy on the balcony of a villa. They engage in a fandango dance before parting. The sequence shows rather than tells viewers the lengths to which Joe would be willing to go to win Suzy's affection.

The indefatigable Gene was forced to stop shooting for a few days due to an injury he sustained in the middle of filming the fantasy sequence. At one point during the scene, Kathryn Grayson throws him a rose from her balcony. "There was a little wire in the stem," explained Gene. "And that punctured my hand. . . . Now I dance all day and soak my hand all night." Gene minimized his injury; in truth, he had a minor case of blood poisoning and endured shivers and fever for several days before he was able to return to work.[55]

Gene had little time to recuperate. He and Donen were in the middle of editing the fourth—and most complicated—dance routine in the film. The number topped the intricacy of Gene's "Alter Ego" sequence in *Cover Girl* and broke new precedents. Stanley Donen was responsible for the innovative idea behind the number. One morning at three a.m., he called Gene with his brainstorm: blending animation and live action. "How would you like to dance with Mickey Mouse?" Donen asked.

Gene was enthusiastic about the idea. But, MGM executives, like those at Columbia in reaction to the double exposure required for the "Alter Ego" routine, declared that a mix of animation and live action could not be done. Joe Pasternak, however, had complete confidence in Gene and Donen and convinced Mayer that if the two men were able to realize their vision, the studio would gain a great deal of prestige. Gene and Donen initially asked Walt Disney to help them create the sequence, but Disney replied that his cartoon department was occupied making films for the war effort. Disney also felt that having Mickey Mouse in an MGM picture would be a conflict of interest. "He [Mickey] works for me," Disney said.[56] Mayer agreed to commission MGM's cartoon department to work on the number using Jerry the Mouse instead of Mickey. The resulting number endeared Gene even more to children and is what Clive Hirschhorn called "quintessential Kelly."[57]

The sequence occurs when Donald, among his classmates at school, begs Joe to tell them how he won his naval medal. The scene then portrays Donald's imagination as he sees Joe's words come to life in a four-minute routine entitled "The King Who Couldn't Dance." The king (Jerry the Mouse) of a depressed cartoon kingdom cannot sing or dance, and so he has forbidden all the other animals in his land to do so. Joe enters the castle and serenades Jerry with "The Worry Song," which convinces the mouse to try dancing and singing. At the end of the routine, Jerry exclaims, "Look at me, I'm dancing!" and pins a medal on Joe's shirt. "The Worry Song," a tune penned by Arthur Freed's brother Ralph and composer Sammy Cahn, was a simplistic way of encouraging anxious wartime audiences. A sampling of the lyrics shows its unsubtle message:

> If you worry . . .
> If you bother your head,
> It won't help you . . .
> It will hurt you instead.
> You could laugh and sing and dance
> As gaily as an elf, but
> Don't expect to get much help
> If you won't help yourself.[58]

With the concept of the cartoon dance worked out in their minds, Gene and Donen were pleased to be granted $100,000 to execute the sequence. "The next job was to photograph Kelly plus space, the space to be filled with animations at a later date," one visiting reporter from *Theatre Arts* magazine explained. "When the dance called for the mouse to cross over, run back and then forward through Kelly's legs, the cameraman was expected to pan sufficiently to allow for these as yet invisible activities." Ultimately, ten thousand painted frames were required to synchronize with Gene's movements. The animated figures were then photographically superimposed on the film. The *Theatre Arts* reporter stated that Disney's film *The Three Caballeros* (1944) was one of the only pieces of cinema to date comparable to "The King Who Couldn't Dance." However, the Disney film was less advanced in that it did not show the performer interacting with the cartoon characters. "The progress from *Three Caballeros* to *Anchors Aweigh* is not merely a measure of time elapsed. It is also an indication of the light that an active imagination can always turn on established forms," the *Theatre Arts* critic concluded.[59]

"The King Who Couldn't Dance" took two months to complete. Stanley Donen finished the editing and technical details. Gene said, "I get all the credit for this [the number] but it would have been impossible without Stanley. He worked with the cameramen and called the shots in all those intricate timings and movements."[60]

Anchors Aweigh, released on July 19, 1945, met with overwhelmingly positive reviews. The film was the fourth-highest grossing film of 1945. Raking in $7,475,000 (it had cost $2,580,000 to produce), the movie beat the record set by *Meet Me in St. Louis* ($6,566,000) the year before as Metro's biggest moneymaker. In his review, Howard Barnes of the *New York Herald-Tribune* praised Gene for "keeping the proceedings spinning around a flimsy central idea. The sequences in which he dominates the screen are altogether the best in the production. . . . The Sinatra voice still makes the bobbysoxers squeal with delight, but the kid himself cannot hold a candle to Kelly as a performer."[61] A critic for *Time* magazine concurred that Gene's acting was "rock-solid."[62] Both the *Time* critic and Bosley Crowther of the *New York Times* ventured to say that Gene's dancing had surpassed Fred Astaire. Crowther made special mention of the cartoon sequence, calling it "trickily fanciful."[63]

Reflecting on his experience in *Anchors Aweigh* in 1947, Gene did not comment on how it had advanced his career. Instead, he gave a very different reason for its importance in his life: "It gave me an inkling of how I'd look and feel in a sailor suit."[64]

Gene had yet to don an official sailor suit, but he remained politically active and socially conscious. Along with dozens of other performers, including Judy Garland, Rita Hayworth, John Garfield, Jimmy Durante, and James Cagney, Gene was called upon by the Democratic National Committee to speak on a radio broadcast entitled *The Roosevelt Train*. The program aired on September 13, 1944, on CBS. Gene's statement on the show was short and to the point but very aggravating to the ultra-conservative Louis B. Mayer. "This is Gene Kelly, Army bound, but not before I vote for Roosevelt." Gene's statement was a bit perplexing given his long-held plan to join the navy. Biographer Alvin Yudkoff hypothesized that Gene used the wording he did because the bluntness of "Army bound" was "quicker, faster, had more energy—Kelly hallmarks in any public presentation."[65]

The Roosevelt Train proved to be highly effective in helping win the president enough votes for a fourth reelection. Republican radio strategists were displeased with the broadcast's threat to their own campaign and persuaded Jimmy Durante to withdraw from the show, thus leaving four minutes of empty airtime at the end of the broadcast. Gene and fellow Roosevelt supporter Humphrey Bogart believed that the result—four minutes of a "dreary medley of organ music" at the show's close—would actually help their cause: listeners would turn off their radios before the Republicans' scheduled hour of campaigning began.[66] This is precisely what happened.

On November 7, 1944, Gene and Betsy threw a special celebration of Roosevelt's election win at their home (during which they actually refrained from playing their divisive game of charades). Judy Garland and Lena Horne sang, and everyone present enjoyed champagne. The guests were primarily Gene's cronies; Betsy's group would have considered Rooseveltians on the conservative side. She had begun attending performances at the Actors Lab in Hollywood, a far left theater group comparable to New York's Group Theatre (whose famous members included Elia Kazan and Arthur Miller). Gene took his Hollywood work as seriously as actors in the legitimate theater, but when Actors Lab performers came to his parties, "it was difficult for Gene to debate the redeeming social value of *Anchors Aweigh* as against the urgent plays of Clifford Odets."[67]

Gene was dealing with his own personal sense of urgency. For nearly three years, he had been ready to join the war. *Anchors Aweigh* was not slated to premiere for eight months and Gene had no immediate assignments coming his way; now seemed the ideal time to enlist.

Only a week and a half after Roosevelt's victory in November 1944, Louis B. Mayer finally acceded to Gene's insistent requests for a leave of absence. The delighted but anxious dancer told a *Los Angeles Times* reporter: "I'm asking for the Navy. Now the question is, will the Navy ask for me?"[68] Fortunately, the navy did ask for him. Gene reported for induction at the end of the month. Appearing at the recruiting office, he still wore the bandage around his hand from the injury he had received from the rose stem in *Anchors Aweigh*. "I can just see the faces of those . . . guys when I walk in with my mitt all bandaged up," Gene said, embarrassed. Jokingly, he alluded to the manner in which his character in *For Me and My Gal* evaded the draft. "They'll take one look at my hand and say, 'Oh, no ya don't. We saw that picture!' Any movie-going sergeant might, that is."[69]

Gene was assigned to thirteen weeks of basic training in San Diego. Betsy stated that he "didn't want to be in the film unit or the entertainment group. . . . Gene was afraid Metro would pull strings to protect their property. He didn't want that; he wanted to do his bit like everyone else."[70] Betsy and Kerry were also packing their bags, preparing to move in with Betsy's parents in New Jersey for the duration of Gene's service. It was painful for

Betsy to sell their home and their "honeymoon car." The Kellys also said good-bye to their beloved housekeeper, Mamie, who planned to go to work in a munitions factory.

On Gene's last night in Hollywood, he and Betsy threw a farewell open-house party. Saul Chaplin and Phil Silvers performed a forty-five-minute song recounting Gene's life from his birth in Pittsburgh to his triumph in *Anchors Aweigh*. Phil then sang a song specifically for Betsy: "Betsy with the Laughing Face." Chaplin claimed it was the type of memorable "entertainment that could not be paid for or planned."[71]

Chaplin admitted that other parties he had attended at the Kelly home had not been so touching. During the infamous "Game," cracks often showed in the otherwise idyllic Kelly marriage. "Friends who had been chatting and laughing amicably five minutes earlier were now snarling at each other because of a missed word or phrase. . . . The reason for the hostility became obvious: the savage competitiveness of Betsy and Gene. . . . It was scary watching our easygoing hosts turn into veritable storm troopers right before our eyes. . . . It was as if we had suddenly been transplanted into a house of horrors." On one occasion Chaplin and several other guests played a trick on Gene: as he acted out the song title "Tramp, Tramp, Tramp, the Boys Are Marching," everyone on his team purposely shouted out wrong answers. Gene became so enraged that he pounded the floor. His opponents won the game, and Gene began rebuking his team members. They laughed, revealing that they had set him up to lose. He joined in the laughter, but not "very willingly. Our moment of glory was short lived. He reverted to his abusive attitude in the very next game. . . . [He was] the master of the merciless put down."[72] Gene was not without guilt over his behavior. Years later when he spoke of his regrets, he said: "I wish a lot of things I wanted to do could have been done with less temper, without so much fighting."[73]

Chaplin may have interpreted Betsy and Gene's bitter rivalry as a sign of marital tension, but Betsy made no mention of such strife in her memoir. However, she did acknowledge that the reason she acted with such competitive zeal in charades or ping-pong was because these were areas in which she *could* compete. "My unconscious seems to have a strong realistic streak, and I think I recognized there was no contest in the movies or the theater if Gene were the competition. He would win." She may have experienced a certain degree of relief to be apart from him during his training in San Diego. Without the studio and her husband "taking care of everything," Betsy admitted that she felt she was "back in real life."[74] And back in real life, she wanted nothing more than to return to the theater.

Based in New Jersey, Betsy found work in New York as an understudy to Julie Haydon, who was currently playing Laura in Tennessee Williams's *The Glass Menagerie.* Betsy's "a wonderful actress," Gene told *Movieland,* "and I want her to continue her career." He paused and added, with meaning, "as long as she can manage her family along with it."[75] Gene championed and aided Betsy in her career ambitions from this time on. Their separation allowed her to grow up and prove she could be a homemaker and actress at the same time.

Gene, on the other hand, could not be a sailor, father, and film star simultaneously. "I'm in the Navy now, the branch of the service I wanted. Sure, I'm going back to Hollywood someday, but right now, the business of becoming a bluejacket is all I can handle," Gene told the San Diego naval newspaper *The Hoist.* "Hollywood, as far as I'm concerned, is in mothballs for the duration."[76]

If fans believed everything they read in film magazines, they would fancy that Gene relished every moment of boot camp. A reporter in *Movieland* quoted him: "It freed me from all responsibility. I had only to do what I was told to do without any initiative on my part. It was almost like being in school again, and I feel it was really a mental refresher."[77] In truth, Gene was horrified by the experience. Biographer Clive Hirschhorn recounted Gene's real impressions: "He was shocked by the way the men were 'dehumanized' and treated like cattle. Worse, he was amazed at the complacency with which the men accepted their rough-house treatment."[78] The handling of low-ranking soldiers brought back disturbing memories of hazing rituals he had witnessed at college fraternities. He saw no justification for humiliating another human based on his rank.

What Gene found of equal difficulty was the regimentation of his schedule, which he likened to living "in a police state."[79] Ever since he had left home in 1938, Gene had been his own boss in all aspects of his life and work. It is no surprise, then, that the strict schedule of the military chafed him. According to his daughter Kerry, Gene found release through physical activity. "He was an extraordinary all-around athlete and very strong and vigorous . . . pretty much a guy's guy. And so one of the things he did at boot camp was he boxed. And, of course, the studio was horrified that he was boxing."[80]

One might think Gene would have rejoiced to leave boot camp, but he departed with some trepidation. "It was a big discussion about where he was going to be posted," Kerry recalled. "And they decided to put him in the Navy photographic unit to make training films. And he, . . . I think, had mixed feelings about that. On the one hand it was a proper use of his talents and capacities and he wasn't that young at that point."[81]

Gene's new post put him in a photographic division of the Naval Air Force in Washington, DC.[82] Now that he was so close to Betsy and Kerry, they decided to again live under the same roof. "Gene was . . . very dashing in his uniform. We were together whenever it was possible. . . . The Navy assigned him to the film unit [based in the Anacostia district of] Washington, D.C. . . . Kerry and I were going with him. He could live off base, and there was a house for us in Georgetown," Betsy explained in her memoir. The Kellys' new home was elegant but infested with fleas. The navy promptly sent an exterminator. Gene and his family stayed at the house for six months, long enough to warrant Betsy giving up her job as understudy in *The Glass Menagerie*. Though disappointed, she planned to return to work after the war ended. Observing established actors perform gave her a "new modesty and seriousness" in regard to her own abilities, forcing her to shed what she called her "vainglorious" ideas about herself.[83]

Betsy again took on the role of homemaker, keeping "house like a new bride. I burned biscuits, I cried over lumpy gravy." Gene did all he could to help. He fixed breakfast most days and did the dishes while Betsy bathed Kerry.[84] She admitted that "it was bliss" being with her daughter full-time again. Stanley Donen, who was 4-F on account of hypertension, came east to visit Gene and Betsy and, for a few weeks, "dedicated his life to helping them out."[85]

Gene, though happy to be with his family, was "utterly disgusted" with his assignment to a film unit. He could not help but notice as well that his fellow servicemen were disgruntled over what they saw as his easy assignment. "He had thought that at least the hellish [boot camp] training had qualified him to fight his country's enemies in the Pacific. Had he known his military service would consist of making movies, he would have stayed in Hollywood and made them for a lot more money," historians James E. Wise and Anne Collier Rehill remarked.[86] Musicals may have been selling in Hollywood, but if Gene thought that he was going to fulfill his term in the navy through singing and dancing, he was mistaken. He soon discovered that the films he was commissioned to produce were of "critical importance." "They [Gene's peers] were making the same mistake I made to begin with. I also thought that what I was expected to do was 'cushy.' But I was wrong," Gene stated. "Boy, was I wrong."[87]

10

The American Line

Gene Kelly once called himself the "Brando of dance." Without bragging, he could have taken his statement one step further and named himself one of the first Method actors. His work in the Naval Photographic Unit required him not only to play parts in his given assignments but to actively inhabit his roles. Thus, his duties in the unit became not only a service to his country but also a training ground for his future as an accomplished actor/director.

After he realized the true value of the training films he was commissioned to produce, Gene's initially negative evaluation of his assignment changed. His first film, *Combat Fatigue Irritability* (1945), was a thirty-five-minute docudrama dealing with a sailor undergoing therapy for what is now known as post-traumatic stress disorder. Gene did not feel he could give an accurate depiction of PTSD if he did not gain a comprehensive understanding of the illness first. "In order to get authentic material for this one I lived, for some weeks, in Swarthmore Convalescent Hospital, near Philadelphia, where many of the combat fatigue cases are treated." An opportunist at the hospital took a picture of the celebrity, and the shot found its way into the papers with a story alleging that Gene had fought overseas and was now suffering from battle fatigue. "Imagine my poor wife's consternation when she heard the rumor that I was at Swarthmore suffering from psycho-neurotic trouble, due to too many shells in my ears!" Gene told a reporter for *Movie Show* in 1946.[1]

The misunderstanding aside, Gene's research for the film paid off handsomely. *Combat Fatigue Irritability* is now regarded as one of the highest-quality military productions of World War II. It boasts an above-average script, score, and direction, as well as seamless editing and convincing acting by an uncredited cast (Jocelyn Brando, Marlon's sister, portrays Gene's girlfriend). Gene plays the lead role of Seaman Bob Lucas, a troubled and angry fireman (a sailor who works belowdecks in the boiler room). When Lucas's ship is torpedoed, he witnesses his shipmates burning or drowning as the ship sinks. Subsequently, he suffers from "survivor's guilt" and PTSD; his symptoms are a burning feeling in his guts, shaking hands, and an easily ignitable temper.

He recounts to his psychiatrist in the navy hospital the troubles he encountered visiting his parents and his girl while on leave. Over the course of the home stay, he lashed out, accusing them of treating him like a stranger. He reached a crisis point when his father took him rabbit hunting, and he found that he could not pull the trigger. The moment he raised his gun, the rabbit seemed to disappear, and instead he envisioned his mates drowning in the water all around him. "For Christ's sake, what'd you bring me out here for? Goddamn it! Goddamn it! Goddamn it! Goddamn it!"[2]

Lucas is at first resistant to treatment, although he eventually agrees to share his story with his fellow sailors. While speaking, he breaks down in tears—the first time he has been able to release his emotions since his trauma. The film then cuts to the doctor giving a lengthy summary of what led to Lucas's breakdown and what he can do about it. Occupational therapy and physical training, he explains, will provide Lucas with outlets for his feelings and teach him that he can work while solving his problems. Here, the film shows Lucas first woodworking and then happily goofing around with his fellow sailors in a pool. The doctor concludes, somewhat simplistically, "When you can do with your problems what Lucas has done with his, you will be free of all your symptoms."[3] The film's portrayal of PTSD may seem quite mild compared to more extreme depictions in modern movies, but one must keep in mind that *Combat Fatigue Irritability* was unusual in its time in even addressing the problem.

The film's message that the war was not an individual but a group effort harkened back to *Thousands Cheer*, in which Kathryn (Kathryn Grayson) told the nonconformist Eddie Marsh (Gene) that nothing was difficult "if we all work together." In *Thousands Cheer*, as well as in previous roles in *For Me and My Gal*, *The Cross of Lorraine*, and *Christmas Holiday*, Gene played lone wolves who, according to Kerry Kelly, "were all guys with at the very least a chip on their shoulder or a nasty side or a shady side." Gene's real-life shoulder chip may have been only a small one, but he did share other commonalities with the shadier men he portrayed: he was a rugged individualist and had a temper. However, unlike his "nasty" characters, he cared a great deal about others even if, when his temper flared, he verbally abused them (most conspicuously during "the Game" at his house parties). Gene may have drawn upon his own moodiness in his portrayal of Seaman Lucas, but more so, he used the frustration he had felt with MGM for deferring his enlistment. Kerry believed her father was able to get into the part because he well knew "what it feels like to not be sure that you're completely pulling your weight or doing what is expected."[4] That being said, Gene never went so far as to play himself in any picture, no matter how much he drew upon his own feelings. "Professionals are acting," Kerry remarked. "It's not them."[5]

Kerry, a clinical psychoanalyst, offered unique insight and concluding thoughts on her father's involvement in *Combat Fatigue Irritability*. She was quick to note that Gene was the only adult she knew during her childhood who was not in analysis. "He was certainly not opposed [to therapy], but he was a very self-sufficient, active person. . . . I think that he was busy with his creative work and his various hobbies of sports and reading and history. So, he basically had no need or no time," she explained. "I think the context and content of the film was what was significant to him, more than the making of [it]. . . . But I think he really enjoyed the experience of directing the film. He was a very take-charge sort of person."[6]

Along with his performance in *The Cross of Lorraine*, Gene considered his acting in *Combat Fatigue Irritability* the best he had ever done. One would be hard-pressed to disagree; his performance is heartrending and natural. Modern audiences may find it bizarre to hear Gene Kelly, star of squeaky-clean MGM musicals, literally cursing like a sailor. But he performs this and the scenes in which he breaks into tears without self-consciousness or exaggeration. Betsy described the film as "beautiful . . . simple, compassionate, and hopeful. It was another side of Gene, and made us both believe that after the war he should try his hand at serious drama."[7]

After *Combat Fatigue Irritability*, Gene worked on a succession of assignments, but none were as intense as his first production. According to journalist John Maynard: "The motion pictures he makes for the Navy concern such subjects . . . [as] amputees and radar, and he is very proud and pleased at having a part in the work. His greatest thrill, he says, was a 'well done' from Secretary [of the Navy James] Forrestal over a contribution he made."[8] The titles he produced in 1945 include *Submarine Warfare: Now It Can Be Told* (Gene was narrator for this short), *What's the Matter with Steve?* (a film about the difficulties faced by a soldier who, though he never sees combat, still deals with trauma), and *The Names on a List* (a production telling the story of a wounded GI).

Gene and the rest of America paused in the midst of their work to grieve over the shocking news of Franklin D. Roosevelt's death on April 12, 1945. America's future had seldom been fraught with as much uncertainty as it was in the weeks following the passing of the nation's beloved president. Gene, a staunch Roosevelt supporter, continued to put forth his utmost effort into the service he had begun under Roosevelt's leadership.

On April 26, 1945, a mere two weeks after Roosevelt's death, Gene was promoted to lieutenant, junior grade. Some of his peers presumed that Gene became a lieutenant so quickly because of his celebrity status, but this was far from true. He had performed admirably in boot camp, earned a reserve officers training diploma in college and, most important, produced work for the Naval Photographic Unit that had proved "a significant contribution to the understanding and treatment" of servicemen.[9] John Maynard noted: "The . . . ruckus over his abrupt elevation to one-and-a-half stripes hurt him some. He . . . doesn't to this day blame other enlisted men who might have been disgruntled."[10]

Gene did not wish to be regarded or treated as a celebrity, but whether he wanted it or not, he could not escape the attention his fame brought him. He was still incredulous that teenagers often approached him for his autograph. He felt that the sole reason he was popular with teens was that he was Frank Sinatra's co-star. Not everyone recognized him as a star, however. One evening, he was refused admittance at an upscale restaurant "that regarded ordinary sailors with horror and distrust." "He was ready to leave gracefully, but his friends would have none of it. They identified Kelly to the headwaiter, who got very friendly indeed," a columnist for *Motion Picture* recorded. "Kelly thought that was funny too, but not so funny that he gave the headwaiter anything more than a dirty look for his trouble."[11]

Gene's celebrity in no way interfered with his productivity. In the spring of 1945, he received a commission to make a top-secret film showing the efficacy of the navy's new fire-fighting equipment against Japan's deadliest weapons, baka bombs (manned flying bombs). As props, Gene employed twenty-four gasoline-soaked aircrafts filled with lit explosives. His thirteen cameramen caught the swiftness with which the "experimental foam" extinguished the flames. Fleet Admiral Ernest J. King ordered thousands of tons of the new equipment on the strength of Gene's film.[12]

On May 8, 1945, shortly after Gene completed his film on baka bombs, the Allies announced victory in Europe (V-E Day). The country's new president, Harry Truman, reminded Americans that the peace was not yet won. He proclaimed: "We must work to finish the war. Our victory is only half over."[13] With the war in the Pacific an ever-present anxiety, Americans continued to find considerable comfort in the silver screen; approximately 1.7 million people poured into theaters every week. Shortly after V-E day, *Anchors Aweigh* premiered. The country's unquenchable thirst for the consolations films offered aided the popularity of *Anchors Aweigh*—and Gene.

However, it seemed that audiences would have to wait quite a while before Gene returned to Hollywood films. To Gene's delight, his next command turned out to be what he had been all but begging for since his induction: "Gene [got] his wish. He was to go to the Pacific battleground to join a fighting unit."[14] Betsy and Kerry packed up their home in Georgetown, planning to move back to Hollywood until Gene's return. He flew to San Francisco, from where he would travel to Hawaii and on to Japan with eleven other men. A reporter for *Photoplay* recorded Gene's reaction to finally being deployed: "For a year I've been bucking to go. I'm heading a combat photographic unit that'll be taking pictures in actual combat—of demolition squads, bombs, guns, fighting. Then we'll bring 'em back to be used for training films. But anyway, it's action on the fronts!" The reporter ruefully noted: "However, everything happens to Kelly. The date of this speech was August 6, and the atomic bomb fell on [the same day]. This is one time the curtain went down before Kelly got on stage."[15] A week later, on August 15, 1945, Japan surrendered and the war was over. "Gene . . . was coming home," Betsy recalled. "I burst into tears when I heard this—it was only then that I realized how frightened I had been."[16] The three days between the dropping of the first atomic bomb on Hiroshima and the second on Nagasaki were, for Gene, "a drunken nightmare."[17] The sudden declaration of peace left him feeling that he had not truly done his part for the war effort, but his superiors told him that he still had work to do.

Gene was sent to New York to complete two directorial projects before receiving his discharge. As soon as she discovered that Gene was not being shipped overseas, Betsy abandoned her plans to return to Hollywood, instead remaining on the East Coast. She joined her husband in New York, and they rented an expensive apartment overlooking Central Park South on 59th Street. They left Kerry with Betsy's parents in New Jersey; father and daughter saw each other only once a week. In 1974, Gene called this one of his greatest regrets. He felt it was "selfish, unfatherly neglect. Betsy and I fancied ourselves as Zelda and Scott Fitzgerald and just wanted to have a good time. A child would have been in the way."[18]

Gene and Betsy's neglect in this period clashes with their initial insistence that they raise Kerry themselves. But Gene's navy service paired with Betsy's return to work (though temporary) reminded them of what their lives had been like before the domesticity they had established on the West Coast. The fact that they had reunited in New York returned them, in a sense, to the days of their courtship, including late-night suppers at Louie Bergen's bar.

However, Gene was a different person than the struggling dancer/choreographer from Pittsburgh he had been when he first came to New York. Now, with his recent ascent to superstardom in *Anchors Aweigh*, he could live like a stereotypical film star if he so wished. He had earned Hollywood's accolade: an Academy Award nomination for Best Actor (*Anchors Aweigh*). Based on the fan mail he received, MGM reckoned him among its top five male actors. Even more thrilling to Gene than an Oscar nomination, however, was Elia Kazan's suggestion that Gene play the role of Biff in a stage production of *Death of a Salesman*. Gene had grown increasingly interested in drama since his work for the navy and yearned to accept the role. Betsy shared his enthusiasm, particularly because Kazan had been a member of New York's Group Theatre. But the studio refused to release Gene from his contract for the six months required for the project. "Gene accepted their decision, albeit with difficulty because of the big plans being made for him in the Arthur Freed Unit . . . but I think he always remembered and regretted that missed challenge," Betsy remembered.[19] *Death of a Salesman* eventually premiered in February 1949 with Arthur Kennedy in the role of Biff.

In truth, Freed had no concrete plans for Gene. He had wanted the actor to play composer Jerome Kern in his new musical biopic, *Till the Clouds Roll By* (1946), but at the time of its production, Gene was not yet discharged from the navy. The press was filled with rumored projects. Among the most bizarre was *Futurosy*, a musical set in the year 2046. Talk of a sequel to *Anchors Aweigh* also made the news; it was to be titled *All Ashore*. Gene found promising roles harder to secure because his agent, Leland Hayward, had given up his work in Hollywood to become a producer on Broadway. Beginning in 1946, Gene was under the management of MCA (Music Corporation of America), which was the largest talent agency in the world, having expanded into film, radio, and television from its inception as a music company. Such a mammoth corporation lacked the personal touch Gene had enjoyed with Hayward and, before him, Johnny Darrow.

Gene's only immediate movie work was still for the US government. His first postwar production required him to make "an indoctrination film" with the Silent Service (submariners) about the raids American submarines had made on the Japanese coast. Gene experienced much anxiety at the thought of going underwater in such a confined space. His fear bore a remarkable resemblance to Seaman Lucas's in *Combat Fatigue Irritability*. Yet, once below the water, he was pleasantly surprised to feel a sense of tranquility. The resulting film, produced in 1946, was "inspired" and a "valuable recruiting vehicle" for men considering the submarine service.[20]

In short order, the navy assigned Gene to another film. This one dealt with the brutality of kamikaze pilots in their bombing of the US aircraft carrier *Benjamin Franklin*. Gene and his crew stayed a week on the damaged ship, which was docked at Brooklyn Navy Yard. Gene spent hours interviewing survivors of the attack to ensure authenticity.

Gene again relocated to Washington after completing his work in New York. In the nation's capital, he was engaged in far less stimulating work. He edited "seemingly endless footage of film," some from the US Navy, some that had been captured from the Japanese. Occasionally he came across a "riveting battle," but for the most part, the job was a dull one.[21] He was then put in charge of the weekly short films for the navy, which showed commentary on successful methods of warfare and important footage illustrating their execution. The shorts did give Gene some creative opportunity. He narrated the films and penned the voice-overs himself, allowing him to revisit the inclination toward writing he had shown in high school and college.

While in Anacostia, Washington, Gene met an attractive, sturdily built WAVE with a girlish pageboy haircut named Lois McClelland who was working at the Naval Photographic Science Laboratory. "We [she and the other WAVEs] were thrilled when we heard that Gene Kelly was coming to join our outfit. . . . There were so many letters from his fans that he couldn't fit into his office. . . . He tried to answer each one with something personal, cheery and upbeat," Lois recalled. "I offered to help him and he hired me as a secretary to work for him off duty."[22] After a short time, Gene treated her as if she were a member of his own family. "What impressed me most was the fact that he was so human, so natural, so absolutely lacking in affectation. . . . Whatever I had in mind, he made me forget completely," Lois reflected in 1950, adding that he was "really quite a guy."[23]

Only once in the history of the Academy Awards up to this time had an actor won for a performance in a musical film: James Cagney in *Yankee Doodle Dandy* (1942). The year 1946 would not mark a second win for a song and dance man. On March 7, 1946, Gene lost the Oscar to Ray Milland, who took home the award for his haunting portrayal of an alcoholic in *The Lost Weekend.* Gene's loss plus the disappointing receipts of his most recently released picture, *Ziegfeld Follies,* filled him with uncertainty as to how his career would proceed upon his discharge from the navy.

In spite of his dubious prospects, Gene told a reporter for *Movie Show* magazine: "I'll be very glad to get back to the land of dreams and sun and orange juice and make-believe again."[24] At least one aspect of his future was certain: his place of residence at 725 North Rodeo Drive. In May 1946, shortly before Gene's discharge, Betsy and Kerry returned to Los Angeles. Within two weeks, Betsy had found the home that was to be Gene's for the rest of his life. Built twenty years earlier, it was considered old for Beverly Hills. With its white exterior accented by red shutters, it resembled a quaint Connecticut farmhouse. Avocado trees grew plentifully in the backyard. Betsy phoned Gene immediately after viewing it. When he heard the enthusiasm in her voice, he told her, "Go ahead." She wrote out a check for $42,500. "I felt pretty important and grown up," she said.[25]

Aiding Betsy in the move to her and Gene's new home was Lois McClelland. Gene's faithful secretary had left the naval service to work for him full-time. "Lois McClelland came into our lives and stayed forever. . . . She quickly became a friend to all three of us," Betsy wrote in 2003.[26] Lois's description of her duties in the Kelly household reflected her indispensability. "Being secretary to Gene Kelly is really being a little bit of everything: bookkeeper, cook, chauffeur, governess, hostess, housepainter, dressmaker, shopper, nurse-maid. . . . [It is] impossible . . . to share one facet of their [the Kellys'] lives without getting into every other part of the act."[27] Lois ultimately stayed at the Kellys' home for two and a half years before moving into her own apartment.

In summer 1946, Gene returned to civilian life after receiving his discharge papers. The moment he was released, he began to get himself back into condition. A writer for *Movieland* observed that he "promptly reported to the nearest gymnasium to work off the twenty pounds he had gained in service—what he lovingly refers to as 'the Tony Galento [a heavyweight boxing champion] look.'"[28] Gene was brimming with ideas for film projects. "I am very happy . . . that my contract with MGM reads 'producer-director,' as well as actor because, first to direct, and then to produce is what, when I begin to creak, I want to do," Gene explained. "Happy for the time, however, to act and, most of all—to dance. Would like to do fantasy. Would like to do a child classic—*Heidi*, for example, with Margaret O'Brien. Would like to dance again with animated cartoons."[29]

A large part of Gene's challenge in his future career lay in the fact that Americans were split by an urge to return to the past—"go back to normal"—and a simultaneous desire to make way for new ideas and ways of life. Forceful films rose in popularity after the war. William Wyler's *The Best Years of Our Lives* and Edward Dmytryk's *Till the End of Time*, like Gene's 1945 short film for the Navy, *Combat Fatigue Irritability*, addressed the travails of returning veterans. Hard-boiled film noirs, which had remained box office draws during the war, gained in popularity in 1946. *The Postman Always Rings Twice* and *Gilda* are just two examples of chart toppers. However, audiences still craved nostalgia above all. The year's number one film, an idealized vision of the antebellum era, Walt Disney's *Song of the South*, was, like Gene's number with Jerry the Mouse, a musical blend of live action and animation. Freed's *Till the Clouds Roll By* was a purely romanticized vision of a less troubled past and ranked as the eighth most popular film of the year.

Given that Gene's "position in pictures is unique" in that he had "less, rather than more competition than when he went into the service," his unemployment problem was a puzzle. His closest musical rivals, Fred Astaire and George Murphy, had both "virtually turned in [their] dancing shoes."[30] Dan Dailey Jr., one of Gene's potential rivals, had also served in the war and did not begin making films again until 1947. Gene ruefully stated: "I thought MGM would be waiting for me with open arms, with a script, something real solid."[31] Biographer Clive Hirschhorn hypothesized that Gene's temporary joblessness "may have had something to do with his image, which was inextricably linked to war pictures . . . and audiences by then had had enough. It may also have been connected with the return of the studio's most popular male stars such as Clark Gable, Robert Montgomery . . . and James Stewart."[32] As Gene had once noted, the greatest threat to MGM musicals came not from other studios but from MGM's own dramatic productions, which almost invariably outgrossed all other genres.

Not one to remain idle, Gene occupied himself with renovations for his and Betsy's home. He put on a new roof, built furniture, and painted the walls. A reporter for *Movieland* commented that "Gene begged, borrowed and wheedled enough lumber to build some cabinets and shelves. . . . He's a wizard with fixtures, plumbing and odd jobs."[33] While renovating, Gene suggested a swimming pool for the backyard. Betsy firmly said no. What could be more "Hollywood" than a pool? Gene sighed and compromised on a volleyball court instead. The house was as free of Hollywood pretensions inside as it was out. Rather than hire a decorator, the Kellys chose all their own drapes and furniture. Many items came from yard sales or antiques shops, which helped create a comfortable, lived-in atmosphere. The living room walls were lined with shelves brimming with books Gene and Betsy spent their leisure time reading. Gene preferred tomes on history while Betsy read anthologies of Chekov, Ibsen, Odets, Tolstoy, and Sinclair.

Though Gene and Betsy wanted to be as self-sufficient as possible, they did hire a housekeeper, Bertha. Betsy described her as a "round, cheerful, energetic woman [who] loved Kerry." Bertha and her husband, a postman, had a room and bath at the back of the house while Lois had a room, bath, and office on the first floor. "Our life became normal . . . that is, normal rich," Betsy stated. Gene slept until noon when he was not working while Betsy brought four-year-old Kerry to nursery school. She also kept busy with work. In July 1946, Betsy made her film debut in the Rosalind Russell drama *The Guilt of Janet Ames.* In early 1947, she had a cameo as a hat-shop girl in George Cukor's *A Double Life* starring Ronald Colman and Shelley Winters. Though the role required only two days' work, Betsy was hooked; she had abandoned her ambitions for theater work. "By now I was dying to be in the movies," she admitted.[34]

Gene was still a staunch supporter of Betsy's efforts. He had become accustomed to being surrounded by dynamic, talented women—Lois, Betsy, and, as of late 1946, Jeanne Coyne. Twenty-three-year-old Jeanne, a former pupil from his Johnstown dance studio, arrived in Hollywood shortly after Gene's discharge. Her talent had grown with the passing years.

She had appeared as a dancer in two Broadway shows, *Mexican Hayride* (1944) and *Are You with It?* (1945). As well as dancing, she had a great talent for choreographing that meshed with Gene's sensibilities. "When I arrived in the film capital I called Gene, trembling a little in my shoes, for he was a big star and I was someone who'd known him years ago," Jeanne later wrote. "Well, you would have thought I was the President's daughter the way Gene boomed, 'I'm so glad you're here. . . . It's not good for a young girl to live by herself. Come and stay with us.'" The Kellys' invitation, like the one they had given to Lois, extended indefinitely.[35]

Gene and Betsy had, for the most part, returned to the domestic way of life they had established before the war. Again living with her parents, Kerry became a part of their social life. Gene had expressed regret over his "unfatherly neglect" of Kerry during his time in New York, but Kerry's memories were happy ones. "They [Gene and Betsy] were both around a lot and they brought me with them a lot. . . . It was a lucky childhood, there were lots of good times," she reminisced.[36] Nonetheless, the Kellys' world still retained elements of Gene's self-described "Scott and Zelda Fitzgerald" lifestyle.

"I grew up as an only child, in a house full of very active, lively grownups," Kerry explained. "There were always lots of other grownups living in our house, either transiently or permanently: other artists, dancers, musicians, writers. I was around a lot, listening to the grownups, being part of what was going on."[37] "I wouldn't even call all those people guests. They were just friends who were always around. . . . Their [Gene and Betsy's] whole group of friends were all the people he worked with. . . . There was a lot of back and forth of people. . . . [Gene's professional and personal lives] didn't feel split off or somehow unknown. . . . It was a very small community. All the local intellectual types knew each other very well."[38] The rotating group of artists coming in and out of the Kelly home became a permanent feature after Gene announced: "Let's bring back open house parties at the Kellys'!"[39] If his and Betsy's home had been a haven for artists before the war, now it was poised to become the ultimate center for Hollywood's intelligentsia.

"That red front door [of the Kelly home] became rather famous," Betsy recalled. "Because it never locked until we went to bed."[40] Jeanne Coyne remarked that at the end of each party, "I've never seen people leave as reluctantly as they do the Kelly household."[41] To Jeanne and regular guests like Judy Garland, Roger Edens, Kay Thompson, Van Johnson, Saul

Chaplin, and Stanley Donen, the door was always open. Other entertainers or musicians, such as Leonard Bernstein, Hedy Lamarr, Peter Lawford, Charlie Chaplin, George Cukor, and Robert Walker, found their way through the red door as well. Composer André Previn later recalled, "You never knew who was going to be there. . . . I've never met so many extraordinary people in one room, on so many occasions in my life." Van Johnson offered his own reminiscence: "Every Saturday, everybody would meet . . . for franks, beans, and brown bread and play volleyball." Choreographer Bob Fosse had a less rose-colored view of Gene's parties. When Gene went on the volleyball court, he remarked, "I'd never seen anyone so fierce about a so-called friendly game in my life—before or since. He had a competitive streak in him that was quite frightening."[42] Kerry recalled her father on the court as "a very intense guy. . . . He was a great, great athlete. . . . Those games were intense but they [Gene and his guests] were having a ball. I don't think 'mean' captures the flavor [of Gene on the court]. I imagine people who were not athletic found [the game] a bit mysterious. The ones who were smart but equally athletic found it fun."[43]

Betsy did not find amusement on the volleyball court. She claimed that her husband and the rest of the men on the court were being unfair to their female teammates, except "Lois, who was tall and strong as any of them." In her memoir, Betsy stated that after "months of irritation," she withdrew from the court, just as she had withdrawn from substantial stage and film work because she knew that, if Gene were the competition, he would always win.[44] Clearly, two aspects of the Kelly house parties had remained unchanged since the war: the fiercely competitive games and Gene's requirement that his guests be endowed with talent and intelligence. After over a year in the navy, Gene yearned to again be among peers with whom he could engage in heated discussions. Indeed, he seemed to thrive on the competition and argument his less outspoken friends found so off-putting. "I can outshout anyone on theater or politics," Gene told a writer for *Screen Album*. The columnist added, "But you can bet that before he tried any hot-shot shouting, he's done plenty of heavy thinking."[45]

Gatherings at the Kelly home were not always composed of arguments; to a large extent, they consisted of laughter and, above all, people showing off for each other. The gatherings frequently served as Gene's opportunity for a commingling of ideas that served as inspirations for a dance step or a line of clever dialogue. "He must have wanted this way of life, this house full of friends every weekend, or it wouldn't have happened," Betsy concluded. "Of course he was older than a few of us, but as I look back he seems older than everyone. He was the patriarch. . . . Those Saturday nights at our house on Rodeo Drive *were* special."[46]

In 1946, the Kellys' parties became meaningful for another, far more serious reason: they became a haven for those affected by new developments in Hollywood's political climate. The Kellys' home was a natural gathering place for political fund-raisers and benefits. But Gene's open support of liberal causes did have its limits. Gene could no longer defend Betsy's activities for the Progressive Party and her friendliness with card-carrying Communists without putting himself and his family in danger. In her memoir, Betsy reflected with regret: "The atmosphere in Hollywood turned from one of innocence and fun to fear and suspicion."[47]

With the fall of the Third Reich in 1945 came the rise of a new threat—Communism. Hollywood, with its highly concentrated population of liberal artists, inevitably was seen as a hotbed for Communist propaganda. As early as 1944, the Motion Picture Alliance for the Preservation of American Ideals (MPA) was created by high-profile, politically conservative members of the Hollywood film industry for the purpose of defending the entertainment world and the entire nation against Communist and fascist infiltration. At the same time, the House Un-American Activities Committee (HUAC), which had been created in 1938, originally intended to target Nazi sympathizers, became active in Hollywood. On July 29, 1946, William R. Wilkerson, publisher and founder of the *Hollywood Reporter,* published a column entitled "A Vote for Joe Stalin" that named alleged Communist sympathizers, including screenwriters Dalton Trumbo and Ring Lardner Jr.; the group became known as the Hollywood Ten.

Betsy had attended meetings of the Communist Party and worked for the Independent Progressive Party (IPP), aiding in campaigns (such as Henry Wallace's run for president in 1948) and acting as what she called a "foot soldier." Her soldiering often took her to the Mexican community in downtown Los Angeles, where the infamous "zoot suit riots" had recently taken place between Mexican American youths and European American servicemen stationed in the neighborhood. Betsy, struck by the poverty in the area, began to feel guilty about the upper-class life she and Gene led. She, Gene, and everyone else she knew lived in a "happy, safe, productive enclave." On a more personal level, Betsy saw her work for the IPP as "staking a claim for myself as a person apart from Gene."[48] The new friends

Betsy made through her political activities were for the most part liberal European refugees, including blacklisted director Jules Dassin and writer Salka Viertel (who made her home a sanctuary for any European refugee in Hollywood). She also befriended Oona Chaplin, wife of socialist Charlie Chaplin, as well as Orson Welles, an outspoken liberal who openly condemned racism and segregation. Although many of the Europeans Betsy invited home as guests were not Communists, the Kellys' association with socialist foreigners meant that they were opening themselves up to the scrutiny of conservative forces in Hollywood.

Betsy was in fact actively trying to gain membership in the Communist Party. Gene was relieved when her mentor, Lloyd Gough, took her aside to tell her, "The Party has decided it is not a good idea [for you to join], because you are married to a very important man who is not a member. . . . You can be just as useful outside." Although Gene had not forbidden Betsy to pursue her political ideals or even to become a Communist, he had asserted: "All regimentation is bad." He had added, with a smile, "And you'll be the worst Communist in the world." The conformity of Communism did not appeal to Gene. However, he "never turned into an anti-communist," Betsy explained. "He believed in unions, freedom of thought, social justice, and racial equality. . . . He acted on his beliefs, he signed petitions after reading them thoroughly. . . . [He helped] several of the blacklisted writers, gave them money for their families, and tried to get them jobs under the table."[49]

Gene may have seemed like a maverick among the conservatives of Hollywood, but he was an oxymoron in himself. He made it his mission to raise his daughter with everyday values, giving her a limited allowance and making her save her money for a toy she might want. At the same time, he "could comfortably live in Beverly Hills, surrounded by some of the 'wickedest' capitalists in the world." His ability to live in a town that contradicted his philosophies came back to his singular focus on his art, and Hollywood, "wicked" though it may have been, was his means to make his ideas realities. Kerry believed that "his reason for being in Hollywood was to acquire a sort of perfection never before achieved."[50]

Gene's political and social activity became his full-time job while he waited for a film to come his way. During Gene's absence from the screen, his friend Van Johnson (who had not gone to war due to a traumatic head injury he suffered in a 1943 automobile accident) had emerged as Metro's top box office draw and starred in five pictures over the course of 1946–

1947. Johnson was far less choosy in which parts he accepted; a "company man," he took what was offered. Gene, on the other hand, was much more particular and was not as easy to place in a picture as Johnson. MGM finally called him with a firm project after several fleeting proposals for pictures, including a remake of *Roberta,* costarring Kathryn Grayson and Frank Sinatra, and a Judy Garland musical titled *Cabbages and Kings* (the former was eventually produced with Grayson and Howard Keel as *Lovely to Look At* in 1952; the latter never saw the light of day). Gene's assignment came from producer Pandro S. Berman, best known for the Astaire-Rogers films of the 1930s.

At first, the movie seemed the perfect project for Gene because it had him playing Leo, a "regular Joe" who returns home from war and finds himself at odds with his wife Margaud's wealthy lifestyle. Margaud's family sees Leo as a "sensible addition" to the family and perfect for their daughter, who has grown "spoiled and pampered."[51] But Leo regrets his impetuous marriage and wishes for a divorce. The judge refuses to grant it, a decision the couple eventually comes to appreciate. Leo finds more purpose when Margaud's grandmother backs his idea to construct housing for returning veterans—a project that allows Margaud to see his true worth. This particular plot twist paralleled events in Gene's own life. In May 1946, he had presided as chairman at two events, one for the Independent Citizens Committee and one for the American Legion, in which veterans and nonveterans rallied together to protest housing shortages for returning servicemen.

Though elements of the film's plot did have relevance for contemporary Americans, the manner in which the picture was executed threatened its potential appeal. Part of this was due to the director. Gregory La Cava had established his career with fast-paced comedies of the Depression era, his best one being *My Man Godfrey* (1936). Screwball comedy, fluffy millionairesses, and disdain for the wealthy were the rage in 1930s films by La Cava and other directors such as Frank Capra. In the newly prosperous, postwar America, such films were distasteful. From the bits of the unfinished script the director deigned to show him and the fact that it was to be shot in black and white, Gene could immediately see that the film did not reflect its title: *Living in a Big Way.*

When *Living in a Big Way* went into production on a hot July day in 1946, Gene found a horseshoe-shaped wreath waiting for him on the set. The gift came from George Sidney, who had directed him in his two biggest successes to date, *Thousands Cheer* and *Anchors Aweigh*. Attached was a note wishing Gene luck. He would need it.

"Originally Gene's role in his newest picture was listed purely as a dramatic part, but letters from moviegoers throughout the nation soon changed that. They pleaded that a picture in which Gene Kelly doesn't dance is hardly fair. . . . 'So I'll dance in the picture,' said Gene. 'Somehow, somewhere a couple of dance routines will be fitted into the script,'" journalist Paul Marsh recorded for *Screenland* magazine.[52] Because the film had begun as a straight picture, Gene admitted that creating last-minute dance additions for the film intimidated him. The haphazard fashion in which the picture was directed presented another challenge to Gene: "The director, who also does much of his own writing, has a unique system in shooting a picture. To achieve spontaneity in performance he gives his actors their script piecemeal, only a day's pages at a time and only twenty-four hours ahead," a writer for *Silver Screen* recorded.[53]

Gene tried to boost his confidence as well as the film's quality by exerting his influence not only on the dance routines but also on the screenplay. From his experience as a returning veteran, he caught a false note in a particular scene set in a men's clothing store. Leo is trying to purchase civilian clothes, and the salesman shows him the store's complete stock of three suits. "I haven't been able to find one suit since I've been out of the Navy," Gene declared.[54] La Cava changed the scene so that Leo comes away from his shopping trip in a mismatched suit three sizes too big.

In creating his three dance sequences, Gene requested the aid of Stanley Donen. The men's collaboration had never failed in the past; their effort in *Living in a Big Way* was no exception. They modeled the first routine after an Astaire-Rogers number, with Gene and leading lady Marie McDonald slow-dancing to "It Had to Be You." The latter two sequences are more reflective of Gene. One, entitled "Fido and Me," shows Gene dancing with a small dog while serenading a Grecian statue. Gene's character performs the number in an attempt to impress his wife and, in essence, encourage her to let him out of the "doghouse." He does Spanish dance moves at one point in the number, utilizing the training he had received from Angel Cansino in Chicago in the 1930s. Juvenile extras make the second number spontaneous and lively, and also demonstrate Gene's athleticism. He climbs and swings from metal rings and stepladders at the construction site of the veterans' housing project, then jump ropes and plays ring around the rosy with neighbor children. "If someone else had done the picture he wouldn't have been dancing with kids," Stanley Donen noted. "But it was done because it was Gene."[55]

Gene put forth all of his creative ingenuity to help elevate the picture, but he felt that its subpar quality nullified "everything he had achieved before the war." His decision to remain with the pallid film was largely due to MGM executive Benny Thau's persuasion. Marie McDonald was just starting out in pictures, and Thau told Gene that he should give her a chance, just as Judy Garland had given him one in *For Me and My Gal*. Ultimately, Gene found McDonald to be a sort of model for Lina Lamont in *Singin' in the Rain*. He later called her a triple threat—she could not dance, sing, or act. To a man who required those in his social circle to have talent and intelligence, working with such an actress was a nightmare. She was known mainly for her curvaceous figure and was nicknamed Marie "the Body" McDonald. Gene concluded that the film was "a monumental waste of time."[56]

The picture monopolized far more of Gene's time than he had anticipated. It had a longer shooting schedule (nine months) than the big-budget films in which he had starred during the war because of one factor: a strike. Beginning in late August 1946, picketers from more than fifty unions marched in front of Hollywood's major studios. A writer for *Photoplay* reported: "The [strikers] are fighting because two international presidents of American Federation of Labor unions cannot agree on which union should have jurisdiction over about 350 jobs. . . . The livelihood of 30,000 American workers . . . is endangered and an entire industry thrown into chaos and confusion."[57]

Many actors refused to work until the strike was resolved, but others, like Van Johnson, "crossed picket lines" and remained "loyal . . . untouched by social issues of the time."[58] Gene, on the other hand, refused to be complacent. Along with dozens of other actors, he traveled to Chicago to aid in the resolution of the strike. Because of his known sympathy for unions, Metro's executives asked Gene to serve as the mediator between the International Alliance of Theatrical Stage Employees and the Conference of Studio Unions. Gene worked day and night until the rival unions agreed to meet in the same room for the first time in forty years.

J. Parnell Thomas, head of HUAC, viewed Gene's involvement in the strike negotiations as a sign of possible subversive political activity in his private life. However, Gene did not choose a side during the strike; his goal was for both sides to reach a compromise fair to everyone. Gene told reporters, "If we, all Americans, can't get together and arbitrate our differences and problems, then how can we expect nations that don't even speak the same language to do it?"[59] He insisted, "My only line is the American line."[60]

Gene's involvement in the strike ended in his disillusionment with politics—both of Left and Right. On one side, Hollywood's major studios accused him of being too sympathetic to the strikers. On the other, the unions he aided were not fully honest with him. To his disgust, he learned that union leaders had accepted bribes from a slush fund held by the studios for the express purpose of offering "sweetheart" contracts to buy them off and prevent further strikes.[61]

Disenchanted though he was, Gene continued to participate in politics. He became an active member of the Screen Actors Guild board of directors and still worked for veterans' affairs at the Independent Citizens Committee. He managed to do political campaigning as well. "I'm a Democrat and I made speeches for the Democrats in the fall campaign. . . . A good thing too. Imagine an Irishman named Kelly not wanting to make a speech about something or other!"[62] he quipped. "I believe in doing anything I can to better the lot of my family—and the other guy's family. This country is my country, and I intend to keep my mind and my eyes open, and my voice loud, to help make it run smoothly, efficiently and democratically."[63]

Gene's political activities kept his name in the news more than his comeback film, which was hardly a triumph. Filming completed on *Living in a Big Way* in January 1947 with re-takes continuing into the spring. The picture was released with no buildup or fanfare on June 10, 1947. Budgeted at $2,839,000, it grossed only $1,513,000. Critics paid little attention to the film; however, one reviewer for the *Daytona Beach Morning Journal* noted that the pro-veteran storyline "should restore Gene Kelly to the good graces of the House Un-American Activities Committee."[64] What saved the experience of *Living in a Big Way* from being a total loss for Gene was that a dancer he truly admired, Martha Graham, singled out the "Fido and Me" and construction-site dance numbers as great art. In an interview for the *Los Angeles Times*, Gene commented: "Let's face it, it [the film] was a stinker. However, Martha Graham told me, 'Oh boy, I liked those numbers.' . . . I don't care if anybody else saw or liked the picture—it's enough that she did."[65]

Never in his life had Gene worn so many hats, so to speak, as he had in the last two years. He was a veteran, father, husband, political activist, director, producer, choreographer, dancer, and actor. Considering the lack of enthusiasm he had felt working on his latest film, Gene was uncertain of which hats to discard and which to keep. Dancing, which had always come most naturally to him, began to seem a piece of his past. He once likened the ability to dance to sex: as a young man he was at his best physically but knew little about it. At thirty-five, he knew all there was to know but was not as physically able to do it.

In a letter to *Motion Picture* magazine in February 1947, Gene asked his fans to answer his question: should he be a dancer or a dramatic actor? "It's my contention that perhaps I ought to stick to either one or the other," he wrote.[66] An avalanche of mail came in begging him to choose dancing. In addition to his fans, two highly influential people were unconvinced that Gene's best dancing days were behind him. For nearly three years, Gene's close colleagues Vincente Minnelli and Arthur Freed had been toiling over an adaptation of the S. N. Behrman farce *The Pirate*, which on Broadway had costarred legendary acting couple Alfred Lunt and Lynn Fontanne. They hoped to bring the play to the screen as a musical for Judy Garland. And they could see no one as Serafin—a strolling player masquerading as a roguish pirate—but Gene Kelly. Before *Living in a Big Way* had even finished shooting, Minnelli and Freed had already persuaded him to take the role.

The Pirate, a big-budget Technicolor production, carried plenty of prestige and revived any sagging motivation Gene felt toward dancing. In the picture, he sought to prove his ongoing thesis that "dancing is much more than mere exhibition. It's a complete art in itself [and can be used to] aid the plot . . . by a series of dances which reveal the inner thoughts of the players."[67] He came to the conclusion that one could be both a dramatic actor and a dancer. Never did this hold truer for him than now he had proved himself as a serious actor in *Combat Fatigue Irritability* as well as reaffirmed his credentials as a song-and-dance man in the Oscar-nominated *Anchors Aweigh*. The role of Serafin was a "wonderful, multifaceted role for him" that promised to "rejuvenate his film work and take it in new directions."[68]

11

A Flaming Trail of Masculinity

The Pirate—a fantastical and most improbable musical comedy—seemed to cater perfectly to Americans' tastes in 1947. "Musicals made shortly after World War II that emphasized fantasy and spectacle had a chance of doing very well" if executed correctly, film historians Earl J. Hess and Pratibha Dabholkar explained in their 2014 study of *The Pirate*. Escapist fare with incredible comedic plots were still popular in "a country just beginning to put itself back together after the war."[1] The film also promised to click with moviegoers due to its showcasing of Gene's dancing. Audiences clamored to see more of his footwork after *Living in a Big Way*, which was only a teaser for what Gene had to offer. As Gene's first major motion picture after the war, *The Pirate* marked the start of a new era in the thirty-five-year-old dancer's career. The film allowed him to broaden his acting range, play an active role in developing his onscreen character, refine his choreographic work, and learn camera tricks that furthered the art of cinedance.

Though *The Pirate* promised to catapult Gene's career forward, it went into production at a most inopportune time. The country was experiencing a second Red Scare (the first took place after World War I) that alienated a number of moviegoers and prompted many talented writers and actors to relocate to Europe. More obviously detrimental to the movie industry was the sudden drop-off in attendance. Once servicemen returned home, they and their families relocated from the city to new suburban subdivisions; they focused more on feeding and clothing their children than attending the cinema three times a week.

The biggest financial blow to Hollywood, however, came in the form of a law passed on December 31, 1946. For over twenty years, the

Department of Justice had been battling against a practice known as block booking. Major Hollywood studios, including MGM and Warner Bros., were allowed to control their own theater chains, thus securing the power to produce and distribute their own films. Because the studios controlled their films' distribution, they were able to force independent theater owners to buy an entire package, or "block" of films. Invariably, the package included some excellent films with mediocre B pictures sprinkled in. Such a system worked in favor of the studios, but the Department of Justice declared the block-booking system a monopoly. Two years later, the US Supreme Court ruled that the Hollywood film studios could still produce but no longer distribute their own films.

Louis B. Mayer reduced his own salary and MGM staff by 25 percent after the enactment of the new law. He retained only the crème de la crème in his employ—including all members of the Freed Unit. Arthur Freed realized that his unit would have to change along with postwar America. "I wanted a fresh start from what had been before, a combination of new ideas that had been happening on stage and what could be done with film."[2] Freed saw Gene Kelly, Judy Garland, and Vincente Minnelli as indispensable even if they did not signify a "fresh start." Most of the regulars he had employed before and during the war (including composer Hugh Martin, screenwriter Fred Finklehoffe, and actor Mickey Rooney) were struggling to find their place in modern America. Freed had to face that many of his former go-to talents were producing work that Americans had simply outgrown (the fall of backstage musicals and the Andy Hardy series marked a major downturn in Rooney's film career). Freed hoped that *The Pirate* would act as a springboard for the clean start he was seeking.

Finding the right screenwriters to create an acceptable treatment for *The Pirate* was a problem. Eleven writers tried and failed, including Anita Loos (famous for writing the book *Gentlemen Prefer Blondes*) and Joe Mankiewicz (best known for his work on *All about Eve*, 1950). The scripts they presented were perhaps too fresh. Finally, Freed engaged the husband-wife team Albert Hackett and Frances Goodrich. They were not new to Hollywood, but they were versatile and seasoned writers; seldom did they write films that failed. Indeed, they had penned the entire Thin Man series. But even the optimistic Freed had his doubts that the duo could save *The Pirate*. After all, its exotic and avant-garde flavor bore resemblance to the 1946 MGM film that had sent Fred Astaire into retirement, Minnelli's *Yolanda and the Thief*.

The Broadway show on which *The Pirate* was based tells the story of a young woman named Manuela (Judy Garland) who is married to Don Pedro (Walter Slezak), the staid mayor of the West Indies town in which she lives. Manuela dreams of being romanced by a famous pirate, Estramundo. A strolling player, Serafin (Gene), learns of Manuela's fantasy and pretends to be Estramundo in hopes of winning her love. Don Pedro, in a shocking twist, reveals that he is actually the pirate. Still, Manuela leaves the real pirate in favor of Serafin and the gypsy life of an actor. The first change Goodrich and Hackett made to the story, mainly to pacify the censors, was to make Manuela engaged rather than married to Don Pedro.

As Goodrich and Hackett were well on their way to bringing *The Pirate* to the screen, the film faced a major problem. Its star, Judy Garland, was on the verge of her most severe nervous breakdown to date. Minnelli tried to summon enthusiasm from his wife, promising that the part of Manuela would show her flair for comedy and allow her to break from the wholesome girl-next-door type she had played for so much of her acting career. According to Gene: "MGM bought it [*The Pirate*] because they needed a picture for Judy Garland very, very badly."[3] To be sure, Judy did need a project. She had not enjoyed a starring role since *The Harvey Girls* in 1945. Judy, Minnelli, Freed, Gene, and MGM as a whole could not afford for *The Pirate* to lose.

In *The Pirate*, Minnelli wanted to tap previously unexplored areas of Gene's talent, specifically the ability to carry a story that contained comedy, parody, camp, and farce. Minnelli and Gene wanted to expand on these elements and agreed that the film would have to differ from its Broadway counterpart in more aspects than simply changing Manuela from a married girl to an unmarried one. Gene became focused on molding the character of Serafin to suit his own personality. Gene had seen Lunt and Fontanne in *The Pirate* and found the play "delightful, but he considered Lunt a bit too old to *pretend* to be a dashing pirate as Serafin does and he . . . commented that it had been the only Broadway failure in the illustrious career of that acting couple." Gene thought Serafin should be played with "more youthful vigor."[4] When Serafin was being himself—the actor—Gene decided to play the character in the style of John Barrymore. On the other hand, when Serafin is pretending to be the pirate, Gene would take on the persona of his boyhood hero, Douglas Fairbanks, with all his swashbuckling bravado.

In further developing his character, Gene explained, he made Serafin "a thoroughly imitative man. . . . [He's] such a ham and he's so false." From the first scene in which audiences see Serafin, he is depicted as an overly theatrical "consummate performer and promoter." Serafin's assertive and charismatic personality mirrored Gene's own tendency to take charge and stand out in any group. "Kelly's hyper-energetic projection of self . . . so dominated his performance that the perspective shifts to a narcissistic indulgence by a supremely gifted performer who cannot help but love himself," Hess and Dabholkar asserted.[5]

Gene did have confidence in his abilities, but he always viewed his work with a critical eye. Thus, he was eager to have Minnelli's feedback. Gene and Minnelli's collaboration on the production became so close that it extended outside the studio. They lived near enough that on many evenings after dinner, Gene would say good night to Betsy and Kerry and stroll across his yard to Judy Garland and Minnelli's home. There, they worked late into the night. The two men's talents and insistence on perfection melded together seamlessly. Yet, they were far from identical. Gene saw their divergence as an advantage, allowing for a better-rounded product. According to Minnelli, Gene was "more earthy and romantic and in all of the things that Gene does, he has the same sense of reality that never leaves." Lela Simone, who worked as music editor and Freed's assistant on the film, revealed that Gene and Minnelli's differences were not always convenient. She claimed that they had difficulty working together because, in temperament, they were "*very, very* contrary. . . . Gene Kelly is wide away from serious arts and Minnelli is so close to serious arts that one has to be careful not to be run over with it." Simone further stated that she often heard both men "raving" at each other over aesthetic differences.[6] Simone is the only colleague of Gene and Minnelli ever to mention any heated arguments between the two men.

Gene and Minnelli worked especially well together on technical aspects of *The Pirate*. Minnelli not only taught Gene tricks of the camera but also how to manipulate color on film. Part of the magic in *The Pirate* is undoubtedly its sophisticated use of color and atmosphere. Minnelli utilized a mix of styles from South America, the Bahamas, and the West Indies to create the film's provincial Caribbean town. Minnelli even ensured that the extras in the film were of different skin colors. In crowd scenes, black, Hispanic, and white men and women bustle together along the streets. Gene was fascinated with the entire process of Technicolor. He became a constant presence in the editing room. "We could sit down in the lab *with* the Technicolor people and *control* the color so it's almost like a painting."[7] Gene went so far as to cite *The Pirate* as one of the best examples of color combinations in film history.

With the help of his friend and fellow choreographer Robert Alton, Gene carefully planned his dances in *The Pirate,* paying special attention to the use of light and color. Gene was so involved in choreographing that Freed approved adding his name beside Alton's in the film's credits. Alton ultimately handled groups of dancers while Gene worked on solos. He created two for the picture, one of which was a ballet.

The film and its dance routines could not truly take shape until its chosen composer, Cole Porter, completed the original score. Gene was excited to be working with Porter again, fondly recalling their friendship during the run of Gene's first Broadway show, *Leave It to Me!* "We have to change the pirate's name from Estramundo to Macoco. I have a dear friend with the same name who I call Mack the Black. He would be so pleased if I wrote a comic song about him," Porter explained effusively to Freed when he agreed to pen the score.[8] "Mack the Black" became the theme song for the film, though the number accompanying it was primarily designed for Judy Garland. However, Gene personally worked with Porter on what is arguably the best number in the film, a circus-themed routine that he requested be inserted to lighten the mood and quicken the pace of the picture's concluding scenes. When Porter played Gene his composition, tears of happiness came to the actor's eyes. The name of the song? "Be a Clown."

Gene anticipated designing a dance to accompany the number, but first he worked on another solo routine, "Nina." According to film historian John Cutts, "Nina" was perfect evidence of Gene's renaissance as a dancer. The sequence mixed "his own zestful style of humor and fancy . . . with a fantastic gymnastic display . . . [and resulted in dances that were] astonishingly flamboyant, most exciting, beautiful to watch, and extremely difficult to describe."[9] Gene designed "Nina" to utilize an entire plaza as Serafin's playground. As usual, Gene called for dozens of props, or "toys," as Arthur Freed called them, to be employed in the routine. Handholds and footholds on the sides of walls, diving boards, and climbing vines hidden on the set allowed him to jump from place to place. Art director Jack Martin Smith marveled, "He [Gene] was like a monkey. . . . He could run up and down it [the set] like a cat."[10]

"Nina" characterizes Serafin as a fancy-free womanizer who uses his body as a means of winning the affections of any female he sees. The suggestive content of the song and its execution (particularly when Serafin transfers a cigarette from his mouth to a woman's and then dances sensually beside poles in a gazebo) was tasteful enough to get past the censors. More than lyrics or dialogue, Gene's movements convey his character and carry the story along. Though the number put to rest any thoughts that Gene was more of a balletic artist than a straight hoofer, the dancer himself still felt that his work was not as good as it had been. In an interview with Philip Scheuer of the *Los Angeles Times,* Gene said self-effacingly, "Two years in the Navy, three years off the screen. . . . No, I'll never be the dancer I was." However, Gene proved himself wrong after the interview, when a gymnastic rehearsal of "Nina" elicited applause from even "hardened studio employees."[11]

Gene put so much into his solos partly because four of the six major musical numbers in the picture were showcases for Judy Garland in which Gene was a bystander rather than an active participant. Judy's numbers were "Mack the Black," "Voodoo," "Love of My Life," and "You Can Do No Wrong." The former two take place while Manuela is under Serafin's spell, the latter two after Manuela discovers that she loves Serafin in spite of the fact that he lied to her about being Macoco. The rendition of "Love of My Life" that appears in the film is subdued in comparison to the original version. The first fell under heavy scrutiny from the film industry censors at the Breen Office. "We were doing a little bit of over groping," Gene explained. "It was a sensual and sensuous experience . . . but I think it was too long and said too much. I didn't mind that they cut a piece of that out."[12]

In the "Mack the Black" number, Judy is much livelier, though her energy borders on manic rather than exultant.

Through all the Carib-be-an or vicinity
Macoco leads a flaming trail of masculinity
And suddenly I feel I've got a big affinity
And I'm loco for Mack, Mack, Mack the Black, Macoco![13]

Judy shakes her waist-length hair free and covers her arms in gold costume jewelry bracelets as she falls into the arms of one man after another. At the number's close, she is swinging her arms about wildly as men leer around her and other townspeople simply gaze, agog. The final version of the song used only three of the nine verses Porter wrote. The other six were strewn with inappropriate violent imagery such as "Mack will wack yuh and he'll wack yuh in half." Freed was insistent that even while Serafin pretended to be Macoco, he retain a "comparative innocence."[14]

Louis B. Mayer found Gene and Judy's next number together, "Voodoo," highly offensive. Freed and Minnelli were not thrilled with it either, describing the music as uninteresting and dissonant. Additionally, the filming of the sequence provoked intense paranoia in Judy, for it required her to dance around open fires. "I'm going to burn to death! They want me to burn to death!" she cried. Minnelli, rather than attempt to soothe her, watched passively as Judy—laughing and weeping at the same time—was led away by her on-set psychiatrist. Lela Simone went so far as to allege that when Judy fell into a frenzy, she heard the actress cry, "Give me marijuana!"[15]

Judy's extremes of emotion both on- and offscreen, whether it was aggression, passion, or hysterics (including hair pulling and feet stomping) reflected her growing animosity toward MGM and Minnelli. In Judy's mind, Minnelli and the studio had melded into a single ogre. Judy further communicated her increasing resentment toward her husband by asking Gene to stage her dance numbers exclusively, without Minnelli's help. In another move against her husband, Judy purposely delayed filming, calling in for both real and invented illnesses.

Gene, who normally tolerated unprofessionalism from no one, remained nonjudgmental of Judy's scattered work ethic. In the early stages of filming, he claimed, Judy was pleasant to work with. In a 1990 interview, Lela Simone provided a different view. She stated that Gene was aware of Judy's issues but had decided to "shrug his shoulders" over them. "He had no choice. He had a choice to walk out or be philosophical about it."[16] However, after her hysteria during the "Voodoo" number and her repeated absences, Gene faced that his friend was really ill. He began to call in sick on days he knew Judy was going to be absent, just to relieve her of a portion of the blame. Gene's absenteeism also may have been due to guilt he felt for monopolizing Minnelli's attentions during shooting; he also sensed that Minnelli was emotionally closed off to his wife. "Judy . . . became jealous of the time Gene and I were spending together. We'd been so concerned with getting the choreography right and broadening the Serafin character that we excluded her from our discussions," Minnelli confessed.[17]

For a woman with an unquenchable need for approval, watching Minnelli favor Gene acted like poison on Judy. Minnelli later stated that working with Gene "was the most intense professional association I've ever had with an actor."[18] And although film critics now agree that the film gave Judy a unique role showcasing her comedic talent, the truth was that at this time her screen career was declining from its zenith while Minnelli's, and even more so Gene's, were still ascending.

In spite of Gene's insistence that he was secondary to Judy in the film, Judy felt that her character fell to the sidelines. Manuela's scenes, while they did give Judy ample opportunity to prove her wit, were dependent on interplay with Serafin. Equally, without Manuela to play off of, Serafin's comedy would have been lost. For example, when Manuela and Serafin first meet in the seaside town of San Sebastian, she gives him a caustic rejection that the cocky actor refuses to accept.

Serafin: I can tell you your past, your present, and your future.
Manuela: You don't have to tell me my future; I know my future.
Serafin: Am I in it?
Manuela: No!
Serafin: Then you don't know your future.

Later, when she tricks Serafin into believing that she has fallen for his masquerade as Macoco, she continually insults his acting abilities. "I should have known the minute I saw you on the stage that you didn't know anything about acting. . . . I despise actors!" she says with an ironic chuckle and goes on to call the profession "unspeakably drab."[19] Serafin follows her as she leaves the room with a coquettish grin, believing her charade as much as she has feigned to believe his. As soon as he steps outside, Manuela attacks him with what seems to be every object in the room. She shatters a bust over his head, smashes a canvas across his face, and hits him with a sword.

Manuela's tantrum was allegedly inspired by Judy's real actions at home. Her daughter Lorna claimed that "she was amazingly strong. . . . She could hurl almost anything across the room with deadly accuracy."[20] To keep the scene comedic, Minnelli made sure that none of the objects actually hurt Serafin.

Gene was not afraid of filming dangerous scenes. He insisted on performing all his own stunt work. His impressive feats in the picture made him, as Judy intuited, the center of the film. His most nimble footwork, along with his catlike climbing of balconies in the "Nina" sequence, was his walk across a tightrope to Manuela's room. Gene practiced for hours on the tightrope, but MGM was not about to jeopardize his safety. Wires were attached to his back and mattresses were beneath the rope at all times.

Most strenuous physically for Gene were the two musical sequences he choreographed: "Be a Clown" and "The Pirate Ballet." Both were among the last parts of the film to be shot and proved to be the most time con-suming to complete. To perform with him in the clown number, Gene engaged a pair of light-footed African American dance stars, the Nicholas Brothers, who were popular even in parts of the South, where their films were screened illegally. (Incidentally, the Nicholas Brothers were the act for which Gene and his brother Fred filled in at Cab Calloway's club over ten years before.) "Be a Clown" was a landmark number not only because it introduced Porter's new song (one that was destined to become a show business staple), but also because it marked the first time a white man and black men danced together onscreen. Louis B. Mayer's objection to the routine did nothing to soften Gene and the mogul's tense relationship. "It [dancing with blacks] was strictly taboo in those days. L. B. Mayer was really upset about it," Gene reflected.[21] Mayer finally consented but warned Gene that the number would be cut in many southern cities. He proved to be correct, much to Gene's chagrin.

It was the South's loss. "Be a Clown" begins with a delightful bit of jux-taposition. A hangman's noose, awaiting Serafin after his performance, remains at the center of the dance floor. The three dancers pirouette about it with carefree steps as if the prospect of death is something comedic. "No noose is good noose!" Serafin quips only moments before launching into his performance. The number employed more athleticism and gymnastics than any Gene had yet achieved, utilizing "splits, handsprings, and turn-overs" and Gene's trademark move in which he "bounces sideways on his hand and toes—body extended in push up position."[22] Harold Nicholas asserted that Gene had learned this move from him and his brother in New York. In actuality, Gene had developed the move with the Revuers in 1939 before he ever saw the brothers perform it.

The weight disparities between the three men posed problems when they danced together. Gene was so much more muscular that in one part of the dance when he and the brothers are holding hands in a circle and take turns "being lifted off the studio floor, Kelly seems to be leaping to help the struggling Harold pull him along. In contrast, Fayard seems to fly off the floor when Kelly pulls him pretty easily."[23]

The challenges the brothers faced in "Be a Clown" notwithstanding, Harold allegedly deemed the routine "too simple" and consequently "slacked off." Such behavior infuriated Gene.

"Harold, what are you doing? Your brother and I are rehearsing like mad and you are just there moping around."

"Oh, I already got it," Harold insisted.

"Alright, let me see you do it."

Harold went through the entire routine without one mistake. Fayard recalled that "Gene was so mad . . . he [said]: 'Stop everything, let's go to lunch.'"[24]

Gene may have become impatient with his dancing partners in *The Pirate* (with the exception of Judy Garland), but he did take pleasure in designing collaborative dances almost as much as solos. Novelist and critic John Updike claimed that Gene, "as the middle son in his own family enjoyed dancing in the middle of three men in the many numbers through-out his films. . . . Male partners seemed to free him up to be his most cheer-fully spectacular and inventive self."[25] Composer André Previn concurred: "Kelly always liked to dance with a trio of men; they could play off of each other but preferably [they did] not dance better than him."[26] "Be a Clown" was an impressive example of Gene's work with male colleagues, but even he admitted it was perhaps an example of too much "vanity." Remembering "Be a Clown" in 1994, Gene admitted, "The mistake we made was that . . . we did enough bravura endings for fifty numbers."[27]

Gene and Minnelli decided to reprise "Be a Clown" for the film's finale—sans the overblown endings. This time, Serafin and Manuela per-form it together after the real Macoco is arrested and Manuela joins Serafin's troupe as his wife and stage partner. The sequence is the only part of the film in which Judy truly enjoyed herself. She wore huge, baggy pants, a cap that covered all her hair, and a black painted smile on her face. She so loved performing in the inelegant costume that in her famed concert tours in the 1950s and 1960s, clown garb became a staple in her act. Gene shared Judy's fondness for the persona and later professed that he had always wanted to be a clown. The reprise included a number of slapstick tricks, most conspicuously when eighteen Indian clubs pop out one by one from the wings to hit Serafin on the head. Then, all at once, they cascade upon him and Manuela as they duck for cover. Critic Joel Siegel commented in 1971, "Suddenly their eyes meet and both dissolve into gales of what must be unrehearsed laughter. This final shot, which combines the statement that the artistic imagination is the source of happiness with Garland and Kelly's very obvious love of performing together ends the film on a blissfully high note." In 1989, film curator Stephen Harvey provided a unique insight into the ending of the picture: "It's teamwork not passion that is celebrated in *The Pirate*'s upbeat fadeout."[28] Such a message seemed to be a running theme in the best of Gene's films and one that he could personally espouse.

After "Be a Clown," Judy's work was basically done on the film. The rest of the work fell to Gene and Minnelli as they prepared the "Pirate Ballet." The ballet is a prime example of Gene and Minnelli's joint ingenuity. Minnelli's taste for the bizarre and his flair for awesome color meshed with Gene's sense of excitement and athleticism to create a "psychologically charged, surrealistic framework" for the ballet.[29] The sequence depicts Macoco's ruthlessness in an indirect, stagy manner that leaves no doubt it is a product of a young, repressed, and enamored girl's (Manuela) fantasies of a pirate's life. Jeanne Coyne, along with a troupe of five dancers, helped Gene rehearse the ballet. Jeanne did not appear in the film, but by the end of production she had become Gene's full-time assistant.

The number was the most elaborate in the picture, requiring the use of explosives, smoke canisters, swords, and swinging ropes. The "Pirate Ballet" drew heavily from Douglas Fairbanks's *The Black Pirate* (1926), particularly in a shot where Serafin slides down a rope in the same manner Fairbanks had employed when "sliding down the sails of a ship by slicing them with a knife." His costume, too (a short black tunic) was almost a replica of Fairbanks's. The number, however, departs from *The Black Pirate* in its incorporation of dance as a storytelling device. The ballet begins when Serafin twirls around a white mule, the only being left in the town square after Serafin (pretending to be Macoco) scares away the villagers and policemen. Manuela watches him from her window. She sees the mule transform into herself; its ears morph into the points of a headdress. She then envisions Macoco waving a sword as he dances around her, cutting off the points of her headdress, climbing up a mast of a ship, and swinging on a rope toward the camera. Minnelli held that the stunt was the most dangerous of Gene's feats in the film and, as expected, he insisted on doing it himself. The stunt was all the riskier because it required him to throw fiery clubs to the deck below him, setting off explosives. "We pretty near burned down the studio putting it on," art director Jack Martin Smith recalled. "It was a helluva number, savage, beautiful, piercing music."[30]

Choreographer Beth Genné wrote that Gene conceived the dance completely "with the camera in mind," which allowed the scene to transport the audience "freely through a space that seems almost limitless."[31] The primary innovation in the number was Gene's use of a device called a Ubangi—a long, mechanical arm that placed a mirror at a desired location. The camera then could shoot into the mirror, recording its target image from a much lower angle than would normally be possible. The device became essential equipment for musical routines thereafter.

The ballet was striking in its technical innovation as well as in its use of color, especially a purple/scarlet shade that MGM later christened "Minnelli red." The director had first used the hue in a fantastic toreador ballet titled "Death in the Afternoon." The ballet, which had appeared on the Broadway stage in the revue *At Home Abroad* (1935), was widely lauded, though it did contain a controversial element of "homoeroticism."[32] Hints of homoeroticism are also evident in the "Pirate Ballet"; Sheryl Flatow of *Biography* magazine wrote that Gene "was aware of his sex appeal and consciously exploited it . . . in black cut off shorts and black t-shirt that showed off his compact muscular body."[33]

Gene's costume, which just barely passed the censors, was completely Minnelli's design. The fact that Minnelli gave such a suggestive costume to Gene only heightened Judy's jealousy of her husband and Gene's "chummy little club," as she called it. Members of the cast and crew noticed "the crush" Minnelli had on Gene. At several open-house parties at the Kelly home, Judy and others noticed that Minnelli would stand very close to Gene, looking "straight into his eyes" when they talked, and that he seemed to be "always embracing him."[34]

Gene's heterosexuality has seldom been questioned; modern scholars hold that Gene had no problem with the concept of gayness, but he did fight if anyone cast doubt on his masculinity. Screenwriter Arthur Laurents, who carried on a semi-open affair with actor Farley Granger, wrote in his memoir that Gene constantly made "faggot jokes" yet "flirted with men as well as women—which, never mind unfair, was disgusting, however much due to his overblown narcissism." Laurents believed that Gene felt he had to act more "macho than John Wayne" because many men in his profession were deemed "sexless . . . [like] Fred Astaire."[35]

Gene's other homosexual (or possibly homosexual) friends, such as

Danny Kaye, Charles Walters, and Minnelli, never spoke of being offended by him. Minnelli had only awe for his colleague. His marriage to Judy had become quite uncomfortable long before *The Pirate*. Still, Judy and Minnelli had no plans for a divorce yet. Minnelli's primary concern was that Judy regain her health. After her nervous breakdown during *The Pirate*, Judy entered a sanitarium where she received help for her depression as well as addiction to barbiturates.

In July 1947, the tumultuous voyage of *The Pirate* finally came to an end—a quarter million dollars over budget, with a final cost of $3,768,014. Even the indefatigable Gene was glad to see the strenuous project come to a close. "Sometimes I wonder why I didn't become a bus driver."[36]

Arthur Freed looked past the difficulties involved in making *The Pirate;* he had such confidence in the Minnelli-Kelly-Garland triumvirate that he had already assigned them all to another project together before *The Pirate* even finished filming. Entitled *Easter Parade,* the new film would boast a score entirely by Irving Berlin. Freed again assigned Frances Goodrich and Albert Hackett as screenwriters and Robert Alton as choreographer. Judy, who felt stronger after her rest, was ecstatic about *Easter Parade*. "Her resentment over the time Gene and I spent together had long since dissipated," Minnelli wrote in his memoir. "I know you two have something great going," Judy told him.[37]

What everyone thought was going to be a trouble-free film swiftly became muddled. Shortly after *Easter Parade* went into production in November 1947, Freed received a phone call from Judy's analyst informing him that she did not wish Minnelli to act as director because he symbolized "all of her troubles at the studio." Minnelli was devastated. He had become engrossed in *Easter Parade* and envisioned making it into a "kind of Tin Pan Alley *Pygmalion*" while also "imbu[ing] it with the same emotional nostalgia" as *Meet Me in St. Louis*.[38] With or without Minnelli, Freed forged ahead with his expensive new project.

He enlisted as director Charles Walters, who had just completed a film that brought Gene's friends from the Revuers, Betty Comden and Adolph Green, to Hollywood. *Good News,* a collegiate romance set in 1927, had come in under budget and on time due to Walters's streamlined yet exceptional directorial skills. Walters commented that after working on the comparatively small *Good News,* landing a picture with Judy and Gene was "like passing one day to the next from the Bronx to the Palace

Theatre."[39] Gene and Judy were as pleased to be working with Walters as he with them. Walters sealed Gene and Judy's approval by inserting a "fun" number in *Easter Parade* that was similar to "Be a Clown." Set to Berlin's new composition, "A Couple of Swells," the sequence allowed Gene and Judy to wear their favored garb—tramp costumes. They sing in feigned high-society accents about their imaginary life among the "swells" on Fifth Avenue.

To further lighten the film, Walters demanded that Gene's character be softened. In the initial script, Walters claimed, Gene "verbally beat the shit out of Judy," and he feared the audience would hate him for it. Over lunch, "the trio charted a plan of action" and put in a call to Freed, to whom Judy and Gene "fed lines" provided by Walters. "The ploy worked," Walters's biographer Brent Phillips wrote.[40] With the help of a third screenwriter, Sidney Sheldon, the film subsequently became lighter in tone.

Gene could not wait to begin working with Robert Alton on staging his dance routines. In August 1947, two months before Judy was ready for filming, Gene began choreographing his solos. The first routine he tackled accompanied another new Berlin song, "Drum Crazy." Gene used many elements of his signature style in the routine. The setting of the number, a toy store, allowed him to use various props as springboards for dance moves. Additionally, the scene involved children, as had his most success-ful numbers in *Anchors Aweigh* and *Living in a Big Way*. *Easter Parade* appeared to be progressing exactly on schedule—and then a setback far worse than the sudden replacement of Vincente Minnelli occurred.

"The day I handed [Freed] the final script he said, 'Gene Kelly broke his leg last night,'" Sidney Sheldon explained. "I thought it was a joke. It only happens in movies that the leading man breaks his leg."[41] In truth, Gene only broke his ankle, not his leg. But this still meant he would not be able to work for six to eight weeks. Freed managed to remain calm even after Louella Parsons gossiped that Gene's doctor was not very encourag-ing, claiming that he might never dance again.[42] Freed did not listen to such speculation. However, one wonders if he would have remained cool had he known the true cause behind his leading man's injury. Gene later explained that he told Louis B. Mayer he had hurt himself practicing a complicated dance step "because I didn't think he'd respond too well to the truth." In reality, Gene broke his leg in a fit of temper during a volleyball game. Arthur Laurents described how the accident happened in his memoir:

The more points we [Gene's volleyball team] missed, the more infuriated he got. . . . But the tension was too great and we began to laugh like bad kids. . . . Laughing made it difficult to score. . . . Then the ball flew off the court and hit him [Gene]. That ended the game and life in his backyard. He sprang up like a geyser. We were a bunch of lousy spoil sports! . . . Roaring at the top of his high tenor, he thrashed his way back to the house, flung open the kitchen door, and swiveled for one final curse . . . and like Rumpelstiltskin stamped down so hard on the doorsill that he broke his ankle.[43]

Easter Parade, already exorbitant in budget, could not wait six weeks or longer to get under way. Gene, trying to atone for his unfortunate and inconvenient loss of temper, suggested, "How about getting Fred Astaire to take my place?" Fred was hesitant to accept the role. He telephoned Gene and asked him if he was absolutely sure he could not do the picture. "You'll be doing me a favor 'cause they think I'm a bum," Gene said. "L. B. Mayer thinks I broke my [ankle] on purpose. *Please* do it!"[44] Fred accepted the role, and the experience was ultimately a rewarding one for him.

Gene, though highly disappointed to lose the chance to work with Judy, Irving Berlin, and Charles Walters, kept himself occupied while his leg healed. As he had done immediately following the war, he made politics his full-time job.

According to Betsy Blair, the Red Scare had been slow to fully take hold of Hollywood. But, by late 1947, it had become all encompassing. "In hundreds of homes . . . there were fears, tears, battles," Betsy described.[45] Vincente Minnelli recalled an evening he and Judy Garland were guests at a masquerade party hosted by Groucho Marx. "[It was] bizarre to say the least. . . . Here we all were dressed in clown costumes talking of our imminent death . . . [and what] the implications the House Un-American Activities Committee held for . . . us."[46]

In spite of repercussions they might face, Minnelli and Judy, along with Gene, joined the Committee for the First Amendment. The CFA was established by screenwriter Philip Dunne, actress Myrna Loy, and film directors John Huston and William Wyler in response to HUAC's allegations against the Hollywood Ten. Other members included Lauren Bacall, Lucille Ball, Humphrey Bogart, John Garfield, Ira Gershwin, Kay

Thompson, Katharine Hepburn, Lena Horne, Danny Kaye, and Frank Sinatra. On October 27, 1947, a number of the group's members—Gene included—boarded a plane bound for Washington, DC, to support the Hollywood Ten during their HUAC trial. Judy and Minnelli were not among those on the plane. Neither was Betsy. She was in the midst of shooting *The Snake Pit*, a film in which she had a small part as a defensive mute girl in a psychiatric ward.

At every stop the plane made en route to Washington, photographers flocked to snap shots of the stars. The flight and its coverage became less like a political crusade and more like a press tour for an upcoming movie extravaganza. Speaking to the press, Gene tried to draw attention to the group's purpose rather than its members' celebrity status and, as he had during the 1946 union workers' strike, willingly served as the CFA's leader and spokesperson. However, in Pittsburgh (the last stop before Washington), Gene dropped his leadership role. His family was the first to greet him at the airport, and he decided at the last moment to leave the group for a visit. His brother Fred, now out of the army, and sister Louise were still running the Gene Kelly School of Dance. Gene planned to catch up with them and stay with his parents overnight, thus arriving in Washington on Monday morning. His decision concerned the rest of the stars. He was the most persuasive speaker in the group and if he were not present, journalists and radio listeners would be more apt to condemn the Hollywood Ten. Gene's flight, as his colleagues feared, did arrive late, so late, in fact, that he was absent when photographers took a group shot of the CFA. The photograph quickly spread to newspapers across the nation and became the poster representative of the committee. Betsy, seeing the picture sans Gene, was angry that he had "missed it for Mama."[47] Still, Gene arrived in ample time for the hearings.

As proceedings commenced, Gene and his friends' enthusiasm for their cause began to sag. The leader of the Hollywood Ten, John Howard Lawson, was in fact a Communist Party member. The missions of Lawson and the Committee for the First Amendment were no longer in alignment; the people from Hollywood were for free speech, not Communism. Lawson found more disfavor when he engaged in a shouting match with Chairman Parnell Thomas. According to director Edward Dmytryk (one of the Ten), his haranguing alienated the support of those in the CFA.

Though the careers of a number of the CFA's members, such as John

Garfield, Larry Parks, and Edward G. Robinson, were nearly destroyed by their political involvement, Gene emerged unscathed.

A depressed Gene flew back to California after the HUAC trial. Though he remained politically conscious, he again made work his primary focus. He already had another project lined up at MGM with the reliable director George Sidney and producer Pandro S. Berman. The picture allowed him to actually reprise a role Douglas Fairbanks had played in 1921, that of D'Artagnan in *The Three Musketeers*. The lush, Technicolor remake was to go into production in January 1948, giving Gene's ankle ample time to mend.

Betsy, meanwhile, had no intentions of distancing herself from leftist causes even if Gene appeared to be pulling out. "Don't waste your fire. Save it for a big issue, and then come on with your big guns," Gene advised his outspoken liberal colleagues.[48] Even though Gene managed to escape formal accusations from HUAC, both he and Betsy were investigated by the Tenney Committee (a fact-finding group for HUAC that was active from 1941 to 1949). Beginning in 1949, the FBI kept files on Betsy and Gene's activities. Not until 2004 were their files declassified. According to Gene Kelly researcher Susan Cadman, the contents of the files make "very interesting reading," but the lack of incriminating evidence in them "does not inspire confidence" in the FBI.[49]

Betsy, to a certain degree, did hold her fire, as Gene advised. "The Cold War was real," she wrote in 2003. "There were spies and stolen atomic secrets. . . . Perhaps we were 'useful idiots' as Stalin so disdainfully labeled the left outside the Soviet Union. But, I believe we were a force for good and that what we were fighting for still needs to be fought for today."[50]

In September 1947, Gene, Judy Garland, Vincente Minnelli, Arthur Freed, Irving Berlin, and Cole Porter united to view a rough cut of *The Pirate*. "We shall see," Porter murmured the moment the film ended. What Porter really thought was that the picture was "unspeakably wretched, the worst that money could buy."[51] However, Berlin as well as Lee and Ira Gershwin, who saw the movie shortly afterward, thought *The Pirate* represented the best work anyone involved in it had ever done. It remained to be seen what critics would say about the project.

If the reactions of preview audiences were to be believed, the filmmakers had little to worry about. According to one comment card, MGM had "a terrific team in these two [Gene and Judy]." On November 7, 1947, at another Los Angeles preview, viewers praised Judy's comedic skill, but Gene emerged as the undisputed favorite. One enamored filmgoer gushed: "I want Gene Kelly for Christmas!"[52]

Though MGM's profits were still down at the close of 1947, cinema attendance was again rising—a promising sign for *The Pirate*'s box office potential. After its premiere on June 11, 1948, the film actually broke records during its first four weeks on the screen. But few people went to see it a second time, which resulted in a highly disappointing net loss of $812,496. The picture marked the first time a Judy Garland vehicle did not yield a profit. But this did not mean *The Pirate* was an artistic failure. On the contrary, reviews, like preview comment cards, were mostly positive. A critic for the *Hollywood Reporter* wrote: "The simplest way to describe *The Pirate* is wow! . . . Bright, fast, witty and wonderfully entertaining." Other critics liked the film but pointed out its flaws. A writer for the *New York Times* considered the story "larded with bizarre production qualities." James Agee of the *Nation* deemed Gene's Barrymore-Fairbanks imitation "ambitious but painfully misguided." Overall, reviewers concluded what Judy Garland had seen from the beginning: the picture "is Mr. Kelly's . . . and he gives it all he has, which is considerable and worthy of attention."[53]

Historians Earl Hess and Pratibha Dabholkar were of the same mindset. *The Pirate* "proved Gene Kelly's ability to dance any possible mood on the screen" and marked his "coming of age as a dancer, choreographer, and innovator."[54] Gene himself did not feel he had yet come of age. In his view, there was still much work to be done in mastering the blend of dance and story onscreen. In a later interview, Gene took the bulk of the blame for *The Pirate*'s failure to click with a wider audience: "We [Gene and Minnelli] just didn't pull it off. . . . The sophisticates grasped it, but the film died in the hinterlands. It was done tongue in cheek and I should have realized that never really works."[55]

Audiences of 1948 had trouble accepting such a sophisticated satire, but modern critics consistently rank the film among the top ten products of the Freed Unit. In a 1985 interview with *American Film* magazine, Gene explained: "Vincente and I felt that we had the world licked on that [*The Pirate*]. [The humor] . . . was an inside joke, but we thought the public would grab it. . . . Now, when *The Pirate* plays, it is a cult picture."[56] To be sure, the film is a cult favorite, particularly in the gay community. "[The film is] loopy, knowingly campy, brightly colored, ambitious, and absolutely unique," historian Victoria Large commented. Film curator Stephen

Harvey saw *The Pirate* as the best of Gene and Minnelli's collaborations. In 1989, after the film had undergone decades of analysis, Harvey concluded, "There's an innocence to *The Pirate*'s artifice that Minnelli never quite summoned up again. [The film] represented Minnelli's last moment as a freewheeling fabulist, and for all the backstage angst and turmoil, it was a lovely time while it lasted."[57]

Yet despite critical appreciation for the film and its merit on artistic fronts, postwar moviegoers continued to favor more conventional musicals like *Good News* and *Easter Parade*. The latter picture became the sixth-largest grosser of 1948, bringing MGM $5,803,000. Fred Astaire now had no intentions of going back into retirement. After the enormous success of his comeback film, he good-naturedly told the press: "My compliments to Gene Kelly. I'm glad he broke his ankle last year."[58] Gene took the loss and the fact that he again had formidable competition with grace. "I was pleased to be responsible for getting Fred back," Gene told the press. Then, with a wistful grin, he added, "But every time I see him and Judy singing 'A Couple of Swells,' I do get a twinge of regret."[59]

After the lackluster reception of *The Pirate,* Gene realized that his greatest immediate challenge was to redefine his screen persona in a world that was less innocent and more guarded after the war. What he needed were projects that drew upon his own personality. *The Three Musketeers* again placed him in a historical time, but it provided him with a part, like that of Serafin, that reflected his own brashness and athleticism. The picture's similarities to *The Pirate* make it seem an unlikely follow-up picture for Gene. However, the movie bore no artistic pretensions or sophisticated, witty repartee as did the former film. Also, it was a classic, tried-and-true tale audiences still responded to, even though it had already been adapted to film four times. Writing of her impressions of Gene in 1948, journalist Alyce Canfield did not miss the signs of strain the unusually stressful past year had put upon him: "There is only one change in Gene Kelly from the man of a few years back that you wish could have been averted [and that is] a certain weariness when speaking of the past few years."[60] Gene's secretary, Lois, was also attuned to the serious bent her boss's personality had taken. "He would just sit there in one of the two large red chairs in the living room . . . just thinking and thinking. That's how I remember him."[61]

12

The Renaissance Man

Over the course of 1948, Gene embarked upon three demanding but vastly different projects that utilized every talent he possessed: acting, dancing, singing, choreographing, and even writing. "When Gene Kelly says, 'The thing I like to do most is work,' he's not kidding," a columnist remarked in September 1948.[1]

Gene's year brimmed with work as well as changes and transitions in his personal life. Betsy became increasingly involved in her acting career and political causes while Kerry, now six, was away for much of each day at school. He also faced changes in his professional life; at MGM, Gene and his colleagues grew anxious over the news that Louis B. Mayer was soon to be dethroned as head of the studio. It was uncertain what effect such a change would have on the Freed Unit.

Though 1948 was a year of uncertainty in many respects, Gene did not let its ambiguity taint his zeal for his work. Indeed, he was so eager to begin on his first project—a straight dramatic picture, *The Three Musketeers*—that he began preparing for it six weeks in advance of its January 25 starting date. He welcomed a second chance to "be Douglas Fairbanks" and remedy any mistakes he may have made in his homage to the actor in *The Pirate*. Gene told journalist Alyce Canfield: "If I'm half as good as he was, I'll be satisfied."[2]

The Pirate had proven that Gene's sense of rhythm, graceful movement, and bravura were appealing traits. All he needed to learn was to emote with more sincerity and tone down his tendency to overdo satire. Going into *The Three Musketeers,* Gene recognized the task before him. Though described by numerous colleagues as an egotist, Gene was aware of his shortcomings and honest about them. "My main fault is, I still act as if I were on the stage," he said. "I'm still too broad in gestures and facial expressions. Same way with the voice. I hit the back row in a close-up. Keep forgetting there's a microphone that catches every whisper."[3] Further, Gene had the self-awareness to know that he could not "register his satisfaction after completing a dazzling trick without . . . being smug about it. . . . It always came out taunting."[4]

As well as working to perfect his acting, Gene tackled the physical training required for the swashbuckler role. Each day, he had a two-hour session with Jean Heremans, five-time national fencing champion of Belgium, followed by hours of acrobatic work in the studio gym. As in *The Pirate,* Gene refused to use a double. "I think up a lot of those stunts," he said. "I feel responsible."[5] One stunt, however, was beyond Gene—and that was the seemingly relatively easy task of riding a horse. "The horses threw a lot of the riders. I was too chicken to get on a horse, so I used a double," he admitted.[6] He knew that if he were thrown, he could sustain injuries that would prevent him from ever dancing again.

Gene's training in swordsmanship offered him valuable skills. Dueling came easily to him; he likened the sport to balletic dancing. In dueling and ballet, he argued, "the feet are always placed outward, making it possible to move quickly from side to side" so that the body is not exposed and the dueler has a long reach.[7] One duel between Gene's character, D'Artagnan, and Jussac, captain of the guard, ran five minutes (the longest filmic duel on record at the time). Gene's exertions in the art of dueling proved to be so demanding that he lost twelve pounds before *Musketeers* went into production. "I'd just like to see the guy who says acting isn't strenuous work," Gene told columnist Dorothy Kilgallen.[8]

His training completed, Gene was ready to begin filming. The picture was a typical star-studded MGM extravaganza with a near-record budget of $3 million. Van Heflin, Gig Young, and Robert Coote played the three musketeers. Heflin was the only actor to give a lively performance; the other two are pallid spectators for much of the film. The glamorous Lana Turner appeared as Lady DeWinter, the mistress of the Duke of Buckingham who endeavors to discredit the queen. Aiding her in her plot is Prime Minister Richelieu, portrayed by Vincent Price. June Allyson played Constance, one of the queen's wide-eyed ladies in waiting and D'Artagnan's love interest.

The basic plot of the picture follows the chaotic adventures of D'Artagnan, a noble youth from the French provinces who travels to Paris to become a musketeer. His self-assurance and impetuosity complicate his missions, but throughout his travels, he learns of love, hate, loyalty, and friendship from the three musketeers (Athos, Porthos, and Aramis), who help him successfully thwart the villains' plans to usurp the king and queen's power.

The adaptation, though handsomely mounted, suffered from a case of schizophrenia. As Gene's biographer Sheridan Morley put it, the picture could not decide "how seriously to take itself" due to the "comedic, tongue-in-cheek slant that screenwriter Robert Ardrey took." Biographer Tony Thomas asserted that musical arranger Herbert Stothart's decision to use Tchaikovsky's popular theme from *Romeo and Juliet* as a "surging accompaniment" to love scenes between D'Artagnan and Constance made for a "ludicrous" effect. The scenes of swordplay also have comedic elements: the tumbling, leaping, and flipping "tended toward burlesque." For all its shortcomings and attempts at clever comedy, the film did not cross the line into highbrow satire as did *The Pirate*. Overall, Tony Thomas claimed that under George Sidney's direction, the picture offered excellent pacing of action to counteract the "languid dialogue passages."[9]

Gene's performance is as schizophrenic as the screenplay. For instance, when he first sees Constance through a crack in his upstairs floorboard, his exaggerated reaction to her beauty is almost cartoonish. He flails on the floor, bites a handkerchief, and audiences can all but see his heart pumping out of his chest. In other scenes, mainly those with Lady DeWinter, he performs with all seriousness. When he is with his fellow musketeers, the film becomes most appealing; in these sequences, Gene's personality shines through. He is at once a ruthless competitor to his comrades and a loyal confidant.

In Gene's dramatic scenes, he performed with perhaps more intensity than the light script called for. Lana Turner was at the receiving end of his overzealousness. Gene later explained how he inadvertently injured the actress: "I had a fight with her [Lana] in a scene. She said to throw her down harder. I said, 'Lana, if I throw you down harder I'm gonna bounce you.' She said, 'throw me down as hard as you can.' Like a fool, I broke her elbow. . . . We shot around her for six days, then she came back with a little cast on. Did she cry? Yes, but I cried worse. I worried a lot."[10] No evidence suggests that Lana bore a grudge. Gene often seemed unaware of his own strength with his female costars. Cyd Charisse, later his leading lady, once claimed that her husband always knew she had been dancing with Gene Kelly if she came home with bruises and with Fred Astaire if she came home unmarked.

Filming wrapped for *The Three Musketeers* in April 1948 (with some re-takes in May). The picture may have had its faults, but overall, it was a superior piece of cinema that allowed Gene to display his multifaceted talents. In later years, he named it as his favorite of all his nonmusical pictures. People around the world seemed to share his fondness for the film. During his world travels in the 1960s, he was surprised to find that many of his international fans remembered him most for *Musketeers* rather than for *An American in Paris* (1951) or *Singin' in the Rain* (1952).

After the film premiered on October 20, 1948, Gene emerged as the victor in the all-star cast. According to Bosley Crowther in the *New York Times*, "Not since Douglas Fairbanks . . . has a fellow come along who compares with that robustious actor in vitality and grace. And even though he [Gene] is given more than he should have to do and often is permitted to clown in a rather childish way, he carries his heavy role lightly."[11] Why did Gene find such success in *Musketeers* and not *The Pirate* when both were costume pictures heavy with displays of physical agility and satire? *The Pirate* was far more intellectual and subtle in its humor and avant-garde in its execution; *The Three Musketeers* was much more accessible to the mainstream. According to MGM accounts, *Musketeers* grossed $4,507,000, making a total profit of $1,828,000. It was the second-highest-grossing film of 1948.

On paper, 1948 appeared to be MGM's most lucrative year in history, with total revenues amounting to $185 million. But in real terms, the studio made a profit of only $5 million due to excessive studio overhead. Nick Schenck, Mayer's boss in New York, ordered the mogul to find himself a new head of production—a title no one had claimed since Irving Thalberg's death a decade before.

Thalberg's successor came in the unlikely form of RKO's former head of production, Dore Schary. Schary, a vocal Democrat, had recently spoken before HUAC, declaring that RKO would never purposely hire a Communist. MGM, on the other hand, had a "Don't ask, don't tell" policy. Gene and Betsy invited Schary and his wife to one of their house parties and the couple played the Game, but Gene and Schary never became close. Schary was largely inaccessible to anyone but high-ranking executives and other Hollywood elite and held regular black-tie soirees at his home to which people were summoned, not invited.

From the moment Schary took office as vice president and head of productions at MGM, on July 1, 1948, Louis B. Mayer's position became increasingly honorific—a job in name only. Mayer and Schary were on opposite ends of the spectrum when it came to moviemaking. Mayer was all about spectacle and showcasing star quality. Schary preferred featured players over movie stars and, according to Esther Williams, liked "bizarre message pictures." If Mayer had seen Schary's preferred type of films, she argued, they would have sent him "rolling on the floor in one of his famous tantrums."[12] Schary surprised everyone by allowing Freed, Joe Pasternak, and Jack Cummings to operate independently, claiming he knew nothing about musicals and would leave their production to the experts. Freed's assistant, Lela Simone, recalled of Schary: "As far as the Freed Unit went, he didn't exist at all. . . . I can tell . . . you that nobody functioned [over] the Freed Unit. Nobody."[13]

Gene was quick to remark that musicals were not without the social relevance and deeper meaning Schary sought in message pictures. "The way I look at a musical, you are commenting on the human condition no matter what you do."[14] Fortunately, Schary approved of Gene's type of work. "It's fantastic! We'll make more like it," he told Gene after viewing *The Three Musketeers*. In spite of his success as D'Artagnan, Gene intended to keep musicals rather than dramas as his primary work. The future of the genre looked bright: the top-grossing film of the year was *The Red Shoes*, a British picture about a ballerina. Its US premiere in October 1948 was met with overwhelmingly positive public and critical reception, particularly for its twenty-minute ballet sequence. The sleeper hit ushered ballet into the mainstream and left film audiences clamoring to see more—a desire Gene would jump to fulfill if given the chance.

Gene managed to find time between projects to take a much-needed vacation. Precipitating the trip was MGM executives' rejection of a project he had been determined to make his next starring vehicle. Gene was so pleased with the outcome of *The Three Musketeers* that he thought it would naturally segue into another period piece, a musical version of *Cyrano de Bergerac*. However, the studio argued that an unattractive role such as Cyrano would destroy Gene's box office appeal. When Schary had declared, "We'll make more like it" after *Musketeers*, Gene had been certain that the new head of production would back his plans for *Cyrano*. But such was not the case. In 1950, Columbia Pictures adapted *Cyrano de Bergerac* into a straight drama with José Ferrer in the lead; he won an Academy Award for his performance.

After filming on *Musketeers* finished in April 1948, a disgruntled Gene took ship with his family for what would be the first of their many European excursions. "We were in the most luxurious cabin, we had consommé served in our deck chairs at eleven each morning, we dressed up for dinner and danced in the ballroom every night," Betsy recalled in her memoir.[15]

The destination was Klosters, Switzerland. There, Gene braved ski slopes and mingled with literary elites including Irwin Shaw, author of *The Young Lions*. Shaw introduced the Kellys to the "Klosters that counts"— creative, talented people who "firmed up Gene's intention to be treated as a serious filmmaker."[16] He made ample use of his French during the vacation and enlisted local tutors to teach Kerry the language. Graham Fuller, in an interview with Gene in 1994, stated, "Kelly, of course, is a Francophile. . . . I'd contend though that the French respond to something in the Kelly persona . . . that, emotionally and intellectually, reminds them of themselves. . . . His pushiness, his sexual vigor, and his nervous energy are redolent of the boulevardier or the testosterone-driven matelot."[17] Gene would have liked to make the jaunt from Switzerland to fully explore France, but the holiday ended all too quickly. He had to be back by mid-April to begin work on a new picture and finish re-takes on *The Three Musketeers*.

Gene's imminent work did not keep him from remaining attentive to his friends and family. Indeed, they became his primary concern in spring 1948. All at once, he had to face a rapidly emptying house. Lois McClelland was the first to go, moving into a small cottage of her own. She was sorry to leave her roommate at the Kelly home, Jeanne Coyne, who had become a close confidante over the past two years. Jeanne had confessed to Lois that she had been in love with Gene since her adolescence in Pittsburgh. Lois was startled, then, by the news that Jeanne Coyne was going to marry none other than Gene's friend Stanley Donen on April 14, 1948. The sudden union of Gene's two most valued assistants seemed to come from nowhere. "You know it was a close-knit group, a very affectionate group; I don't think there was anything going on, as it were," Kerry Kelly recalled of her father, mother, Jeanne, and Donen. "It was very proper, actually. There was a very fast crowd in Hollywood, but my parents and their friends weren't among them."[18] Gene still treated Jeanne like a daughter; indeed, he gave the bride away and threw a champagne-soaked party to celebrate her wedding.

"Proper" though Gene and Betsy were with their shared friends, both Lois and Jeanne had been conscious for some time that Betsy was becoming interested in other men outside of her and Gene's circle. Gene's biographer Alvin Yudkoff alleged that she and Anatole Litvak, director of *The Snake Pit* (1948), were lovers. However, in Betsy's candid memoir, she did not admit to engaging in any affairs until 1953.

If Gene knew of his wife's infatuations, he gave no evidence of it, unless one views his increasingly violent competition on the volleyball court as an expression of anxiety over his marriage. The games now began sometimes as early as eight a.m. Gene's newest competitors were basketball players from nearby colleges. Though all of them were taller and younger than he, Lois recalled that Gene more than held his own and "ran them ragged."[19] Frequent guest André Previn stopped attending Gene's parties, claiming that the incessant "competition for center stage . . . precluded having fun, and I realized . . . it was an expendable part of my life. . . . He [Gene] always had this desperate need to be the best."[20]

For the most part, however, Gene's increasing competitiveness did not drive away his guests. Those closest to him saw through his narcissism on the volleyball court and knew of his deep-seated modesty and even shyness in social situations. When he had first arrived in Hollywood, Gene shunned the nightclub scene and still rejected it nearly a decade later. "I've always been awkward at them [Hollywood parties]. They bring out the worst in me," he explained.[21]

Lois believed that the endless activity at the North Rodeo Drive home was Gene and Betsy's way of avoiding one another. In Betsy's memoir, she asserted that she seldom voiced or even consciously felt any discontent. Gene continued to encourage what he hoped would keep her from brooding: her fledgling acting career. Though proud of Betsy's accomplishments, Gene did at times inadvertently minimize them. Betsy recalled that at the November 1948 premiere of *The Snake Pit*, "just before the lights in the theater came up, when Anatole Litvak and I would have taken a bow, Gene grabbed my hand and said to Litvak, 'Tola, we have to run. I'll be mobbed. See you at '21.' And we ran. . . . It was years later in my analysis that I allowed my anger for that moment I'd missed to come up to the surface, the moment I would have stood up to the sound of applause."[22]

Gene's point of view was likely that he was trying to protect his wife as well as himself from being mobbed. And in some situations and to a certain extent, Betsy still relished his protection. It relieved her of everyday responsibilities. Lois described Betsy as captivating and generous but disorganized and unpunctual. Lois and the Kellys' housekeeper, Bertha, took care of what Betsy overlooked. Often, when Betsy was involved in political or theatrical activities, six-year-old Kerry saw more of Lois than of her mother. But she was by no means neglected; in interviews as an adult, Kerry had nothing but positive memories to share, though she seemed to have more memories of her father than Betsy. Gene's relationship with Kerry reveals a touching, gentle man free from the volatility and anger he expressed in other areas of his life.

After dinner every night, his daughter reminisced, Gene would help her with her homework and they would often choose a topic and read about it together in the encyclopedia. If he used a word she did not know, he would ask her to look it up in the dictionary and explain it to him. "We [would] talk about whatever it was he thought I ought to know. . . . We were a great family for discussing things from volleyball to the more abstract qualities of life. . . . I was always treated like a 'little adult.' He always thought of me as someone he could reason with. . . . He never talked down to me," Kerry remembered.[23] As much as Gene treated Kerry like an adult, he was determined that she have classic childhood experiences as well. He shared his love of the outdoors with her, giving her a taste of the idyllic summer vacations he had spent on the lake as a boy. "I remember a lot of trips to the mountains where we would go fishing and do some climbing. He would take me roller skating and skiing."[24] He even invented "father-daughter work days" when Kerry would accompany him to the studio and watch the activity on the set before lunching with him at the commissary. "If it was school vacation, I'd be around a fair amount. I think he kept professional and personal separate in the sense that being a movie star wasn't how it felt around the house," Kerry explained in 2015.[25] Gene's biographer Clive Hirschhorn said that Gene "was determined to become a model father" and, in Kerry's words, "he was. . . . I had a great gift from my father in the sense he really enjoyed doing stuff with me. It was very lucky for me. It was a very strong relationship."[26]

Gene kept Kerry in mind when it came to his visions for future film projects. In an interview with Hedda Hopper, he explained: "One of my pet projects is to direct a series of films for children between the ages of four and ten. Except for occasional cartoons, they have almost nothing in the way of film fare. . . . The graphic quality of the screen medium could be turned to advantage if we made films especially for children."[27]

Gene's ideas for making children's pictures showed no signs of becoming reality in the immediate future. His work in his next picture, Arthur

Freed's revue-style biopic of Rodgers and Hart entitled *Words and Music* (1948), was not family-centered entertainment. Gene got his chance to bring more ballet to the moviegoing public, but the concept he had in mind was far from the fairy-tale dancing of *The Red Shoes*. Indeed, the modern ballet Gene created for the production was, by 1948 standards, the most provocative and sexually charged dance ever to be caught on film.

Gene added a grain of authenticity to the otherwise fictionalized *Words and Music*. Not a decade ago, he had worked intimately with the film's subjects in New York. The same could not be said for the cavalcade of other performers in the production. Like *The Three Musketeers, Words and Music* was studded with stars. Tom Drake portrayed Richard Rodgers and Mickey Rooney was Lorenz Hart. Perry Como, Mel Torme, Lena Horne, Cyd Charisse, June Allyson, and Judy Garland were among the many guest performers.

For his segment in this music biography film, Gene chose to dance to the bluesy instrumental "Slaughter on Tenth Avenue." The number had originated in *On Your Toes* (1936) as a darkly comic ballet in which Ray Bolger dances with the corpse of a girl to avoid being shot. With the aid of Robert Alton and Roger Edens, Gene transformed it into "a jazz ballet tale of Love and Death set among Manhattan's demimonde . . . a raw, exciting, and sexy dramatic scenario." In a discussion with a reporter for *Interview* magazine in 1994, Gene concisely explained the story as one of a "girl vamping the guy, and the bad guy coming in trying to get the girl and shooting her."[28] The number, at seven and a half minutes, was among the first "attempts to show a lengthy stretch of ballet, indeed a complete dramatic story, in a major Hollywood film" since Fred Astaire, Robert Alton, and Vincente Minnelli's "Limehouse Blues Ballet" in *Ziegfeld Follies* (1946).[29]

To play the femme fatale of his piece, Gene selected a dancer he had first noticed in New York when she hoofed with Betsy in 1940's *Panama Hattie*. Vera-Ellen had since found modest success in Samuel Goldwyn screen musicals featuring Danny Kaye. The blond, lithe ballerina was an unlikely choice given her relative inexperience in film, but Gene insisted MGM give her a screen test.

Vera-Ellen welcomed the challenge. "Until I got the part of the Bowery girl in the number with Gene Kelly, I had just danced in a thoughtless, easygoing way." Gene also revamped her look, teaching her to showcase what she termed "a sort of earthy, sexy quality toward modern [dance]."[30] Gene and Vera-Ellen both departed from their wholesome images in their costumes for the number. Gene dressed in a skintight purple T-shirt, form-fitting black pants, and a beret. Vera-Ellen wore a platinum blond wig (almost identical to Barbara Stanwyck's in *Double Indemnity*, 1944), a tight yellow and red striped blouse, and a red skirt with a long slit running up the side.

"Slaughter on Tenth Avenue" is supposed to take place on a stage; thus, Gene tried to make the scene look as if it were in an actual theater. To accomplish this, he utilized a revolving set rather than cutting from scene to scene. However, to ensure the dance was also cinematic, Gene employed risky camera angles. At one point during the fight scene, Gene hurls a chair that lands within inches of the camera, "almost in the viewer's face."[31] For the final shot, Gene used a wide-angle twenty-eight-millimeter lens—a technique unprecedented in a musical number. Cinematographers generally agree that a forty-millimeter lens shows what the human eye perceives as the most correct perspective; anything less appears warped. Undeterred, Gene placed the camera with the twenty-eight-millimeter lens in a pit at the bottom of a staircase. When Vera-Ellen falls to her death, she lands close to the camera, which shows her face distorted in a sort of fishbowl effect. "There was a rule at MGM that you could not shoot a woman star with less than a 40mm lens. . . . It was a good rule: MGM was thinking commercially. The executives raised a little hell about it, and then they forgot about it," Gene explained in 1979.[32]

Filming for *Words and Music* completed on October 1, 1948, at a cost of $2,799,970. The picture opened a month after *The Three Musketeers,* on December 9, 1948. A critic from *Picturegoer* magazine commented on Gene's ballet: "From the moment . . . Gene Kelly struts out to meet his girl, the sequence has the stamp of 'difference.' . . . It could have been so easily cheap and nasty, but some queer amalgam of music, choreography and mood lifts it to a strange perfection of its own."[33] *Dancing Times* ranked "Slaughter on Tenth Avenue" as second only to "The Red Shoes"; *Words and Music* as a whole did not gain such a high honor, but it did gross a respectable $4,552,000.[34]

Arthur Freed's films, like *Words and Music,* may have lacked weighty plotlines, but they were heavy in original dance concepts, wit, and fluid execution. Gene's next film for Freed, *Take Me out to the Ball Game,* began shooting immediately after *Words and Music* in July 1948. The picture gave him the ideal opportunity to test dance as a means of storytelling in a non-balletic setting. His challenge lay in creating a fine balance between story and dance without weakening one at the expense of the other.

The idea for *Take Me out to the Ball Game* had been on Gene's mind since 1946. Part of his inspiration for the picture came from MGM's softball team, which bore the same name as the team in the film: the Wolves. Gene, though he was passionate about athletics, did not always relish being a part of the team. He claimed with bitterness (specifically during periods when he was without any promising assignments) that the studio wanted him less as a leading man and more as an athlete. He was especially annoyed by Dore Schary's boasting in MGM games about what a great player he had been in high school. Moreover, Gene was still smarting over the studio's veto of *Cyrano de Bergerac*. Thus, he could not resist razzing Schary, one of the men who had rejected the proposal, on the field. Eying Schary's spiked shoes, he quipped: "Just wear sneakers and you won't hurt yourself."[35] Schary scoffed, but he ultimately never made it into the game. Because of his spiked shoes, he tangled his foot in the grass as he left the batter's box, fell, and tore a thigh muscle. The times Gene most enjoyed on the field were those spent with fellow team member Buster Keaton. Keaton had been one of his boyhood heroes, and he had never lost his admiration for the comedian. Gene later noted that he used to see Keaton nearly every day for a chat. Keaton's film performances were now few and far between, but he still worked at MGM as a gagman, especially for Red Skelton vehicles.

Gene may have used Keaton's slapstick antics as inspiration for the comedic scenes in *Take Me out to the Ball Game*. The rest of the story stemmed from his childhood dream of being a player for the Pittsburgh Pirates as well as from the true story of Nick Altrock and Al Schacht, baseball players who moonlighted as vaudevillians. Finally, the picture was born from an instinct for, in Gene's words, "self-defense." Thirty years after *Take Me out to the Ball Game* completed filming, Gene revealed that the film would never have been made had it not been for his vehemence against doing a picture for Joe Pasternak.[36] The plot of the proposed Pasternak film, which had shades of the dated backstage musical, would have had him and Frank Sinatra converting an aircraft carrier into a nightclub. It was then that he developed, with Stanley Donen, the scenario for *Take Me out to the Ball Game*, which Arthur Freed bought at a cost of $25,000.

"At heart I'm something of a frustrated writer myself," Gene told a columnist for the *Schenectady Gazette*. "MGM is finding that out. Stanley Donen and I banged out a story and managed to sell it to the studio. . . . Now we're making it into a musical. . . . We think it's going to be a lot of fun."[37]

The premise of *Take Me out to the Ball Game* hinges on the tension between the Wolves and the team's new owner, K. C. Higgins. Higgins, to the team's shock, is not a man but a beautiful young woman who intends to take an active role in managing the players. Eddie O'Brien (Gene) tries to woo K. C. so she will soften her discipline of the team, but she is unyielding. Dennis Ryan, Eddie's friend and teammate, is infatuated with K. C., much to the amusement of Eddie and first baseman Nat Goldberg. During the first game of the season, Dennis catches the eye not of K. C. but of Shirley, a man-crazy fan of the team. Unbeknownst to Shirley, her escort to the game, Joe Lorgan, is an underworld figure with a heavy bet against the Wolves. Lorgan convinces Eddie to perform in his new nightclub after every game, knowing the work will make him too tired to play ball. Lorgan's scheme works. After Eddie's exhaustion causes the team to lose a number of games, K. C. discovers his extracurricular activities and suspends him. Eddie, who now has feelings for K. C., confronts Lorgan and quits his job at the nightclub. With Dennis and Shirley's help, Eddie plays in the final game of the season. In the end, Shirley finally wins Dennis, Eddie wins K. C., and the Wolves win the big game. With no shortage of humor and dance, the film stressed the American way of life and glorified the nation's favorite pastime during the height of HUAC's nationwide influence.

Though Gene and Donen created the scenario, they did not write the screenplay. That task was completed by Harry Tugend (writer of many Shirley Temple films and, most recently, the Danny Kaye musical comedy *A Song Is Born*, 1948) and George Wells (writer of numerous Red Skelton comedies as well as Freed's *Till the Clouds Roll By*, 1946). To round out the musical aspects of *Take Me out to the Ball Game*, Gene's friends Betty Comden and Adolph Green came on board as lyricists for the bulk of the score. The two had proved their skill not only on Broadway with the hit show *On the Town* (1944) but also through their recent work on Freed's *Good News* (1947). The duo's screenplays and song lyrics ideally encapsulated the postwar feel of MGM musicals. They were witty and hard-edged while still retaining unshakeable idealism. Freed's assistant, Lela Simone, remarked that the writers "were very smart people" and "adapted themselves to everything very rapidly."[38]

While Comden and Green penned the lyrics, Roger Edens composed the music for most of the songs with the exception of an Irish-themed tune, "The Hat My Dear Old Father Wore" (by Jean Schwartz and William Jerome), and the title song (by Jack Norworth and Albert von Tilzer). Edens was both composer and lyricist of one song: "Strictly U.S.A." Arthur Freed chose the past master of the musical picture, Busby Berkeley, as director. Berkeley had freshly graduated from an Alcoholics Anonymous program and Freed, "essentially a caring person, . . . [was] eager to salve his own guilt feelings" about having fired Berkeley from the Judy Garland vehicle *Girl Crazy* five years before.[39] Gene and Donen had been campaigning to be co-directors on the film, but Freed decided that his friend needed the boost more than the younger men.

After assigning Berkeley as director, Freed began to assemble the rest of the cast. Frank Sinatra played Dennis, a role almost identical to that of the girl-shy sailor in *Anchors Aweigh*. Betty Garrett (wife of blacklisted actor Larry Parks and frequent guest at Gene's parties) portrayed Shirley and Jules Munshin, an eccentric Broadway comic, played Nat Goldberg.

Frank Sinatra was not happy with his unchallenging role. He was sulky and troublesome on the set; he felt he did not need rehearsals and attended only when the mood struck him. However, Frank did love working again with Gene, his former mentor. He also befriended Betty Garrett—though she did make him the butt of a joke. In one scene, Frank faints and Betty must carry him to the sidelines of the playing field. A double had been engaged to do the scene, but Betty said, "Believe me, I can carry him." For the rest of the picture, the joke on the set was that "Betty Garrett can carry Frank Sinatra any day." In general, Betty found production on the film a "loose and friendly" experience.[40]

Betty was alone in her feeling. The atmosphere on the set became unpleasant after Gene and Donen were forced to accept aquatic musical star Esther Williams, a leading lady they never would have chosen, for the part of K. C. Higgins. Esther's position on the set was not helped by the fact that she was fourth choice for the role of K. C. Kathryn Grayson was originally slated for the female lead and then, at Freed's suggestion, Judy Garland was to fill the role. However, Judy was still experiencing major emotional ups and downs and arrived each morning in a drug-induced haze. June Allyson, yet another contender, proved unavailable due to pregnancy.

Freed turned to the Pasternak Unit and chose Esther, one of MGM's top moneymaking stars. On the surface, she and Gene seemed well suited to one another. Next to him, she was the most accomplished athlete on the Metro lot. Yet the two performers' commonalities became their source of animosity. Both were stubborn, outspoken, and accustomed to getting their way on a set. At five feet eight, Esther towered over most of the executives at MGM and, if she wore a hat and heels, was a head taller than Gene. Gene stated that she was "very different" from the other three actresses considered for the part. "Different meant not in his league," Esther explained. "A dancer I was not. . . . I felt clumsy on dry land."[41]

Esther had anticipated having a strong leading man in Gene. Each was disillusioned with the other when they began working together. Esther recalled that Gene behaved like "nothing less than a tyrant behind the camera—at least with me. He had to see that I was doing the best I could— and suffering through it." Truth be told, it was Esther's height and not her lack of dancing skills that seemed to be at the root of their problem. Even in scenes when both stars were seated, her stature was obvious.

"That son of a bitch even sits tall!" Gene allegedly declared.

"It would help if you would just sit up straight. Try tucking one foot under your ass," Esther told the incensed Gene.

"Gee Esther," he said. "The way you just said that, you surprise me. I think you really *would* like to learn to act."

Esther concluded in her memoir: "That's the way it was with Gene. There was always that little zinger."[42]

Esther was no fonder of Stanley Donen. In aesthetic endeavors, Gene and Donen brought out the best in one another. On a personal level, they had long brought out the worst. "They were joined at the hip—and the mouth," Esther declared.[43] Just as Frank Sinatra and Kathryn Grayson had been victims of Gene and Donen's antics on the set of *Anchors Aweigh*, now they made Esther Williams their target.

One afternoon, Gene and Donen stationed themselves beside the actress's new blue Cadillac El Dorado convertible. When she neared the car, the two boys were "merciless, mincing around the car, dropping sarcasm with every step."

"Oh my," said Gene with make-believe admiration. "Stanley, do you see what Esther has?"

"Look Gene! See what you get from splashing around in a pool?"

Esther retaliated by making it known around the studio that playing scenes with Gene gave her a severe case of scoliosis from having to "make herself short."[44]

Esther also sought revenge by going to Freed, lamenting that Donen especially did not respect her acting. Freed ordered the young man to make a public denial. "I can't do this, Arthur. She's absolutely right," Donen admitted.[45]

Gene Kelly researcher Susan Cadman hypothesized that part of Esther's dislike for Gene had to do with her association with Arthur Laurents. "She was friendly with Arthur Laurents . . . who for some reason did not like Gene, and had a poisonous tongue."[46] Laurents, who resented Gene's occasional jokes about homosexuals, could not have taken kindly to his performance in *Take Me out to the Ball Game*. In one scene, Gene (as Eddie) sarcastically behaves in a way that he thinks would be acceptable to K. C. at the dinner table. With dainty gestures, he gushes over fashions in *Vanity Fair* magazine in a feigned effeminate voice. "Have you boys seen the fashion page in this week's *Vanity Fair*? Well, there's the cutest pair of pants with a tank top and a narrow bottom," he says and then brings his hand to his face in a coy manner. "If you'll pardon the expression."[47] Though Gene's mimicry was done purely in fun, Laurents and Esther found his sense of humor offensive.

Adolph Green and Betty Comden, conversely, adored Gene and Donen's company. "Stanley and Gene were terrific storytellers and they were also great with the actors. They too had a terrific sense of humor," Green asserted.[48]

Because of Laurents, Esther may have been predisposed to dislike Gene. Nonetheless, her recollections reveal the truth as she saw it, hard as that truth is for many of Gene's fans to accept. Esther's brief description of Gene on the dust jacket of her book summarized her feelings about him in six words: "a jerk, but he could dance!"[49]

Gene and Esther Williams had a chance to find common ground in their mutual dislike of director Busby Berkeley. Esther disapproved of Berkeley's indifference to actors' safety and his refusal to use stunt doubles. All he cared about, she argued, was seeing that his overblown visions for a given sequence came to fruition. Nonetheless, Esther wanted Berkeley, not Gene, to choreograph her musical numbers. She owed much of the success of her aquatic musical numbers to Berkeley and hoped he could do the same for her in *Take Me out to the Ball Game*. Berkeley envisioned a sort of dream sequence in which Eddie would reach out to K. C. as she swam in a rushing river. His failure to grab hold of her would reflect her elusive affections toward him. Freed and Esther were enthusiastic, but Gene turned down the idea.

"Are you sure it isn't because you don't know how to swim, Gene?" Esther quipped.

"I can swim, smart ass," he retorted.[50]

A fantasy sequence, albeit an underwater one, seems like a concept that would have sparked Gene's imagination, given that he helped pioneer the concept of dream ballets on film. Esther later conjectured that Gene's rejection had more to do with his reluctance to turn the film into an Esther Williams picture. "In retrospect, Gene was right. The movie does just fine without an Esther Williams aqua special. . . . However, at that time in my career, I wasn't used to a backseat and Kelly and Donen knew how I felt."[51]

Esther and Berkeley both came to accept that the film was essentially Gene's. Berkeley's biographer Jeffrey Spivak mused, "Kelly was a choreographer, Berkeley was, most assuredly, not. . . . They did clash a bit on *Ball Game,* but it was Berkeley who gave him [Gene] his start in *For Me and My Gal.* One might have thought Gene Kelly would have been a bit more respectful to the man who gave him his film career, but he wasn't."[52]

For one scene, Berkeley envisioned filming in a bird's-eye view reminiscent of his kaleidoscopic style of the 1930s. "Back, back . . . take the camera back!" he shouted to his cameramen. Gene looked on with his arms crossed, realizing that the shot, if executed in Berkeley's way, would be so long and wide that the movements of the two actors in the frame would be lost. "Yeah, back to 1930," Gene murmured audibly.[53] While Gene considered Berkeley's cinematography style outdated, he did eventually admit, "Anybody who ever used a camera owes a debt to Berkeley. To laugh at his films is like laughing at Chaucer's *Canterbury Tales* because it's in Old English."[54] Berkeley never disparaged Gene's work. In fact, when asked to name his favorite musical sequence of all time, he answered without hesitation: "Gene Kelly's 'Alter Ego' dance in *Cover Girl.*"[55]

Though Gene did ultimately express admiration for Berkeley's work, the musical numbers in *Take Me out to the Ball Game* were mainly small scale and inappropriate for the elder director's sweeping visions. Historian Martin Rubin noted that the musical sequences place "the major emphasis on comedy, transitions to the narrative, the cleverness of the lyrics, and the personalities and performance skills of the stars, rather than on spectacle and group dynamics."[56] The songwriters' creations clearly favored the

Kelly-Donen style. Indeed, every song reflects the character performing it so well that the movie, when viewed in total, seems lopsided. Singing and dancing do considerably more for characterization and storytelling than the dialogue.

Most of the film's musical numbers did serve to further the plot and characterization, but others, like "The Hat My Dear Old Father Wore" and "Strictly U.S.A.," were purely for show. The numbers most indicative of the new direction in Freed musicals were those penned by Comden and Green, including "O'Brien to Ryan to Goldberg" and "Yes Indeedy." In both numbers the performers and cameras are in constant movement.

In "Yes Indeedy," Eddie and Dennis reunite with the Wolves after their season playing on vaudeville. As they sing, they establish themselves as consummate showmen, recounting five outlandish romances they enjoyed during their travels. The song ends with a twist and a laugh:

> We're hot as electric wires
> Twice as hot as forest fires,
> And the biggest pair of liars . . . in the U.S.A.![57]

The second major number in *Take Me out to the Ball Game* succeeds in further establishing Eddie's and Dennis's personalities as well as Nat Goldberg's. The sequence concludes with the three friends standing in a pyramid formation, crooning that they are "the Three Musketeers of the bat and the ball!" The routine fills the requirement for the "teamwork" message conveyed in the bulk of Gene's films.

Gene's solo dance, "The Hat My Dear Old Father Wore," is inessential to the plot but is arguably the most memorable number in the film. Taking place at a clambake, the sequence allows Gene ample opportunity to employ items around him as props. He uses his cane as everything from a flute to a gun, effortlessly dances from picnic table tops to the steps of a bandstand, and struts across the deck in a George M. Cohan fashion. All the while, a cocked green top hat on his head covers one eye. The sequence is the best example of cinedance in the picture; at one point when he slows his pace, Gene wears a dreamlike expression as he hears a distant playback of his voice, as if from a memory nearly faded. Fred Astaire used the same technique of a disembodied singing voice in his "Shoes with Wings On" number from Freed's *The Barkleys of Broadway,* which was filming simultaneously to *Take Me out to the Ball Game.*

The picture's finale, a reprise of "Strictly U.S.A." (it is first sung at the clambake before Gene's solo), was the only piece in the film that held no relevance to the story and bore no uniquely cinematic qualities. The routine ranks as the most bizarre ending of any Freed production. Apparently, the writers on the picture met for a number of fruitless sessions to discuss ways to conclude the film. Finally, Roger Edens wrote a new verse for "Strictly U.S.A." to serve as a slapdash finish. The finale shows Shirley, K. C., Dennis, and Eddie dressed in red, white, and blue, all presumably having joined forces as a vaudeville team (what became of Goldberg is anyone's guess). The scene is odd not only because the new stanza describes modern America in a film taking place roughly between 1909 and 1912 but also because the lyrics have the actors referring to each other by their real names:

> Sinatra gets Garrett and Kelly gets Williams,
> for that's the plot the authors wrote . . .
> Like a Ford or a Chevrolet,
> like potato chips or comic strips, it's strictly U.S.A.[58]

Betty Comden and Adolph Green were not responsible for those verses, but nonetheless, they were not proud of their work on the picture. "That's one we'd like to forget," Comden later stated.[59] Shooting wrapped for *Take Me out to the Ball Game* in late September of 1948. The movie may have failed to find an ideal balance between story and song, but Freed saw that what saved the picture were Gene and Donen's choreographic contributions and Comden and Green's clever lyrics. As a reward, the producer announced his plans to give the duo a solo directorial project with Comden and Green as screen/songwriters.

On March 9, 1949, Gene and Donen saw their first (uncredited) effort as directors premiere at New York's Loew's State Theatre. *Take Me out to the Ball Game* received few accolades except in the area of dance and music. Bosley Crowther of the *New York Times* bemoaned the film's "plotted humor" as "bush-league stuff" and claimed it "lacked consistency and style." Only during the musical sequences did he feel that Frank and Gene were "on firm ground."[60] He singled out Berkeley's only major contribution to the film, the first version of "Strictly U.S.A," for the highest praise. Other critics aside from the almighty Crowther agreed that the musical numbers trumped any other aspect of the picture. Given that Gene's and Berkeley's individual contributions received praise, it appeared that both men's styles still had their place in film. Berkeley's biographer Jeffrey Spivak elaborated that Berkeley was not outdated in "the moviegoing public's opinion. . . . Kelly got his chance to show what he could do (with Stanley Donen) . . . in [*Take Me out to the Ball Game*] . . . and he did an excellent job. Different from Berkeley? Yes. Better? No."[61]

Take Me out to the Ball Game was an audience pleaser, yielding $4,344,000 at the box office. In response to the observation that his recent films had been popular rather than critical sensations, Arthur Freed remarked, "I think a critic too often rests on his own tastes and appetites. . . . It is mass tastes that determine our culture, and whether the culture is a good one or a bad one is not the issue. What counts is that it's there."[62]

Mass taste, it seemed, indicated that Eddie O'Brien in *Take Me out to the Ball Game* was the type of role in which audiences wanted to see Gene. Here was the Gene Kelly from *For Me and My Gal* and *Anchors Aweigh*— the Everyman, brash, all-American style.

Because the larger-than-life image he projected in front of the camera was so conspicuous, audiences identified Gene as the intense but essentially lightweight character they saw onscreen rather than the cerebral Renaissance man he really was. His grandson, Ben Novick, enumerated his other talents aside from singing, dancing, acting, and choreographing: "He liked fine art and could speak foreign languages and could speak with you very intelligently."[63] However, from his beginnings as a dance instructor in Pennsylvania, what Gene cherished most was the concentrated, intellectually demanding work he completed behind the scenes.

Gene held a unique place in the film industry; at this juncture, he was the only actor who was also choreographing, directing, and writing. He embodied everything MGM, but particularly the Freed Unit, sought to accomplish in pictures. He maintained a can-do attitude before and behind the camera, appealed to both mass and aesthete audiences, Democrats and Republicans, Americans and foreigners. As 1948 turned to 1949, Gene emerged as the undisputed leader of the Freed Unit—a highly creative group that had now earned the reputation of MGM's royal family.

13

You Can Count on Me

"We made better pictures than that, but that was the apex of our talent. That was it," Gene remarked. "I think [it was] maybe my biggest contribution to the film musical."[1] What picture did Gene grant such an honorific position? *On the Town.*

Few films evoke as much excitement in their first minutes. From the instant three sailors rush from their ship and announce in song, "New York, New York, it's a wonderful town!" the picture's momentum does not wane for a moment. *On the Town,* based on Betty Comden and Adolph Green's Broadway hit of World War II, took on new life in the hands of Gene Kelly, Stanley Donen, and the Arthur Freed Unit. The film could not have gone into production at a more opportune time. Indeed, the Freed Unit and MGM as a whole were enjoying an unparalleled renaissance.

"MGM studio in the year 1949 was the most glamorous, most glorious place in the motion picture industry," Debbie Reynolds recollected.[2] In the course of that year, Fred Astaire and Ginger Rogers reunited after a decade in *The Barkleys of Broadway,* Esther Williams and Ricardo Montalban sang "Baby, It's Cold Outside" in *Neptune's Daughter,* and Spencer Tracy and Katharine Hepburn starred in one of their most successful collaborations, *Adam's Rib.* Additionally, 1949 marked the triumphant return of Vincente Minnelli as one of the studio's top directors through his artful rendering of Gustav Flaubert's *Madame Bovary.*

MGM's boost in creativity was in part triggered by the emerging medium of television. With more Americans living in the suburbs, home entertainment held vast appeal for men and women exhausted after an eight-hour workday. From 1946 to 1949, the number of television set owners skyrocketed from 44,000 to 4.2 million. However, the small, grainy black-and-white screens and static live programs could not compare to the Technicolor, exciting locales, special effects, and impeccable scoring of motion pictures. Yet television, like film, could evolve. Thus, studios continually increased their efforts to give audiences novel and vibrant products. *On the Town* promised to be both. "I really believed it would be a masterpiece because I set out to make it so," Gene commented in 1993.[3]

Gene had been hoping to bring *On the Town* to the screen since he himself was a sailor. While in the navy, he had phoned Arthur Freed about his wish and the producer "said that MGM [already] owned the rights to the play. I told him I wanted to make it as soon as I got out of the service."[4] It is easy to see why Gene, with his passion for ballet, so loved the show. The 1944 production was inspired by a ballet produced in spring of the same year entitled *Fancy Free* with choreography by Jerome Robbins and a score by Leonard Bernstein. Comden and Green's comedic two-act play married ballet, hoofing, and American musical comedy into a cohesive whole—something Gene hoped to retain and perfect in his film adaptation.

Louis B. Mayer and other MGM executives did not share Gene's enthusiasm for the project; rather, they had a case of buyers' remorse. Gene gave an idea for the reasons behind the executives', particularly Mayer's, regrets: "Here was this play set in New York City with . . . chorus people representing blacks and Japanese and whites and Hispanics. . . . I found out later that Louis B. Mayer had gone to see it and didn't like the melting-pot idea. . . . All these people touching and dancing with each other."[5] Mayer also disliked the suggestive content of many of the songs, especially "Come Up to My Place" and "I Can Cook, Too." Distasteful as well to Mayer was the use of *helluva* in the play's opening—and most famous—number, "New York, New York, It's a Helluva Town."

Nonetheless, Freed told Gene and Donen to forge ahead. Because *On the Town* was decidedly a Gene Kelly picture, Comden and Green knew that their primary task in adapting the play for the screen was to make his character, Gabey, more prominent in both musical and nonmusical scenes. In the stage show, another sailor, Ozzie (portrayed by Adolph Green himself), far overshadowed Gabey. Betty Comden noted that "with Gene as the leading character . . . he couldn't be a helpless, naïve type."[6]

Though Gene approved of the shift in character emphasis, he argued that more of Bernstein's score should be kept. But Freed considered the music too avant-garde and claimed it included nothing that resembled a hit. The producer also felt the stage show had "been done in a campy manner, which he felt would be offensive to movie audiences."[7] Camp, even when executed with wit (as evidenced in Gene and Vincente Minnelli's *The Pirate*), might have impressed highbrow critics, but it failed to click with average American moviegoers.

Gene may not have had his way when it came to the score, but he proved influential in the process of adapting the new music and altered script for the screen. Adolph Green explained, "If they [Gene and Donen] were going to change a number . . . then of course there'd have to be a different lead-in to the scene. We had to stay very close in touch on those things. . . . We were . . . fortunate to have a guy [at MGM] as ambitious as Gene, who had real feelings about the dance and the movies." Stanley Donen, as Gene's co-director, rivaled Gene in ambition as well as, in Green's words, "taste and intelligence and feeling for show business."[8]

On the Town had to embody all of these characteristics, for its success or failure would determine the futures of Comden and Green as lyricists and writers in Hollywood and of Gene and Donen as directors and choreographers. In spite of the high pressure surrounding the film, Comden and Green fondly termed it a "comfortable" experience. After all, two of their closest friends were directing it and were in the same boat, so to speak, as the writers. "We knew we all understood each other. . . . We put things in the script that might have puzzled a lot of other directors, but knowing us as well as they did, they knew exactly what we wanted. . . . They knew our kind of humor, our craziness," Comden recalled.[9]

Comden and Green felt lucky to be members of the Freed Unit, which by 1949 was firmly established as an exclusive club that rarely had "creative exchange" with other MGM writers. Betsy Blair described the Freed Unit as a world unto itself. In her estimation, the insidious blacklist had taken a "blithe confidence" away from Hollywood that was "never to reemerge."[10] Yet the Freed Unit had remained virtually untouched.

"One day in particular comes back to me. Nothing extraordinary happened. . . . Betty Comden, Adolph Green, Stanley Donen, and Roger Edens were arriving [at the Kelly home] to work with Gene. Bertha, the housekeeper, provided orange juice and coffee and tea," Betsy reminisced. "Adolph, as always was irrepressible. There were jokes and laughter. They went into the study to work. . . . As I left they were all in the living room with Roger at the piano. . . . I walked to Santa Monica Boulevard. . . . As I waited [for a trolley] in the sun, I had a moment of that special bliss. I'd just left a perfect place, where talented people that I loved were doing great work. . . . Gene was wildly successful and at the height of his creative life."[11]

By 1949, the adventures and misadventures of amorous sailors on leave had been the basis of countless motion pictures. Even Gene claimed that with *On the Town,* he and his colleagues "took a lot of the clichés" from previous movies. Why, then, was *On the Town,* in the words of film writer John Cutts, unequalled in its "invention and ingenuity"? The answer lay not only in its execution but in its warm, honest characterizations. Cutts explained that the picture "was about people rather than puppets. It proved Kelly and Donen could work wonders with a tired old formula and [add to it] an abundance of ideas."[12]

The picture follows three carefree sailors, Gabey, Chip, and Ozzie, on their twenty-four-hour leave in New York City. When the boys ride on a subway, Gabey sees a poster featuring Ivy, the winner of that month's "Miss Turnstiles" contest. Immediately, he makes it his goal to find the girl before his leave is over. During his and his friends' search, bashful Chip meets a man-crazy female cab driver, Hildy, and Ozzie meets Claire (a role originated on Broadway by Betty Comden) at the Museum of Anthropological History. She explains she's studying anthropology to get her mind off men. "Dr. Kinsey, I presume," Hildy quips when introduced to Claire. In the museum, Ozzie accidentally knocks over a reconstructed dinosaur skeleton and has to dodge the police in increasingly zany ways (including hanging off the side of the Empire State Building) for the remainder of his leave.

Meanwhile, Gabey finds Ivy at a dance studio and makes a date to meet her atop the Empire State Building. During their date, Ivy slips out of one of the many nightclubs she attends with Gabey and his friends to fulfill her duties as a "cooch dancer" on Coney Island. Noting how depressed Gabey is over Ivy's disappearance, Hildy asks her homely, sneezy roommate, Lucy Schmeeler, to act as his blind date. Lucy asks Gabey over a drink: "Have you seen *The Lost Weekend?*" "I feel like I'm living it," he mutters.

After saying good-bye to Lucy, the group discovers Ivy's whereabouts and heads to Coney Island, eluding a speeding police car all the way. The law catches them at the precise moment Gabey sees Ivy performing her cooch dance. Mortified, she explains that she has to do such work to pay for dance lessons. Hildy and Claire then make a rousing speech to the police and the crowd that has gathered, declaring that it is a citizen's duty to see that boys in uniform enjoy themselves in New York. The police sergeant, overcome with emotion, convinces the crowd to take up a collection to pay the sailors' fine. Their leave now over, the boys rush to their ship, but not before they kiss their girls good-bye.

With the script complete, next came the casting of the film. As Gene's two sailor pals were Jules Munshin (as Ozzie, who, in the altered screenplay, took on the part of the clumsy comic relief) and Frank Sinatra, reprising his customary girl-shy screen persona as Chip. Freed had been so pleased with the onscreen chemistry between Frank, Gene, and Jules in *Take Me out to the Ball Game* that he was eager to see them together again in *On the Town*.

The picture also found Frank Sinatra reunited with Betty Garrett, who filled the romantically aggressive role of Hildy. "The rehearsal periods were a joyous period in my life," Betty recalled. She did, however, note that Frank was far moodier, even with her, on the set of *On the Town* than *Take Me out to the Ball Game*. "We [on the set] thought nothing of hugging each other, pinching, or even giving a friendly pat on the behind, until one day when we were shooting . . . and I tried it with Frank. 'Don't do that,' he said to me very sharply. 'Gees, what's the matter with him?' I thought. 'Don't you know?' Gene asked. Frank was upset because he was wearing 'symmetricals,' which was padding that he had to use in the rear."[13]

Frank's displeasure with his part went beyond alterations to his physical appearance. For the first time in any film in which he costarred with Gene, he received second billing. Because he felt he was being "outshone by Kelly," he was "just along for the ride" throughout filming. Freed's assistant, Lela Simone, called Frank's sullen behavior on the set "atrocious."[14]

Vera-Ellen, cast as Ivy Smith, could not have had a more different demeanor than Frank. Her cheerfulness was enough to impress even the moody Frank, who said of her: "God, she's so lovely and so sweet."[15] Despite Gene's attempt to change Vera-Ellen into a sultry dancer in *Words and Music*, she was again the image of wholesomeness in *On the Town*. Leggy tap dancer Ann Miller was chosen to portray Claire.

With the cast in place, Freed then "turned them [Donen and Gene] loose on *On the Town*." Freed recognized that Gene thought more like a director than an actor; therefore, choosing Gene to take charge of the picture "was no haphazard thing. . . . The picture will show Gene and Stan have contributed something really fresh."[16] One novel device was how the film showed the passing of time. At scene transitions, a digital reading of a clock scrolls across the screen, much like the headlines one might see on the side of a building in Times Square. Most innovative was Gene and Donen's idea that the film's opening sequence be shot on location—something unprecedented in a Hollywood musical. "It was tough getting them to let me shoot in New York. I had to stamp my foot and act like a movie star," Gene recalled in a 1970 interview.[17] As usual, Freed championed his "kids," and Mayer and Dore Schary finally agreed to give the crew five days of funding to shoot on location.

Five days was a painfully short time to shoot what promised to be the highlight of the picture. Lela Simone explained that such a tight shooting schedule warred with Freed's usual modus operandi: "We never did things quick, quick, quick, quick, quick like the other productions do. That didn't happen."[18] However, it had to happen if Gene and Donen were to realize their vision. Location shooting began on March 28, 1949. The first scenes filmed were the opening and closing sequences at the Brooklyn Navy Yard, the very location where Gene had made a military service film in 1946. "I got permission from the Navy [to use one of their ships in *Town*] because I was one of their boys," Gene explained.[19]

Gene and Donen shot the rest of the location scenes in a seemingly chaotic fashion that, in the end, fit together like a puzzle. Simone summarized the trip to New York as a "madhouse. . . . We could barely shoot anywhere [because of] the . . . thousands of people everywhere we went. . . . We had to go through an underground passage and people . . . chased us. . . . It was absolutely horrifying." In total, thirty thousand bystanders gathered to watch the actors film their scenes. Police almost had to carry the cast and crew through the crowd, but after a certain point, the police grew so exhausted that, Simone asserted, "they didn't care anymore who [got] run over."[20]

The location shooting (all done with "New York, New York, It's a Wonderful Town," as an accompaniment) was, according to Simone, "the most important thing" to shoot because it packed a dizzying tour of New York into less than ten minutes. Gene later reflected: "When I think that we managed to shoot stuff at Brooklyn Bridge, Wall Street, Chinatown, the Statue of Liberty, Greenwich Village, Central Park, Columbus Circle, Rockefeller Center, and Grant's Tomb, I still can't believe it."[21]

Gene and Donen worried that they would not be able to complete the shooting in time partly because of issues involving Frank Sinatra and Jules Munshin. Gene and Jules were always ready on time, but Frank "[held] up the parade," often appearing so late that the sun had moved to an inopportune angle that made filming impossible. Though Jules Munshin was punctual, he refused to rehearse a scene atop the Loew's Building because of his crippling fear of heights. Lela Simone recalled that Jules was "an absolute wreck. We finally had to put him on a rope . . . around his waist. . . . But in one [scene] . . . where we shot on a roof, I thought he was going to commit suicide. . . . This man suffered hell. . . . He got through it, but he was very unhappy on the picture, very unhappy."[22]

Another reason for Jules's unhappiness was that he found himself inexplicably shunned by Gene and Donen during the remainder of filming. Though the full explanation for the men's shift in attitude toward their colleague is unclear, Simone asserted that much of it had to do with Donen, who "was impossible as usual." Just as Donen and Gene had brought out each other's immaturity on the set of *Take Me out to the Ball Game,* so did they again on the set of *On the Town.* Jules's open display of vulnerability may have been at the root of Gene's lessened regard for him. "I can't explain why," Lela Simone said. "They [Donen and Gene] are not very polite and nice people, you know."[23]

Simone eventually had the opportunity to see Gene's more generous nature. At the last minute, Gene and Donen decided they needed another sixteen bars for the "New York, New York" sequence atop Loew's Building. Simone frenziedly supplied them with the extra bars despite the fact that she had no current playback with which to work. And yet, "it worked perfectly," Simone said. She acknowledged that Gene was not "dumb technically. He realized that it was terribly difficult [to add the extra bars]. That is why he didn't say anything [when I delivered them]. . . . He didn't want to start discussing this . . . [but] he was delighted when I delivered them."[24]

Gene had a different way of expressing his gratitude. "Would you mind going to the very top of the roof and be in the shot?" he asked Simone.

"Why? It's so high that it's like the Alps. What do you want me to do there?"

"I think you should be up there like a tourist would be and just turn around slowly as our truck with the camera goes by so that you can see that everything is okay."[25]

Though at times Gene exercised his authority in negative ways, his demand for perfection had less to do with his ego and more to do with his mission to see everybody in the picture reach their full potential. Ann Miller recalled him being temperamental in a constructive manner; he expected nothing from others he did not expect from himself.

Gene could not be docile in his role as director. During the film's brief one hundred minutes, he had to ensure that eleven musical sequences, which boasted "a bewildering variety of ballet, soft-shoe, ethnic, tap, and comic hoofing," seamlessly moved the characters along in their adventures.[26] Lennie Hayton, Johnny Green, and Saul Chaplin aided Edens, Comden, and Green in scoring the lively, humorous new songs for the film. Chaplin had just begun working for MGM after leaving Columbia, where he and Gene had worked together on *Cover Girl*.

Leonard Bernstein briefly came to Hollywood to help adapt his pieces for the film, but he found the entire experience of *On the Town* less thrilling than the rest of the musical crew. It pained Bernstein to see only a handful of his compositions make the cut. Three of his creations, however, accounted for the most important numbers in the film: "New York, New York" and two ballets, "Miss Turnstiles" and "A Dream Ballet." "New York, New York" retained Bernstein's music but the lyrics were cleansed to read: "it's a wonderful" rather than "it's a helluva" town. "Miss Turnstiles" was purely instrumental and required no changes to appease censors.

In creating a dance to accompany the music, Gene utilized a technique that set a precedent for future ballets he choreographed: a type of fantasy in which a boy describes to his friends how his love interest might behave in given situations. During his descriptions, the screen shows the girl acting out his visions through dance. The climactic number in the film, which Gene renamed "A Day in New York," is a reverie recapturing the events of Gabey's day, conveying the emotions he experienced in the short hours during which he met and lost Ivy. The number ends quietly with Gabey slumped beside the poster of Ivy he found during his first subway ride. The ballet follows the formula of Gene's "Alter Ego" sequence in *Cover Girl*—it escalates in passion, color, and movement before concluding on an introspective note. The stage ballet was more abstract and symbolic than Gene's, but the thesis of both was lost love.

Gene, taskmaster though he was, did not push Jules Munshin, Frank Sinatra, Betty Garrett, and Ann Miller to work eighteen hours a day learning ballet. Rather, he engaged four professional dancers to stand in for them during the "Day in New York" sequence. He felt that only he and Vera-Ellen were experienced enough to perform the number. Betty Garrett's stand-in was a pixieish, twenty-five-year-old dancer named Carol Haney. Gene fondly described her as "a clown with curves."[27] He saw Carol as a real asset and persuaded her to join him as a full-time choreographic assistant. Like Jeanne Coyne, Carol seemed to possess an almost telepathic knowledge of what Gene wanted from a scene. Though Gene's decision not to use the film's cast in the ballet led him to Carol, in hindsight, that choice was his primary regret concerning *On the Town*. "It [using stand-ins] never works in films," he remarked. "The public won't buy it."[28]

The most effective part of the dance involves the two actual cast members, Gene and Vera-Ellen. The sequence uses a bright red background and a spotlight trained on Gene (in his sailor suit) and Vera-Ellen (in a tight black leotard). They continually elude one another in a pas de deux on either side of a ballet barre, and audiences can feel the romantic tension. The sequence fell under scrutiny from MGM's censors. As Gene explained in 1979, "I never laid a glove" on Vera-Ellen. "There was nothing the censors could say. If they did, I could have said, 'What? Do you have a dirty mind?' But yes, it was very sensual, and the colors did it."[29]

Viewing a rough cut of the film, Arthur Freed had no qualms about the ballet, which he thought was better than "The Red Shoes Ballet" in the 1948 picture. Despite the merits of Gene's ballet, it was not an artistic breakthrough, nor was it integral to the plot. According to Donen's biographer Stephen M. Silverman, it "emphasized the weak storyline" and served as a cue for the audience to go out and get popcorn.[30]

The remaining musical sequences in *On the Town* were less artistic but more entertaining. Two of the most notable songs were new compositions by Roger Edens, Comden, and Green: "You Can Count on Me," a tune rich in wordplay emphasizing the teamwork theme of the picture, and the title song, "On the Town." The latter follows the six principals from the top of the Empire State Building to the streets of New York. The execution of the number is reminiscent of "Make Way for Tomorrow" in *Cover Girl*; the camera remains trained on the cast members, linking arms as they rush forward toward the lens, singing:

> We're going on the town
> New York
> We're riding on a rocket
> We're going to really sock it . . .[31]

Though Edens's music is not as complex as Bernstein's, it nonetheless captures the "get up and go" quality of the film. The screenplay, music, and choreography cooperate to such a degree that the frequent dance numbers and songs do not cause the audience to roll their eyes and shift in their seats, grumbling, "Get on with the story!" Gene expounded on how *On the Town* achieved this: "In the old musicals, they just said, 'I love you' and started singing. Finally, the public said, 'This isn't real.' That's something we changed a lot at MGM. You have to stay in character or come out of that character in some kind of fantasy way, but not *lose* the character."[32]

Filming for *On the Town* wrapped in mid-July of 1949, totaling forty-seven days of shooting and $2,111,250 in production costs.[33] After *On the Town,* Gene said, he and Donen were no longer teacher and pupil but co-creators. That assessment, as well as Gene's reliance on others, like Roger Edens, Saul Chaplin, and Lela Simone, was evidence of how he thrived on collaboration. In fact, biographer Clive Hirschhorn asserted, without his colleagues, "Gene's work would have come to a standstill. . . . He needed people behind the camera to make sure he hit a certain mark on a certain beat and this took expertise."[34]

But Gene could not be certain that the film was his and the Freed Unit's "apex" until he witnessed its reception. At the movie's first preview in Pacific Palisades, moviegoers began applauding at the film's finale. Freed turned to the relieved Gene, Edens, and Donen and declared, "If it were a show, it'd run a year!"[35] (An ironic statement, considering that *On the Town* had been a show, and it had actually run for two years.) The picture was experimental in a sense, yet it was successful because, unlike *The Pirate,* it was "ambitious [but not] spoiled by any signs of ambitiousness."[36]

When *On the Town* was released at New York's Radio City Music Hall on December 8, 1949, New Yorkers met it with the same enthusiasm as preview audiences. The line waiting outside stretched for nine blocks. With a gross of over $4,428,000, the picture broke box office records and more than recouped its budget. The film proved to be just as much a critics' darling as an audience favorite. Even Bosley Crowther of the *New York Times* was ecstatic: "Gene Kelly and Stanley Donen . . . have cleverly liberated action . . . and . . . have engineered sizzling momentum by the smart employment of cinema techniques."[37] A critic for *Time* magazine deemed the "Day in New York Ballet" as "clumsily inserted," but otherwise considered the picture a breakthrough in its genre. The reviewer credited Gene and Donen with turning "out a film so exuberant that it threatens at moments to bounce right off the screen. . . . It also leaves a happy impression that MGM has hit upon a bright new idiom for cine-musicals and a bright new directing team that knows how to use it."[38] *On the Town* set a precedent not only for future pictures in the Freed Unit but for later on-location musicals such as *The Sound of Music* (1965), *Sweet Charity* (1969), and other dance-heavy films, including *Seven Brides for Seven Brothers* (1954) and *West Side Story* (1960). Louis B. Mayer, who had been against the project since its inception, stopped Gene one day at the studio barbershop and murmured: "I was wrong about that picture. You fellows did a good job."[39]

On the Town earned only one Oscar nomination, but it took home the award at the twenty-second ceremony on March 23, 1950. The statuette went to Lennie Hayton and Roger Edens for Best Scoring of a Motion Picture. Fred Astaire, though deserving of the honorary Oscar he earned this year, stole the spotlight from Gene and Donen's choreographic achievements. Gene and Donen's superior cinematography received a nomination at the Golden Globe Awards, but did not win the prize (which went to Walt Disney's animated *The Adventures of Ichabod and Mr. Toad*). *On the Town* earned Betty Comden and Adolph Green their first Writers Guild Award for Best Written American Musical, sealing their futures as Hollywood screenwriters. Adolph Green wrote to Leonard Bernstein, "I hate people who go to Hollywood" but, he confessed "I have a grisly feeling that we've [he and Comden] really got a future in this place, Lord help me."[40]

The success of *On the Town* established Gene as a formidable director. Because it was the first film to truly give him the opportunity to do what he loved best—direct—he never lost his regard for the milestone *On the Town* marked in both his career and the history of film. "It's a bit dated now, but that film still has a warm place in my heart," he said decades later.[41]

How to follow the success of *On the Town* was no easy question for thirty-seven-year-old Gene Kelly. If he believed he had reached the height of his talent in the picture, then the only direction to go, he feared, was down. Gene's daughter Kerry recalled her impressions of her father at this time: "Though he was always surrounded by people who believed him to be as outgoing in his private life as he was on the screen, he was very complex and really rather lonely. He was always restless, trying to prove something to himself all the time. . . . He wanted to make one perfect film, and then he would be happy."[42] Gene loved *On the Town,* but he did not see it as the perfect picture, particularly because of the ballet stand-ins and a soft shoe between him and Vera-Ellen, "Main Street," which he believed never came to life. "When I see myself on screen," Gene explained, "I'm never satisfied."[43]

Though the ability to completely relax seemed perpetually to evade him, Gene's home life remained a haven to which he could retreat and enjoy the privacy he rarely found elsewhere. He was still the content family man he had been since marrying Betsy Blair and was never above pitching in to help with household chores. "One of Gene's characteristics is neatness," Betsy explained in a 1949 article. "Whenever he leaves a room, it's infinitely more orderly than when he entered. . . . He's always been a spic-and-span gentleman." Gene kept his intellectual pursuits as well ordered as his home. "Gene seems to remember every book he has ever read," Betsy said. "[He] loves to read in bed, mostly biographies [and history]. He's a restless sleeper . . . and keeps chocolate bars on his night table to munch on when those tossing periods start."[44] Gene was also interested in fine art and began collecting impressionist paintings.

Despite Gene's fame, he and Betsy remained down to earth, as did their daughter. She was untainted by the Hollywood lifestyle. "They had a very conscious attitude about it and they talked to me about it growing up . . . the phrase was that I was not going to be allowed to become what they called a Beverly Hills kid," Kerry explained. "That meant I had chores and much less allowance than most kids I knew. Shopping was not what we did together. It was a real conscious effort on their part for me to have an ordinary upbringing. We climbed trees, we ran up and down the alley, and had a gang of kids who built forts and stuff." Kerry also recalled "another ordinary family thing" about the Kellys: their many pets. "We had a lot of dogs and cats and fish and hamsters, a horned toad and god knows what. . . . We had a lot of pets! [Our] cats . . . started having babies and they kind of took over my playhouse in the backyard. . . . We gave them to some of the neighborhood kids."[45]

Gene passed on his love for reading and culture to Kerry as well. He told her stories of his own invention each night, which he made either frightening or romantic, depending on the girl's mood. They maintained their nightly reading of the encyclopedia, but now that Kerry was older, Gene and Betsy took her on educational field trips. "My parents took me to a lot of museums and historical places. . . . I really enjoyed [doing] that stuff together, but, you know, sometimes I thought it went on a bit long," Kerry said with a chuckle. Added to outdoor sports such as roller-skating, bike riding, camping, and skiing, Kerry summarized the activities she did with her parents as a "pretty well-rounded set."[46]

Gene's insistence on keeping Kerry and Betsy safe from the prying eyes of columnists grew in the wake of his elevated success. In a revealing interview, Gene told journalist Alyce Canfield that he was now "more of a recluse. I notice that I sometimes dodge public eating places. . . . My life is out of my hands. The moment you step out of the house . . . you're public property."[47] Ben Novick, Gene's grandson, reflected that Gene "resented the fact that the public, perhaps understandably, portrayed him or saw him only through his roles."[48] Most reviewers assumed that the extroverted personality he projected into his roles was his own. Asked what acting method he used, Gene simply replied that he pretended to be as much like his character as possible. Thus, the conception that he was the same person onscreen as he was off was in truth a testament to his remarkable ability to make his characterizations believable. The extroverted, dominant behavior Gene often displayed at house parties or at MGM was possibly his way of denying his shyness or the feelings of inadequacy that he dealt with through his work.

Betsy, unlike her husband, enjoyed getting out of the house. Her social activities kept her away from home a great deal. Her friendship with screenwriter/actress Salka Viertel had intensified; Betsy explained that, having "withdrawn from the volleyball games [at the Kelly parties], I was free to jump in my car and spend the afternoon at what I was sure was the most fascinating place in the world [Salka's home]. Sometimes Kerry would come with me, but mostly she chose the fun of [Salka's] backyard."[49] At Salka's home, Betsy found an ideal outlet for her interest in socialism and enjoyed innocent flirtations with Salka's guests, including playwright and poet Bertolt Brecht.

Gene accepted Betsy's increasingly independent life outside the home, although it made him uneasy. But having witnessed the dissolution of Jeanne Coyne and Stanley Donen's union, he put more effort into keeping his family together—even if it meant resigning himself to the fact that Betsy's outside interests at times outweighed her domestic ones.

The root of the problem in the Donen-Coyne marriage was Donen's immaturity and callousness, characteristics also evident in his behavior with colleagues at MGM. He eventually married four times, admitting that his motto may as well have been "Eat, drink, and re-marry." Jeanne later called her years with Donen the "black spot of her life."[50] In an article

Harriet Kelly with (*left to right*) two-year-old Gene, Harriet Joan, baby Louise, and James Jr. in 1914. (Courtesy of the Everett Collection.)

Youngsters James Jr., Gene, and Fred Kelly don police uniforms for a local neighborhood revue, 1922. (Courtesy of the Everett Collection.)

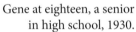

Gene at eighteen, a senior in high school, 1930.

Gene the college graduate, 1933. (Courtesy of the Everett Collection.)

Gene as Harry the Hoofer in William Saroyan's *The Time of Your Life*, 1939. (Courtesy of Photofest.)

The program for *Pal Joey,* 1940, Gene's breakthrough show on Broadway.

Gene with another future MGM star, Van Johnson, and a chorus girl in *Pal Joey.* (Courtesy of Photofest.)

Gene in an early publicity shot for MGM, 1942. The caption calls him a "male magnet." (Courtesy of Media History Digital Library.)

Gene hoofing with Judy Garland in his first film, *For Me and My Gal*, 1942.

Gene and Judy Garland performing the lively "Ballin' the Jack" in *For Me and My Gal*.

Gene and
Betsy Blair;
inset, Gene and
newborn daughter,
Kerry, 1942.
(Courtesy of
Media History
Digital Library.)

A debonair profile shot
of Gene, 1943. (Courtesy
of Media History Digital
Library.)

Gene in his first stand-out
solo, the "mop dance," in
Thousands Cheer, 1943.
(Courtesy of Photofest.)

Gene showing off one of his trademark moves, bouncing across the stage on the balls of his hands (while wearing a tuxedo, no less), in *Du Barry Was a Lady*, 1943.

Gene dancing with Rita Hayworth to the emotive "Long Ago and Far Away" in Columbia's *Cover Girl*, 1944.

Gene's famed
double-exposure
"Alter Ego"
dance routine
in *Cover Girl*.

Gene, Phil Silvers, and Rita Hayworth making use of props to the tune of "Make Way for Tomorrow" in *Cover Girl*.

Advertisement for *Anchors Aweigh*, 1945. (Courtesy of Media History Digital Library.)

Gene singing "The Worry Song" to Jerry the Mouse in *Anchors Aweigh*.

Betsy, Gene, and their two-year-old daughter, Kerry, in a series of publicity photos, 1944. (Courtesy of Media History Digital Library.)

Gene begs rides from pals to save gas, but whips out the convertible for those Thurs. eve baseball sprees with the Garfield, Barry Sullivan gang.

Gene and close friend Danny Kaye at a rally for President Harry Truman, 1945. (Courtesy of Media History Digital Library.)

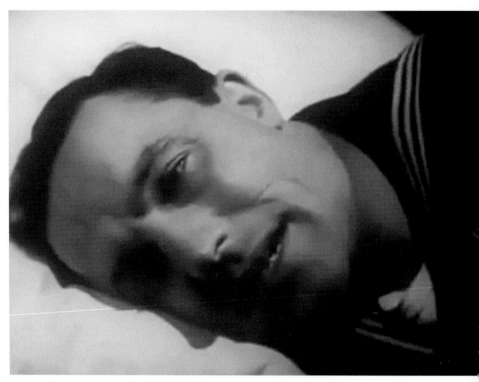

Gene in his pioneering short film for the US Navy addressing post-traumatic stress disorder, *Combat Fatigue Irritability*, 1945.

Gene with Betsy during his service in the US Navy, 1945. (Courtesy of Media History Digital Library.)

Left, I
husban
above,

The screen's masters of dance, Gene Kelly and Fred Astaire, performing "The Babbitt and the Bromide" in *Ziegfeld Follies,* 1946. (Courtesy of Jerry Ohlinger's Movie Material Store.)

Gene's home on North Rodeo Drive, where he lived from 1946 until his death in 1996. (Courtesy of Media History Digital Library.)

Gene dancing with a dog to "Fido and Me," a number he choreographed with Stanley Donen for *Living in a Big Way*, 1947.

The neutral walls and beige shag sofas in the living room strikingly set off the carnival painting above the mantel, and the vivid Indian figurines. All the furnishings are interchangeable. The coffee table was cut down from a dining room table.

The Kellys' home was the site of famous and at times raucous house parties. The lower image shows Betsy in the extensive library. (Courtesy of Media History Digital Library.)

Executives of the Conference of Studio Unions and the Screen Actors Guild engage in a telephone conference regarding an impending strike: *from left,* James Skelton, Herbert Sorrell, Ronald Reagan, Edward Arnold, Roy Tindall, George Murphy, and Gene Kelly, October 26, 1946. (Courtesy of the Everett Collection.)

Gene dancing in the
sensual "Nina" routine,
The Pirate.

Gene acting out Judy
Garland's fantasy in the
elaborate "Pirate Ballet"
in *The Pirate*, 1948.

Gene dancing with Harold and Fayard Nicholas in the athletic "Be a Clown" routine, *The Pirate.* (Courtesy of Jerry Ohlinger's Movie Material Store.)

Gene and Judy in their favored "tramp" attire in *The Pirate.*

Gene, Betsy, and Stanley Donen entering Ciro's restaurant, 1947. Gene broke his ankle during a fit of temper on his volleyball court. (Courtesy of the Everett Collection.)

Gene as D'Artagnan in
The Three Musketeers,
1948.

Gene and Vera-Ellen in the controversial "Slaughter on Tenth Avenue" in *Words and Music,* 1948. Notice the "fishbowl" effect of the twenty-eight-millimeter camera lens.

Gene performing "The Hat My Dear Old Father Wore," an Irish-themed tune in which he wears a kelly green hat in *Take Me out to the Ball Game*, 1949.

Gene, Jules Munshin, and Frank Sinatra sing on location in *On the Town,* 1949.

Gene and Vera-Ellen in the "Day in New York Ballet," *On the Town.*

Gene and Kerry skiing in Klosters, Switzerland, Gene's favored vacation resort, 1950. (Courtesy of Media History Digital Library.)

Gene in his favorite solo dance of those he choreographed, *Summer Stock,* 1950. (Courtesy of the Everett Collection.)

Gene dancing atop a table in the rousing "Dig, Brother, Dig" routine in *Summer Stock.* Jeanne Coyne is seated in the front left corner. (Courtesy of Jerry Ohlinger's Movie Material Store.)

Director Charles Walters, Judy Garland, and Gene behind the scenes of *Summer Stock.* (Courtesy of the Everett Collection.)

Gene rehearsing with Leslie Caron on the set of *An American in Paris,* 1951. (Courtesy of Jerry Ohlinger's Movie Material Store.)

Gene with Vincente Minnelli and Leslie Caron between takes of *An American in Paris.* (Courtesy of the Everett Collection.)

Leslie Caron and Gene in the "American in Paris Ballet."

Gene singing "I Got Rhythm" with a group of children in *An American in Paris*.

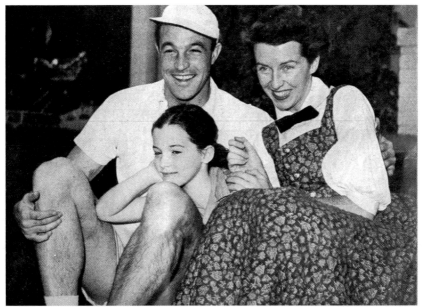

An informal family picture, circa 1951. (Courtesy of Media History Digital Library.)

Gene and Donald O'Connor wreak havoc in the "Moses Supposes" number in *Singin' in the Rain,* 1952. (Courtesy of Photofest.)

Gene in arguably the most iconic number ever i

...llywood musical, "Singin' in the Rain."

Gene and Cyd Charisse in the "Broadway Ballet" in *Singin' in the Rain*.

Donald O'Connor, Debbie Reynolds, and Gene in the "Good Morning" number in *Singin' in the Rain*.

Gene in the climactic sequence to the "Broadway Ballet" in *Singin' in the Rain*. (Courtesy of Jerry Ohlinger's Movie Material Store.)

Gene, the debonair American in London, living abroad in 1952. (Courtesy of Media History Digital Library.)

Gene singing "It's Almost Like Being in Love," a high spot in the ill-fated *Brigadoon*, 1954.

Cyd Charisse, Gene, his choreographic assistant Carol Haney, and producer Arthur Freed on the set of *Brigadoon*. (Courtesy of the Everett Collection.)

Gene at the piano, rehearsing with his brother Fred on the set of *Deep in My Heart,* 1954. (Courtesy of the Everett Collection.)

Michael Kidd, Gene, and Dan Dailey Jr. dancing with garbage can lids on their feet in *It's Always Fair Weather*, 1955. (Courtesy of Jerry Ohlinger's Movie Material Store.)

Gene dancing on roller skates in *It's Always Fair Weather*. (Courtesy of Jerry Ohlinger's Movie Material Store.)

Images from each vignette in Gene's all-dance film, *Invitation to the Dance*, 1956.

Gene directing on the set of *Invitation to the Dance*. The caption reads: "Through films, Gene Kelly is teaching the world to know what dancing can be when it's freed from the bounds of convention." (Courtesy of Media History Digital Library.)

Gene dressed as the tragic clown in *Invitation to the Dance*. (Courtesy of Jerry Ohlinger's Movie Material Store.)

Young French actress Brigitte Fossey at her tenth birthday with Gene on the set of *The Happy Road* in 1956. Hairdresser Jean Clement is cutting her hair for the film. (Courtesy of the Everett Collection.)

Gene (*second from left*) spoofing Marlon Brando in *Les Girls,* 1957. (Courtesy of Jerry Ohlinger's Movie Material Store.)

"*Marjorie Morningstar*"...GENE KELLY · NATALIE WOOD

A lobby card depicting a serious moment between Natalie Wood and Gene in *Marjorie Morningstar*, 1958.

Gene directing Pat Suzuki and Miyoshi Umeki on the set of the Broadway Rodgers and Hammerstein show *Flower Drum Song*, 1958. (Courtesy of Photofest.)

Gene rehearsing with a group of athletes on the set of the television special *Dancing: A Man's Game*, 1958. (Courtesy of Photofest.)

Gene with Jeanne and Kerry, circa 1960. (Courtesy of Media History Digital Library.)

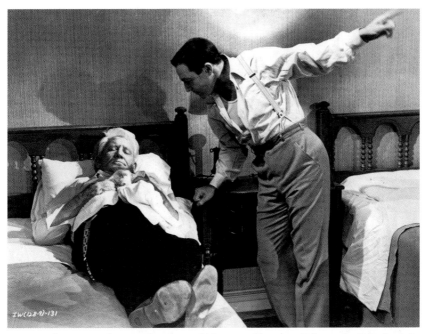

Gene with an actor he greatly admired, Spencer Tracy, in *Inherit the Wind*, 1960. (Courtesy of Jerry Ohlinger's Movie Material Store.)

Gene spoofing an old-style production number with Shirley MacLaine in *What a Way to Go!* 1964.

Gene in his superior television special, *Gene Kelly in New York, New York* in 1966. (Courtesy of Jerry Ohlinger's Movie Material Store.)

Gene demonstrating his dancing skill with a group of French youngsters on the set of *The Young Girls of Rochefort* in 1967.

Gene and Bobby Riha on the album cover of Gene's Emmy Award–winning *Jack and the Beanstalk*, 1967.

Gene with Walter Matthau and Barbra Streisand during a rare moment of fun on the troubled set of *Hello, Dolly!* 1969. (Courtesy of the Everett Collection.)

Gene and Fred Astaire reunite thirty years after their first onscreen pairing to narrate and dance in *That's Entertainment! Part II,* 1976. (Courtesy of Jerry Ohlinger's Movie Material Store.)

A lobby card showing Gene as the has-been actor in *40 Carats,* 1973, wearing a false mustache that Natalie Schafer seems to be examining.

A Fantasy,
A Musical,
A Place
Where Dreams
Come True

XANADU

XANADU

UNIVERSAL Presents A LAWRENCE GORDON Production
OLIVIA NEWTON-JOHN · GENE KELLY · "XANADU" · Also starring MICHAEL BECK
Written by RICHARD CHRISTIAN DANUS and MARC REID RUBEL   Director of Photography VICTOR J. KEMPER, A.S.C.
Songs for OLIVIA NEWTON-JOHN by JOHN FARRAR   Songs for ELECTRIC LIGHT ORCHESTRA by JEFF LYNNE
Musical Scoring by BARRY DeVORZON   Executive Producer LEE KRAMER
Co-Producer JOEL SILVER   Produced by LAWRENCE GORDON   Directed by ROBERT GREENWALD

Gene in a nostalgic number with Olivia Newton-John on a lobby card for *Xanadu*, 1980.

Gene and his third wife, Patricia Ward, in 1990. (Courtesy of Photofest.)

Gene Kelly, eighty-two, in *That's Entertainment! Part III*, 1994, his final film appearance. (Courtesy of Photofest.)

describing the couple's divorce proceedings, one reporter recorded: "Miss Coyne testified that she had wanted a home and children, but that they [she and Donen] only had dinner alone at home about three times during their three-year marriage."[51] The couple separated in December 1949; their divorce was not finalized until 1951.

Gene and Betsy resumed their roles as Jeanne's surrogate parents. They ensured that she drank the ginger ale and cream her doctor prescribed to restore her weight and included her in their yearly trips to Europe. Because he was so close to both Jeanne and Donen, Gene found himself in an uncomfortable position. Both of them were necessary to him in his work, and thus he tried not to let their personal differences interfere with his professional activities. Donen, however, was showing signs that he wished to dissociate himself from Gene. Asked to describe how he and Gene co-directed, Donen replied, "If you substitute the word 'fight' for co-direct, then you have it. It wasn't always like that with Gene, but it gradually came to be that."[52] Donen was delighted when Arthur Freed granted him his first solo directorial project in 1950, *Royal Wedding,* a plum assignment starring Fred Astaire. The film made Donen one of Hollywood's top musical directors, primarily due to its iconic "Dancing on the Ceiling" routine.

Jeanne Coyne also took on more responsibility at MGM. Once she went under contract, she began to act as assistant to many stars during rehearsals. Jeanne was indispensable not only as an assistant but as a source of perspective for Gene. Betsy explained, "Most of the women who worked with Gene seemed to adore him unquestioningly; Jeannie, for all her sweetness, was often rather sharp and curt with him, and would think nothing of deflating him if she thought he needed it."[53] For a man who had difficulty admitting he was wrong, Gene found Jeanne's honesty at once unnerving and refreshing.

Gene especially needed Jeanne's support in his next musical project, which to him was a rather depressing step down. Though he later observed that after *On the Town,* MGM let him do virtually anything he wished, his new picture, *Summer Stock,* was not something he would have chosen. A second-tier film by producer Joe Pasternak, it was a blatant throwback to the dated backstage genre of musical. Simultaneously with *Summer Stock,* the studio assigned him to *The Black Hand.* The picture, though a mere programmer, actually enthused Gene; in fact, he had requested the straight dramatic role after fretting that he had done musicals and light comedies for too long.

Gene applied his customary perfectionism to both forthcoming parts, his restlessness and need for constant mental stimulation propelling him into action. In a 1950 interview, Gene elucidated his passion for his work, no matter if it matched his expectations: "I . . . don't believe anyone is really alive unless he is connected with it [show business] in some way."[54]

After the release of *The Black Hand* in March 1950, a writer for the *Saturday Evening Post* commented that "a number of folk have phoned the Pittsburgh Kellys to say, 'I didn't know that your family was Italian.'"[55] Such assumptions attested to the conviction Gene put into his role in *The Black Hand,* a film that biographer Clive Hirschhorn asserted was not one for which Gene or anyone else involved would be remembered.[56] The picture, set in 1908, cast Gene as Johnny Columbo, an Italian immigrant from New York's Little Italy seeking revenge after his father is murdered by the Mafia. Richard Thorpe directed.

Gene's first concern was whether he could pass as Italian. Jack Dawn, head of makeup, suggested he wear a curly wig. It was not the first time Gene had worn such an item. Since *The Pirate,* he had worn a toupee to cover his thinning hair (a similarity he shared with Fred Astaire; the elder dancer had worn a hairpiece since the early 1940s). Though the wig helped make Gene appear more Mediterranean, his knowledge of both the Italian language and Italian immigrants were what truly aided him in his performance. A journalist visiting the set during rehearsals observed, "He was rattling off Italian dialogue when I entered the set."[57] Gene had picked up much Italian from the owner of his old hometown haunt Bakey's.

The public more readily associated Gene with Ireland rather than Italy, but Kerry asserted that in his personal life, "Irish identity wasn't enormously important for him." His grandson Ben explained that professionally his Irish identity held even less importance. "He wanted to avoid being typecast as a drunk or as comic relief." Though he did not identify himself as an Irishman, in the 1940s and 1950s, Gene did donate money to Ireland as well as other sidelined countries, including Israel. Ben remarked, "He was motivated by . . . helping the underdog."[58]

Whether he played an Irishman or an Italian, Gene's characterizations, as ever, were credible. According to a writer for *Newsweek,* Gene was "as graceful when throwing a knife as when hoofing. . . . [He shows] a dramatic restraint and facial vocabulary that exceed the requirements of either dancer or comedian."[59] Though admirably acted and executed, *The*

Black Hand failed to turn a profit. Budgeted at a mere $774,000, it grossed only $1,210,000. On paper, the picture turned a profit, but MGM actually lost $55,000 on the project due to publicity and other overhead costs.

Audiences still preferred to see Gene sing and dance, which he did plenty of in *Summer Stock*. Gene went into rehearsals for the musical in August 1949 directly after filming wrapped on *The Black Hand*. *Summer Stock* follows the story of a farmer, Jane Falbury (Judy Garland), whose stagestruck sister, Abigail (Gloria DeHaven), invites her theater troupe to put on a show in Jane's barn. When Abigail runs off to New York with her leading man, the show's director, Joe Ross (Gene), persuades Jane to take over her sister's role.

The light musical comedy that Gene thought would be a quick filler between better assignments monopolized almost six months of his life. Though Gene was pleased to be working with old friends like Charles Walters (as director), Saul Chaplin, and Phil Silvers (cast as Gene's comic sidekick), his affection for Judy Garland remained his primary reason for accepting and sticking with the assignment when other cast and crew members began leaving. She had recently suffered another nervous break-down and *Summer Stock* was her last chance to "prove she could function through the grueling shooting schedule of an entire musical." As Saul Chaplin noted: "This was an opportunity for him [Gene] to show his grati-tude. As it turned out, he was really put to the test." Judy, initially certain that she could do the picture without any trouble, fell into the same erratic behavior patterns she had displayed on the set of *The Pirate*. She "obviously could not cope with the daily demands of shooting a film," Chaplin com-mented. "Her absences became more frequent and of longer duration. Gene, who was forced to endure all kinds of inconveniences, never said a word."[60]

Being surrounded by people who believed in her was not enough to make Judy feel prepared for work. Charles Walters explained that during shooting, "together, we [Gene and himself] literally tried to keep her on her feet."[61] If Judy was aware of the pains Gene and Walters took to help her, she felt guilty rather than comforted. During a wrap party that was, oddly, held in the middle of shooting, Judy threw herself into Saul Chaplin's lap, put her head on his shoulder, and began crying uncontrollably "about how ugly and untalented she was."[62]

Pasternak was ready to abandon the film, but Louis B. Mayer stepped in, declaring, "If we stop production now, it'll finish her [Judy]."[63] Gene concurred and encouraged Pasternak to be patient. "I'll do anything for this girl, Joe," he told the producer. "If I have to come here and sit and wait for a year, I'd do it for her."[64] Film critic Pauline Kael later observed that "there was a vulnerability both Gene and Judy brought out in each other and which neither had with anyone else."[65] Indeed, the empathetic Gene that Judy knew and loved was a far cry from the sarcastic, belittling Gene that Esther Williams had known. Lela Simone found it remarkable that Gene and Judy, who, she claimed, were "absolutely impossible temperaments," got along "relatively well." Perhaps this was because both were temperamental, although "in totally different ways."[66]

Walters dealt with Gene's temperament on *Summer Stock* with great diplomacy. Gene rearranged many dance sequences so that he would never be dancing beside Carleton Carpenter, a young and handsome member of the theater troupe who happened to be six foot three. "Gene is quite short, so I went through the entire picture never standing up straight," Carpenter recalled.[67] "Mr. K. didn't like me and was mean to me for [the] entire film. Always with a strange smile! Very odd. Judy loved me."[68] (Nevertheless, Gene admired the young man's talent. Forty years later, Gene came backstage to congratulate Carpenter on his performance in *Crazy for You*.) Walters recalled that Gene and the film's official choreographer, Nick Castle, engaged in such heated arguments that he thought they would come to "fisticuffs." But in the end, Lela Simone asserted, "Kelly did what Kelly wanted."[69]

Gene was not always in an argumentative mood. During Judy's frequent absences, he kept busy organizing brisk games of basketball in the rehearsal hall or concocting ideas for a solo dance. The solo he eventually produced saved the picture from being what he termed "a piece of crap."[70] As was his custom, Gene created a dance inspired by the environment in which it takes place (a barn). He employed a squeaky floorboard as a basis for his rhythm. Then, he stepped on an old newspaper and experimented with the sounds it made. The number grew in complexity when Gene noticed that the newspaper he used did not tear easily and could not be synchronized with his dance steps. He became obsessed with finding just the right consistency of paper and spent hours on his quest. "We found one year [of newspaper] that was perfect and we sent the poor prop man around town looking for something like 1935 copies of the *L.A. Times*. . . . They thought we were crazy," Gene recalled with a grin.[71]

Kerry Kelly explained the ingenuity behind her father's routine: "He would make music out of objects and space. . . . It was weeks and weeks of experimenting . . . to make it work . . . [but] all that behind the scenes work [made it look] fortuitous and easy."[72] Like the "Day in New York Ballet" and the "Alter Ego" sequence, the "squeaky floor" routine ended quietly with Gene as a lone, lit figure. A prime example of cinedance, the number would lose all effectiveness if performed on the stage not only because of its subtle use of sound but also because of its camera angles. From the back row of a theater, no one would be able to see Gene dividing newspapers into smaller and smaller squares with his dancing feet. Years hence, Gene chose the dance as his favorite of all his solo routines.

The part of Joe Ross in *Summer Stock* proved to be superior in more areas than dance. It gave Gene an opportunity to play a character with a job that mirrored his own. As dance director of his company, he puts his troupe through grueling rehearsals—demanding perfection even if it takes all night. In one scene, viewers can see hints of Gene the notorious task-master. "Your job is to do what I tell you and do it right for a change. . . . You're gonna buckle down and get to work like everybody else. You're gonna play it the way I want it if I have to drag a performance out of you with my two hands!" Joe yells at a whining Abigail.[73]

Composer André Previn described the real-life Gene as a man almost identical to Joe Ross: "I don't think it ever occurred to him that he was wrong."[74] However, Joe and Gene were not without their tender sides. Before a nervous Jane goes onstage for opening night, Joe is much like Gene in his treatment of Jane/Judy. He rubs her feet, gives her a bouquet of wildflowers, and softly says: "Remember, if you get nervous, I'll be there right by you . . . every second."[75]

Gene's soft side was also apparent in his generosity to Jeanne Coyne. Still in a fragile emotional state after her separation from Donen, Jeanne found welcome diversion as Gene's assistant and an extra in the film. She is present in almost every scene in which Joe's troupe is featured. Always clad in either rehearsal shorts or a pair of denim pedal pushers, she is seldom far from Gene. He even takes her on his left arm during "Dig Brother Dig" (the film's obligatory teamwork number).

After the principal photography was completed in spring 1950, Judy Garland left Hollywood for a vacation in the rarefied resort town of Carmel, California. Under the guidance of a holistic healer, she took a rest cure at a spa and after only three weeks had shed twenty-five pounds. Her miraculous transformation coincided with the creation of what became one of her most iconic numbers, "Get Happy." Vincente Minnelli suggested that for the number Judy dress in a black tuxedo jacket, a man's fedora tipped over one eye, and black nylon stockings. The number was a smash.

In spite of the film's old-fashioned story line, Gene's and Judy's irrepressible screen presences and the film's above-average dance routines made *Summer Stock* surprisingly successful among both critics and audiences. Upon its premiere on August 31, 1950, Bosley Crowther claimed that Gene's squeaky board dance was the "best spot in the show" aside from Judy's "Get Happy," calling the dance "a memorable exhibition of his beautifully disciplined style."[76] Budgeted at $2,025,000, the picture grossed $3,357,000, but overhead costs resulted in an $80,000 loss.

Sadly, *Summer Stock* was Judy's last film for Metro. "They [at the studio] loved her and they wanted her to be happy, to be able to go on to bigger, greater things [so they severed her contract]," Joe Pasternak wrote. "And she did go on, and her appeal has become even more universal."[77] Gene and Judy's relationship had come full circle; she had seen him through his first film at MGM, and he had seen her through her last. Judy's marriage to Vincente Minnelli ended shortly after her break with the studio. For the next four years, she found a new beginning through her record-breaking concert tours at such prestigious venues as New York's Palace Theatre and London's Palladium.

Gene, too, went on to greater things. His next assignment put him under Vincente Minnelli's direction for the third time in his career. The picture, a Technicolor Arthur Freed production entitled *An American in Paris*, boasted a full George and Ira Gershwin score and an original screenplay by the young writer and lyricist Alan Jay Lerner. Lerner had won acclaim as the writer and lyricist of the 1946 Broadway hit *Brigadoon*.

The promise of his new screen project reinvigorated Gene and he approached the assignment with as much, if not more, excitement than *On the Town*. He explained to biographer Clive Hirschhorn: "I combined the energy I still had with an intelligence and an awareness of my capabilities that I certainly could not have had when younger. . . . Not only did I know exactly what I was striving for in pictures, but I felt that I now knew how to achieve it. . . . I can only be grateful that when I finally matured as an artist . . . I had the physical stamina to explore my ideas to their fullest."[78] Gene saw *An American in Paris* as his opportunity to achieve the level of perfection he had been seeking for nearly a decade in Hollywood.

14

Who Could Ask for Anything More?

In 1950, Gene fell in love, a passion akin only to "art or faith; it can't be explained, only felt."[1] The object of Gene's ardor was a locale synonymous with love: Paris. Gene's words could not have been more eloquent had they been penned by Alan Jay Lerner himself as part of the screenplay for *An American in Paris*.

Klosters, Switzerland, had been the Kellys' only intimate experience with Europe before 1950. Gene and Betsy had seen Paris only briefly when they had attended a ballet two years before. In 1950, they finally took the grand tour of Europe. Betsy reminisced: "We were out for culture and history. We weren't corny enough to say it out loud, but that's what we were doing." The couple went on their tour alone, leaving Kerry with Betsy's mother in New Jersey. They sailed from New York on the *Queen Mary*, bound for Southampton. Among the sites on their itinerary were the Stratford Theatre in London and the city's bombed-out East End. Then came Paris. Gene "adored Paris and learning French and learning French songs," Kerry later reminisced. Betsy fancied the city just as much as her husband. "It is now, has been, and always will be the most beautiful, romantic place in the world. . . . We knew we'd come back often."[2]

In Italy, the couple admired the beauty of Venice and Rome. Gene and Betsy were both surprised by the class disparity they witnessed: less than a mile from the pope's opulent summer residence, Castle Gondolfo, the people in the surrounding countryside lived in poverty. Gene had witnessed similar excess in the Catholic Church during his trips to Mexico in the late 1930s. Indeed, the disparity was what had led him to embrace atheism in college. Still, Gene claimed that his mother would never forgive him if he went to Rome without seeing Pope Pius XII and obtaining a medal for her blessed by His Holiness. Betsy could hardly conceal her disdain. She recalled, "Good little Marxist that I was, the Pope himself represented the enemy." When the pope blessed a silver medal for Kerry, it gave Betsy pause and she found herself thinking: "If I am wrong about everything [her political ideologies], at least Kerry will be okay."[3]

The pope and Gene shared a genial conversation while Betsy stood back, medal in hand.

"I understand you are an actor and dancer and you bring happiness to people in your work. For that, heaven awaits you."

"Thank you, your Holiness," Gene replied and went on, "I think a friend of mine came to see you last year. Frank Sinatra."

The pope gave him a blank stare, at which point a cardinal whispered, "He's a singer."

"Yes, my son. I love the opera," the pope replied obliviously.

Before leaving the castle, Gene bought a medal for his mother, murmuring to Betsy that she would never know the pope had not actually blessed it. "I wasn't about to give up Kerry's," Betsy concluded.[4]

Although Gene was not a regular churchgoer, both Betsy and Kerry emphasized that he lived his life free of scandal and upheld moral and ethical convictions. "He felt very deeply and strongly about women and children . . . and for anything that was threatening to them . . . he would be very fierce about," Kerry explained in 2015.[5]

Gene and Betsy's trip was all too brief, for Gene had to return to Hollywood to fulfill two minor obligations. He had agreed to make a cameo appearance in Stanley Donen's second solo screen project, *Love Is Better Than Ever*. Gene also served as advisor for sequences in the film set at a dancing school. The picture went into production in December 1950 but was not released until March 1952. The lightweight romantic comedy starred a teenage Elizabeth Taylor, with whom Stanley Donen allegedly had an affair during filming, though his and Jeanne Coyne's divorce was not yet final. In Gene's cameo, he runs into Taylor and her beau (Larry Parks) at the restaurant 21 and patiently listens as Parks brags about Taylor, proclaiming her to be the best dancing teacher in New England. Unfortunately, Gene's cameo did little to boost the film's popularity at the box office. It lost $362,000.

Next, Gene appeared in *It's a Big Country: An American Anthology* (filmed from April to September 1950). The patriotic film, a series of eight unrelated stories, was designed to showcase the diversity of the nation.

Boasting a star-studded cast including Gary Cooper, Ethel Barrymore, and Van Johnson, the ambitious film was marred by a weak script and flawed execution. Gene's "chapter" in the film, "Rosita, the Rose," placed him in the role of a breezy young Greek named Icarus Xenaphon. He has a long-standing dislike of Hungarians until he falls in love with Rosa (Janet Leigh), the daughter of a Hungarian shopkeeper. As Rosa's little sister was Sharon McManus, who had so memorably danced with Gene in *Anchors Aweigh*. However, even the considerable talents of Gene, Janet, and Sharon could not make the tale of love triumphing over prejudice effective. The film was a major financial disaster, grossing only $655,000 when it had cost $1,013,000 to produce.

Gene, because he had no creative influence over *Love Is Better Than Ever* or *It's a Big Country*, easily put their failures behind him. His only thought now was how best to pour his newfound love of Paris into the production awaiting him.

From its inception, an unparalleled amount of creativity, innovation, and camaraderie infused *An American in Paris*. The idea for the picture came about during one of the many evenings Arthur Freed spent dining with Lee and Ira Gershwin. Over dessert, Freed asked Ira if he would sell him the title "An American in Paris." "I'll sell it to you under one condition—the picture uses only Gershwin music," Ira replied. Freed readily agreed. Very early in the project's evolution, Freed considered it as a vehicle for Fred Astaire, but after formulating a plot around which to center Gershwin's music, Gene Kelly emerged as the more appropriate candidate.

The story, about a former American GI turned painter, was a concept for which both Freed and Gene Kelly took credit. The two men had read the same article in *Life* magazine detailing the lives of painter-soldiers living in Paris to study art, thanks to funds from the GI Bill of Rights. Alan Jay Lerner, with Gene's personality and sex appeal in mind, added much-needed romantic elements and intrigue to the story line. As he explained, he decided to write of "a kept man [who] falls in love with a kept woman."[6]

The film tells the story of Jerry Mulligan (Gene), who, after years as a struggling artist in Paris, finds a patron in the person of wealthy heiress Milo Anderson. She is interested in him for more than his art and proceeds to buy him a private studio. In short, she plans his life for him. Jerry has other ideas. He falls in love with a young shopgirl, Lise, who happens to be engaged to his friend Henri, a popular musical performer. Inevitably,

Henri discovers Lise and Jerry's love for one another and gives them his blessing. Milo is left crushed and without a struggling artist to indulge. An objective observer of all the drama in the film is Jerry's confidant, Adam Cook, who dubs himself the world's "oldest child prodigy" on the piano.

Gene was ecstatic to resume his fruitful professional relationship with Vincente Minnelli. He also found a new friend in Alan Jay Lerner, whom Minnelli deemed "an artist with none of the artist's pretensions."[7]

The film, because it was directed by Minnelli, was more dreamlike and subtle than Gene's cocksure, literal execution of On the Town. Gene had hoped to film on location, but the mayor of Paris as well as the city council imposed so many restrictions that shooting would have been impossible. Minnelli biographer Stephen Harvey considered it a blessing in disguise that the picture was filmed instead on the MGM lot. "Had they [the film's creative team] been bound to the notion of dancing through a succession of Parisian parks and boulevards, the result might well have been . . . a kind of On the Town in berets. Instead, the need to conjure up a dream Paris with lights and canvas prompted a far bolder leap of the imagination."[8]

As imaginative as the picture promised to be, Minnelli realized it had to be approached as a commercial entertainment free of the pretensions that marred Yolanda and the Thief and The Pirate. But being commercial did not mean the film lacked ingenuity—or talent. Those engaged for the picture so far were only the best. They included Johnny Green (head of MGM's music department), Conrad Salinger and Saul Chaplin (both musical arrangers), Irene Sharaff (as costumer for the dance sequences), and Jeanne Coyne and Carol Haney as Gene's choreographic aides.

Though casting posed some challenges, Minnelli had only one man in mind to play Adam: Oscar Levant. Levant, the foremost player of Gershwin songs in America and one of Gershwin's closest friends, "lent the enterprise a sort of legitimacy."[9] According to Arthur Freed's assistant Lela Simone, Minnelli and Freed "adored Oscar. . . . [Freed] absolutely worshipped Levant and vastly exaggerated his talent." Simone claimed that Freed paid for Levant to live in a mansion in Beverly Hills with three servants on the premises.[10] Minnelli called Levant "a sponger of the first order . . . and the second and the third."[11]

The rest of the cast members were newcomers to the Freed Unit. Cool blond Nina Foch was placed in the role of Milo, winning the part over Oscar nominee Celeste Holm. Minnelli had originally envisioned Maurice Chevalier as Henri. When the actor proved to be unavailable, suave French entertainer Georges Guetary, younger and far more believable as Lise's fiancé, was cast.

For the role of Lise, Gene made one thing clear: he wanted a genuine French girl. Freed tried to persuade him to accept either Cyd Charisse or Vera-Ellen, but Gene was adamant. He already had one dancer in mind as his leading lady: Leslie Caron. He had first seen her two years before when he and Betsy had attended the Ballets des Champs-Élysées. As casting was under way, he flew to Paris and arranged a meeting with her at the Hotel Plaza Athénée. "He was gentle and respectful and spoke of doing a film test," Leslie later wrote.[12] Of Gene's choice, Lela Simone said: "Leslie is not exactly a beauty, you know? . . . But [for the ballet technique needed in the film], she knew a great deal . . . and was able to do that very well." Aside from her ballet training, the nineteen-year-old's broken English and hesitant manner perfectly suited the shy, unassuming girl Lerner had characterized in his script. Simone remarked that Gene often preferred working with beginners whose looks and abilities did not detract from his own. "[He] shied away successfully not to get into people who were shining above him. He never sought after a star."[13] Simone's observation is consistent with Gene's pattern of working best with young and impressionable female partners. Though his previous leading ladies Kathryn Grayson and Esther Williams had been ten years his junior, both were their own bosses; they did not need, nor did they want, Gene as their supervisor. Leslie Caron, nineteen years younger than Gene and completely new to America and films, did not balk at Gene's guidance.

By the time Leslie received a phone call from MGM, she had all but forgotten about the screen test she had made the year before. She still had her heart set on a classical ballet career. But she could not turn down an offer from Hollywood's greatest studio. When she agreed to play Lise, however, she was not signed to a long-term contract. As Leslie packed her trunks for America, her mother gave her a bit of parting advice: "Be careful they don't put you in a sarong . . . and whatever you do, don't marry Mickey Rooney!"[14]

Leslie's mother need not have worried; Mickey Rooney was no longer a member of the Freed Unit. Gene Kelly and Fred Astaire were now the definitive actors of the group, and Leslie ultimately found herself dancing with them both by the decade's end. She entered the Freed Unit at an ideal time; by 1950, the group had hit its stride after the monumental successes of *Easter Parade* and *On the Town*. "There was nothing in the phone book that said 'Freed Unit,'" Stanley Donen explained in 1982. "The Unit was a myth created by the fact that he had brought these people to the studio more or less. . . . All worked with him more than anyone else, so we just seemed to be a unit. . . . [Other] producers . . . were all envious of Freed. . . . He WAS a god, with the sort of power he accumulated."[15]

The unit's table in the MGM lunchroom was an object of both awe and scorn among those at the studio who worked outside what Freed termed his "own little Camelot." Johnny Green elaborated: "We were the laughingest bunch of people in Hollywood. . . . We were so loud and raucous and behaved as if we owned the place that a lot of people couldn't stand us. . . . The Freed boys and girls weren't liked. Talent frightens people . . . but all we were doing was making MGM money."[16]

What was the secret of the Freed Unit's success? Gene mused, "I think we liked working together and I think we did have camaraderie. But everything wasn't easy. We always had to deal with the different personalities and creative instincts of each individual, but we sat down and talked everything out."[17] Johnny Green concluded, "Those years with Arthur Freed were among the richest of our lives."[18]

Americans in 1950 needed the lighthearted yet intelligent products Freed offered. The early 1950s bore little resemblance to the latter half of the decade which, in contrast, was characterized by "a glow of a new optimism and unprecedented prosperity." According to the authors of Time-Life's *The American Dream: The 50s*, "The escalating Cold War with the Soviet Union cast such deep shadows that some Americans considered 1950 the darkest time since early World War II."[19] When Communist North Korea declared war on South Korea in June 1950, President Harry S. Truman sent in troops and approved the development of a superbomb designed to be far more destructive than the atomic bomb.

But in spite of its dark political climate, America was nonetheless a nation to be envied in 1950. The country was entering the beginning of its consumer culture and was still experiencing the baby boom that had begun in 1943. Suburban living continued to grow—and that equaled a continual rise in television sets as well. Stories reminiscent of those unfolded in the Andy Hardy series found a new audience thanks to TV. Called "situation comedies," they were popularized by such shows as *I Love Lucy* (1951) and *The Adventures of Ozzie and Harriet* (1952).

As much as the Freed Unit's musicals promised to fulfill the average American's wishes, the group still faced numerous obstacles in producing universally appealing products. Youths in particular presented a problem. The rise of a new type of idol, the antihero, crashed into pop culture with passionate intensity. Montgomery Clift in *A Place in the Sun* (1951) and Marlon Brando in *A Streetcar Named Desire* (1951) were just two early antiheroes. Brando and Clift subscribed to the Stanislavsky or "Method" style of acting and *became* the characters they portrayed. Musical stars at MGM knew they were acting in a land of Technicolor make-believe; Method actors mimicked the harshness of the real world.

But what about Gene Kelly? He professed to become as much like the characters in his films as he could. He immersed himself in the character of Jerry Mulligan. In preparation for his role, he took daily painting lessons (often using Oscar Levant as a model). He already dressed more or less like the starving artist he was portraying; his entire clothing budget for the picture totaled $50. Gene certainly held a special place in the film world: he was the musical antihero. However, according to Kerry, no matter how convincing he was in his roles, he never lost sight of the fact that he was pretending. "I think that's a false assumption about actors," she observed, that they are like "the characters they portray."[20]

An American in Paris had the potential to be that rare work of cinema to appeal to Americans of all ages in all regions of the country. Gene as leading man and a teenage girl as leading lady would attract younger people while older Americans would relate to the Gershwin score on a nostalgic level.

An American in Paris was finally ready to begin filming on August 1, 1950—but not before it experienced a few hiccups.

On her first day in Hollywood, Leslie Caron's first stop was not MGM but a gathering in Gene's backyard. She recalled in her memoir: "Gene and Betsy Kelly offered the warmth of a . . . dinner at home, *en famille* with their daughter, Kerry. 'She's brighter than you,'" Gene teased Leslie.[21]

Gene was jesting. In truth, Leslie had passed his test for admission into his home, for she possessed talent and intelligence. Though Lela Simone claimed that the Freed Unit had initially approached Leslie with the attitude of "well, let's hope for the best," everyone soon recognized Leslie's remarkable dancing skill.[22]

However, she made a serious faux pas on the first day of rehearsals. Leslie told Sidney Guilaroff, Metro's head hairdresser, that she wanted a "modern French girl's hairdo, short as a boy's and straight." He did not understand her meaning, so she took up a scissors and cut her hair herself. Leslie recalled the frenzied scene that ensued: "Everything stopped . . . until the executive hierarchy could be summoned. There were frantic phone calls. . . . I found myself back against the outside wall of the building, facing the firing squad." "They fire girls for less than that, you know," Gene told her.[23]

Arthur Freed sent Leslie home, and plans for filming had to be rearranged for the next three weeks to allow her hair to grow. Leslie did not regret shearing her hair; she reasoned that she was ahead of her time. Audrey Hepburn and Shirley MacLaine made that look fashionable a few years later in *Roman Holiday* (1954) and *The Trouble with Harry* (1955).

When she returned to MGM, Gene, to familiarize her with his style, showed her a forty-five-minute montage of dances he had choreographed at MGM "performed with cocky charm and apparent facility."

"What tremendous fun you must have had!" Leslie exclaimed.

"Fun?" he retorted. He then gave her five minutes "of dressing-down as he pointed out the hard work all this represented."[24]

Gene could be abrupt with the young dancers he trained to be his partners, but he also knew when to praise them. Leslie described his way of working: "He had a sense of fair play and would indicate in measured tones his approval. . . . His rebukes were feared by one and all in the studio. . . . Although he was very encouraging, I could lose my confidence in front of him." Leslie fast discovered that Gene's lectures were born not from anger but tough love. "Gene guided me in front of the camera with patience and good humor," she explained. "I spoke my first lines phonetically. He would say to me, 'Lester'—that was his affectionate nickname for me, 'Lester, de pester'—. . . 'if you want your grandmother to see you in this scene, you'd better turn toward the camera to speak your line.'" Leslie, accustomed to the presence of an audience when she performed, felt the camera was cold and thus could not act convincingly before it. Eventually, she solved the problem by playing to the director, Vincente Minnelli, who was always sitting under the camera. Despite his notorious inarticulateness when giving direction, Leslie claimed that she understood him. "There was a quality in him that pushed you to surpass yourself in order to surprise him."[25]

The atmosphere on the set became a familial one after the cast and crew overcame their initial hurdles. Leslie wrote in her memoir: "Gene Kelly, who kept his car in front of his bungalow, very democratically walked to and from rehearsals. . . . He was saluted with familiarity by one and all: 'Hi Geno, how ya doin'? See ya!' He wore the same kind of informal clothes every day . . . and on his head, what was then called a beanie—a baseball cap to cover his baldness."[26]

More bumps arose as production went on. This time they involved Oscar Levant. From the beginning of the filming, his dejected expression had been more pronounced than usual. He felt certain that Gene would not support his idea about including a concerto sequence in the movie. He had performed two in his previous film for Freed, *The Barkleys of Broadway* (1949), but Freed had different ideas for *An American in Paris*. "We won't have any concert music. I don't want any lulls in this picture," Freed decreed, a declaration Levant felt was "directed at me."[27]

Freed's none too subtle comment did not stop Levant from pitching his idea to Gene and Minnelli: he would perform Gershwin's "Concerto in F" for what he termed an "ego fantasy." In Levant's number, Adam would play all the instruments in the orchestra and act as the conductor. To top it off, everyone in the audience would be a twin of himself, cheering him on with endless calls of "Bravo!" Gene and Minnelli, to Levant's surprise, consented.

Gene may have been a supporter of Levant's "ego fantasy," but their egos clashed when it came to another number, "By Strauss." A comical sequence devised by Gene, it centered on Jerry waltzing through the bistro he and his friends patronize each morning. There is a piano in the establishment, which Adam commandeers. Gene puts a checked napkin over his head, pretending to be a Parisian belle as Henri serenades him. Jerry then drops his clowning and does a dainty waltz with the old woman who runs the bistro. Minnelli later wrote of Gene's interpretation of the number: "He's one of the rare people who can get away with such cute touches."[28] Levant, who concurred that Gene was "not averse to a good dose of corn now and then," asked Jack Cole, the famed dancer and choreographer, how he liked the choreography in the picture. Cole replied, "rather bitterly," "With old women and children, how can you miss?"[29] Levant had his own reason to be bitter about the number. As Saul Chaplin explained, Levant wished to play "By Strauss" as "a true Viennese waltz with all its hesitations and accents. Gene objected. It didn't fit what he had in mind. What started as a normal discussion soon turned into a shouting match with Gene threatening to hit Oscar, who threatened to sue Gene if he did. Now it seems quite laughable, but not then." Though Levant stormed out of the rehearsal, he came back the next day as if nothing had happened. "What is surprising," Chaplin concluded, "is that neither of them won or lost the argument. From then on, they were friends and the incident was never mentioned again."[30]

Gene tried to avoid arguments on the set because they impeded the collaboration necessary to create the film. And he certainly spoke on behalf of the entire cast and crew when he stated that he hoped audiences would find the film to be a fresh and distinctive musical.

The moment the film begins, one can almost taste its freshness. The opening character introductions are executed with a twist, adopting the "subjective camera" technique used to much acclaim in noir films like *Dark Passage* (1947) and *Lady in the Lake* (1947). The camera acts alternately as the eyes of Adam, Henri, and Jerry, yet the actors do not remain invisible behind the lens. Rather, they observe themselves and narrate their doings. The "subjective camera" technique ends as Henri and Adam meet for breakfast. Henri is unusually cheerful because he is in love with Lise, whom he describes variously as exciting, sweet, shy, bookish, and vivacious. "Look, let's start all over again, shall we? What's she like?" a frustrated Adam asks.[31]

Throughout their exchange, viewers watch a series of vignettes portraying Lise in each persona. "Embraceable You" provides the background music, changing in tempo and mood with each scene change. She is shown as a flapper, a ballerina, a beatnik, and a vamp. The entire sequence is like the sophisticated older sister of the "Miss Turnstiles Ballet" in *On the Town*. The earlier ballet did not employ the saturated colors or the creative interpolation of the same tune throughout, nor did its closing shot take on the form of a puzzle with each piece showing an alternate personality.

Leslie Caron had not realized how demanding working on the picture would be. Coming from a background of classical ballet, she had assumed that a light Hollywood film would be easy in comparison. When the physical pressure of filming plus a strict diet caused Leslie to become sick with anemia and mononucleosis, Gene turned from taskmaster to father figure. Lela Simone's interpretation of Gene's kindness was not flattering. A good director has to excel at "handling unsure new people," but Gene was "very often not good" at this—however, she remarked sardonically, "if a young actress had talent and technique and falls in love with him, she has it made."[32]

Leslie may not have been in love with Gene, but she did possess the talent and technique required to win his favor and, at times, leniency. "Gene was my defender, he'd say to me: 'If you're too ill just tell me and stand by me, and I'll say you're too ill, and we will collect insurance and go off one day, and you can lie in bed all day and rest up.'" With Leslie, as with Judy Garland, Gene displayed an empathy that he did not allow everyone. Leslie "thanked God" for the aid of Carol Haney and Jeanne Coyne, with whom she did most of her rehearsing.[33]

Minnelli was, for the most part, equally understanding. He was known for his ability to calm even the most frayed of actors by taking them aside and whispering comforting words. Still, a number of his colleagues wondered if his concern was genuine. Gene's empathy, if given, was always sincere. He was not afraid to blow up at people; consequently, they seldom questioned where they stood with him. "He was dictatorial but in a nice way," Leslie explained.[34] Minnelli, on the other hand, would just purse his lips and keep his feelings to himself.

Though Minnelli's dominance was less obvious than Gene's, Leslie Caron aptly summarized his crucial contribution to the picture: "He could express poignancy in dramatic situations but was never cloying and he always respected the limits of elegance."[35] The most dramatic, albeit low-key, musical number in the picture takes place during Jerry and Lise's first date along the Seine. With elegance and simplicity in perfect tandem, Jerry gives Lise a single red flower and begins to sing "Our Love Is Here to Stay." Their languorous dance is so natural that their balletic movements seem merely an extension of walking. Leslie Caron recalled only one thing that made the filming of the sequence unpleasant: "The water [used to imitate the Seine] was becoming very stagnant—it smelled moldy—but once the lights were on . . . and Gene was singing and we were dancing . . . it was very tender and a moment of great closeness."[36]

In addition to touches of elegance, Minnelli lent the other numbers "what I call the great Hollywood sense of humor, which was in fact a blend of Hollywood and New York humor," Leslie said.[37] Minnelli used Levant to embody this humor; Levant, with his "curiously sad charm," acts as the film's moderator in two of the film's "cute" numbers, "Tra La La La" and "S'Wonderful."[38] In the former routine, Jerry enters Adam's apartment singing: "This time it's really love, tra la la la." Adam brings him down to earth, bellowing in a baritone, "To me you're full of bla bla bla!" During the latter number, Jerry and Henri both torture Adam with dreamy-eyed declarations of love, crooning how wonderful it is that "she should care for me." Adam, who has not informed them they love the same woman, sits between the men with a look of doom on his droopy face that is in comic juxtaposition to the toothy grins of his friends.

The routine most reflective of Gene, "I Got Rhythm," could have been condemned as saccharine if not for its novel execution. Gene invented a most unexpected approach to the old tune by using it as an English lesson for a group of French children. Jerry points to a child and prompts him or her to say, "I got," after which he sings, "rhythm." His well-known Pied Piper quality was never conveyed more brightly than in this number. Claude and André Guy, two of the children in the routine, recalled: "Gene Kelly wanted children who weren't professional. . . . [He] was terrific. He was so nice to the kids, loved playing with us even off the set. He'd tap dance round us and he would give us candy. He was like sunshine when he came into the studio."[39]

Gene's love for children especially shone through whenever four-year-old Liza Minnelli, the daughter of Vicente Minnelli and Judy Garland, visited the set. Gene became a mentor to Liza in her adolescence, but his affection for her began during the making of *An American in Paris*. Minnelli recounted Gene's rapport with her in his autobiography: "On a previous Halloween I'd had a witch costume designed for Liza. . . . I took her round the neighborhood. 'Will I scare the people?' she asked. 'You'll frighten them to death,' I assured her. . . . We stopped at Gene Kelly's. His was an award-winning performance. 'A witch! A terrible witch! Save me!' Liza walked home with her pointed witch's chin held high."[40]

Liza found another encounter with Gene less pleasant. According to Leslie, one day when she came to visit the set, Gene and Minnelli were "kidding around and pretending to have an argument." Liza started to cry and scream, "Don't fight!" Leslie observed, "She obviously was a very highly strung child who had witnessed scenes that were too emotional for her age." Whether the argument Liza witnessed was truly in jest or real is uncertain. Both men had definite opinions about their art and though "they both allowed for each other's sensibilities," when "Gene [took] over, Minnelli had a way of circumventing opposition and eventually getting his way."[41]

Gene and Minnelli were in sync in their vision for the film's major ballet sequence. After Nina Foch caught chicken pox from one of the youngsters on the set, rather than shoot around her, Gene, Minnelli, and Freed used their time to discuss the ballet in detail. Freed insisted on placing it at the end of the picture because nothing else could top such a production number. Minnelli showed a rough cut of the picture, sans ballet, to Irving Berlin before proceeding. Berlin asked dubiously, "You say you're going to film a seventeen-minute ballet at the end of the picture?" Minnelli nodded. "I hope you fellows know what you're doing," Berlin murmured.[42]

Minnelli, Freed, and Gene received no more encouragement from Betty Comden and Adolph Green. After viewing the same rough cut as Berlin, they were full of accolades.

"Release it now," Comden insisted.

"But the best is yet to come," Minnelli told her.

"Do you really think you need a ballet? I don't," she said.[43]

Berlin, Comden, and Green had a solid foundation on which to base their doubt. In *Yolanda and the Thief,* Freed and Minnelli had included a sixteen-minute fantasy sequence using only the language of dance. The film had failed. But that was five years ago; since that time, the phenomenon of *The Red Shoes* had taken place, not to mention *On the Town.* Thus, Freed, Gene, and Minnelli were unmovable in their conviction to forge ahead with the ballet. Minnelli, Gene, and costumer Irene Sharaff for all intents and purposes lived in Minnelli's office for a week making sketches and plans.

Before long, head of production Dore Schary and other members of the art department joined the group's meetings about the ballet. The noncombatant Minnelli had to "sell them" on the idea or admit defeat—which he was not willing to do. "It's an emotional nightmare which alternates with great moments of joy," he explained. "Then the hero returns to sad reality. He thinks of Lise. He searches for her throughout Paris. He finds her, then loses her again. Paris loses its color and excitement. The ballet doesn't review what's happened in the picture so far like *On the Town.* It shows the hero's inner conflict."[44] Gene offered his own words of persuasion, explaining that their goal, through choreography, was to emulate what French Impressionist painters created through their use of color, light, and form. He insisted that the ballet must re-create the musical mood of Gershwin's "An American in Paris." The ballet should suggest rather than narrate. It was more abstract and Minnellian than concrete and linear, as was Gene's style. This did not mean the ballet lacked Gene's stamp. He planned to keep Leslie's balletic style in the sequence strictly classical in order to accentuate his modern all-American moves.

The man who ultimately convinced Metro's executives to endorse the half-million-dollar experiment was none other than Louis B. Mayer. When Minnelli showed Mayer sketches for the ballet imitative of Toulouse-Lautrec and Edgar Degas works, Mayer declared, beaming, "My daughters will like that." Alan Jay Lerner asserted that Mayer's approval of the ballet "was probably one of the last major picture-making decisions he was to make."[45] Mayer knew that Schary and his New York boss, Nick Schenck, wanted him out of the studio. But as long as he held any power, he was going to advocate for Freed. One wonders if Gene would have revised his opinion of Mayer had he known of the mogul's influence on the inclusion of the pivotal ballet. In 1994, Gene was still declaring he "hated the man. I thought he was bizarre, and he never liked me."[46]

With the ballet approved, Gene, Saul Chaplin, and Minnelli made themselves "thoroughly familiar with every note and nuance of Gershwin's 'An American in Paris.'"[47] Then the group held nightly meetings with Jeanne Coyne and Carol Haney during which they began to match the sections of the music with the painters who had been selected.

The group decided to employ a single red rose as the starting and ending image in the ballet. The ballet begins with Jerry at the annual Beaux Arts Ball—a rowdy but colorless affair at which everyone is dressed in black-and-white harlequin attire. The rose, then, not only symbolizes Jerry's lost love but acts as the springboard for Paris, a "fickle city" drained of color, to come alive.[48]

In Jerry's first reverie, he sees the bustling Place de la Concorde, one of Paris's major public squares, appear in the vibrant style of Raoul Dufy. Jerry appears doing what Freed insisted be a "George M. Cohan strut" that would immediately identify him as American. Jerry attempts to join the crowd but goes unnoticed. Suddenly, Lise appears in the throng. Jerry dodges past cars and people only to find that she has disappeared. The scene then dissolves to the quiet flower market of Madeleine at dawn, executed in the style of Pierre-Auguste Renoir and Édouard Manet. Lise appears, ethereal, and she and Jerry dance together around a fountain bathed in blue light. The scene is more fantasy than reality; Lise is still unattainable. The dance is infused with a feeling of emptiness. Here, Gershwin's haunting instrumental "Blues" plays from a lone trumpet in a style Gene insisted must be "sexy and sensuous."[49]

The stillness of the scene is immediately juxtaposed by the next image, done in the style of Maurice Utrillo, a French painter specializing in bright cityscapes. A group of American servicemen dancing down the street cheers Jerry. He joins them until they come to the Zoological Gardens, styled after Henri Rousseau. Jerry, "purged of sadness and resentment," again finds Lise and they dance together in a carefree manner. Paris pulsates with vibrancy as Jerry's "dream expands." He indulges in fantasies reflecting "temptations that mirror [those in] the plot," including becoming a café singer at the Moulin Rouge. He is dressed in a skin-tight, flesh-colored body suit like one pictured in Toulouse-Lautrec's poster *Chocolat Dancing in Achilles' Bar.* Emanuel Levy claimed that the scene evoked the plot point that money "turns artists into gigolos." In a surreal twist, Lise appears as a provocative can-can dancer as the scene changes to the Place de l'Opéra, shown in the style of Vincent van Gogh. "Their hysteria becomes an orgy of fulfillment when, without warning, the nothingness returns. . . . Color drains out of everything. . . . He's left again, hopeless and alone."[50] Jerry stands with only the red rose in his hand. The camera zooms in close to the bud before he drops it on the ground amid piles of confetti and streamers thrown by the revelers at the ball. Among the only gloomy faces at the party are Milo, Lise, Adam, and Henri, whose paths cross unexpectedly.

The camera shows a trail of cigarette smoke and follows it to the smoker's face (Henri), revealing that he has overheard Lise tell Jerry she loves him but cannot be with him (a confession she made immediately before he falls into his reverie). Jerry looks over the balcony moments later to see Henri's car, which he assumed had left earlier with Lise in tow, pull up downstairs. Henri emerges and kisses Lise good-bye; she runs up the stairs to Jerry. They embrace and walk off together into the night as the camera pans upward to show a panoramic view of Paris.

The original screenplay included a scene to wrap up the stories of Milo and Adam. Immediately before the ballet, the scene showed the two "slightly drunk, feeling sorry for themselves" and suggested "that [Milo] would go on to sponsor him after [Jerry's] defection." In a rare case of poor judgment, Minnelli ordered the scene cut, feeling that it ruined the flow of the film and made Jerry's character less likeable. One critic claimed it was omitted because of Minnelli's devotion to his "morbidly beautiful *mise en scène.* In other words, the unresolved feeling we're left with . . . is an expression of Minnelli's essential melancholy."[51] The lack of closure for Adam and Milo is one of the picture's major weaknesses; the other is the fact that Lise's character is not intriguing enough to convince audiences that Jerry's desire to win her would be so intense. Director Stanley Donen summed it up: "You look at the movie and you just don't care."[52]

Though the screenplay had its flaws, the ballet saved the production from being, as Dore Schary put it, "just a cute and nice musical."[53] The ballet remains the primary reason people still watch *An American in Paris* today, and yet it is not essential to the momentum of the plot. In fact, few of the musical sequences are fully integrated into the story line. Roger Ebert remarked in 1992 that the picture "was essentially a clothesline on which to hang recycled Gershwin songs."[54]

Though no one in 1951 could guess how critics and audiences might react to the picture, Gene and Minnelli had the approval of at least one viewer: Judy Garland. Shortly after the movie completed principal filming in January 1951, Judy caught a preview of it. She put in a call to her ex-husband in spite of the late hour. "Well, I've seen your little picture," she said. "Not bad. Only a masterpiece."[55]

Gene's back-to-back movie projects, as ever, did not impair his active social life. Leslie Caron, now a regular guest at the Kelly house parties, never failed to be surprised at the simplicity of her hosts' abode. The front door opened straight into the living room, which featured an L-shaped sofa, a baby grand piano, and a bar. The bar was "a serious affair with barstools, professional enough for the real Irishman Gene was. The back wall was all glass and looked over a volleyball court. . . . There were no locks on the front door—you just walked in—and you never locked your car either."[56] Kerry, now age eight, had become more interested in her parents' parties. "I was around all the time. I would help set the table . . . and get the food organized. . . . Then it would be my bedtime and I'd pretend to be asleep and then I'd sit on the stairs and peek through the banisters because I could see the piano from there. Very fond memories."[57]

Some aspects of the parties, however, were strictly for the adults, particularly when a guest was outside the Kellys' normal social circle. One such guest was a young San Francisco filmmaker, Kenneth Anger, who had written a letter to Gene about his recently completed sixteen-millimeter movie entitled *Fireworks*. Sundays were typically reserved for screenings of films at the Kellys', so one weekend Gene invited Anger to show his film. "I don't know how he [Anger] happened to write to Gene," Betsy Blair commented. "I do know that none of us had any idea what we were about to see. . . . We watched in stunned silence this fascinating, surreal, homoerotic essay on film." At the film's conclusion, Gene "leapt to the rescue, put his arm around Kenneth Anger's shoulders, and took him into the study, where he congratulated and thanked him." Anger shook Gene's hand and left the house, at which point the rest of the guests fell into hysterical laughter "at the memory of the cascades of candle sparks from the sailor's crotch" in the film.[58] Everyone fell silent in embarrassment when they glanced up to see that Anger was in the hallway, having forgotten his overcoat. He left with a backward wave of his hand. He never appeared at another Kelly party. Betsy claimed that Gene was the politest to Anger of the group and found it difficult to restrain himself from lecturing his guests about their childish behavior.

Gene could have lectured himself for his own unfortunate behavior one evening when Noël Coward was the guest of honor. Arthur Laurents, who persisted in sarcastically calling Gene and his friends the "Real People," claimed that when Coward arrived, the guests "sprawled on the floor more than usual, ostensibly to make us more Real than ever by displaying indifference to superficiality." Coward, according to Laurents, was not a Real Person because he represented the upper classes. But once Coward began to engage in self-deprecating humor and satiric song, he turned Gene's "plaid-and-shag rumpus room into his own elegant drawing room [and] he turned us into his guests, then he turned the room into his shrine and us into his worshipping sycophants." Gene could not stand Coward's dominance; before the applause had ended, he "was on his feet, taking over the floor . . . in his own house on a shaggy rug he knew was not for dancing . . . but he tried to dance because that was what he could do best and Noel Coward couldn't do very well." Jeanne Coyne and Carol Haney, whom Laurents called Gene's "secretary-fans," danced with him. Laurents elaborated that Coward "wanted it to work. . . . Gene was so needy that even I wanted it to work. If it weren't for the rug it might have. . . . It was very embarrassing." Betsy finally "saved him" by calling it a night, and the party ended.[59]

More successful, if odd, was a special dinner the Kellys' housekeeper, Bertha, suggested they host. "I know a salesman—you have to invite him. He sells waterless cookers. He'll prepare dinner for twenty people. . . . All you have to do is provide drinks, dessert, and coffee," Bertha declared. Betsy agreed. But, not trusting that the waterless cookers would produce edible food, she surreptitiously informed her guests that the affair was a potluck. The salesman—a fellow navy veteran, much to Gene's delight— appeared to have no knowledge of the movies. He failed to recognize Gene or any of the guests he saw, including Hedy Lamarr, John Garfield, and

Lena Horne. Only a few moments after the salesman arrived, Gene opened the door to two unexpected visitors: George Cukor and Greta Garbo. A flustered Betsy, "grinning ear to ear," ushered the luminaries into the already crowded kitchen, where the salesman was "extolling the merits of cooking without water and the wonders he was going to perform when he finally got around to cooking our meal."[60] Garbo seated herself on the counter next to the sink. The salesman did not recognize her either, so, unlike the other partygoers, he was not dumbstruck by her presence. In blissful ignorance, he prepared a giant rice pancake full of nuts and mushrooms that was "unsalted, oversteamed, and tasteless." Garbo was the only one to eat the pancake with relish. Then the salesman urged everyone to buy "Reverewear." Garbo bought the whole set of his waterless cookers for $150. Hedy Lamarr and Gene, "out of embarrassment," took sets of their own. When the salesman left, Betsy recalled that a general uproar arose over the hideous meal and the overpriced cookers. "This brought on one of Gene's lectures—they were quite well-known and regarded with tolerant amusement by our friends," she said. "Don't laugh at a fella trying to earn an honest buck!" he chided.[61]

The rest of the evening became a dedication to Garbo. Comden and Green did numbers from their nightclub days with the Revuers for her, plus "assorted bits of indescribably cuckoo nonsense." Garbo laughed during their performance. As always, the Kellys' party, according to Comden, "winded up with everyone who felt like it getting up and performing, not to be 'on,' not to impress anyone, but out of sheer exuberance and just for the hell of it."[62]

On March 21, 1951, Gene, Vincente Minnelli, Arthur Freed, and Lela Simone paced the lobby of the Crown Theatre in Pasadena. The first preview of *An American in Paris* was under way—and people were filing out of the theater halfway through the film. Minnelli declared he felt "downright suicidal." With his colleagues, he went to a bar across the street and drank several martinis. Fortunately, Minnelli's death wish vanished after he discovered that the reason for the audience's mass exodus was that the projectionist had neglected to raise the volume to an audible level. "The second preview at Bay Theatre in Pacific Palisades was a triumph," Minnelli reported.[63] Satisfied movie patrons called the picture "outstanding" and the controversial ballet garnered a round of applause at the film's close.

Critics and moviegoers shared the enthusiasm of preview audiences when the picture opened in New York on October 4, 1951. After its nation-wide release, *An American in Paris* became the sixth-highest-grossing film of the year. The production received mixed reviews, but Freed, Minnelli, and Gene all considered themselves victors where the ballet was concerned. Bosley Crowther of the *New York Times* commented: "[The] ballet . . . is, beyond question—a truly cinematic ballet—with dancers describing vivid patterns against changing colors, designs, costumes and scenes. . . . It is the uncontested high point of the film."[64]

Though Crowther did not single Gene out for praise, the vast majority of other critics named him as the artist who elevated the film. A reviewer for *Time* magazine rhapsodized, "Throughout, the film breathes the buoyant spirit of Gene Kelly. In 1949's *On the Town* . . . Kelly staked his claim as the most original talent in Hollywood musi-comedy; the new picture makes his claim secure."[65]

The success of *An American in Paris* acted as a sort of barometer of the country's growing hope for the decade. True, it had begun on a black note, but it could still have splashes of color. As shown, albeit symbolically, in the "American in Paris Ballet," it was possible that a colorless world could come back to life. *An American in Paris,* then, was a most timely film for the country in 1950–1951. According to author Barbara Wolf in a 1976 critique, the picture's "setting of idealized artifice [was] a never-never land of sheer delight and wish-fulfillment. . . . Yet the sunny surface of the film is a veneer. Its underlying story tells of compromised lives and hopes, amid false promises of fulfillment."[66]

Gene's life, too, concealed an underlying tension. Outwardly, he was at the top of his art and enjoyed a steady home life. But twenty-eight-year-old Betsy Blair was no longer the child-wife he had taken in 1942. She had grown up and no longer needed Gene's guidance and protection. Though she was still very much a part of the Kellys' everyday family life, more and more often she was receiving offers to further her career that she could not resist—and sometimes they required her and Gene to be a continent apart.

Gene's next picture, *Singin' in the Rain,* a virtual ode to optimism, was precisely the film he needed at this point in his life. Arthur Freed commissioned Betty Comden and Adolph Green to write the screenplay. He gave them no instructions except to use his and Nacio Herb Brown's tunes of the 1920s and 1930s and take the film's title from their cheeriest composition, "Singin' in the Rain."

No one involved in the project foresaw that it would take on more significance than their previous efforts. Gene later claimed that if he had had to guess in 1952 which of his pictures would endure through the decades, he would have chosen *An American in Paris, The Pirate,* or *On the Town.* "We [the Freed Unit] did our best on every picture," Gene declared. "But we never said, 'Now this one will last.'"[67]

15

Laughing at Clouds

Gene Kelly had grown from child to man during what F. Scott Fitzgerald fondly dubbed the Jazz Age. In his formative years, he absorbed the vivid characters that flickered on the silver screen: swashbuckling pirates, cowboy heroes, fearless aviators, and mustachioed matinee idols. Young Gene heard American music find its own sound and saw American dance break free from European influences. After World War I, his country became a world power and trendsetter. Flappers and philosophers danced side by side, artifice and realism commingled. Gene had lived through all of this; thus, in the summer of 1951, he delved into his next project, *Singin' in the Rain,* with added gusto. In its final form, the screen musical was less a fond look back at the 1920s and more a modern satire with the 1920s as a backdrop.

The moment Betty Comden and Adolph Green finished their script in October 1950, they clearly saw Gene as the leading man, Don Lockwood. In an earlier draft, they had made the main character a cowboy screen star and had considered Howard Keel for the role. But in the final draft, the cowboy was instead a hammy matinee idol much more suited to Gene's talents than Keel's. Indeed, the part bore similarities to that of Serafin in *The Pirate.* According to Green, "Gene was not afraid of ridiculing himself. That is one of the wonderful qualities in *Singin' in the Rain.* He caught the spirit of the spoiled movie star and exploited it like mad. He loved every second of it, I know he did."[1]

Gene's role in *Singin' in the Rain* has become so iconic that it is almost impossible to imagine him not being part of the picture. But Gene initially could not even consider participation in the film—at the time of the script's completion, he was still entrenched in *An American in Paris.* Nevertheless, Comden and Green as well as director Stanley Donen had Gene in mind as they formed the scenario. Green recalled, "We were running old movies, things of that sort, saying, 'Gee, how about doing this?' Stanley was *in* on the genesis, in that sense, worrying along with us both, as friends, and hopefully as a future co-director with Gene of whatever evolved."[2]

At first the story wouldn't come together. As Comden and Green recounted: "We had endless conferences [with Arthur Freed] the first month and a half. We were tempted to go up to the front office and say, 'Here's your money back. . . . The whole thing's off. We can't write this god-damned thing.'" But finally, with the aid of Arthur Freed and Nacio Herb Brown's catalogue of Jazz Age hits, Comden and Green hit upon an idea of making the picture the story of a matinee idol's (and his leading lady's) struggle to make the transition from silents to talkies. The rest of the plot flowed easily. "It's a conglomeration of bits of movie lore."[3]

"We did an 'audition' for him [Gene], and we read him the script. . . . He fell in love with *Singin' in the Rain* right away," Comden said. It was now January 1951 and, with *An American in Paris* completed, Gene could not wait to get started on *Singin' in the Rain* and reunite with Stanley Donen as his co-director. With Comden and Green, the two men did extensive rewrites that greatly improved the final script. (Gene's personal copy of the script with his edits was burned in a 1983 house fire, so his precise contributions to the film have been lost to history.) "I can't complain; the studio . . . let[s] me act, direct, design dance numbers, everything else. It could hardly be said that I'm suffering from a lack of variety," Gene told a *Los Angeles Times* reporter, leaning back in a contour chair Betsy had bought him for his office at MGM as a gift for their tenth wedding anniversary.[4]

Singin' in the Rain gave Gene the job of actor, director, choreographer, dance coach, singer, and screenwriter (to an extent). From his first time as director in 1949, Gene admitted, "I never prided myself that I could jump in front of the camera and direct a whole picture alone." Now, as then, he found Donen invaluable. "When I am in front of the camera, Donen . . . directs. His is the last word. If he doesn't like a bit of business, particularly comedy, out it goes. . . . Stan and I divide the work when I am not in the scene. Then I direct the actors and he the lighting and camera angles."[5]

Though Gene and Donen could still bring out the worst in one another personally, in their work, they continued to achieve new levels of excellence. In the case of *Singin' in the Rain,* they toned down the more obvious comedy evident in *On the Town* to create an unflinching yet warm satire. "I think its uniqueness is the comedy," Betty Comden commented in a 2002 interview. "Most musicals aren't very funny at all."[6]

The film tells a well-drawn story of an egotistical screen actor, Don Lockwood, his obnoxious leading lady, Lina Lamont, his clever but down to earth pianist friend and former partner in vaudeville, Cosmo Brown, and Kathy Selden, the young ingénue who threatens to take Lina's place when talkies come into vogue in Hollywood in the late 1920s. Like *An American in Paris,* the picture introduces the primary characters in a novel fashion: via a live radio broadcast at the premiere of Lina and Don's latest picture at Grauman's Chinese Theatre. Over the air, Don narrates for his fans a falsified account of his rise to stardom. He declares that his life's motto has been "dignity, always dignity"—though, in truth, his career has been strewn with indignity.[7] As he speaks, the camera shows scenes of him and Cosmo performing in shoddy vaudeville houses, followed by Don taking any and every bit of degrading stunt work film studios offered him. The fact that Lina does not speak for the entire sequence only heightens the shock—and ensuing laughter—when she utters her first words at a post-premiere party, revealing that she possesses a truly ear-splitting voice.

On his way to this party, Don leaps into Kathy's passing car to escape a group of rabid fans. Kathy feigns disgust for the movies, though she actually adores pictures and wishes to be in them herself. Don falls in love with Kathy, much to Lina's dismay. An exasperated Don tells her: "Now Lina, you've been reading all those fan magazines again! . . . Try to get this straight: there is nothing between us. There has never been anything between us. Just air."

At the height of Lina and Don's screen success, *The Jazz Singer* (1927) is released and suddenly, the powers that be decree that their present picture must be turned into a talkie. Lina's screechy voice jeopardizes the film's success—and Don's future if she remains his leading lady. The first-night preview of Lina and Don's talking picture, *The Dueling Cavalier,* is a debacle. The sound is out of sync on several parts, making it sound as if Lina is speaking the lines of the film's villain and vice versa. Cosmo and Don decide to reshoot the entire film as a musical with Kathy dubbing Lina. When the jealous Lina discovers their stratagem, she does not want to share credit with Kathy. Nonetheless, she tries to force the studio to use Kathy's voice in all her future productions. "What do they [Don, Cosmo, and studio executives] think I am? Dumb or something? Why, I make more money than—than—than Calvin Coolidge! Put together!" she shouts.

At the premiere of *The Dancing Cavalier,* the audience demands a speech and a song from Lina. Don and Cosmo are delighted at this opportunity; they gleefully lift the stage curtain to reveal Kathy singing into a microphone behind Lina. A distraught Kathy tries to flee the theater but Don cries: "Ladies and gentlemen, stop that girl. . . . That's the girl whose voice you heard and loved tonight. She's the real star of the picture. Kathy Selden!" He launches into "You Are My Lucky Star." Next, the camera cuts to a movie poster depicting him and Kathy as costars, in love on- and off-screen; it is, presumably several months later.

In writing the script, Comden and Green were not exaggerating when they said it was a conglomeration of movie lore. Freed provided a number of tidbits, including the awkward positioning of microphones to capture the actors' voices in the early days of talkies. Lina Lamont's painful transition from silent movie queen to talking picture actress was based on Mae Murray's fall from stardom—not, as is commonly believed, John Gilbert's decline. Still, Comden and Green included an allusion to John Gilbert in Don Lockwood's character. In one scene, Don ad-libs dialogue during a first recording for his and Lina's picture. Kissing her arm, he repeatedly says, "I love you," just as Gilbert did in his first talkie, *His Glorious Night* (1929).

Directing the new flurry of talkies, including Don and Lina's, is a spastic, eye-patch-sporting director, Roscoe Dexter, a character Comden and Green modeled after both Busby Berkeley and Erich von Stroheim. Other characters were also based in reality. The sometimes-indecisive studio head, R. F. Simpson, is modeled after Freed himself, though Comden and Green claimed this was unintentional. The female lead, Kathy Selden, falls into the mold of the innocent troupers portrayed by Ruby Keeler in early musicals, though her wit and ability to supply quick comebacks closely parallel Ginger Rogers's roles in the early 1930s. Cosmo, Don's sidekick, had no real-life counterpart.

To depict the boom of musical pictures that accompanied the advent of sound, *Singin' in the Rain* uses a lively montage set to a medley of Freed's tunes including "Wedding of the Painted Doll," "I've Got a Feeling You're Fooling," and "Beautiful Girl." The latter number depicts a series of chorines posing as life-size cover girls, a device that had been popularized in the sensational *Ziegfeld Follies* revues of the 1920s and had often been used in film, including Gene's 1944 *Cover Girl*. The number concludes with a Busby Berkeley–inspired aerial view of the girls in a kaleidoscopic configuration. Adolph Green rightly stated that *Singin' in the Rain* was particularly beautiful to look at. "They [Gene and Donen] were in charge of the entire project, [and] they were naturally involved with visual design as well." In the evenings, Gene, Comden, Green, and Donen would meet at Gene's home to discuss "structure and go over the film shot-by-shot." "Everything pulled together perfectly," Comden recalled.[8] Roger Edens, assigned by Arthur Freed as associate producer and musical arranger, was also integral to the making of the picture.

All was not perfect for one person: Jeanne Coyne, who worked on the film as Gene's dance assistant. Her divorce from Donen had just gone through, and she could not have found it easy to be in such close proximity to him. By this time, Donen was already planning a second marriage, to actress Marion Marshall. However, no accounts exist of tension between the former spouses during filming. Gene, a friend to them both, maintained an air of neutrality. Jeanne had the moral support of Carol Haney, Gene's second assistant, throughout the filming.

Gene was nonplussed by Freed's casting suggestions of Oscar Levant as Cosmo and Nina Foch as Lina Lamont. Casting Levant and Foch would make *Singin' in the Rain* virtually a remake of *An American in Paris*. "I don't want to work with Oscar again. This is a different kind of movie, and I need somebody who's more of an entertainer—somebody I can dance with," Gene told Freed.[9] Gene got his way. Twenty-six-year-old dancer Donald O'Connor won the role of Cosmo. Gene's choice was somewhat unusual, considering that Donald's previous work had been mostly in B pictures for Universal Studios. A talented performer of tap, ballroom, and eccentric dance, Donald O'Connor never aspired to be balletic. His zany yet wholesome persona lent itself well to straight hoofing and tap dancing.

Comden and Green (if not Levant, who was extremely distraught not to be chosen for the role) came to agree that Gene was wise in insisting that Donald O'Connor play Cosmo. Donald had a far lighter style of humor than the mordant Levant. As well as being a hoofer, he was also an acrobat of sorts. He could contort his face in seemingly any expression and could climb up a wall and do a somersault in the air before landing on his feet. Donald later stated that Gene "tried to incorporate a lot of my personality outside his own, and then he got himself in there as Kelly. I think that's the great director that he is."[10]

Freed also heeded Gene's request to replace Nina Foch with Jean Hagen. Jean was primarily a dramatic actress, having made her name in

The Asphalt Jungle (1951), but she had also proven herself a fine comedienne in the Spencer Tracy–Katharine Hepburn vehicle *Adam's Rib* (1949). Jean had a rich and deep voice, but she perfectly put on a Judy Holliday–like shriek as Lina. Stories conflict as to who chose Debbie Reynolds, a nineteen-year-old starlet, to play Kathy. Debbie had most recently appeared as Jane Powell's kid sister in the period musical *Two Weeks with Love* (1950). Debbie outshone Powell in the film and made a hit singing the popular tune "Aba Daba Honeymoon" with Carleton Carpenter. Her performance in the picture was what made Louis B. Mayer decide she should have the part. He called her into his office and told her: "You are a very talented little girl and I have a surprise for you today. You are going to make a movie with Gene Kelly and Donald O'Connor."[11] Debbie was thrilled because every picture she had seen and loved most as a girl had starred Gene.

When Mayer called Gene to his office one afternoon, the actor did not know he would be meeting Debbie.

"So here's your leading lady," Mayer told him.

"Whaaat?" Gene cried and stared, scrutinizing Debbie.[12]

Debbie remembered that Gene opposed her casting. Gene's and Stanley Donen's remarks on the subject are contradictory. In 1974, Gene asserted that after seeing her in *Two Weeks with Love* he immediately knew he had found the right girl to play Kathy. Donen agreed: "We couldn't wait to get her. . . . I thought she was adorable."[13] Yet in a 1991 interview, Gene claimed that after the meeting with Mayer where he met Debbie, he recalled thinking: "What the hell am I going to do with her?" And Donen called Debbie "a royal pain in the ass" who "thought she knew more than Gene and I combined."[14]

Debbie was aware of Gene's and Donen's ambiguous feelings about her. "I soon found out I should have been thinking 'just go take gas, turn on the carbon monoxide and just close the door.' Because I was about to start something more difficult, more exhausting, more horrendous than any experience I'd ever known," she reflected in her memoir in 1988. In a mere three months, she had to become a dancer who could hold her own against Gene and Donald O'Connor. Carol Haney and Jeanne Coyne worked with her for up to eight hours a day. Unlike he had with Leslie Caron during shooting of *An American in Paris,* Gene did not seem to relent in his role as taskmaster over Debbie. "Gene would come into rehearsals, look at . . . the steps they were teaching me. He was never satisfied," Debbie explained. "I never got a compliment. Ever."[15]

Debbie offered a different perspective on Gene in a 1996 interview. "He taught me how to dance and how to work hard, to be dedicated and to be loving—as he was to his family and friends."[16] Kerry Kelly recalled that Gene did in fact appreciate Debbie's efforts and even included her in his social life. "She [Debbie] let me come with her on a cookout trip. I . . . thought that was so great."[17]

In one respect, the dueling stories regarding Debbie match: Gene enforced almost impossibly high standards on the ingénue. He was the first to admit it: "I can be very mercurial, but also patient with slow learners. . . . It is only when they are dogging it that I can become mean. I don't like amateurs."[18] However, Kerry was quick to remark that her father "never asked anyone to work harder than he did."[19]

On one especially demanding day, Debbie became so dispirited that she crawled under the rehearsal piano and cried. Fred Astaire, passing by, found her there and invited her to watch him practice. She discovered that he too grew frustrated and tired, but he was able to keep calm. "His gesture was an enormous help to me."[20] In part thanks to Fred's encouragement, Debbie threw herself back into rehearsals with Gene.

The situation improved by the end of the filming; Debbie grew to have a friendlier relationship with her costar/director. When she had difficulty with a dance step, rather than lose his temper with her, "he'd just smile and say 'I guess we'll have to work a little harder.' . . . I owe more to him than I can ever repay. He literally willed me to dance."[21] Years later, Gene declared that he was surprised Debbie would still speak to him after the harsh drilling he put her through.[22]

After weeks of preproduction and grueling rehearsals, shooting began in earnest on June 15, 1951. The dialogue sequences were simple to film; the majority of shooting time was spent on the song and dance portions of the picture. Stanley Donen observed that part of what made *Singin' in the Rain* different was that more than half its running time was composed of musical sequences. Debbie's dance numbers, "Good Morning," "All I Do Is Dream of You," and "You Were Meant for Me," required the most rehearsal time due to her inexperience. In execution, the latter scene harkens back to a sequence between Gene and Judy Garland in *Summer Stock*, "You Wonderful You." In both films, Gene's character uses stage scenery, lighting, and props to create a romantic setting, and the scene begins "tentatively" and ends with a "comfortable parting."[23] Though the number appears calm and romantic onscreen, an unfortunate mishap occurred during its filming. Before the cameras began to roll, Debbie remembered she had forgotten to remove gum from her mouth. She quickly did so and stuck it under the ladder on which she was to stand during Gene's serenade. "When Gene leaned back, his head somehow caught the gum, and when he straightened up, he left a nice clump of hair behind. Well, he let out a yell, and I just turned pale. . . . That was very nearly the end of me," Debbie recalled.[24]

Another flare-up took place after Gene relentlessly went through a tap routine with Debbie and Donald that was to accompany "Good Morning." The scene takes place at Don's mansion and depicts him, Cosmo, and Kathy brainstorming ideas of how to save Don and Lina's disastrous talkie. To cheer themselves, they sing and dance everywhere from the counter of Don's bar to his sofa. As Debbie and Donald rehearsed, Gene continually told them they were out of step. "You're so stupid, you're not doing the step right. You're stupid," he told Donald. Thirty-five years later, Donald told Debbie that Gene picked on him because he was in fact always mad at her. But Gene knew that if he kept yelling at the young actress, she would hold up production with her tears. "So he screamed at Donald, who wouldn't cry," Debbie concluded.[25] Finally, Gene realized it was he who was tapping the dance steps incorrectly. This only fueled his temper; he chided his costars, who had noticed his fault all along, for not informing him of it.

After all the suffering involved in "Good Morning," Gene was still unhappy with Debbie's dancing and decided someone should dub her taps. He went into the recording room to dub the sound of her feet as well as his own. Gene's lifelong drive for perfection and incessant dissatisfaction (which, Debbie intuited, was largely directed at himself) could not help but transfer to his costars. He did not take long to apologize to Donald O'Connor for using him as a whipping boy. "That's okay, Gene. But next time you do it, I'll kick you in the balls," Donald told him, with no trace of his usual clowning.[26] There is no record that Gene ever unleashed his frustration on Donald again.

The friendship—and generosity—Gene showed to Donald O'Connor went far in compensating for his inconsiderate treatment of the dancer. The first musical sequence in the film, "Fit as a Fiddle," does not spotlight either actor more than the other; they are completely equal. Dressed in gaudy, green, checked suits, they perform a comic number with violins that garner "boos" from their unreceptive audience. (The routine was a true joy for Gene. He later claimed it was almost autobiographical, reminiscent as it was of his and his brother Fred's early attempts to please audiences.) But the best evidence of Gene's thoughtfulness was his giving Donald a solo comic number that took up a considerable slice of screen time. Donald's routine ultimately outshone all other sequences in the film with the exception of the title number. Gene's need to be in the spotlight while playing charades or volleyball at his own home clearly did not always extend to his work on the Metro lot. "I had always felt badly for Donald. . . . Nobody before ever seemed to know how to show him off properly," Gene explained.[27] Gene sometimes exploded at Donald, yelling at him to stop clowning on the set. But he realized the value of Donald's fooling around—the spontaneous stunts Donald performed whenever he saw Jeanne Coyne and Carol Haney kept them in constant hysterics. Gene noted what made the two women laugh most uproariously and employed Donald's tricks into "Make 'Em Laugh."

"[Gene's] main contribution [to "Make 'Em Laugh"] was his ability to see something very good and utilize it. And his only other contribution was where I hit the wall and screw up my face. He thought that was funny. I didn't," Donald recalled.[28] Gene insisted that the sequence of Donald's face contortions be in close-up; his knowledge of what would work not only in cinematic comedy bits but in cinedance proved just how much he had learned during his decade in pictures. Donald offered a concluding thought on his costar/director: "Gene and I had a relationship like George Burns and Jack Benny. We'd just look at each other and start to laugh."[29]

Donald performed the comic sequence to an original tune Arthur Freed had composed for the film. "Make 'Em Laugh" serves as Cosmo's effort to cheer Don after a dismal rehearsal for his first talking picture. It employs nearly every slapstick gag in show business. One of the most amusing bits in the number is Cosmo's use of a headless dummy as his "partner." He pantomimes that he is flirting with it until the situation reverses and the dummy gets fresh with him. The scene also includes Donald's trademark stunt of walking up a wall and doing a somersault.

The cast and crew were amused that the melody of "Make 'Em Laugh" bore an uncanny resemblance to Cole Porter's "Be a Clown," which Porter had written for Freed's The Pirate. The plagiarism was apparently unintentional on Freed's part. Betty Comden recollected that on the day the number was to be shot, Freed brought Irving Berlin to the soundstage. "He [Freed] was very proud of both the song and the number," she said. "[Then] Irving walks onto the set, and we were all horrified. We were all thinking,

'My God, Irving's going to hear the song and recognize the similarity! What's going to happen?' . . . So Irving's listening, and he's listening, and then you could see his face changing."

"Well that's 'Be a Clown,'" Berlin declared. Freed "suddenly got very flustered and said, "Oh, well, we . . . that is, the kids . . . we all got together and . . . Well, let's move along!" Freed pulled Berlin away from the set, and everyone "fell on the floor laughing."[30] Lela Simone remembered that it "was one of those things Freed did not want to have anything to do with discussing. . . . It [just] slipped by."[31] Cole Porter never came forward with an accusation of plagiarism.

The other original tune composed for the film bore no similarities to any existing compositions: "Moses Supposes." Roger Edens wrote the music and Comden and Green supplied the tongue-twisting lyrics. The song, performed by Cosmo and Don, takes place in an elocution classroom and acts as a springboard for the young men to lampoon the professor's pretentious verbal flourishes. The two dancers behave like naughty schoolboys throughout the entire number, rolling the puzzled teacher about in his chair, dumping over his trashcan, and putting a lampshade over his head. The energetic number is a textbook example of synchronized dance onscreen.

The most intricate number in the picture was a ballet. By 1951, ballet in musicals had become virtually mandatory though, in Comden's view, the medium "didn't really fit in [Singin' in the Rain]. But we had no control over it."[32] Gene and Donen managed to make it fit. As a lead-in to the sequence, Don and Cosmo approach R. F. Simpson to explain their vision for the big production number in Don's first talkie: it takes place before the film's hero is knocked on the head and dreams that he is living during the French Revolution (a scenario strikingly similar to that in *Du Barry Was a Lady*). Rather than employ a dialogue-dense explanation of all that occurs in the ballet, Gene and Donen followed the first rule of good writing— show, don't tell. Thus, they treat viewers to a twelve-minute ballet depicting their conception. Immediately after Don and Cosmo's description of the number, R. F. states: "I can't seem to visualize it, I'd have to see it on film first." The line was an in-joke; Arthur Freed often spoke such words when listening to ideas for production numbers.

Freed was, however, able to visualize one idea for the sequence. Cyd Charisse had recently returned to MGM after a maternity leave, and he wanted her to appear in the ballet. "Gene wanted [Carol Haney], but

Arthur asked me if I'd do it. . . . I told Arthur I'd be delighted," Cyd wrote in her memoir. Gene and Cyd began rehearsals with Carol Haney as an assistant. "She [Haney] was the epitome of unselfishness. Even though she must have been consumed with disappointment, she did everything she could to make things easy for me," Cyd recalled.[33]

Cyd Charisse's experience on the set of *Singin' in the Rain* was far different than Debbie Reynolds's. She concurred with her peers that Gene "was such a hard worker, such a perfectionist. . . . He was always intense. Everything was just the way he wanted it to be."[34] However, she saw this as a plus, later calling *Singin' in the Rain* "the justification of my career as a dancer."[35] Lela Simone once asserted that Gene did not take well to leading ladies outshining him; Gene refuted her statement. "I believe it's my duty and also the way the film should be that you direct everything toward the girl, make her look good. If she looks good, the *pas de deux* looks good," he explained.[36]

Gene's relationship with Cyd was not compromised by her stunning looks or her size. At five feet seven, she was at or above Gene's height in heels. In a 1972 interview, Gene said of Cyd: "Now there was a big girl. We had a beautiful relationship, but she was a big girl. Every time I lifted her over my head Fred Astaire would say: 'How can you do that, kid? That's the way you get a hernia.'"[37] Cyd declared that when Gene "lifts you, he lifts you! Fred [Astaire] could never do the lifts Gene did and never wanted to." Gene "didn't want" Cyd to "look like a ballet dancer on the screen."[38] This was quite the opposite of Gene's methods when working with Vera-Ellen or Leslie Caron, whose balletic styles he endeavored to enhance. Gene's intention was to bring out a sexier side to Cyd's dancing because her character was a sensuous vamp.

The ballet, like the film, is a hodgepodge of movie lore. Historians Earl Hess and Pratibha Dabholkar described it as "a purposely designed kaleidoscope of show business clichés, particularly those relating to early sound pictures." The ballet follows a naïve young dancer's climb to stardom; when first seen, he is dressed in a suit too small for him, a pair of horn-rimmed glasses, and a straw boater, all of which bring to mind silent film comedian Harold Lloyd. He pounds the pavement of New York exclaiming, "Gotta dance!" or "Gotta sing!" until one agent finally likes what he sees and pulls the dancer into a speakeasy to negotiate a contract.[39] The dancer's eyes are drawn to a mobster's girlfriend (Cyd), who sports the angular brunette bob of 1920s actress Louise Brooks. The mobster, who has a prominent scar on his cheek and flips a coin in his palm, resembles George Raft in his early gangster pictures. The girl rejects the young dancer and teases him in an alluring dance during which she takes off his glasses, polishes them on her stocking, and kicks them across the floor. The dancer dejectedly leaves the speakeasy and pursues his career, but he does not forget the girl.

A montage follows, showing him climbing the show business ladder, always performing the song "Broadway Rhythm." Adolph Green credited Gene and Donen for the concept of showing "the hoofer go[ing] from vaudeville to the Palace to the *Ziegfeld Follies* . . . and [having] the costumes and arrangements [get] classier and classier though [he is] singing the same lyric."[40] Also attributable to Gene and Donen are the film's costumes, shown most vibrantly in the ballet. Arthur Freed apparently hated Jazz Age garb and suggested that the picture instead use "interpretations" of 1920s clothing. "Gene and I stuck to our guns and went for the real look of the times," Donen explained.[41]

The scene then shifts to the dancer attending a high-class speakeasy, apparently for a party held in his honor. Upon entering, he freezes in the doorway. At the top of a staircase leading into the dining room is the girl from long ago. She appears angelic, clad in white. He drifts into a "fantasy within a fantasy" in which he and the girl are separated by a long billowing scarf later dubbed "the crazy veil."[42] They dance in each other's arms for a moment, only to be separated again by the lengthy veil. Gene later claimed the dance with the veil was among the most challenging he ever created. The wind machine used to make it billow was so strong that Jeanne Coyne and Carol Haney had to (out of the camera's view) hold down Cyd's ankles to prevent her from being knocked over by its force.

As the dancer comes out of his reverie, he sees a coin flipping before his eyes. Scarface extends a diamond bracelet to the girl, and she promptly follows him out the door. The dancer is left in the dark, his back to the lights of Broadway flashing merrily behind him. Suddenly, a hoofer identical to himself when he first came to the city waltzes by. "Gotta dance!" the boy exclaims. The dancer shrugs, snaps back into reality, and animatedly follows the young hopeful. He launches into "Broadway Rhythm" and is soon surrounded by a chorus of brightly clad flappers amid the neon marquees of Broadway's most iconic theatres. The ballet's thesis is the age-old adage "The show must go on"—most appropriate for a film that is all about how show business must continue in spite of love woes, changing times, and technology.

Though cleverly inserted in the film and one of Gene's finest pieces, the "Broadway Ballet" strays from his long-standing stance that dance must further a film's plotline. The ballet is, as historians Hess and Dabholkar describe it, "a self-contained entity, complete with its own story and characters."[43] Researcher William Baer noted that it "doesn't fit that well into the narrative of such a tightly-structured and fast-paced film."[44] Gene and Donen had their own qualms; they considered the piece too long. The sequence was expensive: it cost $100,000 more to put on film than the "American in Paris Ballet."

In direct contrast to the lavish ballet is the simplest, least assuming number in the picture: "Singin' in the Rain." It consists of one performer—Gene—using an umbrella, rain puddles, and a streetlamp as props. Gene had devised the number to come after Don and Kathy's first kiss, the point when his character is most blissful. "The idea was to be so much in love and so ecstatic and joyous that you reverted to childhood and splashed about. You know all kids do that," Gene explained in a 1975 interview.[45]

To fluidly transition into the number, Roger Edens wrote an introduction to the song that served as a bridge. Don dreamily strolls down the street, looks at the rain, shrugs, and closes his umbrella before quietly singing Edens's interlude: "Doodle, doo, doo, doodle, loodle, doo, doo . . ." Next, he tap-dances—one foot on the sidewalk, one in the gutter—stands under a spurting drainpipe, and swings off the side of a lamppost. As the scene's climax, he jumps into the biggest, deepest puddle he can find in the middle of the street and proceeds to twirl in a circle with his open umbrella held out before him. He stops abruptly when he comes face-to-face with a somber policeman. He looks sheepish only for a moment, then smiles and sings an explanation for his behavior: "I'm dancing and singing in the rain." The number closes on a quiet note, as do all Gene's best solos. He silently turns, heads down the street, and hands his umbrella to a grateful man hurrying past him. The policeman stares after Don, crossing his hands behind his back in puzzlement.

The number was not simple to create even if it appeared so onscreen. MGM used so much water to simulate the rainstorm that the water pressure in Culver City was lower for a few hours because of it. To create a night sky, a black tarpaulin was stretched across the set—creating a greenhouse effect. Watching the exuberant Gene in the number, one would not guess that he was in fact suffering greatly during the filming. He had recently caught the flu and had a temperature of 103; the humid air under the tarpaulin must have been torture. Gene was able to stay on beat thanks in part to Stanley Donen's strategic placement of rain puddles as markers for his feet. On a lighter note, the moisture in the air caused Gene's tweed suit to grow tighter and his pants shorter as the scene progressed. Donald O'Connor remembered that it was "really hysterical."[46]

With Gene's illness, "the studio will take care of it" phenomenon sprang into action. The day after filming the title number, Gene had Betsy call the first assistant on the film to alert him he would not be coming in that day. Before long Betsy spotted MGM's doctor coming up the front path. "Ah they're spying. Lock the door and tell Bertha not to answer it," Gene said. He and Betsy giggled while the "poor man knocked and rang and rang." When the doctor started to move toward the rear entrance, Betsy made a mad dash to lock the back door. Gene smiled weakly and told her, "Good work."[47] The next day, he was better.

Filming, complete with re-takes, for *Singin' in the Rain* came to a close on December 26, 1951. As soon as shooting completed, Debbie Reynolds fled to Lake Tahoe and promptly slept for eighteen hours. The cost of the production totaled $2,540,800, $620,996 over budget. The final print of the movie was delayed several weeks because the technicians working with the footage "were so confused by the non-synchronization" scene. "They kept trying to make it match. . . . They finally admitted, 'We can't get this thing in sync,'" Betty Comden recalled. "So Gene and Stanley had to explain to them that that was the point. It shouldn't be in sync!"[48] Such was the comical end to Gene Kelly's most comical film.

At the time *Singin' in the Rain* was being shot, genuine storms brewed behind the scenes at MGM. Tensions between Dore Schary and Arthur Freed had escalated after Louis B. Mayer's exit from the studio, which occurred during production in August 1951. The end came for Mayer after Schary received one hundred thousand shares in the Loew's corporation— more than any other employee. Mayer gave Metro's New York boss, Nick Schenck, an ultimatum: either Schary went or he would. Schary won the showdown. Mayer resigned with the declaration: "I shall pursue projects at a studio and under conditions where I shall have the right to make the right kind of pictures."[49]

Many believed that when Mayer left, Freed would follow him. Though Freed stayed, his assistant, Lela Simone, recalled that "ice cold air blew through the third floor [of the Thalberg Building]. Freed detested Schary

. . . and vice versa."[50] Under Mayer's reign, the name of MGM was synonymous with elegance and taste in all genres, but above all in musicals. When Mayer left, leading man Turhan Bey claimed, "In every meaningful way, it was the end of Hollywood."[51] Schary succeeded in temporarily keeping the studio solvent, but overhead costs remained high and, with his lack of finesse, the quality of future Metro productions was in severe jeopardy. How the Freed Unit would continue under Schary's aegis left all its members unsettled. Schary's preference was for films that, rather than being sheer escapism, contained social content. "He would sell his soul for a pot of message," one detractor grumbled.[52]

Arthur Freed still operated more or less independently at MGM. As long as he could, he was going to keep his "little Camelot" together. He went forward with plans to produce a musical adaptation of what he considered the greatest American novel, Mark Twain's *The Adventures of Huckleberry Finn*. *Huck* had been on Freed's mind since 1945, but the project had been continually shelved. Now, in 1951, Freed resurrected it. He hoped to make the film, in his words, the "kind of picture Mark Twain would have loved."[53] He wanted it to be a Gene Kelly picture, and Gene was eager to do it. After all, the dancer had long expressed his wish to make films that would appeal to children.

Freed chose composer Burton Lane to pen music for Alan Jay Lerner's lyrics. He had already tapped Vincente Minnelli as director, Irene Sharaff as costume designer, Gene as "the Duke" and choreographer, Danny Kaye as the King, Dean Stockwell as Huck, William Warfield as Jim (Warfield had played Joe in Freed's *Show Boat*, 1951), and Margaret O'Brien and Louis Calhern as two members of the Grangerford family. Suddenly, plans for the production came to a standstill. Freed called Minnelli to his office and somberly informed him that Gene Kelly had decided *Huck Finn* was not going to be his next project. Still, Freed, Lerner, and Minnelli planned to resume the film at a later time when Gene told them he was ready.

Freed questioned why Gene would put off such a promising role. The answer? Gene and his family had decided to become expatriates. The author of a 1953 article in *Modern Screen* explained the motivating forces behind Gene's decision to leave America: "Gene Kelly's first contract with MGM was scheduled to expire. . . . Loew's, Inc. had no intention of letting Kelly go. In seven previous years the studio had paid him relatively little, especially when one realizes that Gene worked not only as an actor but as a director, choreographer, and writer as well. As a matter of fact, he was regarded by the studio as a one-man unit."[54] Gene decided to remain at MGM after an executive of Loew's informed him of a new tax law Congress had just passed on December 30, 1951. The law mandated that a person could work outside the United States for eighteen months, during which time all his earned income would be tax-free. "Look," the Loew's executive explained. "MGM has millions abroad in blocked currency. The only way they can use that money is to make pictures in foreign countries. It is no legal sin to make a film in London or in Paris or in Italy."[55] In Europe, Gene would be earning a healthy $5,000 a week.

Gene was not the only artist to take advantage of working abroad. Soon, Gary Cooper, Ava Gardner, Kirk Douglas, Clark Gable, Claudette Colbert, and Lana Turner packed their bags, too. "Because of this Hollywood exodus, Kelly is bearing the brunt of public griping," the *Modern Screen* columnist recorded. "The law [is] . . . proper and legal. I would sooner cut off my right arm than do anything shady," Gene defended himself. "Actors don't have very lengthy careers; that's particularly true of dancers. . . . In saving some money for my old age and providing for my family, I don't see anything morally wrong."[56]

Gene and Betsy planned to rent out their Rodeo Drive home while they were in Europe. Accompanying Gene, Betsy, and Kerry were the three women Gene could not live without: Lois McClelland, Carol Haney, and Jeanne Coyne. Betsy embraced the move. "I was enthusiastic . . . and thought it would be good for Kerry. And it was a fine joke on the IRS. . . . The commonly held view of the left was that as long as capitalism is there, we should get as much as we could out of it," Betsy remarked.[57]

In truth, the reason behind Gene's decision to uproot was less pecuniary and more aesthetic. Considering the overwhelmingly positive reception of his ballet in *An American in Paris,* he saw no reason why he should not make an all-dance picture. The idea, Gene claimed, "almost resulted in a psychiatrist being called . . . to examine me. . . . I was prepared to fight. I had the most important of assets to help me—sheer unadulterated enthusiasm." He continued that the reason he had "taken up a film career" in the first place was so he could eventually make an all-dance picture. "It was a dream of mine almost since the first day I ever went to a cinema."[58] Arthur Freed, although doubtful about the project, could not resist Gene's eagerness. He agreed to produce it at MGM's London studio under the condition that Gene complete two low-budget pictures for Metro overseas. One of the films, *The Devil Makes Three,* was set to start production in late

January 1952 at Bavaria Studios, Geiselgasteig, Germany. The other, *Crest of the Wave,* was to be filmed in the United Kingdom but would not begin production until 1953.

Doing two less prestigious pictures seemed a small sacrifice given that Gene had the green light on his dance picture and would have the experience of living in Europe. There, he felt, he could truly expand and refine his art and bask "in the respect and recognition that Europe accords artists."[59]

If Gene believed that Hollywood and America as a whole did not grant him the recognition he deserved, he was soon to be proven wrong. The honor Hollywood lavished upon Gene after he left for Europe confirmed that his artistry was far from overlooked in his native country. Never in the history of film had a musical ever received as many Oscar nominations as Gene's *An American in Paris.* The picture received nods in eight categories: Best Picture, Best Director, Best Screenplay, Best Musical Score, Best Art Direction and Set Decoration, Best Color Cinematography, Best Costume Design, and Best Film Editing.

Most significant, Gene was announced as the recipient of the annual Honorary Oscar. The category, created in 1948, acknowledged cinematic achievements not covered by existing Academy Awards. Gene was only the second dancer to receive such recognition (Fred Astaire received one at the 1950 awards ceremony). Though pleased with the award, Gene still voiced regret that he had not been nominated as Best Actor. "The idea that musical [actors] are less worthy of Academy consideration than drama[tic ones] is a form of snobbishness."[60]

In truth, the honorary Oscar did pay tribute to Gene's acting ability as well as his dancing talent. On March 20, 1952, the night of the awards ceremony, the president of the Academy, Charles Brackett, stated that Gene had earned his statuette through his "extreme versatility as an actor-singer, director, and dancer . . . and because of his specific and brilliant achievements in the art of choreography on film."[61] From Europe, Gene requested that Stanley Donen accept the Oscar for him. Vincente Minnelli admitted that Gene's decision hurt his feelings, particularly because Donen had had no part in the production of *An American in Paris.*

Gene was not the only one to receive an honorary Oscar that night. Arthur Freed took home the Irving Thalberg Memorial Award, given to a different producer each year. The Freed Unit was sweeping the Oscars;

before Best Picture was announced, *An American in Paris* had already won two honorary awards plus Best Costume Design, Best Color Cinematography, Best Art Direction and Set Decoration, and Best Screenplay (not to be confused with Best Adapted Screenplay, which went to *A Place in the Sun*). However, in the Best Picture category, *An American in Paris* faced heady competition. In a year that sported such prestigious titles as *A Streetcar Named Desire, The African Queen,* and *A Place in the Sun,* a musical picture with a thin story line seemed the least likely to win the award. Presenter Jesse Lasky could not conceal his surprise when he opened the envelope. "Oh my!" he exclaimed. "The winner for Best Picture is *An American in Paris*." The audience was silent except for a few gasps of shock. But slowly, hearty applause erupted, which only became more vigorous when Freed trotted up to the stage, clearly moved. As he cradled the statuette with the honorary one he had already received, he quipped, "It's a double header!" He continued on a more serious note: "Thank you. And thank you from my brilliant associates who made this possible: Vincente Minnelli, Gene Kelly, and a great studio with real courage and leadership who supported me. Thank you."[62]

For the present, it appeared that everything Gene Kelly and the Freed Unit touched equaled acclaim. The reaction to *Singin' in the Rain* upon its premiere on March 27, 1952, was no exception. Metro's New York boss, Nick Schenck, remarked: "Everyone loved it. I was delighted with every scene and it will bring a pleasant glow to everyone who sees it. Kelly's singing in the rain number should become a musical classic."[63]

However, the formidable Bosley Crowther of the *New York Times* had a number of complaints about the film, the dominant one being that the title had nothing to do with the plot. He asserted that the picture was mostly nonsense but did concede that the "nonsense is generally good and at times it reaches the level of first-class satiric burlesque." Crowther deemed the "Broadway Ballet" nothing but a lot "of eye-filling acrobatics against a mammoth production splurge."[64] Though opinions were mixed about the "Broadway Ballet," its contribution to the art of cinedance was virtually undisputed. A critic for *Nation* magazine remarked: "His [Gene's] . . . ballet becomes something more than ballet screened—a dance brilliantly designed for the camera."[65] The title number was, in most reviews, crowned as the high spot of the film. Crowther wrote that it was "by far his [Gene's] most captivating number . . . a beautifully soggy tap dance performed in the splashing rain."[66]

Singin' in the Rain should have outshone *An American in Paris* due to its superior cohesive plotline, witty screenplay, strong characterizations, and infectious musical numbers. Though *An American in Paris* did have a laudable screenplay and inventive musical numbers, it lacked the comedy, fluid story, and fully developed characters that made *Singin' in the Rain* so superb. *Singin' in the Rain* did gross $5.6 million at the box office, more than recouping its $2.6 million budget. Still, *An American in Paris* had grossed $1.2 million more. As Adolph Green aptly put it, the earlier picture was "considered Art" and thus "got so much publicity and so many favorable notices."[67] The reasons behind the lack of buildup for *Singin' in the Rain* also had much to do with Dore Schary. Donen's biographer Stephen M. Silverman explained that Schary, to capitalize on "the windfall" of honors *An American in Paris* received, decided to re-release it in theaters at the same time *Singin' in the Rain* was playing, thus sabotaging the latter picture. In fact, in many movie houses, *Singin' in the Rain* was "yanked to accommodate the Oscar winner."[68]

An American in Paris had been nominated for eight Oscars; *Singin' in the Rain* for only two: Best Supporting Actress and Best Original Music Score. On the night of the ceremony, March 19, 1953, the picture took home neither statuette. Gloria Grahame won over Jean Hagen for her role in Vincente Minnelli's *The Bad and the Beautiful* and Alfred Newman won over Lennie Hayton for his work on *With a Song in My Heart*.

However, the picture was not bereft of honors. At the Golden Globes ceremony on February 26, 1953, Donald O'Connor received a Best Actor award and the picture itself was nominated for Best Musical or Comedy, although it lost to the well-executed but somewhat stilted Jane Froman biopic, *With a Song in My Heart*. Betty Comden and Adolph Green received a Writers Guild of America prize for Best Written American Musical.

"Our picture didn't seem as important [compared to *An American in Paris*]. Mainly because it was full of laughter—that sinful, superficial thing called laughter," Adolph Green said facetiously.[69] However, *Singin' in the Rain* cannot be said to be less important than *An American in Paris* because of its lighter mood. Film critic Elvis Mitchell went so far as to say that "*Singin' in the Rain* may be the smartest musical comedy ever made."[70] And of course the film has delighted audiences for decades; it is perhaps the most beloved and revered film to come from Hollywood's golden era.

Singin' in the Rain appealed to audiences all over the world not only because of its contagious energy and irresistible wit but also because of its timeliness. The film's script rang especially true to audiences in 1952; the transition from silent to sound was an analogy of the transition from film to television. (Incidentally, the twenty-fifth Academy Awards, at which *Singin' in the Rain* was nominated, was the first televised Oscar ceremony. It aired on March 19, 1953.) Reflecting on *Singin' in the Rain* decades later, Stanley Donen thought that it hadn't remained relevant; it looked "creaky."[71] Gene Kelly was of the opposite opinion. "I've made a lot of films that were bigger hits and made lots more money, but now they look dated. But this one, out of all my pictures, has a chance to last. The picture was made with love."[72] What keeps the film pertinent is its essential innocence and lack of pretension. As Leonard Bernstein put it, the film is truly "a reaffirmation of life."[73]

Singin' in the Rain should have propelled Gene's career forward, marking as it did the third in a triumvirate of masterpieces, preceded by *On the Town* and *An American in Paris*. Indeed, *Singin' in the Rain* came closest to being the perfect picture Gene was forever striving to create. Gene, however, remained dissatisfied. He felt, for the time being, that he had done all he could with the conventional format of the Hollywood musical. Hence his compulsion to pursue his all-dance picture; here was new, unexplored territory to master. The picture could very well mark a new beginning in his career—and his life. Betsy observed that Gene "knew . . . making a plotless film in a balletic form might be overstepping the mark, but he did it from serious artistic ambition, not for any pretension." Those Gene left behind at MGM—even the steadfast Arthur Freed—may have seen Gene's dual decision to move overseas and proceed with his experimental film as a sort of death sentence for his career, but in Betsy's observation, her husband "was altogether happy. . . . He knew what he was doing."[74]

16

What a Day This Has Been

For Gene Kelly, living and working in Europe in the early 1950s gave him ample room for exploration in his directorial and choreographic career. For Betsy Blair, living abroad allowed for a different kind of exploration. Indeed, away from the familiar "Gene and the studio will take care of it" environment in Beverly Hills, "the time had come to grow up. . . . I was strong enough to change myself, but I was not strong enough to confront him and make him see me as a woman, not as a little angel."[1]

The new opportunities Gene and Betsy found abroad were decidedly not shared ones. Gene's naysayers in Hollywood had predicted that his move to Europe would sound the death knell for his career; none predicted that it could presage the end of a marriage that so far had been free from conflict.

Betsy began to accept offers of work from fellow expatriates and black-listed artists. Gene, she said, was often "so busy he [didn't] notice my absence." She began to garner many admirers among her mentors and comrades, admitting later, "I can see now that I wanted every man to sort of fall in love with me. . . . I'm sure this behavior was directly related to Gene and his fame. With the whole world admiring him, I had to find my own circle of admirers."[2]

Gene's incessant activity did in truth put emotional distance between him and his wife. He took on as much, if not more, responsibility for his nascent dance picture as Arthur Freed, the titular producer of the film. Far from the scrutiny of MGM executives, Gene felt his power and position. His new picture was completely in his hands and not a collaborative effort, as had been his best films to date.

As he had in Hollywood, Gene did try his best to keep Betsy involved in his work. "Gene asked me to come along when he was running screen tests or to see a set and have lunch," Betsy recalled. "But I wasn't part of the action in the way I always felt I was in Beverly Hills." In Europe, she came to miss members of the Freed Unit coming in and out of the house, playing games in the living room or singing at the piano. Though she had no part in the professional aspects of their meetings, Gene always ushered her and Kerry in to hear new songs by Comden and Green or Roger Edens. "We were never shut out," she commented. "The study had no door."[3]

At the dawn of 1952, Gene and his family did not ring in the New Year together. Gene was in Paris to begin work on *The Devil Makes Three* while Betsy and Kerry were still in Hollywood; they did not set sail for Europe until March 5, 1952. When the ship docked at Le Havre, Gene was eagerly awaiting his wife and daughter with three cars and a van to accommodate their forty-seven suitcases. They stayed at the chic Hotel Lancaster overnight before traveling to Munich so Gene could complete location work on *The Devil Makes Three*—a picture for which he felt little but apathy. A thriller, it deals with an air force captain (Gene) in postwar Germany who loves a girl (starlet Pier Angeli) used by neo-Nazis to smuggle gold. Gene had long yearned to do another straight role, but the flat dialogue of the B picture came as a depressing anticlimax to the sharp and witty banter in *An American in Paris* and *Singin' in the Rain*.

Filming for *The Devil Makes Three* continued until April 1952. But only four days passed before Betsy decided that she could not stay with Gene, and she and Kerry removed to Paris. Betsy confessed that she had difficulty even pretending to tolerate the Germans, whom she viewed as fascist enemies. Gene did not share his wife's ill will. On his film sets, Gene brought a spirit of openness and amity. Knowing he was a guest in a foreign country, he went further to show his goodwill. One evening while enjoying a drink in a beer cellar, he overheard two American ex-GIs muttering insults about the Germans. He flew into a rage and engaged in a fight with the men. Kerry later reflected that he "must have been going through a terrible crisis of conscience because, after all, only a few years ago we were at war with the Germans. . . . I remember it was a very painful thing for him to punch an American over a German—but he did."[4]

Gene's swiftness to anger not only was an example of his lifelong tendency to defend the underdog, but was also prompted by his misgivings regarding his career potential in Europe. Shortly before the fight, he had heard news of his Honorary Academy Award for *An American in Paris*. Now, halfway across the world, he saw what a disaster of a movie he was making compared to the film that had merited him the Oscar. *The Devil*

Makes Three was certainly an inauspicious beginning to his work in Europe, one he feared would cast "an indelible blot" on his career.[5]

Fortunately, Gene's fears were unfounded. The picture premiered, virtually unnoticed, four months later. Upon its New York release on August 29, 1952, a *New York Times* critic panned the picture as "on the whole, a synthetic, pallid and erratic endeavor," but spared the film's players, who emerged "unscathed." "Mr. Kelly proves once again that dancing shoes don't necessarily make the actor in a fine, restrained characterization."[6] According to MGM records, the film made $743,000 in the United States and Canada and $742,000 elsewhere, resulting in a loss of $57,000.

With the picture forgotten almost the moment it was released, Gene forged ahead with plans to travel to London and get back in shape for his dance picture. He had put on twelve pounds thanks to his relative inactivity and consumption of rich German food. "I'll get trim again as soon as I start practicing. Dancing is like boxing. Only you don't get hit."[7] He elaborated on his goals: "I would like to be twins or quadruplets. Then I could produce and direct films and at the same time could develop film choreography and dancing. . . . I could scour the world to discover new talents. . . . I could be working in Munich and Rome and Paris and London and Hollywood, absorbing all the various techniques."[8]

When summer 1952 came and the starting date for the picture edged closer, Gene realized at least one wish as he embarked on an international search for dancers. He hoped to show the world—everywhere from Senegal to Hackensack, New Jersey—that dance in film was not defined only by himself and Fred Astaire. Despite Arthur Freed's wariness over the picture, he had enough faith in it to finally give it a title: *Invitation to the Dance*. Still, the producer stated in no uncertain terms: "I am *not* for making this film."[9] Gene was unfazed. In fact, Freed's doubts about the film's potential only spurred him to work harder. Betsy observed that he "worried and fumed a bit because he felt responsible for every detail of the film. This film was his baby."[10]

Betsy was experiencing creative stimulation of her own; Orson Welles had made her the tantalizing offer to come to Rome and play Desdemona in his cinematic production of *Othello*. She accepted Welles's proposal, brimming with excitement. To her supreme disappointment, Welles ultimately lost funding for the picture, and she flew back to Gene and Kerry in London. (Almost two years later, Welles completed *Othello* with a different actress, Suzanne Cloutier, in Betsy's part.)

Betsy still had plenty to keep her occupied. She and Gene were busy finding lodgings in London. Until they could find a more permanent home, they were living at the Savoy Hotel. Kerry came down with the flu, but she did not seem to mind being ill. Every night until she was well, Gene's friend Danny Kaye came to tell her comical stories, complete with his crazy vocal intonations and facial contortions. As soon as she was well, Gene enrolled Kerry at the Royal Ballet School. But the lessons did not last long. Kerry's ballet instructor informed Gene that the low arch of the child's foot would prevent her from ever being a ballerina. Gene proceeded to remove his shoes and peel off his socks. He held his foot beside his daughter's. "They're identical!" he declared. He took Kerry by the hand and exited, proud that neither of their feet conformed to stereotype. Kerry, who had no real interest in dance, was unmarked by the incident. Gene was far more affected by it, taking the ballet teacher's criticism as a personal affront. Such judgment reinforced his "distaste for conventional rules where dancing was concerned."[11]

The Kellys soon found a homey abode on Chapel Street. They hired a married couple to look after the home and see to errands, including the ordering of their food from Harrods. Soon after they settled in, Betsy's mother came from New Jersey to enjoy a lengthy stay with the Kellys. Mrs. Boger's arrival could not have come at a more opportune time, for Betsy had landed a job that would take her to Paris. Director Anatole Litvak asked Gene if he and Kerry could spare Betsy for two weeks so she could coach the French leading lady of the Kirk Douglas picture, *Act of Love* (1953), he was making in Paris. Sydney Chaplin was performing the same service for the actor playing the second male lead. In Paris, Betsy could be part of Litvak's crew, part of something in which she could immerse herself. "I think I was playing at being someone else—or maybe just me if I hadn't gone to Hollywood with Gene," Betsy later reflected.[12]

In Paris, Betsy engaged in the first of what became a series of extramarital affairs, despite the fact that she claimed she and Gene were still "happy in bed." Her first affair was with a young French man who, she claimed, was a hero of the French Resistance affiliated with the Communists. "None of it was secret. I always said where I'd been," Betsy said. "Gene seemed busy and amused by my adventures."[13]

True, Gene always knew where Betsy had been—but he did not know whom she had been with—or what she had been doing.

With *Invitation to the Dance* at the serious planning stage, Gene became engulfed in the project. He returned to France with Kerry and his assistants Lois, Carol, and Jeanne. There, he rented a small, converted mill in a quaint village six miles from Chartres. The quiet getaway proved the ideal locale for creative inspiration. Betsy did not live with Gene and Kerry at the mill, having taken another job in Paris. Kerry and her father took a train each morning to Paris, where Betsy would then take the girl to a progressive day school. "It was all fascinating," Kerry said of her time living abroad.[14]

Gene and Betsy, though apart for much of the time, still enjoyed a convivial and stimulating social nightlife together. Directors Anatole Litvak, Alexandre Trauner, Jules Dassin, photographer Robert Capa, and screenwriter Paul Jarrico were just a few of their friends. "We had a great time," Betsy recalled. "I have to say we were a pretty flashy couple on the dance floor. . . . They [the clubs] were like 'raves' but without the drugs. Come to think of it, we were incredibly wholesome." Wholesome the clubs may have been, but Betsy's life away from the family continued to diverge from the clean-cut image Gene had of her. In her memoir, she confessed to having another affair with a man she did not name; she referred to him only as an "uncle" figure.[15]

After several weeks in Chartres, Gene and his assistants had drafted several ideas for sequences in *Invitation to the Dance*. By August 1952, the Kellys all returned to their Chapel Street home. Gene was finally ready to begin shooting the project at London's Elstree Studios. Although they were now living together, Gene and Betsy saw less of each other. Gene's work consumed him; technical problems that would have taken no time to remedy at MGM took days to fix at the modest London studio. Betsy commented that "he tackled the problems with determination—even joy."[16]

Gene's sense of joy in the picture diminished after it became virtually a one-man show. "I . . . didn't want to appear in the film as much as I did, but this was at MGM's insistence. They were investing a million dollars and wanted some protection for their money. My name was about all they could gamble on," Gene explained.[17] He expressed his concerns to Arthur Freed in a six-page letter, declaring that he feared he would glut "the public with the sight of Kelly slowing it up like a dancing Orson Welles."[18] But Gene heeded MGM's request and worked himself into more sequences in the picture.

More difficulties arose due to the fact that Gene's selected dancers came from several different continents and had other commitments that limited the flexibility of their schedules. As a consequence, Gene had to film their routines in bits and pieces. Among the cast were the gamin Claire Sombert and Tamara Toumanova, the latter the only freelance ballerina Gene knew of who did not belong to a company. He also persuaded Russian-Ukrainian dancer Igor Youskevitch, who had become an American citizen in 1944, to come to London. Gene had originally planned for Youskevitch to perform a completely balletic number, but when the artist who was to perform with him dropped out, Gene had to step in to complete the scene with the great dancer himself. "That meant I had to invent something that I could do," Gene explained, noting he could not match Youskevitch's balletic finesse. "The only thing I could think of was to play the clown who's tragically in love with a young woman."[19] Thus, the film's first sequence, set at a circus, was born.

Even after his and his assistants' intensive work at the Chartres house, Gene still had no concrete plans for the rest of the film. A reporter from *Screenland* who asked him how a script would be written for a film composed entirely of dance, received the answer: "It's all in there." Gene pointed to his head. "And I work from day to day. . . . It's an awful strain, directing the picture as well as dancing in it. It means no parties, no shows—I haven't had a chance to read a book in weeks. There's a constant strain. [But] it isn't as if I had to do this," he added with a rueful smile.[20]

Gene ultimately decided to construct the film into four separate sequences. He already had the circus dance planned. The second number he envisioned as a modern dance accompanied by popular songs of the past decade. Gene's solo would use "Sunny Side of the Street"; Carol Haney, in her first film spotlight, would dance to "St. Louis Blues." Gene planned for another segment, "Ring around the Rosy," to be set to original music by frequent Freed Unit contributor André Previn. It tells a series of romantic stories woven together by the exchange of a gold bracelet. Gene plays a Marine in the sequence. The fourth segment, "Sinbad the Sailor," is a fantasy that, like Gene's acclaimed routine in *Anchors Aweigh* with Jerry the Mouse, mixes live action with cartoons. This time Gene dances with a genie in a scene set in a casbah. Gene, playing a sailor for the fourth time in his career, buys a magic lantern, which sets into motion conflicts with animated sword-carrying villains. Also part of the story is the sailor's love for a harem girl, who is also animated. Carol Haney acted as a live-action reference for the girl, to help the animators better simulate her movements. As well as Previn, other regular Freed Unit members, including Roger Edens, Johnny Green, Conrad Salinger, and Lela Simone, worked on the musical arrangements.

Despite the contributions of these talents, Gene soon realized the film lacked something: passion. Gene put every ounce of energy into the creation of the picture, but the other dancers did not share his enthusiasm. Without Freed's encouragement and a spirit of teamwork behind the picture, Gene's customary exuberance failed to translate onscreen. He realized that the film could never live up to what he envisioned in his mind. He constantly drilled the dancers, as if by working them hard enough his vision would somehow materialize. Youskevitch later said: "There were times, I think, when [Kelly] overdid things. He rehearsed us all so rigidly—and on cement floors!—that it required superhuman energy not to collapse. . . . He worked . . . until finally I injured my knee, and he realized he was wrong."[21] Overall, the performers simply did not take the film to heart as Gene did. In the death scene at the end of the circus sequence, for instance, dancer Claire Sombert and Youskevitch "were suddenly struck by the phoniness of the situation in the studio" and burst into laughter. Gene, "to his eternal credit," did not lose his temper, although the entire scene had to be reshot.[22]

By winter 1952, *Invitation to the Dance* had already been in production for four months but seemed far from completion. Gene became more depressed and not a little discouraged when Metro executives informed him that the popular songs number, which had promised to be the most accessible and lively of the picture, would have to be dropped due to production costs. The bulk of the expenses were related to the lengthy "Sinbad" sequence. The number was the weakest in the film: overly long and devoid of charm. Gene decided he could not finish the intricate animation needed for the sequence in London; the MGM animation department took over the job and spent a year completing it.

A dejected Gene temporarily brightened during the holidays. First, he took his brood on a short jaunt to his ancestral stomping ground. According to one reporter, "All the Kellys headed for Dublin. From the moment they started, Gene and Kerry were like nine-year-olds. . . . The mere name of the place thrills them. They prowled the countryside for hours. They haunted ancient castles."[23] After leaving the Emerald Isle, Gene took the family to his favorite resort, Klosters, where they were joined by Lois McClelland, Jeanne Coyne, and Carol Haney. "It was a storybook Christmas with snow and sleigh bells and hot chocolate," Betsy recalled.[24]

But even during Gene's break from *Invitation to the Dance*, he did not leave work completely behind. Arthur Freed traveled to the United

Kingdom, and he and Gene went to Scotland to scout out locations for *Brigadoon,* a film based on the 1947 Alan Jay Lerner and Frederick Loewe Broadway musical. Freed had already assigned Vincente Minnelli as director and Lerner as screenwriter. Given that Gene had worked so well with the two men on *An American in Paris,* Freed instantly thought of giving the lead role to Gene once the actor returned to Hollywood.

Freed would have to wait quite a while. Gene's work on *Invitation to the Dance* as well as filming on the second low-budget drama he was required to complete kept him in England for ten more months. Upon returning to London, Gene and his family found yet another new lodging. Their rented abode, located off Hyde Park corner, happened to be the townhouse of British film star Robert Donat. A columnist for *Screen Stars* magazine described the scene thus: "Like something out of an historical novel, it is a cobbled street, with old-fashioned attached houses on both sides, and an arched exit at the far end that leads into a regular street." Gene saw the quaint lodging as an especially stimulating "storybook" locale for Kerry. Exciting though London was for Kerry, the girl could not help feeling homesick. However, Gene's ongoing support and love had made the transition from Beverly Hills to Europe far easier than it might have been. Time spent with Kerry seldom failed to buoy Gene's spirits. "Gene and Kerry have found a meeting of minds, as it were, an understanding and pleasure in each other's company. Together they enjoy the same simple things—steeple rides in the park, a visit to London's Zoo, or quiet evening walks down narrow winding streets," the *Screen Stars* reporter observed.[25] Gene occasionally brought Kerry to the set of *Invitation to the Dance* as well. In the studio commissary, they would enjoy ice cream between Nabisco wafers. Gene, ignoring the English tradition of delicately using a spoon and fork to eat dessert sandwiches, picked his up with his fingers. "It's the American way," he said. A visiting reporter noted, "At home or abroad it's . . . the Kelly way, to be simple and simply American. To love his work, his family and above all—his home."[26]

With Kerry, Gene's happiness was genuine. But the moment he left his family each morning, his confidence flagged. He despaired over the degree to which his dance film was being cut, edited, and cleansed—robbing it of the originality and excitement he had tried to instill. In the "Ring around the Rosy" sequence, for instance, Gene explained: "I'm walking down the street and a prostitute comes up to me. The censors got real up in arms about it. . . . I don't believe in letting children see things that aren't good for them. There are certain pictures I wouldn't let my daughter see. It's okay to show scenes of murder and guys getting beaten to a pulp. The censors approve that, but they worry about how close the girl stands to me in the street scene."[27]

Despite his misgivings about how his picture was taking shape, Gene still felt it was an important contribution to the art of cinedance. MGM did not share his view, and Gene now harbored well-founded fears that the studio would either shelve the project or fail to properly promote the finished film. Inadequate advertising would spell certain box office failure for such an avant-garde film. "I don't think I want to direct another picture; not unless it's something very special," an exhausted Gene confided to a reporter in October 1952.[28]

Gene began to spend much time after hours at his favorite haunts in London. In the relaxing atmosphere of the Star Tavern in Belgravia, one of the most exclusive areas of the city, Gene was hidden away from autograph seekers and reporters. In the elegant pub, adorned with mahogany walls, blood-red leather seats, gold mirrors, and a chandelier, Gene enjoyed a pint with actor-friends including Robert Taylor, Errol Flynn, Humphrey Bogart, and Lauren Bacall. Les Ambassadeurs Club, the chief hangout for expatriate Americans, became his and Betsy's place to meet any night they could. After closing time, the owner of the club would drive the stars to "an illegitimate watering hole on the outskirts of London," where they would continue their discussions early into the morning.[29]

By summer 1953, *Invitation to the Dance* at last reached completion, its final cost an astounding $2,822,000. Gene admitted that the picture was not great, but wanly told reporters: "I think they'll [the public] like it. . . . So it's an experiment, so *somebody's* got to experiment. You can't leave an art form static."[30] MGM executives' feet grew colder and colder regarding the film, and they continually postponed its release. A year later, a writer for *Picturegoer* observed: "So far as MGM is concerned . . . it has been dropped from the list of past, present and future productions of the company."[31] Nonetheless, the film underwent endless cuts and recuts, dubs and redubs, until MGM decided whether or not to release it.

Almost immediately after completing principal photography on *Invitation to the Dance,* Gene went into shooting for his second B picture. Entitled *Crest of the Wave* (aka *Seagulls over Sorrento*), the film was based on a West End show that had run for five years in London but only twelve nights on Broadway. The fact that it had not appealed to American theater audiences made its failure as a picture seem predestined. The film tells the story of a US Navy lieutenant who works for the British to supervise torpedo experiments after an English scientist is killed. Gene, with deadpan humor, remarked that *Crest* was "torpedoed and sank with all hands."[32] The film was not released until November 10, 1954. A critic for the *New York Times* called "Gene Kelly's portrayal . . . smooth if not exciting" and concluded that the movie was "largely a tempest in a teapot."[33] Like *The Devil Makes Three, Crest of the Wave* failed to make a profit. It lost $58,000 upon its release.

The encouragement—and recognition—Gene needed to lift his spirits came at a most unlikely venue: Queen Elizabeth's coronation parade. The great event took place on June 2, 1953, in the midst of the shooting of *Crest of the Wave*. Gene's agents at MCA gave him and his family the opportunity to gain a better view of the parade. It was before seven in the morning, and Gene carried his umbrella up, with Kerry and Betsy huddled beneath it. They eventually went down to the street and stood on Hyde Park Corner. Onlookers spotted Gene and began to serenade him with "Singin' in the Rain." The dancer was moved to tears. The crowd then cleared a path for the Kellys, who ran and skipped to the door of their building. Then Gene grinned at his fans and did an impromptu pirouette.

Just as Betsy had harbored ill will toward the Germans, Gene confessed that when he had first visited England several years before, he had, "for no particular reason, felt hostile towards the 'limeys.'" After his eighteen months working and living among the English, he had completely changed his mind. Decades later, Gene still had nothing but praise for England and its people, claiming that taxi drivers in London especially were the friendliest in the world.

To end his tumultuous stint in Europe on a pleasant note, Gene took a boat trip up the River Thames, truly relaxing for the first time in over a year. With Betsy, Kerry, Lois, and assorted friends, he stopped for tea at intriguing old towns along the river. At the end of each day's excursion, Gene and Kerry cooked, camping style (often in the rain), at a riverside inn. Betsy was immune to the appeal of such rusticity and chose to drive back to London during these adventures. She met Gene and Kerry at the end of each of their day trips to drive them back to London.

In spring 1953, Gene and his family returned to Hollywood, $370,000 richer, tax-free.[34] After nearly two years away from America, Gene could not help but worry if his name held the same draw at the box office. Arthur

Freed had no such fears that Gene had lost popular appeal. He had two projects lined up for him, the long-postponed *Huckleberry Finn* and *Brigadoon*. For the latter film, Gene would be choreographer as well as star.

"It is . . . fascinating to see how Freed continued to push his team to produce new material even in the face of the imminent collapse of the movie musical as a commercial genre," historian Dominic McHugh commented.[35] The Freed Unit—and Gene—had reached the apex of their careers at the moment musicals began to slip as foolproof moneymakers. Film studios had to face the fact that television had become more exciting to Americans than virtually anything on a movie screen. On the night of January 19, 1953, two-thirds of the country's population tuned in to watch the birth of little Ricky on *I Love Lucy*.

The other third watched President Dwight Eisenhower's inauguration. Eisenhower ushered in a conservative era marked by prosperity for manufacturers and corporations but not for filmmakers. Studio executives wrung their hands when Congress repealed the tax exemption law that made income earned overseas untaxable. Now, any money overseas films had made was retroactively taxed—and so was the income of the actors, including Gene. For the average American, however, the Eisenhower era was generally one of relative peace and comfort. One writer called the 1950s an age of "the bland leading the bland."[36]

If those in the movie industry hoped to triumph over television, they had to produce films that were anything but bland. The industry's most conspicuous effort was the creation of CinemaScope, a new technology that used three projectors and a wraparound screen to create a 3D effect. Especially effective for epics with lush landscapes, CinemaScope dazzled audiences upon its debut in the biblical story *The Robe* (1953). However, cameramen and directors of the old guard were displeased with the way the new camera lens forced them to shorten and widen the sets and reevaluate how to zoom in and out without causing distortion. CinemaScope may have given audiences a spectacle they could not get from their televisions, but it also made the intimate shots and settings of the 1930s and 1940s obsolete. How it would change choreography for musical numbers remained to be seen.

Gene was not immediately confronted with filmdom's many changes upon his return to America. Gene and his family arrived quietly in New York, where Harriet Kelly met them and drove them to Gene's boyhood home in Pittsburgh. "We didn't want people to know [we had arrived] because Gene needed a little rest," Betsy told a writer for the *Pittsburgh Press*.[37] Gene was still in a state of melancholy after his unsuccessful efforts in Europe and would often slip "blackly out of a conversation to stare unhearing at his shoes and chew on some obscure worry."[38]

Betsy was in a state of crisis as well. In her memoir, she recalled that after settling back into her and Gene's Rodeo Drive home, she "woke up," literally and figuratively. "I was all alone. I wandered downstairs . . . went into the backyard, [and] looked at the avocado trees and Kerry's play-house. . . . This was my house, this is where I live, this is where I belong. But I suddenly couldn't hide the truth. That 'I,' the good little girl who lived there, was no longer me." Betsy tearfully told Gene her feelings of desperation. "He was indulgent and concerned as always—whatever I needed, he just wanted me to be happy." She began seeing a "Marxist Freudian psychoanalyst" weekly. Gene did not believe in analysis and was not pleased by her decision. "He probably felt threatened," Betsy said, "but again, he didn't interfere." The first words she uttered to her analyst were, "I think I should get a divorce."[39] However, she kept divorce solely in the realm of thought—for the time being.

In addition to worries in his home life, Gene looked to *Brigadoon* with increasing frustration. With the repeal of the tax exemption law, MGM was scrimping in every way possible, rendering location shoots out of the question. "We had the vision of shooting *Brigadoon* as you'd shoot a western—out on the moors of Scotland," Gene said. "But the studio didn't have the money. . . . Vincente and I . . . were very disappointed."[40] The project presented more challenges for Gene; as choreographer, he had to find a way of effectively designing dances for CinemaScope.

According to Minnelli, "I remember him [Gene] telling me that he hadn't liked the Broadway show [*Brigadoon*] at all, and I loved it. I think he only took on this assignment because we all asked him to, because we felt we needed him badly."[41] Minnelli's statement conflicts with an observation made by his biographer, Emanuel Levy, that "early on, Minnelli made a mistake and confessed to Kelly that he hadn't really liked the Broadway show." To further complicate matters, Gene and Minnelli were not "in sync . . . in terms of their musical conception." Nevertheless, the two colleagues worked closely together to "improvise" and "touch up" the Lerner script—with little success.[42] Minnelli's and Gene's lack of passion for the project could not help but infuse every aspect of the picture. Yet, Gene needed to make a "comeback" in Hollywood, and so continued toiling on *Brigadoon*. "Show business is all I know," Gene stated. "Take it away from me and you've taken everything."[43]

Throughout his career, Gene had utilized dream ballets to resolve conflicts in his films. As fantasies, they were clearly separated from the real story. *Brigadoon*, then, was an atypical project for the man who brought the musical film into the real world. The story was pure whimsy. In Gene's words: "It's a moody fantasy . . . and that is the most difficult type of show to stage."[44]

Brigadoon tells the story of two New York businessmen, Tommy Albright (Gene) and Jeff Douglas, on a hunting vacation in Scotland. They discover a quaint and remote village, Brigadoon, that does not appear on any map. In time, Tommy and Jeff discover why from a wise village elder, Mr. Lundie: Brigadoon is enchanted; it appears only once every hundred years, and only for one day. Then it vanishes back into the mists, waiting another century to awaken again. When Tommy falls in love with Fiona, a village girl, he is shattered that she can never be part of his world. He must choose, then, whether he wants to be a part of hers. He ultimately returns to New York but remains haunted by memories of Fiona. Four months later, he breaks off his engagement to his fiancée, Jane, and returns with Jeff to the site of Brigadoon. As Tommy mourns the loss of Fiona, the village suddenly emerges. Mr. Lundie explains to Tommy that when one loves deeply enough, miracles are possible.

One promising aspect of the film was its cast. Gene's old friend Van Johnson was to play Jeff and Cyd Charisse, who had made such a hit with him in *Singin' in the Rain*'s "Broadway Ballet," was to portray Fiona. "I was excited about being in it [*Brigadoon*], but it started off badly," Cyd remarked.[45] From the start, tension and melancholia plagued the set. Gene was accustomed to having the time and resources to experiment. But Dore Schary, cutting expenses, had ordered musical producers not to shoot extravagant numbers unless they were certain they would be included in the final picture. Schary's new rule was like a physical blow to Gene. He could spend weeks working on a number that was not used, yet such numbers often served as springboards for masterpieces. "The studio betrayed us," Gene stated years later. A musical that "could have been magical" became a victim of tight finances.[46]

It was unfortunate also that the picture couldn't be shot on location.

Instead, the film's art directors painted backgrounds and built mounds and elevations with realistic-looking heather and vegetation as well as full reproductions of thatched-roof Scottish cottages. Cyd Charisse asserted that "from the lavishness of the sets, it would have been cheaper to send the whole company to Scotland. . . . But with Scotland's weather, we could've been there a year and a half."[47] Gene's hope to give the film "great movement and the look and feel of fresh air" was virtually impossible to reproduce on a soundstage.[48]

Unlike the vital and emotive dance collaborations Gene and Vincente Minnelli had created in *The Pirate* and *An American in Paris,* the choreography in *Brigadoon* was as uninspired as the simulated sets. Minnelli was continually changing Gene's choreography to conform to the picture's wide-screen format, adding dozens of dancers to fill the sides of the elongated screen. Gene, who had pioneered intimate production numbers that used only one or two dancers as their focal point, bristled at the alterations. *Brigadoon* was a thoroughly stage-bound musical, negating the strides Gene had made in the art of cinedance. Minnelli remembered that "Gene . . . seemed remote and slightly down. . . . I had many talks with him, trying to impress on him the need . . . to light up the sky. . . . Gene delivered as much as he could."[49] Gene's best show of vivacity in the picture occurs when Tommy sings to Jeff of his newfound love. He prances from hill to heather-laden hill, crooning:

What a day this has been
What a rare mood I'm in
Why, it's almost like being in love.

The tune is now a standard in the American songbook and has been revived by many artists over the decades, but Gene's rendition of the song is perhaps the most arresting.

Though his delivery of "It's Almost Like Being in Love" was convincing, Gene's spirits offscreen were still dejected. His depression made him less affable on the set, even toward costars he considered valued friends and colleagues. Cyd Charisse was especially taken aback by his moodiness. She claimed that the only time she became truly angry at Gene was one day when he instructed her and Carol Haney (she and Jeanne Coyne were again acting as his assistants) to stand on a mound of dirt for a number. But then he simply muttered, "You two work something out," and left. The mound of dirt was supposed to be covered in heather, but the studio land-scaping department hadn't installed it yet. "So we were dancing in plain old dirt and we would get dirtier and dirtier. For several days, Carol and I worked on that dirt, trying to create something pretty. . . . Kelly had appar-ently abandoned us." When Gene appeared several days later, his lips were drawn tightly together and his eyes blazed. "He was in what I call his Irish mood. Something had gone wrong. . . . And he was about to explode," Cyd recalled. He told Carol and Cyd that what they had created was "no good."[50]

As he stood criticizing the women, he heard the clicking heels of two secretaries on their way to lunch. "He was at that point where anything would set him off." Gene turned to the two secretaries. "I don't come to your office when you're working so don't come here when I'm working!" he shouted. Frightened, the girls fled from the soundstage. Gene then turned back to Carol and Cyd and "really told us off." Cyd, exhausted and covered with dirt, began weeping and ran to her dressing room. She promptly packed her bags. "Then Kelly came in, all contrite and apologetic. He didn't mean it, he said, he was tired himself, he said, and overworked and it was a hard time for all of us. 'Please excuse me,' he said. When he turned on the charm, nobody could refuse him anything. I realized that his apology had been a genuine one and that we were all tense from the work. . . . I accepted his apology and the whole incident was forgotten."[51]

That Gene had left part of the choreography in *Brigadoon* to Carol Haney and Cyd Charisse was in direct opposition to his usual hands-on approach to his work. According to Minnelli, Jeanne Coyne took over many duties and was the "perfect intermediary with the crew. . . . Her patience was superhuman."[52] Carol Haney, on the other hand, had lost her patience. Her spotlight number had been cut from *Invitation to the Dance*, and she was dispirited and discontented with remaining behind the scenes for the rest of her career. Unbeknownst to Gene, she had already begun looking for a different job.

Carol discovered during shooting that she had landed the job for which she had auditioned—a supporting but important role in a new Broadway show, *The Pajama Game*. "I remember the afternoon when I was on a stage and Carol came around to talk to me because she had been offered the part," Lela Simone recalled. "And she said, 'I can't do it. I can't leave Gene. It's impossible.'"[53] However, after many tears and some cajoling from Simone, Carol took the part. At MGM, everyone began greeting her as "The Star."

Gene, in Simone's memory, did not share the sense of celebration over Carol's good fortune. "There was a big blow up [when Gene found out]. Gene said, 'You are not grateful to me and to what I did for you, because without me you would never have gotten or been offered a part like this.' . . . And finally Gene said, 'Well, okay, why don't you go and do it. Try it.' He thought she could never make it. . . . There was nothing gracious" about their farewell. Carol left for New York immediately. *The Pajama Game* premiered on May 12, 1954, and ran for an astounding 1,063 performances through 1956. Gene recovered from losing the invaluable Carol and eventually saw that her decision had been the right one. "It [Carol's leaving] did not ruin their friendship. It sort of slowly repaired itself and Gene got used to the fact that his little assistant became a star and it all went all right," Simone concluded.[54] The ever-loyal Jeanne Coyne remained to aid Gene in his choreographic work.

On March 9, 1954, filming for *Brigadoon,* mercifully, came to a close. Throughout shooting, Freed, Minnelli, and Lerner had never ceased planning for *Huckleberry Finn* as their next project with Gene, hoping it would prove better than *Brigadoon.* "From my experience with you and Vincente, it's only when the three of us are working together for immediate production that a really final script can be prepared," Lerner wrote to Freed.[55] Lerner and Minnelli were determined to create another film on a par with *An American in Paris.* Both men, as well as Gene, realized that *Brigadoon* had not been up to their usual standards.

Despite Lerner's enthusiasm, *Huckleberry Finn* died in November 1954, shortly after the release of *Brigadoon.* Gene explained the reasons behind its cancellation: "Danny [Kaye] quit the picture because he wasn't very enthusiastic about it. . . . I couldn't quit. But I wouldn't have anyway, because I loved what was being done with it. . . . This is the only time in my career I got sick from overwork. . . . Kaye wouldn't come back. The studio shied away from it. They couldn't see it without Kaye. It's a crime, because this was probably the best score [by Lerner and Burton Lane] ever written for films." In spite of the work he'd put into the project, Lerner was ultimately relieved to see it end. He flew to New York, where he proceeded to "have the most fun I've had writing in a long time" as he collaborated with Frederick Loewe on what became the sensational *My Fair Lady.*[56]

Although musicals still boomed on Broadway, the year 1954 marked the veritable end of the great film musical. But the genre did not leave without a bang. The top-grossing picture of the year was the tuneful Irving

Berlin film, *White Christmas*. At number ten was the first CinemaScope musical to hit Hollywood. Warner Bros., partnered with Transcona Enterprises, had produced the biggest, most expensive musical to date—*A Star Is Born*. The picture starred Gene's first champion in Hollywood, Judy Garland. Like a Freed Unit film, it boasted a score by MGM alums Harold Arlen and Ira Gershwin, special material by Roger Edens, costumes by Irene Sharaff, and an eighteen-minute musical sequence that, like the ballet in *Singin' in the Rain,* acted as a film within a film. Because of the movie's running time (over three hours), film exhibitors sliced a half hour from it, robbing it of many effective scenes that could have won Judy Garland her first Best Actress Oscar. *A Star Is Born* was for Judy what *Singin' in the Rain* was for Gene. While representative of her best work, it became like an obituary to her screen career.

One musical film of 1954 did not spell death for those involved in it. Stanley Donen, Gene's protégé and frequent collaborator, had truly arrived as a director with the Jack Cummings production *Seven Brides for Seven Brothers.* The sleeper hit of the year, the film utilized CinemaScope to advantage and included lively choreography by Michael Kidd. Released in July 1954 shortly before *Brigadoon*, it grossed over $9 million. *Brigadoon,* which premiered on October 22, 1954, grossed just over $2 million, resulting in a loss of $1,555,000. Jane Powell, star of *Seven Brides,* concluded: "[It] was a big hit and *Brigadoon* seemed to disappear."[57]

Reviewers were as disenchanted with *Brigadoon* as Gene, Lerner, and Minnelli had been. Bosley Crowther of the *New York Times* called it "curiously flat and out of joint." He commented on the sets' artificial appearance and criticized the star and the director. "Mr. Kelly's [performance] is as thin and metallic as a nail. . . . Vincente Minnelli's direction lacks his usual vitality and flow. . . . 'Brigadoon' on the screen, we must say, is pretty weak synthetic Scotch."[58] A critic for *Newsweek* had similar insults to hurl at the picture, declaring that it was an example of Hollywood putting its worst foot forward.[59]

Gene's next project showed little promise of reinvigorating his career. Rather, it seemed, according to his biographers Sheridan Morley and Ruth Leon, more a way to "retrieve some kind of [the] family life" he felt slipping away.[60]

Gene's forthcoming assignment called for him to play himself in a skit for the musical biopic of composer Sigmund Romberg, *Deep in My Heart.* The picture, old-fashioned in its construction, harkened back to revue-style biopics of the previous decade. In a reversal of roles, Gene found himself under Stanley Donen's direction. It could not have been easy for him to relinquish his role as mentor, but no record exists that he voiced any complaints over it. However, in 1988, he intimated that Donen had never wished to be a solo director, which was untrue. "We finally got Stanley to do his own pictures," Gene explained. He followed with sincerer words: "a blessing, I think, for the cinema in general."[61]

To make his number in *Deep in My Heart* a retrieval of family life, so to speak, Gene requested his brother Fred as his dance partner. The brothers, as had been the case since childhood, felt no sense of rivalry. Fred's career had progressed well, even if he had not won the international fame of his brother. Since 1948, Fred had been working in New York City, mainly for NBC to direct television shows. Additionally, he choreographed and directed the Ice Capades for three years and served as dance director at the Latin Quarter nightclub for star acts. Apparently, at the nightclub Havana Madrid, he helped to introduce and popularize the cha-cha.

In *Deep in My Heart*, the two Kellys danced together for the first time since they had played in cloops nearly two decades before. The number begins with them wearing 1910s-style white pin-striped suits and straw boaters (garb almost identical to that worn by Gene and Fred Astaire at one point in their 1946 skit in *Ziegfeld Follies*). A crowd of bathing beauties surrounds them and they change into striped swimsuits, all the while zealously singing "I'd Love to Go Swimmin' with Wimmin." The number, strictly vaudevillian in style, did not require any great innovation, but it did require more than a little "expended energy and boisterous clowning."[62] As much as Gene enjoyed hoofing with his brother, the breathless pace of his work took its toll on him. He admitted that his body had given out, though his mind was still so active that at times it worked half the night.

When *Deep in My Heart* premiered on December 10, 1954, Bosley Crowther claimed the picture "calls for a strong digestive system and a considerable tolerance for clichés." However, he saved complimentary words for Gene and Fred's performance as the high point of the film, deeming their number "just about as funny as it sounds."[63]

At the close of 1954, forty-two-year-old Gene had fallen to the lowest point of his career. He saw himself lagging behind as his friends and family diverged from him, going on to greater things. Stanley Donen thrived.

Carol Haney was a star. Vincente Minnelli, with whom he never again teamed, went on to direct several masterful works in all genres of film throughout the latter half of the 1950s. And Betsy had come into her own as a screen actress, thanks to another sleeper hit: *Marty.*

In February 1954, fan magazine columnists were all atwitter with the news that the Kellys were headed for divorce. Gene, most claimed, was straying—not Betsy. "The talk that he and his wife, Betsy, had separated and were planning to divorce because of his so-called extra-curricular ramblings, makes Gene laugh—and then get angry," a writer for *Movie Pix* reported. The writer concluded: "Gene is as dedicated to Betsy as he is to his wonderful, creative work."[64]

Gene was indeed as dedicated to Betsy as ever. Indeed, had it not been for him, Betsy would not have landed her breakthrough role. After her small part in the Ethel Barrymore drama *Kind Lady* (1951), she had been blacklisted and unable to find work in American pictures. Now, hearing that she was being considered for the role of the awkward schoolteacher Clara in Paddy Chayefsky's *Marty,* Gene was determined to see that she got it—blacklist or no blacklist. His first step was to invite Chayefsky to dinner.[65] After meeting her, Chayefsky knew Betsy was Clara. But there still remained the pesky fact that she was blacklisted.

The film's producer, Howard Hecht, asked Betsy to write a letter to HUAC that would clear her. She attempted to write one but realized that it would not "pass muster" because she had not named any names. Betsy was miserable—until Gene "rode to my rescue. . . . With kid gloves off [he went] raging into Dore Schary's office; 'You know her. You know she's not going to overthrow the government. You have to do something. She really wants this part. . . . Do something, Dore or I'll stop shooting.'"[66] Gene was presumably shooting *Deep in My Heart* at this time. Schary heeded Gene's request and called the American Legion in Washington, using his influence to remove Betsy from the blacklist. Betsy got the part and was spared writing the dreaded letter to HUAC.

Marty was in production from September to November 1954. The picture was slated for release in March 1955. At this point, Gene was vying for a role in a new picture—one that he felt would do for his film career what *Pal Joey* had done for his stage reputation. The part was that of professional gambler Sky Masterson in Samuel Goldwyn's film adaptation of the Broadway hit, *Guys and Dolls.* "I was born to play Sky the way Gable was born to play Rhett Butler," Gene declared. All he needed was permission from MGM. "It was a part that would have meant a lot to me. But . . . those new bastards at MGM refused to loan me out."[67] Goldwyn was unhappy about losing Gene, but he recovered faster than the actor. "If I can't borrow you from MGM then I'll get the best actor I can get," he told Gene. "So he got Marlon Brando! I was very sad I wasn't able to do it."[68] Gene was so devastated by MGM's inconsiderate treatment of him after his years of loyalty that he began to make serious plans for leaving the studio. Fourteen years later, reflecting on this, one of the darkest periods of his life, Gene remarked, in a wry understatement, "I've had my fair bundle of disappointments."[69]

17

The Unhappy Road

It's Always Fair Weather, the title of Gene's next film, in no way reflected the climate in the actor's professional or personal life in the fall of 1954. MGM offered the picture as a consolation prize to Gene after denying him the part of Sky Masterson in Samuel Goldwyn's *Guys and Dolls.* At the outset, *It's Always Fair Weather* seemed a worthy prize; in fact, Gene's reformed heel character in the new film heavily resembled Sky. Overall, the picture was more a quasi-sequel to *On the Town* than MGM's answer to *Guys and Dolls.* Like *On the Town, It's Always Fair Weather* boasted Arthur Freed as producer, Betty Comden and Adolph Green as screenwriters/songwriters, and Stanley Donen as Gene's co-director. Gene, who had professed that he wanted to stay away from directing after the debacle of *Invitation to the Dance,* embraced the distraction from his personal woes such responsibility would give him. In spite of its sunny title, *It's Always Fair Weather* is largely considered a "downbeat" film. Green explained the premise: "Three guys meet during the war, they think they'll be friends forever, and years later, when they're reunited for a day, they have to deal with a lot of disillusionment, in the others and in themselves." Comden elaborated that it "just seemed like a wonderful theme—the corrosive effect of time."[1]

The harsh toll of time was all too evident both in Gene's marriage and on the set of his new picture. Stanley Donen summarized the experience as a nightmare; off set, Gene's daughter Kerry described her father as a shattered man.[2] Gene went through the "nightmare" alone; when the film went into production on October 13, 1954, Betsy was in New York doing on-location shooting for *Marty.* Though Gene immersed himself in the making of *It's Always Fair Weather,* his colleagues failed to approach it with the same dedication. Arthur Freed, finally losing the optimism that had kept him so prolific for over a decade, had come to the realization that musicals would never hold as high a place in the entertainment industry as they had in his heyday, from the Depression through the postwar years. Like Louis B. Mayer, who had turned his attention to racehorses when he fell from his throne at MGM, Freed began to disengage, focusing on his impressive orchid collection. He did not have to answer to orchids as he had to answer to studio head Dore Schary, a man Adolph Green termed "uncivilized."[3]

While Freed chafed under Dore Schary's authority, Donen chafed under Gene's. "I really didn't want to co-direct another picture with Kelly at that point. We didn't get on very well and, for that matter, Gene didn't get on very well with anybody."[4] Gene may have been irritable but, according to Gene's biographer Clive Hirschhorn, Gene was eager to start the project and claimed it was "what he had been searching for during the last few years."[5] He envisioned making the picture as magical as their previous joint efforts, *On the Town* and *Singin' in the Rain*.

It's Always Fair Weather certainly had the potential for magic, given that it was essentially a combination of those two films. In *Singin' in the Rain,* Comden and Green had satirized Hollywood and the film industry; now, they were ready to poke fun at what they termed "the dreaded tube": television.[6] Still, the picture more closely resembles *On the Town.* Like the earlier film, the plot centers around three buddies and their adventures during a twenty-four-hour period—but ten years have passed since they last met. Originally, Comden and Green hoped to see Frank Sinatra and Jules Munshin return as Gene's costars. However, Sinatra, now an Oscar winner, had outgrown his naïve, boyish persona and Munshin had simply lost popularity. The actors who filled their places, though not big names, were both talented dancers. Michael Kidd plays the Sinatra character, Angie. Kidd, who had choreographed *Seven Brides for Seven Brothers* with Donen only months before, was a fine choice for the part because he could match Gene's dancing skills. Portraying the Munshin character, Doug, was tap dancer Dan Dailey Jr., most famous for his screen musicals with Betty Grable at Twentieth Century-Fox. Gene was delighted to have Dailey on board for the picture. "Fred [Astaire] and myself were pretty good at comedy," he later said, but "Dan Dailey was far better than we were—he was just marvelous."[7] Gene portrays Ted, a no-account gambler and playboy. The three men are forced together by a female TV producer, Jackie (Cyd Charisse), who works in the same office as Doug. Ted eventually falls for Jackie and "goes straight," despite the fact that she tricks them all into walking on her show's set, where their reunion is caught on candid camera.

The television program inadvertently bonds the three friends. Not only do they share disgust for the show but during the live recording, they join forces to defeat a gang of thugs with which Ted is involved. The over-zealous, insincere champion of the TV program's sponsor, Klenzrite, is convincingly played by Dolores Gray. During the unexpected mayhem, she remains ridiculously buoyant and ingratiating. Perhaps the most comical aspect of the film is encapsulated by her character—in Comden and Green's merciless satire of TV they capture the "bread and circuses" feel of the medium and take glee in portraying advertisers as little more than glorified snake oil salesmen. Gene's character makes a speech while on camera dripping with facetiousness: "I'm mixed up with some of the shadiest characters in town. As a matter of fact, knowing the inspiring and uplifting work you do on this program, I—I feel terrible showing my face in decent homes across the country. Boys, don't be like me. Live clean. Use Klenzrite."[8] At the film's conclusion, Ted, Angie, and Doug walk off the television set to share a last drink together. Though no longer bitter, they all know they will never see each other again as they part.

From the moment shooting began on the picture, few on the set felt as if they were making a comedy. Stanley Donen stated, "We had to struggle." Though Gene was pleased to be working with Dan Dailey and Cyd Charisse, he butted heads with Kidd. He was especially unreceptive to a ten-minute solo Kidd had planned for himself and a group of children entitled "Jack and the Space Giants." A melding of the Jack and the Beanstalk story with space exploration, the fantastical sequence shows Angie explaining how he escaped being devoured by giant space ants by cooking a gourmet dinner for them. "It doesn't come across," Gene argued. Donen and the composer of the film's score, André Previn, felt otherwise. Previn believed Gene's distaste for the number was born of jealousy. He, after all, was usually the one to dance with children. Gene ordered the scene cut, which Kidd took as a "personal insult" that afterward led him to "vehemently criticize Gene as a dancer, actor, and person." According to film historians Earl Hess and Pratibha Dabholkar, Gene's call was judicious. The number was "less a dance and more of a comic shtick with none of the comic genius of [Donald] O'Connor, and complete lack of chemistry between Kidd and the three children."[9] Additionally, the number was unrelated to the plot of the film. In truth, the film has few integrated numbers.

Gene's cutting of the number, according to Hess and Dabholkar, resulted in the "breaking off of his collaboration and friendship" with Donen. Donen took Kidd's side in this and other disputes, and both men made "repeated sophomoric reactions to Kelly's attempts to direct the film in serious and thoughtful ways."[10] For instance, Kidd and Donen banded against Gene in what they deemed his overattachment to the film's climactic scene during the TV program. Donen complained that Gene talked about it "ad nauseam . . . until we were all sick of hearing about it." When the time finally came for the scene to be shot, Donen said, Gene was again "espousing lofty homilies about [its] motives and meanings." Kidd asked Gene what he should say when he finds that one of the thugs has beat up his "beloved friend, Ted."

"You just look at me and you say 'Ted!'" Gene told him.

Kidd looked at Gene with disbelief that, after all Gene's buildup of the scene, all he wanted from Kidd was a single word to declare his character's regard for his friend. "Can I spell it?" Kidd asked sarcastically.[11]

Gene was not completely unreceptive to his colleagues' ideas. He accepted one of Donen's brainstorms that used CinemaScope technology to its best advantage. Donen, who had already proved his finesse with the wide-screen format in *Seven Brides for Seven Brothers,* devised a completely original idea for a musical number that takes place when Doug, Ted, and Angie are dining together. He split the screen into three blocks, with each of the three star's faces filling one. Each man's inner thoughts are musically articulated in his own block to the tune of the "Blue Danube Waltz." Comden and Green did not fail to give their lyrics much-needed comedy:

Old pals are the bunk
This guy's a cheap punk
And that one's a heel
And I'm a schlemiel.[12]

The scene is not only the best integrated in the film, it also set a precedent for the use of a split screen. Avant-garde in 1954, the method became ubiquitous by the 1960s and 1970s.

Gene's primary contribution to the film was no less original. As usual, he created a standout solo for himself. This time, he roller-skates down the streets of New York singing "I Like Myself." The number immediately follows his realization that he loves Jackie and no longer wishes to lead the seedy existence of a gambler. The idea of having Gene roller-skate through busy city streets came to Comden and Green after they witnessed him skating on the tennis court in Comden's backyard. "We've got to use that in the movie somehow," Comden said.[13] But it was Gene's refinement that elevated the roller-skating idea to something remarkable: he tap-dances while wearing the unwieldy footwear.

Gene designed another particularly inventive number for the film, this time involving himself, Dailey, and Kidd. It, too, used another unique form of footwear: tin garbage can lids. The lids, strapped to the men's feet by their handles, seemed as if they would create only dissonant noise. However, Gene perfectly synchronized the beats of the dancers' feet so that the noise was more akin to cymbals in a parade. The number takes place near the beginning of the film when the three men, playful after a drinking binge, celebrate the end of World War II. Their conflicts are in the future; their bond is intact and joyful. In execution, the number is typical Kelly in that it showcases a threesome and makes ample use of props (similar numbers include "Make Way for Tomorrow" in Cover Girl and "New York, New York" in On the Town).

Though Gene again found Donen's expertise in the wide-screen format invaluable in choreographing the number, Donen still felt that Gene minimized his efforts. "Co-directing . . . is a nightmare," he stated. "To work with somebody, particularly somebody who is so concerned with his image, was impossible."[14] However, Donen finally won his moment in the spotlight after years of being outshone by Gene. At the Academy Awards, held on March 30, 1955, his Seven Brides for Seven Brothers was up for Best Picture, Best Cinematography, Best Screenplay, Best Score, and Best Film Editing; it won for Best Score. Brigadoon was nominated for Best Sound Recording, Best Art Direction, and Best Costume Design but took home no statuettes.

Betsy Blair also finally achieved renown for her own work. Two weeks after the Academy Awards, her picture Marty was released to overwhelming acclaim. Bosley Crowther of the New York Times wrote, "Miss Blair is wonderfully revealing of the unspoken nervousness and hope in the girl who will settle for sincerity."[15] The picture, budgeted at $350,000, grossed $2 million. The film was received just as warmly at the Cannes Film Festival. It took home Golden Palms for Best Picture, Best Actress, and Best Actor. Gene and Kerry caught a plane to Paris late on the night of April 8, 1955, in order to be present at the ceremony. "I just can't find words to tell you what it meant to me. . . . Gene gave a press conference [while in Cannes]. . . . You know how he started it off? 'I am the husband of Betsy Blair.' . . . Everyone smiled and the tears came to my eyes and I thought I'd just pass out with happiness," Betsy told a reporter.[16] In her memoir, she deemed her triumph with *Marty* as "one of the most wonderful times of my life."[17]

While Betsy may have been enjoying the best of times, Gene was still in a slump—and he was fast realizing that *It's Always Fair Weather* was not going to pull him out of it. The picture completed filming in May, one month after *Marty* premiered. Gene and Donen did not part on amicable terms. Donen reflected in 1992: "I'm grateful to him [Gene], but I paid the debt ten times over and he got his money's worth out of me."[18] Gene never spoke with such antipathy about Donen. In 1979, he reflected, "I thought we complemented each other very well. On the last picture we made . . . we were . . . so used to each other, that we didn't need each other. It was almost dull . . . we could have phoned the shots in. It wasn't a bad picture . . . [but it's] the only picture we didn't have fun on."[19]

The film's final budget was $2,771,000, an amount that, only five years before, an MGM musical seldom failed to recoup. But the picture, meant to be a satiric romantic comedy, came across as bitter and hard-edged. It was devoid of the light touch and escapism audiences expected from a Kelly film. Gene commented: "We wanted to make an experiment by treating a serious subject in the context of a musical comedy. It was a good story for which we needed a little bit of realism, but we missed our goal, because we didn't succeed in giving it the feeling of nostalgia."[20] Unfortunately, Gene's words were all too true. Upon its release on September 2, 1955, the film grossed only $2,374,000. In total, MGM's ledgers revealed that the film lost over $1 million.

Part of the picture's failure was due to MGM's lack of buildup. *It's Always Fair Weather* played as the second half of a double bill in many towns. Also, numerous exhibitors didn't have the technology needed to screen the film in its wide-screen format; thus, the dancers' feet and the sides of the scenes were cut off, negating the pains Gene and Donen had taken to tailor the choreography to CinemaScope. Even at the film's first preview, the theater was ill equipped. Furthermore, as Comden explained, "I don't think Gene was quite the star he was. I don't think he was that popular anymore and neither were musicals."[21]

This being said, *Guys and Dolls* and the film adaptation of *Oklahoma!*

ranked as two of the top five moneymaking pictures of 1955. Why were they popular when *It's Always Fair Weather* was not? The answer lies in the fact that the vast majority of popular musicals in the mid- to late 1950s were adaptations of Broadway shows. When Arthur Freed first began producing musicals, his goal had been to create original films rather than rely on Broadway hits as movie material. When he did take from Broadway, he, with the help of artists like Gene, Minnelli, Comden, and Green, changed the shows enough to make them uniquely cinematic. However, screen musicals like *Oklahoma!* and *Guys and Dolls* were virtual copies of their Broadway counterparts—yet they succeeded while *Brigadoon,* another virtual copy, did not. In the hands of another unit, perhaps *Brigadoon* would have done well. But Freed and his team were innovators who languished within the strictures of the stage-bound musical. The problem with the Broadway musical, done Hollywood style, was that the stories became watered down and cleansed, making for weak and uninspired films. Bland or not, audiences trusted Broadway adaptations over original Hollywood musicals because they were preapproved hits.

It's Always Fair Weather, though not an audience favorite, resonated with critics who appreciated originality. A reviewer for *Time* magazine called the picture "a sunny example of a Hollywood rarity—a song-and-dance movie with enough plot to justify its dialogue and enough needling satire to make some points. . . . For its superb dancing, inventive musical numbers . . . *Fair Weather* rates as one of the top contenders for the year's lightweight title."[22] Bosley Crowther gave Gene this stamp of approval: "[His] sly eyes and nimble feet are measured among the happiest adornments of the screen."[23]

On March 21, 1956, at the twenty-eighth annual Academy Awards ceremony, *It's Always Fair Weather* was considered for one award: Best Story and Screenplay. However, it lost to the soapy MGM biopic of singer Marjorie Lawrence, *Interrupted Melody.* At the same ceremony, Betsy lost the Best Supporting Actress award to Jo Van Fleet, who portrayed a madam in Warner Bros.'s *East of Eden.* But Betsy felt like a winner; indeed, *Marty* swept the Oscars. It won in nearly every major category: Best Picture, Best Actor, Best Director, and Best Screenplay (not to be confused with Best Story and Screenplay). Betsy commented that afterward she became something of a favorite among the press. As her confidence soared, she increasingly longed for a divorce—to begin a completely new life, one that she might have had if she had not married Gene at seventeen.

For ten years, gossip columnists had been dropping hints that Gene and Betsy's marriage was in trouble. In 1945, a reporter falsely claimed that Gene had left his wife and baby daughter and moved to a hotel. Six years later, Hollywood columnists still remembered Gene's livid reaction to the erroneous report. Reflecting on Gene's reaction, writer John Maynard recorded: "Kelly exhibited the first pronounced symptoms of . . . Celt ferocity and independence. . . . One was an earnest effort to slug a widely read and heard commentator on movie doings. After which, Kelly proposed to stuff him into a wastepaper basket. . . . Gene knew exactly what he was doing. He was inviting professional suicide to preserve his conceptions of human dignity and integrity."[24] In 1954, one commentator asserted that though Gene was now "quieter, more dedicated—and more fulfilled— than when, ten years ago, he was charging everything from windmills to Sherman tanks with whatever lance he had in hand," he was "in no respect . . . any different. The lance is still in the closet for the time being but he still keeps the grip oiled."[25]

When new reports sprang up about Gene and Betsy's shaky union in 1956, Gene did not pull out any lances. This time, he could not deny the gossip. In spite of Betsy's discretion, Gene was aware of her affairs; however, he did not bring up the possibility of divorce and Betsy still kept her wish for one to herself. After viewing *It's Always Fair Weather*, she wailed to her analyst: "How can I even think of resistance and rebellion, I mean divorce, when he's [Gene] up there in close-up thirty-two times larger than life and irresistible?"[26]

Asking Gene for a divorce, as Betsy well knew, would be no painless task—particularly because her husband was already depressed. MGM had finally decided to take the risk and release *Invitation to the Dance* to international audiences. When the film made its premiere in Zurich on April 1, 1956, audience reactions temporarily buoyed Gene's spirits. One Swiss reporter called Gene the "Diaghilev of motion pictures" while a writer for London's *Daily Mirror* declared that the film was not "merely art but sheer enjoyment. . . . The Technicolor perfection of [its] sequences represents an accomplishment that should rate serious Academy Award consideration."[27]

With such praise heaped upon the picture, MGM executives felt safe in releasing it to American audiences on May 23. But they realized immediately that they had waited too long. By this time, US television audiences had been inundated with dance shows and ballets, nullifying the enlightening effect Gene had hoped his film would have. In Europe, on the other hand, television was still in its infancy and *Invitation to the Dance* was a novelty. Decades after the picture's release, reviewer Pauline Kael darkly observed: "The film bollixed the career of Kelly, and probably broke his heart as well. . . . Practically no one saw it."[28] The appeal of Gene's work had long lain in the fact that it was accessible to the average Joe. The ballets in *Invitation to the Dance,* unlike those beautifully executed in *On the Town, An American in Paris,* and *Singin' in the Rain,* made little sense to audiences, likely because they were not part of a fluid story. The picture, which had cost $2,822,000 to produce, made a dismal $615,000 at the box office, making it MGM's biggest flop of the year.

Though a financial disaster, the film did receive a degree of praise from US critics. Bosley Crowther wrote in his piece for the *New York Times:* "Mr. Kelly deserves some admiration. . . . This film represents a brave experiment, but it would have been more commendable if Mr. Kelly had been more fertile with ideas and less inclined to overdo."[29] *Dance* magazine complimented the film for its "obvious artistic sincerity" but concluded: "The librettos that Kelly has provided for his three ballets are of a kind that have long been superseded in the ballet, dance narratives designed to touch or amuse but affording no moments of either eloquence or revelation."[30]

Gene, seeing the success of *Guys and Dolls* and the failure of his own film, lost all loyalty to MGM. Fueling Gene's anger at the studio was its refusal to cast him in two pictures that could have given him the chance to resuscitate his career: MGM's *Teahouse of the August Moon* and a cinematic adaptation of *Pal Joey* for Columbia. The role in *Teahouse of the August Moon,* as in *Guys and Dolls,* went to Marlon Brando; the title role in *Pal Joey* went to Frank Sinatra. Gene requested to be released from his contract, but Nick Schenck refused. "They [MGM] had nothing on tap for me and I'd been sitting around for months [waiting] for an assignment. I couldn't stand not working so I suggested to them that we come to terms," Gene related.[31] Arthur Loew, one of MGM's highest executives, agreed to Gene's terms: he would complete two more pictures. One would be a property of Gene's choice in which he served as star, co-producer, and director.

Gene's selected project, *The Happy Road,* was a property he had originally hoped to independently produce and release in France. He had not planned to star in it. "The whole idea of making *The Happy Road* was that television had just come in and everybody was worried. They were saying they couldn't make huge pictures any more, and it was true," Gene explained. "So my determination was to show everyone in the business that I could do a nice, small-budget picture in Europe."[32] Gene's second project, *Les Girls,* was not slated to begin until January 1957. The picture was to be directed by George Cukor, scored by Cole Porter, and choreographed by Jack Cole. *Les Girls* was the antithesis of *The Happy Road*—lavish, sophisticated, and Technicolored in comparison to the simplicity, innocence, and black-and-white photography of the other picture.

The Happy Road centers on two children who run away from their Swiss boarding school and trek together to Paris in hopes of convincing their parents (the little boy has only a widowed father and the girl has only a divorced mother) to let them stay at home. In the parents' joint search for their children, the mother and father fall in love, and the children find the home and security for which they have been searching. Gene returned to his first love—writing—when he also took on the role of songwriter for the film. During the picture's opening credits, Maurice Chevalier croons Gene's wistful, melancholic lyrics to the title song:

> Time hurries by
> Youth goes so fast
> Don't rush down the road of life
> Soon youth will be past.[33]

As preparation for filming began in the spring of 1956, Gene rented the same home he had used in France when shooting *Invitation to the Dance.* He scouted for children to cast as leads, ultimately choosing two relatively unknown actors: Brigitte Fossey (a French girl) and Bobby Clark (an American boy). Brigitte had won some notice in René Clair's *Forbidden Games* (1952). She did not relish the prospect of having her hair cut for the film, but Gene, to assuage the pain of losing her locks, arranged for the deed to be done on her tenth birthday. Immediately after the haircut, Gene led her to a group of her friends surrounding an enormous cake, which she promptly dug into.

The Happy Road was the closest Gene had yet come to his longtime dream of making a film for children. Shown from the viewpoint of the boy and girl, the film is unpretentious and even naïve yet still manages to be highly effective and poignant. Perhaps what lent the film its sincerity was the fact that Gene lost his own family unity during its production.

When Betsy and Kerry joined Gene in France for a weekend, Betsy soberly asked Gene to meet her alone at her hotel in Paris. She had fallen in love with a French actor and socialist, Roger Pigaut, and was finally ready to ask Gene for a divorce. "I had found what I needed to give me the strength to escape," Betsy explained.[34] Gene and Betsy sat on the balcony overlooking the Champs-Élysées, he drinking a beer while she sipped hot tea. Such a romantic setting could have come straight from *An American in Paris.*

"I want a divorce," Betsy told him.

Gene put down his beer and gave her a slight paternalistic smile, then surprised her by saying, "I've known about your affairs. I thought since you never had a true adolescence, it'd pass. I'll wait it out."

They stayed up all night talking. "I cried, I thought about Kerry and felt that my heart was breaking," Betsy said. "But I had to do it. We had to divorce." Three or four times during their conversation, Betsy repeated: "But Gene, you couldn't have been faithful these fifteen years. You're a sexy movie star. You must've had all kinds of women throwing themselves at you." Gene resolutely answered no each time she asked the question. "Come on, Gene," Betsy prodded.

"Never while you were there," he told her at last. Betsy remembered, "Somewhere inside me I knew this was funny. At the time I only felt relief."[35]

No infidelity of Gene's has ever been disclosed, and it remains a point of debate whether he ever had had any affair at all. It is possible that Gene told Betsy he'd been unfaithful merely to assuage her guilt.

As the lights of Paris faded in the morning sun, they decided on a trial separation rather than immediate divorce. Betsy agreed to the plan, but she knew it would end in divorce. True, this would mean leaving behind her beloved Beverly Hills home, convenient charge accounts, and friends like Comden, Green, and Jeanne Coyne. On the positive side, however, the divorce and her planned relocation to Europe would be good for her career. She had been allowed to appear in *Marty,* but the entertainment industry still knew of her Communist sympathies, and future ostracism was a certainty.

As Betsy had matured, she had become a far different woman than the one Gene had married. Though a private person like Gene, Betsy was more socially inclined, and Gene's lack of deep friendships puzzled her. "I tried desperately to introduce him to people," she recalled. "But . . . after fifteen years of marriage and hundreds of people passing through our lives, I had to face the fact that Gene was a loner and was somehow going to have to get through the divorce on his own."[36] Betsy concluded that "Gene's character, the creator, the patriarch, the boss in a way, was too set. . . . He saw no reason to change."

Informing fourteen-year-old Kerry of their separation was more difficult than Gene and Betsy had anticipated. They told her the news one weekend at Gene's rented home in the country. The girl broke down and fled to the bathroom, refusing to come out for twenty-four hours. She had had no clue there was anything amiss between her parents. She knew they were seldom home at the same time, but she had assumed it was due to their working schedules. "Would it help if I called Jeannie [Coyne]? Could you talk to her?" Gene pleaded through the closed door. Kerry murmured yes; Jeanne was, as she had been for most of the girl's life, "like a second mother to me."[37] Jeanne arrived only a day later.

Gene took the divorce as hard as Kerry. According to Kerry, he was "utterly helpless, couldn't cope with the situation, and was of no use to anybody. [He never] quite regained his unassailable self-confidence. . . . He became much more reflective and down-to-earth, developed a sense of reality about life which he never had before."[38] Betsy offered further insight: "This [the divorce] was one of the few failures in Gene's life, but it was a personal failure. Gene did not take well to personal failure."[39]

In the middle of such turmoil, Gene received more bad news: his father had died. Gene quickly traveled to Pittsburgh before completing *The Happy Road*, a film whose title seemed to become more mocking by the day. Before he arrived, Harriet was upset for more reasons than her husband's death. She had read a piece in the *Pittsburgh Post-Gazette* reporting: "If the story-book romance of Gene Kelly and Betsy Blair is heading for the rocks, it's a complete surprise to his mother. . . . Kelly's studio announced yesterday he and his wife, who are in Paris, are trying a trial separation. It gave no details. Mrs. Kelly scoffed at the report, saying, 'I've been hearing that for ten years. . . . I think it's just publicity.'"[40] Not wishing to cause more upheaval in the family, Gene did not disclose that the report was indeed true.

A despondent Gene returned to France a week later to complete *The*

Happy Road. The picture was swiftly becoming a nightmare. Shot on location in the Burgundy wine country, the picture was subject to the whims of the weather. It rained incessantly for six weeks, holding up production on a film that MGM had explicitly instructed Gene to keep under its budget of half a million dollars. Additionally, technical problems cropped up almost every hour. Gene found himself overwhelmed without the help of a co-director behind the camera and second guessed his every choice without a partner to concur that a given scene worked or did not work. Biographer Clive Hirschhorn surmised that the movie failed to be the success it might have been because Gene's "heart and soul" failed to match the light mood of the film.[41] Gene's performance comes across as uneasy and strained, unlike his breezy, confident performances in his best films.

However, upon the film's release on June 20, 1957, the vast majority of reviews were positive. Gene even began to feel fond of the project again, remarking, "I particularly enjoyed the making of *The Happy Road*. I liked being on location in the French countryside and meeting the people."[42] One of the most perceptive reviews of the picture came from the *Age*, a paper based in Australia: "Mr. Kelly's is a world where everyone badly needs each other. . . . It is a world of irony, in which the forces of law fluster and blunder and disorganize so fast that only an army of children are left to co-operate to a common humanitarian goal. . . . All the time, I was scared Mr. Kelly would go too far and consistently he managed to avoid doing so."[43] Gene's "little film" merited a BAFTA United Nations Award as well as a Golden Globe for Promoting International Understanding. The film earned $325,000 in the United States and Canada and $625,000 internationally, thus losing $117,000. "It won all kinds of awards," Gene reflected in 1968. "It was hailed as a sweet family picture—but nobody came to see it."[44]

Upon his return to Beverly Hills, Gene was immediately beset with more challenges. Among the first was the news that Kerry wished to go away to school. She could not cope with a broken household and felt she would benefit from attending a boarding school in Switzerland. Gene and Betsy did not argue with her; they enrolled her at the Geneva International School. "The hopes of their good friends that the meeting this week between Gene Kelly and Betsy Blair in Switzerland preparatory to entering their daughter Kerry in school there may lead to a reconciliation," one reporter wrote.[45] No such reconciliation took place; Gene realized their separation had become permanent.

He and Betsy both hired lawyers to handle their divorce and division of property. Gene retained Greg Bautzer, one of the most prominent lawyers in Hollywood, while Betsy hired a green left-wing lawyer. Both spouses agreed upon joint custody of Kerry. Betsy did not foresee that she and Gene would have anything to argue about. "I was wrong," she stated. "The day came when my lawyer told me, 'Mr. Bautzer says that Mr. Kelly doesn't agree to the community property division of assets. . . . [He] says he will accuse you of adultery and of giving $10,000 to the Red Chinese. Did you give $10,000 to the Red Chinese?'" Shocked, Betsy explained that she was a partner in a Parisian film company planning to shoot a movie in China. She had invested money in the film, but this did not mean she was donating to the Red Chinese. "For the first time in my life, I was so angry I couldn't think straight. I went home and when Gene came in I told him to get out. I was ashamed of him. Wasn't he ashamed of himself? . . . Wouldn't he be ashamed in front of his friends? 'What friends?' Gene asked and left the room."[46]

After litigation, Betsy received $18,000 a year for ten years, though she claimed that her legal share should have been $250,000. Unwilling to wait the year California law required for a divorce, she flew to Las Vegas. There, she had six weeks to calm down. She admitted that she called Gene one night after six weeks. Sad and frightened she had made the wrong decision, she began to sob.

"Betsy, just come back," Gene said, a note of pleading in his voice.

"I can't. I promised," Betsy replied.[47] Whom she had promised—herself or Roger Pigaut—is unclear. What was clear was that she could not and did not come back.

Betsy chose Paris as her new home base. She was pleased that Kerry had decided to attend high school in Europe; their proximity allowed them to see each other every other weekend. Betsy lived with Pigaut, who she said was wise enough "not to intrude on Kerry . . . just to be friendly and there." Betsy and Pigaut did not marry, but they remained lovers and business partners. Betsy felt "sexy in Paris. . . . I had changed. . . . I wasn't pleasing my other. I wasn't pleasing Gene. I was free, just living, just being."[48]

Gene did not share Betsy's joyous sense of domestic freedom. Along with his own feelings of personal failure, he had to contend with his mother's disappointment. Harriet Kelly was stunned by her son's divorce and the attention it received from the press. She did not blame Betsy for the dissolution of the marriage—she pointed her finger at Gene. Betsy believed that to Harriet, "anything unfortunate in any of the Kelly lives was Gene's fault—it was heaven's retribution for his success."[49]

Without the extroverted Betsy at home, Gene's open-house parties went extinct. Betty Comden, decades later, surprised Betsy by saying, "The atmosphere in the house . . . came from you." Betsy explained that Gene was "the dominant figure" at their parties, but he was "slightly removed . . . always pleasant and amused and attending to drinks, but not entirely there."[50]

Only Jeanne Coyne remained by Gene's side throughout the ordeals of the divorce, the dissolution of his social life, and the heartbreaks in his work. Betsy remarked that during one of the last dinners she and Gene attended as a couple with Adolph Green, his wife, and Jeanne, she had noticed that each time Jeanne laughed at Green's many jokes, she put her head on Gene's shoulder. "I never guessed she was in love with Gene because she never flirted with him while our marriage was still working. She wasn't that sort of woman." After the dinner with Green, however, Betsy suspected Jeanne's feelings went deeper than she'd realized and had a four-hour "heart to heart" talk with her. Betsy asked Jeanne whether she was waiting to marry Gene. "Yes," Jeanne replied. "That's great, but it won't work until he gets analyzed. He'll treat you like a child, like he did me," Betsy told her. Jeanne said nothing. Years later Betsy understood that she had been wrong: Jeanne was already a grown woman and thus did not need to establish herself as an adult with Gene as Betsy had. Not long after Gene and Betsy's divorce was finalized, on April 3, 1957, Jeanne moved back into Gene's home.[51]

More changes took place on North Rodeo Drive. Gene, in an act of rebellion against Betsy's long-standing hatred for the Hollywood lifestyle, broke ground on a swimming pool in his backyard. Kerry explained that "he suddenly woke up to the fact that it would be rather nice to have a swim . . . as his whim decreed. . . . A swimming pool suddenly became a fun thing to have. It also gave the house a new 'toy' which in no way could be related to Betsy."[52]

Gene could not help but relate his career at MGM, which began with his marriage and ended with his divorce, to Betsy. Now, he had only one more commitment left to complete for the studio. After that, he could truly begin anew and direct what course his career and life should take—and with whom.

Les Girls (1957) is not a great film, but it is notable in Gene Kelly's career as the great dancer's final picture for MGM. The atmosphere in the MGM musical department was no longer familial; many of Gene's trusted colleagues, including Donen, Comden, Green, and Roger Edens, were no longer under contract. The fact that yet another new studio head had been appointed exacerbated the changed mood at Metro. In November 1956, Dore Schary was ousted. Executive Benny Thau took his place, but he was ultimately as unsuccessful as Schary in keeping the studio solvent. He approved a massive budget for *Les Girls* (over $3 million) despite the fact that musicals were no longer surefire moneymakers. The film faced heady competition—and not just from television. Now filmmakers had a new phenomenon with which to contend: rock and roll. How could *Les Girls*, with its score by an old master like Cole Porter, win young audiences' attention when MGM had slated teen idol Elvis Presley's third film, *Jailhouse Rock* (1957), for an almost simultaneous release? Aside from Broadway adaptations, the most original musicals now coming from studios were those in the emerging genre of rock musicals. The advent of rock and roll divided young and old Americans as much as jazz had in the 1920s.

While Broadway musical remakes were merely bland and uninspired, rock musicals showed little semblance of artistry or wit. Hastily put together films like *Shake, Rattle, and Rock!* (1956, starring Bill Haley and His Comets) were vehicles for rock and roll stars rather than for viable screen personalities. Rock musicals brought forth no talents as exciting as Judy Garland and Mickey Rooney, with the one exception of Elvis Presley, who had charisma and whose films were more substantial than the average teen flick.

In spite of rock and rollers, Cole Porter was still a strong presence in Hollywood. His song "True Love," written for the Bing Crosby–Frank Sinatra–Grace Kelly picture *High Society* (1956) became a gold record and the film was the ninth-biggest grosser of the year. *Love Me Tender*, Elvis's screen debut, came in at number sixteen. *High Society*'s success was largely due to its powerhouse cast; audiences were as fascinated to see Crosby and Sinatra share screen time as they were to see Grace Kelly, in her last film appearance, sing. *Les Girls* had only one A-list member in its cast: Gene. And he could not hold the weak picture together by himself—particularly since he was not as popular as he once was.

Les Girls tells the story of Sybil Wren (portrayed by British actress Kay Kendall), who pens a tell-all book about her time in the dance troupe Barry Nichols and Les Girls. Fellow dancer Angele (Taina Elg) sues Sybil for libel. The narrative then shows the story from three points of view:

Sybil accuses Angele of having an affair with Barry (Gene); Angele insists that it was Sybil who was having the affair. Last, Barry gives his side of the story, revealing that all along he was in love with an American dancer in his troupe, Joy (Mitzi Gaynor). The film ends on a comic note; Joy, who has listened to the other women's testimonies from the back of the courtroom, suspects that Sybil and Angele did not completely invent stories of their relationships with Barry, which leads to another circuitous romantic dispute. The screenplay was lopsided; the three viewpoints failed to balance, and Gene's character was virtually lost in the shuffle. The score, too, was unimpressive. Though Saul Chaplin declared that Cole Porter was as "alert, articulate, and witty as ever," the truth was that his compositions were not up to his usual standard.[53] Not surprisingly, *Les Girls* was the last film Porter ever scored.

Les Girls, whatever its faults, did not suffer from lack of talent. Aside from Cole Porter, other behind-the-scenes greats included George Cukor as director, Saul Chaplin as associate producer and musical arranger, Orry-Kelly as costume designer, and Jack Cole as choreographer. Sol C. Siegel, who had a fine track record for backing superior musicals such as *Gentlemen Prefer Blondes* (1953) and, most recently, *High Society* (1956), served as producer.

From the moment *Les Girls* went into production, Gene felt miscast. Indeed, Jack Cole described the film as "the essence of chic," and Gene could not conform to Cole's vision of staging numbers that were "more sophisticated" and enacted "with less bravura."[54] Jeanne Coyne, Gene's assistant on the film, told Cole it was useless to attempt to make Gene into a Fred Astaire. Ultimately, the dance routines were as scattered as the script itself. Cole, ill with hepatitis, left the picture before its completion. Gene took over as best he could. As a consequence, the numbers serve as examples of Cole's and Gene's styles of choreography warring with each other.

Gene enjoyed a friendly relationship with George Cukor, though he found the director's lengthy shoots even more maddening than Vincente Minnelli's. Cukor could spend two hours explaining uncomplicated scenes. "For Christ's sake George, let's just shoot the goddamn thing!" Gene often exclaimed. Cukor and the rest of the cast would laugh and then "everything would be fine."[55] Gene also enjoyed a genial—if curious—relationship with Kay Kendall. She was the only nondancer in the cast yet was the only one of "les girls" who, according to Saul Chaplin, had the magnetism to keep all eyes riveted on her. Gene and Kay had, up to this time, known each other only personally, having first met when he was working in London. They were friends, yet Saul Chaplin recalled that Gene seemed to bring out Kay's occasional "violent temper." "They [Gene and Kay] would disappear into one of their dressing rooms and scream at each other, using the foulest language imaginable. I never knew what prompted the arguments, but I'm quite certain they had nothing to do with the film. Just when we thought that there would be no more shooting that day, they would emerge arm-in-arm, laughing and joking as though what they had indulged in was normal behavior. For them it was."[56]

Given their electric chemistry, it is unfortunate that Gene's most enjoyable number in the picture, a spoof on the rock and roll/motorcycle culture epitomized in the Marlon Brando picture *The Wild One* (1954), paired him with Mitzi Gaynor rather than Kay. The routine, "Why Am I So Gone about That Girl?" has Gene dressed in a black leather jacket and cap. The rest of his performance lacks the "charm" and "vitality" evidenced in this number.[57] The very fact that Gene had declined the role of choreographer indicated that he was not invested in the film. In his mind, he was already gone from MGM. Filming wrapped in April 1957.

Upon its release on October 3, 1957, *Les Girls* did surprisingly well, not only in the United States but in England. Reviewers did not seem to sense Gene's underlying lack of enthusiasm for the picture. Bosley Crowther wrote a glowing account: "Mr. Kelly is more winning in this picture than he was in *An American in Paris*—which is some!"[58] A critic for *Picturegoer* expressed similar appreciation for the film and made conspicuous mention that Queen Elizabeth chose it to be screened for the Royal Film Performance at London's Odeon Theatre in Leicester Square.

> At last Kelly's back! And, fittingly, in right royal fashion. . . . But Gene Kelly BACK? Who says he's been absent? Haven't we seen him recently in *Invitation to the Dance* and *The Happy Road?* Well, some may hold the view that the star in those two pictures was indeed Kelly. But not the majority of picturegoers. . . . In *Les Girls,* out have come the straw hat and the dancing shoes. . . . This is the bubbling, full-of-life Kelly we know. Welcome back! Which, by the way, is a sentiment with which the Queen will probably agree.[59]

The review, though complimentary, minimized the attempts Gene had recently made to broaden the scope of his work and dancing technique.

The critic may have thought Gene was back, but his performance was truly a farewell. What the writer saw as the real Gene was merely a projected personality. *Les Girls* ultimately grossed $3,865,000, but because of its high production costs, it lost $1,635,000.

Gene's tenure at MGM was at its end, but Benny Thau had one last favor to ask of him. Would he agree to direct *The Tunnel of Love?* A Doris Day vehicle sans music, it seemed a simple task. Gene agreed because, in his words, he "just couldn't take sitting around with nothing to do."[60] The picture was not slated for production until January 1958. In the meantime, Gene received an offer from a most unexpected source: Warner Bros. After Danny Kaye and Paul Newman turned down the role of Noel Airman for the studio's adaptation of Herman Wouk's best-selling novel *Marjorie Morningstar*, Jack Warner suggested Gene as an ideal choice for Airman, a dance teacher and producer of amateur theatricals who can also sing, compose, and speak several languages. The picture would not begin filming until August 1957.

As he waited for production to start, Gene watched his protégé Stanley Donen again triumph in a solo directorial project, Paramount's *Funny Face* (1957), starring Fred Astaire and Audrey Hepburn. The same year, the singer Gene had taught to dance, Frank Sinatra, made a hit in the role Gene originated on Broadway, *Pal Joey*. Both films ranked in the top twenty highest-grossing movies of 1957.

The year Gene left MGM, the studio was $445,000 in debt, with gross receipts $18 million less than the year before.[61] Though *Les Girls* won an Academy Award for Best Costume Design and Golden Globes for Best Musical/Comedy and Best Actress (shared by Kay Kendall and Taina Elg), it did not help relieve the studio's debt. After Benny Thau's brief reign ended, Sol C. Siegel, producer of *Les Girls*, appeared to be MGM's savior. Under his aegis, the studio released Arthur Freed and Vincente Minnelli's Best Picture winner, *Gigi* (1958), starring Gene's discovery Leslie Caron. MGM nevertheless continued to lose money because of high overhead costs. Regardless of Metro's tumult, Gene later expressed regret over not having fulfilled the original terms of his contract. "Had I hung on a few years longer, I would have qualified for several thousands of dollars [$25,000] a year for life," he explained.[62] Gene left after sixteen years under contract, which was not long enough to qualify for an MGM pension.

Instead, Gene was now his own boss, earning money largely through freelance work in all mediums: stage, film, and even television. During filming for *Les Girls,* Gene had already begun venturing into television. "I find myself getting ready for a TV debut," Gene told a columnist in January 1957, "in a voice sounding as if he still didn't believe it."[63] Indeed, a writer for the *Los Angeles Times* had only the month before called Gene "one of the real hold outs against TV."[64] However, he succumbed to the "dreaded tube" in "The Life You Save," an episode of the CBS-TV anthology series *Schlitz Playhouse* (which began in 1951). The episode was set to air on March 1, 1957. Gene maintained a positive attitude about his transition to the small screen: "In Europe, television is still an experiment. It is shunned as a career handicap by most of the top stars there . . . already I find myself getting ready for a TV debut. . . . What makes it more unique, they didn't even ask me to dance. I'm just playing a straight dramatic role."[65]

Gene's television debut revealed an actor far different from the Gene Kelly the columnist for *Picturegoer* had rhapsodized over in his review of *Les Girls.* The teleplay tells the story of a beautiful deaf-mute girl whose mother (Agnes Moorehead) encourages a one-armed bum (Gene) to marry her daughter. "Unfortunately, Mr. Kelly was burdened with a lot of nonsensical lines and did not show up very well in his first TV appearance," wrote a critic for the *New York Times.*[66]

Gene's inauspicious beginnings on television led him to refocus his attention on his upcoming film projects. But, as his biographer Clive Hirschhorn observed, the brutal fact remained that "everything [Gene] did couldn't match up to [his] glory days."[67]

Part 3

Still Going Strong

1957–1972

18

A Hundred Million Miracles

"Everything for me has been happenstance. The good parts have been the luck of the Irish and the bad parts I generally worked out for myself," Gene reflected in 1980.[1] For him, the period 1957–1959 was more a time of fortune than adversity.

The first instance of Gene's Irish luck was winning the role of Noel Airman in Warner Bros.' *Marjorie Morningstar,* directed by Irving Rapper. The part was the first substantial dramatic assignment Gene had received in a prestigious picture (as compared to his other dramatic films, which had been strictly programmers). "It's hard to play a fellow of charm who falls apart," Gene admitted when he accepted the role.[2] Though a few Warner Bros. executives gave Gene only "begrudging acceptance," arguing that he was "too old, too dark, too much the dancing man" for the part, Gene changed their minds once the cameras started rolling.[3] Forty-five-year-old Gene was convincing as the thirty-two-year-old Noel, even when shown beside his leading lady, twenty-year-old Natalie Wood.

Gene's primary challenge in playing Noel was the fact that the character's struggles, in a number of ways, were too similar to his own. At the beginning of the picture, Noel is the idol of young hopefuls at a summer camp in upstate New York. There, he choreographs and composes annual musical revues that are far too good for an amateur venue. He eventually tries his luck on Broadway, but his experimental play fails to garner any attention. He takes to drinking to soothe his hurt ego but eventually returns to the summer camp. There, a new group of wide-eyed young performers consider him the last word in show business.

At the beginning of the picture, the one at the summer camp who most idolizes Noel is Marjorie Morgenstern, an eighteen-year-old Jewish girl who aspires to be an actress. She and Noel are virtually the same ages as Gene and Betsy Blair were when they first met at Billy Rose's Diamond Horseshoe in 1940. Parallels between Noel and Gene end, however, in their levels of ambition and energy. Gene described Noel as a brilliant fellow "people think will take Broadway by storm. But he lacks . . . the ability or the confidence to push himself . . . [to the] top. . . . Those who succeed in this business are not necessarily those with the most talent, but those with the most stamina and the most luck."[4] Gene had been blessed with the stamina, confidence, and luck to make it to the top. But in light of his recent professional downturn, Gene had learned that luck was not something he could depend on. All he could control was the effort he put into his endeavors. Kerry Kelly once remarked that her father had drilled into her that life was essentially nothing but hard work.

Marjorie Morningstar's primary focus is Marjorie's rise to fame and Noel's simultaneous decline. But the secondary plotline follows the girl's struggle to stay true to her strict Jewish upbringing. In another parallel with Gene, Noel is ambivalent about religion. A nonpracticing Jew, he is, in Marjorie's words, "not very religious. He doesn't believe in those things." Nonetheless, he attends a Passover Seder at Marjorie's home. Halfway through the meal, he rises from the table. Marjorie follows him. She assumes he was bored, but he tells her, "I wasn't bored. I was disturbed, deeply. I couldn't help thinking of all the things I've missed in life. Family, your kind of family. Faith, tradition."[5]

At this point in Gene's life, he was still a firm agnostic. However, he had raised Kerry as a Catholic so as not to deprive her of tradition, although unlike his parents, he had not been strict about his or his daughter's observance of church strictures. "I was married in the Catholic Church. I was later divorced . . . so [I was prohibited] by Church law from taking Communion," Gene explained. "My point is this: if you can get absolution for murdering a guy, or for adultery, or any other offense, why can't you get absolution for being divorced? I think a change is needed." Gene felt compelled rather than inspired to attend Mass on major holidays, though he found the consistency of the ceremonies reassuring. The church was an institution he felt he could "lean on" in difficult times, but he continued to "defend the need of individuals to follow their own sincerely found convictions."[6]

Although *Marjorie Morningstar* dealt with heavy issues and could not be called a musical, it did give Gene some opportunities to show off his singing and dancing skills in scenes taking place at the summer camp. His rendition of the film's theme song, "A Very Precious Love," is especially effective and moving. The movie allows audiences to glimpse all Gene's talents: he sings, dances, and gives, arguably, the best dramatic performance of his career. One of the most striking scenes in the film occurs when Noel, after a group of potential backers for his show reject his avant-garde concept, breaks down, near tears, and shouts that he will not sacrifice his artistic integrity to make the production a commercial success.

Marjorie Morningstar was, on the whole, a pleasant experience for all involved. As filming commenced in August, Gene was approaching his forty-fifth birthday—a fact that the cast and crew did not ignore. During the three-week location shooting at Scaroon Lake in upstate New York, the film's company stayed at the Scaroon Manor, a lavish resort. On Gene's birthday, the cast celebrated with a champagne lunch, after which the party relocated to an onsite open-air theatre. A ping-pong table on the second floor of the theater immediately drew Gene's attention and he initiated a ping-pong tournament on the spot. "At first, theatre patrons complained about the noise made by the plunk plunk of the balls. When they heard who the players were, many in the audience came to watch the ping pong games in lieu of the movies. . . . Hotel guests were recruited as extras for the picture," a visiting reporter noted.[7]

Filming wrapped for *Marjorie Morningstar* in November 1957. Released on April 24, 1958, it received favorable reviews, particularly for Gene's performance. A writer for *Time* magazine commented: "Gene Kelly sings and dances too well to be a convincing second-rater, but he gives an agile performance as the camp's entertainment director."[8] A. H. Weiler of the *New York Times* singled out Gene's scene of "impassioned defiance of his prospective backers" as one of the high points of the film.[9] *Marjorie Morningstar* was up for Best Song at the thirty-first Academy Awards (for "A Very Precious Love," by Sammy Fain and Paul Francis Webster). However, Alan Jay Lerner and Frederick Loewe's "Gigi," the theme song of Arthur Freed and Vincente Minnelli's final masterpiece, won. It is regrettable that Gene's dramatic turn in *Marjorie Morningstar* did little to advance his career and is not better remembered in modern times. Gene was proud of the picture and later stated: "I haven't liked all my roles, more often than not I wince when watching myself, but I had some good scenes in this one."[10]

Almost immediately after filming ended on *Marjorie Morningstar,*

Gene left for his annual sojourn to Switzerland. Jeanne Coyne, from whom he was now nearly inseparable, accompanied him to San Moritz. Gossip columns ran items that Gene was dating "dozens of women" during this period, but in truth, he was dating Jeanne "exclusively."[11] Kerry, on vacation from school, joined the couple on the ski trip, but Gene still felt their little party was incomplete. Though they'd been divorced for only seven months, Gene was already on amicable terms with Betsy again. "Gene called whenever he was coming to Paris . . . and strange though I now think it was, for the first few years [after our divorce], I went to [Switzerland] for Christmas," Betsy recalled. "You're the Christmas fairy. Kerry can't have Christmas without you," Gene told her. "I believed him and Roger [Pigaut] made it easy, so I went to a tiny single room [at the resort] and put a happy face on the awkwardness I felt."[12]

Betsy and Gene remained connected throughout their lives. On her first trip back to California to visit a friend in 1958, Betsy was crestfallen to see that one of the three birch trees she and Gene had planted in the front yard of their home on Rodeo Drive was dead. The trees, she stated, had seemed to represent her, Gene, and Kerry. Betsy went on to say that although she did not have to pass by the house each time she visited Beverly Hills, she wanted to. "This is my house—I found it—I bought it—I made it our home—and I left it. . . . I finally understood that nothing ever goes away. You can't leave it behind or erase it. Everything you live is forever part of you."[13]

Though the thought of selling his and Betsy's home had crossed Gene's mind after the divorce, he was strongly attached to the house. He did not plan to relocate to Europe, although he intensely enjoyed his sojourns there and he intended to travel overseas after his directorial assignment on *The Tunnel of Love*, which was drawing near to its January 1958 starting date. Gene, in embarking upon his first stint as director rather than director/performer, was entering what could be the most promising avenue for his future in show business.

Gene returned to his old studio to shoot *The Tunnel of Love*, but it did not feel like a homecoming. The atmosphere at MGM was so changed that it bore little resemblance to the great dream factory he had known less than ten years ago. Parsimony was the rule in producing anything that was not an epic or prestige picture. Going into his project, Gene had to juggle several restrictions. Studio head Benny Thau (before Sol C. Siegel took his place) had stipulated that the film must be done in black and white and use only one primary set. Additionally, it had to be shot in three weeks for less than $500,000. Gene surprised everyone by completing the picture well within Thau's confines.

The MGM picture, based on a Broadway hit, follows a married suburban couple who are unable to conceive a child and must overcome countless obstacles in their mission to adopt one. The tension of the plot hinges on the fact that the baby the couple wishes to adopt is actually the husband's illegitimate child. Doris Day filled the role of the wife and Richard Widmark played her husband.

Gene's first strictly directorial experience was a pleasant one; the atmosphere on the set was easy and congenial. Elizabeth Wilson, who filled a supporting role in the film, recalled: "Gene Kelly was really gentle and very supportive. . . . I can remember [him] . . . trying to keep a sense of humor. . . . Kelly told both Day and Widmark that they looked Swedish and took to calling Day Brunhilda."[14] A reporter for the *Los Angeles Times* elaborated: "[Gene] didn't merely tell his stars how he wanted them to act—he showed them. And so, bouncing in and out of character like a rubber ball, Kelly acted every part in the movie. . . . Said star Richard Widmark: 'Movie actors often complain they miss the audience. But not with Gene around. He's not only an actor, producer, and director. He's a whole audience too.'"[15]

In spite of the positive feedback for the film from preview audiences, it did not perform well upon its New York premiere on November 21, 1958, and ultimately lost MGM money. Doris Day blamed the picture's failure on a weak script; Gene offered the explanation that audiences could not accept Widmark in a "light, sexy part," given that he was usually cast in noir films.[16] Bosley Crowther was unimpressed by the film's casual invocation of controversial subjects and terms (for example, Alfred Kinsey and *aphrodisiac*) that, ten years before, would never have passed censors. "It's a 'Little Accident,' updated just a bit," the bored Crowther concluded, referring to the 1928 Broadway hit *The Little Accident,* which bore a few plot similarities to *The Tunnel of Love.* He conceded that the actors, "under the direction of Gene Kelly," did a "competent" job.[17]

Gene did not consider the film a failure and neither did studio executives. In Gene's words: "Every studio in town [began to offer] me straight directing jobs, but I don't want to stay away from acting. They soon forget you in this age of specialization."[18] As much as Gene wanted to remain in acting, he later expressed that he did wish for more recognition in the areas of directing and producing. "The public couldn't care less [that I've directed pictures]. They want to see you. It's love. I don't mind. It's only my ego that says gee, I wish they knew I did something else. . . . Even after you're recognized all over the world this doesn't give you the thrill of knowing you've done a good job."[19] As Gene waited for a new assignment and mulled over what the next step in his career should be, he resumed his travels at home and abroad, visiting Paris, London, and occasionally New York.

For Easter 1958, Gene, Jeanne Coyne, and Kerry took a skiing holiday in Zermatt, Switzerland. Gene, still the competitive sportsman, was excited to learn that a group of Olympic champions was also staying at the resort. He joined them in their escapades but soon accepted that he was not in their league. Exhausted, Gene left the slopes early and made his way to the hotel for a hot bath. On his journey, he hit slush, fell, and ripped apart the cartilage in his leg. For half a mile, he staggered in excruciating pain until he reached the hotel and was rushed to the hospital. A doctor in Zermatt wanted to operate, but Gene refused. He later commented that if he had let that "quack cut me up I'd probably never have danced again." Instead, he hobbled around in bandages until after Kerry returned to school. He then traveled to Zurich for more intensive treatment. His leg healed as well as it could, and Gene felt ready to resume dancing. Still, he later admitted that the accident "was the end of serious dancing for me."[20]

Gene was delighted, then, to receive a challenging new job offer that did not require him to dance; instead, he would be telling others how to dance. During one of his stops in New York, he had received a call from Richard Rodgers and Oscar Hammerstein II. The duo asked him if he would like to direct what the two called the "Chinese *Life with Father*," their new stage show entitled *Flower Drum Song*. According to Gene's biographer Alvin Yudkoff Gene's "relaxed attitude about people of color and his 'couldn't-care-less' feelings about ethnicity were well known to Rodgers and Hammerstein. He was one of the very few who could direct a story about the clash of a gentle, ancient Asian culture against the bruisingly modern American way, without patronizing or insulting."[21]

The story centers on a father, Wang Chi-yang and his son, Wang Ta. The father, a wealthy refugee from China, clings to traditional values in San Francisco's Chinatown. The son is torn between loyalty to his father's traditions (specifically, going through with an arranged marriage to a

Chinese refugee) and assimilation into American culture (exemplified by his desire to marry a Chinese American nightclub performer). While the show was not Rodgers and Hammerstein's strongest, it included notable songs such as "A Hundred Million Miracles," and "I Enjoy Being a Girl."

Gene thought the "whole thing sounded charming" and it would be a "nice change" after seventeen years in the movie business. "It had a warmth about it and a sweet sentimentality. . . . I knew that as long as I crammed the show brim-full of every joke and gimmick in the book, I could get it to work."[22] Preproduction began in May 1958, shortly after the Easter holidays. By August 29, 1958, Gene, Jeanne Coyne, and Lois McClelland had rented and taken up residence in Milton Berle's Manhattan apartment on Park Avenue for the duration of rehearsals.

Gene's entire experience working on the show was, in a sense, a homecoming as well as a reunion. "The stage door I walked through when we began auditions for *Flower Drum Song* at the Shubert Theatre was the very same stage door by which I had left Broadway [after *Pal Joey*] for Hollywood in 1941," Gene told *Theatre Arts* magazine. The experience had a further element of déjà vu in that he was again working with Richard Rodgers, who had written the music for *Pal Joey*. Gene reconnected with his former assistant, Carol Haney, engaging her as choreographer, while another Freed Unit alum, Irene Sharaff, was engaged to do the costumes. "What makes the New York theatre so wonderful . . . is the handful of people— writers, composers, choreographers and others—who create for it. They are the people who can bring one back to Broadway. And here I am," Gene stated.[23]

As usual, Gene strove for as much realism as possible. With Jeanne Coyne, he made a special trip to San Francisco to recruit authentic Chinese actors who could also sing and dance. The show ultimately starred Miyoshi Umeki, Pat Suzuki (who was actually Japanese American), Keye Luke (Charlie Chan's "Number One" son), and Juanita Hall (a light-skinned African American who somehow passed as Asian).

When rehearsals began in September 1958, Gene was basically left to hold the show together by himself. Oscar Hammerstein was absent, still recovering from a surgery. Rodgers was present in body but not in mind. He had recently completed an unsuccessful twelve-week alcohol addiction program and was now suffering from major depression. He was often asleep during rehearsals. James Hammerstein urged his father to get out of bed right away; Gene was confused and unconfident as a director, he asserted. "Things are a hodgepodge." At the show's Boston tryout, review-ers complained that Larry Storch (who portrayed a nightclub comedian) "had gotten off on the wrong track in his role and Gene Kelly seemed unable to get him back on the right one."[24] Larry Blyden replaced Storch before the New York premiere. Despite the troubled rehearsals and tryout period, Rodgers later wrote in his memoir that he and Hammerstein were "confident that he [Gene] could do a beautiful job. He did."[25]

James Hammerstein's initial poor estimation of Gene may have been because the director left the show to take a brief trip to London only a week after rehearsals for *Flower Drum Song* commenced. Gene had received an offer from the eminent film production company the Rank Organization to direct and choreograph an Edwardian period piece titled *Gentleman's Gentleman*. The picture was to be a lavish musical starring Moira Shearer of *Red Shoes* fame. Gene was intrigued by the prospect and accepted the offer. The film was not slated for production until the follow-ing year. Gene rushed back to New York and finished his work on *Flower Drum Song*.

The show opened on December 1, 1958. It seemed a certain hit; advance ticket sales amounted to $1 million. However, New York critics favored *Flower Drum Song* with only tepid reviews. Brooks Atkinson of the *New York Times* called it merely "pleasant" but not intelligent. He did at least give a nod to Gene's directorial skills: "Gene Kelly has organized a warm, radiant, fluid performance [from the actors]."[26] Audiences, how-ever, adored the show. It ran for six hundred performances, until May 7, 1960. Richard Rodgers declared that in Gene, "we got a man who was not only experienced and professional to the very marrow of his bones, but also hard-working and inspired. Without him, who knows how it all would have turned out!"[27] Rodgers even stated that the success of the play enabled him to overcome his depression. Gene's melancholy lifted as well. In an interview with Edward Murrow in 1958, he concluded: "It's been a won-derful experience . . . coming back to Broadway after fifteen or sixteen years. It wasn't a chore, and that's an understatement."[28]

Flower Drum Song won Tony nominations for Best Musical, Best Actor and Best Actress (for Larry Blyden and Miyoshi Umeki), Best Costume for Irene Sharaff, and Best Choreography for Carol Haney. Salvatore Dell'Isola won the award for Best Musical Direction. Though Gene won no nominations or awards, *Flower Drum Song* proved to be an invigorating experience for him. Carol Haney may have been the choreographer for this show, but Gene was eager to resume the combined tasks of choreographing and directing in his future projects. "I actually love to create the dance more than I love to dance it. So naturally I got into directing. That was my greatest joy," he reflected in 1990.[29] As it turned out, Gene's next assignment gave him the jobs of performer, choreographer, and director—for a television program, no less.

Though Gene did intend to resume his life in Hollywood, he was not ready to return just yet. He took no respite between the premiere of *Flower Drum Song* and his next project, *Dancing: A Man's Game,* to be filmed in New York's NBC Studios and aired on December 21, 1958. The show was to be an episode of *Omnibus,* a TV series hosted by Alistair Cooke. A superior example of early television, the program featured a wide range of specials about cultural arts and science. Among the show's past guests were Gene's old friends William Saroyan and Leonard Bernstein. In Bernstein's appearance, he explained the structure of Beethoven's Fifth Symphony and drew the orchestral score on the floor so that the various instrumentalists could walk along it to illustrate their contribution to the sound. Gene's special was to be similar to Bernstein's in that he, too, explained the structure of his art. *Dancing: A Man's Game* sought to illustrate Gene's career-long goal to prove that dance is as masculine a sport as football or boxing. For the *Omnibus* special, Gene called upon great athletes of the time to perform alongside him, among them legends Sugar Ray Robinson, Mickey Mantle, and Johnny Unitas.

As the program opens, the camera shows dancers and athletes alike warming up in a gym with balletic movements. "All these men share skill and rhythm. An athlete's goal is to win the game; his aim is competition. A dancer goes further, he conveys emotion, he tells a story visually. A dancer must have something to say or he's in real trouble," Gene explains as he walks through the gym.[30] Again and again Gene, in one reviewer's words, "returned to his thesis that the dance was the property and prerogative of men, not women, illustrating with the tremendously masculine and virile dances of Spain and Russia."[31] The show closes with a balletic vignette showing a group of street toughs fighting and loafing. Gene set his ballet to the music of Gershwin's "Concerto in F."

Dancing: A Man's Game was unanimously well received, with numerous critics hailing it as a masterpiece. The entire hour, as described by *Variety,* was a "stunning production, expertly directed and executed . . . as high on entertainment value as it was informative."[32] The *St. Petersburg Times* called it "a wonderful mixture of education and sheer visual fun, showing what TV can do in this line when it half tries."[33] In 1976, Gene still spoke with pride about his show, highlighting its honest acknowledgment of issues that hitherto had been carefully avoided in television and film:

> I talked about homosexuality—and this was before everyone went overboard with sexual frankness—saying that an artist in any form . . . is the custodian of a certain gift, and his sexual preferences have nothing to do with his art. I said that we in America are still afraid to say that a man is graceful, and pointed out that John Wayne is graceful. John phoned me the next day . . . and I wondered what was coming. . . . But he was grateful to me. I'd picked out the toughest guys I could think of at the time, and he saw the point I was making immediately.[34]

Gene's program went far in helping *Omnibus* earn an Emmy statuette as 1958's Best Public Service Program or Series. Gene himself received an Emmy nomination for Best Choreography for Television and won *Dance* magazine's yearly award for Best Television Program. (Incidentally, the show to receive the most wins—nine in all, including Most Outstanding Single Program of the Year—at the eleventh Emmy awards was a special by Gene's colleague and alleged rival, Fred Astaire. NBC aired the musical variety program, *An Evening with Fred Astaire,* on October 17, 1958. The special was the first television program to ever be taped in color.)

Even if his special did not receive the deluge of awards Astaire's program had, Gene considered *Dancing: A Man's Game* his first professional victory since *Singin' in the Rain.* True, *Flower Drum Song* was a hit, but Gene's television program was a product of his own creation and thus its success validated him on a personal and professional level. No longer wary of television, Gene accepted an offer from the *Pontiac Star Parade* to choreograph and perform in two specials, the first of which was to have the honorific title *The Gene Kelly Show.*

Before production began, Gene went on his yearly holiday trip to Switzerland with Kerry and Jeanne. A disappointing bit of news, however, made the holiday less sweet. He received a phone call from the Rank Organization informing him that *Gentleman's Gentleman* had been cancelled. Gene flew to London for two days, hoping that the project could be salvaged. But his hopes were fruitless, and he found himself on a plane to New York after taking a consolatory whirlwind trip to Paris.

As Gene laid his head back on his seat, the plane suddenly dropped thirty thousand feet over the icy waters of the North Atlantic. Gene clutched his seat, certain he was about to die. "I felt as if all the blood was being drained out of my body and my lungs were tearing to shreds. . . . My first thought was 'Should I pray or not,' and I decided I wouldn't because I hadn't been in a church or prayed for several years, and the last thing I wanted to be was a deathbed Catholic and a coward. . . . My next thought was whether I'd paid my insurance and whether Kerry would be sufficiently provided for," Gene recalled in 1974. In a Hollywood-style ending, the plane leveled out at six thousand feet—just in time—and was flown to Gander, Newfoundland, for inspection. The plane had apparently developed a fault in its automatic pilot setting while the captain was outside his cabin hobnobbing with the passengers. A second plane safely transported Gene and the 113 other passengers to New York within five hours. The same day, another plane had crashed into the East River and Jeanne Coyne, who was to meet Gene at the airport, was near tears; she was sure it was Gene's plane and that he had been killed. "It was about the most unpleasant experience in my life," Gene concluded.[35]

Gene's brush with death did not turn him into a religious man; nor did it make him believe in miracles. But his recent successes, his blossoming romance with Jeanne, and the fact that his plane had not crashed made him again believe he was, as he stated numerous times throughout his life, a lucky man. His next project also proved to be lucky, if not as prestigious as *Dancing: A Man's Game*. *The Gene Kelly Show*, filmed in Hollywood, was a pleasant revue that gave Gene the opportunity to showcase almost every medium of dance.

The show opens with Gene singing "I Got Rhythm," appearing youthful and trim, dressed in a straw hat and bow tie and twirling a cane. "This is a dancing show with lots of music and lots of songs and we hope lots of fun," Gene begins in a soft voice. "It comes to you from Hollywood, but it could be coming from anywhere, for every song and dance man is a traveling man."[36]

Gene then begins to sing "Les Girls" as ballerinas from France, Germany, and Sweden spring into view. Next, he does a soft-shoe with Cherylene Lee, a five-year-old girl who had appeared in *Flower Drum Song*. Next is the "Coffeehouse Ballet" (scored by Henry Mancini), which seemed like a burlesque of Fred Astaire's "Girl Hunt Ballet" in Arthur Freed and Vincente Minnelli's *The Band Wagon* (1953). Later in the show, Gene impressed audiences with a technically advanced, split-screen sequence that was a virtual reprisal of his acclaimed "Alter Ego" number from *Cover Girl*. In the most unexpected sequence in the special, Gene dances to a poem written for him by Carl Sandberg. Gene acts like Sandberg's puppet, moving in whatever way the poet tells him to. The number is both childlike and striking in its originality.

For the finale of the special, Gene surprised audiences by dancing with a teenage girl unnamed in the credits: Liza Minnelli. Gene had been intent on having Liza make her screen debut after attending a party at Ira Gershwin's house at which the girl was singing. Minnelli was enthusiastic, but he advised Gene to obtain Judy Garland's blessing first. Gene called Judy the next day. She agreed: "I'd like to see what Liza could do with the number." Liza was thrilled; one of her lifelong dreams had been to dance with Gene. "I went to the studios every day [as a child], and I loved to dance." Sometimes during breaks, she remembered, Gene would say, "C'mere, I'll teach you a step."[37]

On the night of the special, Gene was stricken with anxiety that Liza would freeze. However, when the cameras started rolling, Liza was as calm as could be. Gene was the one whose stomach churned. "I was so concerned that . . . I almost blew it. But [it was] as if this was [Liza's] fifty-fourth show. I don't know where it came from. It had only been a couple of years since she'd come and played in our back yard."[38]

Gene and Liza performed a sweet, gentle tap dance to "For Me and My Gal," a poignant choice, for it was the first dance Gene had performed on film with Judy Garland. Their routine was flawless, and Gene was swift to compliment his young partner: "Every once in a while, you see flashes of Judy [in Liza] that you can't escape. . . . I don't think it harmed her having two talented parents, but I don't think you can say it gave her her talent."[39] Gene remained a mentor to Liza into her adulthood.

After Liza and Gene's dance, Gene closed his special twirling an umbrella while crooning "Singin' in the Rain." Hearty applause rang from the audience. The show, which had been prerecorded, aired on NBC-TV on April 24, 1959. It was nearly as well received as *Dancing: A Man's Game*. Robert Lewis Shayon, a critic for the *Saturday Review*, had nothing but accolades for Gene: "Mr. Kelly is a dancer who dares to have an idea. . . . He is an artful satirist with taste and distinction. . . . If he and Pontiac [the special's sponsor] chose to be partners in a weekly dance show . . . they could make some very significant contributions to this nation's understanding of the mind behind the dance."[40]

Gene had no intention of turning television into his primary mode of work yet. He held that "television isn't really a dancer's medium. . . . The limitation in the size of the screen is obvious. The viewer doesn't want to see a close-up of the ballerina's face: he wants to see the movement of her whole body, and her relationship to the other dancers."[41] Nonetheless, he did agree to do a second special for Pontiac in the fall.

In the meantime, Gene received the honor of sitting on the jury of the Cannes Film Festival during the summer of 1959. After participating, he and Kerry visited a family of genteel Greek ship owners they had met in Klosters at their home on an island off the mainland of Greece. However, even on a secluded island, offers of work still found their way to Gene. He welcomed one with unusual anticipation: Stanley Kramer asked him to appear in *Inherit the Wind,* a film based on the famed Scopes Monkey Trial. Gene would play the part of E. K. Hornbeck, a character based on reporter H. L. Mencken, who had covered the trial in 1925. "When I learned that Spencer Tracy and Fredric March were in it [the film] I didn't even call my agent. I just scooped up my family and flew back" to Hollywood.[42] Since entering the film business, Gene had often stated that Tracy and March were two actors he particularly admired and whose unpretentious styles of acting he strove to emulate.

Gene seemed an unlikely choice for the part of the ironic Hornbeck, who professes that "it is the duty of a newspaper to comfort the afflicted and afflict the comfortable."[43] When he announced Gene as his pick for the role, Kramer said it was "hard for some people to digest." But Kramer had a precedent; the previous year, "against conventional wisdom," he had placed Fred Astaire in a serious role in the dystopian drama *On the Beach* (1959). The director argued that he wanted Hornbeck to be a "complicated and incredibly vital character . . . in every way an American original. Gene Kelly . . . was an excellent actor who could convey the combination of intelligence and devilish humor the character needed."[44]

The Hornbeck character's beliefs meshed well with Gene's own agnostic convictions. The target of his unflinching monologues is Tracy, who portrays Henry Drummond, the man defending a jailed teacher's right to teach evolution: "Why don't you wake up? Darwin was wrong! Man's still an ape," he declares at one point. Hornbeck and Drummond's love/hate relationship is one of the more intriguing aspects of the film, lending it depth and much-needed humor. Gene gets the last word in the picture as he and Drummond leave the sweltering, empty courtroom.

> Drummond: When you go to your grave, there won't be anybody
> to pull the grass up over your head. Nobody to mourn you.
> Nobody to give a damn. You're all alone.
> Hornbeck: You're wrong, Henry. You'll be there. You're the type.
> Who else would defend my right to be lonely?

Budgeted at $2 million, *Inherit the Wind* went into production on October 21, 1959, at Universal Studios and wrapped in mid-December 1959. It made its premiere seven months later, on July 21, 1960, in Dayton, Tennessee—the very state in which the film takes place. Reviewers were complimentary, but the film's highly controversial subject matter caused audiences to stay away. *Variety* commented that a "good measure of the film's surface bite is contributed by Gene Kelly. . . . Kelly demonstrates again that even without dancing shoes he knows his way on the screen."[45] Bosley Crowther of the *New York Times* summarized Gene's performance in one line: "There's a nimble newspaper reporter, played briskly and glibly by Gene Kelly." Overall, Crowther hailed the movie as "a triumph."[46] Triumphant though it may have been, it grossed only $2 million, resulting in a loss of $1.7 million due to publicity and other overhead costs. "It was a very high class picture—for that reason, not too big a hit," Gene stated in 1994. "But that was I think the great climax to my career, doing a straight part with these two guys [Tracy and March]."[47]

Then and now, Gene's brilliant performance as Hornbeck has been too little appreciated. According to his biographer Tony Thomas: "Some critics hastened to comment that Gene was miscast without explaining why. His Hornbeck is in fact precisely what the script calls for—a superficially amusing, hard-hearted, and somewhat lost soul."[48] Note that even Gene called the picture the climax of his career because he worked with Tracy and March—not because he thought his performance was special. Patricia Wilson, a Broadway performer, recorded in her memoir that when she complimented Gene on his acting in *Inherit the Wind,* he said, "I wanted to hide under the seat when I saw that film! I walked like a damn ballet dancer, turn-out and all!" "Well," Patricia's brother David remarked, "there goes the man's credentials as a megalomaniac!"[49]

At forty-seven, Gene had become a humbler and significantly mellower man. As Kerry Kelly had observed after her parents' divorce, he was not as self-confident or social as he had been in years past. Jeanne Coyne's constancy seemed to limit his famous temper. According to biographer Clive Hirschhorn, Gene, "the erstwhile innovator who had taken the movie musical by the scruff of its neck and shaken it free of cobwebs seemed content now to spend his time appearing in lucrative specials . . . recapping his career in musicals for the benefit of a new generation of Americans."[50]

Gene's second Pontiac special included recaps of dances he had been performing throughout his career. He enlisted Carol Lawrence (who originated the role of Maria on Broadway in *West Side Story,* 1957) and, in a much-anticipated reunion, Donald O'Connor as his partners. Filmed entirely in color, the *Pontiac Star Parade* aired on NBC-TV on November 21, 1959. The finale was a "sit down dance medley" which favored O'Connor, who professed to primarily use his feet rather than his entire body while dancing. After engaging in comedic banter, they challenge each other in a sort of "name that tune" game, tapping out rhythms with their feet.[51] Throughout the entire number, Gene and Donald seem to be holding back sincere laughter, infusing the number with an air of spontaneity and camaraderie. In truth, Gene, his costars, and the dance chorus had rehearsed for a month to ensure the numbers were perfect.

Most critics admired Gene's second *Pontiac* special. A reporter for the *TV Radio Mirror* deemed the show "light-hearted, light-footed magic."[52] However, Jack Gould of the *New York Times* thought the show fell short of expectations. "Mr. Kelly's singing voice is extremely husky and limited in range. . . . With so much singing he left little time for dancing, most of which did not seem blessed by the verve and imagination the occasion warranted."[53]

To his detractors, Gene may have seemed content to revel in nostalgia rather than create imaginative new dance concepts, but when the right opportunity came along, he had as strong an urge for innovation as ever. In April 1960, Gene found himself again an American in Paris, this time at the request of the Paris Opera Ballet. The company had not yet explored any style but classical and feared it was falling behind the times. Gene accepted the assignment to choreograph a modern ballet with alacrity.

Before leaving for his beloved European city, he grinningly told columnist Hedda Hopper: "The French said at one time we [Americans] were ten years behind in dance. Now they say we're ten years ahead."[54]

The last time Gene had worked in Europe, Betsy had accompanied him and he had been intent on creating an all-dance picture. He had come home from that trip with an air of defeat; both his career and his marriage had all but fallen apart. Now, Gene returned to Europe with Jeanne Coyne on his arm, set on choreographing the first jazz ballet ever staged at the Paris Opera. In Europe, Gene had never lost popularity as he had in America. Thus, it was with a feeling of triumph that he, whom director/performer Jean Louis Barrault fondly termed "the most French of Americans in Paris," took on the most challenging assignment to come his way in almost a decade.[55]

19

"I wear so many hats"

Professional ballet dancer, writer, choreographer, director, and priest: at various times in his life, Gene Kelly had considered all of them as viable career paths and had already mastered three: writing, choreographing, and directing. By 1962, he would essentially master or remaster all five paths through the mediums of stage, film, and television. "I wear so many hats that sometimes I forget where I've been and where I'm going."[1]

He won the position of ballet dancer first, if only in an honorary capacity, via choreographing for the Paris Opera Ballet. Adamant that America now held the lead in dance, he boasted, "Our New York City Ballet is the best in the world."[2] Eager to prove the truth of his claim, Gene now sought to bring New York excellence to Paris. He held an exalted position: he would act not only as choreographer for the ballet company but also as writer and musical supervisor. Gene flew to France in February 1960 to begin preparing the show, although rehearsals did not commence until April 1960.

As late as March, he still had no clue what the plot of the ballet would be, but he kept busy creating dance steps. By May, he had finally devised a story. "[It's] just mythology as written by me. Sort of Amphitryon in reverse. Silly but fun."[3] The tale he created depicted a sort of lovers' quarrel between Aphrodite and Zeus and the drastic means it takes to reconcile them. Aphrodite was portrayed by French ballet star Claude Bessy, whom Gene had used in *Invitation to the Dance*. The story "was good clean naughty fun and Mr. Kelly could use all the flying machines for clouds and chariots that a 19th-century opera house can provide," a reporter for the *New York Times* remarked of the ballet, which Gene titled *Pas de Dieux* (which cleverly substituted the French word for "gods" in the ballet term *pas de deux*, a duet in which two dancers perform steps together).[4] Among the visual effects Gene employed was a large traffic light directing the clouds. Its flashing colors of red, green, and yellow also served to indicate Aphrodite's moods.

As an accompaniment to the zesty, forty-five-minute ballet, Gene selected George Gershwin's Concerto in F. "The paramount problem was to teach the corps de ballet how to dance modern symphonic jazz," Gene commented. "It's been a huge source of satisfaction for me, working with these kids. I think they liked the informal atmosphere of my rehearsals. . . . Every so often when I looked up at this ornate old building and reminded myself of what I was doing, I sort of looked up toward heaven and murmured 'Forgive me, Diaghilev.'"[5] Not all the dancers thought the rehearsals were "informal" or fun; a number of ballerinas complained that Gene's "muscular rehearsals" were "wearing them out."[6]

Pas de Dieux made its Paris premiere on July 6, 1960. When the final curtain fell, the audience was rapturous, applauding like "a Saturday night crowd at a barn dance." The company took an astounding twenty-three curtain calls. "It was hard to tell, however, whether the audience and the majority of critics were applauding the ballet or the man who created it," a reporter for *Newsweek* observed. Gene was pulled from the audience and onto the stage as theatergoers began to shout, "Auteur! Auteur!" His eyes were damp and he wore a "radiantly happy" smile on his face as he took three more curtain calls with the dancers. Among the enthusiastic audience members were a handful of movie folk, including Grace Kelly and Sam Goldwyn.[7]

French and American critics had almost unanimous praise for the show. One French author recorded: "Kelly succeeded in blowing away a half century of dust from the Paris Opera."[8] Gene, ever the perfectionist, was not content to leave the production at its status quo. "This was just the first night. Wait till we get the thing polished up."[9] Negative reviews of the show are difficult to find, but one stands out—a piece written by a critic for *Le Monde*. "It was a bad idea to insist pompously on evening dress for the opening. To have been at one with the other side of the footlights last night, we should have come in jeans."[10] Gene was his own severest critic. Twenty years later, he commented, "Now I feel I could do it better."[11] A. M. Julien, general director of the opera, saw no flaw in Gene's work and presented him with the French government's honorific title Knight of the Legion of Honor.

Though plagued by doubts of the ballet's merit, Gene found his months in France refreshing. He and Jeanne rented an expensive apartment in

Paris that, according to Gene, cost him every franc he earned that spring. The abode was too big for just the two of them, but "he adopted a 'what the hell' attitude (of which his mother would not have approved!) and enjoyed himself." Each night, Jeanne and Gene made it their custom to stop by a nearby bar and play pinball. The couple competed ferociously against each other, but not to the extent Gene and Betsy had years ago. Gene claimed that he usually won because he knew how to "cheat outrageously." One night, Jeanne had had enough of his tricks and kicked Gene on the shin beneath the table. Unbeknownst to Jeanne, she had kicked not her opponent but a stranger observing the game. Gene was apoplectic, then, when the stranger began to hurl insults at Jeanne in French, including the epithet "whore." The man retreated from the bar after Gene punched him on the nose. On the way back to the hotel, Gene wondered aloud why the man had turned against Jeanne. "Is he anti-American? Dirty son of a bitch." Jeanne turned to him with a sheepish expression and confessed, "I think I kicked him in the groin." Several weeks later, the couple passed the man on the street, apologized, bought him a drink, and played a game of pinball with him. "He beat the hell out of me," Gene recalled.[12]

In Paris, Gene and actor Jackie Gleason began discussing a screen project titled *Gigot* that would star Gleason and have Gene as director. Gene and Gleason were "pals by proxy" because the comedian was friends with Gene's colleagues Paddy Chayefsky and Frank Sinatra. Seven Arts Productions was to produce the film and Twentieth Century-Fox agreed to release it. The Gleason project was only in its infancy when Gene, at the behest of producer Jerry Wald at Fox, flew to Hollywood to appear in *Let's Make Love,* a Marilyn Monroe musical directed by George Cukor.

The picture costarred Yves Montand as Jean-Marc Clement, a sort of French Howard Hughes. When he becomes the subject of an off-Broadway satire, he makes a trip to the theater only to be mistaken for a look-alike actor auditioning for the role based on himself. Clement becomes infatuated with the leading lady Amanda (Monroe) and decides to play along with the misconception. To make himself believable as a performer, he hires Milton Berle to teach him comedy, Gene to teach him to dance, and Bing Crosby to teach him to croon. Gene's one line allowed him to espouse his personal dance philosophy: "You see, a dancer expresses with his body what an actor does with words. It's not just the feet."

The high point of the picture is Marilyn Monroe singing a sultry rendition of "My Heart Belongs to Daddy," which Mary Martin had made a hit in Gene's first Broadway show, *Leave It to Me!* (1938). Gene was happy to work with Marilyn. As a starlet, she had been a semi-regular guest at his and Betsy's open-house parties, usually as the date of a director or producer. Gene saw great potential in Marilyn's musical comedy skills and hoped to work with her more closely in the future.

When *Let's Make Love* premiered on September 8, 1960, Bosley Crowther of the *New York Times* bemoaned Montand's leaden performance. "Bing Crosby and Gene Kelly are brought in to give the pupil further lessons. The only humor in their appearance is the idea. The futility of their efforts is more ironic."[13] Though the movie lost money at the box office, Gene viewed it as a positive experience—and an easy one. "I got on a plane and flew over the Pole to Los Angeles. Jerry [Wald] met me in the evening at the airport; we filmed the next day and then he returned me to the airport," Gene explained. "Would that all my jobs had been so well arranged."[14]

Gene hoped his impending directorial job would be as streamlined. However, the importance of *Gigot* paled beside a lively event in Gene's personal life. He was certain he had kept the development a secret, but it came as little surprise to his friends and family. At age forty-eight, Gene Kelly became the husband of thirty-seven-year-old Jeanne Coyne.

"I can't imagine an adult man not wanting marriage. Freedom is lonely. . . . It's sheer boredom. . . . A little variety can't possibly compensate for the joys of solidity, of having someone close by your side. . . . A woman clips your wings a bit, but she's worth it," Gene stated in 1962.[15] By that time, he had been happily married to Jeanne Coyne for two years. Two decades after their first meeting, the couple married at two o'clock in the morning in a small ceremony in Tonopah, Nevada, on August 8, 1960. Gene wished to keep the marriage quiet to protect Kerry, whom he did not wish to be hounded by columnists. Tireless columnist Louella Parsons, however, managed to leak the story. Kerry later said she was "thrilled" about her father's remarriage and "thought it was great."[16] She recalled that Gene had asked her permission to marry Jeanne, thinking it would come as a surprise to his daughter. "I played it very straight and said: 'What a wonderful idea, Dad. *How* did you ever think of it?'"[17]

Now that Gene and Jeanne were ready to begin a life together, Gene considered putting his house on the market to make a completely fresh start. But when he asked his wife what she thought of the house, "she said she loved it and wouldn't dream of making me sell." What changed was not Gene's house but his lifestyle. It had already altered considerably since his divorce from Betsy, but now it became even quieter. The couple was content to stay at home. On the infrequent occasions they went dancing, Gene said, "People expected me to be throwing her around and dancing on tables. All we wanted to do was the foxtrot."[18] Jeanne was not fond of flashy dance, nor did she like volleyball or charades. In spite of their less stimulating social life, they found all the refreshment they needed in each other. Their personalities complemented each other ideally, for they shared the key traits of, in Betsy's words, being "charming, good-natured, straightforward, and energetic."[19]

Gene, as he settled into a semi-retirement, "was not only personally happy but also thought himself the better for having had his temperament and perfectionism cut down to size" by Jeanne.[20] This being said, Jeanne was not dominant. Unlike Betsy, she had no interest in pursuing her own career after she married, and moreover, she was apolitical and "a little puritanical." She believed a wife's place was in the home and, according to Kerry, had an "image of family life . . . she was intent on turning . . . into a reality even if it meant suppressing her actual intelligence in the process." Kerry asserted that Jeanne's only fault seemed to be her "neurotic denial of her intelligence."[21]

Gene was aware of his wife's intelligence, but he seemed to thrive on living with a more self-effacing woman. Nonetheless, he was proud of her abilities—abilities he had seen from the first time he met her when she was his twelve-year-old pupil. "No one I've ever known has such a combination of talents," Gene said of his wife, referring specifically to her skill in assessing any routine he showed her and critiquing a number's effectiveness. One journalist aptly described her as a woman who "became his living answer. . . . He has found someone whose sense of perfectionism matches his. . . . Like Gene, she has one foot in fantasy, and a perennial child's ability to imagine."[22]

One area in which Jeanne did not adapt herself to Gene was in becoming politically active; apolitical, she left campaigning, rallies, and the like to Gene. Gene was especially active in championing John F. Kennedy as the Democratic candidate for president in the 1960 election. Gene's colleagues Frank Sinatra, Judy Garland, and Marilyn Monroe joined him in their support. Kennedy did ultimately win the election, making him, at forty-three, America's youngest president as well as the country's first Catholic leader.

At Kennedy's inaugural gala in January 1961, Gene was among the celebrities who paid tribute to the president via a lengthy musicalized story of his life. Gene sang and danced to "The Hat My Dear Old Father Wore," wearing the green top hat he had worn performing the number in *Take Me out to the Ball Game.* He next did a vaudevillian skit complete with his trademark dance move of hopping along the ground on his hands and feet. The audience met his contributions with lengthy applause and shouts.

America in 1961 was far different from the America Gene recalled in his nostalgic skits. The Cold War was escalating; the US government attempted to halt the spread of Communism, first in an unsuccessful invasion of Cuba's Bay of Pigs and next in Vietnam. On December 11, 1961, the war in Vietnam officially began when American helicopters landed in Saigon. American soil, too, was not free from conflict. Tension brewed when African American Freedom Riders were arrested for allegedly disturbing the peace when they refused to sit in the backs of buses. On a brighter note, America had become a strong contender in the space race against the Soviet Union. Kennedy launched the Apollo program, claiming a man would be on the moon by the end of the decade. As immersed as he was in his family and work, Gene remained in touch with the world around him and was an especially firm supporter of the civil rights movement.

Film reflected the racial tension in the country. *West Side Story,* the number one movie of the year, depicted animosity between whites and Puerto Ricans. Escapist entertainment, however, remained a necessary element in cinema. Doris Day and Rock Hudson delighted audiences in one of their many "sex" comedies, *Lover Come Back,* while Disney found a new star in Hayley Mills in its pleasant family movie *The Parent Trap.* The year's surprise hit was not escapist but experimental: Federico Fellini's *La Dolce Vita.* Its success proved that Americans were now more receptive to foreign, avant-garde cinema. The Italian film, shot completely in black and white and on location in Rome, led Gene to see his impending project, *Gigot,* as a promising one. It, too, was to be shot in black and white and entirely on location.

Gene had little reason to doubt his capability to create an artistic yet accessible picture. On October 5, 1961, his alma mater, Pittsburgh State University, awarded him an honorary doctor of fine arts degree. The title was far more fitting than bachelor of science in economics, the degree he had actually earned there. In late spring 1961, the newly christened "doctor" flew to France to begin shooting on *Gigot*—a film he claimed had the makings of a minor masterpiece.

Gigot was essentially Jackie Gleason's *Invitation to the Dance.* As such, producers viewed it with grave doubt. Already, four directors had tried and failed to bring the picture to life: Orson Welles, José Ferrer, William Wyler, and Fred Zinnemann. What the film needed was a man of sentiment who still had the spark of childhood about him—Gene was a natural choice. Gleason's biographer William Henry III disagreed, asserting that Gene's "genial nice guy humor" and "schmaltzy romantic vision of France" as shown in *An American in Paris* in no way could be reconciled to Gleason's Paris of "rotting suburbs, petty merchants, peasant mores, and stark survival." Gleason, Henry concluded, took Gene on simply because he needed to get his movie made.[23]

Gigot tells the story of an outcast Parisian deaf-mute who can communicate with others only via pantomime. When a prostitute with a baby finds her way to his basement one rainy night, Gigot takes it upon himself to look after them.

Gleason and Gene found that they worked well together in spite of their clashing egos. The comedian remained in good humor even after Gene imposed an exercise regimen upon him that included running up and down flights of stairs. Though Gene put Gleason on a weight-loss plan, he did not seem overly concerned with Gleason's eating habits. They regularly went to LeRoy Haines's restaurant in Montmartre—the only establishment in Paris that listed barbecued pork ribs, Texas chili, and homemade apple pie as its specialties. Gleason was so pleased with the food that he made an embossed certificate for the restaurant reading, "Winner of the First Annual Jackie Gleason Culinary Award."[24]

Three events more significant than Gene and Gleason's delight in finding American cuisine in Paris occurred during the filming of *Gigot*. In August 1961, Gene escaped death when a group of right-wing terrorists attempted to bomb a Parisian police station. The bomb hit Gene's parked sedan instead, blowing it to smithereens. The second event was a happier one: Gene received from Hollywood the offer of a role in a new television series by the makers of *Leave It to Beaver,* Joe Connelly and Bob Mosher. The series was a spin-off of the movie *Going My Way* (1944), which had won Bing Crosby a Best Actor Oscar for his portrayal of the progressive

Father O'Malley. Gene did not relish the idea of committing himself to the twenty-six-week job, but he reconsidered after receiving a special birthday card from Jeanne—the third and most exciting event to occur during shooting of *Gigot*. "I have your present inside me," Jeanne wrote succinctly. Now, the idea of *Going My Way* became vastly appealing. Because it was to be filmed at Universal Studios, it assured Gene that he would be close to home when the baby was due in March 1962. Leo G. Carroll and Dick York (the latter had also appeared in *Inherit the Wind*) signed to be his TV costars. All would report to ABC-TV for work in February 1962.

Gene was eager to return home, but he continued to put his best efforts into *Gigot*. In December 1961, after six months of shooting and editing, Gene agreed with Gleason that the film was Oscar material. They planned to complete the final polishing at Seven Arts Studios in Hollywood. "I was a very proud and happy man."[25] Gene's pride was all too short-lived. After the film's New York preview, Gleason and Gene realized, much to Gene's dismay, that Seven Arts had heavily cut and edited the picture.

Gleason's biographer William Henry III claimed that Gene was at fault for the film's massacre because he departed for another project, presumably *Going My Way*, before completing final edits. "Jackie astonishingly forgave Kelly's . . . departure. . . . Jackie grumbled publicly that the result was not as good as it could have been . . . but he never criticized Kelly."[26] Gene stated years later: "I did have a wonderful time working with Jackie . . . and we are still great friends."[27]

Gigot made its New York premiere on September 27, 1962. Bosley Crowther had little good to say about the picture; he deemed it a failed homage to Charlie Chaplin's brand of silent comedy. "[Gigot] is a ponderous, steamy figure whose maunderings are soggy and gross—and made only more so in the close-ups that Gene Kelly, who directed, has generously employed. . . . True, there is a fast burst of morbid humor and sweet sentiment at the end, but it is awfully late in coming."[28] The picture grossed only $1.6 million.

Americans may have had little appreciation for *Gigot*, but the French revered Gene for again featuring Paris in American cinema. In November 1962, the American Legion cited him for his outstanding contribution to Franco-American relations; Gene received the additional honor of being made a Friend of the City of Paris.

A different sort of honor helped assuage the less than enthusiastic reception of *Gigot* in America. In summer 1962, New York's Museum of

Modern Art hosted a retrospective of Gene's films. The country, in the thick of civil unrest and worry over atomic warfare, needed the optimism and hope Gene's films instilled in audiences.

Gene's reward of becoming a father for the second time trumped any professional accolades he received. On March 3, 1962, Jeanne gave birth to Timothy Kelly, a little boy with the same dark hair and striking eyes as his father. Gene was the archetypal proud father, and columnists were quick to note it. Jane Ardmore of the *TV Radio Mirror* commented: "When I saw him two years ago [1960] . . . something was missing. . . . Well, see him now, stopping to roll son Timothy's baby carriage to a sunnier spot, and you know what was missing." Timothy was baptized in November. Patricia Lawford (wife of actor Peter Lawford) acted as his godmother and TV producer Joe Connelly was godfather. Ardmore observed that at the ceremony "Jeanne and Kerry were radiant—but you should have seen Gene! He was positively misty in the midst of all this. . . . A fulfilled man."[29]

Gene was able to spend ample time with his wife and son now that his work kept him so close to home. *Going My Way* was ready for its premiere on ABC-TV on October 3, 1962. "It's been twenty years since the movie [of *Going My Way*] was produced and we've updated it. . . . Gene Kelly will not play the role Bing Crosby did. He'll be more of a fighter," Joe Connelly told the *New York Times*. "The TV show will have many serious moments. There will be a script about an unwed mother, a couple that can't have a child, and a story about a kid who steals."[30] Though it dealt with sober topics, the show was not without humor. Gene's character, Father O'Malley, has a talent for dancing and singing, causing his superior, Father Fitz, no end of frustration. "I asked the bishop for a hard worker and he sends me Arthur Murray."[31] No one was more pleased with Gene's latest role than Harriet Kelly. "I like seeing Gene doing [this kind of] program."[32]

The first season of *Going My Way* was well received and it appeared that it might be picked up for another. Gene was discontented with the show, however, considering his role passive in spite of Connelly's assertion that O'Malley was a fighter (particularly after the Catholic Church and the TV studio put restrictions on the program, cleansing it of much of its initial edge). Furthermore, Gene found "the weight of the lines he was expected to learn sheer drudgery."[33] The shooting schedule was fast paced even for Gene, leaving him only two days to memorize each script. The rigidity of the daily routine also made him balk. One worker on the set, commenting on working with Gene, snorted: "Holy Father? More like a holy terror!"[34]

Gene may have had his qualms about the program, but he still regretted its cancellation. It could not compete against the popular *Beverly Hillbillies,* a sitcom that shared its time slot. "It was too gentle," Gene said of *Going My Way.* "It was a nice, clean family show."[35] Ironically, when *Going My Way* went into reruns during the summer, its ratings skyrocketed. But it was too late to revive the program; the cast had already been released and had moved on to other projects.

By the beginning of 1963, Gene had agreed to another professional venture that brought him back to the big screen. He signed to become a part of a new company Frank Sinatra formed with Warner Bros. In his contract, he agreed to produce one film, appear in another, and direct a third. Frank would perform in all three pictures. The first project, *Robin and the Seven Hoods,* was designed as a satire on Chicago during Prohibition. In the cast were Bing Crosby and Frank's Rat Pack friends Sammy Davis Jr. and Dean Martin. "I must say they're most agreeable to work with," Gene commented. "Trouble is they've spread themselves so wide that to get them all together at once takes more logistic ability than Eisenhower's on D-Day. For a supposed lazy, drawling group, they're busier than beavers."[36]

Frank, who was living in New York, was a difficult man to pin down. The singer kept postponing rehearsals, leading Gene to lose patience and tell studio head Jack Warner he was going to quit. Warner "kept reminding me how friendly I was with Frank, to which I replied I was more than friendly. I really loved him, and that was the reason I was walking out. . . . If I stayed on as a kind of paid laborer, our relationship would be over."[37] Gene dropped out of *Robin and the Seven Hoods* as well as his other two prospective projects. Frank and Gene remained on good terms; their friendship actually deepened over the years. Frank affectionately called Gene "Shanty," a humorous put-down nickname referring to the most impoverished of Irishmen. He later declared that nothing on earth could change his position as Gene Kelly's number one fan.

Gene may have been experiencing a barren period in his professional life, but he was never one to remain idle; he became more active in politics than he had been since the McCarthy era. In late January 1963, President Kennedy and his wife hosted a gala in Washington, DC, at which many stars, including Gene and Carol Burnett, were honored guests. Gene, serving as emcee, called to Kennedy from the audience: "Sing something Irish!" The president agreed as long as Gene sang with him. They performed a duet of "Wearing of the Green" that listeners called "out of this world."[38]

On November 20, 1963, Gene had an opportunity to entertain the Kennedys on a far more personal level. It was Robert Kennedy's birthday, and Ethel, Robert's wife, invited Gene over as a surprise guest. He arrived wrapped as a gift and plopped in Robert Kennedy's lap. After being unwrapped he entertained Kennedy and his guests with a song and dance. Such goings on were common among Gene and the Kennedys, who shared a warm friendship.

Two days after Robert Kennedy's birthday, on November 22, 1963, Gene was back in New York rehearsing a number he was planning for a surprise party for Jackie Gleason. That night he heard the news that his friend President John F. Kennedy had been shot by Lee Harvey Oswald in Dallas. He immediately took a flight home to California and his family. They spent the afternoon numbly watching the television, grief-stricken and stunned.

The year 1963 was one of endings in more ways than one. Gene's first two boosters in Hollywood, Arthur Freed and Judy Garland, made their farewells to Hollywood. Freed produced his last picture, *Light in the Piazza*, in 1962. He had dreams of creating more musicals, particularly *Say It with Music*, a biopic of Irving Berlin. None came into being. Judy Garland made her cinematic swan song in 1963's *I Could Go on Singing*. The film won critical praise but failed at the box office. Freed and Judy had given up the struggle to maintain their places in a world and an industry that were unrecognizable from what they had known in the 1930s through the early 1950s. Gene, perhaps more than any Freed Unit alum, persevered to remain a part of the modern film business. But he found it an increasingly Sisyphean task.

Gene landed an opportunity to keep his work with the Freed Unit alive in a most unexpected way: sharing it with the natives of Africa. On December 20, 1963, the US State Department had asked Gene to tour the continent as part of its cultural exchange program. Gene was to speak to university students about American filmmaking and the performing arts, after which he would screen a forty-five-minute clip showing scenes from his movies. Gene planned to leave in early January and return on February 1, 1964. He was enthusiastic about the project but reluctant to leave when he discovered that Jeanne was pregnant again. However, Jeanne encouraged him to go, given that the baby was not due until June.

Gene's adventure took him to Senegal, the Ivory Coast, Upper Volta, and Ghana. The US State Department had prepared Gene to discuss film as well as answer questions on race relations in America. He was surprised that few natives broached the latter subject. "Everyone wanted to know about the assassination of President Kennedy," Gene said. "People over there cannot be convinced it was not a plot." He enjoyed "a wonderful, warm reception" everywhere except in Ghana, where "officials were chilly and he was ignored by the press."[39] Nonetheless, Gene deemed his trip a fascinating one. "I went into the back country every chance I got to see the tribal dances." The dancers, he observed, were very knowledgeable about their craft. Gene was excited to explain to them that Western modern dance actually had its origins in Africa. He especially amused those he met by obliging their requests to learn such modern dances. "In the cities they wanted me to teach American steps, especially the Lindy Hop. It was the favorite," Gene commented, referring to a dance that had become widely popular in the late 1920s.[40]

Gene arrived back in the United States on February 1. Less than three weeks later, on February 18, 1964, Steve Allen asked Gene to be his guest on his television program to share his experiences in Africa. Allen attempted to begin a political discussion about the trip, but Gene brusquely stopped him. He had no political agenda, he stated; he had merely shown diverse groups of Africans film clips and dance steps. After thus defusing any political talk, Gene took questions from the show's live audience. One member asked if the people in Africa were "backward." In education, yes, Gene replied, except in the large cities where there were numerous universities. He went on that he did not view their culture as uncivilized at all. Grinning, he cited as an example the fact that bare-breasted women were the norm in some areas. On a more serious note, he noted that integration was more successful in Africa and that America seemed "backward" by comparison. Africans might be anti-American where the US government was concerned, Gene observed, but they were pro-American in respect to the average US citizen. Allen commented, "People like you are an overlooked weapon in the Cold War."[41]

Another topic Gene discussed with Allen was his current role in a new film to be directed by J. Lee Thompson, *What a Way to Go!* Almost immediately upon his return to America, he began work on the dark comedy, in which he had agreed to appear when it was in the planning stages in 1962. How could he turn it down when it was penned by none other than Betty Comden and Adolph Green? Originally conceived as a vehicle for Marilyn Monroe, its original title was *I Love Louisa*. The project was temporarily shelved after Marilyn's sudden, tragic death on August 5, 1962. Gene revealed to a columnist that he had had a meeting with Marilyn only days before her death "to discuss a . . . musical. . . . She was in excellent spirits—very happy and very excited about her future prospects. I just don't understand."[42] Another sudden death occurred shortly before the release of *What a Way to Go!* that affected Gene on an even more personal level. Taken ill with pneumonia, Gene's former assistant, Carol Haney, died on May 10, 1964, at the premature age of thirty-nine. She had just completed choreographing the Broadway smash *Funny Girl.* Her death was a great blow to Gene and yet another one of the endings that characterized the years from 1962 to 1964.

Production for *What a Way to Go!* resumed with a new leading lady, Shirley MacLaine. Gene saw as much potential in Shirley as he had in Marilyn Monroe. He had followed her career since 1953, when he had noticed her in the chorus of *The Pajama Game,* the show for which Carol Haney had left the Freed Unit. After the play, Gene had elbowed his way backstage to find Shirley. Moving her red ponytail over her shoulder, he had whispered in her ear, "Kid, you've really got something, keep going."[43]

The film's powerhouse cast also included Dick Van Dyke, Robert Mitchum, Dean Martin, Robert Cummings, and Paul Newman. Through a series of flashbacks shown as Louisa Foster speaks with her psychiatrist, the film explains how she became a four-time widow. She claims that she was, in one way or another, responsible for making each of her husbands wealthy. But once the men became rich, they suffered untimely deaths due to their insatiable urge for more money. Gene portrays one of the husbands, a clown in a nightclub whose songs and dances go unnoticed by patrons. Louisa notes his talents and advises him to remove his makeup and sing just as himself. He becomes an instant sensation, and Louisa agrees to be his dance partner. After they are married, he becomes an egotistical movie idol dubbed "Pinky" Benson. He erects a monument to himself—a mansion decorated entirely in pink. At a movie premiere, Pinky opens his arms to welcome his adoring fans—and they trample him to death.

Though not a musical, *What a Way to Go!* gave Gene two song and dance routines: "I Think That You and I Should Get Acquainted" and "Musical Extravaganza" (the latter he performed with Shirley). Gene greatly enjoyed choreographing the numbers. Pinky sings the first tune before becoming a huge star; it is executed quietly and sincerely, similar to the staging of "For Me and My Gal" in 1942. The second number stands in juxtaposition and spoofs some of Gene's old, spectacular dance numbers. If the number can be compared to any in Gene's career, it would be the finale of *Anchors Aweigh*. The number, nautical in setting, shows Louisa, Pinky, and "squads of singers and dancers [cavorting] over the vast deck of a battleship."[44]

Twentieth Century-Fox gave *What a Way to Go!* a staggering $3.75 million budget. When released on May 13, 1964, it more than recouped its costs. In the United States, it earned $6.1 million, making it the eleventh-highest-grossing film of the year. Audiences flocked to see it, but critics condemned the film. An annoyed Bosley Crowther of the *New York Times* commented, "The whole thing . . . lacks wit and grace. . . . Of course, it is in dazzling color and is riotously overdressed."[45] Gene's biographer Tony Thomas called the movie an example of all that was wrong with Hollywood in the 1960s; *What a Way to Go!* sank under its own excesses while, ironically, trying to spoof the dangers of abundance.[46]

Comden and Green never wrote another Hollywood screenplay, instead devoting themselves completely to the theater, the medium they had always preferred. Gene stayed off the big screen for three years. But his reason for taking a hiatus from film was different. He had become a father for the third time, and he was determined to be more present in his young children's lives than he had been in Kerry's.

Bridget Kelly was born on June 15, 1964. "I was in the Cedars of Lebanon hospital waiting for Jeannie to give birth, when I received a phone call from a well-known newspaper columnist who congratulated me on becoming a father again and what, he wanted to know, did I have to say for myself? Well, I had no idea Jeannie had already delivered, and wondered how the hell the guy had heard before me! I knew it was impossible to keep a secret in Hollywood, but this, I thought, was ridiculous!"[47] Jeanne's delivery was not an easy one, and for the first few weeks, the baby's survival was touch and go. When they first married, Gene and Jeanne "intended to have five children and over-populate the earth." However, Bridget was their last. "Well, we never had those five children, after all. We lost [a] third child and the doctors told us Jeannie couldn't have any more," Gene later revealed.[48]

Gene was more than happy with his three children. "Being a parent is probably the most important thing you can do in your life. My kids and I are very close," he reflected in 1996.[49] As well as instituting major changes in his professional life to ensure the stability of his home, Gene also made a concerted effort to become more involved in Kerry's life. After the divorce she felt "betrayed and neglected and withdrew her affections. But her animosity was short-lived."[50] Now twenty-one, Kerry was studying psychology in London. Gene, though never a huge fan of analysis, supported her choice. "One measure of our relationship is that when I told him I was going into this [psychology] and needed a financial hand, he wanted to understand what I was doing, so he read books about analysis and modified his opinion," Kerry related.[51] Kerry was thrilled to have two new siblings as well as three stepbrothers courtesy of Betsy Blair's new husband, Czech-born director/producer Karel Reisz. The couple had married in 1963.

Asked about her relationship with Tim and Bridget, Kerry responded, "I lived in London most of the time when they were little kids. . . . I saw them a few times a year; I was more like an aunt when they were little. . . . Once they were grown up, we were just brothers and sisters, so it was nice, because I was an only child until I was nineteen. . . . And then I've got my . . . three . . . stepbrothers, so suddenly I was one of six, which was fabulous." Kerry acknowledged that Gene's two youngest children had entirely dissimilar childhoods than her own. "My father was older and Jeanne was a different person than my mother. . . . The whole household was very different because Hollywood was very different by then, too. . . . None of that [parties] happened at all, a very different sort of pattern of social life."[52] As part of Gene's stronger focus on domestic life, he gave up numerous opportunities because they would have required him to leave his home base.

The most significant project he turned down was directing Twentieth Century-Fox's cinematic adaptation of *The Sound of Music*. It had been in the works for nearly five years, and William Wyler and Stanley Donen had also been considered for the job. Both declined the offer. Ernest Lehman, screenwriter for the movie, recalled being hopeful and excited as he drove to Gene's home on Rodeo Drive to approach him for the job. "As soon as I walked inside the house, I announced, 'Gene, I came over to ask if you'd like to be our director.'" Gene "walked Lehman back out the door and said,

'Ernie, go find someone else to direct this kind of shit!'"[53] In defense of Gene's judgment, at this point in the film's development, it was little changed from the Broadway production, which many critics deemed saccharine and lacking in vitality and character development. Gene's vehemence against the project was also likely due to the critical failure of the big-budgeted *What a Way to Go!* He may have seen *The Sound of Music* as following in the same vein. Additionally, if he had indeed accepted the directorial job, it would have been necessary for him to be away for months on location shoots in Austria.

Gene was offered but ultimately turned down two more film projects, both for Universal Studios: *Send Me No Flowers* (1964) and *Beau Geste* (1966). *Send Me No Flowers,* directed by Norman Jewison, was a great success upon its premiere in fall 1964. The same year, MGM released *The Unsinkable Molly Brown* (adapted from the Broadway hit). The film, directed by Charles Walters, produced by Roger Edens, and starring Debbie Reynolds, was a virtual Freed Unit reunion. Its considerable success proved that audiences still had an appetite for musicals—if only ones based on Broadway shows. But the success of *The Unsinkable Molly Brown* could not compare to the phenomenon that was *The Sound of Music.* When it made its debut in March 1965, it took *Gone with the Wind*'s place as the highest-grossing film of all time. It swept the Academy Awards, winning five statuettes including Best Picture and Best Director (Robert Wise). The film was a significant lost opportunity for Gene, but if he had any regrets, he never voiced them. He certainly did not regret pulling out of *Beau Geste;* when it was at last released in 1966 with Douglas Heyes as director, it was unremarkable.

Though Gene had lost the chance to work with Julie Andrews in *The Sound of Music,* another job came his way that involved Julie. The project was yet another television special, this time for NBC-TV. Recorded on March 23, 1965 (only weeks after *The Sound of Music*'s release), it aired on November 28, 1965, in full color. Both Julie and Gene had strong associations with umbrellas (Julie because of *Mary Poppins,* 1964, and Gene because of *Singin' in the Rain*). Thus, it was fitting that Julie made her entrance onto the television screen by appearing to float onstage using an umbrella. She sang a medley from *My Fair Lady,* whereupon Gene joined her, umbrella in hand, and crooned "Singin' in the Rain." They concluded by doing an old-fashioned tap routine together.

The program, entitled *The Julie Andrews Show* (indicative of Julie's rise to fame and Gene's decline), merited rapturous reviews. A journalist for the *Pittsburgh Post-Gazette* called it a "pleasing, uncluttered hour of song," with the dance numbers between Julie and Gene "the major winners."[54] The special won two Emmy awards (Outstanding Directorial Achievement in Variety or Music and Individual Achievements in Electronic Production—Video Tape Editing).

The Julie Andrews Show was the last significant project in which Gene was involved for two years. He spent the bulk of his time with Jeanne and his two babies. He referred to playing with the children in the backyard as his daily workout—one far superior to any he could get at a gym. To reflect his pride as a family man, Gene had a vanity plate made for his Chrysler sedan: DADDY. The plate on the Kellys' other car, a station wagon, read, MOMMY.[55] "Even if the [jobs] didn't come in fast enough—well, I could afford to wait and just potter around the house," a contented Gene reflected in 1973. "This is where it's at for me!"[56]

20

Looking for Enchantment

"I'm at an age now when I'm willing to work only when something unusual comes along," Gene said in 1972.[1] Such was his attitude during the entirety of his marriage to Jeanne Coyne. As soon as they wed, Gene vowed to be a family man first and an entertainer second; work would have to be unusual to separate him from his wife and children. Yet, the bulk of Gene's work between 1964 and 1967 was indeed ordinary. His television programs were merely nostalgic glimpses into Hollywood's golden era. As the 1960s progressed, however, Gene's assignments rose in prestige and by the end of the decade, Gene Kelly was once again a hot property. Documentarian Robert Trachtenberg observed: "People really are critical and dismissive of his [Gene's] later years, and it is true that he was not a very good director on his own, but his intentions were good and he was trying, really trying, to get his vision across, to either publicize dance and particularly dance in America or try . . . directing comedies or westerns."[2]

The best of Gene's television specials in the mid-1960s was entitled *Gene Kelly in New York, New York*. Harkening back to Gene's landmark production *On the Town*, it was filmed on location in New York City and was designed as a musical tour of the wonderful town. The program also featured dancer/choreographer Gower Champion and two rising talents, British musical performer Tommy Steele and comedian Woody Allen. Woody wrote his own material for the show. His sketch with Gene is by far the production's high spot. It revolved around Gene's observation that if a person cannot hail a cab in New York, he or she can take the Sardi's bus, a red double-decker like those in Britain. Stopping beside the bus, Gene strikes up a conversation with Woody, who climbs down from the top floor. Woody declares that the top floor is his apartment and it becomes quite crowded at times, but "it's a great way to meet women." Gene, with a straight face, asks: "Did anyone ever tell you you're a little unusual?" "Yes.

After I got out of the army. That's what it says on my file: 'this boy is a little unusual. Don't let him fight for our country.'"[3] Woody enjoyed working with Gene and has often spoken of his great love for *Singin' in the Rain*.

Gene was heavily involved in the television production, in which, as he had done so many times in the past, he filled multiple roles: performer, dancer, and choreographer. Those on the set saw both Gene the taskmaster and Gene the supporter. He was especially encouraging to Tommy Steele. Though he had once stated he disliked amateurs, he contradicted himself by taking extra time with the inexperienced dancer. Tommy was starstruck when he met Gene, later claiming it was like meeting the king of England. When Tommy confessed he could not tap-dance, Gene personally brought him to Capezio's in Times Square and asked the shop to make "the Limey" some suitable shoes. For the next six weeks, he taught Tommy the essentials of tap dancing. In part because of Gene's help, Tommy snagged plum roles, most notably as the leprechaun in Fred Astaire's final picture, *Finian's Rainbow* (1968). Upon viewing Tommy's tapping skills, Fred Astaire allegedly joked: "The Irishman taught you that, didn't he? He never could do it properly."[4] When *Gene Kelly in New York, New York* premiered on CBS-TV on February 14, 1966, reviews were enthusiastic and warm. A writer for the *Chicago Tribune* recorded: "Gene Kelly delivered his own valentine to Manhattan last night. . . . It was a sparkling hour-sized tribute which the whole nation could enjoy."[5]

Now that Gene had mastered the once-intimidating medium of television, he felt ready to bring more innovation to the small screen in the form of a children's program. Since the end of World War II, Gene had spoken of his desire to produce child-friendly shows or movies. He planned to produce, star in, and direct a television special that would take its inspiration from the "Jack and the Beanstalk" fairytale. He tapped Sammy Cahn and Jimmy Van Heusen as songwriters for the program and Freed Unit alum Lennie Hayton as musical arranger. He also secured the services of William Hanna and Joe Barbera (who had done the animation in *Anchors Aweigh* and *Invitation to the Dance*) to do the cartoon segments of the show.

"We haven't changed the story much," Gene explained. "[But we've] taken the fright out of the giant" and "changed the plot slightly so young Jack doesn't steal coins from the giant," an amoral concept in the dancer's mind.[6] Gene added a role for himself: Jeremy Keen, a peddler who accompanies Jack on his adventure. For a dash of romantic interest, Jeremy rescues Princess Serena, who is bound to a harp in the giant's abode.

As Jack, Gene chose an unknown actor, Bobby Riha. The boy had little experience, but Gene thought nothing of spending six weeks giving him dancing lessons. He also wanted Bobby to wear tights to enable free movement during the rehearsals. When Bobby pouted over this, Gene won him over by recounting tales of his own boyhood when he had been teased for dancing. "You don't have to wear tights. Just wear loose fitting pants," Gene compromised.[7]

Because the bulk of the program was shot with only Gene and Bobby before a blue screen, Gene used his storytelling talent to help Bobby envision the animated characters and backgrounds that the animators would draw in later. Less enjoyable for Gene were the sequences in which he and Bobby had to be fitted with harnesses and wires at the hips and lifted in the air. Gene was not at ease with heights. Bobby, on the other hand, relished it and often asked to be lifted up while he ate lunch. Gene ate safely at floor level. Bobby considered working with Gene the highlight of his career. Though he and Gene never had a disagreement on the set, Bobby almost made a misstep when he saw Gene without his toupee. He was about to comment when members of the crew warned him that Gene's baldness was a sensitive subject. Bobby tactfully said nothing.

On February 26, 1967, *Jack and the Beanstalk* made its premiere to receptive audiences and critics. A writer for *Dance* magazine noted that the mix of live action and cartoon exhibited "perfect technical follow-through" and concluded that "there is one personality which leaves its indelible imprimatur for all the public to see. That one, it need hardly be added, is Gene Kelly."[8] At the primetime Emmy Awards for 1967, Gene, as producer, took home the statuette bestowed upon *Jack and the Beanstalk* as Best Children's Program.

Gene, with renewed confidence from his success on television, felt ready to return to the big screen after a six-year absence in a film that would take him back to his beloved France.

At the behest of French director Jacques Demy, Gene accepted a supporting role in a new musical, *The Young Girls of Rochefort*. Gene had been impressed with Demy's pioneering work in *The Umbrellas of Cherbourg* (1964) and the new life it had breathed into the art of cinedance. Demy's films were like operas; they were essentially all song and dance with minimal dialogue interspersed. For his part, Demy had been so intent on having France's favorite American in Paris appear in the film that he had postponed its production for two years, waiting for Gene to be free from other commitments. Though Gene was staunch in his opposition to projects that separated him from his family, he found the prospect of appearing in a French musical irresistible. Accepting the role in *The Young Girls of Rochefort*, he simultaneously agreed to direct a film for producer Frank McCarthy at Twentieth Century-Fox. An ultra-modern spoof on sex entitled *A Guide for the Married Man*, the picture was a chance for Gene to broaden his experience and challenge himself as a director.

At fifty-five, Gene could have gone into permanent retirement, but this was not an option for a man as alert and energetic as he. Gene flew to France for the film's six-week shoot in summer 1967. In *The Young Girls of Rochefort*, he added much-needed zest to the dancing segments of the picture. Those in which he did not appear, choreographed by Norman Maen, came across as stage bound, with dancers clustered before the camera rather than "besporting themselves through the town."[9]

The Young Girls of Rochefort tells the story of fraternal twin sisters Delphine and Solange Garnier, who find love in their hometown, the seaside village of Rochefort. Solange finds her ideal man in American concert pianist Andy Miller (Gene). Andy is visiting a friend in Rochefort when he discovers the manuscript of a masterful concerto that he learns has been composed by Solange. Delphine finds her match in an idealistic young artist/sailor whom she follows to Paris.

Film historian Tony Thomas characterized the film as a "sincere homage to the Hollywood musical."[10] The production does indeed have similarities to the genre. Like *An American in Paris*, *The Young Girls of Rochefort* relies heavily on music, dance, and color to illustrate the characters' personalities and moods. Using pastel hues of pink, yellow, blue, and white, Jacques Demy filmed the entire picture in the real town of Rochefort-sur-Mer. All of the actors' outfits and even hairstyles match to some degree, varying only in color. The complementary colors and styles make the film a cohesive and exalting visual experience. Gene designed his own numbers; the most memorable one, "Andy Amoureux," shows him dancing through the streets of Rochefort, interacting alternately with children and two sailors. The sequence is like a melding of "I Got Rhythm" from *An American in Paris* and "New York, New York" from *On the Town*.

Gene later expressed that he felt the film could have been better had Demy engaged professional singers and dancers for the leading ladies. Catherine Deneuve and Françoise Dorléac were lovely but required dubbing. The dubbed singing of all the principals and the dubbed speaking voices of Gene and his costar George Chakiris (of *West Side Story*, 1961, fame) also detracted from the picture's effectiveness. (Gene did voice a small bit of his own dialogue because of his proficiency in French.) "Dubbing puts a great strain on a musical. And they all made the mistake of assuming that it's easy to learn to dance for a film because it looks so easy. It isn't," Gene explained. "It [the movie] was a good idea . . . but it missed."[11]

Almost a year after production closed, *The Young Girls of Rochefort* made its New York premiere on April 11, 1968. In spite of its flaws, it was a box office hit, grossing $8,008,429. Renata Adler of the *New York Times* was enthusiastic in her review: the "strange, off-beat movie . . . is in French (in which Kelly does admirably). . . . The whole movie [is] . . . fine, eccentric, pastel and dreamlike. . . . The cast is extremely solid and alive."[12] Gene still considered the film a disappointment. Biographer Clive Hirschhorn asserted that it was, in total, "effete" and "boring" and failed to give Gene's film career the boost it sorely needed.[13] However, whatever its faults, the film was an original, which could not be said for the Broadway musical adaptations that still glutted the screen.

Gene regretted that the movie had taken away so much of his time with his family. Upon his return from France, he claimed that Timothy and Bridget looked "twenty years older. In six weeks they had changed enough for me to feel resentful that I had missed out on some vital part of their development and I made up my mind never to spend any time away from home unless I could take them with me. Twenty, or even ten years earlier I wouldn't have given it a thought."[14] Gene kept Timothy and Bridget, even more than he had Kerry, completely sequestered from the prying eyes of the press. He became more guarded with himself as well. In 1976, Gene explained, "The public don't know me at all. My life is a quest for privacy but I know I can never have it except in the quiet and seclusion of this home."[15]

As family oriented as Gene was, his next directorial project, *A Guide for the Married Man*, was hardly kid friendly. The picture was to star Walter Matthau as Paul, whose friend Ed recommends that he should cheat on his wife (without getting caught, of course) in order to maintain his happy marriage. The friend's instructions on how to cheat are illustrated through a series of vignettes enacted by a flurry of celebrities including Jack Benny, Art Carney, Lucille Ball, Phil Silvers, and Joey Bishop. In the end, Ed is caught cheating while Paul flees home without committing adultery. He embraces his wife, realizing he never wanted to betray her to begin with.

Producer Frank McCarthy explained that Gene's good taste as well as his popularity made him an ideal choice as director. He was the only man in show business McCarthy thought could convince enough celebrities to make cameos in the film. Gene directed the film with innovation in mind; he did not want to re-create a romantic comedy in the style of the 1950s. A critic for *Time* magazine wrote that under Gene's direction the film was "one of the niftiest comedies to come out of Hollywood in years. Deftly alternating fast and slow motion, blackouts, flashbacks and stop action . . . Kelly in effect has choreographed the film along the lines of a fast-paced modern dance."[16] In a nightclub sequence, he choreographed moves for a tribal go-go dancer and was not too self-conscious to demonstrate the steps to the girl himself.

Gene was back in his element working on a substantial project. The writer for *Time* noted that "these days he prefers the checkered cap that goes with the director's chair."[17] Gene may not have performed in the film, but he did manage to take on a role of sorts: in one scene, his voice can be heard coming from a television set.

When *A Guide for the Married Man* premiered on May 26, 1967, it was a critical and commercial hit. Bosley Crowther of the *New York Times* called it "the broadest and funniest farce that has come from Hollywood since . . . last year." More than once, he singled out Gene for praise. "He proves himself a swinger with this film . . . [and] has directed with speed and persistent wit."[18] The film, budgeted at $3.25 million, earned $5 million and firmly established Gene as capable of executing a commercially viable modern film.

Twentieth Century-Fox had been on the verge of bankruptcy a mere three years before; now, with the success of *The Sound of Music* and smaller projects like *A Guide for the Married Man*, the studio was in the black and executives, exhibiting not a little hubris, set up production for three lavish musicals: *Doctor Doolittle* (1967), *Star!* (1968), and *Hello, Dolly!* (1969). The first two were unequivocal flops. And yet, the studio forged ahead with *Hello, Dolly!*, ultimately pouring over $25 million into its production. This one, executives were certain, would be a hit. After all, it was based on a Broadway musical that had been running for three years and showed no signs of slowing.

In April 1968, Twentieth Century-Fox handed the multimillion-dollar production to Gene Kelly. Producer Ernest Lehman asked Gene to direct, and this time Gene accepted (perhaps remembering he had dismissed Lehman's last offer, *The Sound of Music,* as "shit"). The producer felt that Gene had both the enthusiasm and the confidence needed to direct the film.

The Arthur Freed Unit at MGM may have been long disbanded, but it was alive and well at Twentieth Century-Fox, if only temporarily. Behind the scenes of *Hello, Dolly!* Gene enjoyed a sort of family reunion with his old colleagues. As costume designer was Irene Sharaff, who had created such memorable garb for the "American in Paris Ballet." Roger Edens, Arthur Freed's "right hand man," served as associate producer while Lennie Hayton acted as musical arranger. Michael Kidd, who had costarred (and clashed) with Gene in *It's Always Fair Weather,* was brought in as choreographer. Harry Stradling controlled the camerawork. Stradling had been responsible for many Freed films including *The Pirate.*

Though surrounded by esteemed colleagues, Gene was not without doubt as to the merits of *Hello, Dolly!* Ernest Lehman aptly noted that Gene's enthusiastic attitude was only "outward." Gene admitted that he "knew it [*Hello, Dolly!*] was old-fashioned" and that it "probably wouldn't have been my first choice."[19] When the film went into production in 1968, the stage show was still running to packed houses, which presented a unique challenge to the film producers. The picture could not be released until the production closed on Broadway or until June 1971, whichever came first. If the picture did sit on the shelf until 1971, it ran the risk of becoming even more dated.

Hello, Dolly! was not a new story. Rather, it was a musicalized version of Thornton Wilder's 1955 Broadway hit *The Matchmaker.* Both plays tell the story of Dolly Levi, a New York matchmaker who merrily arranges others' lives. A widow, she is in love with a "half-a-millionaire," Horace Vandergelder, a Yonkers merchant. She weaves a web of romantic complications around him, two clerks at his store, a fetching milliner, and her assistant. The story ends happily with all characters matched to the people they truly love. As the two clerks at the store were fledgling dancers Michael Crawford and Tommy Tune; Walter Matthau filled the role of Vandergelder. The picture was to be shot in part in Garrison, New York. Before arriving in the small town, Gene ensured that a street had been beautified and made to resemble the gingerbread-style facades distinctive of the early 1900s. Gene was not pleased at traveling east and being away from his family, but much of the film was shot at Twentieth Century-Fox and consequently did not keep him away for long.

The on-location shots added authenticity to the picture, but the casting of the title character did not. Twenty-six-year-old Barbra Streisand portrayed Dolly, a woman meant to be middle-aged. The actress was fresh from her success as Fanny Brice in both the stage and screen versions of *Funny Girl* (1968). "I suppose Barbra was a little young to play Dolly, but after she got through the first couple of reels she did a marvelous job," Gene stated.[20]

Walter Matthau made it clear that he most definitely did not approve of Barbra. His and his leading lady's first run-in occurred in Garrison on June 6, 1968. Only the previous day, the nation was stunned by the news that Palestinian terrorist Sirhan Sirhan had shot and killed Robert Kennedy after the senator won the Democratic presidential nomination in the California primary. Michael Crawford recalled that "Gene was crushed. . . . The set was closed down the day after the tragedy. . . . When production started up again . . . the mood was bleak for cast and crew. Yet Gene Kelly was able to handle it all with great equanimity."[21] Matthau also took the news especially hard, but he was angry rather than depressed over it. The heat of the sun and the overhead lights on the set only enhanced his self-described "mean, foul mood."[22]

After the day of mourning, Gene called Barbra, Matthau, and several extras to rehearse a scene taking place outside Vandergelder's feed store. As Gene explained how he envisioned the sequence, Barbra interrupted to suggest a comic exchange between the characters. Matthau found no humor in her ad-libbing and accused her of assuming the role of director. Gene took hold of Matthau's arm and attempted to pull him away from the escalating argument, but the actor was immovable. He continued to tear into Barbra.

"Why don't you learn your lines! You're just jealous because you're not as good as me!" Barbra shot back.

"Everybody in the company hates you! You're dispensable!" Matthau yelled. Barbra began to sob and fled the set.

Ernest Lehman, Barbra's greatest ally on the set, went to comfort her. Gene murmured, "Cut the lights."[23]

Gene managed to gather the seething actors together again and "straightened it out" in three hours' time. In an interview with columnist Joyce Haber, Gene downplayed the tension on the set. "There was only one major rift," Gene explained. "Walter was saying a line and Barbra was nodding her head at the same time. He told her, 'You're doing that purposely.' I dragged them both off the set and said 'You're not going to do this here.' Walter apologized to her a few days later."[24] Whether or not Matthau actually apologized is uncertain. But tensions certainly remained.

Barbra called her confidant Lehman nearly each day after filming with complaints not only about Matthau but also regarding Gene. Though Lehman respected Gene's work, he was not exactly his biggest fan and could commiserate with Barbra. "Who would get along with Gene Kelly? He's a tough guy. He would grin and smile and laugh and all that, but he was no pussycat," Lehman commented. "Once I made a suggestion to Michael Crawford about how he should play a close-up and Kelly said to me, 'If you ever talk to another one of my actors on the set I'll kick your fucking teeth in.'"[25]

If Gene displayed his temper to Lehman, he refrained from doing so to Michael Kidd. Nonetheless, the friction that had existed between Gene and Kidd on the set of It's Always Fair Weather still remained thirteen years later. Lehman described their relationship as "eggshell time." He would often find Gene "muttering away in the background about something he felt was wrong in the dance direction and I'd tell him to have a word with Michael about it. He said he couldn't and that I'd better do it." Gene held sincere regard for Kidd's work and did not wish his colleague to assume otherwise. His primary concern was that viewers watching the film were likely to conclude that Gene was choreographer and so any imperfections would reflect badly on him. Lehman remarked that Hello, Dolly! was "not a happy film. . . . It's quite amazing what people go through to make something entertaining for others."[26]

Gene balanced his less than amiable moods with shows of gratitude and generosity. For the most expensive number in the film, which included the construction of an entire New York street and the use of thirty-eight hundred extras, Lehman wanted a "rolling shot that would leave Barbra in the center of the screen, and then go wide to show most of the parade around her." Gene insisted on photographing "straight down so all you could see are a few people marching down the center."[27] Barbra and Lehman were adamantly against Gene's plans, and Gene finally shouted over the phone to Lehman: "Why don't you direct the scene tomorrow?" Lehman did exactly that. Viewing the results, Gene turned to him and declared, "Jesus, my shot was awful. I'm glad you redid it."[28]

Gene later expressed regret at the lack of rapport he shared with his leading lady. "If there had been more time, I'd have tried to help her work out a clear-cut characterization. . . . She kept experimenting with new things out of sheer desperation, none of which really worked." He admitted that he felt he had let Barbra down, and as a result the entire picture suffered.[29]

No matter how much tension existed on the set, whenever Walter Matthau brought his eight-year-old son to work, the cast and crew could be assured that Gene would be relaxed and affable. "Let's let Charlie direct today," Gene would say as he took the child's hand. Lehman and Barbra had their issues with Gene, but Matthau claimed that he liked having him as director. "Gene Kelly . . . is charming, intelligent, and has an inordinate amount of patience."[30]

Perhaps the most genial relationship on the set was between Gene and Michael Crawford. Again contradicting his earlier statement that he "hated amateurs," Gene was, according to newcomer Crawford, "enormously understanding and empathetic to his artists." Crawford had come to Gene's attention after Roger Edens arranged an audition for him. Three decades later, Crawford still recalled with remarkable clarity the day he met Gene. "The doorbell rings. . . . I open the door and see that famous genial Irish grin. . . . 'Let's cut the small talk,' he said. 'Can you dance? . . . Just get up and do something. Try this.' He cleared the coffee table, got up on it and did a couple of tap steps. . . . His compassionate eyes were glued to the human rubber band who helplessly flailed away in front of him."[31]

Gene did not shower compliments on Crawford; instead, he used a bit of "put-down humor" on him, which was actually Gene's way of showing esteem. "Siddown," he said to Crawford. "What I'm looking for is someone to play Cornelius Hackl. . . . He's an attractive idiot. Now my wife, well, she thinks you're attractive, and I think you're an idiot."[32]

From that point on, Crawford made Gene his idol. After singing his solo in the picture, "It Only Takes a Moment," Crawford remembered, he glanced at Gene to see his reaction. Gene "was in tears. He came over and put his arm around me. 'That's my boy.'"[33] Crawford never forgot Gene's impact on his career. In 1990, on Crawford's opening night in the legendary *Phantom of the Opera* on Broadway, he stated that he owed "his success to Gene Kelly."[34]

Filming wrapped on *Hello, Dolly!* in summer 1968. Then the agonizing editing process began. Gene took bits and pieces out of the film after its sneak preview but declared, "I wish we could cut more, but we've taken all we can." He found it a challenge to portray on the big screen what he saw as a "very intimate story." "It wasn't the best picture I ever directed, but I was pleased with what we did."[35] The almost workmanlike quality of Gene's solo directorial projects is evidence that he clearly thrived on collaboration and would have benefited from being able to bounce ideas off another, as he had with Stanley Donen. The overlong *Hello, Dolly!* was ready for release, but it sat on the shelf for a year while Twentieth Century-Fox waited for the stage production's run to end on Broadway. Finally, the studio managed to negotiate the release date to December 16, 1969.

On November 24, 1969, shortly before *Hello, Dolly!* premiered, Gene was invited to place his foot- and handprints in the forecourt of Grauman's Chinese Theatre in Hollywood—an honor long overdue. His spirits were high and he was confident that his mammoth picture would break the string of flops Twentieth Century-Fox had produced over the last two years.

At first, it seemed *Hello, Dolly!* would indeed break the curse. In its first two weeks of release, it actually grossed more than *The Sound of Music* had in the same amount of time. A writer for *Time* magazine noted: "If the echoes sometimes blend into a solid chorus, credit must be divided between director Gene Kelly and his choreographer Michael Kidd. . . . The . . . dancing is happily reminiscent of the old MGM musical."[36] As the film continued to sell more and more tickets, Fred Astaire sent Gene and his wife a congratulatory greeting with an effusion of enthusiasm about the film.

What looked like the biggest sensation since *The Sound of Music* plummeted as quickly as it had risen. Vincent Canby of the *New York Times* likened the extravagance of *Hello, Dolly!* to relics such as "D. W. Griffith's Babylon on a Hollywood back lot in 1916." Canby elaborated, "Gene Kelly . . . and Ernest Lehman . . . have . . . been reverential [to the Broadway show] to the point of idiocy, since, by preserving something basically thin and often witless on a large movie screen, they have merely inflated the faults to elephantine proportions." Canby concluded with the remark that "Gene Kelly and Michael Kidd . . . [have] added nothing to the heritage of the musical screen except statistics."[37]

In order to make a profit, *Hello, Dolly!* would have had to earn at least $60 million. Though it was ultimately the fourth-highest-grossing film of the year, earning $38 million in the United States and $20 million internationally, it was still not enough. The film's backers lost approximately $10 million on the venture. Nevertheless, it was not the critical and box office disaster that *Doctor Doolittle* or *Star!* had been. It won Oscar nominations for Best Picture, Best Art Direction, Best Sound, and Best Score (and won the latter three).

Critics and historians largely consider *Hello, Dolly!* the Hollywood musical's last hurrah. The younger generation's idea of what constituted a musical left Gene nonplussed. One of the most popular original musicals among young Americans was the 1968 Broadway hit *Hair*, an antiwar play revolving around a group of hippies and their clash with "normal" society. Gene claimed that the authors of the show approached him about directing a film version. "I said, 'Send me a script.' A script? They had no script. So they finally typed up what people say to each other and they had about three pages. There is very little to say, just . . . some action and yelling against the establishment. And some mild, very mild I thought, put-downs of the middle class and the middle-aged. But it depressed me very much that movies are only making adaptations of old Broadway shows. By the time *Hair* is put on the screen," he said with irony, "it may turn out to be *Blossom Time*. Musical styles change, the world moves so fast now."[38] Gene further stated that the music did "not lend itself to dramatic treatment . . . and you can't adlib a movie musical. . . . You need discipline and coordinated teamwork to make musicals—it's one area of filmmaking where the now popular auteur theory just does not make sense."[39]

In 1969, the trend in cinema, whether the work was a drama or musical, was toward realism—not nostalgia and eye-dazzling spectacles. As the Vietnam War dragged on, a blossoming counterculture (as depicted in *Hair*) infused with ideas of free love, nihilism, and rejection of tradition left no place for *Hello, Dolly!* Gene was not immune to the controversy of the era; in a 2001 interview, his daughter Kerry explained that she had many heated discussions with her father about the war and other major events of the 1960s.[40] Gene continued to be a staunch Democrat and supporter of the Kennedy family in particular. However, one achievement by the US space program John F. Kennedy had supported so strongly was one that weighed heavily on Gene's mind: the moon landing on July 20, 1969. While the bulk of the nation rejoiced over the fantastic achievement, Gene looked upon it with sadness, claiming that the landing took away from the moon's romance. With the mystery of the moon lost, Gene saw yet another ending of innocence and wonder for the younger generation. "Every day was a happy day when I was growing up," Gene later told reporter Nancy Anderson. "Now not even the kids are happy."[41]

The Best Picture winner of 1969 reflected the bleak mood of the times: *Midnight Cowboy*, an X-rated film about a gigolo. The same year saw the release of *Easy Rider*, a dark picture with themes similar to *Hair*. The film became the most iconic counterculture film of the 1960s. Its glorification of drug use and depiction of small-town Americans as little more than prejudiced savages would have sent Louis B. Mayer into seizures if he had been alive to see it (he died in 1957, mercifully before the evolution of hippie culture). Gene saw merit in the picture, however. "*Easy Rider* is a musical," he asserted. "Just because they weren't doing numbers didn't make it less a musical. . . . Although I can't like two bums who bring cocaine into the U.S. to ruin lives, I thought *Easy Rider* added up."[42] Overall, Gene did not favor the new trend of musicals, which all but negated the decades of work he had done refining the genre at MGM.

Another event in 1969 was a poignant symbol of the passing of the Hollywood musical. On June 22, Judy Garland was found dead in her London apartment from an accidental overdose of Seconal. Her funeral, held in Manhattan, attracted twenty-two thousand people. Mourners lined the streets; two thousand were eventually turned away for lack of space. Gene was unable to attend his beloved colleague and friend's funeral because he was preoccupied with finishing *Hello, Dolly!* This did not diminish his sadness over her passing, however. "We loved each other," Gene said in 1990. "She was a deep friend. . . . We were very, very close."[43]

Gene's *Hello, Dolly!* can justly be viewed as a tribute to the era in which Judy Garland had been synonymous with the Hollywood musical. In the judgment of Gene's biographer Clive Hirschhorn, the film "brought to life something of the enchantment and innocence of a world since departed. . . . *Hello, Dolly!* has the joyous appeal of Vincente Minnelli's [and Judy Garland's] *Meet Me in St. Louis* (1944). . . . [It] combines all the best elements of the Metro musical and Gene . . . made a contribution to the film whose excellence cannot be overestimated."[44]

The Hollywood musical may have died, but many of the greatest stars of old Hollywood had plenty of vitality left. Gene's next directorial project starred two of the silver screen's most iconic leading men, Jimmy Stewart and Henry Fonda, serving as proof of their enduring audience appeal. The National General film, a quasi-Western entitled *The Cheyenne Social Club*, tells the story of an older cowboy, O'Hanlan (Stewart), who inherits his brother's property. With his pal Sullivan (Fonda), he travels to survey the land only to find that a brothel stands on it. At first, he plans to shut it down but eventually sees the essential goodness of the girls living there. In the end, he writes the deed to the property over to the madam, Jenny (Shirley Jones), with whom he has formed a special attachment. He then, in classic cowboy style, rides off into the sunset with Sullivan.

The picture was unlike other Westerns of the era such as *Hombre* (1967) with Paul Newman or *The Man with No Name* trilogy starring Clint Eastwood, which all had cynical undertones and antiheroes as the main characters. "I don't see any purpose in the modern Westerns where they try to apply things today to the way they were. They're trying to excuse the violence by equating things now with things then. This really bores me," Jimmy Stewart declared.[45]

Though *The Cheyenne Social Club* was not typical of its genre, Gene initially did not want to do the picture. "But I'm a pushover for performers, and how could I go through the rest of my life realizing that I had turned down an opportunity to work with two people [Fonda and Stewart] like that?" He added that he was more than flattered that Fonda and Stewart had handpicked him as director—he was "ecstatic."[46]

Writer James Lee Barrett had infused the screenplay with plenty of "charming" banter between Fonda and Stewart that fully exploited their real-life affection for each other. Still, Barrett believed that "something [about the film] was not working." And the flawed factor in the production was, he claimed, Gene Kelly: "You'd think that with two actors like James Stewart and Henry Fonda a director would find it hard to make a poor Western. I don't say it was a poor film, because I think it had its virtues. But as a Western it pretty much stank."[47] Henry Fonda conceded that Gene "blocks out the scenes like a chorus." But he did not see this as a negative thing. "We had a location scene in which Jimmy and I are doing laundry alongside a track. It called for coordinating action, dialogue, sound, etc. as a train, starting from half a mile away, passed by. Gene worked it like a countdown, with everything happening on count."[48]

Gene endeavored to make the picture as authentic a Western as possible. He used the time spent shooting on location in Santa Fe, New Mexico, to question local cowboys about how to brand cows and saddle horses; he also read thoroughly about the period (1860s) in which the film took place. The assistant director, Paul Helmick, claimed that Gene had not known "a damn thing about Westerns or the West when he started but when he finished there wasn't much you could tell him he didn't already know."[49]

Though Gene tried his best to add realism to the picture, it still came across as a "cinematic time travel to a simpler, happier time . . . a happy dose of theatrical unreality."[50] Even the whorehouse seemed innocent. This is not to say those working on the picture (particularly Gene and Stewart) did not question its morality. In one scene, Stewart enters a girl's room to find her in a see-through negligee. This would not have been an issue for most actors, but because of Stewart's spotless image, the scene gave Gene some concern. "Jimmy and I felt it should come out. But the [film's] owners, National General, insisted it stay in and I think that was a mistake."[51]

The picture's completion was jeopardized when James Stewart's stepson, Ronald, was killed in Vietnam. The devastated actor returned immediately to Los Angeles to arrange the memorial. However, production resumed sooner than anticipated; Stewart returned to the set of *The Cheyenne Social Club* long before anyone expected him. But it was obvious to all that he was still deeply grieving. He was further saddened by the death of his beloved horse Pie during filming. Barrett believed that Stewart needed a tough-love director who would demand that he concentrate on the film, but Gene felt that it was best to accommodate the actor, shooting around him. Whenever he noticed Stewart looking especially gloomy, he would go so far as to cancel filming for the day and take the actor fishing instead. "Gene's heart was in the right place. . . . He was a sweet guy," Barrett declared.[52]

The Cheyenne Social Club wrapped in the fall of 1969 but was not slated to premiere until nearly a year later. Gene had plenty to occupy him in the meantime. In January 1970, he agreed to host and perform in a television special for NBC-TV entitled *Gene Kelly's Wonderful World of Girls*. "The show," Gene explained, "will reveal the foibles of the American woman. It will be satirical, done with love and affection in song, dance and comedy sketches." Gene insisted the show be filmed without a laugh track. "We're playing straight to the living room," he said. "If you hear any laughter, it'll be strictly because *you* thought it was funny."[53] Upon the show's premiere on January 14, 1970, *New York Times* critic George Gant heralded Gene as a "free-wheeling and engaging link" between his guests and their antics. "While women were the butt of the show," Gant concluded, "most would agree that it was a tasteful exploration of one of nature's masterpieces."[54]

The show so impressed the proprietors of the International Hotel in Las Vegas that they requested Gene adapt it as a live attraction for their establishment. Gene was reluctant, remembering the pact he had made with himself long ago never again to work in nightclubs. He still vividly recalled the humiliation of working cloops as a young hoofer and being ignored or talked over by inebriated audiences. After the International Hotel's owners virtually begged him to come to Las Vegas, Gene relented, with two conditions. First, he demanded higher pay than any entertainer had ever received at the hotel. Second, he demanded that the date be set for the Easter holiday, which would allow his family to travel with him. After going on location for both *Hello, Dolly!* and *The Cheyenne Social Club,* he was reluctant to leave Jeanne and the children again even for a brief time. The proprietors agreed to his stipulations, and Gene signed for a four-week engagement.

His production was a novelty in town: he managed to make a "girlie show" kid friendly. He gave two performances nightly; the earlier show attracted entire families while the second attracted primarily tipsy gamblers. Frank Sinatra, a seasoned Las Vegas entertainer, sent Gene a fond telegram on his opening night, addressing Gene with the nickname he had given him: Shanty.

Gene's show proved to be so popular that the hotel's owners extended the engagement to eight weeks. His family returned to Beverly Hills while he fulfilled the rest of his commitment. Gene found that playing to a nightclub audience was not the demoralizing experience he assumed it would be. Gene even interacted with some of the theatergoers, "flirting with older women in the later show and playing with children in the earlier one." During one week of the engagement, a hotel strike closed the production down. That same week, Jeanne fell ill with pneumonia. Gene rushed back to North Rodeo Drive to be at her side. When he returned to Las Vegas, he was homesick and exhausted. Because he did not gamble, he swiftly tired of Las Vegas. Nonetheless, at the close of eight weeks Gene came away grateful that he had at least overcome his "distaste for nightclub audiences."[55]

Several months after his return home, *The Cheyenne Social Club* made its New York premiere, on September 16, 1970. It managed to make a small profit and won a nomination for Best Comedy Written Directly for the Screen from the Writers Guild. The film received favorable reviews, though critics noted its old-fashioned feel. An author for *Time* magazine called the picture "a wonderfully outdated odyssey of bawdy innocence."[56] Only after

The Cheyenne Social Club aired on cable channels years later did it gain a larger appreciation. It was ultimately the last major motion picture Gene directed.

After taking a short jaunt to London to promote *The Cheyenne Social Club,* Gene took a much-needed break. His vacation spot of choice was Ireland, which he decided his younger children needed to see as Kerry had when she was young. Before leaving the United States, Gene and his family stopped in Pittsburgh to visit his mother and siblings. The visit was one of the last times Gene ever saw Harriet Kelly. The woman who had virtually willed Gene to be a dancer passed away on June 1, 1972, leaving behind five children who all attributed the roots of their success and veneration for family to her.

Before Gene and his brood arrived in Ireland on June 15, 1971, Gene's aide, a Mr. Tobin from Shannon Free Airport, sent him a humorous wire, assuring him that the Ballyvaughan area would be amply supplied with whiskey before Gene's arrival. After a voyage around Loch Derg, the family rented a traditional Irish cottage in Ballyvaughan. The Kellys also made a stop in Portroe, a village in North Tipperary. There, Gene visited scenic designer Sean Kenny. The meeting proved to be more than a friendly one. As ever, even when Gene tried to rest, he could not keep his mind completely off work. Gene and Kenny had become acquainted in Los Angeles during early preparations for a live family theater show. Entitled *Clownaround,* it was to be imitative of *Disney on Parade.* The show's producers and investors, Harry Lishinsky and Franklin Roberts, had approached Gene in early 1971 to act as director. Kenny, as set designer, had plans for "a giant 'clown machine' . . . in, on, and around which the entire entertainment was to take place. To Gene the idea was utterly irresistible. . . . The show had a circus feeling to it which he relished. . . . It appealed to his sense of fantasy and wonderment."[57]

On July 3, the Kellys, refreshed and invigorated, left the scenic Emerald Isle, made a brief stop in London to visit Kerry, and then returned to Beverly Hills. The serenity of Ireland made the constant reports of violence in the American media all the more overwhelming. In December 1971, popular culture's portrayal of the brutality that seemed to be the norm onscreen and off hit Gene at a personal level. Stanley Kubrick (once a guest at Gene and Betsy's house parties and now a cutting-edge director) released his controversial dystopia of an ultra-violent future: *A Clockwork Orange.* The film is a veritable masterwork of dark comedy blended with nightmarish, surreal scenarios. The primary character in the film, a teen thug named Alex, is an aficionado of music and song, favoring especially Ludwig van Beethoven—and none other than Gene Kelly. In one of the first scenes of the film, he dances and croons to "Singin' in the Rain" while his buddies brutally rape a woman and beat her husband. After each line of the song, Alex kicks the husband or cuts a piece of the wife's clothing off. The scene came about in a moment of improvisation on the part of Malcolm McDowell (Alex). "I jumped up and started singing 'Singin' in the Rain' . . . on the beats, slapping, kicking, boom. And why did I do that? Because [that song is] Hollywood's gift to the world of euphoria. And that's what the character is feeling at the time."[58] The movie was the ninth-top-grossing film of 1971.

Gene was not thrilled with the use of "Singin' in the Rain" in the film, but he was not one to stand in the way of creativity, whatever form it took. What he did object to, however, was any lack of compensation for the imitation of his song and dance moves in the film. In 1972, a year after McDowell had moved to Hollywood, the actor recalled that Gene "cut him dead at a party." McDowell assumed that Gene was offended by the use of "Singin' in the Rain" in such a perverse manner. Only after Gene's third wife, Patricia Ward, addressed the Academy of Motion Picture Arts and Sciences at the fortieth anniversary of *A Clockwork Orange* in 2011 did McDowell discover the true reason behind Gene's snub. She explained that Gene was angry that he was not compensated for the use of his dance routine that accompanied "Singin' in the Rain." McDowell elaborated, "He [Kubrick] was cheap. . . . He thought it was enough that 'Stanley Kubrick' was going to use the song."[59]

Gene, determined to create euphoria in a nondystopian sense, plunged into work on *Clownaround* with blithe enthusiasm. It tapped into his creativity for original concepts as no project had since *Jack and the Beanstalk.* But during rehearsals, suddenly a dystopia seemed far more real than the colorful world of entertainment he had been trying to create. Jeanne Coyne Kelly discovered she had leukemia.

Part 4

Ambassador of His Art

1972–Present

21

True Talent Shows Itself in Kindness

The early 1970s were a time of both loss and revival for Gene. While tragedy tainted his personal life, the rediscovery of his movie work, borne by a wave of nostalgia that swept over America, gave him hope and encouragement.

Such comfort, however, seemed a long way off in the spring and summer of 1972. Gene's new pet project, *Clownaround*, was not living up to his expectations in spite of the great effort he initially poured into it. He spent weeks touring the country in search of dancers who were also gymnasts who could navigate scenic designer Sean Kenny's intricate, multilevel set. The ingenious design was like a circus in and of itself; it could be transformed into a jungle, a ship, or a fairground if rotated.

On March 11, 1972, in the midst of Gene's cross-country talent scouting, Jeanne grew concerned over several large bruises on her body. She showed Gene's faithful secretary, Lois McClelland, the contusions, explaining that she had neither fallen nor bumped herself. Lois advised her to call a doctor, which she did. The following day, Gene returned home and drove to the studio as usual with Lois. Jeanne went to the doctor without telling her husband or children. Lois expected her to call a few hours later with news of the outcome of her exam, but it was not until two-thirty in the afternoon that the phone rang.

"I need to talk to Gene," Jeanne said, frantic. Lois handed the phone to him. A few minutes later, she recalled, Gene "disappeared into a dark corner of the stage and wandered up and down. Jeanne had leukemia and could be dead within three weeks."[1]

Gene tried to use work as a distraction but he could not think of anything but Jeanne. *Clownaround* became a chore rather than a joy. It pained

Jeanne to see how fully Gene's heart had gone out of the project; but it made her more determined to keep life as normal as possible. Frank McCarthy, who had become a friend of the family since producing *A Guide for the Married Man,* commented that her "spirit was incredible. . . . I never saw her with sadness in her eyes and I never heard her complain."[2] Nonetheless, Jeanne's illness, compounded with injuries sustained by actors in *Clownaround* during performances, caused Gene's faith in the show to all but disappear. *Clownaround,* which the producers had planned to tour forty cities until closing in New York's Madison Square Garden, never made it out of California. It shut down after two weeks when the producers' funds ran dry and Sean Kenny became ill.

Gene was somewhat relieved to be free of the show. All he wanted was to be close to Jeanne. He refused to accept any work more than thirty minutes from home. Jeanne had to cajole him into taking a supporting part in what would be his first film in ten years. Entitled *40 Carats,* it was a cinematic adaptation of a popular Broadway romantic comedy about a forty-year-old woman who falls in love with a twenty-two-year-old man. When producer M. J. Frankovich approached Gene to portray the leading lady's ex-husband (an aging, has-been actor), Gene remembered, Jeanne "said it would be good for me to get out and be occupied. She was right."[3] Another deciding factor for Gene was the opportunity to work with two top-notch actresses, Liv Ullman and Binnie Barnes. "I haven't regretted a minute of the filming," Gene told the *Toledo Blade.* He was happy to have only one role in the film—that of actor. "My God, it was nice to have someone else shouldering the responsibility [of directing]!" he exclaimed.[4] Gene did not escape the film without performing an obligatory dance, however. The dance, which takes place in a hip nightclub, was unlike any he had ever done. Gene is hilarious trying to dress and dance like the paisley- and polyester-clad young people on the floor.

The picture was in production from October 1972 to January 1973. When released on June 28, 1973, it grossed a modest $2.1 million. The film received mixed reviews, but the majority of critics seemed to agree that Gene added vitality and humor to the endeavor. A reviewer for *Variety* stated that he "projects superbly the intricacies of a showbiz character, an aging gypsy so to speak, whose head and heart are together though his career is erratic. It's made to order for his mature abilities in both comedy and drama."[5]

Gene did not have the heart to start another project after finishing his work on *40 Carats*. Illness and death seemed ubiquitous in his life. As he watched Jeanne rapidly weakening, he received news that the man who had made him a star at MGM—Arthur Freed—had died, on April 13, 1973. In May, Gene was honored to be the first recipient of an award named after the great producer. At the awards show, a series of classic film clips featuring Gene was screened.

In the same spring, Gene watched Liza Minnelli take home an Oscar for Best Actress in *Cabaret*. The previous year, shortly after Gene had discovered his wife was ill, he had turned down the tantalizing offer to direct and choreograph *Cabaret,* which was to be shot on location in Berlin. He wanted neither to leave Jeanne nor take his family with him, as that would mean uprooting the children. Gene recommended Bob Fosse (who used to be a frequent visitor at the Kelly house parties) for the job. The innovative young choreographer had found success in his work with the stage and movie versions of *The Pajama Game* (1957, film) and *Sweet Charity* (1969, film). According to *Cabaret*'s producer, Cy Feuer, Gene "could have made the movie, but it wouldn't have been the same picture. It would have been more . . . frivolous. It wouldn't have Fosse's dark side."[6]

The morning after the Academy Awards ceremony on March 27, 1973, "one of the earliest calls" Vincente Minnelli got "was among the most heartwarming." "It was Gene Kelly, who'd been a part of Liza's life for such a long time. . . . His cheery voice gave no indication he'd been under the weather. 'Wonderful! Judy would have been thrilled!' he said."[7]

Liza's victory was one of the few positive events that dismal spring. Jeanne spent her days in and out of hospitals. She had been trying to keep her illness secret from Tim and Bridget, but after Christmas, that had become impossible. Tim, looking through a magazine one day, stumbled upon an article on leukemia and asked Gene if it was what his mother had. The eleven-year-old had heard the word whispered around the house and make the connection. Tim then asked Jeanne if leukemia was fatal. It was, she told him. "Is there any medicine to make you better?" Tim asked, staring at the many prescriptions on her nightstand. Jeanne admitted there was nothing that could make her better, but that her medicines would keep her around a bit longer. Though Jeanne rarely allowed her fear to show, Tim once saw her in her bedroom, looking out the window and sobbing.

Jeanne was eventually confined to the house to prevent her from catching infections. The Kellys' social life, already limited, dwindled even further. Jeanne remained very practical and discussed with Gene whether the children should be allowed to see her "when the end came and the sort of services she wanted held. She did not, she said, want an open casket and everything was to be as simple as possible. In truth she did not want a service of any kind, but because her children attended a Catholic school, she felt she would have to have one 'as a gesture.'"[8] She even gave Gene specific instructions about which of her friends would be best to take Bridget shopping, how to put corrections (such as arch supports and heel wedges) in the children's shoes, and even what placemats should be used for what meals. Basically, she wanted the house to continue running as it always had.

Jeanne Coyne passed away on May 10, 1973—nine years to the day after Gene's onetime assistant Carol Haney's death. Her strong will to live and her unflagging optimism went far in allowing her to live fifteen months although her doctor had projected three weeks. The death of the woman many deemed Gene's one true love—sweet, selfless, intelligent Jeanne— was the "sad climax" to the most depressing year of Gene's life. From spring 1972 to summer 1973, he saw the death of his mother, Arthur Freed, Jeanne, and Sean Kenny (in June 1973). A despondent Gene termed the next two years of his life "a siege. I didn't feel much like working or doing anything."[9] Kerry Kelly recalled that Gene's everyday existence became a struggle. The loss changed his life "enormously. . . . He was a quieter guy."[10] Tim elaborated, "He was crushed. Later in life he would get psychosomatically sick around the time of her death. It was like clockwork."[11]

For weeks after Jeanne's death, Gene spent the early morning hours watching television and drinking beer, which he termed his sleeping pills. He went into professional seclusion, devoting himself to being both a mother and father to his two young children. He had enough in savings to live on for the rest of his life and could, if he chose, never work again. When asked about raising Tim and Bridget alone, Gene replied: "I don't think I had any choice. I never felt sorry for myself. It was a very tough job, but it made me appreciate the woman's role in the house. Anyway, sing no sad songs for me."[12]

Though Gene found life as a single dad intimidating, he had no intention of remarrying. He still had Lois McClelland to help him and, bereaved as he was, he firmly insisted on raising the children himself. Gene decided the best thing for him and his family was a change in surroundings. He appreciated the outpouring of sympathy in Hollywood, but he needed a place to grieve and heal in quiet. That place was Ireland. Gene took Tim and Bridget to the Emerald Isle for the entire summer of 1973. "When Jeannie was alive we'd spend many happy days in County Clare. . . . We'd take a boat out on the loch and live off the fish. . . . They were such happy days," Gene later reminisced.[13]

Gene, Lois, and the children first arrived in London. There, Gene visited Kerry at her home. Kerry had recently given birth to a baby girl—Gene's first grandchild. Gene beamed with pride to see his eldest daughter settled into married life with a fellow psychologist, Jack Novick. He affectionately called them a pair of "eggheads."[14]

Gene, Lois, and his children then headed to Puckane with plans to remain a month. In Ireland, Gene rented two cars. Lois drove one with the children while Gene and the luggage occupied the other. He deliberately acquired two cars for the lengthy journey from the airport to Puckane because, when cooped up in an auto for too long, he claimed, children "grew fangs and claws!"[15]

Gene rented an unassuming, white-walled thatched cottage in Puckane, one of three recently constructed holiday homes that were made to resemble abodes one would have seen in the 1830s. The locals gave the Kellys a warm welcome. "A lovely, lovely man," "a wonderful man" seemed to be the general consensus of the townspeople. Locals often saw Gene make his nightly stop at Paddy Kennedy's pub where he would enjoy two whiskies and a Guinness before returning to his cottage. One local, Willie Slattery, approached Gene one night, telling him that three starry-eyed young ladies were dying to meet him but feared invading his privacy. Gene, without hesitation, said he would meet them. He gave them all hugs and, according to witnesses, the girls' knees buckled and they all fell to the floor.[16]

The trip to Ireland proved so medicinal to Gene that he corresponded with Paddy Kennedy for a time with plans to build his own cottage there. He apparently never broke ground, but the fact that he entertained the idea evidenced his earnest love for Ireland. Gene explained, "With my good Irish name, I feel at home in the old country. I'm accepted there."[17]

Back in Beverly Hills, Gene was not the bleak man he had been when he left. He may have been sixty-one years old, but suddenly no one could possibly imagine that Gene Kelly could ever be elderly. One film was responsible for making the work of Gene and his colleagues new again: *That's Entertainment!*—a mammoth collection of scenes from MGM's greatest musicals. In 1947, Gene had said, "I think there's nothing sadder than to see an artist who keeps capitalizing on his former reputation."[18] By 1966, his opinion had changed: "Before I die . . . I would like to have a clip of the whole thing—everything I've ever done and watch it all."[19] Now, he had his chance.

Gene once referred to Metro-Goldwyn-Mayer as a "Grand Duchess."[20] However, the studio was more like nobility fallen on hard times after 1970. By 1974, MGM was in major financial peril and had produced only four movies over the course of the year. Beginning in May 1970, James Aubrey, the new head of MGM, had begun to systematically destroy what used to be the most enviable studio in Hollywood by liquidating its history in an attempt to keep the company solvent. What he could not sell, he ordered to be leveled or auctioned. Among the saddest losses were "Andy Hardy Street," where the trolley and house in *Meet Me in St. Louis* stood, and the Cotton Blossom Show Boat. Aubrey next sold the studio's sixty-acre back lot to the Levitt housing developers. Finally, he ordered the burning of the Metro music department's library. The only remnants saved from his reign of terror were the script library, whose contents were donated to the University of Southern California. Some props and costumes did survive as well but were either stolen or sold at massive auctions. Film lovers did not see such cheapening of the studio's history as a crime until after the release of *That's Entertainment!* in 1974.

One woman had the foresight to save as much of Hollywood's history as she could. Gene's costar Debbie Reynolds bought many of the items at the MGM auction and acquired over the decades what was regarded as one of the finest collections ever assembled, valued at $26 million. Asked why she began collecting, Debbie explained, "It was mostly emotional. I couldn't believe that they were getting rid of all these iconic pieces that I considered to be historical and should be saved."[21]

In 1973, Jack Haley Jr., the son of the actor who portrayed the Tin Man in *The Wizard of Oz* (1939), planned to write, direct, and produce a celebration of MGM's fiftieth anniversary. It was more than a retrospective—it was an anthology of the Hollywood musical. With enormous changes taking place in society during the early 1970s, Americans yearned for the simpler times reflected in such films. Popular culture reflected America's growing nostalgia for the not-so-distant past. In 1971, the 1950s-themed *Grease* opened on Broadway. In Hollywood, George Lucas and Francis

Ford Coppola produced a fond look back at the early 1960s, *American Graffiti*, which became the third-highest-grossing film of 1973. Contemporary songs also expressed longing for the old days, such as the Carpenters' "Yesterday Once More" and Elton John's "Crocodile Rock."

With the impeachment and resignation of President Richard Nixon in 1974 and the ongoing Vietnam War, Americans did not have much to sing and dance about. The planned tagline for *That's Entertainment!* was, appropriately, "Boy, do we need it now!" Even Gene, who had once called himself a cockeyed optimist, was feeling less positive, admitting to biographer Tony Thomas that he was going through a period of cynicism, which he could only hope would be brief. The time seemed ripe for reintroducing America to the optimistic musicals of the 1940s and 1950s.

"There is always a great deal of nostalgia about those days," Gene observed. "Certainly at the time, we felt part of a Golden Age."[22] Any lingering bitterness he may have had toward MGM had vanished by 1973. He had also gained insight into the positive aspects of the studio system. "I could not have done those pictures without [it]. It would have taken too long. By the time you wheel and deal and get financing today, you're practically an old man."[23]

As much as Gene now appreciated MGM, he was hesitant at first when Jack Haley Jr. approached him to be part of *That's Entertainment!*, admitting that he still had little motivation to get involved in a project. However, helping to preserve the contributions he had made to film history was enough to spur Gene to action. With colleagues and friends like Frank Sinatra, Peter Lawford, Liza Minnelli, Donald O'Connor, Debbie Reynolds, Mickey Rooney, Elizabeth Taylor, Jimmy Stewart, and Bing Crosby, he threw himself into what had long been his emotional outlet: work. The film covered all MGM musicals but paid special homage to those starring Gene and Fred Astaire.

Though the two men still endured endless comparisons to each other, Gene emerged as the dominant dancer in the film. "It was Gene Kelly who was the crown prince of the Hollywood musical during its golden era at MGM—not just in front of the camera but behind it as well," a columnist observed.[24] The finale of *That's Entertainment!* proved Gene to be bearer of the crown. "We have saved the best for last," Frank Sinatra narrated. "*An American in Paris* starred Gene Kelly . . . and [his] . . . ballet is as timeless as when we first saw it. It can only be described as MGM's masterpiece."[25] As presented in the film, though, the ballet seemed less a tour de force because it was cut down from seventeen to seven minutes. Such ruthless editing left Gene with "mixed feelings" about the picture. "The best things in [the ballet] are not shown," he said unhappily.[26]

That's Entertainment! premiered on May 17, 1974, in Los Angeles. Audience reaction was akin to that of rabid fans at a Beatles concert. A writer for the *Chicago Tribune* recounted that "thousands of screaming fans packed the bleachers that lined the area between the Beverly Theatre and the Beverly Wilshire Hotel, hoping to catch a glimpse of the stars. . . . Most applause [went] to Gene Kelly."[27] The film's production costs totaled approximately $1.1 million, but it more than recouped that amount, grossing an eye-popping $19 million at the box office.

After *That's Entertainment!* premiered, Gene's period of cynicism abated somewhat. Nevertheless, certain aspects of the film's reception gave him pause. "At the Hollywood premiere of *That's Entertainment!,* no one was interested in any contribution I may have made as a choreographer and director, which I felt in my immodest Irish way, was perhaps a major one as far as the musical went, but no, all they wanted was . . . 'Get up and do a little dance,'" Gene remarked. Yet, he felt that the timing of *That's Entertainment!* was fortuitous for him, both personally and professionally. "Life is very much alive for me now."[28]

Gene's buoyed confidence led him to accept an offer to play a part in another bit of nostalgic entertainment: *Take Me Along.* The show, a musical, was based on Eugene O'Neill's ode to his youth, *Ah! Wilderness.* Arthur Freed had produced a musical version of the play in 1948, *Summer Holiday,* with little success. The play presents a sentimental story of the Millers, a New England family, at the turn of the nineteenth century. Producer John Kenley tapped Gene for the role of the alcoholic but loveable Uncle Sid, arguably the most three-dimensional character in the play (Jackie Gleason originated the role in the 1959 Broadway show).

Gene's part in *Take Me Along* marked his first appearance on the stage in over thirty years. A reporter for *People* magazine asked Gene why he had chosen to return to live theater. "I am working for pleasure, not for financial reasons," he said.[29] *Take Me Along* was to be a touring show with a seven-week run. The six planned stops included Dallas, Columbus, and St. Louis. According to Gene, his reasons for accepting the job were due in large part to Tim and Bridget. "It offered Pop Kelly a see-America vacation with his children," one reporter stated. "We're going to hire a van or something, so instead of seeing America from 5,000 feet, we'll ride around it, like I was able to do when I was growing up," Gene explained.[30] "We got a cabin in the Black Hills of South Dakota over Easter for ten days. We split logs for the fire and had to use an outhouse. In four hours they had adapted and wanted to live there forever. That trip made me see they can do a lot of things. . . . They're so protected in Beverly Hills—it isn't the way it was in the Pittsburgh neighborhood I came from. We fought our way to and from school every day."[31]

Forty-five-year-old Patricia Wilson, Gene's love interest in the play, wrote extensively of her and Gene's friendship in her 2009 memoir. When she first met Gene in June 1974 for rehearsals in Dallas, Patricia recalled, he appeared at her door "in a white polo shirt and chinos, a can of beer in each hand."

"I want to show you a few dancer's steps on—ahem—on how you can appear shorter on stage!" he said.

"Does my height concern you, Mr. Kelly? I'm quite a good method actress. How tall do you want me to be?" Patricia quipped.

Gene "laughed out loud, stood, and clicked his beer can against mine."[32] From that time on, Patricia and Gene were allies.

Patricia was just as pleased to make the acquaintance of twelve-year-old Tim and ten-year-old Bridget as she was to meet Gene. She found them "lovely, well-behaved children, unlike the spoiled, monster-progeny of many Hollywood stars."[33] The children even became part of the show, acting as extras in a picnic scene. Bridget would throw her arms around Gene as soon as he stepped in the wings. Seeing Gene with his children made Patricia miss her own two daughters all the more. Gene suggested that she send for them, arguing they would make perfect playmates for his children.

The day the girls arrived, Gene told Patricia that he needed a favor. "I should've done this right after my wife died, but I wasn't thinking clearly. Would you witness my new will? I have someone coming to notarize your signature."

Patricia, though shocked, agreed. "Oh gosh, Gene—you've made me think . . . ," she stammered.

"Just get it done," he said gruffly.[34]

Though outwardly Gene was back to the man people expected him to be—charismatic, charming, and energetic—he was still deep in mourning for Jeanne. Gene later said: "You see, people think you get over them [the aches of losing a loved one]. But you don't always. They stay with you. It's hard to explain. . . . But you have to adapt to it. You can't mope around. The kids can't mope around."[35]

Neither Gene nor his children moped during the tour. Bridget quickly befriended ten-year-old Kate Wilson and the two often "made mischief backstage" while they awaited their entrances. When they were onstage, Gene would beam at the children from the wings and comment to Patricia, "Look at those hambones out there!" Patricia's other daughter, seven-year-old Penelope, inadvertently made mischief herself when, one morning, she spotted Gene without his toupee. "Momma! All of Mr. Kelly's hair fell out last night!" she cried.[36]

Another member of the cast, aspiring actress Colleen Lester, found an ally in Gene. A young understudy, she had had many scarring experiences with ill-tempered stars and back-stabbing colleagues. She was thinking of packing up her bags and returning home until, on opening night, Gene approached her in the wings and asked her why she looked so melancholy. "I ended up pouring out all the fear and bitterness I felt," she recalled. "Don't let them bother you," he told her. "The ones who are the most insecure are the ones who are the meanest. True talent seems to show itself most often in kindness."[37] Buoyed by Gene's compassion, she decided to stay in show business.

It was a bittersweet moment when *Take Me Along* ended its tour. Gene and Patricia Wilson were aware of—and amused by—Bridget and Kate's plot to become sisters by convincing Gene and Patricia to marry. "Gene Kelly and I were never more than friends, each of us like a wounded pup kicked into life's corner," Patricia, smarting from marital difficulties, stated. "We were both insomniacs. We'd talk on the phone for hours in the middle of the night about books, work, the children, the sweet mystery of life."[38]

In a 1976 interview in *Woman's Weekly,* Gene elaborated on why he intended to remain single, maintaining that his children were "my whole life right now. They gave me the will to carry on when I didn't know what to do with my life." Gene kept his professional life less active to ensure that his primary role remained that of Dad. Gene was not sorry to turn down more opportunities for work. "Me and the kids . . . [have] so much fun together. . . . For sheer contentment I really [don't] have to do anything else but just be with them," he remarked.[39] On Father's Day of 1975, Tim and Bridget presented Gene with a well-earned certificate naming him Father of the Year. Gene kept it for the rest of his life and today it is among his preserved papers at the Gottlieb Archive in Boston.

As Gene grew older, he especially enjoyed going to Sunday Mass with his growing children. He had recently become more interested in Catholicism; up to this time, his observance had been intermittent at best. The Catholic Church, he explained, "has sustained me, and I have helped sustain the Church, not just with money and sending my children to Catholic schools, but by working with the Church in other ways."[40]

When Gene did agree to another substantial project in 1976, it did not take him from Los Angeles. Saul Chaplin and Daniel Melnick approached him to direct *That's Entertainment! Part II*, which they were producing. They hoped Gene could persuade Fred Astaire to perform in new sequences Gene would direct. The question was, could Gene convince his friend to put his dancing shoes back on?

Gene and Fred had both, on numerous occasions, announced their formal retirement from dancing. Yet, both men had time and again been persuaded to perform again. As had been the case in 1948 when he had to drop out of *Easter Parade*, Gene was again responsible for pulling Fred out of retirement in 1976. He wanted to include segments of song and dance men recapturing classic moments from their careers in *That's Entertainment! Part II*, and without Fred, Gene knew the segments would be sorely lacking. "I simply said, 'Fred, I need you!'" Gene recalled. "Told him what for and he started shouting 'No, no! I don't want to dance.' So I said, 'Let's have a quiet drink together tonight and discuss it.' So we met, and we talked, and eventually we did those scenes! And we loved doing them."[41] Another factor in coaxing Fred to appear was Gene's assurance that neither of them would "kill themselves." He arranged numbers they could execute with as little physical demand as possible. Gene was aware of Fred's dislike for nostalgia, which had served as another obstacle in getting him to agree to do the film. "Nostalgia is just not my bag. I live for today," Fred explained. Gene completely understood, defending his colleague with: "He won't be compared now with what he was then. And who's to blame him?"[42]

Gene did not see the picture as a look at the past through rose-colored glasses. "It's a historical record we're preserving here. Some of these obscure dance routines never get seen on TV, or if they are, they're cut beyond recognition." "You see, it's not just nostalgia. . . . It's kids seeing all this for the first time. It's delight in something new. They can't go out and see joy and fantasy on the screen today—I wish they could."[43]

If observers hoped to see the two men butt heads on the set, they were

385

disappointed. Gene tailored the new numbers more to Fred than to himself; he even submitted to wearing a top hat, tie, and tails. Fred appreciated Gene's efforts and, though thirteen years his senior, did not chafe at being directed by Gene. "I used to say, 'Go ahead and direct me.' He is a damned good director," Fred explained.[44]

The film closes with Gene seated on a ladder in the dark. Fred sits below on a smaller one (unintentionally reflecting Gene's dominance in the picture). They begin singing "That's Entertainment" and end by climbing up and down the ladders, enumerating the names of the stars who appeared in the film. The camaraderie between the two dancers onscreen was not a scripted part of the narration; it was genuine. "Gene and Fred had become very, very close in those years," said producer Daniel Melnick. "Gene would pick up Fred to have dinner because Fred had gotten very frail and didn't like driving at night. Gene was devoted to him. . . . It was very sweet to see him almost at the seat of the master. He respected him because he knew he had led the way."[45] Gene called himself and Fred a "fraternity of two." Gene's reverence for Fred and his protection of him increased after shooting for the film was finished. Knowing Fred's dislike of the promotional duties involved, he asked the film's producers and promoters to put out the word: "Fred doesn't want to talk to anybody—he's had it. Send everyone to Gene."[46]

That's Entertainment! Part II opened at New York's Ziegfeld Theatre on May 16, 1976. It was not as big a box office draw as its predecessor. Part of this may have been due to the fact that the Vietnam War had finally ended in 1975 and the nostalgia craze that had sprung up during the conflict was slowly waning. However, *That's Entertainment! Part II* did decent business and received critical acclaim. "They [Gene and Fred] . . . are still vital talents, but they should not use the make-up men who have attempted to erase the years of their careers under layers of paint and borrowed hair," *New York Times* critic Vincent Canby remarked.[47] Norma McLain Stoop of *Dance* magazine noted Gene's elation at the rediscovery of his films and the fact that *That's Entertainment! Part II* was chosen to open the 1976 Cannes Film Festival. Stoop claimed that European directors considered the Hollywood musicals to be "the acme of the effective use of the medium, a peculiarly American art form that has raised the spirits and gladdened the lives of many." In the opinion of the Cannes judges, the sequel outdid the original because it linked "yesterday with today by employing the present."[48]

Fred remarked that he was "glad people enjoyed it, but it didn't mean anything to me."[49] Gene's enthusiasm compensated for Fred's apathy. With a broad "Irish grin," he told one columnist: "A thousand letters a week have been coming in. A lot of mail is from kids who seem to think we made those musicals only a couple of years ago. And I'm surprised at the romantic notes I'm getting from girls who weren't even born when I made those pictures."[50]

Gene's work on *That's Entertainment! Part II* inspired filmmakers and performers all over the world. In 1977, director Martin Scorsese departed from his usual gritty style of filmmaking to pay homage to the big band era in a Liza Minnelli vehicle, *New York, New York*. The film included a "show within a show" in the style of the "Broadway Ballet" from *Singin' in the Rain*. However, the picture lost money at the box office; it had strong competition from the first disco musical, *Saturday Night Fever,* starring heart-throb John Travolta. The picture became the fifth-highest-grossing film of the year. Younger audiences now began to veer toward pictures featuring disco rather than films showcasing the songs their parents and grandparents had loved. Interestingly, John Travolta was actually taught at the Kelly School of Dance, though not by Gene. "Fred Astaire with Gene Kelly . . . really supported my debut, if you will, and really wanted me to succeed. I could feel it from them," Travolta later reflected.[51] Another notable dancer/pop star who called Gene one of his major inspirations was Michael Jackson.

Pop stars admired Gene for his pioneering work in Hollywood's golden era, but over the next five years, his final two feature film performances proved that he could not remain such a pioneer forever. Indeed, they represented pop culture at its campiest. His stage work, too, lacked innovation, instead following the now-familiar formula of his best-received television and film specials: nostalgia, nostalgia, nostalgia.

The Hollywood system of the late 1970s was "obsessed with capturing the current pop culture zeitgeist," but the sad result was that films appeared dated a few years after their release.[52] Gene's next film, *Viva Knievel!* was a case in point. A biopic of the famed daredevil motorcyclist, it had Gene playing his drunk, grease monkey sidekick. Gene initially rejected the role. "I turned down the part when my agent called to ask if I was interested," said Gene. "But then my kids heard about it."[53] Tim had his own trail motorcycle and begged his father to do the picture, arguing that Knievel was a "folk hero." Bridget, too, wanted Gene to take the role. "Bridget gasped when I told her I had refused the part," Gene explained. "So I changed my attitude. I sent for the script and liked it."[54] Gene called his part as Knievel's mechanic his "first real character role. . . . This Knievel picture is a lark," he said. "I don't dance, I don't shave, I don't wear make-up. And I don't get the girl. I'm having so much fun that I can hardly wait to go to work in the morning."[55]

Critics panned the film upon its release in summer 1977. One reviewer for the *Ottawa Citizen* said the movie was for Knievel's fans, "but they'll probably wonder why he bothered." The writer deplored Gene's participation as the "saddest" part of the film because it showed what he had "been reduced to . . . but Knievel seems grateful to have [him] around because of the suggestion of class he brings with him."[56]

Following *Viva Knievel!* Gene returned to television in a special called *An American in Pasadena,* set to air on CBS-TV on March 13, 1978. The show guest-starred a swath of Gene's former colleagues plus a group of young tap dancers and sixteen-year-old Bridget. To get in shape for the show (Gene professed to be ten pounds overweight), he upped the amount of time he spent skateboarding with his kids and also reduced indulgences such as beer and desserts. The show, a benefit for homeless children, had Gene re-creating songs and dances from over the years and sharing with the audience "special moments from a life that has been truly blessed with the luck of the Irish."[57]

Gene's next endeavor was not for television but for the stage. Having overcome his distaste for nightclub audiences, he agreed to perform at the Superstar Theatre, an Atlantic City supper club, for a show termed a "trip down memory lane." Gene admitted he spent little time in preparing his act, which he agreed to do mainly so he could visit his family in Pennsylvania. The *Levittown Courier Times* noted, "At 66, Kelly has trouble holding a note, seems uncomfortable with one-liners, and dances rather sparingly . . . but he retains that one lasting gift that money can't buy: Charisma."[58] The show went well enough for him to be invited back on St. Patrick's Day of 1979. "They . . . literally overpaid me. So I did one show a night. Then they asked me back by popular demand. So I went back. Then I said 'To hell with this.' I was only doing it for the money, and I was doing easy routines," Gene reflected in 1985.[59]

Gene again performed almost effortless routines in what proved to be his final motion picture role that was not part of a retrospective. Though the film's producer, Lawrence Gordon, was a tremendous fan of the classic Hollywood musical, he structured the film as a disco musical. A Universal Studios picture titled *Xanadu,* it tells the story of Sonny, a frustrated young artist who falls in love with one of the nine muses (Terpsichore, who renames herself Kira, played by Olivia Newton-John, fresh from her success in the film adaptation of *Grease,* costarring John Travolta). She comes to life and mysteriously enters his world. He also meets Danny McGuire (Gene), a former big band clarinetist. Sonny and Danny team to revamp a dilapidated building into a nightclub that offers a blend of disco and swing music. The most interesting part of the movie is the fact that Kira is identical to Danny's flame from the 1940s. An effective scene depicts Danny dancing with her in his imagination, shown via a translucent projection in the lavish but sorely empty living room of his mansion. The dance they perform is similar to the intimate routine he and Judy Garland did to the title song in *For Me and My Gal.* The translucent special effect element of the number harkened back to the "Alter Ego" sequence in *Cover Girl.* By no coincidence, Gordon gave Gene's character the same name as the character he had played in *Cover Girl,* also a nightclub owner. Gene called his work in the picture "unambitious" and was pleased that his "supporting part ... allows him to leave the set most days in time to pick up his daughter when school lets out. Kelly enjoys his evening jog with her more than any residual hoofing he does in front of the cameras."[60]

The picture went into production in September 1979. Though Gene respected those involved in the movie, particularly the fledgling choreographer Kenny Ortega, the project nonetheless became an embarrassment to him as he saw it take shape. Critic Janet Maslin stated that "director Robert Greenwald has filled the movie with bright colors—people often turn into beams of light or are surrounded by neonlike coronas. . . . *Xanadu* is desperately stylish without having any real style."[61] Gene was not immune to being made a part of the gaudier aspects of the film. In one sequence, Kira and Sonny help Danny choose a snazzier wardrobe to wear at the nightclub. Gene is shown emerging from dressing rooms in increasingly embarrassing costumes, the worst being a cowboy suit dripping with sequined fringe. Later, he roller-skates about the nightclub with a swarm of young disco dancers following behind (an obvious if ill-conceived homage to Gene's number in *It's Always Fair Weather*).

Xanadu premiered on August 8, 1980, to mostly negative reviews. "Too many different things are going on here, and they don't have much to do with one another. . . . Mr. Kelly . . . is forever charming, but why this movie needed him is unclear," Janet Maslin of the *New York Times* wrote.[62] The $20 million picture failed to turn a profit, though its soundtrack was an international best seller.

"I have to admit it's a terrible picture," Gene stated. "But I must say it was fun working with Olivia. And for that reason alone I do not regret that experience. It also showed me just how little today's crop of youngsters actually know about making musicals and that was kind of depressing."[63] If he were to continue in the film industry at all, directing, he explained, would be his choice of work. "Dancing . . . for me, isn't satisfactory or very exciting anymore," Gene said in 1983. "I'd rather be playing coach than be the short stop."[64]

And playing coach was just what Gene had the opportunity to do when, at age sixty-eight, the "plum job of all time" came his way.[65]

Fred Astaire may have been against nostalgia, but one prestigious artist was determined to keep it alive. Producer/director Francis Ford Coppola, who had co-created the wistful *American Graffiti* (1973) as well as the Oscar-winning Mafia saga, *The Godfather* (1974), approached Gene about heading a musical unit at Zoetrope Studios, which he had founded with George Lucas in 1979. Coppola hoped to expand it and create a group under Gene's aegis not unlike the Freed Unit at MGM. Gene, "over the moon" with joy, accepted the offer with alacrity. To him, it was an opportunity to pass on all he had learned from his decades in musicals. "At this stage in my career, I couldn't have asked for anything more."[66]

Zoetrope Studios was, according to production head Lucy Fisher, "an updated version of the old studio system, complete with contract players, contract writers, senior filmmakers on hand such as Gene Kelly, and a distinctive studio signature on each film it makes." One screenwriter described the fledgling studio as "the small college we all wanted to go to."[67]

Gene's first assignment, titled *One from the Heart* (directed by Coppola), dealt with a couple that breaks up to find their dream mates but eventually realize they are ideal for each other. The plan was to produce it in the style of a Broadway musical. The film had a whopping $27 million budget, but, when released in 1981, it grossed only $900,000. Gene stated that he felt he did not contribute much to the film, deeming it "Francis' baby all the way." Gene asserted he would have done many things differently from Coppola but he nonetheless saw the producer as a rare man who took the musical seriously enough "to create a workshop in which it would have been possible for a young choreographer to look over an older, more experienced guy's shoulder and learn his trade through a process of trial and error. But I guess it was not to be and that's that." In a sober tone, he concluded: "It's another two years of my life that have to be written off."[68]

Gene's dispiritedness could not have been helped by the fact that, during this two-year period, he had not one professional failure but three. After *One from the Heart* was *Satchmo,* a lavish Broadway musical telling the story of Louis Armstrong. The show came so close to going into production that Gene had already cast the leads and was auditioning actors to play Armstrong as a boy. Gene was also preparing a movie musical to be produced by David Niven Jr. about the life of Santa Claus. Neither *Satchmo* nor *Santa Claus* ever came to fruition. No satisfactory scripts or funding came through to make the projects possible.

Gene, in his words, resigned himself to being "the ambassador of his art form whose duty it is to explain my trade to the initiated, and to help keep modern dance alive and active."[69] One avenue through which he achieved this "duty" was through *Dancing Is a Man's Sport, Too,* a TV program for NBC-TV similar to Gene's award-winning 1958 special. Choreographing the show was up-and-coming young dancer Twyla Tharp. Gene continued to support new ideas in dance and said of Tharp: "I think Twyla has a lot to say. The great thing about Twyla is that she continues to explore. . . . She's not just doing her own thing."[70]

A man who, in the course of only seven years, had lost his wife, become a single parent, appeared in and helped create three major films, and performed in a successful theater production, Gene had more than earned the privilege to take on the less demanding job of being the primary ambassador of his art.

22

Contemporary
Yet Timeless

By 1982, Gene had watched so many retrospectives of his work that the magic of his films had begun to wear thin—if only for him. Audiences all over the world could not get enough of his movies. "I don't watch my films too much, because when I do, I do a lot of wincing," Gene explained. "[I] say, 'Did I look like that?' . . . When I see myself often in a big close-up, I do one of those big winces." His son, Tim, observed that Gene was still "a perfectionist" about his films. "The only thing he won't criticize is the ballet scene in *An American in Paris*."[1]

Gene did not delude himself into thinking he still had the lean, catlike figure he had had at the height of his career. "I am going downhill physically—gradually—and I don't care," he admitted.[2] His figure had thickened and he indulged in his lifelong taste for cakes, candy bars, and hamburgers with guilt-free pleasure.

Gene remained instantly recognizable, however. "You know you can't walk down the street anymore without being recognized," Gene said ruefully. "It's often quite upsetting, to be honest about it, but you can't escape it. . . . But then, nobody begs you to be in the movies or on Broadway. It's our own choice. I can't understand all the crying I hear about it. If you have to take that to do what you want in life, you take it."[3]

Throughout the 1980s, Gene was the recipient of various honors and continued acting as an ambassador of his art. He received the Cecil B. DeMille Award on January 31, 1981, a lifetime achievement statuette bestowed at the annual Golden Globes ceremony. The following year, President Ronald Reagan and First Lady Nancy Reagan invited Gene to Washington, DC, to appear on a PBS program, *Young American Artists in Performance at the White House*. He served as host, introducing young dancers to America. "True to his word, he neither sang nor danced," columnist Irvin Molotsky commented. He quoted Gene: "I'll be seventy years old in August. And when you get to that age, you don't jump over tables. Every dancer and every athlete stays too long. I hope I didn't."[4]

Gene saw the Reagans again in December 1982, this time for a program showcasing not young hopefuls but himself. The event bestowed upon Gene arguably the most coveted award an artist can receive: the Kennedy Center Honors. Gene received his award on Christmas Day with fellow honorees George Abbott (producer of *Pal Joey*), actress Lillian Gish, bandleader Benny Goodman, and conductor/violinist Eugene Ormandy. Walter Cronkite, anchorman of *CBS Evening News,* hosted the event. When Gene's "Singin' in the Rain" dance was screened, the audience (which included the Reagans) gave him a standing ovation. Gene appeared proud and pleased, but then waved his hand as if to signal: "That's enough adulation."

A reprise of "Singin' in the Rain" began to play and a chorus of dancers appeared, along with Donald O'Connor, Cyd Charisse, Betty Comden, and Adolph Green. They sang a spoof of "Singin' in the Rain" tailored to Gene:

What fabulous eyes, what a smile, what a face
His fame will remain, a star with a brain
He's dancing and acting, and directing, and choreographing,
   and making love
And singin' in the rain.

Gene chuckled, wiped tears from his eyes, and shook his head. One chorus member stepped forward and spoke: "Mr. Kelly, on behalf of all the gypsies everywhere, we thank you."[5] After the dancer's simple statement, Gene began to weep openly. He then stood and took a bow. On this occasion, it seemed, he embraced his image as an inspiration to the next generation.

Indeed, Gene wished that the new generation of aspiring dancers would take *more* inspiration from his work. He despaired of the state of the musical film as it stood in 1983: "The dances in today's movies feature lots of nearly nude, sexy bodies, male and female. . . . Fred Astaire . . . could dance with an overcoat on, and you'd still watch him. . . . A lot of lovely art forms have practically disappeared."[6]

One new trend in musical films disturbed Gene more than any other:

dance doubles. The popular *Flashdance* (1983) made ample use of them. When asked about the picture, Gene stiffened and said: "I don't even want to discuss *Flashdance*. . . . I don't understand the whole concept of doubles. . . . From my point of view it is bad for the art. But obviously the public doesn't seem to care. They like it—and they're stuck with it." With the use of dance doubles, Gene explained, the camera does not shoot the performer from head to toe. "When they do let them sustain on screen from head to toe, though, then you know they must think the person is a good dancer."[7]

Though Gene may have sounded curmudgeonly in his views of the youth-oriented musicals being churned out in the 1980s, he was optimistic that young dancers would "start going back to romantic numbers." Romance was what he missed most in modern musicals, he insisted. "I keep saying this over and over again, but dance follows music. . . . And if the accent today is percussion and rhythm and loudness, then that is the way the dance numbers will be. . . . I love rhythmic dancing—I'm not derogating it at all. It's just that sometimes you want to whisper, '*I adore you.*' And for that you need strings and woodwinds."[8]

On December 21, 1983, a fire broke out in the Kellys' home due to a faulty Christmas tree light. Tim was the first to notice it and roused his pajama-clad father from sleep. The blaze spread swiftly and destroyed their beloved home. Gene lost a lifetime collection of treasures, both expensive and intimate. Numerous works of art and a painting that Kerry had made for his fortieth birthday turned to ashes. His honorary Oscar from 1952 and an old French poster that had been a family joke were also lost to the flames.

Kerry, who now lived in Michigan with her husband and children, called Betsy Blair with the news at two in the morning. Betsy, although still based in Paris, was in Beverly Hills at the time with her husband, Karel, who was shooting a film. Betsy decided she had to go to Gene. As she approached North Rodeo Drive, she saw Tim trying to get past the firefighters, begging to be allowed to enter the house to save things. The firefighters forbade him. Lois McClelland stood beside Gene with Bridget (who was home for the holidays). Gene caught sight of his first wife and said in a broken voice, "Oh Bets, oh Sweeney." They hugged each other and both began to cry. "The 725 North Rodeo Drive that was part of me was gone. It was no longer 'mine,' but in its proper place as a memory," Betsy wrote.[9]

Though the fire was disastrous, Gene did not fall into despair: he and his children were safe. Asked what he would do now, Gene said without a pause: "Rebuild." He did just that, ordering a replica of the home to be constructed. Unlike Betsy, he was unwilling to let the house be a memory. In coping with his staggering loss, Gene's positive attitude and (if intermittent) faith remained intact. As he had said in 1980, "Cheerfulness and good humor have always been important values for me. Gloom doesn't help anyone. My religious faith that God is good and doesn't abandon his own—as well as my faith in life and in other people—sustains me in stormy times."[10]

Gene had reason to be cheerful as he watched his children flourish into adulthood. Forty-year-old Kerry now had two children and was a successful child psychologist in Ann Arbor, Michigan. Twenty-year-old Bridget was studying art in Gene's beloved Paris. Twenty-two-year-old Tim, showing the entrepreneurial spirit Gene had exhibited as a young man beginning his own dance studio, operated his own nightclub. From June 1983 until late April 1984, Tim (who now bore a striking resemblance to his father) and a friend ran the Nairobi Room which, almost overnight, became the hippest spot in Los Angeles. One night, Tim asked Gene to come and see the club in action. "It was a big surprise to him," he explained. "[He said] 'Gosh, this is a great time, but some of these kids need dancing lessons.'"[11]

Gene encouraged self-reliance in his children, but this did not mean he refused to help them financially. He lent Tim money to buy a used Porsche, but he made the boy sell it when he could not keep up with the payments. He paid Tim's tuition at the University of Southern California's film school while allowing his son to stay rent-free in a room above the garage. Tim did not let his father's star status make him complacent. He worked two jobs, one at the Nairobi and the other as a production assistant. "I work twice as hard as anybody else. It's best if someone doesn't know who I am. When they do, they expect the worst from me, thinking 'Oh, Daddy got him the job,'" Tim explained. Like Gene, he was more interested in working behind the camera. For a time, he dabbled in photography.[12]

Tim ultimately pursued work behind the scenes in the film industry, as did Bridget. After graduating from the American College in Paris, she became a costume designer for motion pictures. The lives of Gene's children were, for the most part, kept private from the public—just as he had always wished. The same could not be said for Gene.

On May 7, 1985, he was again the center of attention when the American Film Institute chose him as the recipient of the Lifetime Achievement Award. Shirley MacLaine hosted the event, which was televised on CBS-TV. Guests included Fred Astaire, Leslie Caron, Cyd Charisse, Betty Comden, Betty Garrett, Kathryn Grayson, Adolph Green, Lois McClelland, Vincente Minnelli, Harold and Fayard Nicholas, Olivia Newton-John, Donald O'Connor, Debbie Reynolds, and James Stewart. Gene made his way through a cheering crowd to join his family; his sister Louise, his brother Fred, his nephew, Kerry and her family, Bridget, and Tim waited for him at his table. Gene's two eldest siblings, Jay and James, were not present. Shirley MacLaine began by recollecting her first meeting with Gene after *The Pajama Game* and how he had encouraged her to persevere. Thirty years later, she asked him how long she should keep going; he advised her to remain active as long as she found fulfilment in helping others see their dreams become realities.[13]

When Gene stood to receive his award, he was quick to deflect honor from himself. "You need a lot of talent around you. There are no auteurs in musical movies. . . . All these people [behind the scenes] who knocked themselves out so that we could look good. . . . They don't get enough credit," he said. "It [the movie business] was . . . fun, we had the best of times. And I think it was because we all thought we were trying to create some kind of magic and joy."[14]

In conclusion, Shirley asked everyone to join in singing "When Irish Eyes Are Smiling" to Gene. Gene waved his award above his head and sang loudly with the crowd.

Gene's seemingly unflagging vitality began to wane as the 1980s neared their end. According to Kerry: "His last years were sad. Satisfying in some ways but also very sad. For someone whose physical prowess had been so central to his identity to be old . . . and not able to do all the things he loved doing was very limiting and very hard."[15]

One satisfying aspect of his later years was seeing the appreciation that continued to be accorded to his work. In July 1985, *Singin' in the Rain* was adapted into a Broadway extravaganza. Transferring a cinematic musical to the confines of a stage was no easy task. Choreographer Twyla Tharp was at the helm of the production. The show ran for over three hundred performances but failed to garner positive notices. Frank Rich of the *New York Times* pointed out: "Once transposed to the stage in realistic terms, the fantasy evaporates. . . . Because Miss Tharp has failed to meet—indeed, even to consider—the central challenge of transposing a quintessentially cinematic work to the theater, her show usually flattens out in exactly this way."[16] Gene did not disapprove of Tharp's attempts. He commented, "I [don't] agree with everything she has done. . . . But Twyla's still experimenting, probing new ground."[17]

Gene was now funneling less energy into show business and more into one of his first passions: writing. He began redrafting his autobiography, the first version of which had burned in the house fire. Throughout the process, he enlisted four different authors to aid him in writing the book, but all failed to meet his expectations. Then he met twenty-six-year-old Patricia Ward, a graduate student, Melville scholar, researcher, and author.

They first met at Washington's Air and Space Museum, where Patricia was working as screenwriter for a documentary on the Smithsonian. The documentary was supposed to be narrated by Gregory Peck, but when he withdrew from the project, Gene was asked to take his place. Apparently, Patricia was not sure if Peck's replacement was a female Jean or a male Gene. She had never seen a Kelly film or heard his name, something Gene found quite refreshing. Gene, then seventy-three, liked the fact that the young woman could not compare him to his past celluloid image. They shared an immediate rapport, mostly over their shared love of languages and writing. Of course she went to the nearest video store and rented his movies, but rather than becoming disenchanted with the Gene she had met compared to the young and vital dancer she saw on the screen, she only became more fascinated. Next, she read a biography of him, most likely the first comprehensive book written on Gene, by Clive Hirschhorn in 1974 (updated and re-released in 1984). The book, to her, failed to capture the essence of the man she had come to know.

Six months after meeting Gene, Patricia was surprised to receive a call from Gene asking her to help him write his autobiography. The job was only supposed to last two weeks; she accepted. However, she swiftly found that the job would be far lengthier. It was no simple task to get Gene to open up to her, particularly when he saw her tape recorder continually running. After what turned out to be several years, Gene's trust in Patricia grew, and so did the depth of his stories. He was not the easiest subject; his stories could be inconsistent, but they never bored his young biographer.

As they worked together, Patricia and Gene fell in love. She saw him not as a man nearly eighty years old, nor as a young man. Rather, he was ageless. They paused their work to take time out for dates to "regular guy" activities such as baseball games, where they would enjoy hot dogs and soda pop.

Gene and Patricia's budding romance may have been one of the forces behind his buoyed spirits and subsequent flurry of professional activity in the mid-1980s. He made several forays back into television. He appeared on two episodes of the popular sitcom *The Love Boat* in 1984, and the following year, he appeared as a senator in six episodes of a Civil War miniseries on ABC, *North and South*. In 1986, he costarred in a soapy Joan Collins miniseries on CBS, *Sins,* as a Gershwinesque composer. On the big screen, he hosted a film documentary entitled *That's Dancing!* (1985). An attempt to recapture the magic of *That's Entertainment!* it was yet another retrospective produced by Jack Haley Jr. for MGM. The picture traces the origins of dance for the camera, starting in the late 1920s and ending with break dancing and the rise of music videos in the 1980s. Other hosts included Ray Bolger and Liza Minnelli.

Gene also acted as host for local events, including the annual Beverly Hills St. Patrick's Day Parade in 1986. The parade rolled down thirty-two hundred square yards of kelly green carpet before 250,000 spectators and TV cameras. "For twenty years I've had a house party on St. Patrick's Day," Gene said. "This is just a bit more involved."[18] Though the day of the parade was besieged with rain, Gene refused to perform "Singin' in the Rain." Parade spokeswoman Gail Block asked Gene whether he would sing the iconic tune, but Gene snapped, "No, no, no," and declined to comment further.[19]

Though at times frustrated by such incessant expectations that he relive the past, Gene ultimately relished being the "elder statesman of his genre," a role he took on after the deaths of his beloved friends and colleagues Vincente Minnelli and Fred Astaire.[20] Minnelli succumbed to pneumonia in July 1986; Fred died of the same ailment the following year.

As his social circle shrank, Gene began to entertain ideas of marriage. In 1990, after five years of working with Patricia on his manuscript, Gene caused a minor sensation by marrying his thirty-one-year-old girlfriend. Gene and Patricia's wedding ceremony, held in Santa Barbara, was a small one. His children did not attend. However, Betsy Blair stated that Kerry, Tim, and Bridget welcomed Patricia "as an intelligent companion for him."[21] Gene, still a romantic at age seventy-seven, left Valentine's cards and love notes around the house at midnight for Patricia to find the next morning. "It was the epitome of romance," she said. "He'd wake me up in the middle of the night just to go outside and look at the full moon."[22]

Ten years earlier, Fred Astaire had caused a similar sensation by marrying Robyn Smith, a female jockey forty-five years his junior. Also like Gene, he had remarried after the devastating loss of his beloved wife, Phyllis, to cancer. However, the two men's marriages to much younger women did not receive negative press—probably because both dancers had such spotless reputations that it seemed almost libelous to speak against them.

Though Gene seems to have genuinely loved Patricia, his union with a woman young enough to be his granddaughter also gave him much-needed companionship and someone to look after him in his old age. In his new marriage, there was also the Pygmalion-Galatea dynamic he had enjoyed with seventeen-year-old Betsy Blair. As he had done with Betsy, he molded Patricia into his ideal woman. She appeared to be patient and adaptable to Gene's likes and dislikes. One of his first orders of business was teaching her how to dress. He advised her to wear glasses and to never leave the house without a stylish scarf and hat. After his death, she looked back at the gowns she wore during this period as matronly. Not that Gene forced Patricia to be a plain Jane. Several photographs of Patricia on Gene's arm at black-tie events show her in strapless gowns, her brown hair long and arranged in curly buns, her face fully made up. Many women might have bristled at having such alterations imposed upon them. But Patricia seemed amenable to Gene's "teachings," accompanied as they were by his warmth and trust.

Gene was content to stay home with Patricia, as had been the case with his two other wives. He was still an intensely private person. When he and Patricia did go out, Gene was often barraged by autograph seekers at restaurants, but he dealt with the attention with great modesty. He obliged fans, but would try to turn attention from himself if he was present at someone else's performance.

According to Stanley Donen, Gene was not always so gracious to fans. In 1991, Gene and Donen were both present at a ceremony honoring Betty Comden and Adolph Green at the Kennedy Center—the first time the former co-directors had seen each other face-to-face since their bitter experience on *It's Always Fair Weather*. As Gene made his way into the center, fans waving poster and autograph books bombarded him from the sidelines. Gene was annoyed. "I'm late," Gene shouted, and, in the words of Donen's biographer Stephen M. Silverman, was "loud and ferocious enough to send chills through the bones of bystanders." "L-A-T-E," Gene rat-tatted. "Late, late, late, late, late, *late, late, late!*"[23] Silverman did not mention if Patricia was present to see Gene's display of anger. Indeed, Patricia seems to have rarely seen Gene's temper; no stories exist of any friction between the couple.

Betsy Blair's memoir painted Patricia and Gene's union in a far different light. Betsy only met Patricia a few times. She suspected the younger woman of gold-digging: "It's hard for me to believe that Gene with his realistic attitude and his discerning insight could have turned into a vain old man, but perhaps he did. He would not be the first man to believe that a clever young woman loved him for himself alone."[24] Friends noticed with some concern that Gene, whom Phil Silvers had once chided as being "tight fisted" with money, bought his new wife an expensive car and, it was rumored, a separate condominium for her use alone. According to Gene's biographer Alvin Yudkoff, Patricia was not a gold digger and "turned out to be a sturdy support for him and his cronies."[25] One evening, Patricia found herself responsible for getting a tipsy Frank Sinatra, with whom she and Gene were dining, home. Frank cried that he loved Gene, and told her that they were just like brothers.

In 1993, Gene agreed to make one last contribution to the cinema. He signed to host a second sequel to *That's Entertainment!* His desire to keep the art of dance and the musical film alive became more ardent as honors continued to be bestowed upon him. In 1991, his alma mater, the University of Pittsburgh, created an annual Gene Kelly Award for outstanding high school musicals in Allegheny County. In 1994, the same year *That's Entertainment! Part III* premiered, President Bill Clinton awarded him the National Medal of Arts at a ceremony held in the White House.

When *That's Entertainment! Part III* went into production in spring of 1993, columnist Kevin Thomas described Gene as "[making] light of the passing years. . . . [He was] the model of polite professionalism. . . . The sense of camaraderie was very much like that on his own sets."[26] The third installment of the series proved far less effective than its predecessors. *New York Times* critic Caryn James said of the picture: "With the best material used up, *That's Entertainment! Part III* cleverly focuses on outtakes. . . . Many of the clips are extremely short. . . . Over the course of a two-hour film, the effect is jarring, like stop-and-go driving in heavy traffic."[27]

Although the movie did not match the quality of the first two, it achieved the series' goal of introducing new generations to classic movies. As they had in the 1970s, young people responded. Nostalgia was back in the 1990s, especially for the big band era. New groups, particularly the Brian Setzer Orchestra, released albums of neo-swing tunes, and films such as *Swing Kids* (1993) and *The Mask* (1994) featured swingy soundtracks that became best sellers. Classic movies were more easily accessible due to the expansion of video rental stores and the creation of Turner Classic Movies in 1994. The channel, whose owner, Ted Turner, had acquired Metro-Goldwyn-Mayer studios in 1986, screened nothing but uncut and commercial-free films from Hollywood's golden age.

Classic style was also revived in the early 1990s—perhaps as a rebellion against the grunge look that also dominated the era. In 1993, Gap introduced a series of advertisements for khakis that showed vintage artists including Marilyn Monroe and Rock Hudson wearing khakis. The tagline for the ad featuring Gene was misleading in that it was in the past tense ("Gene Kelly wore khakis"), leading some to assume he had passed away. Gene insisted during an interview: "I'm alive all right, as you can tell. . . . I have a pair [of khakis] on right now." Gene's Gap ad was done in good taste, much to his approval. "I won't do anything peddling anything," he declared. "[But] this is very classy, and I like it."[28] Gene, who had referred to himself as a "walking slum" throughout his life, suddenly found himself a fashion icon. Columnist Hal Rubenstein stated, "In his wardrobe's renewed popularity, Kelly sees a hopeful sign that men's wear is maturing." Gene expounded on his distaste for contemporary trends. What most disgusted him were baseball caps worn backward. "On grown men, it's so stupid."[29]

Just as Gene was enjoying the latest appreciation of his legacy, he suffered a serious stroke on July 24, 1994. He was hospitalized for seven weeks. Betsy Blair related, "Kerry and Tim called and left messages of love and concern. They had the impression Gene didn't know about these calls"—Patricia, Betsy alleged, kept the messages from him. "Bridget was told that her presence in the hospital was 'embarrassing' for him. But she could see the joy in his eyes when she arrived, so she just showed up every day."[30] Gene remained largely homebound for the next eight months and received few visitors. He did not wish for anyone, even his family, to see him in such an altered state. In February 1995, he endured a second stroke. He was admitted to Cedars-Sinai Medical Center under an assumed name.

"He is neurologically stable," Ron Wise, a hospital spokesman, said. "He's aware and conversational."[31]

After his second stroke, Gene was bedridden for a year and a half—a nightmare for a man who had been active his entire life. Betsy asserted that Patricia made the difficult situation an impossible one: "[He was] paralyzed down one side. He was cut off from everything familiar: Lois, his secretary for fifty years, was no longer welcomed in the house; the locks were changed, there was a new housekeeper. His doctor, his business manager, and his lawyer were fired and replaced. The telephone was never answered. Old friends who left messages over a period of months received no calls back. They assumed he was too ill and therefore incommunicado." Betsy claimed that Gene's children had only limited information on their father's state. Betsy further alleged that Patricia required the children to make an appointment if they wished to see Gene. "But [Bridget] has her mother Jeannie's spirit—she could not be stopped so she barged in anyway," Betsy wrote.[32] Though Gene was half paralyzed, he was still able to speak. It is unknown whether he asked Patricia to dismiss his longtime staff and keep his family and friends at a distance. Gene had a strong sense of pride, and, as after his first stroke, it is likely he did not wish for anyone to see him incapacitated. Gene's brother Fred did state that Gene did "not want anybody to see him unable to walk and in poor health."[33] Betsy commented, "I'm sure he wanted no pity. . . . He never complained."[34]

Among the few people who did see Gene was Betsy Blair. Hearing of his "incommunicado" status from Kerry, she determined that she "would not be stopped. I *was* going to see Gene." She was surprised to receive an exceedingly formal invitation from Patricia inviting her for tea at four o'clock on a Friday afternoon. Gene, paralyzed only on one side, was able to sit up in a chair to receive his guest. "All his old charm was there in a low-key way. . . . He was wry and funny," Betsy recalled. "Tea was served to the three of us by a uniformed housekeeper. . . . When he saw my empty cup, good old Gene said with an Irish brogue, quoting his father and grandfather as he always had 'A little hot, hon.'"[35] Gene and Betsy shared a fond laugh, and Betsy held out her cup for a refill. Patricia did not take it; instead, she rang a bell on the tea trolley beside her and the little group waited in awkward silence for the maid to come from the kitchen to pour.

Betsy drove home from the visit blinded by tears. Gene extended several more invitations to Betsy after that occasion, asking her to come by and bring old friends to visit. Betsy claimed that Patricia cancelled each one, leaving terse messages that it was "too much for Gene."[36] Betsy never saw Gene again.

Betsy, as well as all three of Gene's children, had permanent homes outside of California; Gene had no family close at hand. His eldest sister, Jay, still lived in Pittsburgh, and his younger sister, Louise, was in Alabama, where she had set up a new location of the Gene Kelly School of Dance. His elder brother, James, had moved to California and become an aeronautical designer before his death in 1989. His youngest brother, Fred, had retired in Tucson after a fruitful career as a dancer and producer. Fred, who lived nearest to Gene, came to visit him in January 1996 when he heard of his brother's rapid deterioration. "All the life supports had been removed," Fred remembered. "The last day we saw him, we shared about a half-hour of wonderful chatter."[37]

Facing his own mortality, Gene gave directives for his burial—or lack thereof. According to Patricia, he did not want his grave to be a stop on a bus tour; consequently, he wrote out notarized instructions that his ashes not be placed anywhere public. Gene's mind remained sharp, and he was more intent on preserving his memory through words than through an urn or a tombstone. After his strokes, he was still dictating notes to Patricia for his autobiography.

On Friday, February 2, 1996, Gene suffered a third massive stroke and died in his bed with Patricia by his side. On the night of his death, the lights of Broadway, where he had first become a star, were dimmed. "There can only be one Astaire in a generation, maybe in every several generations," Adolph Green remarked. "And one Gene Kelly."[38]

Gene Kelly's death was peaceful, but it was followed by pain and controversy. Patricia notified Kerry, Tim, and Bridget in their respective homes in Michigan, New York, and Montana. "Gene's widow told them there was so much to do that she couldn't have them stay in the house they had all grown up in. Besides there was no reason to come—it was all over," Betsy related in her memoir.[39] Patricia had had Gene cremated the very day he died. The children insisted that they were going to fly to Beverly Hills anyway, and Patricia agreed for them to come to the house on Saturday evening.

Grieving and in states of shock, the children (in Betsy's words) "passed a most bizarre half hour. There were no friends, no food, no tears, and no embraces. They were given a tour of flowers from famous people as if they were strangers. . . . Kerry later told me that they all felt as if she [Patricia] threw him away—as if he were garbage. . . . His children, who loved him, never got to say goodbye to their father."[40] They turned to Lois McClelland for comfort, as Betsy was living in London at the time. Because there was no marker for Gene's remains, his children planted a tree in his honor in the Will Rogers Memorial Garden on Rodeo Drive in Beverly Hills.

Betsy asserted that the lack of closure for the children would have saddened and "I imagine enraged [Gene] because he loved his children deeply. . . . I cannot forgive his widow, not because she got almost all of the children's inheritance, but because I don't think he had the happy ending he deserved."[41] Twenty years after Gene's death, his children still hesitate to speak of Patricia Ward. Though Patricia's decision to have Gene cremated was apparently in keeping with his wishes, the speed with which she had it completed was understandably upsetting for his family. The impersonal way Betsy claimed Patricia acted during the children's visit may have been due to shock and was her way of maintaining composure during the grieving process.

Patricia did not arrange a formal memorial for Gene, but his death did not go unnoticed. Hundreds of news broadcasts showed clips of him singing and dancing, and movie channels ran marathons of his work. Dozens of his friends and colleagues gave interviews expressing what Gene had meant to them. His closest collaborator, Stanley Donen, offered effusive words about Gene's talent and infectious optimism.

Yet sadly and, according to Betsy, "mysteriously . . . Stanley, over the years, has been less than generous about Gene."[42] In the years after Gene's death, Donen often spoke disparagingly of him as a tyrannical co-director and egotist. When director Robert Trachtenburg contacted him to speak about Gene in a 2002 documentary, he "essentially . . . relayed a message saying he had nothing nice to say, so he'd rather not say anything at all."[43] Donen had been nonplussed by the speech Gene gave when the two met at the event honoring Comden and Green at the Kennedy Center in 1991, resenting Gene's words: "Stanley needed me to grow up with. He came to me when he was . . . maybe sixteen," even though Gene went on: "I always wanted to be a . . . choreographer. I needed Stanley behind the camera."[44]

After Gene's death, Donen took his place as elder statesman of the genre that he, Gene, and their colleagues had helped to create. With the deaths of virtually all the members of the Freed Unit, the golden days of the MGM musical have passed into legend. From 1998 to 2008, five people who played major parts in Gene's career passed away. Frank Sinatra was the first to leave, in May 1998. Adolph Green died in October 2002, followed by Donald O'Connor in September 2003. Betty Comden passed away in November 2006 and Cyd Charisse in June 2008. Debbie Reynolds died suddenly in January 2017. Gene's siblings also died within this period: Fred in 2000, Harriet Joan Kelly Radvansky in 2002, and Louise Kelly Bailey in 2008. Betsy Blair died in March 2009—but not before, at Kerry's urging, she penned a candid memoir. "I wanted to write something that tells Gene's children [especially Tim and Bridget] about our life, to give them something about the time of Gene Kelly," Betsy explained.[45] Her honest and tasteful book, *The Memory of All That,* was released in 2003.

Gene's third wife and widow, Patricia Ward, had similar plans for a memoir. As of 2016, she has not completed it—or the biography of Gene for which she took such assiduous notes. But she has made it her career to protect, celebrate, and preserve Gene's legacy. As the sole owner of the Gene Kelly Image Trust, she has been for the most part successful in keeping Gene's image and name untarnished.

However, in 2005, Volkswagen released an advertisement for the newest model of Golf GTI that bordered on defaming Gene's most enduring creation: the "Singin' in the Rain" dance. The advertisement "metamorphosed" the original footage of Gene's dance to make it look as though he were "rapping and breakdancing to a club-mix of 'Singin' in the Rain.'" The ad remastered the scene "using masks, wigs and digital techniques to impose Kelly's face on the dancers." The ad ended with the slogan: "The original, updated." Advertising agent Martin Loraine defended the commercial: "Even though [Gene] was from the 1940s he was very interested and approved of modern dance."[46] Loraine's assertion is specious; Gene did approve of modern dance, but he deemed certain styles uncreative and undisciplined. Additionally, many rap songs boast lyrics that glorify drugs or use derogatory terms for women. Gene was adamant against drugs and even more ardent in his views of protecting women.

The explosion of the Internet from the mid-1990s to the present day has inevitably given Patricia less control over information about or photos of Gene. Hundreds of fan sites have popped up, the vast majority harmless. The largest is a beautifully designed, comprehensive archive entitled Gene Kelly: Creative Genius. The founder of the website, Susan Cadman, had the opportunity to meet Betsy Blair in London during an open-air showing of *Singin' in the Rain.* The show was sold out, but "I was very surprised to get a phone call from Betsy, asking if I would like her to secure tickets for my friends and myself for the film!" Cadman stated. "Betsy was so warm and funny and actually seemed interested and thrilled that people still loved Gene so much. . . . It was clear that Betsy still loved Gene very much, and had no bad word to say about him."[47]

After Betsy's death, Patricia became Gene's primary publicist and spokesperson. Though Kerry has given countless interviews about her father, Gene's other children have mostly remained silent, although Tim made an appearance in the 2002 PBS *American Masters* special, *Gene Kelly: Anatomy of a Dancer.* Patricia, on the contrary, is seldom out of the public eye. She has traveled the world giving talks to audiences of all ages about her late husband's life and work. Beginning in 2012 for the centennial of Gene's birth, Patricia launched a one-woman show titled *Gene Kelly: The Legacy* that has been a sensation in every town it hits.

The show consists of Patricia's memories of Gene, film clips, a display of memorabilia, and a discussion of his impact on film. She stresses his wish to be remembered not as just a dancer but as a pioneering choreographer. The show also seeks to continue Gene's lifelong goal of passing a love of dance to younger generations.

Audiences young and old flocked to see *Singin' in the Rain* upon its re-release in 2012. In the mere eighteen days it played in select theaters throughout the country, it grossed nearly $2 million. As the only surviving members of the cast and crew, Debbie Reynolds and Stanley Donen were present at its screening in Los Angeles for Turner Classic Movie's Annual Classic Film Festival. Though Gene feared his work would become dated and forgotten, audiences are still responding to his films as though they were new.

In spite of the controversy surrounding Patricia before and after Gene's death, she has stayed fiercely dedicated to him and has not remarried.

Gene remains vital today, serving as an inspiration and driving force behind Broadway's most successful shows. Ironically, classic movie musicals dominate contemporary Broadway rather than Broadway dominating Hollywood (as had been the case in Gene's heyday). In 2014, *On the Town* returned to Broadway, blending elements of the original 1944 show with Gene and Donen's 1949 adaptation. The show had been revived twice before, once in 1972 and again in 1999; however, both previous revivals failed, each running under 80 performances. The most recent revival ran for a laudable 368 performances. *New York Times* critic Ben Brantley (a bit unfairly) called Gene and Donen's film "winceably antiseptic," but claimed that director John Rando's stage version "has grown up quite nicely."[48]

Another Broadway artist Gene inspired was director and choreographer Christopher Wheeldon, who is also a gifted ballet dancer. In 2015, he brought *An American in Paris* to Broadway. Unlike Twyla Tharp's *Singin' in the Rain* in 1985, *An American in Paris* met with rave reviews. "Musicals based on classic movies, or not-so-classic movies, have become a familiar staple on Broadway. . . . Dance, on the other hand, has become the wallflower at the Broadway prom in recent decades, which makes Mr. Wheeldon's triumph all the sweeter," *New York Times* critic Charles Isherwood wrote.[49] As a sort of cherry on top for the show, it opened at the Palace Theatre—the very locale at which Gene and Judy Garland aspired to play in Gene's first film, *For Me and My Gal*.

The dance musical is thriving on the stage, but the cine-musical has yet to be resurrected. With a few exceptions, such as *The Artist* (2011), any musical that makes it to the screen is still based on a stage show. Jean Dujardin, star of the (mostly) silent *Artist*, claimed that he took inspiration from Gene Kelly for his character's energy and smile. Screen musicals such as *Newsies* (1992) and *Chicago* (2002), both of which were based on Broadway hits, contain a substantial amount of dance but are highly stage bound in execution. Original dance is more ubiquitous on the small screen. Programs such as *So You Think You Can Dance?* and *Dancing with the Stars* have made the medium more accepted commercially. Both shows premiered in 2005 and, as of 2016, are still running. Both programs, however, fail to demonstrate Gene's thesis that dance should be a means of expressing emotion, character, or storytelling. Thus, he may have regarded the programs with some wariness. But, because the shows do acknowledge the medium as an art, he would likely appreciate their success at getting people to move in new and creative ways.

Whether or not the film musical ever returns, it is apparent that audiences still have an appetite for song and dance Gene Kelly style. The twenty-first century has brought unprecedented changes in technology that have alienated people from each other to a great degree. Warfare and the constant threat of terrorism have dampened spirits—but, unlike in the World War II era, the entertainment industry offers no obvious escapism to boost morale. "Boy do we need it now," the slogan for *That's Entertainment!* would be a most appropriate slogan for the twenty-first century—and this is indeed why Gene Kelly's work has not fallen into obscurity. Gene once said his real challenge was to make something contemporary and yet time-less. If the enthusiastic response each new generation has to Gene's work is any indicator, he overcame his challenge. He danced character, he danced emotions—and neither can ever go out of date.

Epilogue

Think of Him and Smile

Gene Kelly holds the special distinction of being one of the few song and dance men whose films are enjoyable not only to fans of musicals but to those who normally dislike them. He holds an even more exceptional place in the history of film as one of the few entertainers who was talented in almost every aspect of filmmaking and performing. Documentarian Robert Trachtenberg explained his reason for choosing Gene as his subject thus: "I'm . . . drawn to someone who can get up and go to work decade after decade, plugging away at trying to do something fresh and new. When you really look at it . . . there is no precedent for this career."[1]

Another precedent Gene set was his international appeal; he is a uniquely American dancer who is equally revered in his native country and abroad. At Gene's Kennedy Center Honors ceremony in 1984, actor Yves Montand described Gene's unique appeal: "When an artist is as good as Gene Kelly it makes us forget about language. He shows how to find the road to joy in your hearts and that is international. . . . He is in people's hearts everywhere, an American for the whole world."[2]

The world embraced Gene and he, in turn, embraced it. He was never still in his quest to attain more experience and knowledge of people and things. Seldom did a year pass when Gene failed to go abroad and gain new perspectives. Just as he is loved by filmgoers of all different tastes, he is respected by Americans of all different political affiliations because of the honesty and high principles he espoused. "He is a liberal in politics, and when he states his own convictions it sounds as if he were a rebel also," columnist W. H. Mooring observed in 1946. "He is smart enough to make his way on his own merit and Irish enough to command attention whether or not his ideas are approved or disapproved. He is not the kind of fellow who gets ignored."[3]

Alternately seeking attention and shunning it was typical of Gene's often contradictory nature. His life, he once stated, was a quest for privacy, yet he often sulked when he was not the center of attention. Gene's unpredictable moods manifested themselves most notoriously in displays of temperament dreaded by his friends and colleagues. But he was no stereotypical spoiled movie star: that temperament arose out of his perfectionism. And he could erase memories of his angry outbursts with one flash of his charming smile. His zest for life was contagious to those around him, and it was this ebullience that audiences responded to, and continue to relish, in his work. "His buoyant athleticism, naive passion and look-Ma-I'm-hoofing brand of enthusiasm introduced cinematic dance to sweat, lust and earthly delights. Gene Kelly made Everyman believe he could dance, and Everywoman wish that he would," writer Hal Rubenstein stated in 1994.[4]

As merry as he appeared onscreen, Gene as well as his family insisted that he was nothing like the fellow full of bravura he played in his pictures. He was, as it were, an introverted extrovert, an Everyman sophisticate—an intensely private man whose irrepressible personality, ambition, and charisma could not help but thrust him into the spotlight. However, time and again Gene expressed his preference for working behind the camera. "When you're performing you're interpreting someone else's creation," he said. "To me, always, ever since I've been a young man, the creation has been the most satisfying."[5]

Gene's creations revolutionized dance and helped make America the leader in contemporary movement. As one journalist expressed it, "He drew upon the whimsy of tap, the showmanship of the eccentric dancer, the free form of Martha Graham, his own skills as a gymnast and organized all of it with legitimate classical disciplines. The bristling package of rhythm and style hit the dance world with a fallout that is still being felt."[6]

True, Gene took inspiration from other artists, but the skills he borrowed from them he transformed into something unprecedented, and thus his performance was indeed his own. Film scholar Jeanine Basinger aptly stated: "He created a technique. He was his own technique."[7] Author John Updike added: "No one in the postwar era worked harder to expand the musical comedy's boundaries than Kelly. . . . [He is able] to instantly transport the action in his films . . . to a plane of buoyant make believe where singing and dancing are the norm."[8] Gene accomplished this feat by instilling meaning in dance, using the medium to build plot and character. In freeing his routines from ostentation, his dancing flowed naturally with a film's storyline.

The simplicity and charm of Gene's best numbers make him both contemporary and timeless. Liza Minnelli remarked: "He [is] part of all our heritage . . . an American treasure, a friend, an original. For the rest of my life, whenever it rains . . . I will think of him and smile."[9]

Though Gene often balked at being pegged solely as a dancer, he did not reject the title. Kerry Kelly remarked of her father: "He once said he hoped most that he had made people happy."[10] By the end of his life, Gene realized it was his dancing that had accomplished this goal best. And dancing, Gene Kelly style, can never be merely dancing. "You dance love, you dance joy and you dance dreams," Gene said. "And I know if I can make you smile by jumping over a couple of couches or by running through a rainstorm, then I'll be very glad to be a song and dance man, and I won't worry that the Pittsburgh Pirates lost one hell of a short-stop."[11]

Acknowledgments

We would like to thank Kerry Kelly Novick for her invaluable contributions to our research on her father. We are grateful to Janet Lorenz at the Margaret Herrick Library for helping us gain access to previously unpublished archival material. We also extend thanks to Susan Cadman for the exhaustive research she so generously shared on her Gene Kelly tribute webpage, *Gene Kelly: Creative Genius*. We are also grateful to Patricia Towers and Sally Sherman for granting us interviews about Gene Kelly's work with Kathryn Grayson. Thanks to Eve Golden for her help editing our work. Finally, we wish to thank Sally Jervis and Amelia and Mark Brideson for their generosity, encouragement, and support throughout this endeavor.

Appendix A

Selected Stage Work

Due to the breadth of Gene's stage work, this list is only a selection of the most notable productions in which he served as star, director, and/or choreographer. Details as to director, producer, musicians, and cast are included where information is available.

Leave It to Me!
Imperial Theatre, November 9, 1938–July 15, 1939
Produced by Vinton Freedley; directed by Harry Howell; staged by Sam Spewack; choreographed by Robert Alton; music and lyrics by Cole Porter; book by Bella and Sam Spewack
Selected cast: Mary Martin, Sophie Tucker, Victor Moore, and Gene Kelly

One for the Money
Booth Theatre, February 4, 1939–May 27, 1939
Produced by Gertrude Macy and Stanley Gilkey; directed by John Murray Anderson; choreographed by Robert Alton; staged by Edward Lilley; music and lyrics by Morgan Lewis and Nancy Hamilton; music arranged by Hugh Martin; sketches by Nancy Hamilton
Selected cast: Nancy Hamilton, Keenan Wynn, Maxine Barrat, Ray Cavanaugh and His Orchestra, and Gene Kelly

The Time of Your Life
Booth Theatre, October 25, 1939–April 6, 1940; September 23, 1940–October 19, 1940
Produced by the Theatre Guild; directed by Eddie Dowling and William Saroyan; choreographed by Gene Kelly; book by William Saroyan
Selected cast: Charles De Sheim, Eddie Dowling, Gene Kelly, and Celeste Holm

Billy Rose's Diamond Horseshoe Revue
Billy Rose's Diamond Horseshoe Nightclub, Paramount Hotel, Summer
1940
Produced by Billy Rose; directed by John Murray Anderson;
choreographed by Gene Kelly

Pal Joey
Ethel Barrymore Theatre, December 24, 1940–August 16, 1941
Shubert Theatre, September 1, 1941–October 21, 1941
St. James Theatre, October 21, 1941–November 29, 1941
Produced and directed by George Abbott; choreographed by Robert
Alton; music and lyrics by Richard Rodgers and Lorenz Hart; book by
John O'Hara
Selected cast: Gene Kelly, Vivienne Segal, Jack Durant, Leila Ernst, June
Havoc, and Van Johnson

Best Foot Forward
Ethel Barrymore Theatre, October 1, 1941–July 4, 1942
Produced and directed by George Abbott; choreographed by Gene Kelly;
music and lyrics by Hugh Martin and Ralph Blane; book by John Cecil
Holm
Selected cast: June Allyson, Tommy Dix, Jack Jordan Jr., Gil Stratton Jr.,
Rosemary Lane, Nancy Walker, and Stanley Donen

Flower Drum Song
St. James Theatre, December 1, 1958–May 7, 1960
Produced by Richard Rodgers and Oscar Hammerstein II; directed by
Gene Kelly; choreographed by Carol Haney; music and lyrics by Richard
Rodgers and Oscar Hammerstein II; book by Oscar Hammerstein II and
Joseph Fields
Selected cast: Larry Blyden, Keye Luke, Juanita Hall, Miyoshi Umeki, and
Pat Suzuki

Pas de Dieux
Paris Opera House, July 6, 1960
Directed by A. M. Julien; choreographed by Gene Kelly; music by George
Gershwin
Selected cast: Claude Bessy and Corps de Ballet

Selected Stage Work

Gene Kelly's Wonderful World of Girls
International Hotel, Las Vegas, April 1970–June 1970
 Produced and directed by Greg Garrison; choreographed by Jonathan
Lucas and Tommy Tune; music by Lee Hale; written by Stanley Daniels
Selected cast: Gene Kelly, Ruth Buzzi, Kay Medford, and Joy Hawkins

Clownaround
Oakland Coliseum, Oakland, California, April 27–30, 1972
Cow Palace, San Francisco, May 2–7, 1974
Produced by Harry Lishinsky and Franklin Roberts; directed by Gene
Kelly; choreographed by Howard Jeffrey; music and lyrics by Moose
(Morris) Charlap and Alvin Cooperman; book by Alvin Cooperman
Selected cast: Gene Kelly, Ruth Buzzi, and Dennis Allen

Take Me Along
Touring show with stops including Dallas, Texas; Columbus, Ohio; and
St. Louis, Missouri, June 18, 1974–July 31, 1974
Produced and directed by John Kenley; choreographed by Leo Muller
and Gene Kelly; music and lyrics by Bob Merrill; book by Joseph Stein
and Robert Russell
Selected cast: Norwood Smith, Gene Kelly, Patricia Wilson, Russ Thacker,
and Alex Romero

Appendix B

Selected Filmography

For Me and My Gal, 1942, MGM
Produced by Arthur Freed; directed by Busby Berkeley; choreographed by Bobby Connolly, Busby Berkeley, and Gene Kelly (uncredited); musical adaptation by Roger Edens and Georgie Stoll; screenplay by Fred Finklehoffe, Richard Sherman, Sid Silvers, and Howard Emmett Rodgers
Selected cast: Judy Garland, George Murphy, Gene Kelly, Martha Eggerth, and Ben Blue

Du Barry Was a Lady, 1943, MGM
Produced by Arthur Freed; directed by Roy Del Ruth; choreographed by Charles Walters; music and lyrics by Lew Brown, Roger Edens, Ralph Freed, E. Y. Harburg, Burton Lane, and Cole Porter; screenplay by Irving Brecher
Selected cast: Lucille Ball, Red Skelton, Gene Kelly, Virginia O'Brien, and Rags Ragland

Pilot #5, 1943, MGM
Produced by B. P. Fineman; directed by George Sidney; screenplay by David Hertz
Selected cast: Franchot Tone, Gene Kelly, Van Johnson, and Marsha Hunt

Thousands Cheer, 1943, MGM
Produced by Joe Pasternak; directed by George Sidney; choreographed by Gene Kelly (uncredited); music and lyrics by Burton Lane, Lew Brown, Ralph Freed, Walter Jurmann, Paul Francis Webster, Earl Brent, E. Y. Harburg, Harold Rome, Roger Edens, Ralph Blane, Hugh Martin, Thomas Waller, Andy Razaf, Mabel Wayne, Sam M. Lewis, and Joe Young; screenplay by Paul Jarrico and Richard Collins

Selected cast: Kathryn Grayson, Gene Kelly, Mary Astor, John Boles, Judy Garland, Lena Horne, Red Skelton, Lucille Ball, and Margaret O'Brien

The Cross of Lorraine, 1943, MGM
Produced by Edwin Knopf; directed by Tay Garnett; screenplay by Michael Kanin, Ring Lardner Jr., Alexander Esway, and Robert D. Andrews
Selected cast: Jean Pierre Aumont, Gene Kelly, Peter Lorre, Sir Cedric Hardwicke, and Hume Cronyn

Cover Girl, 1944, Columbia
Produced by Arthur Schwartz; directed by Charles Vidor; choreographed by Seymour Felix, Gene Kelly (uncredited), and Stanley Donen (uncredited); music and lyrics by Jerome Kern, Fred W. Leigh, Ira Gershwin, and Henry E. Pether; screenplay by Virginia van Upp
Selected cast: Rita Hayworth, Gene Kelly, Phil Silvers, Otto Kruger, Lee Bowman, and Eve Arden

Christmas Holiday, 1944, Universal
Produced by Felix Jackson; directed by Robert Siodmak; music and lyrics by Frank Loesser and Irving Berlin; screenplay by Herman Mankiewicz
Selected cast: Deanna Durbin, Gene Kelly, Richard Whorf, and Gale Sondergaard

Combat Fatigue Irritability, 1945, United States Navy
Produced by United States Navy; directed by Gene Kelly
Selected cast: Gene Kelly, Jocelyn Brando, Harlan Warde, and Lauren Gilbert

Anchors Aweigh, 1945, MGM
Produced by Joe Pasternak; directed by George Sidney; choreographed by Jack Donohue and Gene Kelly (uncredited); original music and lyrics by Jule Stein and Sammy Cahn; screenplay by Isobel Lennart
Selected cast: Frank Sinatra, Gene Kelly, Kathryn Grayson, Dean Stockwell, Pamela Britton, and José Iturbi

Ziegfeld Follies, 1946, MGM
Produced by Arthur Freed; directed by Vincente Minnelli, Norman Taurog, Robert Lewis, Roy Del Ruth, Lemuel Ayers, and George Sidney;

choreographed by Charles Walters, Eugene Loring, and Robert Alton; music and lyrics by Harry Warren and Arthur Freed, Ralph Blane and Hugh Martin, Roger Edens and Kay Thompson, George and Ira Gershwin, and Earl Brent; screenplay by Peter Barry, David Freedman, Harry Tugend, George White, Robert Alton, Al Lewis, and Irving Brecher
Selected cast: Fred Astaire, Gene Kelly, Judy Garland, Lucille Bremer, Kathryn Grayson, Lena Horne, Fanny Brice, Victor Moore, Hume Cronyn, Keenan Wynn, and Red Skelton

Living in a Big Way, 1947, MGM
Produced by Pandro S. Berman; directed by Gregory La Cava; choreographed by Gene Kelly and Stanley Donen (uncredited); music and lyrics by Louis Alter and Edward Heyman, and Isham Jones and Gus Kahn; screenplay by Gregory La Cava and Irving Ravetch
Selected cast: Gene Kelly, Marie McDonald, Spring Byington, Charles Winninger, and Phyllis Thaxter

The Pirate, 1948, MGM
Produced by Arthur Freed; directed by Vincente Minnelli; choreographed by Robert Alton and Gene Kelly; music and lyrics by Cole Porter; screenplay by Frances Goodrich and Albert Hackett
Selected cast: Judy Garland, Gene Kelly, Gladys Cooper, Walter Slezak, and the Nicholas Brothers

The Three Musketeers, 1948, MGM
Produced by Pandro S. Berman; directed by George Sidney; screenplay by Robert Ardrey
Selected cast: Gene Kelly, Lana Turner, June Allyson, Van Heflin, Gig Young, Vincent Price, and Robert Coote

Words and Music, 1948, MGM
Produced by Arthur Freed; directed by Norman Taurog; choreographed by Robert Alton; music and lyrics by Richard Rodgers and Lorenz Hart; screenplay by Fred Finklehoffe
Selected cast: Mickey Rooney, Tom Drake, Gene Kelly, Vera-Ellen, Janet Leigh, Judy Garland, Mel Torme, Cyd Charisse, Lena Horne, and Betty Garrett

Take Me out to the Ball Game, 1949, MGM
Produced by Arthur Freed; directed by Busby Berkeley; choreographed by Busby Berkeley, Gene Kelly, and Stanley Donen (uncredited); original music and lyrics by Jean Schwartz and William Jerome, Roger Edens, and Betty Comden and Adolph Green; screenplay by Harry Tugend and George Wells (story by Gene Kelly and Stanley Donen)
Selected cast: Gene Kelly, Esther Williams, Frank Sinatra, Jules Munshin, Betty Garrett, and Edward Arnold

On the Town, 1949, MGM
Produced by Arthur Freed; directed by Gene Kelly and Stanley Donen; choreographed by Gene Kelly and Stanley Donen; music and lyrics by Betty Comden and Adolph Green, Leonard Bernstein, Lennie Hayton, and Roger Edens; screenplay by Betty Comden and Adolph Green
Selected cast: Gene Kelly, Frank Sinatra, Jules Munshin, Vera-Ellen, Ann Miller, and Betty Garrett

The Black Hand, 1950, MGM
Produced by William H. Wright; directed by Richard Thorpe; screenplay by Luther Davis
Selected cast: Gene Kelly, J. Carrol Naish, Teresa Celli, and Frank Puglia

Summer Stock, 1950, MGM
Produced by Joe Pasternak; directed by Charles Walters; choreographed by Nick Castle and Gene Kelly (uncredited); music and lyrics by Saul Chaplin, Harry Warren, Harold Arlen, Ted Koehler, Jack Brooks, and Mack Gordon; screenplay by George Wells and Sy Gomberg
Selected cast: Judy Garland, Gene Kelly, Phil Silvers, Eddie Bracken, Marjorie Main, and Gloria DeHaven

An American in Paris, 1951, MGM
Produced by Arthur Freed; directed by Vincente Minnelli; choreographed by Gene Kelly; music and lyrics by George and Ira Gershwin; screenplay by Alan Jay Lerner
Selected cast: Gene Kelly, Leslie Caron, Oscar Levant, Nina Foch, and Georges Guetary

It's a Big Country: An American Anthology, 1952, MGM
Produced by Robert Sisk; directed by Richard Thorpe, John Sturges, Charles Vidor, Don Weis, Clarence Brown, William A. Wellman, and Don Hartman; screenplay by Dore Schary, William Ludwig, Helen Deutsch, Ray Chordes, Isobel Lennart, Allen Rivkin, Lucile Schlossberg, Dorothy Kingsley, and George Wells
Selected cast: Gene Kelly, Janet Leigh, S. Z. Sakall, Ethel Barrymore, Van Johnson, Gary Cooper, Sharon McManus, and George Murphy

Singin' in the Rain, 1952, MGM
Produced by Arthur Freed; directed by Gene Kelly and Stanley Donen; choreographed by Gene Kelly and Stanley Donen; music and lyrics by Arthur Freed, Nacio Herb Brown, and Roger Edens; screenplay by Betty Comden and Adolph Green
Selected cast: Gene Kelly, Debbie Reynolds, Donald O'Connor, Jean Hagen, Cyd Charisse, and Millard Mitchell

The Devil Makes Three, 1952, MGM
Produced by Richard Goldstone; directed by Andrew Marton; screenplay by Jerry Davis
Selected cast: Gene Kelly, Pier Angeli, Richard Egan, and Richard Rober

Love Is Better Than Ever, 1952, MGM
Produced by William H. Wright; directed by Stanley Donen; screenplay by Ruth Brooks Flippen
Selected cast: Larry Parks, Elizabeth Taylor, Josephine Hutchinson, Elinor Donahue, and Gene Kelly (cameo)

Crest of the Wave, 1954, MGM
Produced by John and Roy Boulting; directed by John and Roy Boulting; screenplay by Frank Harvey and Roy Boulting
Selected cast: Gene Kelly, John Justin, Bernard Lee, and Jeff Richards

Brigadoon, 1954, MGM
Produced by Arthur Freed; directed by Vincente Minnelli; choreographed by Gene Kelly; music and lyrics by Frederick Loewe and Alan Jay Lerner; screenplay by Alan Jay Lerner

Selected cast: Gene Kelly, Van Johnson, Cyd Charisse, Elaine Stewart, and Barry Jones

Deep in My Heart, 1954, MGM
Produced by Roger Edens; directed by Stanley Donen; choreographed by Eugene Loring and Gene Kelly (uncredited); music and lyrics by Sigmund Romberg, R. Harold Atteridge, Dorothy Donnelly, Roger Edens, Alex Gerber, Oscar Hammerstein II, Otto Harbach, Ballard MacDonald, Herbert Reynolds, Cyrus Wood, and Rida Johnson Young; screenplay by Leonard Spigelgass
Selected cast: José Ferrer, Merle Oberon, Walter Pidgeon, Gene Kelly, Fred Kelly, Paul Henreid, and Rosemary Clooney

It's Always Fair Weather, 1955, MGM
Produced by Arthur Freed; directed by Gene Kelly and Stanley Donen; choreographed by Gene Kelly and Stanley Donen; music and lyrics by Betty Comden and Adolph Green; screenplay by Betty Comden, Adolph Green, and André Previn
Selected cast: Gene Kelly, Dan Dailey Jr., Michael Kidd, Cyd Charisse, and Dolores Gray

Invitation to the Dance, 1956, MGM
Produced by Arthur Freed; directed by Gene Kelly; choreographed by Gene Kelly; original music by Jacques Ibert, John Hollingsworth, and André Previn
Selected cast: Gene Kelly, Claire Sombert, Igor Youskevitch, Tamara Toumanova, and Claude Bessy

The Happy Road, 1957, MGM
Produced by Gene Kelly; directed by Gene Kelly; original music and lyrics by Georges Van Parys, Maurice Chevalier, and Gene Kelly; screenplay by Arthur Julian, Joseph Morhaim, and Harry Kurnitz
Selected cast: Gene Kelly, Barbara Laage, Bobby Clark, and Brigitte Fossey

Les Girls, 1957, MGM
Produced by Sol C. Siegel and Saul Chaplin; directed by George Cukor; choreographed by Jack Cole; original music and lyrics by Cole Porter; screenplay by John Patrick

Selected cast: Gene Kelly, Mitzi Gaynor, Kay Kendall, Taina Elg, and Jacques Bergerac

Marjorie Morningstar, 1958, Warner Bros.
Produced by Milton Sperling; directed by Irving Rapper; choreographed by Jack Baker; original music and lyrics by Sammy Fain and Paul Francis Webster; screenplay by Everett Freeman
Selected cast: Natalie Wood, Gene Kelly, Ed Wynn, Carolyn Jones, and Marty Milner

The Tunnel of Love, 1958, MGM
Produced by Joseph Fields and Martin Melcher; directed by Gene Kelly; screenplay by Joseph Fields and Jerome Chodorov
Selected cast: Doris Day, Richard Widmark, and Gig Young

Let's Make Love, 1960, Twentieth Century-Fox
Produced by Jerry Wald; directed by George Cukor; choreographed by Jack Cole; music and lyrics by Cole Porter, Sammy Cahn, and James Van Heusen; screenplay by Norman Krasna
Selected cast: Marilyn Monroe, Yves Montand, Tony Randall, Gene Kelly (cameo), Bing Crosby (cameo), and Milton Berle (cameo)

Inherit the Wind, 1960, United Artists
Produced by Stanley Kramer; directed by Stanley Kramer; screenplay by Nathan E. Douglas and Harold Jacob Smith
Selected cast: Fredric March, Spencer Tracy, Gene Kelly, and Dick York

Gigot, 1962, Seven Arts
Produced by Kenneth Hyman; directed by Gene Kelly; screenplay by John Patrick
Selected cast: Jackie Gleason, Katherine Kath, and Gabrielle Dorziat

What a Way to Go! 1964, Twentieth Century-Fox
Produced by Arthur P. Jacobs; directed by J. Lee Thompson; choreographed by Gene Kelly and Richard Humphrey; music and lyrics by Betty Comden, Adolph Green, and Jule Styne; screenplay by Betty Comden and Adolph Green

Selected cast: Shirley MacLaine, Gene Kelly, Robert Mitchum, Dick Van Dyke, Paul Newman, Dean Martin, and Robert Cummings

A Guide for the Married Man, 1967, Twentieth Century-Fox
Produced by Frank McCarthy; directed by Gene Kelly; original music and lyrics by Leslie Bricusse and Johnny Williams; screenplay by Frank Tarloff
Selected cast: Walter Matthau, Robert Morse, Inger Stevens, Lucille Ball, Art Carney, and Jayne Mansfield

The Young Girls of Rochefort, 1968, Warner Bros.–Seven Arts
Produced by Gilbert de Goldschmidt; directed by Jacques Demy; choreographed by Norman Maen, Pamela Hart, and Maureen Bright; music and lyrics by Michel Legrand, W. Earl Brown, Jacques Demy, and Julian More; screenplay by Jacques Demy
Selected cast: Catherine Deneuve, Françoise Dorléac, George Chakiris, and Gene Kelly

Hello, Dolly! 1969, Twentieth Century-Fox
Produced by Ernest Lehman; directed by Gene Kelly; choreographed by Michael Kidd; music and lyrics by Jerry Herman; screenplay by Ernest Lehman
Selected cast: Barbra Streisand, Walter Matthau, Michael Crawford, Marianne McAndrew, and Tommy Tune

The Cheyenne Social Club, 1970, National General Pictures
Produced and directed by Gene Kelly; screenplay by James Lee Barrett
Selected cast: James Stewart, Henry Fonda, and Shirley Jones

40 Carats, 1973, Columbia
Produced by M. J. Frankovich; directed by Milton Katselas; screenplay by Leonard Gershe
Selected cast: Liv Ullman, Edward Albert, Binnie Barnes, and Gene Kelly

That's Entertainment! 1974, MGM
Produced, directed, and written by Jack Haley Jr.; clips in the film include choreography by Gene Kelly, Stanley Donen, Charles Walters, and Busby Berkeley; clips include music and lyrics by George and Ira Gershwin, Arthur Freed and Nacio Herb Brown, and Ralph Blane and Hugh Martin

Selected cast (included are hosts and narrators): Gene Kelly, Fred Astaire, Liza Minnelli, Donald O'Connor, Mickey Rooney, Elizabeth Taylor, Frank Sinatra, James Stewart, and Debbie Reynolds

That's Entertainment! Part II, 1976, MGM
Produced by Saul Chaplin and Daniel Melnick; directed by Gene Kelly; new sequences choreographed by Gene Kelly (uncredited), Alex Romero, and Robin Hoctor; clips in the film include choreography by Gene Kelly, Stanley Donen, Charles Walters, and Busby Berkeley; clips include music and lyrics by George and Ira Gershwin, Arthur Freed and Nacio Herb Brown, and Alan Jay Lerner and Frederick Loewe; screenplay by Leonard Gershe
Selected cast: Gene Kelly and Fred Astaire

Viva Knievel! 1977, Warner Bros.
Produced by Stan Hough; directed by Gordon Douglas; screenplay by Antonio Santillan and Norman Katkov
Selected cast: Evel Knievel, Gene Kelly, Lauren Hutton, and Red Buttons

Xanadu, 1980, Universal
Produced by Lawrence Gordon; directed by Robert Greenwald; choreographed by Kenny Ortega and Jerry Trent; original music and lyrics by John Farrar and Jeff Lynne; screenplay by Richard Christian Danus and Marc Reid Rubel
Selected cast: Olivia Newton-John, Michael Beck, Gene Kelly, and James Sloyan

That's Dancing! 1985, MGM
Produced by Jack Haley Jr., David Niven Jr., and Gene Kelly (executive producer); directed by Jack Haley Jr.; choreographed by Alex Romero; original music by Henry Mancini; screenplay by Jack Haley Jr.
Selected cast: Mikhail Baryshnikov, Gene Kelly, Ray Bolger, Liza Minnelli, and Sammy Davis Jr.

That's Entertainment! Part III, 1994, MGM
Produced, directed, and written by Bud Friedgen and Michael J. Sheridan; clips in the film include choreography by Gene Kelly, Stanley Donen, Charles Walters, and Busby Berkeley; clips include music and lyrics by

Arthur Freed and Nacio Herb Brown, Johnny Mercer and Harry Warren, and Betty Comden and Adolph Green
Selected cast: Gene Kelly, June Allyson, Cyd Charisse, Mickey Rooney, Ann Miller, and Debbie Reynolds

Appendix C

Selected Television Work

The Life You Save, March 1, 1957, *Schlitz Playhouse*, CBS
Directed by Herschel Daugherty
Selected cast: Buddy Joe Hooker, Gene Kelly, Agnes Moorehead, and
Barbara Pepper

Dancing: A Man's Game, December 21, 1958, *Omnibus*, CBS
Choreographed by Gene Kelly
Selected cast: Gene Kelly (as himself), Mickey Mantle, Johnny Unitas,
and Sugar Ray Robinson

The Gene Kelly Show, April 24, 1959, NBC
Directed by Joseph Cates
Selected cast: Gene Kelly (as himself), Claude Bessy, Cherylene Lee, Liza
Minnelli, and Carl Sandburg

Pontiac Star Parade, November 21, 1959, NBC
Directed by Sidney Miller
Selected cast: Gene Kelly (as himself), Carol Lawrence, and Donald
O'Connor

Going My Way (series), 1962–1963, NBC
Directed by Joseph Pevney and Robert Florey
Selected cast: Gene Kelly, Dick York, Leo G. Carroll, and Ed Begley

The Julie Andrews Show, November 28, 1965, NBC
Directed by Alan Handley
Selected cast: Julie Andrews, Gene Kelly (as himself), and the New
Christy Minstrels

Gene Kelly in New York, New York, February 14, 1966, CBS
Directed by Charles S. Dubin
Selected cast: Gene Kelly (as himself), Woody Allen, Gower Champion, and Tommy Steele

Jack and the Beanstalk, February 26, 1967, NBC
Produced and directed by Gene Kelly; original music and lyrics by Sammy Cahn and Jimmy Van Heusen; teleplay by Larry Markes and Michael Morris
Selected cast: Gene Kelly, Bobby Riha, Ted Cassidy, and Marian McKnight

Gene Kelly's Wonderful World of Girls, January 14, 1970, NBC
Directed by Danny Daniels
Selected cast: Gene Kelly (as himself), Ruth Buzzi, Barbara Eden, and Diane Davis

An American in Pasadena, March 13, 1978, CBS
Directed by Buzz Kohan
Selected cast: Gene Kelly (as himself), Frank Sinatra, Lucille Ball, Cyd Charisse, Kathryn Grayson, and Liza Minnelli

The Kennedy Center Honors: A Celebration of the Performing Arts, December 25, 1982, CBS
Directed by Don Mischer
Selected cast: Gene Kelly (as himself), George Abbott, Cyd Charisse, Betty Comden, Adolph Green, Van Johnson, and Lillian Gish

"Hong Kong Cruise," parts 1 and 2, *The Love Boat* (series), February 4, 1984, ABC
Directed by Richard Kinon
Selected cast: Gene Kelly, Gavin MacLeod, Bernie Kopell, and Jill Whelan

North and South (miniseries), 1985, ABC
Directed by Richard T. Heffron
Selected cast: Kirstie Alley, David Carradine, Patrick Swayze, Gene Kelly, Johnny Cash, and Morgan Fairchild

AFI Life Achievement Award: A Tribute to Gene Kelly, May 7, 1985, CBS
Directed by Don Mischer
Selected cast: Gene Kelly (as himself), Fred Astaire, Shirley MacLaine, Mikhail Baryshnikov, Cyd Charisse, Betty Comden, Adolph Green, Leslie Caron, and Stanley Donen

Sins (miniseries), 1986, CBS
Directed by Douglas Hickox
Selected cast: Joan Collins, Gene Kelly, Timothy Dalton, and Capucine

Notes

Introduction

1. "Gene Kelly," *Photoplay,* January 1946.
2. Adolph Green's assessment is in *Gene Kelly: Anatomy of a Dancer,* dir. Robert Trachtenberg, perf. Betsy Blair, Stanley Donen, Kerry Kelly Novick (2002; New York: American Masters, 2002), DVD. For "cocky" and "jaw-jutting," see "Interviews," *American Film,* February 1979.
3. "Interviews," *American Film.*
4. Alyce Canfield, "That Old Black Magic," *Movieland,* May 1948.
5. Ibid.
6. Jane Ardmore, "Holy Man or Holy Terror?" *TV Radio Mirror,* November 1962.
7. "Gene Kelly," *Seventeen,* September 1946.
8. *Gene Kelly: Anatomy of a Dancer.*
9. Ibid.
10. "Gene Kelly," *Picturegoer,* September 1946.
11. Rudy Behlmer, *America's Favorite Movies: Behind the Scenes* (New York: F. Ungar, 1982), 157.
12. "Stanley Donen interview, February 8, 1996," Capitol Public Radio.
13. Tony Thomas, *The Films of Gene Kelly* (Secaucus, NJ: Citadel, 1974), 20.
14. *Gene Kelly: Anatomy of a Dancer.*
15. *Gene Kelly: Anatomy of a Dancer.*
16. "To Dance or Not to Dance . . . and Gene Kelly Wants YOU to Give Him the Answer," *Motion Picture,* February 1947.
17. Thomas, *The Films of Gene Kelly,* 20.
18. Graham Fuller, "And Now, the Real Kicker . . . ," *Interview,* May 1994.
19. David Reiss, "An Interview with Gene Kelly," *Premiere,* February 1981.
20. Michael Singer, *A Cut Above: 50 Film Directors Talk about Their Craft* (Los Angeles: Lone Eagle, 1998), 143.
21. *Gene Kelly: Anatomy of a Dancer.*
22. Ibid.

1. The Reluctant Dancer

1. "Sears Closing a Major Setback for East Liberty Residents," *Beaver County Times,* January 28, 1993.

2. Maxine Garrison, "Kelly's from Pittsburgh and He Is Almighty Proud of the Fact!" *Pittsburgh Press,* October 30, 1944.

3. "Those Were the Days," *Filmland,* February 1951.

4. Kimberly Powell, "Pittsburgh's Scotch Irish Heritage," *About.com,* accessed January 1, 2015, http://pittsburgh.about.com/library/weekly/aa_scotch_irish.htm.

5. Clive Hirschhorn, *Gene Kelly* (New York: St. Martin's, 1984), 5.

6. Gladys Hall, "Gene Kelly Writes a Letter," *Movie Show,* June 1946; Robert Van Gelder, "Mr. Kelly, or Pal Joey: Portrait of a Dancer, from Pennsylvania to the Barrymore Theatre," *New York Times,* March 2, 1941.

7. Betsy Blair, *The Memory of All That: Love and Politics in New York, Hollywood, and Paris* (New York: Knopf, 2003), 18–19.

8. Hirschhorn, *Gene Kelly,* 8.

9. "Sincerity, Unrehearsed Charm Percolated by the Real Gene Kelly," *Sarasota (FL) Journal,* July 20, 1976.

10. Rusty E. Frank, *Tap! The Greatest Tap Dance Stars and Their Stories, 1900–1955* (New York: William Morrow, 1990), 171.

11. Hirschhorn, *Gene Kelly,* 15.

12. John Wakeman, *World Film Directors Book: 1945–1985* (New York: H. W. Wilson, 1988), 602.

13. "Sincerity, Unrehearsed Charm Percolated by the Real Gene Kelly."

14. "Gene Kelly," *American Way,* June 1984.

15. Hirschhorn, *Gene Kelly,* 9.

16. Cynthia Millen Roberts, "Did You Really Smoke Cigarettes? An Interview with Gene Kelly," 1991, *Gene Kelly Fans,* accessed November 7, 2010, http://genekellyfans.com/blogs/%E2%80%9Cdid-you-really-smoke-cigarettes%E2%80%9D-and-other-questions-an-interview-with-gene-kelly/.

17. Hedda Hopper, "Gene Kelly Would Rather Teach," *Los Angeles Times,* July 25, 1954.

18. "André Previn and Gene Kelly," December 21, 1986, BBC Two England, television.

19. "Those Were the Days."

20. "Sincerity, Unrehearsed Charm Percolated by the Real Gene Kelly."

21. "Those Were the Days."

22. Kay Proctor, "Hey, Irish!" *Photoplay,* May 1943.

23. Ibid.

24. Alvin Yudkoff, *Gene Kelly: A Life of Dance and Dreams* (New York: Backstage Books, 1999), 3.

25. Frank, *Tap!* 171.

26. Ibid., 172.

27. John Kenrick, "Broadway in the Gay '90s," *Musicals 101,* 2000, accessed January 4, 2015, http://www.musicals101.com/1890–1900.htm.

28. Ron Weiskind, "Obituary: Harriet Joan Kelly Radvansky, Dancing Sister of Gene Kelly, Longtime West Mifflin Teacher," *Pittsburgh Post-Gazette*, April 10, 2002.

29. "Gene Kelly," *Dallas Morning News,* June 1974.

30. Kevin Thomas, "Gene Kelly Singing the Blues over State of U.S. Musicals," *Los Angeles Times,* August 30, 1966.

31. Sheridan Morley and Ruth Leon, *Gene Kelly: A Celebration* (London: Pavilion Books, 1996), 22.

32. Douglas Martin, "Fred Kelly, 83, a Dancer in a Shadow, Dies," *New York Times,* March 17, 2000.

33. Yudkoff, *Gene Kelly,* 7.

34. Ibid., 16.

35. Danny Shane, "Know This about Dancing," *Screenland Plus TV-Land,* January 1953.

2. A Depression-Era Kid

1. Christopher Rawson, *"On the Town,"* *Pittsburgh Post-Gazette,* May 27, 2000.

2. "Gene Kelly," *Parade,* August 3, 1957.

3. "Interviews," *American Film.*

4. Margy Rochlin, "Old Is New Again," *Interview,* February 1985.

5. Ardmore, "Holy Man or Holy Terror?"

6. "TV Graphic," *Pittsburgh Press,* December 9, 1962.

7. Ibid.

8. Helen Hover, "Popping Questions at Gene Kelly," *Motion Picture,* October 1944.

9. Ibid.

10. "Great Vitality," *Motion Picture,* January 1943.

11. "Gene Kelly," *Saturday Evening Post,* July 1950.

12. Frank, *Tap!* 173.

13. Yudkoff, *Gene Kelly,* 16.

14. Frederick Lewis Allen, *Only Yesterday: An Informal History of the 1920s* (1931; repr., New York: Bantam Books, 1959), 185.

15. Blair, *The Memory of All That,* 19.

16. Van Gelder, "Mr. Kelly, or Pal Joey."

17. Hirschhorn, *Gene Kelly,* 27.

18. Thomas, "Gene Kelly Singing the Blues over State of U.S. Musicals."

19. Hirschhorn, *Gene Kelly,* 28.

20. Fuller, "And Now, the Real Kicker."

21. Rosemary Layng, "Pied Piper," *Modern Screen,* July 1947.

22. Alan Jay Lerner, *The Street Where I Live* (New York: Norton, 1978), 41.

23. Yudkoff, *Gene Kelly*, 13.

24. Morley and Leon, *Gene Kelly*, 27.

25. "Gene Kelly," *Saturday Evening Post.*

26. "Old Faces: Sextuple Threat," *Time*, August 4, 1967.

27. "Gene Kelly," *Allegheny (PA) Times*, November 4, 1990.

28. Pauline Swanson, "Gene Kelly," *Dance*, September 1954.

29. Ardmore, "Holy Man or Holy Terror?"

30. Hal Rubenstein, "An American in Style," *New York Times*, April 17, 1994.

31. "Gene Kelly Goes Legit Again after 33 Years," *People*, July 8, 1974.

3. Kelly Mania

1. "Gene Kelly," *Collier's*, May 19, 1945.

2. Van Gelder, "Mr. Kelly, or Pal Joey."

3. "Gene Kelly," *Saturday Evening Post.*

4. Yudkoff, *Gene Kelly*, 25.

5. Hirschhorn, *Gene Kelly*, 32.

6. "Gene Kelly," *Saturday Evening Post.*

7. "Gene Kelly," *Collier's.*

8. "Gene Kelly," *Saturday Evening Post.*

9. Ibid.

10. Frank, *Tap!* 178.

11. *Dancing: A Man's Game*, perf. Gene Kelly, Dick Button, Mickey Mantle, Sugar Ray Robinson, *Omnibus*, December 21, 1958 (New York: NBC, 2013), DVD.

12. "Gene Kelly," *Irish America*, December 1990.

13. Yudkoff, *Gene Kelly*, 27.

14. ". . . Called It Home," *Gene Kelly: Creative Genius*, accessed March 8, 2017, www.freewebs.com/geneius/calledithome.htm.

15. Hirschhorn, *Gene Kelly*, 35.

16. Randy Whittle, *Johnstown, Pennsylvania: A History, 1937–1980* (Charleston, SC: History Press, 2007), 33.

17. Yudkoff, *Gene Kelly*, 28.

18. Ibid.

19. Hirschhorn, *Gene Kelly*, 38.

20. Jeanne Coyne, "I Knew Him When," *Movieland*, November 1948.

21. Yudkoff, *Gene Kelly*, 29.

22. Frank, *Tap!* 174.

23. Yudkoff, *Gene Kelly*, 29.

24. "Gene Kelly," *Collier's.*

25. Ann Rodgers, "Obituary: Louise Kelly Bailey, Last of Five 'Dancing Kellys,' Dies," *Pittsburgh Post-Gazette*, February 24, 2008.

26. Frank, *Tap!* 174.

27. Rodgers, "Obituary: Louise Kelly Bailey."

28. Frank, *Tap!* 179.

29. Yudkoff, *Gene Kelly,* 30.

30. Hirschhorn, *Gene Kelly,* 41.

31. Ibid., 42.

32. Yudkoff, *Gene Kelly,* 42.

33. Hover, "Popping Questions at Gene Kelly."

34. Jeffrey Spivak, e-mail interview with authors, March 31, 2014.

35. Franklin D. Roosevelt, "Address by Franklin D. Roosevelt, 1933," *Joint Congressional Committee on Inaugural Ceremonies,* accessed January 23, 2015, http://www.inaugural.senate.gov/swearing-in/event/franklin-d-roosevelt-1933.

36. Florence Fisher Parry, "On With the Show," *Pittsburgh Press,* 1933.

37. "Gene Kelly Days," *Pittsburgh Press,* June 24, 1987.

38. Alyce Canfield, "Things I Wish I Knew 10 Years Ago," *Movieland,* September 1945.

4. "It wasn't elegant, but it's me"

1. Steve Sucato, "Chicago National Association of Dance Masters Celebrates Its Past, Looks to Its Future," *Dance Studio Life,* May 1, 2012, accessed January 24, 2015, http://www.dancestudiolife.com/a-century-of-dance-education/.

2. "Gene Kelly," *Chicago Tribune,* January 4, 1970.

3. Van Gelder, "Mr. Kelly, or Pal Joey."

4. Anna Kisselgoff, "Gene Kelly: Ballet Influenced His View of Dance," *New York Times,* January 17, 1985.

5. Hirschhorn, *Gene Kelly,* 44.

6. Ibid., 45.

7. *Dancing: A Man's Game.*

8. "Gene Kelly Interview with Edward Murrow," *Person to Person,* December 19, 1958, CBS.

9. Yudkoff, *Gene Kelly,* 148.

10. *Dancing: A Man's Game.*

11. Hirschhorn, *Gene Kelly,* 46.

12. Ibid.

13. Albin Krebs, "Gene Kelly, Dancer of Vigor and Grace, Dies," *New York Times,* February 3, 1996.

14. Reiss, "An Interview with Gene Kelly."

15. Krebs, "Gene Kelly, Dancer of Vigor and Grace, Dies."

16. Philip C. DiMare, interview with authors, May 9, 2014.

17. Fred Astaire, *Steps in Time* (1959; repr., New York: Dey Street Books, 2009), 6.

18. Krebs, "Gene Kelly, Dancer of Vigor and Grace, Dies."

19. Anna Kisselgoff, "Dance View: Just a Regular Joe Doing Ballet," *New York Times,* February 11, 1996.

20. Dan Callahan, "Gene Kelly Retro at Film Society," *Alt Screen,* July 13, 2012, accessed January 28, 2015, http://altscreen.com/07/13/2012/gene-kelly-at-film-society-thru-jul-26/.

21. "Gene Kelly, Cap and Gown Director," *Pittsburgh Post-Gazette,* March 25, 1935.

22. Thomas, *The Films of Gene Kelly,* 13.

23. Yudkoff, *Gene Kelly,* 37.

24. Ibid., 38.

25. Hirschhorn, *Gene Kelly,* 49.

26. "Child Stars," *Encyclopedia of Children and Childhood in History and Society,* accessed November 10, 2014, http://www.faqs.org/childhood/Ch-Co/Child-Stars .html.

27. Frank, *Tap!* 175.

28. "Gene Returns Tie to Powell," *Pittsburgh Press,* May 16, 1943.

29. Yudkoff, *Gene Kelly,* 41–42.

30. "Short Tour Set for *Trailer Ho!*" *Pittsburgh Post-Gazette,* April 20, 1937.

31. Yudkoff, *Gene Kelly,* 44.

32. Blair, *The Memory of All That,* 3.

33. "Gene Kelly Forum," August 8, 2011, *Delphi Forums,* accessed January 26, 2015, http://forums.delphiforums.com/n/main.asp?webtag=genescene&msg=1906.63.

34. "Merry Tune Revue All Set for Opening at Playhouse," *Pittsburgh Press,* April 14, 1938.

35. Ibid.

36. Kaspar Monahan, "A Salute to the Kellys," *Pittsburgh Press,* April 27, 1938.

37. Frank, *Tap!* 171.

38. "*Hold Your Hats* High Spot of Season," *Pittsburgh Press,* April 24, 1938.

39. "Gene Kelly," *Pittsburgh Post-Gazette,* December 3, 1942.

40. Proctor, "Hey, Irish!"

41. Van Gelder, "Mr. Kelly, or Pal Joey."

42. Coyne, "I Knew Him When."

43. Morley and Leon, *Gene Kelly,* 35.

5. The Time of His Life

1. Hugh Martin, *Hugh Martin: The Boy Next Door* (Encinitas, CA: Trolley, 2010), 57, 59.

2. Stanley Green, *Ring Bells! Sing Songs! Broadway Musicals of the 1930s* (New Rochelle, NY: Arlington House, 1971), 12.

3. Vincente Minnelli, *I Remember It Well* (London: Angus and Robertson, 1975), 52.

4. Ibid., ii.

5. Lerner, *The Street Where I Live,* 42.

6. Kisselgoff, "Gene Kelly: Ballet Influenced His View of Dance."

7. Brent Phillips, *Charles Walters: The Man Who Taught Hollywood to Dance* (Lexington: University Press of Kentucky, 2014), 32.

8. "An Evening with Gene Kelly," *Film 74*, BBC One, November 5, 1974.

9. Yudkoff, *Gene Kelly*, 47.

10. "Gene Kelly," *Movie Stars Parade*, July 1947.

11. Hirschhorn, *Gene Kelly*, 46.

12. Ibid., 56.

13. Yudkoff, *Gene Kelly*, 54.

14. Morley and Leon, *Gene Kelly*, 38–39.

15. Hirschhorn, *Gene Kelly*, 55.

16. Ibid., 56.

17. Ibid., 54.

18. "Gene Kelly Forum," Delphi Forums, August 8, 2011, accessed January 26, 2015, http://forums.delphiforums.com/n/main.asp?webtag=genescene&msg=1906.63.

19. Brooks Atkinson, "The Play," *New York Times*, November 10, 1938.

20. Morley and Leon, *Gene Kelly*, 39.

21. "One for the Money," *Pittsburgh Press*, March 30, 1939.

22. Howard Sharpe, "I Knew Him When," *Modern Screen*, October 1946.

23. Morley and Leon, *Gene Kelly*, 39.

24. Martin, *The Boy Next Door*, 87.

25. Ibid., 85.

26. Brooks Atkinson, "The Play," *New York Times*, February 6, 1939.

27. Yudkoff, *Gene Kelly*, 55.

28. Harold W. Cohen, "The Drama Desk: Local Girl," *Pittsburgh Post-Gazette*, June 29, 1939.

29. Van Gelder, "Mr. Kelly, or Pal Joey."

30. Hirschhorn, *Gene Kelly*, 60.

31. Van Gelder, "Mr. Kelly, or Pal Joey."

32. Hirschhorn, *Gene Kelly*, 62.

33. Ibid.

34. Richard Somerset Ward, *An American Theatre: The Story of Westport Country Playhouse, 1931–2005* (New Haven, CT: Yale University Press, 2005), 286.

35. Lawrence Fellows, "Westport Playhouse, a Stable of Talent," *New York Times*, June 11, 1976.

36. Paul Robeson Jr., *The Undiscovered Paul Robeson: Quest for Freedom* (Hoboken, NJ: John Wiley and Sons, 2010), 18.

37. Lawrence Fellows, "Westport Playhouse: A Stable of Talent," *New York Times*, June 11, 1976.

38. *Gene Kelly: Anatomy of a Dancer.*

39. Hirschhorn, *Gene Kelly*, 63.

40. William Baer, "Singin' in the Rain: A Conversation with Betty Comden and Adolph Green," *Michigan Quarterly Review,* Winter 2002.

41. Morley and Leon, *Gene Kelly,* 40.

42. Blair, *The Memory of All That,* 20.

43. Ibid., 12.

44. Hirschhorn, *Gene Kelly,* 65.

45. Blair, *The Memory of All That,* 12.

46. Yudkoff, *Gene Kelly,* 61.

47. William Saroyan, *The Time of Your Life* (New York: Harcourt, Brace, 1939), 43.

48. Harold Cohen, "The Drama Desk," *Pittsburgh Post-Gazette,* September 4, 1940.

49. Saroyan, *The Time of Your Life,* 95.

50. "Grek Gormick, from Sleeve Notes, Totem Records, *On the Air,* September 1980."

51. Brooks Atkinson, "The Play," *New York Times,* October 26, 1939.

52. "Gene Kelly," *Saturday Evening Post.*

53. Atkinson, "The Play," October 26, 1939.

54. Lerner, *The Street Where I Live,* 137.

55. Murray Schumach, "Score on a Hollywood Music Man," *New York Times,* February 16, 1964.

56. John Kobal, *People Will Talk* (New York: Knopf, 1986), 650.

57. Blair, *The Memory of All That,* 9.

58. Ibid., 8–9.

59. "Gene Kelly and Billy Rose," *Radio Times* (London), October 1972.

60. Blair, *The Memory of All That,* 9.

61. Ibid., 12.

62. Ibid.

63. "Playbill, *Billy Rose Diamond Horseshoe Review,*" circa November 1940.

64. Blair, *The Memory of All That,* 18.

65. Ibid.

66. Ibid., 28.

67. "Gene Kelly Forum."

68. "Musical Revue Opens," *New York Times,* June 25, 1940.

69. "Some New Faces," *New York Times,* July 28, 1940.

6. Bewitched, Bothered, and Bewildered

1. "Pal Joey," *Movieland,* April 1943.

2. Mark Vieira, *Majestic Hollywood: The Greatest Films of 1939* (New York: Running Press, 2013), 5.

3. John O'Hara, *Pal Joey,* in *American Musicals: 1927–1949,* ed. Laurence Maslon (New York: Library of America), 187.

4. Richard Rodgers, *Musical Stages: An Autobiography* (Cambridge, MA: Harvard University Press, 2002), 198.

5. O'Hara, *Pal Joey*, 222.

6. Rodgers, *Musical Stages*, 202.

7. O'Hara, *Pal Joey*, 170.

8. Ibid., 188.

9. Morley and Leon, *Gene Kelly*, 43.

10. Hirschhorn, *Gene Kelly*, 73.

11. "Gene Kelly Talks about *Pal Joey*," *Allegheny (PA) Times*, November 4, 1990.

12. Van Gelder, "Mr. Kelly, or Pal Joey."

13. Blair, *The Memory of All That*, 22–23.

14. Van Johnson, "Just One of Us," *Movie Fan*, July 1954.

15. Hall, "Gene Kelly Writes a Letter."

16. Blair, *The Memory of All That*, 18.

17. Phillips, *Charles Walters*, 57.

18. Blair, *The Memory of All That*, 16.

19. Susan Dominus, "Betsy Blair: An Independent Woman," *New York Times*, December 22, 2009.

20. Blair, *The Memory of All That*, 12.

21. Ibid., 17.

22. Ibid., 57–58.

23. Frederica Boger, "My Kids, the Kellys," *Photoplay*, February 1949.

24. Blair, *The Memory of All That*, 29.

25. "Gene Kelly Reflects on *Pal Joey*," *Pittsburgh Press*, December 16, 1948.

26. "Van Johnson Remembers Gene Kelly," *Movie Show*, October 1947.

27. Van Gelder, "Mr. Kelly, or Pal Joey."

28. Ibid.

29. "A Professional Heel Is Really Man with a Soul," *New London (CT) Day*, February 17, 1941.

30. Harold W. Cohen, "The Drama Desk: Directing His Goal," *Pittsburgh Post-Gazette*, September 4, 1940.

31. Hirschhorn, *Gene Kelly*, 75.

32. Ibid.

33. "*Pal Joey*," *New York Times*, December 27, 1940.

34. Stephen M. Silverman, *Dancing on the Ceiling: Stanley Donen and His Movies* (New York: Knopf, 1996), 30.

35. "*Pal Joey*," *New York Times*; Frank Rich, "*Pal Joey*, 50 Years Older, but Also New," *New York Times*, July 24, 1990.

36. "Gene Kelly," *Saturday Evening Post*.

37. John Martin, "The Dance: Pal Kelly," *New York Times*, June 8, 1941.

38. Ibid.

39. Van Gelder, "Mr. Kelly, or Pal Joey."

40. Silverman, *Dancing on the Ceiling*, 28.

41. "Van Johnson Remembers Gene Kelly."

42. Ibid.

43. "Gene Kelly and Van Johnson," *Picture Show,* September 25, 1943.

44. Phillips, *Charles Walters,* 32.

45. Van Gelder, "Mr. Kelly, or Pal Joey."

46. Gerold Frank, *Judy* (Boston: Da Capo, 1999), 170.

47. Ibid.

48. Blair, *The Memory of All That,* 94.

49. Ibid., 29.

50. Hirschhorn, *Gene Kelly,* 87.

51. Peter Hay, *MGM: When the Lion Roars* (New York: Turner, 1991), 78.

52. Thomas, *The Films of Gene Kelly,* 27.

53. Hugh Fordin, *MGM's Greatest Musicals: The Arthur Freed Unit* (Boston: Da Capo, 1996), 61.

54. Morley and Leon, *Gene Kelly,* 48.

55. Blair, *The Memory of All That,* 30.

56. Ibid., 35–36.

57. Ibid., 26.

58. Hirschhorn, *Gene Kelly,* 83.

59. Yudkoff, *Gene Kelly,* 87.

60. Blair, *The Memory of All That,* 36.

61. "Actor Gene Kelly to Direct Comedy at Shubert September 11," *Hartford (CT) Courant,* August 31, 1941.

62. Martin, *The Boy Next Door,* 126.

63. Ibid., 145.

64. Silverman, *Dancing on the Ceiling,* 32.

65. Ibid., 35.

66. Gene Kelly, "A Letter to My Daughter Kerry," *Silver Screen,* March 1943.

67. Blair, *The Memory of All That,* 36.

68. Ibid., 36–37.

69. Brooks Atkinson, "The Play," *New York Times,* October 2, 1941.

70. Martin, *The Boy Next Door,* 141.

71. Blair, *The Memory of All That,* 81.

72. "Musical Comedy Is a Serious Business," *Theatre Arts,* December 1958.

73. Martin, "The Dance."

7. At the MGM University

1. Ibid.

2. "'I Never Intended Staying In Hollywood': An Interview with Gene Kelly," *Photoplay,* August 1975.

3. Blair, *The Memory of All That,* 82, 84.

4. Ibid., 84.

5. Ibid., 85.

6. Ibid., 86.

7. Ibid., 90.

8. Ibid.

9. Hirschhorn, *Gene Kelly*, 90.

10. Blair, *The Memory of All That*, 143.

11. Ibid., 105, 204.

12. Ibid., 105–6.

13. Arthur Laurents, *Original Story By: A Memoir of Broadway and Hollywood* (New York: Applause Theatre and Cinema Books, 2000), 92.

14. Blair, *The Memory of All That*, 252.

15. "On *Combat Fatigue Irritability*: Kerry Kelly Novick," *Circulating Now*, March 12, 2014.

16. Blair, *The Memory of All That*, 104.

17. Fuller, "And Now, the Real Kicker."

18. Lerner, *The Street Where I Live*, 42.

19. Minnelli, *I Remember It Well*, 112–15.

20. Fordin, *MGM's Greatest Musicals*, 33.

21. John Updike, *More Matter: Essays and Criticism* (New York: Random House, 1999), 665.

22. Yudkoff, *Gene Kelly*, 103.

23. Scott Eyman, *Lion of Hollywood: The Life and Legend of Louis B. Mayer* (New York: Simon and Schuster, 2005), 303.

24. Neal Gabler, *An Empire of Their Own: How the Jews Invented Hollywood* (New York: Anchor Books, 1988), 79.

25. Eyman, *Lion of Hollywood*, 83–85.

26. Gabler, *An Empire of Their Own*, 80.

27. "Gene Kelly, BBC Interview, 1974."

28. Hirschhorn, *Gene Kelly*, 93.

29. Fredrica Boger, "My Kids, the Kellys."

30. Blair, *The Memory of All That*, 92.

31. Lerner, *The Street Where I Live*, 136.

32. Blair, *The Memory of All That*, 143.

33. Debbie Reynolds, *Debbie: My Life* (New York: William Morrow, 1988), 64–66.

34. Paul Marsh, "Interview with Gene Kelly," *Screenland*, May 1947.

35. Hirschhorn, *Gene Kelly*, 147.

36. Blair, *The Memory of All That*, 93–94.

37. Ibid., 93.

38. Ibid., 159.

39. "Spotlight on the Stars," *Middletown Times Herald*, October 17, 1946.

40. Updike, *More Matter*, 667.

41. John Fricke, *Judy Garland: World's Greatest Entertainer* (New York: Henry Holt, 1992), 70.

42. Hirschhorn, *Gene Kelly*, 98.

43. Updike, *More Matter*, 666.

44. *For Me and My Gal*, dir. Busby Berkeley, perf. Judy Garland, Gene Kelly, George Murphy (1942; Hollywood: MGM, 2006), DVD.

45. "Gene Kelly on Judy Garland," *Picture Show*, September 25, 1943.

46. Blair, *The Memory of All That*, 92.

47. "Gene Kelly," *Liberty Magazine Then and Now*, Summer 1976.

48. Minnelli, *I Remember It Well*, 185.

49. Blair, *The Memory of All That*, 92.

50. John Fricke and Lorna Luft, *Judy Garland: A Portrait in Art and Anecdote* (New York: Bulfinch, 2003), 107.

51. Harold W. Cohen, "The Drama Desk: Going Up," *Pittsburgh Post-Gazette*, June 8, 1942.

52. Fordin, *MGM's Greatest Musicals*, 66.

53. Jeffrey Spivak, *Buzz: The Life and Art of Busby Berkeley* (Lexington: University Press of Kentucky, 2010), 193.

54. Proctor, "Hey, Irish!"

55. Thomas, *The Films of Gene Kelly*, 19.

56. "Cinema: The New Pictures," *Time*, November 16, 1942; Bosley Crowther, "*For Me and My Gal*, a Musical Moving Picture Concerned with Vaudeville, Makes Its Appearance at the Astor," *New York Times*, October 22, 1942.

57. "Gene Kelly on Acting," *TV and Movie Screen*, August 1975.

58. "Gene Kelly," *Chicago Tribune*, January 23, 1944.

59. Updike, *More Matter*, 667.

60. *Gene Kelly: Anatomy of a Dancer*.

61. "*Pilot #5* Press Book," 1943.

62. Thomas, *The Films of Gene Kelly*, 96.

63. "At Loew's State," *New York Times*, June 25, 1943.

64. Phillips, *Charles Walters*, 57.

65. Fuller, "And Now, the Real Kicker."

66. Phillips, *Charles Walters*, 57.

67. Fordin, *MGM's Greatest Musicals*, 71.

68. Ibid.

69. Bosley Crowther, "*Du Barry Was a Lady* Mirthful Newcomer at the Capitol," *New York Times*, August 20, 1943.

70. "The Shadow Stage," *Photoplay*, July 1943.

71. "Gene Kelly," *Films Illustrated* (UK), August 1980.

72. Silverman, *Dancing on the Ceiling,* 39.

73. Frederick C. Othman, "12 Pounds of False Hair No Help While Dancing," *St. Petersburg (FL) Times,* October 20, 1942.

74. "Gene Kelly," *Silver Screen,* April 1947.

75. Blair, *The Memory of All That,* 109.

76. George Benjamin, "Kelly Is the Name," *Modern Screen,* August 1944.

77. "Gene Kelly: Hottest Thing in Town," *Movieland,* April 1943.

78. Proctor, "Hey, Irish!"

79. Blair, *The Memory of All That,* 113.

8. New Heights

1. "Gene Kelly," *Motion Picture,* January 1943.

2. "Gene Kelly," *Seventeen.*

3. "Gene Kelly, First to Dress Like a Slob," *Nova,* July 1972.

4. Blair, *The Memory of All That,* 112–13.

5. Hay, *MGM,* 165.

6. "Wartime Hollywood," *Digital History,* University of Houston, accessed April 13, 2015, http://www.digitalhistory.uh.edu/teachers/modules/ww2/wartimeholly wood.html.

7. *Gene Kelly: Anatomy of a Dancer.*

8. "Joe Pasternak on Gene Kelly," *Gene Kelly: Creative Genius,* accessed April 3, 2015, http://www.freewebs.com/geneius/moviesthatweknow.htm.

9. Leo Verswijver, *Movies Were Always Magical: Interviews with 19 Actors, Directors and Producers* (Jefferson, NC: McFarland, 2003), 57.

10. *Thousands Cheer,* dir. George Sidney, perf. Gene Kelly, Kathryn Grayson, José Iturbi (1943; Hollywood: MGM, 2009), DVD.

11. "Joe Pasternak on Gene Kelly."

12. Silverman, *Dancing on the Ceiling,* 55.

13. Hirschhorn, *Gene Kelly,* 105.

14. *Gene Kelly: Anatomy of a Dancer.*

15. Howard Barnes, "*Thousands Cheer,*" *New York Herald Tribune,* September 13, 1943.

16. Jeanine Basinger, *Gene Kelly* (New York: Book Service, 1978), 78.

17. Marsh, "Interview with Gene Kelly."

18. Marsh, "Interview with Gene Kelly."

19. "*The Cross of Lorraine* at Loew's State," *New York Times,* December 3, 1943.

20. Philip Scheuer, "Gene Kelly's Real Life Symbolized by Dance," *Los Angeles Times,* April 23, 1944.

21. Hirschhorn, *Gene Kelly,* 107–8.

22. *Cover Girl,* dir. Charles Vidor, perf: Gene Kelly, Rita Hayworth, Phil Silvers (1944; Hollywood: Columbia Studios, 1992), videocassette.

23. Blair, *The Memory of All That*, 115.

24. Silverman, *Dancing on the Ceiling*, 87.

25. Silverman, *Dancing on the Ceiling*, 48.

26. "*Cover Girl*," *Milwaukee Journal*, May 7, 1944.

27. Blair, *The Memory of All That*, 114.

28. Benjamin, "Kelly Is the Name."

29. Saul Chaplin, *The Golden Age of Movie Musicals and Me* (Norman: University of Oklahoma Press, 1994), 87.

30. "On *Combat Fatigue Irritability*."

31. Blair, *The Memory of All That*, 82.

32. Lerner, *The Street Where I Live*, 33.

33. Yudkoff, *Gene Kelly*, 58.

34. Silverman, *Dancing on the Ceiling*, 58.

35. Benjamin, "Kelly Is the Name."

36. Chaplin, *Golden Age of Movie Musicals*, 89.

37. Hirschhorn, *Gene Kelly*, 111.

38. Ibid., 110.

39. Silverman, *Dancing on the Ceiling*, 61.

40. Benjamin, "Kelly Is the Name."

41. Ibid.

42. Silverman, *Dancing on the Ceiling*, 64.

43. "Gene Kelly," *Screen Album*, Winter 1952.

44. *Gene Kelly: Anatomy of a Dancer*.

45. Silverman, *Dancing on the Ceiling*, 64.

46. "Gene Kelly Lecture," *Guardian*, May 1980.

47. Bosley Crowther, "*Cover Girl* with Rita Hayworth and Gene Kelly at the Music Hall," *New York Times*, March 31, 1944.

48. Benjamin, "Kelly Is the Name."

49. "Gene Kelly," *Current Biography*, December 1945.

50. Silverman, *Dancing on the Ceiling*, 64.

51. Hirschhorn, *Gene Kelly*, 119.

52. Jeanine Basinger, "Gene Kelly," *American Film*, March 1985.

53. "Gene Kelly," *Current Biography*.

54. "Theater Gossip," *Evening Independent* (Massillon, OH), July 20, 1944.

55. Bosley Crowther, "The Screen," *New York Times*, July 29, 1944.

56. Hirschhorn, *Gene Kelly*, 115.

57. "Gene Kelly Does a Job for Uncle Sam," *Screenland*, September 1944.

58. "Gene Kelly Does a Job for Uncle Sam."

59. Scheuer, "Gene Kelly's Real Life Symbolized by Dance."

60. *Musicals, Great Musicals: The Arthur Freed Unit at MGM*, dir. David

Thompson, perf. Hugh Fordin, Cyd Charisse, Mickey Rooney (1996; Hollywood: Turner Entertainment, 1996), videocassette.

61. Mark Griffin, *A Hundred or More Hidden Things: The Life and Films of Vincente Minnelli* (Cambridge, MA: Da Capo, 2010), 82.

62. Blair, *The Memory of All That,* 104.

63. Ibid., 95.

64. Maxine Garrison, "Gene Kelly," *Pittsburgh Press,* October 30, 1944.

65. "Gene Kelly," *Screen Album,* Fall 1945.

66. Blair, *The Memory of All That,* 99–100.

67. Ibid., 100–101, 108.

68. "Gene Kelly Talks about MGM," *St. Petersburg (FL) Times,* August 4, 1984.

69. "Gene Kelly," *Screen Album,* Winter 1952.

9. "I'm asking for the Navy"

1. Kobal, *People Will Talk,* 642.

2. Minnelli, *I Remember It Well,* 116.

3. Kobal, *People Will Talk,* 643.

4. Aljean Harmetz, *The Making of "The Wizard of Oz"* (New York: Knopf, 1977), 7.

5. *Musicals, Great Musicals.*

6. Frank, *Judy,* 330.

7. Eyman, *Lion of Hollywood,* 330.

8. *Musicals, Great Musicals.*

9. Gerald Clarke, *Get Happy: The Life of Judy Garland* (New York: Delta, 2001), 209, 210.

10. Eyman, *Lion of Hollywood,* 328.

11. Minnelli, *I Remember It Well,* 96.

12. Ibid., 141.

13. Astaire, *Steps in Time,* 257.

14. Kobal, *People Will Talk,* 645.

15. Minnelli, *I Remember It Well,* 124.

16. Oscar Levant, *Memoirs of an Amnesiac* (Hollywood: Samuel French, 1989), 203.

17. Jack Wintz, "Gene Kelly," *St. Anthony Messenger* (Cincinnati), August 1980.

18. Updike, *More Matter,* 661.

19. *Gene Kelly: Anatomy of a Dancer.*

20. "*Cover Girl,*" *Photoplay,* June 1944.

21. Benjamin, "Kelly Is the Name."

22. Peter J. Levinson, *Puttin' on the Ritz: Fred Astaire and the Fine Art of Panache* (New York: St. Martin's, 2009), 186.

23. Thomas, *The Films of Gene Kelly*, 68.

24. Ira Gershwin, "The Babbitt and the Bromide," in *Ira Gershwin: Selected Lyrics*, ed. Robert Kimball (New York: Library of America, 2009), 35.

25. Kobal, *People Will Talk*, 648.

26. Minnelli, *I Remember It Well*, 144.

27. Hopper, "Gene Kelly Would Rather Teach."

28. Fordin, *MGM's Greatest Musicals*, 137.

29. Griffin, *A Hundred or More Hidden Things*, 84.

30. Edwin Schallert, "'Follies' Splendiferous Show," *Los Angeles Times*, April 9, 1946.

31. Bosley Crowther, "The Screen," *New York Times*, March 23, 1946.

32. Astaire, *Steps in Time*, 167.

33. Wanda Hale, "*Anchors Aweigh*," *New York Daily News*, July 20, 1945.

34. Eileen Creelman, "*Anchors Aweigh*," *New York Sun*, July 20, 1945.

35. *Anchors Aweigh*, dir. George Sidney, perf. Gene Kelly, Frank Sinatra, Kathryn Grayson (1945; Hollywood: MGM, 2000), DVD.

36. Yudkoff, *Gene Kelly*, 148.

37. "Isobel Lennart Brilliantly Word-Paints the Real Gene Kelly," *Screen Stars*, February 1946.

38. James Kaplan, *Frank: The Voice* (New York: Anchor, 2011), 217.

39. Ibid., 218.

40. Ibid.

41. Hirschhorn, *Gene Kelly*, 123.

42. Rubenstein, "An American in Style."

43. Marsh, "Interview with Gene Kelly."

44. Kaplan, *Frank*, 219.

45. Susan Cadman, e-mail interview with authors, January 5, 2015.

46. Marsh, "Interview with Gene Kelly."

47. Verswijver, *Movies Were Always Magical*, 57.

48. Sally Sherman, interview with authors, March 4, 2016.

49. Patricia Towers, interview with authors, March 5, 2016.

50. Hirschhorn, *Gene Kelly*, 119.

51. Silverman, *Dancing on the Ceiling*, 68, 69.

52. Ibid., 70.

53. Yudkoff, *Gene Kelly*, 145.

54. Blair, *The Memory of All That*, 131.

55. Virginia MacPherson, "Gene Kelly Dancing His Head Off," *Pittsburgh Post-Gazette*, November 9, 1944.

56. Silverman, *Dancing on the Ceiling*, 71.

57. Hirschhorn, *Gene Kelly*, 120.

58. Ralph Freed, "The Worry Song," 1944, *Angelfire*, accessed September 3, 2016, http://www.angelfire.com/musicals/thats_entertainment/worrysong.html.

59. "Gene Kelly and the Mouse," *Theatre Arts,* October 1945.

60. Thomas, *The Films of Gene Kelly,* 65.

61. Howard Barnes, "*Anchors Aweigh,*" *New York Herald-Tribune,* July 20, 1945.

62. "The New Pictures," *Time,* July 30, 1945.

63. Bosley Crowther, "The Screen," *New York Times,* July 20, 1945.

64. Marsh, "Interview with Gene Kelly."

65. Yudkoff, *Gene Kelly,* 150.

66. Ibid., 150–51.

67. Ibid., 149.

68. "Gene Kelly Has His Physical at Draft Center," *Los Angeles Times,* November 21, 1944.

69. MacPherson, "Gene Kelly Dancing His Head Off."

70. Blair, *The Memory of All That,* 117.

71. Chaplin, *Golden Age of Movie Musicals,* 66.

72. Ibid., 65, 66.

73. "Gene Kelly, Looking Back," *St. Louis Post-Dispatch,* July 1, 1974.

74. Blair, *The Memory of All That,* 134, 117.

75. "Gene Kelly," *Movieland,* Summer 1946.

76. "Actor's Locks Shorn for Biggest Role in World Drama," *San Diego Hoist,* December 8, 1944.

77. "Gene Kelly," *Movieland,* Summer 1946.

78. Hirschhorn, *Gene Kelly,* 124.

79. Ibid.

80. "On *Combat Fatigue Irritability.*"

81. Ibid.

82. Ibid.

83. Blair, *The Memory of All That,* 121, 122.

84. Ibid., 123.

85. "Where's Kelly?" *Photoplay,* November 1945.

86. James E. Wise and Anne Collier Rehill, *Stars in Blue: Movie Actors in America's Sea Services* (Annapolis, MD: Naval Institute Press, 1997), 185.

87. Hirschhorn, *Gene Kelly,* 125.

10. The American Line

1. "Gene Kelly," *Movie Show,* June 1946.

2. *Combat Fatigue Irritability,* dir. Gene Kelly, perf. Gene Kelly, Jocelyn Brando, Harlan Warde (Washington, DC: United States Navy, 1945).

3. Ibid.

4. "On *Combat Fatigue Irritability.*"

5. Kerry Kelly Novick, telephone interview with authors, June 25, 2014.

6. "On *Combat Fatigue Irritability.*"

7. Blair, *The Memory of All That*, 124.

8. Maynard, "This Is about Gene Kelly."

9. Wise and Rehill, *Stars in Blue*, 185.

10. Maynard, "This Is about Gene Kelly."

11. "On Gene Kelly's Navy Service," *Motion Picture*, February 1951.

12. Wise and Rehill, *Stars in Blue*, 185.

13. "Harry S. Truman: The President's News Conference on V.E. Day," *The American Presidency Project*, accessed May 6, 2015, http://www.presidency.ucsb .edu/ws/?pid=12248.

14. Blair, *The Memory of All That*, 124.

15. "Everything Happens to Kelly," *Photoplay*, November 1945.

16. Blair, *The Memory of All That*, 125.

17. Hirschhorn, *Gene Kelly*, 126.

18. Ibid., 128.

19. Blair, *The Memory of All That*, 124.

20. Wise and Rehill, *Stars in Blue*, 186.

21. Ibid.

22. Yudkoff, *Gene Kelly*, 148.

23. Lois McClelland, "The Neighbors Are Talking," *Motion Picture*, February 1950.

24. "Gene Kelly Returns Home," *Movie Show*, June 1946.

25. Blair, *The Memory of All That*, 125.

26. Ibid., 123.

27. McClelland, "The Neighbors Are Talking."

28. "Gene Kelly," *Movieland*, Summer 1946.

29. Gladys Hall, "Gene Kelly Writes a Letter," *Movie Show*, June 1946.

30. "Gene Kelly," *Photoplay*.

31. Fordin, *MGM's Greatest Musicals*, 203.

32. Hirschhorn, *Gene Kelly*, 130.

33. "Gene Kelly, Handyman," *Movieland*, Summer 1946.

34. Blair, *The Memory of All That*, 126, 212.

35. Coyne, "I Knew Him When."

36. Novick, interview with authors.

37. "On *Combat Fatigue Irritability*."

38. Novick, interview with authors.

39. Yudkoff, *Gene Kelly*, 161.

40. Blair, *The Memory of All That*, 125.

41. Coyne, "I Knew Him When."

42. Yudkoff, *Gene Kelly*, 186, 165.

43. Novick, interview with authors.

44. Blair, *The Memory of All That*, 135.

45. "Gene Kelly," *Screen Album*, Winter.

46. Blair, *The Memory of All That*, 146.

47. Ibid., 196.

48. Ibid., 132.

49. Ibid., 133.

50. Hirschhorn, *Gene Kelly*, 153.

51. Thomas, *The Films of Gene Kelly*, 71.

52. Marsh, "Interview with Gene Kelly."

53. *"Living in a Big Way," Silver Screen*, April 1947.

54. "The Most Natural Guy," *Movieland*, January 1947.

55. Silverman, *Dancing on the Ceiling*, 86.

56. Hirschhorn, *Gene Kelly*, 130.

57. Adela Rogers St. Johns, "Gene Kelly Mediates Strike," *Photoplay*, January 1947.

58. Ronald Davis, *Van Johnson: MGM's Golden Boy* (Jackson: University Press of Mississippi, 2001), 100.

59. St. Johns, "Gene Kelly Mediates Strike."

60. "The Tenney Committee," *Eugene Register Guard*, June 19, 1949.

61. Yudkoff, *Gene Kelly*, 160.

62. "Gene Kelly, Democrat," *Silver Screen*, April 1947.

63. "Gene Kelly," *Movieland*, June 1947.

64. *"Living in a Big Way* . . . Has Lots of Things Which Should Appeal to the Average Moviegoer," *Daytona Beach (FL) Morning Journal*, November 12, 1947.

65. Thomas, "Gene Kelly Singing the Blues over State of U.S. Musicals."

66. "To Dance or Not to Dance."

67. Ibid.

68. Earl J. Hess and Pratibha A. Dabholkar, *The Cinematic Voyage of "The Pirate"* (Columbia: University Press of Missouri, 2014), 58.

11. A Flaming Trail of Masculinity

1. Ibid., xiii.

2. Ibid., 8.

3. "Gene Kelly on *The Pirate*," *Dallas Times Herald*, June 1980.

4. Hess and Dabholkar, *"The Pirate,"* 58.

5. Ibid., 58, 173.

6. Ibid., 61.

7. Ibid., 125.

8. Minnelli, *I Remember It Well*, 179.

9. John Cutts, "Kelly, Dancer, Actor, Director," *Films and Filming*, August/September 1964.

10. Hess and Dabholkar, *"The Pirate,"* 95.

11. Philip Scheuer, "Kelly's Luster as Dancer Undimmed by Absence," *Los Angeles Times,* March 30, 1947.

12. Hess and Dabholkar, "*The Pirate,*" 104.

13. Cole Porter, "Mack the Black," 1947, *StLyrics,* accessed September 3, 2016, http://www.stlyrics.com/lyrics/thepirate/macktheblack.htm.

14. Hess and Dabholkar, "*The Pirate,*" 73, 63.

15. Lela Simone, oral history, 1990, Margaret Herrick Library, Los Angeles.

16. Hess and Dabholkar, "*The Pirate,*" 89.

17. Minnelli, *I Remember It Well,* 186, 187.

18. Ibid., 187.

19. *The Pirate,* dir. Vincente Minnelli, perf. Judy Garland, Gene Kelly, Walter Slezak (1948; Hollywood: MGM, 2007), DVD.

20. Hess and Dabholkar, "*The Pirate,*" 108.

21. Burt Prelutsky, *The Secret of Their Success: Interviews with Legends and Luminaries* (Santa Monica, CA: Expanding Books, 2008), 166.

22. Hess and Dabholkar, "*The Pirate,*" 114.

23. Ibid., 115.

24. *The Pirate.*

25. Updike, *More Matter,* 661.

26. *Gene Kelly: Anatomy of a Dancer.*

27. "Gene Kelly," *Reflections on the Silver Screen,* February 2, 1994, television interview.

28. Hess and Dabholkar, "*The Pirate,*" 118, 167.

29. Ibid., 119.

30. Ibid., 122–23.

31. Ibid., 123.

32. Griffin, *A Hundred or More Hidden Things,* 35.

33. Sheryl Flatow, "Gene Kelly," *Biography,* March 1999.

34. Emmanuel Levy, "*Pirate:* Judy Garland's Paranoia and Breakdown," *Cinema 24/7,* July 5, 2006, http://emanuellevy.com/comment/the-pirate-judy-garlands-paranoia-and-breakdown-7/.

35. Laurents, *Original Story By,* 96.

36. "Gene Kelly," *Deseret News* (Salt Lake City), September 20, 1947.

37. Minnelli, *I Remember It Well,* 194–95.

38. Emanuel Levy, *Vincente Minnelli: Hollywood's Dark Dreamer* (New York: St. Martin's, 2009), 169.

39. Phillips, *Charles Walters,* 96.

40. Ibid., 97.

41. Levinson, *Puttin' on the Ritz,* 158.

42. Louella Parsons, "Gene Kelly May Never Dance Again," *St. Petersburg Times,* October 16, 1947.

43. Laurents, *Original Story By*, 95.

44. "*Easter Parade* Production," *The Judy Room*, 1999, accessed May 20, 2015, http://thejudyroom.com/ep/index.html.

45. Blair, *The Memory of All That*, 196.

46. Minnelli, *I Remember It Well*, 197.

47. Yudkoff, *Gene Kelly*, 173.

48. Patrick McGilligan and Paul Buhle, *Tender Comrades: A Backstory of the Hollywood Blacklist* (Minneapolis: University of Minnesota Press, 1997), 312.

49. Cadman, "We're on the Left."

50. Blair, *The Memory of All That*, 197.

51. "*The Pirate*," *The Judy Room*, 1999, accessed September 4, 2016, http://www.thejudyroom.com/thepirate.html.

52. Hess and Dabholkar, "*The Pirate*," 130.

53. Ibid., 140, 151.

54. Ibid., 153.

55. "Gene Kelly: Profile of a Dance Master," *Shadowsandsatin*, August 2012, accessed September 4, 2016,https://shadowsandsatin.wordpress.com/2012/08/20/gene-kelly-profile-of-a-dance-master/.

56. Basinger, "Gene Kelly."

57. Hess and Dabholkar, "*The Pirate*," xvii, 167.

58. Fordin, *MGM's Greatest Musicals*, 198.

59. Thomas, *The Films of Gene Kelly*, 79.

60. Canfield, "That Old Black Magic."

61. Yudkoff, *Gene Kelly*, 185.

12. The Renaissance Man

1. "Gene Kelly," *Liberty*, September 1948.

2. Canfield, "That Old Black Magic."

3. Gene Handsaker, "Writer Starts Something," *Kentucky New Era*, September 13, 1949.

4. Morley and Leon, *Gene Kelly*, 82.

5. "Gene Kelly," *Liberty*.

6. "Gene Kelly," *Reflections on the Silver Screen*, February 2, 1994, television interview.

7. Morley and Leon, *Gene Kelly*, 83; *Dancing: A Man's Game*.

8. Dorothy Kilgallen, "Guest Today Is Screen Star Gene Kelly," *Schenectady Gazette*, September 14, 1948.

9. Thomas, *The Films of Gene Kelly*, 82, 84, 85–86.

10. "Gene on *Merv Griffin*, 1977," *I Dream of Gene*, accessed May 20, 2015, http://i-dream-of-gene.tumblr.com/post/14037021344/i-worked-with-her-lana-turner-i-broke-her-arm.

11. Bosley Crowther, "Lana Turner and Gene Kelly Top Cast of *Three Muske-teers*," *New York Times*, October 21, 1948.

12. Esther Williams and Digby Diehl, *The Million Dollar Mermaid: An Autobi-ography* (New York: Simon and Schuster, 1999), 185.

13. Simone, oral history.

14. Morley and Leon, *Gene Kelly*, 128.

15. Blair, *The Memory of All That*, 161.

16. Yudkoff, *Gene Kelly*, 191.

17. Fuller, "And Now, the Real Kicker."

18. Novick, interview with authors.

19. Yudkoff, *Gene Kelly*, 189.

20. Hirschhorn, *Gene Kelly*, 148.

21. Ibid., 150.

22. Blair, *The Memory of All That*, 260.

23. Hirschhorn, *Gene Kelly*, 152.

24. Doug Nye, "Gene Kelly's Daughter Recalls 'Wonderful Parent,'" *Chicago Tribune*, March 15, 2002.

25. Novick, interview with authors.

26. Hirschhorn, *Gene Kelly*, 152; Novick, interview with authors.

27. Hedda Hopper, "Gene Kelly Would Like to Appear in Dramas, Make Pic-tures for Tots," *Los Angeles Times*, October 9, 1949.

28. Fuller, "And Now, the Real Kicker."

29. David Soren, *Vera-Ellen: The Magic and the Mystery* (Parkville, MD: Mid-night Marquee, 2003), 76.

30. Ibid., 78–79.

31. Ibid., 82.

32. "Gene Kelly," *American Film*, February 1979.

33. "*Words and Music*," *Picturegoer*, August 6, 1949.

34. Sheri Chinen Biesen, *Music in the Shadows: Noir Musical Films* (Baltimore, MD: Johns Hopkins University Press, 2014), 89.

35. Yudkoff, *Gene Kelly*, 190.

36. Hal Erickson, *The Baseball Filmography, 1915 through 2001*, 2nd ed. (Jef-ferson, NC: McFarland, 2002), 454.

37. Kilgallen, "Guest Today Is Gene Kelly."

38. Simone, oral history.

39. Yudkoff, *Gene Kelly*, 195.

40. Betty Garrett and Ron Rapoport, *Betty Garrett and Other Songs: A Life on Stage and Screen* (New York: Madison Books, 2000), 107.

41. Williams and Diehl, *Million Dollar Mermaid*, 168.

42. Ibid., 168–69.

43. Ibid., 169.

44. Ibid., 170.

45. Silverman, *Dancing on the Ceiling,* 176.

46. Cadman, interview with authors.

47. *Take Me out to the Ball Game,* dir. Busby Berkeley, perf. Gene Kelly, Frank Sinatra, Esther Williams (1949; Culver City, CA: MGM, 1994), videocassette.

48. Tina Daniell and Pat McGilligan, "Betty Comden and Adolph Green: Almost Improvisation," in *Backstory 2: Interviews with Screenwriters of the 1940s and 1950s* (Berkeley: University of California Press, 1991), 77.

49. Williams and Diehl, *Million Dollar Mermaid,* 170.

50. Ibid., 171.

51. Ibid.

52. Spivak, interview with authors.

53. Yudkoff, *Gene Kelly,* 195.

54. Earl Wilson, "It Happened Last Night," *Pittsburgh Post-Gazette,* February 12, 1966.

55. Silverman, *Dancing on the Ceiling,* 94.

56. Ibid., 92.

57. Betty Comden and Adolph Green, "Yes Indeedy" (1948).

58. Roger Edens, "Strictly USA" (1948).

59. Silverman, *Dancing on the Ceiling,* 95.

60. Bosley Crowther, "Frank Sinatra and Gene Kelly in *Take Me out to the Ball Game,* at Loew's State," *New York Times,* March 10, 1949.

61. Spivak, interview with authors.

62. Bob White, "'Music Is a World Language,' Says Noted Film Genius," *Los Angeles Times,* June 2, 1946.

63. Andy Taylor Fabe, "The Return of *Singin' in the Rain,*" *Michigan Daily,* March 28, 2002.

13. You Can Count on Me

1. "An Evening with Gene Kelly," *Film 74,* BBC One, November 5, 1974.

2. Reynolds, *Debbie,* 60.

3. David Parkinson, "Dancing in the Streets," *Sight and Sound,* January 1993.

4. Singer, *A Cut Above,* 145.

5. Ibid.

6. Fordin, *MGM's Greatest Musicals,* 259.

7. Ibid., 258.

8. Daniell and McGilligan, "Betty Comden and Adolph Green," 78.

9. Ibid.

10. Blair, *The Memory of All That,* 99.

11. Ibid., 99–100.

12. Cutts, "Kelly, Dancer, Actor, Director."

13. Garrett and Rapoport, *Betty Garrett*, 110.

14. Simone, oral history.

15. Soren, *Vera-Ellen*, 80.

16. Philip Scheuer, "Top Filmmaker Still Song Writer at Heart," *Los Angeles Times*, July 10, 1949.

17. "Gene Kelly: Looking at the Future of Musicals," *Entertainment World*, March 6, 1970.

18. Ibid.

19. Singer, *A Cut Above*, 146.

20. Simone, oral history.

21. Hirschhorn, *Gene Kelly*, 156.

22. Simone, oral history.

23. Ibid.

24. Ibid.

25. Ibid.

26. Parkinson, "Dancing in the Streets."

27. "Carol Haney," *Milwaukee Sentinel*, May 21, 1954.

28. Norma McLain Stoop, "Gene Kelly," *Dance*, July 1976.

29. "Interviews," *American Film*.

30. Silverman, *Dancing on the Ceiling*, 118.

31. Betty Comden and Adolph Green, "On the Town" (1949, *Allthelyrics*, accessed September 4, 2016, http://www.lyricsmania.com/on_the_town_lyrics_gene_kelly.html.

32. "Gene Kelly," *Interview*, May 1994.

33. Fordin, *MGM's Greatest Musicals*, 267.

34. Hirschhorn, *Gene Kelly*, 158.

35. Fordin, *MGM's Greatest Musicals*, 268.

36. Updike, *More Matter*, 670.

37. Bosley Crowther, "*On the Town*, Yuletide Picture at Radio City, Is Musical to Please the Family," *New York Times*, December 9, 1949.

38. "*On the Town*: A Fast Moving Song and Dance Show," *Time*, January 2, 1950.

39. Basinger, "Gene Kelly."

40. Dominic McHugh, *Alan Jay Lerner: A Lyricist's Letters* (New York: Oxford University Press, 2014), 142.

41. Silverman, *Dancing on the Ceiling*, 119.

42. Hirschhorn, *Gene Kelly*, 153.

43. Hess and Dabholkar, "*The Pirate*," 211.

44. Betsy Blair, "I Married a Dynamo, 1949," *The Gene Scene*, accessed September 4, 2016, http://genescene.blogspot.com/2008/02/genes-eternal-verities.html.

45. Novick, interview with authors.

46. Novick, interview with authors.

47. Canfield, "That Old Black Magic."

48. Fabe, "The Return of *Singin' in the Rain.*"

49. Blair, *The Memory of All That,* 140.

50. Silverman, *Dancing on the Ceiling,* 98.

51. "Dancer Wife Divorces Elizabeth Taylor Escort," *Los Angeles Times,* May 18, 1951.

52. Silverman, *Dancing on the Ceiling,* 106.

53. Blair, *The Memory of All That,* 166.

54. "Gene Kelly," *Saturday Evening Post.*

55. Ibid.

56. Hirschhorn, *Gene Kelly,* 161.

57. Handsaker, "Writer Starts Something."

58. Fabe, "The Return of *Singin' in the Rain.*"

59. "The Black Hand," *Newsweek,* March 27, 1950.

60. Chaplin, *Golden Age of Movie Musicals,* 125.

61. Hirschhorn, *Gene Kelly,* 162.

62. Chaplin, *Golden Age of Movie Musicals,* 129.

63. Hirschhorn, *Gene Kelly,* 162.

64. Joe Pasternak, *Easy the Hard Way: The Autobiography of Joe Pasternak* (New York: Putnam, 1956), 231.

65. Hirschhorn, *Gene Kelly,* 167.

66. Simone, oral history.

67. Marion Kabaker, "A Charmed Life," *Chicago Tribune,* November 7, 1993.

68. Carleton Carpenter, interview with authors, October 20, 2015.

69. Phillips, *Charles Walters,* 125.

70. Hirschhorn, *Gene Kelly,* 162.

71. *Gene Kelly: Anatomy of a Dancer.*

72. Ibid.

73. *Summer Stock,* dir. Charles Walters, perf. Judy Garland, Gene Kelly, Phil Silvers (1950; Hollywood: MGM, 1992), videocassette.

74. *Gene Kelly: Anatomy of a Dancer.*

75. *Summer Stock.*

76. Bosley Crowther, "Metro Musical, *Summer Stock,* with Judy Garland and Gene Kelly, Opens at Capitol," *New York Times,* September 1, 1950.

77. Pasternak, *Easy the Hard Way,* 233.

78. Hirschhorn, *Gene Kelly,* 160.

14. Who Could Ask for Anything More?

1. Sue Harris, *An American in Paris* (Basingstoke, UK: Palgrave Macmillan, 2015), 22.

2. Blair, *The Memory of All That*, 161.

3. Ibid., 162.

4. Ibid., 163–64.

5. Novick, interview with authors.

6. Griffin, *A Hundred or More Hidden Things*, 136.

7. Minnelli, *I Remember It Well*, 230.

8. Stephen Harvey, *Directed by Vincente Minnelli* (New York: Harper Collins, 1989), 163.

9. Minnelli, *I Remember It Well*, 229.

10. Simone, oral history.

11. Minnelli, *I Remember It Well*, 64.

12. Leslie Caron, *Thank Heaven: A Memoir* (New York: Plume, 2010), 54.

13. Simone, oral history.

14. Caron, *Thank Heaven*, 54.

15. "I've Got a Studio."

16. Hirschhorn, *Gene Kelly*, 146.

17. Singer, *A Cut Above*, 144.

18. Thomas, *The Films of Gene Kelly*, 130.

19. Loretta Britten and Sarah Brash, *The American Dream: The 50s* (Alexandra, VA: Time-Life Books, 1998), 24, 22.

20. Novick, interview with authors.

21. Caron, *Thank Heaven*, 65.

22. Simone, oral history.

23. Caron, *Thank Heaven*, 69–70.

24. Ibid., 61.

25. Ibid., 62, 70.

26. Ibid., 61.

27. Levant, *Memoirs of an Amnesiac*, 200.

28. Minnelli, *I Remember It Well*, 231.

29. Levant, *Memoirs of an Amnesiac*, 201.

30. Chaplin, *Golden Age of Movie Musicals*, 133.

31. *An American in Paris*, dir. Vincente Minnelli, perf. Gene Kelly, Leslie Carson, Oscar Levant (1951; Hollywood, MGM), film.

32. Simone, oral history.

33. Caron, *Thank Heaven*, 73.

34. Ibid., 70.

35. Ibid.

36. *S'Wonderful: The Making of "An American in Paris,"* perf. Leslie Caron, André Guy, Claude Guy (2008; Hollywood: Trailer Park, 2008), DVD.

37. Caron, *Thank Heaven*, 70.

38. Roger Ebert, *"An American in Paris," Roger Ebert.com*, October 2, 1992,

accessed June 24, 2015, http://www.rogerebert.com/reviews/an-american-in-paris-1951.

39. *S'Wonderful.*

40. Minnelli, *I Remember It Well,* 267.

41. Caron, *Thank Heaven,* 71.

42. Minnelli, *I Remember It Well,* 240.

43. Ibid.

44. Ibid., 236.

45. Eyman, *Lion of Hollywood,* 440.

46. James Robert Parish and Michael Pitts, *Hollywood Songsters: Singers Who Act and Actors Who Sing,* 2nd ed. (New York: Routledge, 2003), 452.

47. Chaplin, *Golden Age of Movie Musicals,* 137.

48. Minnelli, *I Remember It Well,* 241.

49. *S'Wonderful.*

50. Levy, *Vincente Minnelli,* 214, 242.

51. Minnelli, *I Remember It Well,* 235, 327.

52. Silverman, *Dancing on the Ceiling,* 132.

53. Fordin, *MGM's Greatest Musicals,* 321.

54. Ebert, *"An American in Paris."*

55. Minnelli, *I Remember It Well,* 242.

56. Caron, *Thank Heaven,* 65.

57. Novick, interview with authors.

58. Blair, *The Memory of All That,* 160.

59. Laurents, *Original Story By,* 94–95.

60. Chaplin, *Golden Age of Movie Musicals,* 67.

61. Blair, *The Memory of All That,* 158, 159.

62. Betty Comden, *Offstage* (New York: Limelight, 1996), 173.

63. Minnelli, *I Remember It Well,* 243.

64. Bosley Crowther, *"An American in Paris,* Arrival of Music Hall, Has Gene Kelly and Leslie Caron in Leads," *New York Times,* October 5, 1951.

65. *"An American in Paris," Time,* October 8, 1951.

66. "Barbara Wolf, 'An American in Paris,' Film Buff 1976," *Gene Kelly: Creative Genius,* accessed June 25, 2015, www.freewebs.com/geneius/bygollythesearegood.htm.

67. Singer, *A Cut Above,* 146.

15. Laughing at Clouds

1. "Adolph Green," *Gene Kelly: Creative Genius,* accessed July 5, 2015, http://www.freewebs.com/geneius/bygollythesearegood.htm.

2. Daniell and McGilligan, "Betty Comden and Adolph Green," 82, 83.

3. Earl Hess and Pratibha Dabholkar, *"Singin' in the Rain": The Making of an American Masterpiece* (Lawrence: University Press of Kansas, 2009), 57.

4. Edwin Schallert, "In the Movie Field, Gene Kelly Proves a Quintuple Threat," *Los Angeles Times,* October 7, 1951.

5. "Gene Kelly and Stanley Donen," *Deseret News* (Salt Lake City), December 20, 1949.

6. Baer, "Singin' in the Rain."

7. *Singin' in the Rain,* dir. Gene Kelly and Stanley Donen, perf. Gene Kelly, Donald O'Connor, Debbie Reynolds (1952; Hollywood: MGM, 1992), videocassette.

8. Daniell and McGilligan, "Betty Comden and Adolph Green," 80.

9. Baer, "Singin' in the Rain."

10. *What a Glorious Feeling* (Los Angeles: Turner Entertainment, 2002), film.

11. Reynolds, *Debbie,* 86.

12. Ibid.

13. Hess and Dabholkar, *"Singin' in the Rain,"* 52.

14. Silverman, *Dancing on the Ceiling,* 152, 157.

15. Reynolds, *Debbie,* 87, 88.

16. Phil Roura and Jane Furse, "Gene Kelly, Famed Hollywood Dancer, Dies at 83," *New York Daily News,* February 3, 1996.

17. Doug Nye, "Anatomy of a Father," *Beaver County (PA) Times,* March 4, 2002.

18. Pat York, *Going Strong* (New York: Arcade, 1991), 157.

19. Novick, interview with authors.

20. Reynolds, *Debbie,* 89.

21. Ardmore, "Holy Man or Holy Terror?"

22. Daniel Bubbeo, "Gene Kelly's Widow Patricia Chats about Her Late Husband and *Singin' in the Rain,*" *Newsday,* July 11, 2012.

23. Hess and Dabholkar, *"Singin' in the Rain,"* 106.

24. Hirschhorn, *Gene Kelly,* 186.

25. Reynolds, *Debbie,* 90.

26. Silverman, *Dancing on the Ceiling,* 162.

27. Prelutsky, *The Secret of Their Success,* 186.

28. Mindy Aloff, "Remembering a Hoofer: An Interview with Donald O'Connor," *Dance View Times,* October 13, 2003.

29. Hess and Dabholkar, *"Singin' in the Rain,"* 196–97.

30. Baer, "Singin' in the Rain."

31. Simone, oral history.

32. Baer, "Singin' in the Rain."

33. Cyd Charisse and Tony Martin, *The Two of Us* (New York: Mason Charter, 1976), 200.

34. Bernard Weinraub, "A Portrait of the Dancer, Perfectionist and All," *New York Times,* February 28, 2002.

35. "Cyd Charisse," *Gene Kelly: Creative Genius,* accessed July 7, 2015, http://www.freewebs.com/geneius/icouldencourageyou.htm.

36. York, *Going Strong,* 158.

37. "Gene Kelly," *Nova,* July 1972.

38. Hess and Dabholkar, *"Singin' in the Rain,"* 160.

39. Ibid., 168.

40. Baer, "Singin' in the Rain."

41. Silverman, *Dancing on the Ceiling,* 156.

42. Hess and Dabholkar, *"Singin' in the Rain,"* 165, 164.

43. Ibid., 169.

44. Baer, "Singin' in the Rain."

45. Parkinson, "Dancing in the Streets."

46. Hess and Dabholkar, *"Singin' in the Rain,"* 135.

47. Blair, *The Memory of All That,* 164–65.

48. Baer, "Singin' in the Rain."

49. Hay, *MGM,* 282.

50. Simone, oral history.

51. Eyman, *Lion of Hollywood,* 447.

52. Hirschhorn, *Gene Kelly,* 205.

53. Fordin, *MGM's Greatest Musicals,* 369.

54. Tom Dancy, "At Home Abroad," *Modern Screen,* July 1953.

55. Ibid.

56. Ibid.

57. Blair, *The Memory of All That,* 164.

58. A. H. Frank, *The Girls' Book of Ballet* (London: Burke Publishing, 1953), 95.

59. Blair, *The Memory of All That,* 183.

60. Levy, *Vincente Minnelli,* 216.

61. Fordin, *MGM's Greatest Musicals,* 344.

62. Ibid., 346.

63. Hess and Dabholkar, *"Singin' in the Rain,"* 175.

64. Bosley Crowther, *"Singin' in the Rain,* Starring Gene Kelly, Ushers in Spring at the Music Hall," *New York Times,* March 28, 1952.

65. Hess and Dabholkar, *"Singin' in the Rain,"* 185.

66. Crowther, *"Singin' in the Rain."*

67. Baer, "Singin' in the Rain."

68. Silverman, *Dancing on the Ceiling,* 169.

69. Baer, "Singin' in the Rain."

70. *Gene Kelly: Anatomy of a Dancer.*

71. Silverman, *Dancing on the Ceiling,* 171.

72. James Robert Parish and Gregory Monk, *The Best of MGM: The Golden Years, 1928–1959* (Westport, CT: Arlington House, 1981), 185.

73. *Gene Kelly: Anatomy of a Dancer.*

74. Blair, *The Memory of All That,* 183.

16. What a Day This Has Been

1. Blair, *The Memory of All That,* 223.

2. Ibid., 203.

3. Ibid., 190–91.

4. Hirschhorn, *Gene Kelly,* 194.

5. Ibid., 195.

6. *"Devil Makes Three,* Melodrama Filmed on Location in Europe, Is Globe's New Feature," *New York Times,* August 30, 1952.

7. "Gene Kelly," *Sydney Morning Herald,* March 30, 1952.

8. "Traveling Man, Magazine Article 1952."

9. Fordin, *MGM's Greatest Musicals,* 370.

10. Blair, *The Memory of All That,* 189.

11. Hirschhorn, *Gene Kelly,* 195.

12. Blair, *The Memory of All That,* 190.

13. Ibid., 227–28, 183.

14. Novick, interview with authors.

15. Blair, *The Memory of All That,* 180, 231.

16. Ibid., 189.

17. "Film Article: *Invitation to the Dance,*" *Turner Classic Movies,* accessed July 17, 2015, http://www.tcm.com/this-month/article/154948|0/Invitation-to-the-Dance.html.

18. Fordin, *MGM's Greatest Musicals,* 393.

19. Fuller, "And Now, the Real Kicker."

20. *"Invitation to the Dance,"* *Screenland,* January 1953.

21. "Film Article: *Invitation to the Dance.*"

22. Hirschhorn, *Gene Kelly,* 193.

23. Linet, "An American in London."

24. Blair, *The Memory of All That,* 184.

25. "Gene Kelly in London," *Screen Stars,* June 1953.

26. "Gene Kelly," *Motion Picture and Television,* January 1953.

27. "Dancer Has Confidence in His No-Dialogue Film," *Victoria (TX) Advocate,* December 23, 1953.

28. Hugh Samson, "My, This Kelly's Keen," *Picturegoer,* October 11, 1952.

29. Hirschhorn, *Gene Kelly,* 203.

30. "Gene Kelly," *Motion Picture,* May 1954.

31. "Anybody Here Seen Kelly?" *Picturegoer,* July 17, 1954.

32. Morley and Leon, *Gene Kelly,* 121.

33. *"Crest of the Wave,* British Film, Opens at Guild," *New York Times,* November 11, 1954.

34. "Dancer Benefits, Salary Tax-Free," *Spokane Daily Chronicle,* March 5, 1953.

35. McHugh, *Alan Jay Lerner,* 44.

36. Britten and Brash, *The American Dream,* 36.

37. "Gene Kelly Back Home," *Pittsburgh Press,* June 1953.

38. "Gene Kelly," *Motion Picture and Television,* May 1954.

39. Blair, *The Memory of All That,* 232.

40. Stoop, "Gene Kelly."

41. Fordin, *MGM's Greatest Musicals,* 427.

42. Levy, *Vincente Minnelli,* 248–49.

43. "Gene Kelly," *Screen Album,* November 1954.

44. Hortense Morton, "Gene Kelly Talks about *Brigadoon,*" *San Francisco Examiner,* October 10, 1954.

45. Charisse and Martin, *The Two of Us,* 206.

46. Morley and Leon, *Gene Kelly,* 126.

47. Charisse and Martin, *The Two of Us,* 203.

48. Bosley Crowther, "*Brigadoon:* Cyd Charisse, Gene Kelly Are Starred Musical Fantasy Seen at the Music Hall," *New York Times,* September 17, 1954.

49. Minnelli, *I Remember It Well,* 281.

50. Charisse and Martin, *The Two of Us,* 207.

51. Ibid.

52. Minnelli, *I Remember It Well,* 281.

53. Simone, oral history.

54. Ibid.

55. McHugh, *Alan Jay Lerner,* 39.

56. Ibid., 41, 54.

57. Silverman, *Dancing on the Ceiling,* 197.

58. Minnelli, *I Remember It Well,* 280–81.

59. Ibid., 281.

60. Morley and Leon, *Gene Kelly,* 131.

61. Singer, *A Cut Above,* 150.

62. Thomas, *The Films of Gene Kelly,* 158.

63. Bosley Crowther, "The Screen in Review: Romberg Film, Mostly Music, at Radio City," *New York Times,* December 10, 1954.

64. "Gene Kelly's Marriage on the Rocks?" *Movie Pix,* February 1954.

65. Blair, *The Memory of All That,* 218.

66. Ibid.

67. Morley and Leon, *Gene Kelly,* 132.

68. Ken Ferguson, "Why Fred and I Rarely Starred Together," *Photoplay,* August 1976.

69. "Gene Kelly," *Observer,* November 10, 1968.

17. The Unhappy Road

1. Daniell and McGilligan, "Betty Comden and Adolph Green," 84.

2. Hess and Dabholkar, *"Singin' in the Rain,"* 202; Hirschhorn, *Gene Kelly,* 214.

3. Silverman, *Dancing on the Ceiling,* 207.

4. Ibid., 206.

5. Hirschhorn, *Gene Kelly,* 209.

6. Daniell and McGilligan, "Betty Comden and Adolph Green," 84.

7. Singer, *A Cut Above,* 149.

8. *It's Always Fair Weather,* dir. Gene Kelly and Stanley Donen, perf. Gene Kelly, Cyd Charisse, Dan Dailey Jr. (1955; Hollywood: MGM, 2006), DVD.

9. Hess and Dabholkar, *"Singin' in the Rain,"* 202–3.

10. Ibid., 202.

11. Silverman, *Dancing on the Ceiling,* 212.

12. Victoria Large, "Clouds and Scattered Sun: Kelly and Donen's *It's Always Fair Weather,*" *Bright Lights Film Journal,* August 1, 2006.

13. *Gene Kelly: Anatomy of a Dancer.*

14. Silverman, *Dancing on the Ceiling,* 212.

15. Bosley Crowther, "Screen: A Butcher in Love in the Bronx; *Marty,* Adapted from TV, Stars Borgnine," *New York Times,* April 12, 1955.

16. Nate Edwards, "I Am the Husband of Betsy Blair," *Modern Screen,* November 1955.

17. Blair, *The Memory of All That,* 264.

18. Silverman, *Dancing on the Ceiling,* 213.

19. "Gene Kelly," *American Film,* February 1979.

20. Fordin, *MGM's Greatest Musicals,* 436.

21. Silverman, *Dancing on the Ceiling,* 206.

22. "Cinema: Current and Choice," *Time,* October 24, 1955.

23. Bosley Crowther, "Screen: Kidding Video," *New York Times,* September 16, 1955.

24. Maynard, "This Is about Gene Kelly."

25. "Gene Kelly," *Motion Picture and Television,* May 1954.

26. Blair, *The Memory of All That,* 233.

27. *"Invitation to the Dance,"* *Schweitzer Rotes-Zeitung* (Zurich), April 1, 1956; *"Invitation to the Dance,"* *Daily Mirror* (London), May 23, 1956.

28. Pauline Kael, *5001 Nights at the Movies* (New York: Picador, 1982), 369.

29. Bosley Crowther, "Screen: Twinkle-Toes; Gene Kelly Performs in All-Dance Film," *New York Times,* May 23, 1956.

30. *"Invitation to the Dance,"* *Dance,* June 1956.

31. Thomas, *The Films of Gene Kelly,* 170.

32. Singer, *A Cut Above,* 195.

33. Gene Kelly, "The Happy Road," *The Happy Road,* dir. Gene Kelly, perf. Gene Kelly, Brigitte Fossey, Bobby Clark (Hollywood: MGM, 1957), film.

34. Blair, *The Memory of All That,* 233.

35. Ibid., 234.

36. Hirschhorn, *Gene Kelly,* 215.

37. Ibid., 214.

38. Ibid.

39. *Gene Kelly: Anatomy of a Dancer.*

40. "Gene Kelly, Wife in Trial Separation," *Pittsburgh Post-Gazette,* August 11, 1956.

41. Hirschhorn, *Gene Kelly,* 216.

42. "Gene Kelly on *The Happy Road*," *Film Show Annual,* 1959.

43. "*The Happy Road,*" *Age* (Melbourne), January 22, 1957.

44. Peter Evans, "Gene Kelly," *Observer* (London), November 10, 1968.

45. "Reconciliation Possible," *St. Petersburg (FL) Times,* September 26, 1956.

46. Blair, *The Memory of All That,* 234.

47. Ibid., 235.

48. Ibid., 245.

49. Ibid., 239.

50. Ibid., 145.

51. Hirschhorn, *Gene Kelly,* 217.

52. Ibid., 221.

53. Chaplin, *The Golden Age of Movie Musicals,* 165.

54. Hirschhorn, *Gene Kelly,* 219.

55. Ibid., 220.

56. Chaplin, *The Golden Age of Movie Musicals,* 166.

57. Thomas, *The Films of Gene Kelly,* 173.

58. Bosley Crowther, "The Screen: *Les Girls,*" *New York Times,* October 4, 1957.

59. "Gene Kelly's Back," *Picturegoer,* November 2, 1957.

60. Thomas, *The Films of Gene Kelly,* 22.

61. Hay, *MGM,* 313.

62. Thomas, *The Films of Gene Kelly,* 22.

63. "Gene Kelly's Television Debut," *Toledo Blade,* January 26, 1957.

64. Walter Ames, "Gene Kelly Stars in Drama; Films Change TV Habits," *Los Angeles Times,* December 3, 1956.

65. "Gene Kelly Makes Television Debut," *Toledo Blade,* January 26, 1957.

66. "Gene Kelly in Debut on Schlitz Playhouse," *New York Times,* March 2, 1957.

67. *Gene Kelly: Anatomy of a Dancer.*

18. A Hundred Million Miracles

1. "Gene Kelly," *Films Illustrated,* August 1980.

2. "Gene Kelly in *Marjorie Morningstar,*" *Toledo Blade,* April 12, 1958.

3. "Gene Kelly," *Screen Album*, May 1958.

4. Thomas, *The Films of Gene Kelly*, 190.

5. *Marjorie Morningstar*, dir. Irving Rapper, perf. Gene Kelly, Natalie Wood, Ed Wynn (1958; Hollywood: Warner Bros., 2002), DVD.

6. Wintz, "Gene Kelly."

7. "Gene Kelly's Birthday Celebration," *Screen Stories*, April 1958.

8. "Cinema: The New Pictures," *Time*, April 28, 1958.

9. A. H. Weiler, "Version of Wouk Novel Opens at Music Hall," *New York Times*, April 25, 1958.

10. Thomas, *The Films of Gene Kelly*, 190.

11. Dorothy Kilgallen, "Gene Kelly Seems to Be Dating Jean Coyne Almost Exclusively!" *St. Petersburg (FL) Times*, April 29, 1959.

12. Blair, *The Memory of All That*, 249.

13. Ibid., 313.

14. "Elizabeth Wilson, 'Miss MacCracken' in the Film," *Gene Kelly: Creative Genius*, accessed August 7, 2015, http://www.freewebs.com/geneius/itllbework-hardwork.htm.

15. Joe Hyams, "The Do-It-Yourself Director," *Los Angeles Times*, September 7, 1958.

16. Thomas, *The Films of Gene Kelly*, 198.

17. Bosley Crowther, "*Tunnel of Love*: Widmark, Doris Day Star in Roxy Film," *New York Times*, November 22, 1958.

18. "Gene Kelly: Director," *Toledo Blade*, April 12, 1958.

19. Don Alpert, "Gene Kelly: Guy without a Trade," *Los Angeles Times*, September 13, 1964.

20. Morley and Leon, *Gene Kelly*, 141.

21. Yudkoff, *Gene Kelly*, 203.

22. Hirschhorn, *Gene Kelly*, 223.

23. "Gene Kelly Returns to Broadway," *Theatre Arts*, December 1958.

24. Hugh Fordin, *Getting to Know Him: A Biography of Oscar Hammerstein II* (New York: Random House, 1977), 342.

25. Rodgers, *Musical Stages*, 295.

26. Brooks Atkinson, "*Flower Song*," *New York Times*, December 7, 1958.

27. Hirschhorn, *Gene Kelly*, 225.

28. "Gene Kelly Interview with Edward Murrow."

29. "Gene Kelly," *Irish America*.

30. *Dancing: A Man's Game*.

31. John Crosby, "Gene Kelly Proved 'It's a Man's Game,'" *St. Petersburg (FL) Times*, December 24, 1958.

32. "*Dancing: A Man's Game*," *Variety*, UCLA Film and TV Archive, Los Angeles.

33. Crosby, "Gene Kelly Proved 'It's a Man's Game.'"

34. "Gene Kelly Talks about *Dancing: A Man's Game*," *Australian Woman's Weekly*, August 1976.

35. Hirschhorn, *Gene Kelly*, 227.

36. *The Gene Kelly Show*, dir. Joseph Cates, perf. Gene Kelly, Liza Minnelli, Cherylene Lee, *Pontiac Star Parade*, April 24, 1959, NBC.

37. "I Could Encourage You," *Gene Kelly: Creative Genius*, accessed August 28, 2015, www.freewebs.com/geneius/icouldencourageyou.htm.

38. Minnelli, *I Remember It Well*, 338.

39. "Liza: Fire, Air, and a Touch of Anguish," *Time*, February 28, 1972.

40. Robert Lewis Shayon, "*The Gene Kelly Show*," *Saturday Review*, May 16, 1959.

41. Bob Thomas, "Gene Kelly Talking: Not Making Musicals So Switching to TV," *Ottawa Citizen*, April 22, 1959.

42. "Gene Kelly: Song and Dance Man," *Films Illustrated*, November 1974.

43. *Inherit the Wind*, dir. Stanley Kramer, perf. Fredric March, Spencer Tracy, Gene Kelly (1960; Hollywood: United Artists, 2001), DVD.

44. Stanley Kramer, *A Mad, Mad, Mad, Mad World: A Life in Hollywood* (New York: Harcourt Brace, 1997), 172.

45. *Inherit the Wind*, *AFI Catalog of Feature Films*, accessed August 11, 2015, http://www.afi.com/members/catalog/DetailView.aspx?s=&Movie=53192.

46. Bosley Crowther, "*Inherit the Wind*," *New York Times*, October 13, 1960.

47. "Gene Kelly," *Reflections*, February 2, 1994, AMC.

48. Thomas, *The Films of Gene Kelly*, 204.

49. Patricia Wilson, *Yesterday's Mashed Potatoes: The Fabulous Life of a Happy Has-Been* (Indianapolis: Dog Ear, 2009), 187.

50. Hirschhorn, *Gene Kelly*, 230.

51. *Pontiac Star Parade*, dir. Sidney Miller, perf. Gene Kelly, Donald O'Connor, Carol Lawrence, November 21, 1959, NBC.

52. "*Pontiac Star Parade*," *TV Radio Mirror*, November 1959.

53. Jack Gould, "TV: In Song and Dance," *New York Times*, April 25, 1959.

54. Hedda Hopper, "The Toast of Paris," *Chicago Tribune*, October 9, 1960.

55. Susan Heller Anderson, "Tout Paris Offers Its 'Hommage a Gene Kelly,'" *New York Times*, September 19, 1981.

19. "I wear so many hats"

1. "Old Faces: Sextuple Threat," *Time*, August 4, 1967.

2. "Our Ballet Is Best, Says Gene Kelly," *Indianapolis Star*, October 14, 1959.

3. "Gene Kelly's Paris Ballet," *Newsweek*, July 7, 1960.

4. Kisselgoff, "Gene Kelly: Ballet Influenced His View of Dance."

5. "Gene Kelly's Paris Ballet."

6. "Ballet by Kelly Cheered in Paris," *New York Times*, July 7, 1960.

7. "Gene Kelly's Paris Ballet."

8. "Gene Kelly's French Frolic," *Life,* August 1960.

9. "Ballet by Kelly Cheered in Paris."

10. Hirschhorn, *Gene Kelly,* 232.

11. Kisselgoff, "Gene Kelly: Ballet Influenced His View of Dance."

12. Hirschhorn, *Gene Kelly,* 234.

13. Bosley Crowther, "The Screen: Milton Berle Steals Show in *Let's Make Love,*" *New York Times,* September 9, 1960.

14. Thomas, *The Films of Gene Kelly,* 206.

15. Ardmore, "Holy Man or Holy Terror?"

16. Novick, interview with authors.

17. Hirschhorn, *Gene Kelly,* 235.

18. "Gene Kelly Prefers the Foxtrot," *Times Daily* (London), March 15, 1986.

19. Blair, *The Memory of All That,* 166.

20. Barbara Wolf, "The Art of Gene Kelly," *Film Buff,* February 1976.

21. Hirschhorn, *Gene Kelly,* 236.

22. "A Man and His Loving Memories," *Woman* (London), December 15, 1973.

23. William Henry III, *The Great One: The Life and Legend of Jackie Gleason* (New York: Doubleday, 1992), 208.

24. James Bacon, *How Sweet It Is: The Jackie Gleason Story* (New York: St. Martin's, 1985), 156.

25. Hirschhorn, *Gene Kelly,* 237.

26. Henry, *The Great One,* 209.

27. Bacon, *How Sweet It Is,* 155.

28. Bosley Crowther, "The Screen: Gleason's *Gigot:* Story of Parisian Mute Opens in Music Hall," *New York Times,* September 28, 1962.

29. Ardmore, "Holy Man or Holy Terror?"

30. John P. Shanley, "*Going My Way,*" *New York Times,* September 30, 1962.

31. "*Going My Way,*" *Gene Kelly: Creative Genius,* accessed August 12, 2015, www.freewebs.com/geneius/cantyouseeimbusy.htm.

32. Ardmore, "Holy Man or Holy Terror?"

33. Hirschhorn, *Gene Kelly,* 238.

34. Ardmore, "Holy Man or Holy Terror?"

35. Vince Leonard, "Kelly: Pittsburgher in New York," *Pittsburgh Press,* February 11, 1966.

36. Philip Scheuer, "Gene Kelly, 51, Still Has That Stardust in His Eyes and Twinkle in His Toes," *Los Angeles Times,* September 8, 1963.

37. Hirschhorn, *Gene Kelly,* 240.

38. Betty Beale, "JFK, Gene Kelly Sing Irish Song," *St. Petersburg (FL) Times,* January 27, 1963.

39. "Gene Kelly Back from Africa Tour," *Los Angeles Times,* January 29, 1964.

40. "Kelly Returns," *St. Petersburg (FL) Evening Independent*, January 29, 1964.

41. "Gene Kelly," *The Steve Allen Playhouse*, Westinghouse TV, February 18, 1964, television.

42. Bob Thomas, "Shock Is Worldwide on Marilyn's Death," *Toledo Blade*, August 6, 1962.

43. "American Film Institute Lifetime Achievement Award, 1985," CBS, March 7, 1985, television.

44. Thomas, *The Films of Gene Kelly*, 216.

45. Bosley Crowther, "Poor Little Rich Girl's Woes," *New York Times*, May 15, 1964.

46. Thomas, *The Films of Gene Kelly*, 214.

47. Hirschhorn, *Gene Kelly*, 243.

48. "A Man and His Loving Memories."

49. "Gene Kelly on Being a Parent," *Star*, February 1996.

50. Hirschhorn, *Gene Kelly*, 243.

51. "Kerry Kelly," *Gene Kelly: Creative Genius*, accessed August 12, 2015, www.freewebs.com/geneius/ohiknowyou.htm.

52. Novick, interview with authors.

53. Julia Hirsch, *The Sound of Music: The Making of America's Favorite Movie* (New York: McGraw-Hill, 1993), 13.

54. "*The Julie Andrews Show*," *Pittsburgh Post-Gazette*, November 27, 1965.

55. "Gene Kelly Goes Legit Again after 33 Years."

56. "A Man and His Loving Memories."

20. Looking for Enchantment

1. "Kelly Jumps at Opportunity to Play Part," *Sarasota (FL) Herald-Tribune*, December 28, 1972.

2. "Gene Kelly: Filmmaker Interview," *PBS.org*, June 8, 2006, accessed October 4, 2015, http://www.pbs.org/wnet/americanmasters/database/kelly_g_interview.html.

3. *Gene Kelly in New York, New York*, dir. Charles Dubin, perf. Gene Kelly, Woody Allen, Tommy Steele, February 14, 1966, CBS.

4. Julie Carpenter, "Tommy Steele: I'm 75 and My Palladium Comeback Shows That I'll Never Retire," *Express*, November 2012.

5. "Gene Kelly in *New York, New York*," *Chicago Tribune*, February 15, 1966.

6. "Gene Kelly," *Pittsburgh Post-Gazette*, February 21, 1967.

7. "Gene Kelly, *Jack and the Beanstalk*, and an Interview with Bobby Riha," January 18, 2013, *Gene Kelly Fans*, accessed October 2, 2015, http://genekellyfans.com/television/beanstalk/.

8. "*Jack and the Beanstalk*," *Dance*, February 1967.

9. Thomas, *The Films of Gene Kelly*, 220.

10. Ibid., 219.

11. Ibid., 222.

12. Renata Adler, "Screen: Offbeat, Dreamlike Musical; Demy's *Young Girls of Rochefort*," *New York Times*, April 12, 1968.

13. Hirschhorn, *Gene Kelly*, 244.

14. Ibid., 244.

15. "Gene Kelly, a Private Man," *Daily Express* (London), October 13, 1976.

16. "Old Faces: Sextuple Threat."

17. Ibid.

18. Bosley Crowther, "Screen: *Guide for the Married Man;* Matthau and Morse in Farce on Infidelity," *New York Times*, May 27, 1967.

19. "Gene Kelly," *Day* (London), January 1970.

20. Ferguson, "Why Fred and I Rarely Starred Together."

21. Michael Crawford, *Parcel Arrived Safely: Tied with String* (New York: Arrow, 2000), 154.

22. James Spada, *Streisand: Her Life* (New York: Crown, 1995), 216.

23. Ibid., 212–13.

24. Joyce Haber, "Gene Kelly Now Tapping out New Career as a Producer," *Los Angeles Times*, December 7, 1969.

25. Spada, *Streisand*, 218.

26. Hirschhorn, *Gene Kelly*, 257.

27. Spada, *Streisand*, 219.

28. Thomas, *The Films of Gene Kelly*, 219.

29. Ibid.

30. Rob Edelman and Audrey Kupferberg, *Matthau: A Life* (Boulder, CO: Taylor Trade, 2002), 274, 193.

31. Crawford, *Parcel Arrived Safely*, 152, 158.

32. Ibid., 158.

33. Ibid.

34. "Star of *Phantom* Gives Gene Kelly Full Credit," *Los Angeles Times*, April 11, 1990.

35. Ferguson, "Why Fred and I Rarely Starred Together."

36. "Cinema: Echolalia," *Time*, December 26, 1969.

37. Vincent Canby, "On Screen, Barbra Streisand Displays a Detached Cool," *New York Times*, December 18, 1969.

38. Harry Clein, "Is There a Future for the Hollywood Musical?" *Entertainment World*, March 6, 1970.

39. Thomas, *The Films of Gene Kelly*, 28.

40. "On *Combat Fatigue Irritability*."

41. Nancy Anderson, "Gene Kelly Wears Own Cockeyed Optimism," *Deseret News* (Salt Lake City), November 18, 1972.

42. Clein, "Is There a Future for the Hollywood Musical?"

43. "Gene Kelly," *Irish America*.

44. Hirschhorn, *Gene Kelly*, 261.

45. Gary Fishgall, *Pieces of Time: The Life of James Stewart* (New York: Scribner, 1997), 317.

46. "Gene Kelly," *Films Illustrated*, 1974.

47. Michael Munn, *Jimmy Stewart: The Truth behind the Legend* (Fort Lee, NJ: Barricade Books, 2006), 266.

48. Norman Dresser, "*The Cheyenne Social Club* is at Colony," *Toledo Blade*, January 4, 1970.

49. Hirschhorn, *Gene Kelly*, 265.

50. Marc Eliot, *Jimmy Stewart: A Life* (New York: Harmony, 2006), 371.

51. Thomas, *The Films of Gene Kelly*, 238.

52. Munn, *Jimmy Stewart*, 268.

53. "*Gene Kelly's Wonderful World of Girls*," *Los Angeles Herald-Examiner*, January 1970.

54. George Gant, "TV: A Satire about Shameful Secrets," *New York Times*, January 15, 1970.

55. Hirschhorn, *Gene Kelly*, 263.

56. Fishgall, *Pieces of Time*, 318.

57. Hirschhorn, *Gene Kelly*, 266.

58. Jeff LaBrecque, "Malcolm McDowell on Stanley Kubrick: An All-Too-Human Artistic Genius," *Entertainment Weekly*, November 24, 2014.

59. Kate Brown, "Stanley Kubrick Too 'Cheap' to Pay for 'Singin' in the Rain,'" *Telegraph* (London), January 2, 2014.

21. True Talent Shows Itself in Kindness

1. Hirschhorn, *Gene Kelly*, 267.

2. Ibid., 268.

3. Ibid.

4. "Gene Kelly Back in Film," *Toledo Blade*, February 17, 1973.

5. "*40 Carats*," *Variety*, June 29, 1973.

6. Keith Garebian, *The Making of "Cabaret"* (New York: Oxford University Press, 2011), 134.

7. Minnelli, *I Remember It Well*, 378.

8. Hirschhorn, *Gene Kelly*, 268.

9. Tom Shales, "Gene Kelly Says He Never Wanted to Be a Movie Star," *Pittsburgh Press*, June 29, 1974.

10. Novick, interview with authors.

11. *Gene Kelly: Anatomy of a Dancer*.

12. "Gene Kelly," *American Way*.

13. "Gene Kelly," *Woman's Weekly* (UK) July 17, 1976.

14. "Sincerity, Unrehearsed Charm Percolated by the Real Gene Kelly."

15. Ibid.

16. Ibid.

17. "Gene Kelly," *Woman's Weekly*.

18. "To Dance or Not to Dance."

19. Thomas, "Gene Kelly Singing the Blues over State of U.S. Musicals."

20. Colin Dangaard, "Dancing Star Gene Kelly a Working Legend at 65," *Ottawa Citizen*, March 9, 1978.

21. "Movie Memorabilia: The Stuff That Dreams Are Made Of," *New York Sunday Morning*, February 22, 2015.

22. "Gene Kelly," *Disney Channel*, March/April 1988.

23. Dangaard, "Dancing Star Gene Kelly a Working Legend at 65."

24. Shales, "Gene Kelly Says He Never Wanted to Be a Movie Star."

25. *That's Entertainment!* dir. Jack Haley Jr., perf. Gene Kelly, Fred Astaire, Frank Sinatra, Liza Minnelli (1974; Culver City, CA: MGM, 2004), DVD.

26. "*That's Entertainment!*" *Lakeland (FL) Ledger*, June 25, 1974.

27. "*That's Entertainment!*" *Chicago Tribune*, May 20, 1974.

28. Shales, "Gene Kelly Says He Never Wanted to Be a Movie Star."

29. "Gene Kelly Goes Legit Again after 33 Years."

30. "Gene Kelly," *Woman's Weekly*.

31. "Gene Kelly Goes Legit Again after 33 Years."

32. Wilson, *Yesterday's Mashed Potatoes*, 236.

33. Ibid., 242.

34. Ibid.

35. Wintz, "Gene Kelly."

36. Wilson, *Yesterday's Mashed Potatoes*, 243.

37. Colleen Lester, "True Talent, Kindness, and *Take Me Along*," *Gene Kelly Fans*, July 12, 2011, accessed September 21, 2015, http://genekellyfans.com/media/take-me-along/.

38. Wilson, *Yesterday's Mashed Potatoes*, 245.

39. "Gene Kelly," *Woman's Weekly*.

40. Wintz, "Gene Kelly."

41. Ferguson, "Why Fred and I Rarely Starred Together."

42. Sally Davis, "Gene and Fred Together Again," *Los Angeles Supplement*, May 1976.

43. Ibid.

44. Bob Thomas, "Movie Musicals Should Be Revived, Says Gene Kelly," *Pittsburgh Post-Gazette*, December 12, 1975.

45. Levinson, *Puttin' on the Ritz*, 376.

46. Davis, "Gene and Fred Together Again."

47. Vincent Canby, "Magical Sequel to *That's Entertainment*," *New York Times*, May 17, 1976.

48. Stoop, "Gene Kelly."

49. Levinson, *Puttin' on the Ritz*, 377.

50. "Gene Kelly Rediscovered," *Boca Raton (FL) News*, July 30, 1976.

51. "John Travolta," *Gene Kelly: Creative Genius*, accessed September 20, 2015, http://www.freewebs.com/geneius/icouldencourageyou.htm.

52. Christian Toto, "Patricia Ward Kelly on Late Husband Gene Kelly's All-American Legacy," *Breitbart* (Hollywood), November 11, 2013.

53. "My Kids Talked Me into the Knievel Movie."

54. "*Viva Knievel!*" *Deseret News* (Salt Lake City), July 28, 1976.

55. "My Kids Talked Me into the Knievel Movie."

56. "Only Fans Will Cheer Knievel Film Featuring Slow Spills," *Ottawa Citizen*, July 20, 1977.

57. "*An American in Pasadena*," *Gene Kelly: Creative Genius*, accessed September 20, 2015, http://www.freewebs.com/geneius/cantyouseeimbusy.htm.

58. "Gene Kelly Still Has Charisma," *Levittown (PA) Courier Times*, August 22, 1979.

59. Rochlin, "Old Is New Again."

60. Bart Mills, "The Dance Today: A Step in Time with Gene Kelly," *Los Angeles Times*, December 21, 1979.

61. Janet Maslin, "Miss Newton-John in *Xanadu*," *New York Times*, August 9, 1980.

62. Ibid.

63. Hirschhorn, *Gene Kelly*, 273.

64. "Gene Kelly: Dancing Isn't Exciting Anymore," *TV Times*, November 1983.

65. Hirschhorn, *Gene Kelly*, 273.

66. Ibid.

67. Gene D. Phillips, *Francis Ford Coppola: Interviews* (Jackson: University of Mississippi Press, 2004), 54–55.

68. Hirschhorn, *Gene Kelly*, 274.

69. Ibid., 275.

70. Rochlin, "Old Is New Again."

22. Contemporary Yet Timeless

1. Susan Peters, "Tim Kelly Doesn't Have Gene's Magic Feet, but He Made Enough on an L.A. Dance Club to Become an American in Paris," *People*, June 18, 1984.

2. "Gene Kelly at Seventy-Two," *St. Petersburg (FL) Times*, August 4, 1984.

3. Ibid.

4. Irvin Molotsky, "Gene Kelly Brings Young Dancers to White House," *New York Times*, March 29, 1982.

5. "Kennedy Center Honors," CBS, December 25, 1982, television.

6. "Dancing Today Dismays Kelly," *Spokane Spokesman Review,* December 16, 1983.

7. Rochlin, "Old Is New Again."

8. Ibid.

9. Blair, *The Memory of All That,* 317.

10. Wintz, "Gene Kelly."

11. Peters, "Tim Kelly Doesn't Have Gene's Magic Feet."

12. Ibid.

13. "AFI Lifetime Achievement Award," CBS, March 7, 1985, television.

14. Ibid.

15. *Gene Kelly: Anatomy of a Dancer.*

16. Frank Rich, "The Stage: *Singin' in the Rain* Opens," *New York Times,* July 3, 1985.

17. Rochlin, "Old Is New Again."

18. "Gene Kelly Heads St. Patrick's Day Parade," *Rock Hill (SC) Herald,* March 16, 1986.

19. "Gene Kelly Does Not Sing in the Rain on St. Patrick's Day," *Rome (GA) News Tribune,* March 18, 1986.

20. *Gene Kelly: Anatomy of a Dancer.*

21. Blair, *The Memory of All That,* 4.

22. Barbra Paskin, "Singin' in the Rain with Gene," *Lady* (London), November 30, 2012.

23. Silverman, *Dancing on the Ceiling,* 214.

24. Blair, *The Memory of All That,* 4.

25. Yudkoff, *Gene Kelly,* 254–55.

26. Kevin Thomas, "Gene Kelly Remembers Golden Age of Musicals," *Pittsburgh Post-Gazette,* May 3, 1993.

27. Caryn James, "Waste Not, Want Not: MGM's Outtakes Are a Movie," *New York Times,* May 6, 1994.

28. Degen Pener, "Egos and Ids; Ads to Die For? To Gene Kelly, It's Yes and No," *New York Times,* August 29, 1993.

29. Rubenstein, "An American in Style."

30. Blair, *The Memory of All That,* 4.

31. Nadine Brozan, "Chronicle," *New York Times,* February 14, 1995.

32. Blair, *The Memory of All That,* 5.

33. Joseph Barrios, "Gene Kelly Admired, Respected by Brother Fred," *Tucson Citizen,* February 3, 1996.

34. Blair, *The Memory of All That,* 5.

35. Ibid.

36. Ibid., 5–6.

37. Barrios, "Gene Kelly Admired, Respected by Brother Fred."

38. Baer, "Singin' in the Rain."

39. Blair, *The Memory of All That,* 5.

40. Ibid.

41. Ibid., 6.

42. Blair, *The Memory of All That,* 116.

43. "Gene Kelly: Filmmaker Interview."

44. Silverman, *Dancing on the Ceiling,* 214.

45. Blair, *The Memory of All That,* 7.

46. Stephen Brook, "Blingin' in the Rain," *Guardian* (London), January 27, 2005.

47. Cadman, interview with authors.

48. Ben Brantley, "*On the Town* Revival Opens on Broadway," *New York Times,* October 16, 2014.

49. Charles Isherwood, "*An American in Paris,* a Romance of Song and Step," *New York Times,* April 12, 2015.

Epilogue

1. "Gene Kelly: Filmmaker Interview."

2. "Kennedy Center Honors."

3. W. H. Mooring, "Gene Kelly Is Home Again," *Picturegoer,* September 14, 1946.

4. Rubenstein, "An American in Style."

5. Alpert, "Gene Kelly."

6. "Gene Kelly: Sex Sells," *Gainesville Sun,* December 16, 1983.

7. *Gene Kelly: Anatomy of a Dancer.*

8. Updike, *More Matter,* 663–64.

9. "Liza Minnelli, 1996," *Gene Kelly: Creative Genius,* accessed October 2, 2015, http://www.freewebs.com/geneius/icouldencourageyou.htm.

10. "*Singin' in the Rain,*" blogcritics.org, July 29, 2015, accessed October 4, 2015, http://blogcritics.org/dvd-review-singin-in-the-rain/.

11. "AFI Lifetime Achievement Award."

Selected Bibliography

Books and Articles

Astaire, Fred. *Steps in Time.* 1959. Reprint, New York: Dey Street Books, 2009.

Baer, William. "Singin' in the Rain: A Conversation with Betty Comden and Adolph Green." *Michigan Quarterly Review,* Winter 2002.

Blair, Betsy. *The Memory of All That: Love and Politics in New York, Hollywood, and Paris.* New York: Knopf, 2003.

Caron, Leslie. *Thank Heaven: A Memoir.* New York: Plume, 2010.

Chaplin, Saul. *The Golden Age of Movie Musicals and Me.* Norman: University of Oklahoma Press, 1994.

Charisse, Cyd, and Tony Martin. *The Two of Us.* New York: Mason Charter, 1976.

Clarke, Gerald. *Get Happy: The Life of Judy Garland.* New York: Delta, 2001.

Comden, Betty. *Offstage.* New York: Limelight, 1996.

Cutts, John. "Kelly, Dancer, Actor, Director." *Films and Filming,* August/September 1964.

Daniell, Tina, and Pat McGilligan. "Betty Comden and Adolph Green: Almost Improvisation." In *Backstory 2: Interviews with Screenwriters of the 1940s and 1950s.* Berkeley: University of California Press, 1991.

Davis, Ronald. *Van Johnson: MGM's Golden Boy.* Jackson: University Press of Mississippi, 2001.

Delameter, Jerome. *Dance in the Hollywood Musical.* Ann Arbor: UMI Research Press, 1981.

Eyman, Scott. *Lion of Hollywood: The Life and Legend of Louis B. Mayer.* New York: Simon and Schuster, 2005.

Fordin, Hugh. *MGM's Greatest Musicals: The Arthur Freed Unit.* Boston: Da Capo, 1996.

Frank, Gerold. *Judy.* Boston, MA: Da Capo, 1999.

Frank, Rusty E. *Tap! The Greatest Tap Dance Stars and Their Stories, 1900–1955.* New York: William Morrow, 1990.

Fricke, John. *Judy Garland: World's Greatest Entertainer.* New York: Henry Holt, 1992.

Fricke, John, and Lorna Luft. *Judy Garland: A Portrait in Art and Anecdote.* New York: Bulfinch, 2003.

Garrett, Betty, and Ron Rapoport. *Betty Garrett and Other Songs: A Life on Stage and Screen.* New York: Madison Books, 2000.

Griffin, Mark. *A Hundred or More Hidden Things: The Life and Films of Vincente Minnelli*. Cambridge, MA: Da Capo, 2010.

Hay, Peter. *MGM: When the Lion Roars*. New York: Turner, 1991.

Hess, Earl J., and Pratibha A. Dabholkar. *The Cinematic Voyage of "The Pirate."* Columbia: University Press of Missouri, 2014.

———. *"Singin' in the Rain": The Making of an American Masterpiece*. Lawrence: University Press of Kansas, 2009.

Hirschhorn, Clive. *Gene Kelly*. New York: St. Martin's, 1984.

Kaplan, James. *Frank: The Voice*. New York: Anchor, 2011.

Kisselgoff, Anna. "Gene Kelly: Ballet Influenced His View of Dance." *New York Times*, January 17, 1985.

Kobal, John. *People Will Talk*. New York: Knopf, 1986.

Laurents, Arthur. *Original Story By: A Memoir of Broadway and Hollywood*. New York: Applause Theatre and Cinema Books, 2000.

Lerner, Alan Jay. *The Street Where I Live*. New York: Norton, 1978.

Levant, Oscar. *Memoirs of an Amnesiac*. Hollywood: Samuel French, 1989.

Levinson, Peter. *Puttin' on the Ritz: Fred Astaire and the Fine Art of Panache; A Biography*. New York: St. Martin's, 2009.

Levy, Emanuel. *Vincente Minnelli: Hollywood's Dark Dreamer*. New York: St. Martin's, 2009.

"A Man and His Loving Memories." *Woman* (London), December 15, 1973.

Martin, Hugh. *Hugh Martin: The Boy Next Door*. Encinitas, CA: Trolley, 2010.

Martin, John. "The Dance: Pal Kelly." *New York Times*, June 8, 1941.

McHugh, Dominic. *Alan Jay Lerner: A Lyricist's Letters*. New York: Oxford University Press, 2014.

Minnelli, Vincente. *I Remember It Well*. London: Angus and Robertson, 1975.

Morley, Sheridan, and Ruth Leon. *Gene Kelly: A Celebration*. London: Pavilion Books, 1996.

Mueller, John. *Astaire Dancing: The Musical Films*. New York: Wings Books, 1991.

Munn, Michael. *Jimmy Stewart: The Truth behind the Legend*. Fort Lee, NJ: Barricade Books, 2006.

"On *Combat Fatigue Irritability*: Kerry Kelly Novick." *Circulating Now*, March 12, 2014.

Parish, James Robert, and Michael Pitts. *Hollywood Songsters: Singers Who Act and Actors Who Sing*. 2nd ed. New York: Routledge, 2003.

Pasternak, Joe. *Easy the Hard Way: The Autobiography of Joe Pasternak*. New York: Putnam, 1956.

Reynolds, Debbie. *Debbie: My Life*. New York: William Morrow, 1988.

Rochlin, Margy. "Old Is New Again." *Interview*, February 1985.

Rodgers, Richard. *Musical Stages: An Autobiography*. Cambridge, MA: Harvard University Press, 2002.

Rubenstein, Hal. "An American in Style." *New York Times*, April 17, 1994.

Selected Bibliography

Silverman, Stephen M. *Dancing on the Ceiling: Stanley Donen and His Movies*. New York: Knopf, 1996.

Singer, Michael. *A Cut Above: 50 Film Directors Talk about Their Craft*. Los Angeles: Lone Eagle, 1998.

Soren, David. *Vera-Ellen: The Magic and the Mystery*. Parkville, MD: Midnight Marquee, 2003.

Spivak, Jeffrey. *Buzz: The Life and Art of Busby Berkeley*. Lexington: University Press of Kentucky, 2010.

Thomas, Tony. *The Films of Gene Kelly*. Secaucus, NJ: Citadel, 1974.

Updike, John. *More Matter: Essays and Criticism*. New York: Random House, 1999.

Van Gelder, Robert. "Mr. Kelly, or Pal Joey: Portrait of a Dancer, from Pennsylvania to the Barrymore Theatre." *New York Times*, March 2, 1941.

Williams, Esther, and Digby Diehl. *The Million Dollar Mermaid: An Autobiography*. New York: Simon and Schuster, 1999.

Wilson, Patricia. *Yesterday's Mashed Potatoes: The Fabulous Life of a Happy Has-Been*. Indianapolis: Dog Ear, 2009.

Wintz, Jack. "Gene Kelly." *St. Anthony Messenger* (Cincinnati), August 1980.

Yudkoff, Alvin. *Gene Kelly: A Life of Dance and Dreams*. New York: Backstage Books, 1999.

Films and Television

Dancing: A Man's Game. Perf. Gene Kelly, Dick Button, Mickey Mantle, Sugar Ray Robinson. *Omnibus*, December 21, 1958. New York: NBC, 2013. DVD.

Gene Kelly: Anatomy of a Dance. Dir. Robert Trachtenberg, perf. Betsy Blair, Stanley Donen, Kerry Kelly Novick. 2002; New York: American Masters, 2002. DVD.

Musicals, Great Musicals: The Arthur Freed Unit at MGM. Dir. David Thompson, perf. Hugh Fordin, Cyd Charisse, Mickey Rooney. 1996; Hollywood: Turner Entertainment, 1996. Videocassette.

S'Wonderful: The Making of "An American in Paris." Perf. Leslie Caron, André Guy, Claude Guy. 2008; Hollywood: Trailer Park, 2008. DVD.

Interviews

Cadman, Susan. E-mail interview with authors, January 5, 2015.

Novick, Kerry Kelly. Telephone interview with authors, June 25, 2015.

Sherman, Sally. Interview with authors, March 4, 2016.

Simone, Lela. Oral history, 1990. Margaret Herrick Library, Los Angeles.

Spivak, Jeffrey. E-mail interview with authors, March 31, 2014.

Websites

Gene Kelly: Creative Genius. www.freewebs.com/geneius.

Gene Kelly Fans. www.genekellyfans.com.
Internet Broadway Database. www.ibdb.com.
Internet Movie Database. www.imdb.com.

Index

Kelly, Gene—FILM CAREER *(cont.)*
Country, 240–41; *It's Always Fair Weather*, 299, 300–303, 304–5; judge at the 1959 Cannes Film Festival, 333; *Les Girls*, 308, 313–17; *Let's Make Love*, 339–40; life and work in Europe in the early 1950s, 273–75, 279–88; *Living in a Big Way*, 177–79, 180; *Love Is Better Than Ever*, 240; *Marjorie Morningstar*, 321–23; Louis Mayer's attempt to hire, 91–93; *For Me and My Gal*, 108–9, 112–16, 121; with MGM (*see* Metro-Goldwyn-Mayer); move to Hollywood in 1941, 98; Donald O'Connor and, 266–67; offer to direct *The Sound of Music*, 351–52; *Pilot #5*, 117; *The Pirate*, 181, 182, 183–94, 198–200, 201, 204; postwar joblessness, 171–72; relocation in Hollywood by MGM in 1942, 109–0; return to Hollywood in 1953, 288–90; Debbie Reynolds and, 264–65; RKO screen test in 1935, 52; *Robin and the Seven Hoods* project, 346; with Selznick International, 94, 101–2; *Singin' in the Rain*, 259–72, 278; social life and parties in Hollywood, 110–12, 158, 173–75, 254–56; stage employees strike of 1946 and, 179–80; on the studio system, 141; *Summer Stock*, 233, 234, 235–38; *Take Me out to the Ball Game*, 210–19; *That's Entertainment*, 379–82; *That's Entertainment! Part II*, 385–87; *That's Entertainment! Part III*, 400–401; *Thousands Cheer*, 121–22, 164; *The Three Musketeers*, 198, 200, 201–4, 205, 206; *On the*

Town, 220, 221–22, 223–31; *Viva Knievel!*, 387–88; *What a Way to Go!*, 348–50; *Words and Music*, 208–10; work with Zoetrope Studios, 390–91; *Xanadu*, 388–90; *The Young Girls of Rochefort*, 356–58; *Ziegfeld Follies*, 143–45, 147–48, 170
—STAGE CAREER: Broadway auditions in 1938, 60–62; Cap and Gown shows at the University of Pittsburgh, 30, 32, 40, 43, 47, 50–51, 53, 55; chief choreographer for the Westport Country Playhouse, 68–70; *Clownaround* family theater show, 370, 371, 375–76; director of *Flower Drum Song*, 326–28; *Gentleman's Gentleman* project, 328, 330–31; *Leave It to Me!*, 62, 63, 64; move to New York City in 1938, 57, 59–60; *One for the Money*, 63–66; *Pal Joey*, 78, 79–83, 87–90; Paris Opera Ballet project, 335–36, 337–38; shows and revues in Pittsburgh in the 1930s, 31–32, 36, 40, 41, 43, 47, 50–51, 53, 55–56; Superstar Theatre performance, 388; *Take Me Along* touring show, 382–84; *The Time of Your Life*, 71–73, 82
—TELEVISION CAREER: *An American in Pasadena*, 388; appearances in shows in the 1980s, 398; *Dancing: A Man's Game*, 329–30; *Dancing Is a Man's Sport, Too*, 391; entry into television, 318; *Gene Kelly in New York, New York*, 354–55; *The Gene Kelly Show*, 330, 331–33; *Gene Kelly's Wonderful World of Girls*, 368–69; *Going My Way* television series, 343–44, 345–46; host for

Screen Classics

Screen Classics is a series of critical biographies, film histories, and analytical studies focusing on neglected filmmakers and important screen artists and subjects, from the era of silent cinema to the golden age of Hollywood to the international generation of today. Books in the Screen Classics series are intended for scholars and general readers alike. The contributing authors are established figures in their respective fields. This series also serves the purpose of advancing scholarship on film personalities and themes with ties to Kentucky.

Series Editor

Patrick McGilligan

Books in the Series

Mae Murray: The Girl with the Bee-Stung Lips
    Michael G. Ankerich
Hedy Lamarr: The Most Beautiful Woman in Film
    Ruth Barton
Rex Ingram: Visionary Director of the Silent Screen
    Ruth Barton
Conversations with Classic Film Stars: Interviews from Hollywood's Golden Era
    James Bawden and Ron Miller
Von Sternberg
    John Baxter
Hitchcock's Partner in Suspense: The Life of Screenwriter Charles Bennett
    Charles Bennett, edited by John Charles Bennett
My Life in Focus: A Photographer's Journey with Elizabeth Taylor and the Hollywood Jet Set
    Gianni Bozzacchi with Joey Tayler
Hollywood Divided: The 1950 Screen Directors Guild Meeting and the Impact of the Blacklist
    Kevin Brianton
He's Got Rhythm: The Life and Career of Gene Kelly
    Cynthia Brideson and Sara Brideson
Ziegfeld and His Follies: A Biography of Broadway's Greatest Producer
    Cynthia Brideson and Sara Brideson
The Marxist and the Movies: A Biography of Paul Jarrico
    Larry Ceplair
Dalton Trumbo: Blacklisted Hollywood Radical
    Larry Ceplair and Christopher Trumbo
Warren Oates: A Wild Life
    Susan Compo
Improvising Out Loud: My Life Teaching Hollywood How to Act
    Jeff Corey with Emily Corey
Crane: Sex, Celebrity, and My Father's Unsolved Murder
    Robert Crane and Christopher Fryer
Jack Nicholson: The Early Years
    Robert Crane and Christopher Fryer
Being Hal Ashby: Life of a Hollywood Rebel
    Nick Dawson
Bruce Dern: A Memoir
    Bruce Dern with Christopher Fryer and Robert Crane
Intrepid Laughter: Preston Sturges and the Movies
    Andrew Dickos
John Gilbert: The Last of the Silent Film Stars
    Eve Golden